Handbook for Training Peer Tutors and Mentors

Editors
Karen Agee, Ph.D., University of Northern Iowa
Russ Hodges, Ed.D., Texas State University-San Marcos

A Publication of the College Reading and Learning Association

CENGAGE
Learning·

Australia • Brazil • Japan • Korea • Mexico • Singapore • Spain • United Kingdom • United States

CENGAGE
Learning·

**Handbook for Training
Peer Tutors and Mentors**

Karen Agee | Russ Hodges

Executive Editor:
Michael Stranz

Senior Project Development Manager:
Linda deStefano

Product Development Editor:
Carrie Carrelli

Marketing Specialist:
Heather Kramer

Production Editorial Manager:
Kim Fry

Content Project Editor:
Peg Hagar

Senior Production / Manufacturing Manager:
Donna M. Brown

Project Coordinator:
Heather Madsen

Sr. Rights Acquisition Account Manager:
Todd Osborne

Cover Image:
© 2009 Larry McGrath

Compositor:
MPS Limited

For product information and technology assistance, contact us at
Cengage Learning Customer & Sales Support, 1-800-354-9706

For permission to use material from this text or product,
submit all requests online at **cengage.com/permissions**
Further permissions questions can be emailed to
permissionrequest@cengage.com

Library of Congress Control Number: 2012934531

ISBN-13: 978-1-133-76944-6

ISBN-10: 1-133-76944-6

Cengage Learning

5191 Natorp Boulevard
Mason, Ohio 45040
USA

Cengage Learning is a leading provider of customized learning solutions with office locations around the globe, including Singapore, the United Kingdom, Australia, Mexico, Brazil, and Japan. Locate your local office at **international.cengage.com/region.**

Cengage Learning products are represented in Canada by Nelson Education, Ltd.

For your lifelong learning solutions, visit **custom.cengage.com.**

Visit our corporate website at **cengage.com.**

Printed in the United States of America

Dedication

The *Handbook for Training Peer Tutors and Mentors* is dedicated to the memory of Gladys Shaw, co-founder of the College Reading and Learning Association's International Tutor Training Program Certification and founder of International Mentor Training Program Certification.

Contents

CHAPTER 1   Theories Underlying Postsecondary Tutoring, Mentoring, and Training   **1**

CHAPTER 2   Modes of Tutor and Mentor Training   **55**

CHAPTER 3 General Training Topics   **103**

Introduction   103

CHAPTER 6   Training Programs   399

Foreword

This exciting new *Handbook for Training Peer Tutors and Mentors* is a labor of love for all involved, especially its two editors, Karen Agee and Russ Hodges. This book builds on the success of two predecessors. The original *CRLA Tutor Training Handbook* was created by Karan Hancock and Tom Gier in 1996, about 10 years after CRLA started certifying tutor training programs, to inform and inspire trainers and program directors. That handbook contained 27 articles. An expanded revision was edited in 2003 by Susan Deese-Roberts and is still available from CRLA as this new handbook is published; some of the 36 articles of the 2003 edition are cited by authors of this new 2011 Handbook. The book in your hands is a new version rather than a revision, containing 111 modules by 106 authors and offering numerous resources for academic support professionals involved in tutor and mentor training. Although mentor training programs have been certified by CRLA since 1998, no materials specifically for training peer mentors have been published until now.

This handbook is designed to address needs in both of CRLA's certification initiatives, International Tutor Training Program Certification (ITTPC) and the International Mentor Training Program Certification (IMTPC). These certification programs are endorsed by the Council of Learning Assistance and Developmental Education Associations (CLADEA) and by each of CRLA's sister organizations in CLADEA (Association for the Tutoring Profession, National Association for Developmental Education, National Center for Developmental Education, and National College Learning Center Association). For information about CLADEA member certification programs, see www.cladea.net.

Information about any current program's ITTPC or IMTPC certification status and the certification process, forms, samples, and contact information are all available on CRLA's website at www.crla.net. Directors of certified programs consistently provide positive feedback regarding the benefits of certification for their training programs. They tell us that using these certification standards brings improved credibility for their program among colleagues, peers, and campus leaders and that employing recognized international standards lends their learning center some well-justified admiration. Because trainers have demonstrated the quality of their training program to attain certification, it is easier to prepare a departmental self-study for institutional accreditation. Because directors receive objective feedback about their specific program in the certification process, they know how to improve their training program. And of course they and their campus leaders value the recognition they can give to their tutors and mentors who complete program certification requirements.

The articles of CRLA's earlier tutor training handbooks were written for trainers but often shared with tutors. This new handbook also is written for trainers to guide their professional practice, and the editors have intentionally not provided materials to be directly photocopied and used in training. To insure quality and appropriate use of materials in CRLA-certified programs, the CRLA Executive Board approved the following copyright policy, effective July 1, 2009:

> *Compliance with federal copyright law is expected of all CRLA members and ITTPC/IMTPC programs. It is our legal and ethical responsibility to give authorship credit for all materials we use in the classroom and for tutor and mentor training. Additionally, it is our legal and ethical responsibility to purchase (or have students purchase) copyrighted materials.*

Programs found to be in violation of copyright law will lose their CRLA certification. Copyright concerns are addressed in all new, renewal, and re-certification applications.

Although copy-ready materials are not provided in the new handbook, readers are invited to revise and adapt the figures and forms and to acknowledge the source of the material in any copies made for training. In addition, CRLA is making available some copyright-free, web-based handouts and other, copyrighted resource materials at www.crla.net/handbook/. Readers should check that site periodically to see what has been added.

By now you are probably eager to begin reading all the theoretical, program, and training modules of this comprehensive new handbook, and so am I. Though I wrote a dissertation on tutor training (*Effects of Training and Experience on Adult Peer Tutors in Community Colleges*), directed an ITTPC-certified program since 1990 (certified at all three levels), served as an ITTPC reviewer for more than a decade, and currently coordinate ITTPC (following esteemed Coordinators Tom Gier, Karan Hancock, Gladys Shaw, Carmen Springer-Davis, Anna Crockett, Tina Barnes, and Penny Turrentine), I look forward to the exciting new ideas, insights, and activities I will find. Please use this handbook as a resource to expand your own knowledge base, repertoire of strategies, and best practices in academic support and learning assistance.

Rick A. Sheets
ITTPC Coordinator
College Reading and Learning Association

Introduction

Since 1989, the College Reading and Learning Association has offered international certification for postsecondary tutor training programs—and since 1998, certification for postsecondary mentor training programs. Nearly 900 programs now use International Tutor Training Program Certification (ITTPC) and International Mentor Training Program Certification (IMTPC) standards of skills and training (based on best-practice research) to ensure the quality of the training they provide at Certified, Advanced, and Master levels of training.

To help trainers develop their programs in preparation for ITTPC certification, Tom Gier and Karan Hancock edited the first *CRLA Tutor Training Handbook* in 1996. Their handbook featured 27 short articles written by learning assistance professional experts—veritable CRLA icons—such as Becky Patterson, Kate Sandberg, Gladys Shaw, Elaine Wright, and many others who offered their best suggestions for tutor training. Susan Deese-Roberts edited a 36-article revision that premiered in 2003; this popular Revised Edition retained some of the original writing but also added fresh training perspectives with a broadened scope.

When the CRLA Board asked for another revision, we (Agee and Hodges) proposed a third edition of the *CRLA Tutor Training Handbook* to the Media Advisory Board (MAB) in fall 2008. Jane McGrath, then CRLA President, sagely suggested that mentor training be included in the same volume, and we complied with a proposal to the MAB in spring 2009 for this combined tutor and mentor training handbook, a totally new publication. After approval by the MAB and CRLA Board, we studied the ITTPC and IMTPC certification requirements, identified 96 training topics for tutor and mentor training, and advertised these topics to prospective authors through open calls to CRLA's membership and LRNASST listserve participants. Prospective authors sent one-page proposals in June 2009; authors of approved proposals sent six-page modules in December 2009. Additional modules were sought to fill some gaps.

To augment the work of the editors, the CRLA MAB, chaired by Jeanne Higbee, provided the expertise for a rigorous, single-blind, peer-review process to assure a focused, scholarly handbook that now includes 111 modules written by 106 authors. The writing, reviewing, editing, and production process was a collaboration among all involved, but we are reminded of the length of time this encompassed when we remember the friends we have lost: Todd Phillips died in March 2011 without getting to see his module printed in Chapter 2, and our cheeriest cheerleader, Gladys Shaw, passed away in September 2011.

This is a big book filled with ideas from many perspectives. Readers will find a variety of approaches on some topics and unique takes on others. As a whole, the book constitutes a wealth of support for trainers of peer tutors and mentors and opens new vistas for exploration. We wish for readers of this handbook the thrill of new discoveries and the joy of continued professional development.

Russ Hodges and Karen Agee
Editors

Preface

Even our very best educational resources at some point become outdated, necessitating the creation of new or revised resources to take their place. We can still appreciate the historical context and contributions of the original yet require more up-to-date material to address the many changes occurring around us on a daily basis. Thus, the leadership of the College Reading and Learning Association (CRLA) recognized the need to replace earlier editions of its *Tutor Training Handbook* (Deese-Roberts, 2003; Gier and Hancock, 1996) with a new handbook that would reflect innovations in such areas as online tutoring and social networking, to name but two. Meanwhile, CRLA was also aware of the need to develop a parallel resource for training peer mentors. At one point two separate new handbooks were proposed, but by combining the two, the editors addressed common themes without unnecessary duplication.

Another significant addition to the handbook is the opening chapter on theoretical perspectives. Meanwhile, the reviews of theory and research included in the training modules provide an understanding of the literature surrounding learning support that will benefit all learning assistance and developmental education professionals. With these additions the editors are modeling the importance of developing best practices that are founded on theory and research. This *praxis* (Freire, 1970/2000) should be evident throughout our educational endeavors.

It is the forward thinking of the two editors, Karen Agee and Russ Hodges, and the engaging writing of the many authors that have enabled this publication to develop into a resource that will be valued by educators working in a wide range of academic support programs and services. On behalf of CRLA and its Media Advisory Board (MAB), I first want to express our appreciation to Karen and Russ. The scope of this project has extended beyond anything any of us could possibly have imagined. I cannot begin to estimate the amount of time that these two scholars have devoted to making this handbook such an extensive resource with applications far beyond the work of those who train peer tutors and mentors. I also want to thank all the authors who have met numerous deadlines and have been so open to feedback. I hope that they are proud to be a part of this project. Finally, I need to express my deepest gratitude to the members of the MAB: Diana Calhoun Bell, Lucy MacDonald, Jane McGrath, Julianne Messia, Maggi Miller, Emily Miller Payne, and Diane Van Blerkom. Their names do not appear on the cover of this volume, and only those who contributed modules are represented in the author list, yet as a service to the profession the members of the MAB performed multiple rounds of review to ensure that our field is well served and represented by the contents of this work.

Jeanne L. Higbee
Chair, Media Advisory Board
College Reading and Learning Association

References

Deese-Roberts, S. (Ed.). (2003). *College Reading and Learning Association tutor training handbook* (rev. ed.). Hastings, NE: College Reading and Learning Association.

Freire, P. (1970/2000). *Pedagogy of the oppressed* (30th anniversary ed.). New York, NY: Continuum.

Gier, T., and Hancock, K. (Eds.). (1996). *College Reading and Learning Association's tutor training handbook*. Anchorage, AK: College Reading and Learning Association.

Acknowledgements

The editors thank the members of the CRLA Executive Board who approved proposals for this handbook three years ago and Board members who supported the book since then without rolling their eyes despite the timeline's running twice as long as planned. Rick Sheets (Paradise Valley Community College, retired) and Vicki Papineau (Central Community College in Nebraska) were unwavering in support of the book. We hope all will find it worth the wait.

Much of the handbook's worth is due to the skilled reviewing provided by CRLA's Media Advisory Board (MAB), members of which are expert editors and much-published authors. Production timelines sometimes required impossible turn-around times for their chapter reviews. Indeed, five MAB reviewers read the entire draft handbook in December 2011, despite demands of their own academic and personal calendars. Our deepest and profoundest debt is to Jeanne L. Higbee, Professor and Director of Graduate Studies in the Department of Postsecondary Teaching and Learning at the University of Minnesota, Twin Cities, who has chaired the MAB since its creation and guided development of the handbook from the beginning. Bountiful thanks go also to MAB members current and past who reviewed the book: Jane McGrath, Professor Emerita of Paradise Valley Community College; Diana Calhoun Bell, Associate Professor of English at the University of Alabama in Huntsville; Emily Miller Payne, Associate Professor of Graduate Studies in Developmental Education at Texas State University-San Marcos; Maggi Miller, Manager for TeamUP at Cengage Learning; Diane Van Blerkom, retired Assistant Professor at the University of Pittsburgh at Johnstown; Julianne Messia, Director of Academic Learning Services at Albany College of Pharmacy and Health Sciences; and Lucy MacDonald, emerita faculty member of Chemeketa Community College.

Without the creativity and patience of 106 authors, this handbook would not exist. These are the authors whose modules survived proposal review and repeated editorial review, the folks who endured—with patience, grace, and good humor—having their stellar ideas forced into our six-page format, like packing a checked-luggage load into a carry-on and hoping it will all emerge beautiful and useful on arrival. Well, we have arrived, and all the rushing to get the whole gorgeous array of training ideas out for people to use is done.

Michael Stranz and Peg Hagar of Custom Solutions at Cengage Learning worked with us to produce the book. We are grateful for their patience and the skill of their team.

The editors are grateful for the support of colleagues and friends during development of the handbook. Texas State University's Debbie Tingey, student worker in the College of Education, checked reference citations and looked up endless Digital Object Identifier (DOI) numbers, and David Stafford, systems support specialist, helped the editors create a useful document management system. (Texas State hosts the TRACS system by which we made sure every document would be accessible to CRLA even if both editors were hit by trucks.) Russ also expresses his gratitude to Santiago "Santi" Ochoa, for his love, support, and for making life all so sweet during this project. And Karen thanks Thom Kline, who only ever asked that dinnertime come before bedtime.

Photo Credits

Neysa Kay Henke from Anoka-Ramsey Community College-Coon Rapids in Minnesota won the student cover design competition in April 2010 with this black and white photograph of treetops in a cloudy sky.

The editors later selected "The Path Ahead" donated by photographer Larry McGrath for the cover as it seems to represent especially well the academic challenge: the path is neither straight nor smooth, yet on it leads.

Theories Underlying Postsecondary Tutoring, Mentoring, and Training

Introduction

To most ancient Greeks, theory (θεωρία) meant watching or observing, especially theatrical performances, but to post-Socratic philosophers the word was used for the kind of cognitive activity that moderns call contemplation or speculation (Liddell, 1889). The result of that speculation might be a general principle (e.g., a Euclidian theorem, Archimedes' principle of displacement) that could be observed in multiple circumstances. That is the use of the word adopted by modern science: a theory explains relationships among observed phenomena.

The best theories are the most explanatory, but even the best cannot yet explain everything. The search for a universal theory of matter and energy continues in physics, and fields like education seem even farther from developing a similar "string theory" (Greene, p. 13) of student learning and development. Professionals in learning assistance and developmental education seem to be making sense of the world by a multiplicity of theories. Lack of a single unifying theory is both evidence of the immaturity of the field and an acknowledgement of the complexity of the enterprise. Because theoretical explanations of training and learning may be analogous to the Harvard Law of Animal Behavior—most briefly paraphrased as "animals under the most precisely controlled laboratory conditions do as they damn please," (Park, 1939, p. 238)—the field has not completely explained why a high school student with a 4.0 grade point average and sufficient emotional and financial support somehow fails to thrive in the first semester of college study or how an astonishingly street-smart student flubs Sociology 101, especially when tutoring and mentoring are offered free of charge on campus.

There is no shame in admitting that the professional wisdom of the field does not yet know it all. Medical science has its germ theory, which explains why a tutor develops strep throat after exposure to a colleague with strep throat but fails to explain why five other tutors likewise exposed to the bacteria did not contract the disease. Lack of commitment to any one perspective as universal, then, may be evidence of wisdom.

Some practitioners may be frustrated with all this attention to theory, but the theoretical underpinnings of a training program are clearly revealed in interaction with staff and students. A mentor trainer who claims to be guided by cognitive theory and andragogy but refers to college students as "kids" and student comments as "feedback" is probably denying an inner pedagogist and behaviorist. The term *training* itself may imply that the College Reading and Learning Association's International Tutor Training Program Certification (ITTPC) and International Mentor Training Program Certification (IMTPC) favor methods that can also be used to condition dogs to heel and cats to stay off the kitchen counters. There certainly is need for training in this sense: preparing peer tutors and mentors to respond quickly and without dithering in situations requiring right action. Readers of this chapter will find, however, that *training* is used in its broadest sense and can be compatible with theoretical perspectives very different from operant conditioning.

Authors of the modules in Chapter 1 have written about theories they consider most salient for tutor and mentor training. They describe perspectives that seem most helpful for deciding not only how to train peer tutors and mentors but also what the content of that training should be and how to explain student learning. All of the perspectives included in this chapter are worthy of contemplation and speculation. The purpose of gathering them into this introductory chapter is not to endorse any one view. On the contrary, it is hoped that readers will meet both familiar explanations and intriguing new ways to think about how best to train peer tutors and mentors.

REFERENCES

Greene, B. (2003). *The elegant universe: Superstrings, hidden dimensions, and the quest for the ultimate theory.* New York, NY: W. W. Norton.

Liddell, H. G. (1889). *An intermediate Greek-English lexicon.* London, United Kingdom: Oxford University Press.

Park, T. (1939). Analytical population studies in relation to general ecology. *American Midland Naturalist, 21,* 235–255. Retrieved from http://www.jstor.org/stable/2420382

Peer Tutoring and Tutor Training: A Historical Perspective

Rick A. Sheets

When marketing for new students is more costly than retaining existing students, budgets are tighter than ever, and campus administrations seek to improve student retention and success, it is important to note what the research says about the history and importance of tutoring and tutor training. Tinto (2004) listed tutoring, mentoring, study groups, and Supplemental Instruction (SI) as academic support services that institutions can provide to enhance retention and graduation rates. He noted how critical it is for academic support programs not to stand alone but rather to be connected and linked to the curriculum. Tinto believed it was crucial that "students [be] able to make meaningful connections between the knowledge and skills they are acquiring in the support programs and those needed to succeed in their credit-bearing curriculum" (p. 8).

Though deplored as a recent problem, student "underpreparedness" for college is not a new phenomenon in higher education in the United States (Sheets, 1994). Many administrators and even academic support professionals may be unaware that the need for tutoring has existed throughout the history of our educational institutions. Tutoring has been provided in some form since Harvard opened its doors in 1636 as America's first college (Maxwell, 1997; Rudolph, 1962/1999; for historical timeline graphic see Sheets, 2011). Many of Harvard's incoming students were not yet proficient in Latin, which was the only language to be spoken in its halls. The college provided tutors to help these elite and wealthy students acquire the proficiency they needed to succeed.

It was the nineteenth century before English was studied in place of the traditional Greek or Latin at U.S. universities, beginning with what is now New York University (Dempsey, 1979). Starting in the 1800s, other changes occurred that opened higher education to the general population. These included the establishment of the Columbia Institute for the Deaf (now Gallaudet College) and the Morrill Acts of 1862 and 1890, which established land-grant colleges and eventually led to creation of historically Black colleges and universities in the U.S. In 1901, the first junior college, Joliet Junior College, was established to provide programs and credits that could be transferred to the University of Chicago (Gutek, 1986). Though opportunity to study at postsecondary institutions was thus broadened, even the elite schools considered their students ill prepared for college; as Maxwell (1997) noted, in 1907 over half the students enrolled at Harvard, Yale, Princeton, and Columbia had failed to meet college entrance requirements.

Until the 1960s, specific tutoring content and circumstances were poorly documented. Tutoring was usually an informal service, often volunteered and privately arranged. Beginning in the 1960s, colleges and universities began to receive government aid to provide higher education to lower-income or minority groups. Campus programs and departments began to establish more formal tutoring services targeted to specific student groups (Maxwell, 1997) like students with low family incomes, students considered underprepared for college, women students, or students of color.

In 1972, at California State University-Long Beach, Christ (1971) created a unique Learning Assistance Support System model "where learners, learner data, and learning facilitators are interwoven into a sequential, cybernetic, individualized, people-oriented system to service all students (learners) and faculty (learning facilitators) of any institution for whom learning by its students is important" (p. 39). This new model transformed the services and support programs offered to students at many colleges and universities. Instead of tutorial support services available only to specific, limited, targeted groups, in this new model, support services were expanded to all. Stanford University opened a new learning assistance center (LAC) in the summer of 1972 for students demonstrating the potential to succeed but needing remedial support. By 1973, its LAC expanded services to include all students (Walker, 1980).

The need to provide tutoring support services for all students continues at many institutions. Despite increases in the numbers of students taking Advanced Placement (AP) courses in high school, nearly one-third (31%) of all entering first-year college students responding to a recent Higher Education Research Institute survey said they believed they would need to get tutoring in specific courses for college (Pryor, 2011). Institutions generally recognize the importance of providing the tutoring students need: nearly 90% of community colleges surveyed by Gerlaugh, Thompson, Boylan, and Davis (2007) offered tutoring.

If the need for tutoring has been long and broad, then equally important should be training tutors to meet that need. Boylan, Bonham, and Bliss (1994) reported that 70% of the nation's tutorial programs surveyed had a training component. Does tutor training matter? Maxwell, in her (1990) review of the literature on tutoring, identified training for peer tutors as essential for successful tutoring programs in colleges and universities. Training is needed to "provide tutors with the information, strategies, and resources to help students become independent learners and attain their educational goals" (Rings & Sheets, 1991, p. 32). Grounded in a theoretical framework of constructivism and metacognition, training can provide tutors with the problem-solving and self-monitoring strategies needed to empower students to build knowledge and learn. Together, constructivism and metacognition build a foundation from which tutors can receive training to help students assess their own needs, identify needed strategies, and evaluate effectiveness in learning new information.

The National Center for Developmental Education at Appalachian State University studied over 6,000 students enrolled in basic skill development courses at 2- and 4-year institutions in the United States (Boylan, Bliss, & Bonham, 1997). Their initial review of the data on tutoring programs found no relationship between tutoring and student grade point average (GPA) or retention. However, when they considered the impact only of tutoring programs with a training component, Boylan, Bliss, and Bonham (1997) concluded that tutor training is one of the best indicators of a successful college developmental education program. Their findings were impressive: compared to students who did not participate in tutoring, students who participated in tutoring were more likely to achieve passing grades in developmental English and also had better grades overall in their first college term. In addition, students of trained tutors at 4-year institutions not only earned higher cumulative GPAs but also demonstrated higher retention rates (Boylan, Bliss, & Bonham, 1997). Tutoring provided by tutors in programs without training programs had no effect on retention or grades.

This study confirmed earlier research studies that also found it essential to train tutors. Casazza and Silverman (1996) stated that solid tutor training that included learning theory, metacognition, motivation, and more) was a key component in most successful development programs. In my own dissertation study of the extent to which training and experience affected peer tutors, I found significant differences in responses of tutors receiving at least 10 hours of training (Sheets, 1994). In the few topics examined, tutors receiving at least 1 hour of active listening training also showed significant differences in their responses from those who did not. This study used ten recommended mentors in the field to calibrate the test instrument used as the pretest and posttest instrument to rate tutor responses.

The need for academic support and appropriate tutor training has been recognized by the Council for the Advancement of Standards in Higher Education (CAS, 2010). For the last 30 years, CAS has been developing, publishing, and promoting standards among its 40 member organizations, which together represent more than 100,000 professionals, and to North American higher educational institutions. In 2010 the new CAS standards for functional areas were made available online to CAS member organizations. The College Reading and Learning Association (CRLA) could post the standards and guidelines for Learning Assistance Programs (LAP) free of charge to CRLA members, including LAC and tutoring management professionals, faculty, and staff. The CAS standards for Learning Assistance Programs require professional learning assistance staff to "ensure that staff members understand their responsibilities by receiving appropriate training" (CAS, 2010, p. 8), and establish procedures for training (p. 9).

CAS standards provided the impetus for CRLA to design standards for tutor training for program certification, known as CRLA International Tutor Training Program Certification (ITTPC; CRLA, 2011b). The concept of certifying the quality of tutor training programs was conceived in 1985 at a CRLA conference, presented in 1986, and developed over a 3-year period, to become CRLA's ITTPC (originally ITCP) in 1989 (Sheets, 2010).

Tutor training program certification has become more widely recognized as a means to provide consistent, high-quality academic support. Tutor training program certification through CRLA is noted as "one of the most effective ways to improve tutor training" (Boylan, 2002, p. 50). CRLA's ITTPC program has continued to grow to over 800 CRLA-certified tutor training programs during ITTPC's first 2 decades within the U.S., and ITTPC now includes programs in six countries outside the U.S. (CRLA, 2011a).

In the next few decades, despite advances in technology, access to information, and more technology options available to all, tutoring and the need to train tutors will continue. In his "learning college" of the future, O'Banion (1997) identified tutor-led groups as a needed learning option for the future. Returning to research by Tinto (2004) about what students need for success, learning assistance professionals can predict that meaningful connections between knowledge and skills acquired in and out of class will continue to be facilitated by well-trained tutors.

References

Boylan, H. (2002). *What works: Research-based best practices in developmental education*. Boone, NC: National Center for Developmental Education.

Boylan, H., Bliss, L., & Bonham, B. (1997). Program components and their relationship to student performance. *Journal of Developmental Education, 20*(3), 2–9. Retrieved from http://www.ncde.appstate.edu/resources/reports/documents//program_components.html

Boylan, H., Bonham, B., & Bliss, L. (1994). Characteristic components of developmental programs. *Research in Developmental Education, 11*(1), 14.

Casazza, M., & Silverman, S. (1996). *Learning assistance and developmental education: A guide for effective practice*. San Francisco, CA: Jossey-Bass.

Christ, F. L. (1971). Systems for learning assistance: Learner, learning facilitators, and learning centers. In F. L. Christ (Ed.), *Interdisciplinary aspects of reading instruction. Fourth Annual Proceedings of the Western College Reading Association* (pp. 32-41). Los Angeles, CA: WCRA. Retrieved from http://www.lsche.net/resources/articles/lass.htm

College Reading and Learning Association. (2011a). *Current certified tutor training programs*. Retrieved from http://www.crla.net/ittpc/current_certifications.htm

College Reading and Learning Association. (2011b). *Tutor training certification: (ITTPC) International Tutor Training Program Certification*. Retrieved from http://www.crla.net/ittpc/index.htm

Council for the Advancement of Standards in Higher Education. (2010). *Learning assistance programs CAS standards and guidelines*. Retrieved from http://www.cas.edu/getpdf.cfm?PDF=E86D2FCA-DBEC-AD47-33AB941E185E1E67

Dempsey, J. (1979). An update on the organization and administration of learning assistance programs in the U.S. senior institutions of higher education (Report No. HE-018-362). Tucson, AZ: University of Arizona.

Gerlaugh, K., Thompson, L., Boylan, H., & Davis, H. (2007). National study of developmental education II: Baseline data for community colleges. *Research in Developmental Education, 20*(4), 1–4.

Gutek, G. L. (1986). *Education in the United States: An historical perspective*. Englewood Cliffs, NJ: Prentice-Hall.

Maxwell, M. (1990). Does tutoring help? A look at the literature. *Review of Research in Developmental Education, 7*(4), 1–5.

Maxwell, M. (1997). *Improving student learning skills: A new edition*. Clearwater, FL: H&H.

O'Banion, T. (1997). *A learning college for the 21st century*. American Council on Education. Phoenix, AZ: Oryx Press.

Pryor, J. H. (2011, January). *The changing first-year student: Challenges for 2011*. Presentation at the Association of American Colleges and Universities Annual Meeting, San Francisco, CA. Retrieved from http://www.heri.ucla.edu/PP/Understanding%20the%20Incoming%20FreshmanAAC&U%202010.pdf

Rings, S., & Sheets, R. A. (1991). Student development and metacognition: Foundations for tutor training. *Journal of Developmental Education, 15*(1), 30–32.

Rudolph, F. (1962/1999). *The American college and university: A history.* Athens, GA: University of Georgia Press.

Sheets, R. A. (1994). *The effects of training and experience on adult peer tutors in community colleges* (Doctoral dissertation). Arizona State University, Tempe, AZ. Retrieved from http://www.eric .ed.gov/PDFS/ED474187.pdf

Sheets, R. A. (2010, February). *International Tutor Program Certification—the beginning.* Presentation at the College Reading and Learning Association Executive Board meeting, Salt Lake City, UT. Retrieved from http://www.crla.net/about/ITPC-Beginnings.pptx

Sheets, R. A. (2011). *Timeline for peer tutoring and tutor training: A historical perspective.* Retrieved from http://www.crla.net/handbook/ch1/sheets

Tinto, V. (2004). *Student retention and graduation: Facing the truth, living with the consequences.* Retrieved from http://www.pellinstitute.org/downloads/publications-Student_Retention_ and_Graduation_July_2004.pdf

Walker, C. (1980). The learning assistance center in a selective institution. In K. V. Lauridsen (Ed.), *New directions for college learning assistance: Examining the scope of learning centers* (pp. 57–68). San Francisco, CA: Jossey-Bass.

A Discourse Mismatch Theory of College Learning

Eric J. Paulson

College learning involves active participation in a series of specialized, academic Discourses, the rules, regulations, and expectations of which are often unfamiliar and largely invisible to students. Specifically the focus is on events and experiences in which students' language usage, expectations, goals, perspectives, identity, ways of being and doing, and more—what James Gee (2005, 2008) termed *big-D Discourse*—conflict with the language, expectations, goals, perspectives, identities, and ways of being and doing of the academic institution. This *Discourse mismatch* between student and academic institution is explored here as a theoretical lens for understanding common aspects of college learning. Brief connections to an apprenticeship model of pedagogy are made, in which one-on-one or small-group peer tutoring and mentoring situations provide ample opportunities for knowledgeable others to scaffold and support students' understanding of these college Discourse expectations.

Big-D Discourse

Though there are potentially many different vehicles for describing differences and conflicts in a variety of learning contexts, Gee's (2005, 2008) work in big-D Discourse is well supported by a large body of articulate, thought-provoking, and solid discourse analysis research. The academic community has acknowledged Gee's theories as having both a solid foundation and a general utility for researchers. Practitioners have made connections between Gee's Discourse theory and student learning in college contexts (Lundell & Collins, 2001; Paulson & Armstrong, 2010), establishing Discourse concepts as informative at the postsecondary level.

Gee (2005, 2008) described the micro-level of language—syntax, morphology, vocabulary, and so on—as *little-d discourse*, in contrast with big-D Discourse, which involves communicating by means of language but not only with language, since attending only to words and their relationships to each other is insufficient for understanding the whole spectrum of communication. Big-D Discourse refers to the integration of "ways of talking, listening, writing, reading, acting, interacting, believing, valuing, and feeling (and using various objects, symbols, images, tools, and technologies) in the service of enacting meaningful socially situated identities and activities" (Gee, 2001, p. 719). Thus Discourses are tightly connected to identity.

Gee (2008) used the example of a person walking into a biker bar, sitting down next to his drinking buddy, and asking "May I have a match for my cigarette, please?" Expressing the question in that way seems out of place and out of character. While the grammar is perfect, it is nonetheless "wrong" from a Discourse perspective, since a more acceptable syntactic construction in this situation would be "Gotta match?" given the "saying-doing" Discourse context described (example from Gee, 2008, pp. 2-3).

Peer tutors and mentors are concerned with an entirely different context—the postsecondary academic scene, not the biker bar—but the point that acceptable language-in-use changes from context to context is relevant for students in college learning situations, where their use of syntactic constructions (to take just one element of language) that are perfect in other contexts could be seen as "wrong" in college classrooms and faculty offices, marking them as outsiders. As Gee (2008) explained, "each Discourse incorporates a usually taken for granted and tacit set of 'theories' about what counts as a 'normal' person and the 'right' ways to think, feel, and behave" (2008, p. 4). When Discourses run counter to each other, the resulting conflict results in an unstable system in which one Discourse emerges as the accepted, or standard, Discourse.

Gee's description of Discourse clarifies that Discourse mismatch is not just an issue of vocabulary (although that may be in the mix) or of dialect or language as traditionally construed (although either may be in the mix). At issue are the larger kinds of expectations, ways of communicating, ways of understanding, value systems, goals, and other aspects of identity that may be in conflict with the implicit expectations, ways of communicating, ways of understanding, value systems, and goals of the academic institution.

Primary and Secondary Discourses

Gee (2008) made an important distinction between primary and secondary Discourses. A primary Discourse is one acquired early in life, usually in contexts centered on family and peer groups, and is usually a nonspecialized, nonprofessional Discourse; this could be considered one's "everyday" identity, which constantly evolves throughout the lifetime. In contrast, a secondary Discourse is one developed in institutions or disciplines that exist in the more public sphere of the wider community. Discourses found in college—like those of the writing classroom, a lecture in Introduction to Psychology, or a visit to a professor during his or her office hours—are specialized, secondary Discourses.

Concepts such as what counts as knowledge, processes that include how meaning is constructed, values such as what is considered "good," and procedures for "being" and "doing" are all part of the specialized Discourse found in college contexts. Where these epistemological ideas, processes, values, and procedures differ from students' primary Discourses, there exists the potential for conflict, a Discourse mismatch. Rogers (2003) explained this mismatch as a "lack of alignment between the culture, language, and knowledge of working-class students and dominant institutions such as schools and other social institutions" (p. 5). When an individual's primary Discourse runs counter to the accepted Discourse of an institution, the resulting conflict usually does not favor the individual, and an emerging body of research has demonstrated that this can set up severe barriers to learning and struggles within the institution's understanding of what it means to be academically successful (Dressman, Wilder, & Connor, 2005; Gee, 2004; Heath, 1983).

One implication of Discourse mismatch theory is that it is not enough to be able to "read" a textbook, because the student must be able to read the textbook with institutionally valued goals, processes, and end products in mind; Ruddell and Unrau have pointed out that "in order to effectively use text in the classroom, the reader must have *knowledge of classroom and social interaction patterns*" (emphasis in original; 2004, p. 1483). These ways of knowing, speaking, being, and doing are numerous. Students are expected to navigate implicit questions about the expectations of, for example, a large Introduction to Psychology class versus those of a 20-student Composition 101 course. In each of those courses, what kinds of norms are there for interacting with the instructor? Is class discussion encouraged, sanctioned, or even allowed? How are comments or questions allowed to be phrased in class? Is there room for divergent viewpoints or explorations of how the sanctioned information became the status quo? What kinds of writing are valued, and what kinds are disallowed? Are there expectations for before- or after-class interaction with instructors or classmates, and what are those expectations? Peer tutors and mentors are especially well positioned to have discussions about these Discourse expectations with students in their tutoring or learning assistance sessions. Without guidance or in the absence of explicit discussion about the different ways of "doing" in college, students whose primary Discourse unintentionally conflicts with the "right" way to approach situations like these will, in the eyes of those already initiated into the Discourse of the academy, get it "wrong."

Dressman et al. (2005) have described this mismatch as eventually producing in students a "sense of detachment and alienation from school tasks and from schooling itself" (p. 45) and situate this as involving issues of identity. When manifested in postsecondary contexts, this mismatch has direct effects on a student's school success. Issues of Discourse mismatch are multivariate: even with success in some aspects of navigation of the specialized Discourse of academia—such as understanding that there are specific and implicit expectations for what is valued as knowledge and behavior that differ from context to context—the student still must understand how to master those Discourses. And if the Discourses can be mastered, there are still issues of identity that are unsolved: if mastering a Discourse involves taking on aspects of a Discourse identity that are in conflict with the student's primary Discourse identity, the tension caused by that mismatch can set up deliberate and nondeliberate resistance behaviors or other actions that can short-circuit students' appropriation of the target Discourse. As Lundell and Collins (2001) noted, acquisition of a new Discourse "depends in large part on the degree to which the new Discourse conflicts with or threatens the primary Discourse and the enduring sense of self it sponsors" (p. 14).

Negotiation of a new specialized Discourse may incur very real identity struggles. In addition, much of what the theoretical lens of Discourse mismatch theory includes is useful in examining how the Discourses of institutions serve a variety of purposes, including the function of effectively excluding those not already exhibiting an institutionally-sanctioned Discourse. These issues are important in understanding the full range of what Discourse mismatch theory can reveal and explain about the relationship between individuals and larger societal institutions, like universities and community colleges.

Discourse Mismatch Theory in Practice

The most appropriate pedagogical model of learning viewed through a Discourse mismatch lens is one of *apprenticeship*. Rather than focusing on discrete skills and decontextualized tasks, the institution's instructors, tutors, and mentors initiate students into a set of culturally appropriate practices. These practices certainly include skills and strategies, but they are never separated from the context— the task, goal, discipline, and more—in which they are found. Reading strategies, for example, are approached in as authentic a way as possible, including, but not limited to, providing metacognitive attention to declarative, procedural, and conditional aspects of the strategies. Strategies are also introduced as both discipline- and task-specific, and adaptable to new tasks and goals. As part of this apprenticeship, knowledgeable others—including instructors, peer tutors, and peer mentors—must work with students to reveal the Discourse of the classroom, institution, and discipline. Such initiation includes explicit discussion and reference to parts of texts, writing, content, processes, and more that are value laden in the particular specialized Discourse. A thorough description of a system of pedagogy that coheres with Discourse mismatch theory and an apprenticeship model is provided in the New London Group's (1996) discussion of four components of pedagogy.

It is important not to assume a mutually-exclusive dichotomy between apprenticing into the specialized Discourses of college and mastering specific, technical tools like reading, writing, problem solving, and study strategies. Street (2001) noted that the sociolinguistic view, for example, "does not attempt to deny technical skill or the cognitive aspects of reading and writing, but rather understands them as they are encapsulated within cultural wholes and within structures of power" (p. 435). What this means in an everyday sense for peer tutors and mentors is that all reading strategies, technical writing skills, and problem-solving strategies that students work on with their peer tutors and mentors should always be situated within a specific academic context for specific purposes and designed to achieve specific goals by a specific person. An apprenticeship model thus focuses on the interrelationship between large, macro-cultural aspects of the institution and small micro-tools that students appropriate and use for specific purposes.

Conclusion

In Discourse mismatch theory, Discourse and identity play an important role in explaining the struggles experienced by students in a variety of learning situations in college contexts. When a student's primary Discourse has many features in common with the specialized, secondary Discourse of academia, that student's mastery of academic practices is facilitated and supported in numerous linguistic, behavioral, affective, and identity-affirming ways. Unfortunately, the opposite also holds: when there is little overlap between a student's primary Discourse and the specialized, secondary Discourse of academia, a host of discursive scaffolds are absent for that student, resulting in a variety of barriers to mastery of academic practices and access and success in college in general. However, the theory lends itself well to pedagogy appropriate to and effective for college students in a variety of learning situations, making a Discourse mismatch theoretical lens one that holds both explanatory power and pedagogical utility for peer tutors and mentors and for the professionals who design their training.

References

Dressman, M., Wilder, P., & Connor, J. J. (2005). Theories of failure and the failure of theories: A cognitive/sociocultural/macrostructural study of eight struggling students. *Research in the Teaching of English, 40*(1), 8–61.

Gee, J. P. (2001). Reading as situated language: A sociocognitive perspective. *Journal of Adolescent & Adult Literacy, 44*, 714–725. doi:10.1598/JAAL.44.8.3

Gee, J. P. (2004). *Situated language and learning: A critique of traditional schooling.* New York, NY: Routledge.

Gee, J. P. (2005). *An introduction to discourse analysis: Theory and method* (2nd ed.). New York, NY: Routledge.

Gee, J. P. (2008). *Social linguistics and literacies: Ideology in discourses* (3rd ed.). New York, NY: Routledge.

Heath, S. B. (1983). *Ways with words: Language, life, and work in communities and classrooms.* Cambridge, United Kingdom: Cambridge University Press.

Lundell, D. B., & Collins, T. C. (2001). Toward a theory of developmental education: The centrality of "discourse." In D. B. Lundell & J. L. Higbee (Eds.), *Theoretical perspectives for developmental education* (pp. 49–61). Minneapolis, MN: University of Minnesota, General College, Center for Research on Developmental Education and Urban Literacy.

New London Group. (1996). A pedagogy of multiliteracies: Designing social futures. *Harvard Educational Review, 66*(1), 60–92.

Paulson, E. J., & Armstrong, S. L. (2010). Postsecondary literacy: Coherence in theory, terminology, and teacher preparation. *Journal of Developmental Education, 33*(3), 2–13.

Rogers, R. (2003). *A critical discourse analysis of family literacy practices: Power in and out of print.* Mahwah, NJ: Lawrence Erlbaum.

Ruddell, R. B., & Unrau, N. J. (2004). Reading as a meaning-construction process: The reader, the text, and the teacher. In R. B. Ruddell & N. J. Unrau (Eds.), *Theoretical models and processes of reading* (5th ed., pp. 1462–1521). Newark, DE: International Reading Association.

Street, B. (2001). The new literacy studies. In E. Cushman, E. R. Kintgen, B. M. Kroll, & M. Rose (Eds.), *Literacy: A critical sourcebook* (pp. 430–442). Boston, MA: Bedford/St. Martin's.

Understanding the Role of Epistemological Beliefs on Student Learning

 Jodi Patrick Holschuh

Epistemological beliefs are an individual's perception about the nature of knowledge and knowing (Hofer & Pintrich, 1997). These beliefs include personal assessments about what knowledge is and where knowledge comes from (Hofer, 2002; Schommer, 1990) and are part of and may direct the cognitive processes involved in learning (Kitchener & King, 1990; Perry, 1970/1999; Schommer, 1990). Thus, epistemological beliefs may directly relate to student learning and academic success. This theory is useful for tutors and mentors to understand, because it may help explain why students appear to be working hard in their courses yet earn poor grades. Additionally, because there is a growing body of evidence suggesting that epistemological beliefs can be changed through training and intervention (Kienhues, Bromme, & Stahl, 2008), tutors and mentors may be able help students develop more sophisticated epistemic stances.

Research indicates that epistemological beliefs may affect the depth to which individuals learn (Schommer, 1990, 1993; Schreiber & Shinn, 2003). There is evidence that students with naïve epistemological beliefs tend to use surface-level strategies, such as memorization, while students with sophisticated epistemological beliefs tend to use deep-level strategies for learning (Holschuh, 2000; Schommer, 1990; Schreiber & Shinn, 2003). Epistemological beliefs may function as a standard against which individuals compare comprehension and learning to task demands, which, in turn, would influence students' strategy selection and use (Hofer & Pintrich, 1997; Ryan, 1984). For example, when encountering a complex task, such as preparing for an essay exam requiring students to pull multiple ideas together, a student holding naïve epistemological beliefs may not understand the necessity of choosing deep-level processing strategies and may select a memorization strategy instead. In fact, individuals with naïve beliefs may not be able to discriminate between surface- and deep-level strategies (Holschuh, 2000).

Five Dimensions of Epistemological Beliefs

One of the leading researchers in the area of epistemological beliefs is Schommer (now Schommer-Aikins). Schommer (1990) conceptualized an individual's epistemological beliefs as consisting of five independent dimensions: certainty of knowledge, simplicity of knowledge, nature of authority, speed of learning, and source of ability. Each of the five dimensions is depicted as a continuum beginning with a naïve perspective and moving toward a mature or sophisticated perspective.

CERTAIN KNOWLEDGE

The first dimension, certainty of knowledge, concerns the extent to which a person sees knowledge as fixed (i.e., set) or changeable. The belief that knowledge is absolute or fixed is common in first-year college students. Because such students believe that there is an answer to every question, they find multiple explanations confusing. Students who hold a strong belief in the certainty of knowledge have a particularly difficult time with assignments to evaluate theories or understand more than one explanation for a concept or theory. They expect the professor to provide the "correct" answer. In addition, they may not be open to exploring or, in some cases, even being exposed to alternative explanations of the world, especially with respect to religious or political beliefs (Schommer, 1990). Conversely, students who believe knowledge is changeable or evolving tend to experience higher levels of academic involvement and achievement in these circumstances (Kizilgunes, Tekkaya, & Sungur, 2009).

SIMPLE KNOWLEDGE

The second dimension, simplicity of knowledge, deals with the discrete or interconnected nature of knowledge. Some students see knowledge as a series of individual facts; others believe that knowledge consists of interrelated concepts. For example, two students who are studying for a mathematics exam but who hold beliefs at opposite ends of this continuum may take very different approaches. The student believing that knowledge is a series of unrelated facts may memorize all of the formulas and key terms to prepare for the exam. The student believing that knowledge consists of interrelated ideas may focus on learning the mathematical processes and underlying theories. The first student may not even attempt to link ideas together because of a belief that each concept is by nature discrete (Schommer, 1990).

Consider these first two dimensions together. Students who hold a belief that knowledge is certain and simple may choose to study using flash cards. This study strategy is a perfect match with their beliefs because it focuses on the facts and keeps each piece of knowledge separate (Holschuh, 2000). After they memorize the cards, according to their beliefs about the certainty and simplicity of knowledge, they achieve knowledge and are prepared for the exam (Nist & Holschuh, 2005). However, given an exam on which students are expected to synthesize ideas or to analyze information, these students are unprepared for the task and baffled by questions that do not match their conception of what counts as knowledge.

OMNISCIENT AUTHORITY

The third dimension, authority, concerns who is in control of knowledge. Some students believe that knowledge is external and is transmitted to individuals from an outside authority such as a teacher or a parent; others believe it is internal and comes from within the individual. Students holding a belief in omniscient authority may be intimidated by professors or may believe that professors are responsible for their learning. These students believe that it is the professor's role to dispense all of the important information and the student's role simply to absorb it. Thus, when students struggle in a course or perform poorly on exams, they may say that the professor is not a good teacher, the book is too difficult, or the exams are tricky. Unfortunately, students holding a belief in omniscient authority tend not to take credit for their successes, either. If they hold the belief that the professor is in charge of their learning, when they experience success, they are likely to credit a good professor, an easy test, or just plain luck—not that they worked hard and studied appropriately (Schommer, 1990). Tutors and mentors may find that these students feel unmotivated for learning because it is difficult to sustain motivation when one cannot take credit for one's successes.

SPEED OF LEARNING

The fourth component concerns beliefs about the speed of learning. Some college students believe that learning happens quickly or not at all, while others believe that learning happens gradually. This belief probably stems from experience with previous academic tasks requiring little time to complete. For example, the majority of math problems that students encounter before college can be solved in less than 2 minutes (Schoenfeld, 1985). A student who fails to solve a math problem in college in this amount of time may become frustrated or give up entirely at that 2-minute marker. Students also hold conceptions about how long it should take to read textbook chapters, write papers, and complete science labs. However, these timeframe notions are largely arbitrary because many of these tasks require more time to complete in college than in high school. Additionally, some students believe that if learning is going to happen it is going to happen immediately, rather than viewing learning as a gradual process requiring persistence. These students find it difficult to stick with a task or to try a different approach when their first does not work (Nist & Holschuh, 2005; Schommer, 1990). This can become an issue for tutors and mentors because students may resist changing learning strategies even when taught new ways to approach the task (Holschuh, 2000).

INNATE ABILITY

The fifth component deals with beliefs about the ability to learn. Some students believe that the ability to learn is fixed at birth, while others believe that people can learn how to learn (Schommer, 1990). For example, if students have always struggled with writing, they may believe that they are not capable of becoming good writers no matter how hard they work at it. Students who hold this belief will not make much effort to learn because they believe that their success in composition classes is related to their inherent lack of ability in writing. These students are apt to give up quickly and are less likely to seek out tutoring when they do not understand something.

Potential Efficacy of Tutors' and Mentors' Beliefs

Research indicates that epistemological beliefs develop as students progress through college (Kitchener & King, 1990) and that making students aware of their own beliefs can help speed this development (Kienhues, Bromme, & Stahl, 2008; Nist & Holschuh, 2005). Although there has been no research to date on the role of tutoring or mentoring on epistemological beliefs, the research on efficacy of teacher beliefs suggests that tutors and mentors can play a role in helping students develop more sophisticated beliefs about knowledge and learning (Hofer & Pintrich, 1997). For example, when tutors pay attention to statements that might give them insight into their students' epistemic stances (e.g., "I studied for a long time, but I think I just can't get this"; "I wish the professor would stop teaching so many theories and just tell us which one is right"), they may be able to guide students to change some beliefs about knowledge that are interfering with academic success.

Just as some teacher beliefs have been shown to result in more effective classroom instruction (Brownlee, Purdie, & Boulton-Gillis, 2001), a tutor's or mentor's beliefs are likely to play a role in the overall effectiveness of the peer session. As peers, tutors and mentors may be able to help students understand the complexity of knowledge as a professor may not, and can impart the wisdom that learning takes time (Topping, 2005). Understanding the role of epistemological beliefs in student learning can help bring a greater understanding of the non-content related struggles many students face in college classrooms. This knowledge may lead to more productive tutoring and mentoring sessions.

References

Brownlee, J. M., Purdie, N. M., & Boulton-Lewis, G. M. (2001). Changing epistemological beliefs in preservice teacher education students. *Teaching in Higher Education*, 6, 247–268. doi:10.1080/13562510120045221

Hofer, B. K. (2002). Personal epistemology as a psychological and educational construct. In B. K. Hofer & P. R. Pintrich (Eds.), *Personal epistemology: The psychology of beliefs about knowledge and knowing* (pp. 3–14). Mahwah, NJ: Lawrence Erlbaum.

Hofer, B. K., & Pintrich, P. R. (1997). The development of epistemological theories: Beliefs about knowledge and knowing and their relation to learning. *Review of Educational Research*, 67, 88–140. doi:10.2307/1170620

Holschuh, J. P. (2000). Do as I say, not as I do: High, average, and low-performing students' strategy use in biology. *Journal of College Reading and Learning, 31*(1), 94–108.

Kienhues, D., Bromme, R., & Stahl, E. (2008). Changing epistemological beliefs: The unexpected impact of a short-term intervention. *British Journal of Educational Psychology, 78*, 545–565. doi:10.1348/000709907X268589

Kitchener, K. S., & King, P. M. (1990). The reflective judgment model: Ten years of research. In M. I. Commons, J. D. Sinnot, F. A. Richards, & C. Armon (Eds.), *Adult development: Models and methods in the study of adolescent and adult thought* (Vol. 2, pp. 63–78). New York, NY: Praeger.

Kizilgunes, B., Tekkaya, C., & Sungur, S. (2009). Modeling the relations among students' epistemological beliefs, motivation, learning approach, and achievement. *Journal of Educational Research, 102,* 243–256. doi:10.3200/JOER.102.4.243–256

Nist, S. L., & Holschuh, J. P. (2005). Practical applications of the research on epistemological beliefs. *Journal of College Reading and Learning, 35*(2), 84–92.

Perry, W. G. (1970/1999). *Forms of intellectual and ethical development in the college years: A scheme.* San Francisco, CA: Jossey-Bass.

Ryan, M. P. (1984). Monitoring test comprehension: Individual differences in epistemological standards. *Journal of Educational Psychology, 76,* 248–258. doi:10.1037/0022-0663.76.2.248

Schoenfeld, A. H. (1985). *Mathematical problem solving.* Orlando, FL: Academic Press.

Schommer, M. (1990). Effects of beliefs on the nature of knowledge on comprehension. *Journal of Educational Psychology, 82,* 498–504. doi:10.1037/0022-0663.82.3.498

Schommer, M. (1993). Epistemological development and academic performance among secondary students. *Journal of Educational Psychology, 85,* 406–411. doi:10.1037/0022-0663.85.3.406

Schreiber, J. B., & Shinn, D. (2003). Epistemological beliefs of community college students and their learning processes. *Community College Journal of Research and Practice, 27,* 699–710. doi:10.1080/713838244

Topping. K. J. (2005). Trends in peer learning. *Educational Psychology, 25,* 631–645. doi:10.1080/01443410500345172

Using Foundational Student Development Theories to Guide Practice

Jeanne L. Higbee and Ellyn K. Couillard

Several years ago a study of developmental educators determined that although many describe the theories that guide their work in terms of their academic disciplines, others cite a foundation in student development theory (Chung & Higbee, 2005). There are numerous situations in which the application of student development theory can assist peer tutors and mentors in understanding student behavior. College student development is a relatively recent field of study, but its roots can be traced to the work of Dewey (1916, 1936) and other educational theorists, as well as to perspectives on *The Student Personnel Point of View* (American Council on Education [ACE], 1937), which proposed that higher education institutions have an "obligation to consider the student as a whole," to focus on "the development of the student as a person rather than upon his intellectual training alone" (p. 39). The provision of services to assist the student with "improvement of study methods" (p. 41) is but one of the recommendations related to "Assisting the student to reach his maximum effectiveness" (p. 41) in this historic document, which was updated by ACE (1949) following World War II to reflect a greater emphasis on social responsibility and the need to consider individual differences. *The Student Personnel Point of View* laid the foundation for further research, evolving theories, and best practices related to college student development. This module will present two early theories of college student development that can contribute to an understanding of student behavior.

Chickering's Seven Vectors of College Student Development

One of the most influential early theories focusing on the whole student was espoused by Chickering in 1969, has stood the test of time (Chickering & Reisser, 1993; Reisser, 1995), and continues to guide postsecondary educators in understanding the many competing challenges faced by college students. Through his research, Chickering identified the following seven vectors of development.

DEVELOPING COMPETENCE

Intellectual competence (i.e., the acquisition of academic knowledge in specific disciplinary areas as well as the development of skills like critical thinking and problem solving) is but one of the foci of college students. Chickering also included physical and manual competence as well as interpersonal competence within this vector. Although peer tutors and mentors are primarily charged with addressing academic knowledge and "habits of the mind" (Conley, 2003, p. 8), it is important to remember that at any given moment students' attention may be diverted to other areas of competence related to their athletic endeavors, artistic interests, social interactions, and so on. Within this vector, Chickering also described the need for a "sense of competence" (Chickering & Reisser, 1993, p. 53), which may be likened to ownership of one's talents and abilities. It is not unusual for students to experience self-doubt. Assisting students in recognizing their own capabilities can be a critical function of the peer tutor or mentor. Even for students with high self-esteem, academic self-concept can be challenged by that first low grade on a college test or paper (Higbee & Dwinell, 1996).

MANAGING EMOTIONS

The first step within this vector is learning to identify emotions—to distinguish among anger, anxiety, and frustration, for example. The misplaced focus of a student's emotions (e.g., a tutee's expressions of anger toward a tutor after failing an exam) may be the result of not really understanding the source of the emotion and simply lashing out at the most convenient target. A tutor who understands this misdirection of emotions is better equipped to respond, realizing that the attack is not personal.

MOVING THROUGH AUTONOMY TO INTERDEPENDENCE

Autonomy involves both emotional independence and instrumental independence. Although Chickering (1969) clearly described vectors rather than stages in his theory, it is readily apparent that it will be difficult for a student who has not yet learned to identify emotions and act on them appropriately to function autonomously. For many first-year college students who are still in their teens, developing emotional autonomy can involve learning to be emotionally self-sufficient rather than looking to parents and others for approval and validation. Similarly, developing instrumental autonomy enables students to move from being motivated by external factors to developing a more internal locus of control (Rotter, 1966) and to engage in self-regulated learning. Finally, as students mature, they are able to understand that becoming more autonomous is not synonymous with not needing others; we are all interdependent and could not survive without our dependence on others to meet some of our most basic needs (e.g., food, clothing, shelter, love). From a peer tutoring and mentoring perspective, achieving interdependence is important because it allows students to seek help without interpreting the need for assistance as a deficiency or inability to be self-sufficient.

DEVELOPING MATURE INTERPERSONAL RELATIONSHIPS

This vector focuses on developing and sustaining close relationships and assumes that in order to do so the student must embrace individual differences. For college students living away from home for the first time, it is critical to supplement long-term relationships with family and friends with new relationships. Because it takes time for these new relationships to mature, initially it is not uncommon for students to call home frequently and to express that they do not have anyone to talk to on campus about more serious issues.

ESTABLISHING IDENTITY

This vector focuses on establishing a realistic and stable sense of self whether considering physical attributes, gender, sexual orientation, culture, spirituality, or any other aspect of social identity. When students are comfortable with who they are, with how they see themselves, they can be more open to new ideas and more receptive to feedback even when in conflict with their self-concept.

DEVELOPING PURPOSE

Before students commit to a major or career path, set long-term goals, or make important life decisions, it is important to have a sense of direction. As students affirm their values and strengthen their sense of identity, they also begin attaching purpose to their lives to guide the years ahead. Students who are indecisive or who seem to take their commitments too lightly may need to focus more of their attention on what they perceive to be their purpose in life. What is most meaningful to them? What do they want to accomplish in their lives? How would they want to be remembered?

DEVELOPING INTEGRITY

Intertwined with developing purpose is developing integrity. Young college students may have acquired their value systems primarily from their families and the communities in which they were raised. College coursework may challenge some of these values, prompting students to reevaluate their system of beliefs within the context of a broader world view, allowing them to affirm or modify their values while also being more accepting of others who do not share their beliefs. The final step within this vector is achieving congruence between values and behavior.

Peer tutors and mentors can provide an environment that fosters student development by encouraging students to examine issues from different points of view. They can enhance students' sense of competence by pointing out students' strengths. They can assist students in articulating emotions such as frustration and anxiety surrounding the learning process. They can promote the development of autonomy by guiding students to make their own decisions. The support provided by peer tutors and mentors can also have an impact on students' sense of belonging at the institution, which research findings support as a key factor in student development (Chickering, 1969; Chickering & Reisser, 1993).

Perry's Theory of Intellectual and Ethical Development

During approximately the same time period in which Chickering was conducting the research that led to his seven vectors, Perry (1968) identified a continuum of positions that reflect student perspectives, ranging from dualism to commitment. Within the position of *Basic Duality*, information is evaluated as right or wrong, good or bad; authority figures provide the correct answers. This position might be likened to the banking concept of education (Freire, 1970), in which students are depositories to be filled with knowledge by the teacher. Students within this position may see peer tutors and mentors as authority figures and expect them to provide the right answers or tell them what to do.

When perceived experts like teachers, tutors, and mentors acknowledge that there may not be a single correct answer and that multiple perspectives may be applied to solving a problem, or when students' values conflict with the knowledge imparted, students are likely to experience cognitive dissonance and begin transitioning to *Multiplicity* (Perry, 1968). Within this position students become more open to different points of view, all of which may be perceived as equally valid. Tutors may experience students in this position who do not understand a low grade on a paper or essay exam because they may reason that if there is no correct answer, then their answer should be just as good as anyone else's.

Peer tutors and mentors can play a significant role in facilitating students' transition to *Relativism* (Perry, 1968). Within this position students learn to support their opinions with facts and acknowledge that although there may be numerous ways to approach a problem, some have more merit than others. Thus, as students move from one position to the next along the continuum, they develop higher-order thinking skills and more meaningful ways of exploring complex issues.

The final positions of the Perry (1968) scheme involve *Commitment*, which requires relativistic thinking. In many ways making commitments from Perry's perspective is not significantly different from developing what Chickering referred to as identity, purpose, and integrity.

Critique

Critics of Chickering and Perry noted that their research was based on populations of affluent, traditional-age male college students at elite institutions. As noted in the next module, some recent contributions to student development theory have considered specific aspects of social identity, while other theorists have embedded consideration of social identity in their construction of more inclusive theories. However, the foundational work of Chickering and Perry can still be traced in more recent theoretical perspectives. The next module in this chapter will present more recent theories of college student development.

References

American Council on Education. (1937). *The student personnel point of view, 1937.* Washington, DC: Author. Retrieved from http://www.myacpa.org/pub/documents/1937.pdf

American Council on Education. (1949). *The student personnel point of view.* Washington, DC: Author. Retrieved from http://www.naspa.org/pubs/files/StudAff_1949.pdf

Chickering, A. W. (1969). *Education and identity.* San Francisco, CA: Jossey-Bass.

Chickering, A. W., & Reisser, L. (1993). *Education and identity* (2nd ed.). San Francisco, CA: Jossey-Bass.

Conley, D. T. (Ed.). (2003). Understanding university success: A report from Standards for Success, a project of the Association of American Universities and The Pew Charitable Trusts. Eugene, OR: University of Oregon, Center for Educational Policy Research.

Chung, C. J., & Higbee, J. L. (2005). Addressing the "theory crisis" in developmental education: Ideas from practitioners in the field. *Research & Teaching in Developmental Education, 22*(1), 5–26.

Dewey, J. (1916). *Democracy and education.* Chicago, IL: University of Chicago Press.

Dewey, J. (1936). *Democracy in education.* New York, NY: Macmillan.

Freire, P. (1970/2000). *Pedagogy of the oppressed* (30th anniversary ed., M. Bergman Ramos, Trans.). New York, NY: Continuum.

Higbee, J. L., & Dwinell, P. L. (1996). Correlates of self-esteem among high risk students. *Research & Teaching in Developmental Education, 12*(2), 41–50.

National Association of Student Personnel Administrators & American College Personnel Association. (2004). *Learning reconsidered: A campus-wide focus on the student experience.* Washington: DC: Authors. Retrieved from http://www.myacpa.org/pub/documents/learningreconsidered.pdf

Perry, W. G. (1968). *Forms of intellectual and ethical development in the college years: A scheme.* New York, NY: Holt, Reinhart, & Winston.

Reisser, L. (1995). Revisiting the seven vectors. *Journal of College Student Development, 36,* 505–511.

Rotter, J. (1966). Generalized expectancies for internal versus external control of reinforcement. *Psychological Monographs, 80*(1), 1–28.

Applying Recent Student Development Theories to Tutoring and Mentoring

Ellyn K. Couillard and Jeanne L. Higbee

The previous module on foundational theories of college student development focuses primarily on the work of Chickering (1969) and Perry (1968). Critics of Chickering and Perry have noted that the samples for their 1960s research are not representative of today's college students. More recent contributions to student development theory have considered various aspects of social identity, including but not limited to gender (e.g., Gilligan, 1977; Josselson, 1987); race (Cross, 1991, 1995; Helms, 1995; Phinney, 1990); and gay, lesbian, bisexual, transgender, and queer identity development (D'Augelli, 1994). Other theorists have embedded consideration of various aspects of social identity in their construction of inclusive theories of college student development. This module will focus on recent theories related to student transitions, epistemological reflection, and self-authorship.

Transition Theory

The transition theory originally posited by Schlossberg, Waters, and Goodman (1995) is one such theory that can be applied to college student development as a subset of adult development. Schlossberg et al. discussed how experiencing transitions—whether anticipated or unanticipated—can have an impact on many intertwined dimensions of a person's life. More recently, Goodman, Schlossberg, and Anderson (2006) built on Schlossberg et al.'s model by addressing *situation*, *self*, *support*, and *strategies* as four Ss related to a person's ability to cope with transitions, as follow:

SITUATION

Situation involves *trigger* of the transition, *timing*, perception of *control* over the transition, potential *role change* resulting from the transition and whether that role change is considered positive or negative, *duration*, *previous experience with a similar transition*, *concurrent stress*, and *assessment*. The situation surrounding an anticipated event like the transition from high school to college can be significantly different from a transition back to school following military deployment, termination from previous employment, or the need for more education to compete in the workplace, especially if the transition is triggered by events outside the student's control and by necessity rather than a desire to learn. Concurrent stressors like financial worries can also play an important role in these transitions. It is imperative that the peer tutor or mentor be aware of how a student's situation may promote or hinder successful transitions to and through postsecondary education.

SELF

Self includes *personal and demographic characteristics* and *psychological resources*. Students' ability to cope with transitions can be influenced by factors such as age, gender, socioeconomic status, health, and cultural background, as well as optimism, self-efficacy, and resiliency. If needed, peer tutors and mentors can work with students to explore referral resources that can facilitate students' development of psychological resources.

SUPPORT

Support can come from four types of social support: (a) *intimate relationships*, (b) *family units*, (c) *networks of friends*, and (d) *institutions and communities*. For students transitioning to college, the support and understanding of friends and loved ones can play a critical role in adjustment to college life. Some members of students' social networks who did not attend college themselves may be supportive of the concept of attending college while having little or no comprehension of students' multifaceted lifestyles. Peer tutors and mentors can play an important role as members of students' new community and as providers of institutional support.

STRATEGIES

Strategies can focus on changing or controlling the situation or on managing the stress associated with the transition. Coping mechanisms discussed by Goodman et al. (2006) include information seeking, direct action, inhibition of action, and intrapsychic behavior. Peer tutors and mentors can assist students in developing multiple coping strategies while also providing information about referral resources.

Thus, transition theory (Goodman et al., 2006; Schlossberg et al., 1995) considers students' different social identities, life experiences, and personal characteristics in providing a model for understanding the complexities of transitions and people's ability to respond effectively to new situations. This is but one of many recent theories that neither ignores social identity nor focuses on just one specific identity group.

Epistemological Reflection

Throughout this handbook there are references to the importance of reflection in the learning process for tutors and mentors as well as for tutees and mentees. Baxter Magolda (1992) has made significant contributions to understanding students' reflective processes. She called educators' attention to students' ways of knowing as socially constructed, context bound, and fluid in nature, and noted that patterns of reflection can be gender related.

Baxter Magolda (2004) defined *epistemological reflection* as "assumptions about the nature, limits, and certainty of knowledge" (p. 31). She identified four stages of epistemological reflection: (a) *absolute knowing* (i.e., the student is certain of the absolute truth of his or her knowledge); (b) *transitional knowing* (the student begins to acknowledge the possibility of uncertainty); (c) *independent knowing* (the student recognizes that much knowledge is uncertain); and (d) *contextual knowing* (the student understands how contexts shape knowledge and realizes the need to provide evidence to support one's point of view). Although not dissimilar in some ways from Perry's (1968) positions of *dualism, multiplicity,* and *relativism,* Baxter Magolda's stages also address gender differences in how students learn and interact with instructors. Her research indicated the tendency for male students to be more competitive and females more collaborative in the first stage, males to use logic and debate while females consider individual differences and use personal judgment in the second stage, and females in the third stage to value their own ideas as well as those of others while males consider the views of others but attend more to their own perspectives. In the early stages, females are also less likely to interact with faculty (or peer tutors and mentors) until they establish a level of comfort in the learning environment. Being aware of these gender differences can assist peer tutors and mentors in engaging more effectively with students as they begin to question the absolute truth of "facts."

Student Self-Authorship

Baxter Magolda's longitudinal follow-up studies (2001, 2004, 2008) with a subset of the sample from her earlier (1992) research led to her definition of *self-authorship* as "the internal capacity to define one's beliefs, identity, and social relations" (2008, p. 269), establishing the critical link between students' epistemological beliefs and their sense of self and others. According to Baxter Magolda (2001), students go through four phases in the evolution from external to internal definitions of self.

At first they are dependent on plans or formulas imposed on them by external authorities. Thus, first-year students often declare majors based on the expectations of others without engaging in significant exploration of the interests and skills or course requirements necessary to pursue these goals. In the second phase, young adults become dissatisfied with the results of *following formulas* and find themselves at a *crossroads*; they begin to realize the need to establish a new life plan based on their own sense of self rather than that imposed upon them by others. Thus, the third phase is *becoming the author of one's life.* Phase 4, *internal foundation*, is characterized by a self-constructed belief system that guides life decisions and commitments.

Baxter Magolda (2001) asserted that to promote student self-authorship, educators must value students' expertise as well as their own and provide safe spaces for students to challenge authority. Doing so requires recognizing the complexity of knowledge, understanding how knowledge is socially constructed and intertwined with a student's sense of self, validating a student's capacity to learn and ways of knowing, situating learning in the experiences of the student, and engaging in mutual co-construction of knowledge.

Critics of Baxter Magolda have noted that although her models for epistemological reflection and self-authorship attend to gender differences, much of her body of work is still based upon a single sample of students from an elite institution, and her more recent studies using a subset of that sample include only White alumni. By contrast, recent research on self-authorship has focused on other populations, including students considered "high risk" (Pizzolato, 2003), first-generation college students (Jehangir, 2010), Latino and Latina students (Torres & Baxter Magolda, 2004; Torres & Hernandez, 2007), and students who self-identify as lesbian (Abes & Jones, 2004). It is interesting to note that some of these studies have found that life challenges and marginalization can lead to earlier development of self-authorship.

Conclusion

Within the context of these two brief modules it is impossible to provide a full introduction to student development theory as it applies to peer tutoring and mentoring. We chose the theoretical perspectives discussed in these modules because of how they have influenced our own work with students. Meanwhile we encourage professionals involved in the work of recruiting, selecting, training, and supervising peer tutors and mentors to explore student development theory in greater depth and apply it to their own work as well as to provide related training for their staff. Numerous texts (e.g., Evans, Forney, Guido, Patton, & Renn, 2010) are available that address theory as it relates to practice.

References

Abes, E. S., & Jones, S. R. (2004). Meaning-making capacity and the dynamics of lesbian college students' multiple dimensions of identity. *Journal of College Student Development, 45*, 612–632. doi:10.1353/csd.2004.0065

Baxter Magolda, M. B. (1992). *Knowing and reasoning in college: Gender-related patterns in students' intellectual development.* San Francisco, CA: Jossey-Bass.

Baxter Magolda, M. B. (2001). *Making their own way: Narratives for transforming higher education to promote self-development.* Sterling, VA: Stylus.

Baxter Magolda, M. B. (2004). Evolution of a constructivist conceptualization of epistemological reflection. *Educational Psychologist, 39*(1), 31–42. doi:10.1207/s15326985ep3901_4

Baxter Magolda, M. B. (2008). Three elements of self-authorship. *Journal of College Student Development, 49*, 269–284.

Chickering, A. W. (1969). *Education and identity.* San Francisco, CA: Jossey-Bass.

Cross, W. E., Jr. (1991). *Shades of Black: Diversity in African American identity.* Philadelphia, PA: Temple University Press.

Cross, W. E., Jr. (1995). The psychology of Nigrescence: Revising the Cross model. In J. G. Ponterotto, J. M. Casas, L. A. Suzuki, & C. M. Alexander (Eds.), *Handbook of multicultural counseling* (pp. 93–122). Thousand Oaks, CA: Sage.

D'Augelli, A. R (1994). Identity development and sexual orientation: Toward a model of lesbian, gay, and bisexual development. In E. J. Tickett, R. J. Watts, & D. Birman (Eds.), *Human diversity: Perspectives on people in context* (pp. 312–333). San Francisco, CA: Jossey Bass.

Evans, N. J., Forney, D. S., Guido, F. M., Patton, L. D., & Renn, K. A. (2010). *Student development in college: Theory, research, and practice* (2nd ed.). San Francisco, CA: Jossey-Bass.

Gilligan, C. (1977). In a different voice: Women's conceptions of self and morality. *Harvard Educational Review, 47,* 481–517.

Goodman, J., Schlossberg, N. K., & Anderson, M. L. (2006). *Counseling adults in transition* (3rd ed.). New York, NY: Springer.

Helms, J. E. (1995). An update of Helms's White and People of Color racial identity models. In J. G. Ponterotto, J. M. Casas, L. A. Suzuki, & C. M. Alexander (Eds.), *Handbook of multicultural counseling* (pp. 181–198). Thousand Oaks, CA: Sage.

Jehangir, R. (2010). *Higher education and first-generation students: Cultivating community, voice, and place for the new majority.* New York, NY: Palgrave Macmillan Press.

Josselson, R. (1987). *Finding herself: Pathways to identity development in women.* San Francisco, CA: Jossey-Bass.

Perry, W. G. (1968). *Forms of intellectual and ethical development in the college years: A scheme.* New York, NY: Holt, Reinhart, & Winston.

Phinney, J. S. (1990). Ethnic identity in adolescents and adults: Review of research. *Psychological Bulletin, 108,* 499–514. doi:10.1037/0033-2909.108.3.499

Pizzolato, J. E. (2003). Developing self-authorship: Exploring the experiences of high-risk college students. *Journal of College Student Development, 44,* 797–811. doi:10.1353/csd.2003.0074

Schlossberg, N. K., Waters, E. B., & Goodman, J. (1995). *Counseling adults in transition* (2nd ed.). New York, NY: Springer.

Torres, V., & Baxter Magolda, M. B. (2004). Reconstructing Latino identity: The influence of cognitive development on the ethnic identity process of Latino Students. *Journal of College Student Development, 45,* 333–347. doi:10.1353/csd.2004.0043

Torres, V., & Hernandez, E. (2007). The influence of ethnic identity on self-authorship: A longitudinal study of Latino/a college students. *Journal of College Student Development, 48,* 558–573. doi:10.1353/csd.2007.0057

Modeling Self-Regulation: Vygotsky and Bloom

Julianne Messia

If there is any agreement about characteristics of successful students, the concept of well-developed metacognition may be one for which there is consensus. Metacognition is knowing what and how one knows; it can take the form of critically thinking about one's knowledge and cognitive skills, or a deep self-awareness that enables one to acquire knowledge and solve problems. In other words, metacognition is a skill that informs and leads to self-regulated learning (Whitebread & Pino Pasternak, 2010). Many students have this skill but take its power and purpose for granted. Many tutors, often successful students themselves who have already mastered metacognition, unconsciously reflect their own metacognitive strategies onto a tutoring session when they ask, "What do you know about this topic already?" "Does this topic remind you of anything you've learned before?" "What do you do next? How do you know?" Verbalizing the metacognitive process between tutor and tutee or between mentor and mentee creates a shared conversation in self-regulated learning from which both parties can develop.

Peer tutoring and mentoring occur through social interactions between two or more people who likely have many shared characteristics, for example, the same school, the same instructors perhaps, the same major, and same generation or age. Often in this relationship the tutor or mentor is seen as the knowledge bearer (either for having advanced knowledge in a subject area or for having more experience at the institution), the keeper of knowledge and experience that the tutee or mentee needs. A fluid and symbiotic exchange develops between peer helper and student, stemming from a conversation guided by questions and modeling, and in which both parties are responsible for the progress of the conversation. In order to foster this conversation successfully, tutors and mentors should strive to create a solid foundation of trust, communication, and challenge.

Current metacognitive theory derives much from Vygotsky's (1978) learning theory and Bloom's (1956) taxonomy of educational objectives. Vygotsky emphasized the importance of the cultural relationship between teacher and student and thus provided theoretical guidance for the knowledge exchange that occurs within the context of tutoring and mentoring. Bloom edited a taxonomy of cognitive processes, one of the most accessible and widely recognized analyses of knowing how to know. This module provides an overview of these theories to inform tutor and mentor training in self-regulated processes.

Vygotsky

Lev Semenovich Vygotsky was a Russian psychologist at the turn of the 20th century who challenged the existing ideas of education and learning, particularly cognitive development theories such as Piaget's (Woolfolk, 2007). Vygotsky (1978) was one of the first to encourage and emphasize the incredible importance of student-teacher interactions, and although most of his work focused on primary and secondary education, it applies to later learning.

In one of Vygotsky's most well-known theories of education, the theory of proximal development, he suggested that students can develop their thinking best when challenged but also supported (Woolfolk, 2007). Higher education is often presented in large classrooms with more lecture than conversation and more challenge than support. Tutoring and mentoring at the college level are supportive interactions for students facing intellectual challenge. Tutors and mentors can act as intermediaries to learning.

Secondly, what people learn and how people learn it is intricately bound up in the culture of the learner (Vygotsky, 1978). Tutors and mentors play a role in teaching students by providing tools to the culture in which they find themselves, in this case the postsecondary academic institution. Indeed, Vygotsky is one of the first educational philosophers to emphasize culture as a tool for learning. Rather like travel guides and translators for travelers to different lands, tutors and mentors can model for students the practical and cognitive skills needed to succeed. They have the experience to say, "This is what you need to know. This is what's important. This citation method is preferred because. . . . This is what is going to help you learn the rest of it." As peers, it is their experience that imparts credibility, which reinforces again the expert-novice relationship between the students.

According to Vygotsky (1978), one of the main ways in which learning is regulated is through verbalizing inner or private speech (Woolfolk, 2007). Tutoring and mentoring interactions create an environment that externalizes both the peer helper's and the student's inner speech through their conversation. The tutor scaffolds the tutee through the thinking process by asking questions, the answers to which the tutee must verbalize in order to participate in the conversation (and therefore solve the problem, or improve the essay, for instance). Through this exchange, tutors learn tutees' cognitive patterns, background knowledge, and problem-solving methods, all which serve to inform tutors of better ways to proceed with tutoring. Tutees, in turn, learn and internalize tutors' cognitive skills and adopt them as their own, thereby developing higher-order thinking skills (Woolfolk, 2007).

Bloom

The concept of *higher order thinking skills* in education derived from use of Benjamin Bloom's taxonomy of educational objectives (Bloom's Taxonomy; Bloom, Engelhart, Frost, Hill, & Krathwohl, 1956), which was developed to help improve educators' instructional objectives (Woolfolk, 2007). Bloom was an educational researcher working in the U.S. who published extensive handbooks to guide the educational process (Bloom et al., 1956). Bloom's research led him to develop a classification system for psychomotor, cognitive, and affective educational objectives. The well-known Bloom's Taxonomy describes the hierarchy of the cognitive domain, but it should be noted that the three domains are interrelated. When viewed as a whole, Bloom's Taxonomy provides practical tools for engaging students in the learning process and modeling self-regulation. It has been persuasively argued that Bloom's Taxonomy is not in fact a theory (a predictive system) but a framework (merely describing characteristics) and that a new taxonomy independent of Bloom's can better model metacognitive processes (Marzano & Kendall, 2007), but Bloom's Taxonomy has nevertheless been widely popular.

The cognitive domain hierarchy describes the development that occurs as students continue through the educational process, acquiring and developing critical thinking skills along the way. Bloom's description of a cognitive taxonomy, often depicted as a set of stairs or a pyramid in which knowledge and cognition become increasingly complex as the levels build upon one another (Anderson & Sosniak, 1994), had six levels—*Knowledge, Comprehension, Application, Analysis, Evaluation,* and *Synthesis* (Bloom et al., 1956) now labeled with verbs to better reflect cognitive activity at each level (Anderson & Krathwohl, 2001). Just as Neptune and Pluto's orbits sometimes change places as further from the sun, *Evaluate* and *Create* (formerly *Synthesis*) are now considered interchangeable in their placement atop the pyramid. The essential definitions remain the same for each level. To illustrate, here is an example from college-level biology: *Remember* (Knowledge): What are mitochondria? *Understand:* What is the role of mitochondria within the human cell? *Apply:* What cell functions could not occur without mitochondria? *Analyze:* How are mitochondria different from other structures in the typical eukaryotic cell? How are they similar? *Evaluate:* What happens if mitochondria are removed from the cell? *Create:* Imagine if mitochondria could also do another function to increase efficiency and reduce waste. How would that change the essential components of the cell? Tutors and mentors can use Bloom's six categories of cognitive skill to think together through higher levels of cognition.

Bloom's taxonomies of the affective and psychomotor domains, though less widely known (Anderson & Krathwohl, 2001), attest to his holistic view of learning and teaching. The affective domain includes the emotional reactions that students can have to learning, eventually leading to personal commitment to the subject (Krathwohl, Bloom, & Masia, 1964). A tutor working with an emotionally distressed student or a student who has a negative reaction to a subject would do well to address the emotional issue first before attempting the cognitive issue. However, the affective domain also includes positive feelings and explains why students are more engaged with subjects they like; the stronger their commitment to the material, the more integrated it will become in their daily life and thinking (Woolfolk, 2007). Helping students to value their challenging coursework and to see applications to majors, careers, and lives is part of engaging the affective domain important to peer tutors and mentors.

Bloom's conclusions regarding the psychomotor domain provide the theoretical foundation for a tenet of many learning assistance programs: the student performs the work. When students write, talk, demonstrate, or play an instrument for themselves, their learning is more positively influenced than when they observe someone else's proficiency (Woolfolk, 2007). Furthermore, varying the learning activity to include physical movement (such as taking a short walk, or standing at the board, or stretching) can also allow new learning connections to form (Medina, 2008). Tutoring and mentoring sessions tend to be less formal than lecture classes, so in peer sessions students can be more physically engaged in learning. Learning center program guidelines that encourage students to do most of the work, most of the talking, and most of the demonstrating are appropriate applications of Bloom's conclusions regarding the employment of the psychomotor domain in learning. Recent research in neuroscience and cognitive psychology (Hannaford, 2005; Medina, 2008) sheds more light on the importance of movement and "doing" in learning, confirming Bloom's research about the importance of the psychomotor domain in subject mastery.

Using Ideas of Vygotsky and Bloom in Training

Tutors and mentors who have developed productive higher-order thinking skills may be completely unaware of how to foster them in others. Bloom's Taxonomy provides a concrete depiction of three domains of learning and an accessible vocabulary that tutors and mentors can use to understand their own metacognitive processes. Training in hands-off techniques, such as having students do the work and allowing student ideas to lead the session, supports Bloom's Taxonomy in action. The taxonomy also allows tutors and mentors to self-manage their own learning, assess their understanding, and seek applications of their knowledge. In turn, they are then able to assist students in thinking through their academic challenges.

Vygotsky believed that learning is guided by the conversation between teacher and student. Trainers can promote this interaction by training tutors and mentors in communication techniques such as questioning skills, active listening, the Socratic technique, and mirroring. Trainees who journal their own inner dialogue as they attempt a challenge or solve a problem are creating their own personal guidebook to metacognition. When trainers observe specific examples of effective dialogue in sessions with student clients, they can point out how speech matters.

Bloom's Taxonomy in both original and revised versions allows tutors and mentors to put into a kind of linear structure the steps toward critical thinking (Anderson & Krathwohl, 2001; Bloom et al., 1956). Indeed, many students seek out the assistance of a tutor or mentor precisely when they are unable to make the leap from application to analysis, or from analysis to evaluation, and have suffered academic consequences for it. With an awareness of Bloom's Taxonomy, tutors and mentors can gently reinforce higher-order thinking skills using rather concrete guidelines and examples. With an understanding of the importance of psychomotor and affective domains, tutors can think about how they can better construct an engaging learning partnership with their tutees.

Moreover, Bloom's Taxonomy offers guidance for trainers to structure training in ways that allow tutors and mentors to experience, categorize, and evaluate their own learning and growth. Trainers should consider using Bloom's own vocabularies to classify training activities by designating portions of the training as Remembering, Understanding, Applying, Analyzing, Evaluating, and Creating, for example; this creates the immersive atmosphere, provides relevant examples, and models the techniques clearly for students. Tutor or mentor demonstrations, group work, and creative projects that engage psychomotor and affective domains can also model for tutors and mentors the active learning environment they should create for their student clients.

References

Anderson, L. W., & Krathwohl, D. R. (Eds.). (2001). *A taxonomy for learning, teaching and assessing: A revision of Bloom's taxonomy of educational objectives* (Complete ed.). New York, NY: Longman.

Anderson, L. W., & Sosniak, L. A. (Eds.). (1994). *Bloom's taxonomy: A forty-year retrospective.* Ninety-third yearbook of the National Society for the Study of Education, Part 2. Chicago, IL: University of Chicago Press.

Bloom, B. S. (Ed.), Engelhart, M. D., Frost, E. J., Hill, W. H, & Krathwohl, D. R. (1956). *Taxonomy of educational objectives. Handbook I: Cognitive domain.* New York, NY: David McKay.

Hannaford, C. (2005). *Smart moves: Why learning is not all in your head.* Arlington, VA: Great River Books.

Krathwohl, D. R., Bloom, B. S., & Masia, B. B. (1964). *Taxonomy of educational objectives. Handbook II: Affective domain.* New York, NY: David McKay.

Marzano, R. J., & Kendall, J. S. (2007). *The new taxonomy of educational objectives* (2nd ed.). Thousand Oaks, CA: Corwin Press.

Medina, J. (2008). *Brain rules: 12 principles for surviving and thriving at work, home, and school.* Seattle, WA: Pear Press.

Vygotsky, L. S. (1978). *Mind and society: The development of higher mental processes.* Cambridge, MA: Harvard University Press.

Whitebread, D., & Pino Pasternak, D. (2010). Metacognition, self-regulation and meta-knowing. In K. Littleton, C. Wood, & J. Kleine Staarman (Eds.), *International handbook of psychology in education* (pp. 673–712). Bingley, United Kingdom: Emerald.

Woolfolk, A. (2007). *Educational psychology* (10th ed.). Needham Heights, MA: Allyn & Bacon.

Integrating Theory and Research With Practice

Martha E. Casazza

The most frequent approach to working with students comes from personal learning experiences—how tutors and mentors were taught and what worked for tutors and mentors in their own academic study. Tutors and mentors are tempted to assume that their own preferred teaching style will align with their students' learning styles. Such assumptions, however, can lead to less than successful outcomes. Rather than making assumptions, it is helpful to consider practice through the lenses of established theory and research. By reviewing and critically reflecting on research related to teaching and learning, tutors and mentors can expand their instructional toolboxes and begin to construct principles to guide their work.

One way to do this is by applying a model that integrates theory, research, principles, and practice (TRPP; Figure 1) and remembering that maximizing student potential is at the heart of what tutor and mentor trainers do (Silverman & Casazza, 2000).

Creating a Framework for Practice

The TRPP model is flexible in that practitioners can begin at any point (theory, research, practice, or principles) that makes the most sense for the instructional challenge they are facing. For instance, if a peer mentor is frustrated that a student is not taking responsibility for learning, the mentor could take a look at the *theory* put forward by Vygotsky (1965) suggesting that instructors conceptualize a zone of proximal development to frame their sessions together. This zone is the distance between what the student is able to achieve independently and what the student can do following the guidance of a mediator, in this case the mentor or tutor. This theory underscores the importance of knowing what the student is currently capable of doing and then constructing a program of guided practice, through collaboration, that leads to a new level of achievement that the student can control independently. Vygotsky's theory underscores the value of social constructivism through guided mediation, working with students to help them construct new ways of thinking, and approaching a difficult subject in ways that make students more successful.

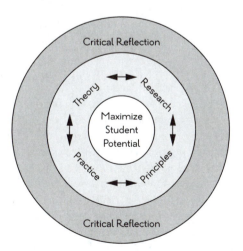

FIGURE 1   TRPP model demonstrating the TRPP framework for making connections between theory and practice and helping students maximize critical reflection potential. From *Learning and Development: Making Connections to Enhance Teaching*, by S. L. Silverman and M. E. Casazza, 2000, San Francisco, CA: Jossey–Bass. Copyright 2000 by John Wiley & Sons. Reprinted with permission.

Vygotsky's (1965) theoretical model was extended by Kegan (1994), who described an "evolutionary bridge" (p. 43). Applying this theory, the tutor would connect to the student's side of the bridge in order to understand how the student makes meaning, and then develop a plan of support that moves the student to more complex thinking. Gradually the tutor is able to release the responsibility for learning to the student. *Research* related to the significance of collaborative learning, schema theory, and social interaction corroborates this theoretical perspective and can be provided to tutors and mentors by their trainer.

By integrating a variety of theoretical perspectives and becoming familiar with related research, tutors and mentors can apply a more eclectic approach to their work, one that has been tested in a variety of settings. This eclectic approach is likely to lead to more successful learning outcomes because it addresses students' wide range of needs and learning styles.

By incorporating theory and research into practice and critically reflecting on the outcomes, tutors and mentors can also begin to develop guiding *principles*. These principles then provide a solid foundation not only for *practice* but for innovation. A peer tutor who is knowledgeable about Vygotsky's (1965) theory of proximal development and Kegan's (1994) theory of creating an evolutionary bridge will most likely take the time to understand a student's current level of understanding and also rely less on being "the expert" and more on the interaction that takes place between tutor and student. After *critical reflection*, an integral component of the TRPP model, the tutor may develop a new principle to guide his or her practice: responsibility for learning should be released gradually to the student who has requested assistance. (For more detailed information on the TRPP model, please see Silverman & Casazza, 2000, Chapter 4.)

Another example of integrating research with theory emanates from an oral history research project conducted by Casazza and Bauer (2006). This study tested assumptions related to the success of students considered underprepared for higher education. Students, practitioners, and pioneers in the field of developmental education were interviewed to look for patterns of variables related to student success. The researchers assumed that the variables would fall into different patterns depending on the category of the interviewees. Surprisingly, they did not; there was strong agreement across the interviewees on what contributes to the success of students who enter the higher education system underprepared. The most powerful finding from this research was the impact of believing in students and, based on that, helping them set high expectations and goals for themselves. Expectations and goals were frequently demonstrated through a relationship of "tough love" and challenging students to stretch their previous boundaries. High expectations were also manifested in time spent outside of structured settings and simply listening to their concerns and helping them identify resources. Students are not always ready to accept this approach from someone in a traditional educational setting; in their experience, the system has too often failed them and failed to believe in them. Consequently they frequently come to tutors and mentors with low self-esteem and expectations of failure. Participants in the Casazza and Bauer (2006) study reported on the transformational effects of individual instructors who cared about students and demanded the best from them.

Integrating this recent oral history research with classic theories exemplifies how the TRPP model can strengthen practice. Bandura's (1977) work on self-efficacy described the impact of one's perceived ability to be successful in a particular situation. Students who have experienced multiple failures begin to lower their expectations for success; they believe they are not capable of succeeding and consequently put forth less effort. In addition, these students are likely to give up completely, develop avoidance behavior, and focus primarily on what they perceive to be their own deficiencies (Bandura, 1986).

Related to self-efficacy are theories that student motivation can be increased by setting the right kinds of goals. Several theorists are known for their work on goals (Maehr & Pintrich, 1995; Schunk, 1991; Weinstein & Meyer, 1986). Goal setting has been related to positive self-efficacy (van Etten, Pressley, & Freebern, 1998), which in turn leads to greater effort and persistence. It is important to note that goal setting alone does not necessarily lead to success; the type of goal is significant, whether a mastery goal (oriented toward self-improvement) or performance goal (oriented toward comparing or competing with others). Maehr and Anderman (1993) concluded that performance goals, directed toward short-cuts and quick payoffs, are less effective than mastery goals, including comprehension monitoring and synthesis, which lead to more engagement in the actual learning process, at least in early adolescence (Maehr & Pintrich, 1995).

Reflecting on Practice

Reviewing relevant research and theory provides a useful framework for beginning a process of critical reflection on current practice. Critical reflection can lead to meaningful change, but only when tutors, mentors, and their trainers are ready to challenge long-held assumptions and question their instructional approaches. Providing training and critical reflection opportunities forces tutors and mentors to leave the comfort zone of their own experiences and try new approaches. After they have made connections among theory, research, and their practice, they begin to develop principles that serve as a framework for future innovation.

References

Bandura, A. (1977). Self-efficacy: Toward a unifying theory of behavior change. *Psychological Review, 84,* 191–215. doi:10.1037/0033-295X.84.2.191

Bandura, A. (1986). *Social foundations of thought and action: A social cognitive theory.* Englewood Cliffs, NJ: Prentice Hall.

Casazza, M. E., & Bauer, L. (2006). *Access, opportunity and success: Keeping the promise of higher education.* Westport, CT: Praeger.

Kegan, R. (1994). *In over our heads: The mental demands of modern life.* Cambridge, MA: Harvard University Press.

Maehr, M. L., & Anderman, E. M. (1993). Reinventing schools for early adolescents. *Elementary School Journal, 93,* 593–610. doi:10.1086/461742

Maehr, M. L., & Pintrich, P. R. (1995). Culture, motivation, and achievement. In M. L. Maehr & P. R. Pintrich (Eds.), *Advances in motivation and achievement* (Vol. 9, pp. 159–181). Greenwich, CT: JAI Press.

Schunk, D. H. (1991). Goal setting and self-evaluation: A social cognitive perspective on self-regulation. In M. L. Maehr & P. R. Pintrich (Eds.), *Advances in motivation and achievement* (Vol. 7, pp. 85–113). Greenwich, CT: JAI Press.

Silverman, S. L., & Casazza, M. E. (2000). *Learning and development: Making connections to enhance teaching.* San Francisco, CA: Jossey-Bass.

van Etten, S., Pressley, M., & Freebern, G. (1998). An interview study of college freshmen's beliefs about their academic motivation. *European Journal of Psychology of Education, 13,* 105–130. doi:10.1007/BF03172816

Vygotsky, L. S. (1965). *Thought and language.* New York, NY: Wiley.

Weinstein, C. E., & Meyer, R. E. (1986). The teaching of learning strategies. In M. C. Wittrock (Ed.), *Handbook of research on teaching* (3rd ed., pp. 315–327). New York, NY: Macmillan.

Strategic Learning: Helping Students Become More Active Participants in Their Learning

Claire Ellen Weinstein, Taylor W. Acee, JaeHak Jung, Jaimie M. Krause, Breana Sylvester Dacy, and Jennifer Kay Leach

Strategic learning is the outcome of students' mindfully and intentionally using knowledge, strategies, and skills to help improve and optimize their learning so they can reach both their short-term and long-term learning goals. Strategic learners are capable of taking more responsibility for their learning because they have relevant prior knowledge, behaviors, cognitive and metacognitive strategies and skills, motivation, and self-regulation needed to manage academic learning. It is important for tutors, mentors, and educational coaches to negotiate the responsibility for helping students learn more effectively and efficiently. Being strategic learners not only aids students in achieving in all types of higher education settings, it also helps these students with life-long learning and the school-to-work transition.

The Model of Strategic Learning

An organizational summary of strategic learning variables and processes is presented in Weinstein's Model of Strategic Learning (Weinstein, Acee, & Jung, 2010; see Appendix). This model places learners and all of their individual differences at the center of strategic learning. Students' prior knowledge, misconceptions, self-concept as learners, self-esteem as learners, personal responsibilities, work responsibilities, expectations of what college will be like for them, and expectations for success are just some of the individual differences students bring with them to college. All of these individual variables have the potential to enhance or interfere with students' reaching their short-term and long-term learning goals; however, although we cannot change the past for students, we can help them to enrich their future. The points of the triangle surrounding the learner are the three major components of strategic learning that are or can be under the learner's control: skill, will and self-regulation (Weinstein, Husman, & Dierking, 2000).

SKILL

Skill refers to what learners need to know about to help them become more strategic learners. It also includes the strategies they need to know how to use in order to learn information more effectively and efficiently. For example, it is important for students not only to know about a variety of cognitive learning strategies but also how to use them. Telling students that creating and answering possible test questions for an upcoming exam is an excellent suggestion but is helpful only if these students know how to create appropriate test questions. Similarly, encouraging students to search for main ideas is important, but merely flipping through students' used textbooks and analyzing their underlining and highlighting reveals that many students have little skill at selecting main ideas and distinguishing them from supportive details or didactic explanations. A review of research on test preparation suggested that college students generally employ "surface-level processing strategies aimed at basic memory or comprehension of the text (e.g., re-reading and rehearsing) and use relatively few deep-processing strategies aimed at transformation or application of information (e.g., generating examples, making connections with prior knowledge" (Broekkamp & Van Hout-Wolters, 2007).

WILL

Will primarily relates to students' motivation, goals, beliefs, attitudes, and emotions about learning. Even after students know about different learning strategies and skills and know how to use them, students also have to want to use them. Few people follow the guidance of the American Dental Association to brush teeth five times a day, though they know brushing often is beneficial and know how to brush their teeth; despite having the knowledge and skills required, most individuals are not motivated enough to brush this frequently. In a similar manner, many students know about or have developed skills and strategies they could use to enhance their studying and learning but do not use these strategies because they are not motivated to use them or do not believe the strategies will work for them. Research has shown that students' motivational beliefs, attitudes, and goals are related to their use of learning strategies (Pintrich & De Groot, 1990; Pintrich & Schunk, 2002).

SELF-REGULATION

The elements in the self-regulation component of the model help students to monitor and manage their use of the skill and will elements. This management function can take place on a macro, or overall, level, such as using time management across the academic term and applying a systematic approach to accomplishing academic tasks. It can also take place on a micro, or more immediate, level, such as maintaining concentration while studying or monitoring understanding while reading a textbook. Other important elements include managing stress by learning to cope with academic worry and anxiety, and creating useful goals and sub-goals for completing both short-term and long-term academic tasks (Boekaerts, Pintrich, & Zeidner, 2000; Schunk & Zimmerman, 2007).

ACADEMIC ENVIRONMENT

The elements in the model outside the rectangle are part of the academic environment. Unlike skill, will, and self-regulation, these environmental variables are not under the direct control of learners but are useful for learners to know about. Peer tutors and mentors can help students to gain the environmental knowledge they need to become more strategic in their studying and learning for a given course or learning task. One element of the academic environment includes knowing about task requirements and how to prepare for and complete the current learning activity (e.g., solving math problems in class), assignment (e.g., writing a paper for biology class), or test (e.g., short-answer or essay exam). If students do not understand what is required to complete a course assignment successfully, how will they know how to accomplish it? How will they know when they have completed the assignment? Understanding the requirements of academic tasks can help students more effectively and efficiently reach their learning goals. The element at the bottom of the model is knowledge of available resources. Help-seeking is an important self-regulation element, but students need to know what types of help are available for them before they can seek help. Is a learning or tutoring center available on campus? If so, what types of assistance are offered? What is the process for setting up meetings with a professional or peer? Social support, another element of the academic environment, is also important to develop so that students feel more welcomed by and engaged with their institutions and with other students. The final element, understanding instructors' beliefs and expectations, helps students to know what is appropriate behavior in each course and what the instructor expects from them as members of the class (Weinstein, Husman, & Dierking, 2000; Weinstein, Tomberlin, Julie, & Kim, 2004).

Strategic learning results from using skill, will, and self-regulation together. Using strategies in only one or two areas is not sufficient. Strategic learning assessments like the *Learning and Study Strategies Inventory* (Weinstein, Schulte, & Palmer, 2002), can help students and educators identify and capitalize on students' strengths and identify and target areas for improvement. The remainder of this module will focus on the learning strategies element of the Skill component, which is a foundational element of strategic learning.

Cognitive Learning Strategies

Cognitive learning strategies help students to build bridges between what they already know or have experienced and the material they are trying to learn. It is this active cognitive processing that is the key to the usefulness of these strategies. Active cognitive processing helps students generate new knowledge and relate it to relevant prior knowledge so it is easier to incorporate into memory and easier to recall when new knowledge needs to be used in higher-order operations such as analysis, synthesis and problem solving (Weinstein & Mayer, 1986).

REHEARSAL STRATEGIES

There are many different types of cognitive learning strategies. At the lowest level are rehearsal strategies, which are surface-level strategies used for simple memorization. An example of a rehearsal strategy is using Roy G. Biv to remember the colors of the visual light spectrum. Although these strategies are useful for remembering bits of information, there is a limit to their usefulness for building knowledge and skills (Ausubel, 1963; Weinstein & Mayer, 1986).

ELABORATION STRATEGIES

Deep-level elaboration strategies are used to understand, learn, and remember new information so that it becomes part of the learner's knowledge base, accessible for future learning or application (Biggs & Moore, 1993; Weinstein et al., 2000; Weinstein & Mayer, 1986). Elaboration learning strategies build meaningful relationships within new ideas students are trying to learn and between this new information and what students already know or have experienced. The simplest level of elaboration is paraphrasing and summarizing. Both of these strategies require some type of mindful transformation of the material to be learned. More advanced forms of elaboration require a greater amount of processing but are also more useful for meaningful, longer-term learning. These include using and applying the new information, concepts, or principles; perspective-taking; generating and answering questions about the material; using visualization; teaching the material to someone else; and using critical and analytical thinking.

ORGANIZATION STRATEGIES

Organization strategies are also deep-level strategies used to organize information into outlines, categories, hierarchies, sequential tree diagrams, or other visual forms so that it can be meaningfully represented, analyzed, and learned (Weinstein, Tomberlin, Julie, & Kim, 2004). Venn diagrams and concept maps, for example, can help learners analyze concepts for similarities and differences (Hilbert & Renkl, 2008; Zahner & Corter, 2010). Like elaboration strategies, organization strategies require deep-level processing. It is this active processing that makes them effective.

Strategic learning requires students to understand and be able to use and modify elements from all three components of the Model of Strategic Learning. The interactions among the components' elements result in effective and efficient learning. Peer tutors and mentors who understand the Model of Strategic Learning can use their knowledge to help students optimize their learning.

References

Ausubel, D. P. (1963). *The psychology of meaningful verbal learning*. New York, NY: Grune & Stratton.

Biggs, J. B., & Moore, P. J. (1993). *The process of learning* (3rd ed.). Sydney, Australia: Prentice Hall Australia.

Boekaerts, M., Pintrich, P. R., & Zeidner, M. (Eds.). (2000). *Handbook of self-regulation.* San Diego, CA: Academic Press.

Broekkamp, H., & Van Hout-Wolters, B. H. A. M. (2007). Students' adaptation of study strategies when preparing for classroom tests. *Educational Psychology Review, 19,* 401–428.

Hilbert, T. S., & Renkl, R. (2008). Concept mapping as a follow-up strategy to learning from texts: What characterizes good and poor mappers? *Instructional Science: An International Journal of the Learning Sciences, 36,* 53–73.

Pintrich, P. R., & De Groot, E. V. (1990). Motivation and self-regulated learning components of classroom academic performance. *Journal of Educational Psychology, 82,* 32–40.

Pintrich, P. R., & Schunk, D. H. (2002). *Motivation in education: Theory, research, and applications.* Upper Saddle River, NJ: Prentice Hall.

Schunk, D. H., & Zimmerman, B. J. (Eds.). (2007). *Motivation and self-regulated learning: Theory, research and application.* Mahwah, NJ: Erlbaum.

Weinstein, C. E., Acee, T. W., & Jung, J. H. (2010). Learning strategies. In B. McGaw, P. L. Peterson, & E. Baker (Eds.), *International encyclopedia of education* (3rd ed., pp. 323–329). New York, NY: Elsevier.

Weinstein, C. E., Husman, J., & Dierking, D. R. (2000). Self-regulation interventions with a focus on learning strategies. In M. Boekaerts, P. R. Pintrich, & M. Zeidner (Eds.), *Handbook of self-regulation* (pp. 727–747). San Diego, CA: Academic Press.

Weinstein, C. E., & Mayer, R. E. (1986). The teaching of learning strategies. In M. C. Wittrock (Ed.), *Handbook of research on teaching* (3rd ed., pp. 315–327). New York, NY: Macmillan.

Weinstein, C. E., Schulte, A., & Palmer, D. R. (2002). *The learning and study strategies inventory* (2nd ed.). Clearwater, FL: H & H.

Weinstein, C. E., Tomberlin, T. L., Julie, A. L., & Kim, J. (2004). Helping students to become strategic learners: The roles of assessment, teachers, instruction, and students. In J. Ee, A. Chang, & O. Tan (Eds.), *Thinking about thinking: What educators need to know* (pp. 282–310). Singapore, China: McGraw-Hill.

Zahner, D., & Corter, J. E. (2010). The process of probability problem solving: Use of external visual representations. *Mathematical Thinking & Learning, 12*(2), 177–204.

Appendix

- - - - - THE MODEL OF STRATEGIC LEARNING

The following diagram for the Model of Strategic Learning (MSL) is from Weinstein, C. E., Acee, T. W., & Jung, J. H. (2010). Learning strategies. In B. McGaw, P. L. Peterson, & E. Baker (Eds.), *International Encyclopedia of Education* (3rd ed., pp. 323–329). New York, NY: Elsevier. Copyright 2006 by Claire Ellen Weinstein. Reprinted with permission.

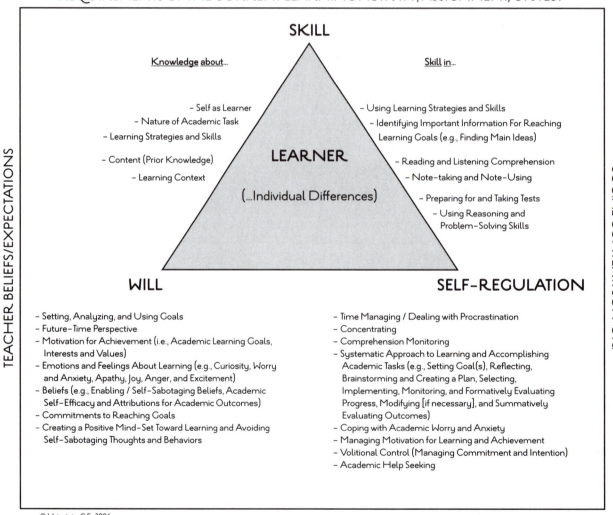

THE MODEL OF STRATEGIC LEARNING

REQUIREMENTS OF THE CURRENT LEARNING ACTIVITY, ASSIGNMENT, OR TEST

SKILL

Knowledge about…
– Self as Learner
– Nature of Academic Task
– Learning Strategies and Skills
– Content (Prior Knowledge)
– Learning Context

Skill in…
– Using Learning Strategies and Skills
– Identifying Important Information For Reaching Learning Goals (e.g., Finding Main Ideas)
– Reading and Listening Comprehension
– Note-taking and Note-Using
– Preparing for and Taking Tests
– Using Reasoning and Problem-Solving Skills

LEARNER
(…Individual Differences)

TEACHER BELIEFS/EXPECTATIONS

SOCIAL CONTEXT/SUPPORT

WILL

SELF-REGULATION

– Setting, Analyzing, and Using Goals
– Future-Time Perspective
– Motivation for Achievement (i.e., Academic Learning Goals, Interests and Values)
– Emotions and Feelings About Learning (e.g., Curiosity, Worry and Anxiety, Apathy, Joy, Anger, and Excitement)
– Beliefs (e.g., Enabling / Self-Sabotaging Beliefs, Academic Self-Efficacy and Attributions for Academic Outcomes)
– Commitments to Reaching Goals
– Creating a Positive Mind-Set Toward Learning and Avoiding Self-Sabotaging Thoughts and Behaviors

– Time Managing / Dealing with Procrastination
– Concentrating
– Comprehension Monitoring
– Systematic Approach to Learning and Accomplishing Academic Tasks (e.g., Setting Goal(s), Reflecting, Brainstorming and Creating a Plan, Selecting, Implementing, Monitoring, and Formatively Evaluating Progress, Modifying [if necessary], and Summatively Evaluating Outcomes)
– Coping with Academic Worry and Anxiety
– Managing Motivation for Learning and Achievement
– Volitional Control (Managing Commitment and Intention)
– Academic Help Seeking

© Weinstein, C.E., 2006

AVAILABLE RESOURCES

Motivational Perspectives on Student Learning

Taylor W. Acee, Claire Ellen Weinstein, Breana Sylvester Dacy, Cheon-woo Han, and Daniel A. Clark

Motivation is a critical component of strategic learning. (See the previous module on strategic learning.) Regardless of differences in students' unique learning strengths and weaknesses, in order to succeed academically, all students must be motivated to do the work that success requires. It is important that tutors, mentors, and educational coaches understand differences in their students' motivation and, when possible, take action to help motivate their students to succeed as well as help students generate their own internal motivation. Unfortunately there is no universally accepted theoretical perspective or set of variables that can be used to explain all facets of students' academic motivation. Instead there are different and often overlapping theories of motivation. In this module we will highlight major ideas from three academic-achievement motivation theories that are particularly relevant for tutoring, mentoring, and educational coaching: expectancy-value, attribution, and goal orientation. (For a more comprehensive review of motivation theories in education, see Schunk, Pintrich, and Meece, 2007).

Motivation

According to Pintrich and Schunk (2002), "Motivation is the process whereby goal-directed activity is instigated and sustained" (p. 5). In the most basic sense, academic motivation refers to students' choices (i.e., decisions about which academic tasks to engage in and how to approach them), effort (the amount of time and energy devoted to an academic task), and persistence (sustained engagement in academic activities, especially in the face of difficulty) in regard to a broad range of academic tasks. However, because motivation is a process that is directly dependent on students' values, beliefs, and goals, these variables are also included in definitions of motivation (Eccles & Wigfield, 2002). For example, students who value learning about politics and set goals to keep up with local politics are more likely to spend time and energy reading and seeking information about local politics compared to students who do not share this value and goal. In other words, students' values and beliefs can directly influence their choices, effort, and persistence. Contemporary motivation researchers have largely focused on students' values, beliefs, and goals in order to predict and explain differences in students' motivation and academic achievement.

Expectancy-Value Theory

Research on expectancy-value theory suggests that individuals are motivated towards tasks that they perceive as being important and expect they can successfully accomplish (Eccles et al., 1983; Wigfield & Eccles, 2000). Believing that success on a task is possible is necessary for motivation. For example, if someone were asked to walk up the side of a wall, would he or she try? Of course not, because it is impossible. That is, one's expectation for success is zero. Many students believe that it is impossible to complete some of their academic tasks, for example that they cannot do math. Their confidence in their capabilities to succeed is so low that to them trying would be as foolish as attempting to walk up a wall. Research on students in K-12 and postsecondary educational settings has consistently shown that students' value perceptions and expectations for success are positively related to academic motivation and achievement (Eccles & Wigfield, 2002; Wigfield & Eccles, 2000).

Students' expectation for success on a particular task is strongly influenced by their past successes and failures on similar tasks (Bandura, 1997). Successes typically raise students' confidence, whereas failures lower it. Therefore, it is important to help students develop a history of successes, beginning with tasks that are easy for them and then gradually increasing the difficulty as they gain expertise and confidence through feedback and successful performance.

The value students place on a task also has a strong effect on their decision to expend time and energy on the task (Wigfield & Eccles, 2000). For example, a college student who enjoys writing and believes that becoming a better writer is important for his or her future career would be more likely to choose writing-based courses and try harder in these courses compared to a student who does not value writing. Students value and devalue academic tasks for different reasons, and it is important to gain a general understanding of students' systems of valuing in order to help them generate motivation. Students may value or devalue a task because of how enjoyable and interesting it is to them, how useful it is in helping them achieve their goals, and how coherent the task is with their identity (Eccles & Wigfield, 2002).

Several strategies have been suggested to help students to value academic tasks (Brophy, 1999; Wolters, 2003). Tutors, mentors, and academic coaches can relate the task to students' interests; make studying into a game; create study groups for students who enjoy working with others; explain to students why learning information or developing a skill is important; have students consider how learning in a particular area is important for achieving their future goals (e.g., career goals); and expose students to role models who value learning.

Attributions

Attributions refer to how people explain the causes of events, behaviors, and outcomes. In research on academic-achievement motivation, attributions tend to refer more specifically to students' beliefs about the causes of their successes and failures on academic tasks (Weiner, 1985, 2000). One student who fails a writing assignment may attribute her lack of success to the difficulty of the assignment and having a bad instructor; another student in the same situation may attribute his failure on the assignment to his lack of effort and not setting up a meeting with his instructor to get clarity on the assignment. Attributions can be categorized as stable or unstable, internal or external, and controllable or uncontrollable (Weiner, 1985, 2000). One dimension that is particularly important to discuss here is controllability. Researchers have discovered that students who tend to attribute their successes and failures to factors that are under their control, such as effort, use of learning strategies, and help seeking, tend to be more motivated, while students who focus on factors that are not controllable, such as innate ability (talent), luck, task difficulty, and the quality of their instructor, tend to be less motivated. (For a more detailed overview of theory and research on the antecedents and consequences of attributions, see Weiner, 1985, 2000). If students believe that the causes of their successes and failures on academic tasks are beyond their control, then they may believe there is no point in trying to improve. Students who believe that they cannot improve their learning are more likely to feel a sense of helplessness; students who believe that they can improve their own learning and achievement, on the other hand, are more likely to learn from their mistakes, identify more effective and efficient methods for learning, and actively generate motivation. In sum, it is important to help students realize that they have control over their learning and achievement, and help them to focus on controllable factors and not dwell on factors that are beyond their control.

Research has shown that attributional retraining programs and interventions can help modify students' attributions and lead to increases in their motivation and performance (Haynes, Ruthig, Perry, Stupnisky, & Hall, 2006; Perry, Hechter, Menec, & Weinberg, 1993). Educators can help students focus on controllable causes of their successes and failures by providing them with repeated attributional feedback that is focused not on innate ability but on factors such as effort and use of strategies (Mueller & Dweck, 1998). For instance, after students succeed on a task, tutors can tell them they did well because of their hard work; or, after students perform poorly, tutors can show them how their study strategies could be improved to increase their chances of success the next time. It is also important to avoid falling into the common pattern of attributing students' performance to a disposition or trait (e.g., innate ability, talent) or consoling them by suggesting that they failed because of bad luck or test difficulty. Another strategy to help students modify their attribution beliefs after an assignment or test is to have students reflect about factors that influenced their performance and analyze their level of effort and the effectiveness of their study methods.

Goal Orientation

Students have different goals and reasons for completing their coursework. Achievement goal orientation researchers have identified three goal orientations that are particularly important for explaining differences in students' learning and motivation: mastery goals, performance-approach goals, and performance-avoidance goals (Elliot, 1999). Mastery goals are oriented towards mastering course content, gaining knowledge, developing skills, and generating meaningful learning. For example, students who complete their biology homework because they want to learn about biology and gain laboratory research skills have mastery goals. Students may also be focused on showing others that they are smart and competent. These are performance-approach goals. For example, students may work hard to get good grades in their algebra courses not because they want to learn algebra but because they want to demonstrate to instructors, parents, friends, and classmates that they are competent. Students with performance-avoidance goals try to avoid looking stupid or appearing incompetent in the eyes of others. For example, students may avoid class participation and working in study groups because they do not want others to think they are incompetent.

Research has shown that both mastery goals and performance-approach goals can help to motivate students and increase their achievement; however, mastery goals are different from performance-approach goals in that mastery goals tend to be positively associated with other important outcomes such as intrinsic (internal) motivation, continued interest, and retention of information studied (Harackiewicz, Barron, Pintrich, Elliot, & Thrash, 2002). Performance-avoidance goals have consistently been found to be negatively related to student motivation, learning, and achievement.

Students' beliefs about whether intelligence is fixed or malleable are also thought to influence students' choice of goals (Dweck & Leggett, 1988). When students believe that they can modify their intelligence through learning and skill development, they are more inclined to form mastery goals. Students who instead believe that their intelligence is fixed and cannot be changed tend to view their performance on tasks as a way to validate their intelligence to themselves and others.

Helping students to view intelligence as something that is modifiable and not fixed is one way to help students to adopt more mastery goals and increase their academic performance (Blackwell, Trzesniewsk, & Dweck, 2007). Students' goal orientations can also be influenced by the goals and expectations conveyed to them on assignments and by others (e.g., teachers, tutors, mentors, coaches, and parents). Other strategies have been suggested to help students adopt more mastery goals. For example, tutors and mentors can convey mastery goals to students; they can express expectations that students should learn meaningfully and retain course content, as opposed to conveying to them that mere completion of a task or earning a good grade is sufficient. Tutors and mentors can introduce assignments with a mastery orientation; they can tell students that the purpose of an assignment is to "learn the following five concepts," not to "complete the following five problems." Tutors and mentors can also help students set goals focused on the methods and strategies they will use to learn information rather than goals focused on the outcomes they want to achieve. Finally, tutors and mentors can help students reflect on and evaluate their learning progress.

Conclusion

Motivation is a complex process because it is affected by and interacts with so many different factors. Students have various values, beliefs, and goals that interact to influence motivation in vastly different ways. At any given moment, students may have a variety of ideas about how to spend their time and energy. Consequently, motivation is often a peace treaty among warring factions.

Given the importance of education to students' future quality of life, economic affluence, and general sense of happiness, it is important to help students make wise choices about how they spend their time and energy during college. Gaining an understanding of the factors that affect students' motivation and practical strategies to influence motivation is an important part of becoming a more effective tutor or mentor.

References

Bandura, A. (1997). *Self-efficacy: The exercise of control.* New York, NY: W. H. Freeman.

Blackwell, L. S., Trzesniewsk, K. H., & Dweck, C. S. (2007). Implicit theories of intelligence predict achievement across an adolescent transition: A longitudinal study and an intervention. *Child Development, 78*(1), 246–263. Retrieved from http://www.wiley.com/bw/journal .asp?ref=0009-3920&site=1

Brophy, J. (1999). Toward a model of the value aspects of motivation in education: Developing appreciation for particular learning domains and activities. *Educational Psychologist, 34*(2), 75–85. Retrieved from http://www.unco.edu/cebs/psychology/kevinpugh/motivation_project/ resources/brophy99.pdf

Dweck, C. S., & Leggett, E. L. (1988). A social-cognitive approach to motivation and personality. *Psychological Review, 95*(2), 256–273. Retrieved from http://www.apa.org/pubs/journals/rev/

Eccles, J. S., Adler, T. F., Futterman, R., Goff, S. B., Kaczala, C. M., Meece, J. L., & Midgley, C. (1983). Expectancies, values, and academic behaviors. In J. T. Spence (Ed.), *Achievement and achievement motivation* (pp. 75–146). San Francisco, CA: W. H. Freeman.

Eccles, J. S., & Wigfield, A. (2002). Motivational beliefs, values and goals. *Annual Review of Psychology, 53*, 109–132. Retrieved from http://arjournals.annualreviews.org/loi/psych

Elliot, A. J. (1999). Approach and avoidance motivation and achievement goals. *Educational Psychologist, 34*(3), 169–189. Retrieved from http://www.psych.rochester.edu/research/apav/ publications/documents/1999_Elliot_Approachandavoidancemotivationandachievement goals.pdf

Harackiewicz, J. M., Barron, K. E., Pintrich, P. R., Elliot, A. J., & Thrash, T. M. (2002). Revision of achievement goal theory: Necessary and illuminating. *Journal of Educational Psychology, 94*(3), 638–645. doi:10.1037//0022-0663.94.3.638

Haynes, T. L., Ruthig, J. C., Perry, R. P., Stupnisky, R. H., & Hall, N. C. (2006). Reducing the academic risks of over-optimism: The longitudinal effects of attributional retraining on cognition and achievement. *Research in Higher Education, 47*, 755–779. doi:10.1007/s11162-006-9014-7

Mueller, C. M., & Dweck, C. S. (1998). Praise for intelligence can undermine children's motivation and performance. *Journal of Personality and Social Psychology, 75*(1), 33–52. Retrieved from http://www.apa.org/pubs/journals/psp/

Perry, R. P., Hechter, F. J., Menec, V. H., & Weinberg, L. E. (1993). Enhancing achievement motivation and performance in college students: An attributional retraining perspective. *Research in Higher Education, 34*, 687–723. Retrieved from http://www.springerlink.com/content/101599/

Pintrich, P. R., & Schunk, D. H. (2002). *Motivation in education: Theory, research, and applications.* Upper Saddle River, NJ: Prentice Hall.

Schunk, D. H., Pintrich, P. R., & Meece, J. (2007). *Motivation in education: Theory, research, and applications* (3rd ed.). Upper Saddle River, NJ: Prentice Hall.

Weiner, B. (1985). An attributional theory of achievement motivation and emotion. *Psychological Review, 92*(4), 548–573. Retrieved from http://www.apa.org/pubs/journals/rev/

Weiner, B. (2000). Intrapersonal and interpersonal theories of motivation from an attributional perspective. *Educational Psychology Review, 12*, 1–14. Retrieved from http://www.springer.com/ psychology/journal/10648

Wigfield, A., & Eccles, J. S. (2000). Expectancy-value theory of achievement motivation. *Contemporary Educational Psychology, 25*(1), 68–81. doi:10.1006/ceps.1999.1015

Wolters, C. A. (2003). Regulation of motivation: Evaluating an underemphasized aspect of self-regulated learning. *Educational Psychologist, 38*(4), 189–205. Retrieved from http://faculty.coe .uh.edu/cwolters/docs/wolters(2003)-edpsych.pdf

Self-Regulated Learning: Helping Students Manage Their Own Learning

Taylor W. Acee, Claire Ellen Weinstein, Michelle E. Jordan, Jeremy K. Dearman, and Carlton J. Fong

Self-regulation is a key component of strategic learning. (See the theory module on strategic learning earlier in this chapter.) Self-regulation refers to how individuals intentionally monitor, manage, and modify approaches to learning and includes management of motivation, perceived stress and negative emotions about learning, use of learning strategies and other skills, and systematic and mindful planning to reach learning goals (Pintrich, 2000, 2004; Weinstein, Husman, & Dierking, 2000; Zimmerman, 2000). The more students know about self-regulation skills and strategies and the more they can use self-management strategies effectively, the more successful they will be in college, work, and other learning situations (Clearly & Zimmerman, 2001; Lynch, 2006; Metallidou & Vlachou, 2007; Pintrich & Degroot, 1990; Zimmerman, Bandura, & Martinez-Pons, 1992).

Self-regulation is the management system that performs the executive functions of thoughts, emotions, and behaviors over which students have some level of control. Self-regulation is involved in inhibiting certain thoughts and emotions, for instance when coping with anxiety or anger. It is involved in setting goals, making plans, managing time, and deciding which learning strategies to use on which academic tasks. Self-regulation helps students generate positive affect and motivation and maintain their focus on academic tasks and goals. These self-management processes are fundamental to monitoring, analyzing, and regulating one's own cognition, motivation, affect, emotion, and behavior and thus are critical for academic success.

In order to help students take control of and successfully manage their own learning, tutors, mentors, and educational coaches should learn and help students learn a systematic approach to studying (Weinstein et al., 2000). There are a number of theoretical and applied models of self-regulated learning (Boekaerts, Pintrich, & Zeidner, 2000; Pintrich, 2000, 2004; Schunk, Pintrich, & Meece, 2007; Weinstein et al., 2000; Zimmerman, 2000). These models use different terminology and draw on different perspectives; however, despite their differences, theoretical and applied models of self-regulation tend to converge around core processes that actively regulate learning. Central to these models are processes involved in setting, pursuing, and evaluating learning and achievement goals.

For our discussion of these core self-regulatory processes we use the conceptual framework and terminology of Zimmerman's (2000) model. There are other conceptual frameworks for aspects of self-regulation, but this model is used most often in the research and applied work for college student learning because of its general nature, cyclic approach, and relationships to models of strategic learning. According to this model, self-regulation involves three cyclical phases: forethought, performance or volitional control, and self-reflection. Forethought involves setting useful learning goals and planning how to reach these goals strategically. The performance or volitional control phase involves a continuing commitment to these goals by implementing the plans generated in the forethought phase and monitoring how well the plan is being implemented. Self-evaluation involves evaluating how much progress has been made toward reaching one's goal and reflecting on successes and failures in order to inform future goal-setting, planning, and implementation.

To illustrate, consider the following hypothetical scenario of a student cycling through the three self-regulatory phases. During the forethought phase, a student sets a goal to earn at least a B on an upcoming algebra test. Then the student creates a strategic plan to study for 3 hours on 3 different days for 2 weeks and to use four different learning strategies (i.e., make flash cards, summarize the main ideas of each chapter, complete all practice problems, and explain the material to a study partner). During the performance or volitional phase, the student implements the plan and through monitoring realizes that the plan needs to be modified because 9 hours a week is not enough time to learn all of the material. Despite modifying the plan to increase study time, the student earns a C. In the self-reflection phase, the student considers issues that led to falling short of getting a B and realizes that visiting the instructor during office hours or seeing a tutor to get help would have been more strategic and that making flash cards was a waste of time. The student then uses this information when creating a study plan for the next math exam by setting up an appointment with a tutor and creating an outline of the material instead of making flash cards. This last part of the scenario illustrates the cyclical nature of self-regulated learning because what was learned in the self-reflection phase was used to inform the forethought phase for the next exam.

Forethought Phase

The forethought phase of self-regulated learning involves setting academic goals and strategically planning how to reach these goals. During this phase it is important that students set goals and create plans that are challenging yet realistic (Alderman, 1999; Locke & Latham, 1990, 2002; Schunk & Zimmerman, 2007). Setting a goal that is too difficult to reach could lead students to view what would otherwise be considered significant progress as failure and thwart their confidence and motivation. Setting goals that are too easy, on the other hand, can lead students to do the bare minimum and become bored. By reflecting about their past performance on similar academic tasks, students can set challenging and realistic goals.

Students' goals and plans are also more useful and effective when they are specific and measurable (Alderman, 1999; Locke & Latham, 1990, 2002; Schunk & Zimmerman, 2007). Goals and plans that are vague will not give students the direction they need to implement action toward reaching their short-term or long-term goals. Furthermore, if students set a goal that is not measurable, it will be difficult to evaluate how much progress they have made toward the goal. For example, a goal to study history more each week is not as specific and measurable, and thus not as useful, as a goal to read the first chapter of a history textbook and answer the discussion questions by next Monday.

When developing strategic plans to reach a goal, students should also select effective and efficient study methods and learning strategies (Weinstein & Mayer, 1986). By reflecting on their strengths and weaknesses as learners, students can develop better-informed and more strategic plans by building on their strengths and targeting areas for improvement. Students should consider their strengths and weaknesses in a variety of areas, including their use of learning strategies, time management, controlling anxiety, generating academic motivation, and managing their concentration (Weinstein et al., 2000).

Before developing a strategic plan, it is also useful for students to generate a long list of potential strategies that they could use to reach their goal (Weinstein et al., 2000). From this list, students can then select several strategies that they will implement. If a strategy is found to be ineffective or inefficient during monitoring, students can then go back to their list of potential strategies and choose a different approach to implement. It is important that students incorporate within their plans a variety of different strategies, including new strategies that they have never used, so that they can learn which strategies are most useful for them in different situations.

Performance or Volitional Control Phase

Following through with a plan can be extremely challenging for anyone, especially for students who are just beginning to develop their self-regulatory strategies. Besides specific and measurable goals, students also need strategies that will help them muster the motivation needed to implement their plans and stay on track toward reaching their goals. These types of strategies are often referred to as volitional strategies or motivation regulation strategies (Corno & Kanfer,

1993; Kuhl, 1985; Wolters, 1998, 2003; Wolters & Rosenthal, 2000). One volitional strategy is to create incentives that are contingent upon implementing the plan successfully. For example, a student could allow herself to watch a video only if she finishes her reading assignment. Self-talk is another type of motivation regulation strategy in which students provide encouraging messages to themselves in order to stay focused, positive, and motivated toward their goals (e.g., "I am making good progress"; "This problem looks difficult, but I can do it!"; "I must keep studying because achieving this goal is important to me"; "There is no reason to be anxious now; I have plenty of time to complete this task"). When tutors, mentors, and educational coaches provide similar messages to students as they work, students can internalize these messages and use them in their own self-talk.

During this phase, students must monitor how well their plans are being implemented and, if necessary, modify plans to be more effective (Weinstein et al., 2000). It is useful for students to keep a written record of their goals and plans so that they can refer back to them to help monitor and evaluate their progress. Students can also set up a series of check points by identifying specific times when they will formatively evaluate the extent to which they are implementing their plan and how well their plan is working. Students need to monitor and evaluate their plans as they implement them so that they can catch major problems and refine their strategies before it is too late. If students notice that a particular strategy is not effective, they can modify their plan by choosing a different strategy. If students observe that their goal is too easy or too difficult to accomplish, they can modify their goal so that it is challenging yet realistic.

Self-Reflection Phase

The self-reflection phase occurs after students have finished implementing their plan and can evaluate whether or not they reached their goal (Zimmerman, 2000). A major part of this phase involves summatively evaluating the overall usefulness of the strategic plan (Weinstein et al., 2000; Zimmerman, 2000). At this point, students evaluate the learning strategies and study skills they used as well as strategies they used to regulate their motivation and emotions and to manage their time and concentration. Students evaluate their strategies based on how effective those strategies were for helping them reach their goal and how much time and energy each strategy required, then use what they learned during this phase to inform how they will approach similar future tasks and goals.

Learning about one's success or failure on a task can bring with it a host of beliefs and emotions that are important to reflect on during this phase. For example, a student who did not reach his or her goal of getting a B on a history exam may become upset and blame the instructor for putting trick questions on the exam. It is important that students become aware of their beliefs and emotions and identify whether these beliefs and emotions are enabling or self-sabotaging. Beliefs and emotions not conducive to successful learning can then be targeted to be modified when working toward future goals. Beliefs and emotions that are conducive to successful learning can be built upon and used to facilitate future successes. (See the module in this chapter on motivational perspectives for a more detailed discussion of students' beliefs related to motivation.)

Using a self-regulatory approach toward learning can help students develop more effective and efficient studying routines and reach their learning and achievement goals; however, students will not see results overnight. Becoming more self-regulated requires commitment, effort, and active reflection. Working through the three self-regulatory phases discussed in this module requires students to spend time and energy breaking down and analyzing their study routines; however, over time, using self-regulatory strategies will become more automatic and require less time and effort. The benefits to students' learning and the time students can save in the long run by developing more effective and efficient studying routines will be well worth their efforts.

References

Alderman, K. M. (1999). Motivation for achievement: Possibilities for teaching and learning. Mahwah, NJ: Lawrence Erlbaum.

Boekaerts, M., Pintrich, P. R., & Zeidner, M. (Eds.). (2000). *Handbook of self-regulation*. San Diego, CA: Academic Press.

Clearly, T. J., & Zimmerman, B. J. (2001). Self-regulation differences during athletic practice by experts, non-experts, and novices. *Journal of Applied Sport Psychology, 13,* 61–82. doi:10.1080/104132001753149883

Corno, L., & Kanfer, R. (1993). The role of volition in learning and performance. *Review of Research in Education, 19,* 301–341. doi:10.3102/0091732X019001301

Kuhl, J. (1985). Volitional mediators of cognition-behavior consistency: Self-regulatory processes and action versus state orientation. In J. Kuhl, & J. Beckman (Eds.), *Action control: From cognition to behavior* (pp. 101–128). New York, NY: Springer.

Locke, E. A., & Latham, G. P. (1990). *A theory of goal setting and task performance*. Englewood Cliffs, NJ: Prentice Hall.

Locke, E. A., & Latham, G. P. (2002). Building a practically useful theory of goals setting and task motivation: A 35-year odyssey. *American Psychologist, 57,* 705–717. doi:10.1037/0003-066X.57.9.705

Lynch, D. J. (2006). Motivational factors, learning strategies and resource management as predictors of course grades. *College Student Journal, 40,* 423–428.

Metallidou, P., & Vlachou, A. (2007). Motivational beliefs, cognitive engagement, and achievement in language and mathematics in elementary school children. *International Journal of Psychology, 42*(1), 2–15. doi:10.1080/00207590500411179

Pintrich, P. R., & De Groot, E. V. (1990). Motivation and self-regulated learning components of classroom academic performance. *Journal of Educational Psychology, 82,* 32–40. doi:10.1037/0022–0663.82.1.33

Pintrich, P. R. (2000). The role of goal orientation in self-regulated learning. In M. Boekaerts, P. R. Pintrich, & M. Zeidner (Eds.), *Handbook of self-regulation* (pp. 452–502). San Diego, CA: Academic Press.

Pintrich, P. R. (2004). A conceptual framework for assessing motivation and self-regulated learning in college students. *Educational Psychology Review, 16,* 385–407. doi:10.1007/s10648-004-0006-x

Schunk, D. H., Pintrich, P. R., & Meece, J. (2007). *Motivation in education: Theory, research, and applications* (3rd ed.). Upper Saddle River, NJ: Prentice Hall.

Schunk, D. H., & Zimmerman, B. J. (Eds.). (2007). *Motivation and self-regulated learning: Theory, research and application*. Mahwah, NJ: Erlbaum.

Weinstein, C. E., Husman, J., & Dierking, D. R. (2000). Self-regulation interventions with a focus on learning strategies. In M. Boekaerts, P. R. Pintrich, & M. Zeidner (Eds.), *Handbook of self-regulation* (pp. 727–747). San Diego, CA: Academic Press.

Weinstein, C. E., & Mayer, R. E. (1986). The teaching of learning strategies. In M. C. Wittrock (Ed.), *Handbook of research on teaching* (3rd ed., pp. 315–327). New York, NY: Macmillan.

Wolters, C. A. (1998). Self-regulated learning and college students' regulation of motivation. *Journal of Educational Psychology, 90,* 224–235. doi:10.1037/0022-0663.90.2.224

Wolters, C. A. (2003). Regulation of motivation: Evaluating an underemphasized aspect of self-regulated learning. *Educational Psychologist, 38,* 189–205. doi:10.1207/S15326985EP3804_1

Wolters, C., & Rosenthal, H. (2000). The relation between students' motivational beliefs and their use of motivational regulation strategies. *International Journal of Educational Research, 33,* 801–820. doi:10.1016/S0883–0355(00)00051-3

Zimmerman, B. J. (2000). Attaining self-regulation: A social cognitive perspective. In M. Boekaerts, P. R. Pintrich, & M. Zeidner (Eds.), *Handbook of self-regulation* (pp. 13–39). San Diego, CA: Academic Press.

Zimmerman, B. J., Bandura, A., & Martinez-Pons, M. (1992). Self-motivation for academic attainment: The role of self-efficacy beliefs and personal goal setting. *American Educational Research Journal, 29,* 663–667. doi:10.2307/1163261

The Brain's Natural Learning Process

Rita Smilkstein

If tutor trainers or mentor trainers sign up for a doctoral-level biology course after a gap of many years since their previous undergraduate science course, they know that they will need much study to bridge that gap. Even well-educated individuals would need to make an effort to learn more concepts, knowledge, and skills to succeed at a level so much higher than any previous course. Students, however, may not realize how great a gap there is between their current knowledge and the higher-level knowledge needed to succeed in the higher-level course. Students need tutors and mentors who recognize that there is a gap to fill and who know how to help students fill in that gap. Tutors and mentors who know that brains are naturally able and motivated to learn and understand how the brain learns are better able to help students understand that there is a gap they need to fill and are better able to help them fill that gap. The neuroscientific view of learning as dendrite growth is particularly useful for tutors and mentors—and their tutees and mentees—because it explains what learners need to do to fill in that gap (Crawford, 2007; Doidge, 2007; Fogarty, 2009; Greenfield, 1997; Hardiman, 2003; Sprenger, 2010; Sylwester, 1995; Wolfe, 2001).

The Brain Is the Learning Organ

Tutors, mentors, and their students all need to know how the brain learns because the brain is the human learning, thinking, and remembering organ. Unless there is a severe brain disability or dysfunction, everyone is a natural-born learner. The human brain "is the most complex object in the universe" (Ratey, 2001, p. 9) with its 100 billion neurons (brain cells) and approximately 40 quadrillion synapses (connections) among them. Fortunately, tutor and mentor trainers do not need to know about all the vast complexities of the brain; they need to know only enough about the brain to train peer tutors and mentors to help their tutees and mentees be confident, successful learners.

When a person experiences, processes, practices a specific skill or concept or area of knowledge, specific dendrites, which look like twigs on a tree (*dendrite*, in fact, means "tree-like"), grow on specific neurons. These neurons then connect with other specific neurons when specific dendrites connect at specific synapses to create a specific neural network that *is* that specific concept, skill, or area of knowledge. The more their brains' dendrites grow, connect, and create larger, more complex neural networks, the more learners know: *the more they grow, the more they know; the more they know, the more they grow* (Bransford, Brown, & Cocking, 1999; McNeil, 2009; Tokuhama-Espinosa, 2010; Zull, 2002). In other words, the brain's learning process, as researched and as described here, is that specific learning occurs when and because the brain constructs specific connections and thus reconstructs itself (Jacobs, 2010; Smilkstein, 2006).

Just as each higher twig on a tree needs to grow on a twig that is already there, each new, higher level of knowledge and skill (i.e., larger neural network) needs to be constructed on a lower-level, foundational, prerequisite, preliminary neural network that is already there. A gap occurs when the prerequisite, lower-level neural network is missing and there is nothing the learner can connect to—nothing the learner can grow on—in order to make sense of and understand the new knowledge, concept, or skill.

By sharing this knowledge with their student clients, tutors and mentors can help them see that, in order to learn, they need to grow the foundational neural network (the foundational knowledge or skill) to fill the gap between where they are (their current neural networks) and the higher level of knowledge and skill (more complex neural network) that they want to develop (Goldblum, 2001; Gopnik, Meltzoff, & Kuhl, 1999; Smilkstein, 2011).

A peer tutor must understand the expectations of the student's course, assess the gap between what the student knows and does not know in relation to those expectations, and help the tutee grow the missing neural network to fill that gap. The length of time or number of tutoring sessions required depends on how large the gap is, that is, how many branches and twigs (dendrites) the tutee needs to grow (learn) in order to construct the higher-level neural network.

A student who has not grown the prerequisite neural network from prior learning will experience some course material as "over my head" (literally and physiologically, "over my neural network"). The expectations of the course are too far beyond this student's current neural network level for the student to catch on with the same amount of time and practice that the prepared student needs. In short, tutors and mentors need to give students the tasks they need to construct their larger tree of knowledge (neural network). Students need to know how their brain learns. This metacognitive knowledge is a powerful motivator for students: "If I do X, I'll grow my neural network for X, and I'll know X." Students have asserted, "I need a bigger neural network. Give me more to do so I can make my neural network grow!"

The Natural Human Learning Process

Research with more than 9,000 students and educators across disciplines, ethnicities, genders, ages, and levels of education (Smilkstein, 2011) found that individuals experience a learning process composed of the same sequence of stages: *motivation* (wanting to or having to know), *beginning practice* (trying it), *advanced practice* (improving, figuring it out), *skillfulness* (developing more fluency or naturalness), *refinement* (further improvement, creativity), and *mastery* (full understanding). Because a similar six-stage learning process has been identified by other researchers (e.g., Bloom & Krathwohl, 1984; Kohlberg, 1981; Piaget & Inhelder, 1969), it strongly suggests that, in fact, there is a natural process of learning, which Piaget described as a "causal sequence."

Peer tutors and mentors may want to do the following research with their own student clients to demonstrate that everyone is a natural-born learner with a brain that knows how to learn:

- Ask students to think of something they learned to do well outside school and to write down how they got from not knowing how to do it to being good at it.

- When students finish writing, ask what happened at the very beginning of learning the new thing. Write their answers verbatim on the board, flip chart, or overhead.

- Then ask, "What happened next to help you learn to do it?" Write their answers as before.

- Keep asking, "What happened next?" until participants have no more stages to report.

Almost every group reports four to six stages. When only four or five stages are reported, the middle stages usually have been consolidated (Smilkstein, 2011). Discussing with students their prior successful learning experiences shows that the students are—and can be—successful learners. Then tutees and mentees are ready and able to learn with confidence, motivation, and success. And they will succeed when their peer tutors and mentors use these sequential natural-learning stages in their work by, for example, providing opportunities for students to practice and figure things out.

Self-Assessment During the Learning Session

After students know about the stages of learning and that learning is the growth of dendrites, synapses, and neural networks, students can do a self-assessment when they are learning something new in a tutoring or mentoring session. The tutor or mentor writes $1 - 2 - 3 - 4 - 5 - 6$ on notepaper or whiteboard and asks the student client about his or her current level of understanding. By marking level 1, the student is indicating that he or she needs the tutor or mentor to provide more for the student to do, at a more fundamental level, so the student has the opportunity to grow the basic, foundational dendrites needed to grow the new neural network (to learn). If the tutor's or mentor's assessment is different from that of the student, evidence for both assessments can be offered and discussed.

After students make the connection between the work they are doing and their brain's neuron network growth, they are ready—and motivated—to construct more knowledge. Then it is up to tutors and mentors to give them the tasks they need to construct their tree of knowledge with the higher twigs—the higher levels of understanding and skill—constructed on the lower, foundational, prerequisite levels.

Peer tutors and mentors need to give students opportunities to do their own thinking, exploring, figuring out, and practicing because simply being shown or being told does not cause someone's dendrites to grow. "The person doing the work is the one growing the dendrites" (Wolfe, p. 187).

Six Principles of Learning

Peer tutors and mentors—and their student clients—need to know the following six principles that foster learning. These principles are derived from neuroscientific research.

- Human beings are born as natural learners with brains that know how to learn. Brains are also naturally motivated to learn because they produce hormones (endorphins, serotonin, and dopamine) that produce feelings of pleasure during learning (Gopnik et al., 1999; Ratey, 2001; Smilkstein, 2011; Sylwester, 1995; Wolfe, 2001).

- People with severe learning disabilities will learn with special help and accommodations (Sousa, 2001). Special learning needs are varied and can be mild to severe. Each person's learning needs may be different from any other person's and therefore difficult to diagnose. For example, a cause of autism might be hypersensitivity to continual, uncontrollable sensory experiences. Doing repetitive actions may help autistic learners overcome the confusion and pain caused by constant and overwhelming sensory experiences. Focusing helps (Grandin, 2008).

- From birth and throughout life, the brain by its nature thinks logically, solves problems, and seeks patterns (Tokuhama-Espinosa, 2010). The only thing ever lacking is the amount and quality of information (from lack of relevant experience) for the brain to think about.

- Brains learn what they practice (Zull, 2002). Practice is making mistakes, correcting mistakes, learning from mistakes, and trying over, again and again. Making and learning from mistakes in order to grow and connect the correct dendrites to form the correct neural network is a natural and necessary part of learning. Learning takes time because a learner needs time to practice.

- The brain has a rule: Use it or lose it. Dendrites and synapses can begin to disappear without practice or use of what has been learned. Dendrites simply get reabsorbed into the brain tissue (Feinstein, 2009; McNeil, 2009).

- Emotions affect the brain's ability to learn, think, and remember. Self-doubt, fear, and other negative emotions prevent the brain from learning, thinking, and remembering. However, confidence, interest, and other positive emotions help the brain to learn, think, and remember (McNeil, 2009; Tokuhama-Espinosa, 2010).

With this knowledge, tutors and mentors can help students gain the self-respect, self-confidence, self-efficacy, and self-responsibility to make it possible for them to achieve the success they desire.

References

Bloom, B. S., & Krathwohl, D. R. (Eds.). (1956/1984). *Taxonomy of educational objectives, Book 1: Cognitive domain*. Reading, MA: Longman.

Bransford, J. D., Brown, A. L., & Cocking, R. R. (Eds.). (1999). *How people learn: Brain, mind, experience, and school*. Washington, DC: National Academy Press.

Crawford, G. B. (2007). *Brain-based teaching with adolescent learning in mind* (2nd ed.). Thousand Oaks, CA: Corwin Press.

Doidge, N. (2007). *The brain that changes itself: Stories of personal triumph from the frontiers of brain science*. New York, NY: Penguin Books.

Feinstein, S. G. (2009). *Secrets of the teenage brain: Research-based strategies for reaching and teaching today's adolescents* (2nd ed.). Thousand Oaks, CA: Corwin Press.

Fogarty, R. (2009). *Brain-compatible classrooms* (3rd ed.). Thousand Oaks, CA: Corwin Press.

Goldblum, N. (2001). *The brain-shaped mind: What the brain can tell us about the mind*. Cambridge, United Kingdom: Cambridge University Press.

Gopnik, A., Meltzoff, A. N., & Kuhl, P. K. (1999). *The scientist in the crib: Minds, brains, and how children learn*. New York, NY: William Morrow.

Grandin, T. (2008). *The way I see it: A personal look at autism and Asperger's* (2nd ed.). Arlington, TX: Future Horizons.

Greenfield, S. A. (1997). *The human brain: A guided tour*. New York, NY: Basic Books.

Hardiman, M. M. (2003). *Connecting brain research with effective teaching: The brain-targeted teaching model*. Lanham, MD: Scarecrow Press.

Jacobs, H. H. (Ed.). (2010). *Curriculum 21: Essential education for a changing world*. Alexandria, VA: Association for Supervision and Curriculum Development.

Kohlberg, L. (1981). *Essays on moral development. Volume 1: The philosophy of moral development*. San Francisco, CA: Harper & Row.

McNeil, F. (2009). *Learning with the brain in mind*. Los Angeles, CA: Sage.

Piaget, J., & Inhelder, B. (1969). *The psychology of the child*. New York, NY: Basic Books.

Ratey, J. J. (2001). *A user's guide to the brain: Perception, attention, and the four theaters of the brain*. New York, NY: Pantheon.

Smilkstein, R. (2006). Constructivism. In S. Feinstein (Ed.), *The Praeger handbook of learning and the brain* (Vol. 1, pp. 154–158). Westport, CT: Praeger.

Smilkstein, R. (2011). *We're born to learn: Using the brain's natural learning process to create today's curriculum* (2nd ed.). Thousand Oaks, CA: Corwin Press.

Sousa, D. (2001). *How the special needs brain learns*. Thousand Oaks, CA: Corwin Press.

Sprenger, M. (2010). *Br@in-based teaching in the digital age*. Alexandria, VA: Association for Supervision and Curriculum Development.

Sylwester, R. (1995). *A celebration of neurons: An educator's guide to the human brain*. Alexandria, VA: Association for Supervision and Curriculum Development.

Tokuhama-Espinosa, T. (2010). *The new science of teaching and learning: Using the best of mind, brain, and education science in the classroom*. New York, NY: Teachers College Press.

Wolfe, P. (2001). *Brain matters: Translating research into classroom practice*. Alexandria, VA: Association for Supervision and Curriculum Development.

Zull, J. E. (2002). *The art of changing the brain: Enriching the practice of teaching by exploring the biology of learning*. Sterling, VA: Stylus.

From Learning Styles to Learning Systems

Patricia A. Maher

Over the past 30 years, a long and elaborate history of learning style instruments can be traced, each attempting to decipher the learning code of the mind. Many instruments and their related constructs have developed on theoretically parallel tracks, sometimes with similar concepts, and at times based on overlapping concepts. As a result, a plethora of learning style models and instruments has been produced along with a wide range of promises by the instrument developers (Coffield, Moseley, Hall, & Ecclestone, 2004b). Unfortunately, this broad array of learning style models in the practice of education has in effect created more confusion than clarity about learning (Bedford, 2004; Cassidy, 2004; Coffield, Moseley, Hall, & Ecclestone, 2004a).

Professionals who prepare academic success tutors and mentors and support their work should apply the most up-to-date and theoretically sound information in their training programs. This module will briefly summarize several comprehensive critiques from the literature on learning styles, suggest an organizational framework of questions intended to assist learning professionals in the selection and application of an instrument or learning model, and briefly describe how one comprehensive learning system may be applied in the tutor or mentor training process.

Critiquing Learning Styles Theory

Many learning professionals agree that such a thing as a learning style or innate preference does appear to exist. It is in fact the unique individuality of each human mind that creates difficulty in creating universal models of how learning occurs. Each mind absorbs and filters experience distinctively and differently and consequently produces, or "learns," something different as a result. So if learning is so individual, how can the process be defined in a way that practically and realistically helps our tutors and mentors work effectively with students as opposed to offering them merely an enjoyable self-awareness exercise that remains isolated from their practice?

A definition of learning style more than 30 years ago has not been seriously challenged and still offers a firm foundation. As reported by Keefe (1979), a national task force in the United States defined learning style as a "composite of characteristic cognitive, affective, and physiological factors that serve as relatively stable indicators of how a learner perceives, interacts with, and responds to the learning environment" (p. 4). Key issues that arose from this work included the idea of an interactive composite of cognitive, affective, and physiological factors, and the recognition that the framework for the way each person perceives (through the individual lens or framework) interacts with the world (utilizes strategies) and responds (presents the results of learning) is relatively stable. To this idea, Curry (1987) added the onion model, supporting the concept of integrating multiple dimensions of personality (emotional/affective), information processing (cognitive), social interaction, and multidimensional/instructional preferences. Based on Curry's model, several professionals (James & Blank, 1993; James & Maher, 2004) advocated for building a comprehensive learner profile through assessments in each dimension: cognitive, affective, and physiological. Although this thinking helped professionals become more aware of the importance of all three dimensions, assessment of each dimension as a separate "function" or "layer" assumed the dimensions lacked interaction, which is not an accurate representation of the brain-mind function.

To better depict the interactive nature of the mind, Johnston (1995) developed the Interactive Learning Model or ILM. While this work continues to evolve, to date it has produced the Learning Connections Inventory or LCI (Johnston & Dainton, 1996) and the Let Me Learn Process® or LMLP® (Johnston, 2006). These theories and associated analytic tools represent a convergence of earlier thoughts on learning as well as more recent developments in deciphering the brain-mind code to produce a comprehensive strategic application system. The system provides an interactive profile along with a lexicon of terms that empowers both instructors (Marcelino, 2003; Osterman & Kottcamp, 2004) and learners (Boyer, Maher, & Kirkman, 2006) to identify learning strategies based first on the inherent demands of the learning task.

The theoretical foundation for the LMLP® rests on the definition of learning as "taking in the world around you and making sense of it" (Dawkins, Kottkamp, & Johnston, 2010, p. 6). Whereas most measures of personality, multiple intelligences, and learning styles categorize or compartmentalize learners, Johnston (2010a) explained the translation process as a filtering system that sifts sensory data through a set of patterned operations termed Sequence, Precision, Technical Reasoning, and Confluence. While all four patterns are available to every learning mind, the individuality of each person's filtering system lies in the unique combination of the degree to which each pattern is utilized.

The mental processes of cognition, (thinking), conation (will to action), and affectation (emotion) are situated within each pattern, further defining the tendencies of each individual mind to think, act, and feel when the patterns are operating. This interaction creates "metacognitive internal chatter" (Johnston, 2010b, p. 26) in the working memory. The LCI (Johnston & Dainton, 1996) yields a profile that measures the level of each of the four patterns, offering each learner an awareness of how and why some demands are comfortably accomplished while others become insurmountable hurdles. In contrast with most other learning assessments, the LCI does not pigeonhole or categorically delineate learners; rather, the LCI describes a flexible and practical learning paradigm aimed at equipping learners with a lexicon of terms that apply to self-awareness, task awareness, and strategic options.

Selecting a Learning System

Although cost and availability are practical factors in choosing a learning style model for learning center use, it is more important to determine if a model is theoretically and empirically sound. Coffield et al. (2004b) reviewed learning style instruments by applying a series of research questions to each instrument in order to address the empirical evidence reported by each model, identify the broad implications for pedagogy, and determine if the model offered proof of an impact on student learning. The more recent and comprehensive framework of Dawkins, Kottcamp, and Johnston (2010) challenges educators to apply four analytical questions (summarized here) as a means to evaluate any learning model for effectiveness:

- Does the explanation of learning include a robust and inclusive conceptualization of the brain, the mind, and the interface between them?

- Does the explanation include a means of communicating an individual's real-time experience with learning?

- Does the conceptualization of the learning process lead to growth in autonomous and independent learning?

- Are the outcomes of the model's implementation measurable?

The weakest aspect of some learning models is actually the most important: whether recommendations for learning can be drawn from the learning profile. Other than in small studies of limited scope, the majority of available learning models lack metacognitive strategies and practical processes for applying the results of the learning profile to enhance learning success (Coffield et al., 2004a). This contention is supported by the results of a large meta-analytic study conducted by Marzano (1998), which indicated that matching strategies with the innate aspects of a learning task, regardless of learner preferences, had the most significant effect on learning outcomes. Concurring with this thinking, Merrill (2000) posited the importance of understanding the strategies inherent in the instructional goals or learning activities. Merrill emphasized that adaptation requires an understanding of task demands together with awareness of individual preferences or style.

Here again the LMLP® can be distinguished from other learning models in that the system offers the learner analytic tools that can be applied directly to learning task demands and thus customized strategies. Further, the learner can return to his or her individual profile to determine which learning tools of the mind will need to be energized or muted in order to apply the right level of each learning process for the task. Hence, the process integrates into the training curriculum as a means to help tutors and mentors understand themselves as learners, to analyze learning task demands, and to determine the most effective strategies for the task. For example, math tutors may determine that a particular math process requires a highly sequential (orderly) and precise (detailed) approach. Therefore, a tutor not naturally inclined to sequential and precise processing can intentionally focus on strategies that will enable him or her to present information to tutees by applying a detailed, step-by-step system representing the intentional use of a more precise and sequential approach, while at the same time deliberately avoiding utilizing the tutor's own preferred approach. As Merrill (2000) indicated, most learners tend to do what comes "naturally" or what has worked in the past, rather than considering what strategies will most effectively deal with the learning task at hand. The analytic tools of the LMLP® offer tutors and learners a framework to use their metacognition more effectively to address each task more intentionally.

In their analysis, Coffield and colleagues (2004a) asked a critical question: "How can we be serious about creating a learning society if we have no satisfactory response to the question, what model of learning do you operate with, and how do you use it to improve your practice?" (p. 1). The work of Coffield et al. in the United Kingdom challenges tutor and mentor trainers elsewhere to be alert to recent advances in understanding of the brain-mind connection and to trainers' responsibility to help student staff take an intentional approach to learning. Learning is complicated, but if the goal is to develop the next generation of problem solvers, critical thinkers, collaborators, and self-reliant lifelong learners, then learning support professionals, tutors, and mentors must offer students the most up-to-date tools available, based on an integrated model of learning.

References

Bedford, T. A. (2004). *Learning styles: A review of literature.* Toowoomba, Australia: University of Southern Queensland.

Boyer, N. R., Maher, P. A., & Kirkman, S. (2006). Transformative learning in online settings: The use of self-direction, metacognition, and collaborative learning. *Journal of Transformative Education, 4,* 335–361. doi:10.1177/1541344606295318

Cassidy, S. (2004). Learning styles: An overview of theories, models, and measures. *Educational Psychology, 24,* 419–444. doi:10.1080/0144341042000228834

Coffield, F., Moseley, D., Hall, E., & Ecclestone, K. (2004a). *Learning styles and pedagogy in post-16 learning: A systematic and critical review.* London, United Kingdom: Learning and Skills Research Centre. Retrieved from http://www.hull.ac.uk/php/edskas/learning%20styles.pdf

Coffield, F., Moseley, D., Hall, E., & Ecclestone, K. (2004b). *Should we be using learning styles? What research has to say to practice.* London, United Kingdom: Learning and Skills Research Centre. Retrieved from https://crm.lsnlearning.org.uk/user/order.aspx?code=041540&src=XOWEB

Curry, L. (1987). *Integrating concepts of cognitive or learning style: A review with attention to psychometric standards.* Ottawa, Canada: Canadian College of Health Service Executives.

Dawkins, B. U., Kottkamp, R. B., & Johnston, C. A. (2010). *Intentional teaching: The Let Me Learn® classroom in action.* Thousand Oaks, CA: Corwin.

James, W. B., & Blank, W. E. (1993). Review and critique of available learning-style instruments for adults. In D. D. Flannery (Ed.), *New directions for adult and continuing education: No. 59, Applying cognitive learning theory to adult learning* (pp. 47–57). San Francisco, CA: Jossey-Bass.

James, W. B., & Maher, P. (2004). Understanding and using learning styles. In M. Galbraith (Ed.), *Adult learning methods: A guide for effective instruction* (3rd ed.). Malabar, FL: Krieger.

Johnston, C. (1995, September). *Dimensions of the interactive learning model.* Paper presented at the European Conference on Educational Research, University of Bath, Bath, England.

Johnston, C. (2006, June). *One in a million.* Keynote address at the Let Me Learn 2006 Summer Institute, Vineland, NJ.

Johnston, C. A. (2010a). *Finding your way: Navigating life by understanding your learning self.* Charleston, SC: CreateSpace.

Johnston, C. A. (2010b). *Strategic learning.* Pittsgrove, NJ: Let Me Learn.

Johnston, C., & Dainton, G. (1996). *Learning connections inventory.* Pittsgrove, NJ: Learning Connections Resources.

Keefe, J. W. (1979). *Learning style: An overview.* In NASSP's student learning styles: *Diagnosing and prescribing programs* (pp. 1–17). Reston, VA: National Association of Secondary School Principals.

Marcellino, P. (2003, April). *Creating communities of learners in higher education.* Paper presented at the American Educational Research Association, Chicago, IL.

Marzano, R. J. (1998). *A theory-based meta-analysis of research on instruction.* Aurora, CO: Mid-Continent Research for Education and Learning.

Merrill, M. D. (2000). Instructional strategies and learning styles: Which takes precedence? In R. A. Reiser & J. V. Dempsey (Eds.), *Trends and issues in instructional design and technology* (pp. 99–106). Upper Saddle River, NJ: Merrill/Prentice Hall.

Osterman, K., & Kottkamp, R. (Eds.). (2004). *Reflective practice for educators: Professional development to improve student learning.* Thousand Oaks, CA: Corwin.

Andragogy and Self-Directed Learning

David L. Reedy

Knowles (1984) stated that andragogy is "the art and science of helping adults learn" (p. 6). Now, nearly 30 years after development of this theory, the principles of andragogy are even more important for trainers to understand and incorporate into staff training because of the ever-growing number of adult learners coming to higher education. Interpreting National Center for Education Statistics data (Snyder, Dillow, & Hoffman, 2008), from 1980 to 2005 there was a growth of nearly 34% in adult learners in postsecondary institutions in the U.S. (Reedy, 2009). Furthermore, the percentage growth between 2000 and 2005 of students older than 24 (12.51%) was at least as great as of students age 18–24 (12.39%) (Reedy, 2009, p. 19). Thus, when providing training for peer tutors and mentors, it is imperative to consider the diverse ways of knowing of students of all ages.

Andragogy and the Adult Student

The theory of andragogy (Knowles, 1984; Merriam, 2001), as distinguished from pedagogy, attempts to model the diversity of learning of postsecondary students and especially of adult students. Knowles (1984) described the role of the learner in the traditional theory of pedagogy:

- The learner is dependent upon the teacher for learning.

- The role of the learner is to accept the expertise of the teacher, textbook, and audiovisual resources and to draw upon them for understanding.

- Readiness of a learner to learn is a function of age.

- Learning is subject-centered, so learning should be organized sequentially in content units within each subject.

- Students' primary motivations to learn are external pressure from parents and teachers, competition for grades, and the consequences of failure. (pp. 8–9)

Andragogic theory assumes a very different role for the adult learner. Following Knowles' (1984) model, Wood (2003) described the adult learner as distinguished by five characteristics:

- Adult learners direct their own learning, make their own decisions, and take responsibility for their own actions.

- Adult learners build their learning on previous experience and life roles.

- Adults are primed to learn. They seek answers to questions and solutions to problems created by changes in task demands or life's circumstances.

- Adults are "oriented to learning" by tasks and problems in their real lives.

- Adults are motivated to learn. Their motivations are internal rather than external and include desires "to gain self-confidence, recognition, improved self-esteem, and a better quality of life." (pp. 89–90)

While each of these characteristics must be discussed in training, basic study skills must also be included in a discussion of how to support adult learners. All learners draw from their past experiences, whether good or bad. Many of the adult students now entering college progressed through the K-12 system with the intention of direct employment following graduation and did not necessarily learn effective study strategies. In light of these students' directional change toward additional education, tutors and mentors should now address strategies for study in a manner appropriate to the coursework students are undertaking. Individual tutoring or mentoring activities begin with an authentic assessment of how the individual student learns. For this reason, learning how to learn must be addressed at the early stages of intervention with the adult student.

Self-Directed Learning and the Adult Student

About the same time that Knowles (1984) identified and refined the concepts of andragogy, a theory of self-directed learning (SDL) was being developed (Knowles, 1984; Merriam, 2001; Mezirow, 2000). There are several different perspectives on what SDL is (Merriam, 2001). According to Knowles (1984), the goal of adult education is to develop the learner to full capacity, that is, to self-direction. Mezirow (2000) built on this theme of development, saying that "transformational learning" arising from attempts to solve problems leads to the goal of self-direction (p. 10); what guides self-directed learning is success in previous attempts to solve a problem. Mezirow (2000) identified this process of solving problems and then critically reflecting on action as characteristic of adult learners. Merriam (2001) reported, however, that self-directed learning is viewed by some writers not as an academic goal for individual learners but something even larger, a step toward "social and political action" (p. 9).

Self-directed learning is certainly the goal for many adult learners. Although student clients may come for assistance with a question about specific content, tutors and mentors must be prepared to help learners to locate answers to questions on their own. Breaking the cycle of dependency is difficult to achieve; however, when systematically removing support, tutors and mentors help learners to become more independent. This independence is necessary so that learners can recognize and internalize the realization that their abilities are adequate to move forward. The self-directed learner is one who uses these advances in independence to strive for additional success.

Applications for Tutor and Mentor Training

These theories and models are useful for tutor and mentor training in several ways. First, tutors and mentors should recognize that a client who makes the effort to attend a session has already overcome some obstacles and demonstrated motivation to learn. A student may have been away from formal learning for a number of years or had unpleasant experiences in school, so the learner's own motivation for seeking assistance and bridging educational gaps will be important. Additionally, something that appears simple to the tutor or mentor may be completely overwhelming for the client. In cases such as these, following the principle that one should acknowledge what is known by the client, the tutor or mentor may need to begin work with a short review of the individual components of a given situation or assignment and ask the client to explain what has already been learned.

As an example, a client who seeks assistance beginning an essay will need to start with the course syllabus and specific assignment to identify the desired outcome. How long should the essay to be? What format must it follow? Has the student thought through past activities and identified similarities? The tutor is able to use these questions as a guide to help in the creation of the thesis statement, brainstorming ideas of supporting points as well as possible concessions, and a conclusion. This type of planning on the tutor's part allows the client to consider life experiences in addition to the class text and lecture, thus validating these life events in an out-of-class learning experience.

A client who has been away from school for some years may need to refresh basic skills. When a tutor recognizes this need, review and practice can assist the development of skills leading to increased retention. Mathematical concepts such as formulas may have been long forgotten due to disuse but may be quickly recalled after a tutor works with the client to show applications to current life situations. For example, a tutor might explain the rise and run of slope by discussing the pitch of a roofline. When math problems are too difficult to grasp easily, a tutor can ask about other situations in which the client persisted and succeeded.

In many cases tutoring is needed for advanced as well as basic courses, so tutors must be trained to appreciate the motivation for success an adult learner brings to the session. Although the client may come to improve a grade from a B to an A, the tutor must be aware of the small points of information that help make this difference and take a very different approach with this student than that taken with someone floundering in major gaps of knowledge or skill.

Knowledge of andragogy and SDL theory can help tutors and mentors to be more creative in their sessions with clients. Rote memory techniques may be inappropriate for some learners and kinds of material; in this case the tutor or mentor will appreciate the need to use a variety of strategies. Also, many adult learners will not be satisfied with the correct answer without knowing how or why it is determined. Rather than misinterpreting these clients' demands for explanation as questioning the knowledge or authority of the tutor or mentor, tutors and mentors who understand andragogy and SDL will recognize the desire to use higher-order thinking skills as a natural way for adult students to learn, and preferable to a rote mastery approach.

Tutors who are expert students in their own field of study and mentors who have much experience to share should be reminded in training of the principles of andragogy and SDL. The needs of individual student clients will vary; however, training need not cover every situation exhaustively. Trainers are encouraged to work collaboratively with tutors and mentors during training sessions to compile a list of activities, techniques for explaining content, and strategies for communicating important ideas, and to allow tutors and mentors to become self-reliant collaborators in service delivery. A shared list of activities, techniques, and strategies accessible to all tutors and mentors also helps staff to provide service in a learning center when a student's usual mentor is away from the center or the usual tutor is busy with another client. Information shared among tutors or mentors can lead to service that is more consistent. As new staff members are hired, the principles of both andragogy and SDL should be reviewed, because the concerns that new clients bring to the center will create a need for more and more knowledge about how adult learners learn.

References

Knowles, M. (1984). *Andragogy in action.* San Francisco, CA: Jossey-Bass.

Merriam, S. (2001). Andragogy and self-directed learning: Pillars of adult learning theory. In S. Merriam (Ed.), *New directions for adult and continuing education: No.89, The new update on adult learning theory* (pp. 1–13). San Francisco, CA: Jossey-Bass.

Mezirow, J. (2000). *Learning as transformation: Critical perspectives on a theory in progress.* San Francisco, CA: Jossey-Bass.

Reedy, D. (2009). *Graduation rates at Ohio 2-year colleges: A comparison of adult students taking and not taking developmental coursework* (AAT 3344448). Retrieved from http://proquest. umi.com/pqdweb?did=1679685971&sid=1&Fmt=2&clientId=3959&RQT=309&VName= PQD

Snyder, T., Dillow, S., & Hoffman, C. (2008). *Digest of education statistics 2007* (NCES 2008-022). Washington, DC: U.S. Department of Education. National Center for Education Statistics, Institute of Education Sciences. Retrieved from http://www.nces.ed.gov/pubs2008/2008022.pdf

Wood, D. (2003). Andragogy: Appreciating the characteristics of the adult learner. In S. Deese-Roberts (Ed.), *College Reading and Learning Association tutor training handbook* (rev. ed., pp. 89–94). Hastings, NE: College Reading and Learning Association.

Modes of Tutor and Mentor Training

Introduction

In the mid–1980s, when Tom Gier first gathered CRLA colleagues to improve tutor training, discussions focused primarily on how many hours of training were offered and what topics trainers covered. Another key concern was *how* training should be provided. Is it necessary for training to be provided in face–to–face seminars? Could trainees be required to read and respond to journal articles and book chapters that conveyed important knowledge, skills, and philosophies of tutoring? Should training incorporate videos and computer programs?

As online options proliferated, standards were developed to reflect the variety of modes of training that could be used to turn good students into outstanding tutors. Twenty–five years later, the current College Reading and Learning Association (CRLA) International Tutor Training Program Certification (ITTPC) requirements continue to specify that of the 10 hours required for training at the first level, at least 6 of them must be "tutor–trainer supervised, interactive, live, and real–time" (CRLA, 2011c, p. 1), as in workshops, seminars, face–to–face or online discussions, or multi–user virtual environments. Any remaining required training time can use other delivery media, such as "videotapes/DVDs/websites; conferences with tutor trainer/supervisor; webquests, podcasts, webcasts, wikis, blogs; texts, handouts, scavenger hunts; special tutor projects; and other" (CRLA, 2011c, p. 1).

Requirements of CRLA's International Mentor Training Program Certification (IMTPC; (CRLA, 2011b) are similar. Of the 15 hours of training required at the first level, most or all must be provided in workshops or academic courses. No more than 3 hours of "individualized, self–paced training" (CRLA, 2011b, p. 1) can be counted toward those 15 hours.

An important principle underlies these limits on individualized modes of delivery: trainers need to verify that training actually takes place. Unless tutor and mentor trainees can demonstrate that they have grappled with a concept, pondered an idea, or modified their behavior as a result of an experience, how can trainers know that learning has occurred? After viewing DVDs or reading journal articles, trainees must then communicate their understanding in some way.

The authors of the modules presented in Chapter 2 describe modes of training that not only provide trainees with the knowledge, skills, and attitudes they need but also give trainers some evidence that learning has occurred. These authors tout some especially productive modes of communication in tutor training: role-played scenarios, weblogs, podcasts, and virtual environments. They also offer interesting structures for training: day camps, campus-wide conferences, academic courses, interactive tasks, staff onboarding, and staff mentoring. Even readers who are satisfied with their own training delivery methods will delight in the variety of options offered in this chapter.

Readers will find additional resources from Chapter 2 authors on the handbook resource pages of the CRLA website (College Reading and Learning Association, 2011a). CRLA will add materials to the handbook resource pages as authors make them available.

REFERENCES

College Reading and Learning Association. (2011a). *CRLA handbook for training peer tutors and mentors.* Retrieved from http://www.crla.net/handbook/

College Reading and Learning Association. (2011b). *IMTPC certification requirements.* Retrieved from http://www.crla.net/imtpc/certification_requirements.htm

College Reading and Learning Association. (2011c). *ITTPC certification requirements.* Retrieved from http://www.crla.net/ittpc/certification_requirements.htm

Scenario Training: Grounding Tutor Preparation in Real-Life Experiences

Pamela Way

Providing exceptional student staff training has long been a priority for learning centers, and The University of Texas Learning Center (UTLC) makes training for new tutors a high priority. Peer tutor training must meet two goals. First, tutors must be trained to deliver content successfully; that is, they need to develop the pedagogical background necessary for effectively sharing their expertise with others. Second, peer tutoring programs are often these students' first employers, so training must prepare peer tutors for the world of work. Therefore, effective training includes elements of common work-related skills such as managing a schedule, providing good customer service, and appropriately relating to people from diverse social and academic backgrounds.

The tutoring program at the UTLC provides tutoring to more than 3,000 students in 15 subject areas, totaling close to 17,000 one-to-one sessions and more than 38,000 hours of drop-in tutoring annually. With 180 tutors—one-third to one-half newly hired each semester—tutor training must be engaging and relevant.

Dissatisfaction With Former Training Program

Prior to spring 2009, tutor training was fairly pedestrian. Morning sessions, delivered by professional staff, consisted of PowerPoint® presentations. One presentation covered the Tutoring Cycle (MacDonald, 2000), while another provided instruction in effective questioning techniques. Although training staff attempted to build relevant activities into these presentations, they were constrained by time limits, attendees' unfamiliarity with each other and with training staff, and sometimes even difficulties with physical space, such as bolted-down chairs and tables. After lunch, new tutors attended a Tutor Round Table: small groups, each facilitated by a veteran tutor, discussed predefined tutoring scenarios (e.g., the tutee just wants to watch the tutor work all the homework problems); discussion was then opened to the group at large. This session was the only real attempt to connect the training directly to the job. During the final 30 minutes of training, professional staff were excused from the room so that a Veteran Tutor Panel could answer any questions.

As a precursor to revising training, the tutoring team generated a list of ideal outcomes. First, direct relevance was essential; for example, what could a new tutor be told about dealing with an unprepared tutee? Good training also requires philosophical relevance: what does a tutor do other than deliver content? It would also be crucial to anchor training effectively to the College Reading and Learning Association (CRLA, 2011) International Tutor Training Program Certification (ITTPC) guidelines, specifically to the 12 Steps of the Tutoring Cycle (MacDonald, 2000). This is important because in their first semester of employment all tutors must complete the Tutor Evaluation and Self-Assessment Tool (TESAT), which is closely linked to the 12 Steps. Training would also need to address diversity and cultural issues. In a survey of UTLC student staff, 62% had expressed an ethnic identity other than White, with more than 20% receiving all or part of their high school education outside of the United States. Although the ethnic make-up of the students using UTLC services mirrors that of The University of Texas as a whole, tutors must be sensitive to both social *and* academic cultural differences. Additionally, such a large student staff tends to self-limit opportunities for collegial interaction, and conducting training in an interactive way would sow seeds for those future interactions. Finally, training must be genuine—providing instruction that effectively modeled all these behaviors for new student-staff.

The Scenario Training Program

After investigation of several training models, *scenario training* (Lesch, 2008) was selected. Scenario training has its roots in preparing specialized personnel (e.g., in the military, law enforcement) by providing situations in which participants are challenged to examine their appraisals of situations. Other employee training models also recognize the need to connect training to the actual actions or outcomes of the job to be performed; frequently, however, training fails because employees have no opportunity either to generate situations or to hypothesis-test potential problems or errors (Beck, Dzindolet & Pierce, 2007; Lesch, 2008). By contrast, the scenario training model requires that training be (a) real-life, based in actual experience; (b) hypothetical, allowing for the generation of "what-ifs" and their possible outcomes; and (c) effective when the employees are on the job.

One key element of the new training program was to provide new tutors with time and opportunity to tell training staff what they anticipated as potential difficulties in their new jobs. The scenario model would allow both new tutors and trainers to generate solutions to problems. New tutors also needed opportunities to generate solutions with those who had themselves been in the trenches, the veteran tutors. Additionally, research suggests that encouraging trainees to generate their *own* diversity issues may be more effective than simply coaching them in diversity issues: directive diversity training is not only ineffective but also actually resented by trainees because it appears to make assumptions about their possible prejudices that in fact may not exist (Kalev, Dobbin, & Kelly, 2006; Paluck & Green, 2009).

Using as a guide the 12 Steps of the Tutoring Cycle (MacDonald, 2000)—paraphrased here as greet tutee, identify task, break task into parts, identify thought process, set an agenda, address the task, tutee summarize content, tutee summarize underlying process, confirm, ask what's next, arrange and plan next session, close—the training team generated ideas, questions, and scenarios to use as training discussion prompts. Generated prompts also emphasized the fluid, recursive properties of the 12 Steps, negating the idea that the "steps" constitute a static, nonvarying progression. The list of generated prompts was not exhaustive, as the scenario training model advocates that training needs to connect to actual job elements. Thus, new tutors had to be provided opportunities to generate novel discussion about the issues they thought they might face.

The most effective way to conduct training in a single day was to turn the entire day into an interactive process that would allow training staff to do several things simultaneously: convey the pedagogical aspects of tutoring; introduce and provide rationale for the 12 Steps of the Tutoring Cycle (MacDonald, 2000); and have tutors explore multiple aspects of tutoring as well as concomitant cultural and academic considerations. A spacious venue was secured for the training event. The room comfortably held 12 large tables (one for each step of the Tutoring Cycle) that could seat five or six tutors each with ample space for the trainees, professional training staff, and veteran tutors participating in the training event.

After a short overview of UTLC services and staff and then attendee introductions, new tutors were introduced to the conceptual ideas underpinning the Tutoring Cycle. Each table was provided with a handout detailing Step 1 of the Tutoring Cycle, as well as the prompts previously generated by staff. Participants were told to (a) discuss the step in their group; (b) generate additional prompts or discussion points; and (c) prepare a presentation—a role play, skit, or other demonstration—that could be presented to the whole group. Attendees were also encouraged to be creative and to have fun with the discussions and presentations. While the new tutors were discussing the step and prompts, professional staff members and veteran tutors rotated among the tables to offer advice, suggestions, and comments. After appropriate time for discussion, participants at a table were asked to volunteer to present to the rest of the group.

Trainees experienced all 12 Steps in the same iterative process: each table was given the same Tutor Cycle step, provided with prompts, asked to discuss and generate additional prompts (with more complex steps receiving more discussion time), and asked to prepare a presentation for the entire group. Every table had the opportunity to present once; after a group presented, discussion was opened to all participants. This whole-group discussion generated rich ideas, and, as expected, Tutorial Services staff members were able to identify misconceptions about the tutoring process as well as reinforce appropriate ideas and even certain policies and procedures.

Evaluating and Revising the Scenario Training Program

Evaluating the new training model was essential, so post-training assessment was administered to both new tutors and veteran tutor assistants. Comments were positive: new tutors frequently commented that they enjoyed the small-group discussion because it permitted them to get to know their new colleagues; they enjoyed generating the presentations, especially when the veteran tutors impelled them to find different ways to approach the Steps. One new tutor commented, "Learning the process of effective tutoring was very useful." Veteran tutor comments were also positive; one commented that "new tutors were given the opportunity to fully understand the 12 Steps of the tutoring cycle because of the active/hands-on approach that was provided." Another said, "I thought it went so much better this year than in the past." However, both groups thought that too much time was devoted to certain steps and suggested consolidation of steps. Both groups also voiced a desire for even more time for peer-to-peer interactions.

Comparing TESAT results generated by a previous training method to the new tutors' post-training TESAT results was also of interest. As previously mentioned, all new tutors are required to complete the TESAT in their first semester of work. After all TESATs were completed in the spring 2009 semester, data analysis was performed to compare this group of TESATs with a previous semester's results. Paired sample t-tests indicated statistically significant changes from the old training model to the new training model in six of the 12 Steps: Step 1 (greet tutee), $t(44) = 3.15$ $p < .002$; Step 2 (identify tutoring task) $t(44) = 3.66$, $p < .001$; Step 6 (address the task) $t(43) = 2.4$, $p < .02$; Step 9 (confirm) $t(44) = 2.02$, $p < .05$; Step 10 (ask what's next) $t(44) = 2.42$, $p < .02$; and Step 12 (close) $t(45) = 3.55$, $p < .001$. Three other Steps—Step 3 (break task into parts), Step 7 (tutee summarize content), and Step 8 (tutee summarize underlying process)—approached statistical significance, with p values less than .07. Results therefore suggest that tutors trained under the new model compared favorably to tutors trained under previous models.

Revision of the new model continues: for spring 2010 training, several of the 12 Steps were consolidated. Veteran tutor assistants developed additional skits that demonstrate both pedagogical and administrative aspects of the job. During break periods, slides presenting the actual evaluative comments made by students about their tutors in previous semesters were rotated, providing new tutors with genuine information about tutee perceptions of "good" and "bad" tutor behaviors. The Veteran Tutor Panel will continue to be part of training day, as new tutors consistently identify this as one of the training highlights. In general, however, the integration of relevant and learner-centered activities and sound pedagogy has already yielded positive results. Additionally, scenario training aligns nicely with the trainers' goals: to prime new tutors to deliver content successfully and to prepare talented young adults for the world of work.

References

Beck, H. P., Dzindolet, M. T., & Pierce, L. G. (2007). Automation usage decisions: Controlling intent and appraisal errors in a target detection task. *Human Factors, 49,* 429–437. doi:10.1518/001872001X200076

College Reading and Learning Association. (2011). *ITTPC certification requirements.* Retrieved from http://www.crla.net/ittpc/certification_requirements.htm

Kalev, A., Dobbin, F., & Kelly, E. (2006). Best practices or best guesses? Assessing the efficacy of corporate affirmative action and diversity policies. *American Sociological eReview, 71,* 589–617. doi:10.1177/000312240607100404

Lesch, M. F. (2008). Warning symbols as reminders of hazards: Impact of training. *Accident Analysis and Prevention, 40,* 1005–1012. doi:10.1016/j.aap.2007.11.009

MacDonald, R. B. (2000). *The master tutor: A guidebook for more effective tutoring* (2nd ed.). Williamsville, NY: Cambridge Stratford Study Skills Institute.

Paluck, E. L., & Green, D. P. (2009). Prejudice reduction: What works? A review and assessment of research and practice. *Annual Review of Psychology, 60,* 339–367. doi:10.1146/annurev. psych.60.110707.163607

Tutor Training Day Camp and Beyond

Darla H. McCann and Jan R. Pomeroy

The word "camp" evokes images of fun, food, camaraderie, and friendly competition. Designing active, high-engagement, activity-based training improves morale, builds team spirit, and can still be content specific to meet the requirements of College Reading and Learning Association (CRLA, 2011) certification. On the assumption that research on effective teaching may apply to effective tutor training, a day camp should follow Smittle's (2003) principles for effective teaching, which include guidelines for promoting cooperation among students and encouraging active learning. Active, relevant, and engaged learning (Wlodkowski, 2008) should be planned. The more actively students are involved in the learning process and the more they take personal responsibility for their learning outcomes, the greater are their learning results (Davis & Murrell, 1994).

Training Framework

In a review of tutoring research, Gordon (2007) found that clients of professionally trained tutors have significantly higher levels of student achievement than the clients of tutors who have little or no training. Hodges and Agee (2009) noted that CRLA's International Tutor Training Program Certification (ITTPC) was developed "on the assumption that tutors require training to be better equipped to assist the broad range of students at their institution" (p. 362). A training camp is one way to provide this training for an entire group. Because a tutor training program accredited by CRLA's ITTPC is considered a best practice for learning support centers in higher education (Christ, 2009), plans for Training Camp should be based on ITTPC certification requirements (CRLA, 2011); that is, Camp should provide at least the 10 hours of training recommended by ITTPC and by Sheets (1994) prior to tutors' working with clients.

In addition to face-to-face training at Camp, interdisciplinary online prerequisites are effective in making sure that all participants have some degree of background knowledge prior to Training Camp. Read's (2009) online tutor training modules can be adapted and enhanced with interactive learning objects. Participants can also be required to view Dartmouth's tutor training videos (Guy & O'Leary, 2004) and complete the Felder-Soloman Index of Learning Styles Questionnaire (Soloman & Felder, n.d.) before attending the face-to-face tutor training day camp.

Research Into Practice

Training Camp should incorporate a variety of training activities based on training research. Handouts or materials should be prepared for each of the activities offered here. It should also be noted that activities like the teamwork tower and minefield obstacle course should not be used when one or more of the trainees has a disability that would limit full participation.

TEAMWORK TOWER

Biech's (2009) recommendations for successful training emphasize the importance of the opening "punch" to engage participants in active learning; *punch* is an acronym for an activity that "promotes interest and enthusiasm, understands participants' needs, notes the ground rules and administrative needs, clarifies expectations and helps everyone get to know each other" (p. 117).

One way to achieve an opening punch is through a team-based tower-building activity. The objectives are to get to know people in the group, review characteristics of a successful tutor, make shared decisions, and illustrate the importance of group collaboration. Small groups are formed by the trainers and given five note cards per person on which to list what they think should be the characteristics of a good tutor. Participants are instructed to design and agree on a tower building plan. Participants may fold, tear, and manipulate the cards or use the masking tape provided. While building the tower, each participant uses just one hand (while the other is held behind the back), recites a characteristic, and places a card on the tower.

After the towers are built, each small group contributes five tutor characteristics until a large group consensus of five characteristics is determined. These characteristics should be recorded because they constitute the shared thinking of the group. Teampedia (2009) has offered some debriefing questions for a similar collaborative tower activity.

ROUND-ROBIN PARAPHRASING

McCarthy, Guess, and McNamara (2009) described paraphrasing as an aid to comprehension, a stimulator of prior knowledge, an assistant to skills development, and a method of transforming written text into a "more familiar construct" (p. 682). Paraphrasing is also recommended by Ray and Belden (2009) in an evidence-based reading approach for adult learners based on the idea that "active readers think aloud" and that students retain material better when they hear themselves think (p. 203).

The trainer creates new small groups for the paraphrasing activity. One member of the group reads aloud a paragraph or a page of the desired material from the training manual. The tutor to the left paraphrases what was heard and adds any insights based on previous experience before continuing the reading aloud. The round-robin reading continues until each member has participated and all of the selections are read aloud and paraphrased.

CASE STUDIES

It is extremely detrimental to a tutoring center's reputation if a question frequently asked of the center's staff is answered differently by different individuals (Valkenburg, 2009). An informative and well-organized training program will minimize this concern. Trainers should use their campus experience to create or select scenarios from situations frequently encountered. Resources to spark ideas for case studies include McCann (2007) and MacDonald (2000).

Case studies provide participants with opportunities to apply higher-level thinking skills, respond beyond open-ended probes, engage more actively in written responses, stimulate problem-solving, and build on background knowledge (Simpson, 2002). Using case studies, the facilitator can review all the elements of training thus far, including how to begin a session, observe body language, ask probing questions, listen, conduct analysis, explore content-specific information, experience the roles of a tutor, and end a session.

MINEFIELD OBSTACLE COURSE

Nist and Holschuh (2000, 2006) divided active learning into three levels of knowledge: *declarative,* knowing what; *procedural,* knowing how; and *conditional,* knowing when and why. The minefield activity follows that framework. Tutors discover some of the most common obstacles they may encounter, then receive suggestions on how to overcome them, and ultimately discover when and why to apply specific strategies during a session. Obstacles to consider would be lack of self-confidence, tutor dependency, cultural differences, lack of preparation, course confusion, lack of personal learning style knowledge, lack of interest, procrastination, passivity, and obstacles that require a tutor to refer a student to another resource. Dzubak's (2009) list of role-modeling problems and solutions contains additional obstacles to include in this activity.

Materials for the Minefield Obstacle Course consist of blindfolds and paper plates with tutoring obstacles written on them. Minefields are created by scattering paper plates in a random pattern at the feet of a blindfolded trainee. The blindfolded player enters the minefield, and team members shout "stop" when the player reaches a plate. The team reports the obstacle and generates solutions to allow the blindfolded player to move further into the minefield. If the player steps on a plate, the remaining plates are rescattered, and a new blindfolded player attempts the minefield. Halverson and Stegge (2009) suggested a similar team-building activity with an emphasis on collaboration and communication.

TRIADS

Learning arrangements such as triads provide for constructive dialogue and deeper engagement in subject matter because "collaboration with others has long been a central form of human activity," (Barron, 2000, p. 403). Rae (2005) described common elements found in successful learning activities accomplished by groups of three: providing immediate feedback, not allowing two speakers to speak at the same time, withdrawal of the observer from conversation, not letting one role monopolize the discussion, and "selective listening" (p. 149).

The training triad uses Gillespie and Learner's (2004) three roles, client, tutor, and observer (p. 83), rotating until everyone in the triad has played all three roles. McGill and Brockbank (2004) advised facilitators to circulate during triad activity to give immediate feedback. If the Tutoring Cycle (MacDonald, 2000) has been covered in training, its 12 steps can be used to evaluate performance of the tutor role (p. 24). Robertshaw (2008) suggested giving observers checklists to note actions such as asking the client to state the problem, thinking aloud, open-ended questioning, active listening, frequently encouraging, reviewing, and concluding.

SOAPIE NOTES

Gordon, Morgan, O'Malley, and Ponticell (2006) encouraged journaling because it allows tutors to "scaffold instruction" (p. 175). When tutors consistently journal, carefully observe, and record skills, behaviors, and thought processes, patterns emerge for subsequent tutoring sessions. Following the Triad activity, each participant in Training Camp practices recording transactions between tutors and (tutors pretending to be) tutees. Applying the medical SOAPIE style of notation (MacDonald, 2000) gives journal entries a predictable structure. SOAPIE notes record six kinds of observations, and the acronym is derived from the initial letters of the observations made: subjective, objective, assessment, plan, intervention, and evaluation. Notes should be written in ink, signed, and dated. SOAPIE notes may also serve as records of actual face-to-face tutoring time required for ITTPC certification and for pay.

GAME SHOW TEMPLATES

The final activity, a game show, provides an active review of all desired training information. Coates (2007) advised that this instructional technique be customized to meet specific objectives. Training games provide speed, action, competition, or achievement in relationship to a goal and allow students to become actively involved and thus are "potentially useful tools for effective teaching" (McKeachie, 2002, p. 202). Murray County Schools (2009) offers a large selection of downloadable templates for creating educational games.

Recommendations and Conclusions

Even a successful Training Camp should be updated and revised annually. One way to establish potential training topics is to conduct periodic SWOT analyses examining the program's strengths, weaknesses, opportunities, and threats (Morrison, 2009). The camp activities presented here can be utilized for a variety of novel topics as needed. For instance, training could include Triads or Case Study activities on such themes as levels of thinking, probing questions, learning styles, diversity, ethics, mock trials, and other CRLA training topics.

Camp training is usually conducted at the beginning of the year, but trainers may want to adapt this structure for training days throughout the year. Trainers are encouraged to devise their own combination of high-energy, high-engagement training activities to make training fast, fun, and fruitful.

References

Barron, B. (2000). Achieving coordination in collaborative problem-solving groups. *Journal of the Learning Sciences, 9*, 403–436. doi:10.1207/S15327809JLS0904_2

Biech, E. (2009). *10 steps to successful training.* Alexandria, VA: American Society for Training and Development.

Christ, F. (2009). *Best practices for learning support centers in higher education.* Retrieved from http://www.lsche.net/aboutLSCs.HO.promisingpractices.htm

Coates, J. (2007). Generation Y—the millennial generation. In *Generational Learning Styles.* River Falls, WI: LERN. Retrieved from http://www2.honolulu.hawaii.edu/facdev/guidebk/teachtip/GenY.htm

College Reading and Learning Association. (2011). *ITTPC certification requirements.* Retrieved from http://www.crla.net/ittpc/certification_requirements.htm

Davis, T. M., & Murrell, P. H. (1994). *Turning teaching into learning: The role of student responsibility in the collegiate experience.* Retrieved from http://www.eric.ed.gov/PDFS/ED372702.pdf

Dzubak, C. M. (2009). Role modeling to under-prepared students. In J. Truschel & M. Zenanko (Eds.), *The ATPs of tutor training* (pp. 72–85). Morrisville, NY: Association for the Tutoring Profession.

Gillespie, P., & Learner, N. (2004). *The Allyn and Bacon guide to peer tutoring* (2nd ed.). Needham Heights, MA: Pearson Education.

Gordon, E. E. (2007, April). *Applying research for best practices.* Keynote address presented at the conference of the Association for the Tutoring Profession, Orlando, FL.

Gordon, E. E., Morgan, R. R., O'Malley, C. J., & Ponticell, J. (2006). *The tutoring revolution: Applying research for best practices, policy implications, and student achievement.* Lanham, MD: Rowman & Littlefield Education.

Guy, J., & O'Leary, T. (2004). *The tutor training video.* Retrieved from www.dartmouth.edu/~writing/materials/tutor/videos/training.shtml

Halverson, L., & Stegge, J. (2009). *Teamwork through a minefield.* Retrieved from http://www.ctlrctc.project.mnscu.edu/index.asp?Type=B_BASIC&SEC={205DA75B-0AF0-41F7-8DAD-2E712A75C156}

Hodges, R., & Agee, K. S. (2009). Program management. In R. F. Flippo & D. C. Caverly (Eds.), *Handbook of college reading and study strategy research* (2nd ed., pp. 351–378). New York, NY: Routledge.

MacDonald, R. B. (2000). *The master tutor: A guidebook for more effective tutoring* (2nd ed.). Williamsville, NY: Cambridge Stratford Study Skills Institute.

McCann, D. (2007). *Understanding and applying an adult learner's learning style.* Unpublished manuscript. Anoka-Ramsey Community College, Cambridge, MN.

McCarthy, P. M., Guess, R. H., & McNamara, D. S. (2009). The components of paraphrase evaluations. *Behavior Research Methods. 41*, 682–690. doi:10.3758/BRM.41.3.682

McGill, I., & Brockbank, A. (2004). *The action learning handbook.* New York, NY: Routledge.

McKeachie, W. J. (2002). *McKeachie's teaching tips: Strategies, research, and theory for college and university teachers* (11th ed.). Boston, MA: Houghton Mifflin.

Morrison, M. (2009). *SWOT Analysis—Matrix, tools, templates and worksheets.* Retrieved from http://rapidbi.com/created/SWOTanalysis.html

Murray County Schools. (2009). *Classroom game templates and more.* Retrieved from http://www.murray.k12.ga.us/?DivisionID=8663&DepartmentID=8975&ToggleSideNav=ShowAll

Nist, S. L., & Holschuh, J. P. (2000). *Active learning: Strategies for college success* (2nd ed.). Boston, MA: Pearson Education.

Nist, S. L., & Holschuh, J. P. (2006). *College success strategies* (6th ed.). New York, NY: Penguin Academics.

Rae, L. (2005). *Techniques of training* (3rd ed.). Aldershot, United Kingdom: Gower House.

Ray, R. D., & Belden, N. (2007). *Teaching college level content and reading comprehension skills simultaneously via an artificially intelligent adaptive computerized instructional system.* Retrieved from ERIC database. (EJ763047)

Read, K. (2009). *Interdisciplinary tutor training.* Unpublished manuscript. Sacramento, CA: American River College. Retrieved from http://www.anokaramsey.edu/resources/Success/TutoringSrvcs/becometutor/TutorTraining.aspx

Robertshaw, S. (2008, March/April). *Problem-solving triads.* Paper presented at the meeting of the Association for the Tutoring Profession, St. Louis, MO.

Sheets, R. A. (1994). *The effects of training and experience on adult peer tutors in community colleges* (Doctoral dissertation). Arizona State University, Tempe, AZ. Retrieved from http://www.eric.ed.gov/PDFS/ED474187.pdf

Simpson, M. L. (2002). Program evaluation studies: Strategic learning delivery model suggestions. *Journal of Developmental Education, 26*(2), 2–11.

Smittle, P. (2003). Principles for effective teaching. *Journal of Development Education, 26*(3), 10–16.

Soloman, B. A., & Felder, R. M. (n.d.). *Index of learning styles questionnaire.* Retrieved from http://www.engr.ncsu.edu/learningstyles/ilsweb.html

Teampedia. (2009). *Teampedia tools for teams.* Retrieved from http://www.teampedia.net/wiki/index.php?title=BuildingtheTower

Valkenburg, J. (2009). A systematic approach to training. In J. Truschel & M. Zenanko (Eds.), *The ATPs of tutor training* (pp. 14–37). Morrisville, NY: Association for the Tutoring Profession.

Wlodkowski, R. J. (2008). *Enhancing adult motivation to learn: A comprehensive guide to teaching all adults.* San Francisco, CA: Jossey-Bass.

Training Conference

Nancy Effinger Wilson, James Mathews, and Carol Dochen

According to the Covey Leadership Center (1996), "Synergy takes place when two or more people produce more together than the sum of what they could have produced separately" (p. 154). This philosophy certainly applies to campus tutor training conferences where two or more programs working together achieve more than any one program could accomplish alone.

The synergy of a training conference manifests itself in obvious ways, as when programs pool their resources—money, staff, networks—to create a conference that none could support individually. But synergy often surfaces in unexpected ways. For example, a few years ago a math tutor from the campus learning center and a verbal tutor from the campus writing center attended a training session on multiculturalism. During the lunch that followed, they began to discuss the relevance of gender and culture in a tutoring session. The verbal tutor argued that power dynamics are always in play when two or more individuals interact. The math tutor argued that all she delivers to her clients are facts: gender and race never enter into the session. Overhearing the conversation, others at the lunch table began teasing the tutors for adhering so closely to the stereotypes of left brains (math) and right brains (verbal). "How funny," they said, "that two people could be so different, so unable to understand one another's perspective."

What happened next is the epitome of synergy. Another student at the lunch table commented that maybe this conflict between left and right brain is at the heart of academic failure. Perhaps clients struggle with math precisely because they are right-brain learners, and clients struggle with writing because they are left-brain learners. Someone observed that if this is true, it is indeed unfortunate that math tutors tend to be left-brain learners and verbal tutors right-brain learners. Tutors' learning styles may be completely mismatched to those of their clients.

Ultimately the tutors concluded that with the training they were receiving, they could accommodate learning styles different from their own. The verbal tutor went one step further and presented her own session at the next conference. She focused on developing tutors' empathy for their clients, but she also gave a nod to her math colleague by conceding that tutors should avoid acting like therapists; after all, ultimately their jobs were to teach. At a tutor conference, one cannot plan or even foresee how synergy will manifest itself, but it will occur.

Primary Benefits of Conference-Style Training

Sheets (1994) wrote that it can be assumed that qualified "tutors can convey their strategies for success to the students they tutor and will gain tutoring techniques with experience. Unfortunately, being successful in their coursework does not necessarily mean they will be successful tutors without training" (p. 3). Because it pools resources, a training conference provides a particularly efficient and cost-effective means of providing such training. In addition, such a delivery model can be especially rich because at every juncture in the preparation process stakeholders from across the campus, across disciplines, and at every level of the academic hierarchy are collaborating to develop a program that reflects institutional goals and tutoring best practices. What follows are specific benefits of conference-style training.

RECOGNITION

Receiving recognition from the people who occupy high administrative positions is always encouraging, and the conference setting provides a valuable opportunity for administrators and faculty members to emphasize tutors' roles in retaining students and enabling students to reach their personal goals. The institution's active support of the training conference shows tutors that they are valued members of the institution's developmental education team.

COMMUNICATION

A significant benefit of a training conference is the delivery of crucial information, such as National Collegiate Athletic Association (NCAA) rules or institutional policies regarding plagiarism, to tutors across campus at the same time. Providing tutors with opportunities to get to know each other and their unique programs is also beneficial because such familiarity encourages tutors to make referrals when necessary. Finally, tutors possess expertise in a variety of disciplines, and their exchanges with each other during training sessions generate new ways of looking at the tutoring process and how students learn.

ECONOMY

Stellar tutor training can be expensive, but pooling resources makes training affordable for programs with even the smallest budgets. Also, because the conference serves programs and students representing the campus as a whole, external funding and give-aways may be easier to solicit from outside sources such as parent, family, or alumni associations, the campus bookstore, or the athletic department.

Planning the Conference

Although the various tutoring programs will come together to set conference goals, one or two individuals should be placed in charge to chart the direction of the conference. These organizers will call planning meetings—preferably throughout the year in order to provide multiple opportunities for individuals to become involved—and supervise the preparations.

SETTING GOALS

Because goals for the conference should parallel the goals of the institution, included in the planning process should be individuals from all levels of the institution—faculty, program directors, tutors, and if possible the disability services office, Student Affairs, athletics, and at least one academic dean.

DECIDING WHOM TO INVITE

Each institution has different dynamics, so planners should thoughtfully analyze the primary goal and the people who should participate. All tutors? Tutors in a specific discipline? Only tutors affiliated with a particular program? Whichever category is chosen, enough tutors should be invited to create a professional conference environment.

FINDING A SUITABLE LOCATION FOR THE CONFERENCE

In addition to being easily accessible to the tutors (and therefore preferably on campus), the conference location should have space for the following:

- An auditorium that will accommodate all attendees for opening and closing remarks and any keynote speaker included in the program.

- Breakout rooms with appropriate seating and instructional technology.

- A large and conveniently located lounge area for sign-in and reception.

- A place for serving food, if any meals will be provided, and areas in which the tutors and presenters can sit down together and eat. Signs should be posted designating any areas in which food and drink are not allowed.

SELECTING THE CONFERENCE DATE AND TIME

Determining the best date for a training conference depends upon its purpose. If the goal of the conference is to train tutors in basic tutoring guidelines, learning theory, tutoring ethics, and so on, as described for Level 1 College Reading and Learning Association (CRLA, 2011) certification, a day early in the academic year should be selected. If these crucial topics are handled via other delivery methods, the training conference can wait.

The highest consideration should be given to when the conference space and presenters will most likely be available. Saturdays generally work well, although if university facilities are used, trainers may have to arrange to unlock the building, classrooms, and media cabinets, and technological support may not be accessible.

As for the day and the length of the conference, preferences of the potential audience should be considered. Especially on a Saturday, tutors will appreciate not having to arrive too early or leave too late. Moreover, to ensure that the tutors remain focused, the number of training sessions should be limited to three or four and thus the entire conference to 4 or 5 hours.

Another factor to be considered in scheduling the conference is the cost of food and drinks. Will meals, snacks, or beverages be provided throughout the day?

PLANNING THE PROGRAM

Determining the shape and content of the conference should be a collaborative process involving representatives from all the stakeholders. If the conference is interdisciplinary, some generic presentation topics to consider include tutoring dos and don'ts, tutoring to different learning styles, avoiding super-tutor syndrome, professionalism, making learning fun, and others from the CRLA (2011) International Tutor Training Program Certification training topics. Of course, presentations require presenters; experienced tutors who lead presentations gain valuable experience, and participants in their sessions observe strong role models. The more popular presenters and topics at the conference should be scheduled for multiple sessions.

A keynote speaker is not required but can help set a professional and inspirational tone for the conference and convey information at one time to all the participants. Ideally the keynote speaker appreciates the importance of tutoring on the college or university campus and can speak enthusiastically about the tutors' value to students and to the institution at large. These goals should be communicated to the speaker.

PREPARING FOR THE CONFERENCE

To ease the workload of any one person or group, tasks should be divided among the planners. Depending on the size of the conference, available resources, and the planning committee's desires, preconference duties may include the following:

- Preparing registration materials (sign-in sheets, nametags).

- Printing conference programs announcing the conference theme, outlining the conference schedule, introducing the conference speakers, detailing the training sessions, thanking sponsors and organizers, and providing any special directions needed to ensure that tutors understand where and when events are taking place.

- Preparing conference bags, folders, or notebooks for the participants.

- Purchasing food and drinks or arranging for catering services.

- Contacting local restaurants, grocery stores, campus bookstores, the athletic department, tourism offices, and businesses for donations such as food, drinks, pens or pencils, notepads, t-shirts, book bags, coupon booklets, and other promotional items.

STAFFING THE CONFERENCE

The following are the general areas in which extra personnel may be needed:

- Registration: Several individuals need to staff the registration table. Their tasks include asking participants to sign in, providing participants with nametags, distributing programs and participant bags, and directing participants to the opening session.

- Refreshments: These individuals will place water in presentation rooms for speakers, set up and replenish participant snacks and drinks throughout the conference day, set up any meal service, and clean up at the end of the conference.

- Substitutes: If a presenter is absent, someone may need to step in to offer the session or to present on an alternative topic.

- Technology: One person should be designated as the technology expert to ensure that all media equipment is working and to resolve any technical problems that may arise.

Feedback on our campus confirms that tutors appreciate the unique benefits of conference-style training. For example, tutors say that they enjoy choosing which sessions they will attend; interacting and networking with presenters and also tutors from other programs; and receiving recognition of their value as part of the institution's academic support system. As one participant explained, "I often feel as though tutors are invisible on this campus, so it's nice to hear a 'thank you.' After all, we're really important to many students' making it out of here."

Certainly a training conference requires a great deal of effort, but involving as many stakeholders as possible in its planning and execution ensures that no one person is over-extended. Even the work that goes into the conference can provide synergistic learning opportunities for tutors.

References

College Reading and Learning Association. (2011). *ITTPC certification requirements*. Retrieved from http://www.crla.net/ittpc/certification_requirements.htm

Covey Leadership Center. (1996). *The seven habits of highly effective people* (Training Manual Version 2.0). Salt Lake City, UT: Author.

Sheets, R. A. (1994). *The effects of training and experience on adult peer tutors in community colleges* (Doctoral dissertation). Arizona State University, Tempe, AZ. Retrieved from http://www.eric.ed.gov/PDFS/ED474187.pdf

Constructing a Training Course: Foundations for Course Development

Jody L. Owen

Training is a critical factor in the success of tutoring and mentoring programs. According to Maxwell, "tutor training is the best programmatic predictor of successful college developmental education [basic skill development] programs" (as cited in Sheets, 2002, para. 3). Training also is considered a best practice for mentoring programs (Arévalo, Boggan, & West, 2004). The quality of the training experience is enhanced through training courses, which develop a standard for tutor and mentor training for the institution and provide a structured framework for application of tutoring or mentoring techniques, buy-in from tutors and mentors, and, over the long term, a cost-effective approach to training.

Sheets (1994) found that the number of hours spent in training also has an impact on the quality of tutoring; "Ten or more hours of training enables tutors to select more appropriate responses to presented tutoring situations" (p. 152). Similar reports for school- and community-based mentor training found that "mentors who receive more than six hours of prematch training and orientation tend to spend more time with their mentees and report having the closest, most supportive relationships" (Herrera, Sipe, & McClanahan, 2000, p. 37). Training courses can cover more topics and include more contact hours than alternate training formats. Additionally, providing a training course concurrently with tutoring or mentoring experience presents opportunities to use contextual material for discussion in the classroom, elicits immediate feedback from the instructor regarding responses to training scenarios, and offers increased incentive for tutors or mentors to apply what they learn in the classroom in their work.

The first step in course development is to consider whether or not the course model is an appropriate training method for a particular program or institution. The following questions can guide that analysis:

- Do trainees request more contact hours or additional training topics?

- Do trainees express that, though training information is helpful, they have difficulty applying training ideas to tutoring situations?

- Are there multiple tutoring or mentoring programs at the institution, and do the training standards for those programs vary?

If, after answering these and other relevant questions, trainers determine that a course is the best method for delivering tutor or mentor training at their institution, they must take several important steps. These include course approval, curriculum development, and the development of an assessment plan.

Course Approval

Before beginning the formal process for course approval, it is critical for the trainer to gain support from various institutional entities. The first step is to identify other campus programs or groups that may benefit from the training course. Demonstrations of collaboration typically increase the likelihood that proposals will be approved. Additionally, these collaborators can assist with developing a proposal and writing letters of support to the administration, if needed. The second step is to determine which academic unit has the strongest connection to tutoring or mentoring and approach department leadership with a plan for offering a training course through their department. Next, trainers must work with that academic department to navigate the institution's course approval process. Documentation typically required for new-course approval includes the rationale for the course, course objectives, and potential outcomes.

Curriculum Development

Upon course approval, the focus shifts to curriculum development. Trainers must first consider the educational theory or theories to use as a foundation for the course, beginning by identifying theories fundamental to the department through which the course is offered and those used by the institution's school of education, if applicable. Based on this information, trainers must determine which theories are the best fit for course content and delivery. One such theory, constructivism, sees learners as creating knowledge by linking new information to their existing knowledge base. Using a constructivist approach, trainers model active learning through questioning, problem-based scenarios, dialogue, and other techniques through which tutors and mentors learn to apply strategies to practical settings.

After a guiding theory has been selected, the next step is to identify which topics must be addressed during the course and compile that information into a training manual, with specific objectives listed for each unit. The course syllabus should articulate important information such as course objectives, policies and procedures, assignments and grading criteria, and the course schedule. Lesson plans can be created that use the selected theory or theories, model effective tutoring or mentoring strategies, and deliver information in a way that meets course and unit objectives. After creating the lesson plans, trainers can develop assignments that meet course objectives and that require students to apply course material. Such assignments include self-assessments, reaction papers, quizzes and exams, and skills portfolios.

Evaluation

After developing course materials, trainers must devise an evaluation plan that will drive curriculum changes in the future. Most importantly, trainers should follow the institution's required evaluation process for courses but also should consider additional assessment methods. Possible assessments include formative feedback from students in the form of 1-minute papers, anonymous written suggestions throughout the semester, and a comparison of pretest and posttest scores to gather information about the impact of the training course. After assessing various aspects of the course, trainers should provide information about course outcomes to trainees, administrators, and other interested parties to gain continued support for the program.

Logistical Considerations

In addition to gaining course approval, developing curriculum, and planning assessment, trainers will need to make logistical decisions that fit their individual programs. Some decisions will be based on institutional policy, while others will be driven by program needs. Topics to consider include the following:

- How many hours per week will the class meet? The number of topics and contact hours incorporated into the course will determine this and may also determine the number of credits for which the course is offered.

- Will the course be offered for academic credit? Institutional policy may dictate whether students take the course for credit and also guide how many credits the course is worth. If the institution does not require that the course bear credit, the trainer will need to make the determination. Trainers may consider a credit option, a noncredit option, or a variable-credit option that allows trainees to choose whether or not they take the course for credit.

- Should enrollment be capped? Are there institutional policies that govern class size based on the type of course? Training courses often are run in seminar format, which requires smaller class sizes.

- Where should training courses be held? The classroom must be appropriate for class size and course activities. Classroom size, set-up, and equipment are key considerations. If possible, it is preferable to hold class in the building where tutoring and mentoring staff and resources are housed to make it easy to incorporate tutoring and mentoring tools into course activities and to build a sense of place for student staff.

- Will all training be offered face-to-face, or will some be offered at a distance? Offering some training modules online may be a good way to get tutors or mentors to interact with different media or tools they can use in their sessions. College Reading and Learning Association (CRLA, 2011) certification guidelines related to course delivery can assist trainers with making decisions about various training formats.

- Will tutors or mentors be paid for time spent in the course? Pay issues quite often are determined by credit decisions and institutional policy. At many institutions, students cannot be paid for time spent in class or working on course activities.

Implementing training as a course can have many positive outcomes if developed correctly. The checklist that follows (see Appendix) will assist trainers with implementing the necessary steps when developing a course. Trainers must determine that this training method is a good fit for the program and then must commit the time and resources to develop a strong training course. By articulating a sound rationale, building the right partnerships, creating a strong curriculum, and using evaluation results to further strengthen training activities, tutor and mentor supervisors can develop a course that sets high standards for institution-wide training of tutors and mentors.

References

Arévalo, E., Boggan, D. V., & West, L. (2004). *Designing and customizing mentor training.* Retrieved from http://www.emt.org/userfiles/DesigningMentorTrng.pdf

College Reading and Learning Association. (2011). *ITTPC certification requirements.* Retrieved from http://www.crla.net/ittpc/certification_requirements.htm

Herrera, C., Sipe, C. L., & McClanahan, W. S. (2000). *Mentoring school-age children: Relationship development in community-based and school-based programs.* Alexandria, VA: National Mentoring Partnership. Retrieved from http://www.ppv.org/ppv/publications/assets/34_publication.pdf

Sheets, R. A. (1994). *The effects of training and experience on adult peer tutors in community colleges* (Doctoral dissertation). Arizona State University, Tempe, AZ. Retrieved from http://www.eric.ed.gov/PDFS/ED474187.pdf

Sheets, R. A. (2002). *Why do we need tutor training?* Retrieved from http://www.pvc.maricopa.edu/lsc/staff/training/why.htm

Appendix

• • • • • CHECKLIST FOR DEVELOPING A TRAINING COURSE

Determine Need

❑   Need for additional contact hours or training topics

❑   Need for increased application of tutoring / mentoring strategies

❑   Need for institution–wide training standards

❑   Other: _____

Seek Course Approval

❑   Develop partnerships with other peer support programs

❑   Present plan to academic department

❑   Work with academic department to apply for course approval

❑   Other: _____

Develop Curriculum

❑   Identify education theories

❑   Develop training manual

❑   Create lesson plans

❑   Create assignments

❑   Develop course syllabus

❑   Other: _____

Develop an Evaluation Plan

❑   Implement standard course evaluations

❑   Implement formative assessments

❑   Compare pretest and posttest scores

❑   Other: _____

❑   Share assessment results

Determine Logistics

❑   Number of contact hours

❑   Number of credits

❑   Enrollment cap

❑   Ideal classroom location

❑   Delivery method(s)

❑   Tutors/mentors paid or unpaid

❑   Course offered prior to or concurrent with work experience

❑   Other: _____

A Three-Credit-Hour Tutor Training Course

Lisa Cradit

The tutoring program at Texas Lutheran University (TLU) began as an informal arrangement between department secretaries and students who felt capable of tutoring a particular subject. When a student inquired about tutoring, the secretary would provide a list of interested tutors, and the student would do the legwork to arrange an appointment. There was little to no training for tutors and no supervision. With the creation of the Academic Support department in 2001, all campus tutoring was centralized and overseen by one supervisor, who developed a pre-semester tutor training program. Regular drop-in tutoring hours were scheduled, and students knew they would be working with tutors who were trained, supervised, and evaluated.

The program became even more effective when a tutor training practicum was developed, conducted in a 3-hour, credit-bearing course titled Practicum in Academic Tutoring, based in the Interdisciplinary Studies division of the university. As a benefit of the training course, student tutors receive a more intensive training experience from assignments that include required conferences with professors, written reflective journals, and compilation of a course portfolio. The training course provides better and more consistent interaction between supervisor and tutors and a more effective method for ensuring that training expectations are met.

Tutor training originally took the form of a 1- or 2-day workshop at the beginning of the semester. Inevitably a few student tutors would be unable to attend the training session because they were out of the country, involved in other university activities, or performing other work. For those tutors the supervisor held make-up training sessions, fitting them into an already-packed schedule that involved directing several other programs in addition to the tutoring program. Logistics became unreasonably complex, and some tutors received inconsistent training. It became clear that if tutors could be trained through a practicum course, they would plan their schedules in order to attend class or risk losing credit. Additionally, the supervisor could (a) keep all the tutors on the same training schedule; (b) require readings, written reflections and online discussions; and (c) better ensure consistent and more thorough training than before.

Course Objectives

The course syllabus sets out the course objectives: By addressing the perspectives and methods of learning theory and disciplines of inquiry, the course orients students to the nature of learning and the development of skills to become effective tutors. Focusing on learning theory topics most applicable to tutoring, role modeling, goal setting, communication, study and referral skills, ethics, and problem solving, the course demonstrates how various tutoring styles can be integrated into helping tutors lead peers to become more active in their own learning while developing study skills and understanding of course materials. Topics on cultural awareness and intercultural communication are also covered, as well as group management skills. All topics are examined and explored through readings, open classroom discussions, role plays, observations, and reflective writing.

The course was developed to meet the university's core Institutional Goals for Graduates (IGGs). Student tutors acquire experience and knowledge in the following areas:

- Knowing: a depth of knowledge in a single discipline sufficient to understand its methods, language, content, history, and value; an awareness of and respect for diverse religions, cultures, and viewpoints; and a breadth of knowledge in the arts, humanities, natural sciences, and social sciences.

- Doing: write clearly and coherently, read with comprehension, speak effectively, and listen with care and openness; use appropriate tools or problem solving and for finding, analyzing, and communicating information; think critically and reflectively and draw reasonable, supportable conclusions both individually and in groups.

- Becoming: a commitment to active community service; an integrated ethical perspective and a sense of moral purpose. (Texas Lutheran University, 2003, p. 1)

It is significant that the course is designed to meet these IGGs—and that the student tutors benefit as well as the students with whom they work—because the course is thus viewed as an important part of the academic curriculum. This practicum course not only contributes to the overall goals of the university but also produces a knowledgeable, professional staff of peer tutors, elevating the status of the tutoring program. Thorough tutor training has become even more important because the university does not offer developmental education courses, meeting needs primarily with tutors and Supplemental Instruction (SI) leaders, so it is critical that these student staff members be well trained and capable of working with students who have various critical needs.

The course uses two texts: Ender and Newton's (2000) *Students Helping Students* and an in-house *Tutor/SI Training Handbook.* Required activities and modes of training meet College Reading and Learning Association (CRLA, 2011) certification requirements as a pilot program.

Course Topics

The first class meeting, which occurs the day before the semester begins, focuses on tutoring guidelines and basic dos and don'ts. Tutors are introduced to the concept of the "independent student," one who is able to assess his or her own knowledge and learning skills and to make changes as needed to learn efficiently and independently of tutoring support. Producing independent students is the goal; all lessons in the practicum focus on teaching tutors to assist students in learning skills that lead to independence. Also covered in the first class are attendance-tracking responsibilities, timesheet information, employee guidelines, some basic referral skills, and the goals of the university's Academic Support Services.

The second class session emphasizes study strategies and includes demonstration and discussion of how to teach study strategies in conjunction with content and an introduction to ethics and philosophy and critical thinking skills. These last two topics recur frequently throughout the course in discussions, role modeling, and online forums. In the online assignment that follows this session, students also read about setting goals and beginning and ending sessions.

For the first month, the class works mostly on Level I topics required for International Tutor Training Program Certification (ITTPC; CRLA, 2011)—those skills and topics that are most critical for tutors when they first begin to work with students. Level I topics include communication skills, critical thinking skills, active listening, problem solving, learning styles, assertiveness, learning theory, and handling difficult situations. In the first month the class also begins working on Level II ITTPC topics such as probing questions and assessing or changing study behaviors because tutors need those early in the process as well. The tutors finish this section with role plays in a group meeting with the experienced tutors who have already taken the course. The experienced tutors also hold a "Panel of Experts" session in which they share advice, tips, and suggestions with the new student tutors who are taking the course.

The next 2 weeks focus on more Level II certification skills, including tutoring in specific content areas. This topic also occurs throughout the semester, as the tutors meet weekly with faculty in their content area to discuss how to tutor any subjects being covered in content-area courses at that particular time. Other topics addressed during these 2 weeks include identifying and using resources, cultural awareness, stress management, and a review of the first month of the course.

In the last 4 weeks of class, topics include working with target populations, group management skills, brain learning, training and supervising skills, and memory strategies. The student tutors research and present a session on the role of learning centers in higher education and a session on self-regulated learning, providing time for questions and answers at the end.

Modes of Training

Throughout the semester, students read chapters in *Students Helping Students* (Ender & Newton, 2000) and the training manual sections appropriate for the current lesson. Class periods rarely include lecture; instead, the students participate in several role plays, discuss hypothetical tutoring situations, teach each other about articles they have read, and work in small groups. A psychology professor conducts the assertiveness session and has the student tutors perform role plays. An education professor teaches the metacognition lesson and includes time for discussion. Students are tested periodically and write journal-style entries on the online discussion board based on prompts from the instructor. Students also observe each other's sessions, discuss observation notes with the person they observe, and write reports based on those observations. In addition to readings from the textbooks, student tutors also access readings and submit assignments online. All of the assignments require application of the principles and topics discussed in class. Tutors meet individually with the trainer at the end of each semester for a one-to-one debriefing evaluation and conference.

To individualize the training the student tutors receive, instructors require that tutors meet every week with professors in their content areas and write journal entries based on their meetings. In those visits, tutors and professors share information about topics with which students in content courses may be struggling that week. Professors can also share ideas about how they teach, what they expect students to learn, and course specifics (e.g., policies regarding calculator use in mathematics classes). Tutors benefit from this rich communication with professors, as do the students with whom they work.

Most of the training in practicum occurs at the beginning of the semester because student tutors need the training sooner rather than later in their work with students. The workload and time spent in class and online are heavier at the beginning of the semester, which allows regular class meetings to end 4 weeks before the end of the semester. After the formal meetings end, tutors are still observed regularly as they work with students. Group meetings of all tutors, both new and experienced, continue through the semester.

Benefits

One of the hallmarks of successful tutoring programs is a well-trained staff (Boylan, 2002). During the semester when tutors are registered in the tutoring practicum class, they are closely observed and have more interaction with the trainer than was possible before the course was created. Additionally, returning tutors observe the student tutors' sessions, and each of the new tutors observes three other tutors' sessions, so there is much more long-term interaction and learning among all the new and experienced tutors. Evaluations for the course consist of end-of-semester written evaluations by the students who are enrolled in it. Additionally, the grades of students who attend tutoring are tracked and compared as a group to the grades of students who do not attend tutoring, written assessments are given to students who attend tutoring, and in-person observations of tutors are performed each semester. Program staff believe that the increased time spent in this interactive training practicum as well as the emphasis on reflection have been beneficial to the training program and will result in more effective developmental as well as overall academic assistance for students.

References

Boylan, H. R. (2002). *What works: Research-based best practices in developmental education.* Boone, NC: National Center for Developmental Education.

Ender, S. C., & Newton, F. B. (2000). *Students helping students: A guide for peer educators on college campuses.* San Francisco, CA: Jossey-Bass.

College Reading and Learning Association. (2011). *ITTPC certification requirements.* Retrieved from http://www.crla.net/ittpc/certification_requirements.htm

Texas Lutheran University. (2003). *Institutional goals for graduates.* Retrieved from http://72.32.196.43/institutional_goals_for_tlu_graduates

Creating an Academic Course for Peer Tutor and Mentor Training

Preston C. VanLoon

The training that peer tutors receive makes a significant difference in the quality of tutoring provided to students (Sheets, 1994). Over the years, different instructional models have been used to train peer tutors. Some programs require tutors to attend training workshops for a specific number of hours, while others have different expectations. Mann (1994) suggested the need for a long-term tutor training curriculum.

Although the philosophy and methods used to train peer tutors may differ from one institution to another, some believe that the most effective way to train peer tutors is through an established academic course (Brewster, 2007; Houston & Johnson, 1993; Szpara, 1994; VanLoon, 2009). A study conducted by Brandwine and DiVittis (1985) found that tutors enrolled in a semester-long training course responded to tutoring situations in a more appropriate manner than tutors who received different training. In another study that examined effectiveness of a tutor-training curriculum, an experimental group of tutors enrolled in a semester-long tutor training course out-performed a control group of tutors who received no training on tutoring outcome measures (Mann, 1994).

Structuring a Training Course

Highly structured tutoring programs tend to experience greater gains in achievement than less structured programs (Cohen, Kulik, & Kulik, 1982; Topping, 1996). In recent decades, some peer tutor training programs have found it beneficial to move to a more structured format by developing an academic course for instruction and training purposes; the same could also occur for peer mentor training. The structure of such a training course may differ depending on the program needs and expectations.

The structure of a tutor training program has a bearing on its success (Brandwine & DiVittis, 1985; Condravy, 1990). For example, after struggling with their tutor training program for several years, Houston and Johnson (1993) created a three-credit elective course in the social sciences at Ohio State University for prospective Writing Lab tutors. At James Madison University, Brewster (2007) developed a structured peer tutoring program that included course credit and a grade for the instruction tutors receive, after previous attempts to operate a tutoring program on a volunteer basis were unsuccessful because of a lack of structure, training, and tutor supervision.

In an effort to build a peer tutoring program that effectively trains and retains tutors, VanLoon (2009, 2011) established two semester-long, one-credit hour, developmental peer tutoring courses at Iowa Wesleyan College that tutors are required to take in their first two semesters of work. The course meets training requirements and certification standards of International Tutor Training Program Certification (ITTPC) of the College Reading and Learning Association (CRLA, 2011b). Colvin (2007) also designed an upper-division course for a large university in Utah that focused on providing to undergraduate students the necessary training for successful tutoring. In a similar manner, tutors at Pennsylvania State University are required to complete a three-credit, semester-long training course before working in the Writing Center (Szpara, 1994).

Benefits

There are several benefits to be gained by training peer tutors or mentors in an academic course. First, such courses need to meet the educational standards and expectations of the institution and have to go through a more rigorous approval process than other training methods. In an academic training course, tutors and mentors are given assignments and receive grades that become part of their collegiate record. Faculty who refer students for tutoring or mentoring services perceive the experience as a much more professional and credible activity in which tutors and mentors are held to the same institutional and academic standards as the students in the courses that faculty themselves teach (Johansen & Bircher, 1992).

Also, when tutors are required to take an established academic course for their training, it encourages instructional content that meets the pedagogical expectations of professional certifying organizations such as the CRLA. Such instruction incorporates appropriate theory, research, and best practices relevant to the specialized services conducted with students (Sheets, 1994). Meeting professional standards also raises the level of accountability for training and enhances the quality of work performed.

A third benefit is the academic credit that tutors and mentors receive for their training (Lidren & Meier, 1991). College students have many demands on their schedules; requesting tutors and mentors to participate in classroom instruction for the work they are hired to do places additional academic pressures and expectations on them. Therefore, offering course credit for the required training not only validates the importance of the instruction but also acknowledges the professional nature of the content tutors and mentors are expected to learn.

Procedure

Establishing an academic course for peer tutor or mentor training demands effective planning, knowledge of institutional procedures for creating a new course, and support of faculty and administration. Important matters need to be addressed early in the planning process: a rationale for establishing the course; the course description, goals, and objectives; content of the course and format (e.g., online, face-to-face classroom); number of credits offered; grading criteria; how often the course will be offered and who will teach the course; prerequisites and other requirements; and resources needed for teaching the course.

When considering the rationale for creating an academic peer tutoring or mentoring course, it is helpful to address topics such as current research, learning theory, the professional nature of tutoring and mentoring, best practices used to train tutors and mentors, and alignment of the training with the professional standards necessary for program certification. The goals and objectives for the course need to be written in behavioral and measurable terms identifying the specific content and skills that tutors or mentors will gain from the training.

Most academic courses are taught in a classroom; thus, it would be appropriate for the majority of the tutor or mentor training to also take place through actual in-class contact with minimal training conducted online. Course credits and grading depend on several factors, such as the time required for training, the number of assignments, and the expectations to which students will be held. A three-credit course may offer all 45 instructional hours over the duration of a semester or be condensed into smaller time frames. The course may be graded or assessed pass or fail. To encourage potential tutors or mentors to apply for the position and take the training course, it would be appropriate that a tuition waiver be granted, if possible.

Possible instructors should be considered while the course is in development. Usually the instructor is the tutor trainer or learning center director. The instructor should meet the appropriate qualifications for teaching academic courses at the institution and have degrees equivalent to those of other faculty.

Prerequisites for students taking the academic training course also need to be examined. Such requirements may include a minimum grade point average, approval of the instructor or program director, and a qualifying grade or demonstration of approved competency in the courses to be tutored. Students enrolled in the course can also be required to complete it with a minimum grade before starting their work as tutors and mentors. Programs might allow tutors and mentors to begin their employment while taking the course, integrating the lessons taught during training in a supervised work setting.

The institution's required form for submitting new course proposals should be used when preparing the draft proposal. Obtaining a copy of this document and developing a thorough understanding of what is expected in the proposal will ensure that the specific issues and concerns of the institution are addressed. Colleagues, supervisors, and appropriate administrators should be invited to review a draft of the proposal to provide feedback and advice on the process for submitting the proposal. The draft should be revised in accordance with the concerns and comments of all readers.

After the final draft has been prepared, the proposal should be presented to the appropriate institutional staff or committee at each stage of the approval process. This can sometimes require attending meetings, providing additional evidence or documentation, making numerous revisions, and integrating additional information. Proposers should be prepared to discuss the proposal persuasively and answer questions effectively.

The structure and content of the tutor or mentor training may differ from one institution to another depending on program goals and needs. Guidelines and training topics that are based on theory, best practices, and recent research are offered through CRLA ITTPC (CRLA, 2011b) and International Mentor Training Program Certification (IMTPC; CRLA, 2011a). Tutors and mentors seeking recognition through these programs are required to have a minimum number of training hours for each certification level as well as a specific number of actual tutoring or mentoring hours. CRLA's ITTPC and IMTPC also offer many benefits for trainers and programs designed to enhance the development of the training curriculum.

References

Brandwine, A., & DiVittis, A. (1985). The evaluation of a peer tutoring program: A quantitative approach. *Educational and Psychological Measurement, 45*, 15–27. doi:10.1177/0013164485451002

Brewster, J. (2007). Peer tutoring: A professional and service opportunity. *Eye on Psi Chi, 12*, 30.

Cohen, P., Kulik, J., & Kulik, C. L. (1982). Educational outcomes of tutoring: A meta-analysis of findings. *American Educational Research Journal, 19*, 237–248. doi:10.2307/1162567

College Reading and Learning Association (CRLA). (2011a). *IMTPC certification requirements.* Retrieved from http://www.crla.net/imtpc/certification_requirements.htm

College Reading and Learning Association (CRLA). (2011b). *ITTPC certification requirements.* Retrieved from http://www.crla.net/ittpc/certification_requirements.htm

Colvin, J. (2007). Peer tutoring and social dynamics in higher education. *Mentoring and Tutoring, 15*, 165–181. doi:10.1080/13611260601086345

Condravy, J. (1990). *Learning together: An interactive approach to tutor training.* Retrieved from ERIC database. (ED341323)

Houston, L., & Johnson, C. (1993, November). *Writing center techniques which foster dialogue in the writing process.* Paper presented at the Annual Meeting of the National Council of Teachers of English, Pittsburgh, PA.

Johansen, M. L., & Bircher, D. F. (1992). Students as tutors in problem-based learning: Does it work? *Medical Education, 26*, 163–165. doi:10.1111/j.1365-2923.1992.tb00143.x

Lidren, D., & Meier, S. (1991). The effects of minimal and maximal peer tutoring systems on the academic performance of college students. *Psychological Record, 41*, 69.

Mann, A. F. (1994). College peer tutoring journals: Maps of development. *Journal of College Student Development, 35*, 164–169.

Sheets, R. A. (1994). *The effects of training and experience on adult peer tutors in community colleges* (Doctoral dissertation). Arizona State University, Tempe, AZ. Retrieved from http://www.eric.ed.gov/PDFS/ED474187.pdf

Szpara, M. (1994). Cross-cultural communication in the writing center and in the tutorial session: A process of sensitization. *Working Papers in Educational Linguistics, 10*(2), 21–32.

Topping, K. (1996). Effective peer tutoring in further and higher education: A typology and review of the literature. *Journal of Higher Education, 32*, 321–345. doi:10.1007/BF00138870

VanLoon, P. (2009, September). *Student and institutional benefits of effective peer tutoring programs.* Presentation at the Annual Conference of the Midwest Regional Association for Developmental Education, Hannibal, MO.

VanLoon, P. (2011). *Syllabus EDUC200.* Retrieved from http://www.crla.net/handbook/ch2/vanloon

Using a Web Dialog Forum to Support Critically Reflective Dialogue

David Hayes and Kathryn Crisostomo

At the University of Rhode Island's Academic Enhancement Center (AEC), the staff challenge themselves to enact peer tutor staff development processes that reflect in practice what they teach in theory. They want staff development to be interactive, to be grounded in the needs of the learner, to enable critical reflection, and to develop skills through practice. Yet conditions such as time, space, group size, staff availability, and the need to work toward prescribed outcomes have often combined to limit the program's ability to bring depth to training sessions. Too often, staff development activities have seemed one-directional, inauthentic, and unable to fully access and address tutors' needs.

AEC tutor training methodology is grounded in social constructivist theory (Vygotsky, 1978) and participatory pedagogy (Freire, 1970/2000), an approach that encourages dialogue and asks student staff to play an active role in developing and facilitating training to ensure that learning is relevant both to their needs and to their level of development. While training sessions are highly interactive, group size, time limits, and other restrictions have historically limited the focus of the sessions and the depth of reflective thought students can express. To address these limitations, the AEC established a web-based dialog forum in 2006.

Web Dialog Forum

A web dialog forum is a model of *asynchronous communication*, a computer-mediated form of communication that enables groups of participants to exchange ideas and information, build community, and teach and learn from one another across time and distance (Gilbert & Dabbagh, 2005). In the AEC forum, tutors and Supplemental Instruction (SI) leaders share questions and stories based on their experiences in practice and dialogue with one another over issues of common concern. Over the years, their discussions have shed much light on the medium's affordances and limitations.

At the AEC, web forum discussions enable a deeper degree of reflective engagement, expand the potential for collaboration, allow for a broader synthesis of ideas and experiences, permit tutors to work at any hour and location, and allow participants to focus on topics that are most meaningful to them. Web forum discussions also broaden the community of practice, enabling tutors to engage with peers who work different shifts or attend different monthly meetings. The web forum may lack much of what face-to-face interaction provides, such as the chance to focus at greater length on a single topic, the opportunity to demonstrate techniques, and the level of comfort some may experience in expressing themselves orally rather than in writing; however, it works wonderfully as a complement to face-to-face training.

Benefits of the Web Forum

A web forum can stimulate critical thought and reflection. Following the constructivist model, web dialogs situate tutors at the center of their own learning by allowing them to reflect and to construct new knowledge through the posting process (Tiene, 2000). At the AEC, tutors typically begin an original thread by describing a significant event in their practice. Through this method of online storytelling, tutors reflect more closely on their experience and encourage feedback, asking other tutors to examine assumptions implicit in the story or offer suggestions for addressing a problem. Thus, posting an original discussion thread furthers the tutor's development not only by compelling additional reflection on the experience but also by engaging others in helping to explore its implications further.

As they respond to one another, tutors reflect not only on the experience of the original poster but also on their own, offering suggestions derived from past tutoring sessions or from their own experience as students. Often respondents with similar experience will collaborate with the tutor who initiated the discussion, trying to predict what could work based on their previous experiences and past training.

Web dialogs enhance AEC staff development planning and assessment by enabling planners to use posts to assess learning and plan for future topics. Within the discussion threads, tutors often make connections back to prior training and may comment directly or indirectly on training-related topics. A tutor may read a post, for example, after thinking back to a previous training session on using open-ended questions and suggest specific types of questions that may be useful in a described situation. Using this type of information, planners can assess tutors' learning and make future training more responsive to the trends emerging in tutors' experience.

Finally, the web dialog allows AEC tutors to construct a learning community that develops through their responses. Peer support grows out of this community organically, as the tutors validate each other's experiences, express empathy, or offer praise or support. Newer staff in particular have found it meaningful to have more experienced tutors suggest that they can relate to the situation because "this has happened to me," or comment that the new tutor handled the situation in a positive way. These responses may further promote a sense of connectedness among the tutors both within the online forum and in their work at the AEC.

Using Web-Based Dialog to Complement Face-to-Face Training

Because participants do not expect immediate answers, web dialogs allow for a deeper reflective engagement with and communication about practice (Hratinski, 2008). Such dialogs can also let training occur at a distance, which makes it convenient for learning assistance center staffs when student tutors work on very limited, very different schedules. It may be tempting, therefore, for a learning center to substitute distance-based training for face-to-face meetings. Administrators should resist this temptation, however. The affordances of web dialog are numerous and unique to the medium, but they do not replace many of the critical benefits of face-to-face interaction (Dow, 2008; Tiene, 2000; Wang & Woo, 2006.).

Web dialog may enable individual tutors to reflect more deeply on elements of their experience and may allow them to focus more closely on what is most important to them, whereas face-to-face interactions may afford greater opportunity to collect a wide range of input on a single topic (Wang & Woo, 2007). A tutor relating a story or posing a problem online may get one or two carefully crafted responses, but a tutor in a group meeting may get feedback from 10 or more people. Such an exchange can serve to open the tutor to a broader range of possibilities, and a dynamic exchange can result in all tutors present arriving at new ways of thinking and working. Similarly, although the act of framing one's experience carefully in a web post may prompt deeper reflection on the details and meaning of the experience, a face-to-face session allows for modeling and rehearsal: tutors can show as well as tell.

Posts in which tutors respond supportively (e.g., encouraging one another to "hang in there," pointing out a job well done) are noteworthy for their poignancy as well as their ideas. Yet face-to-face interactions can address many of the same affective needs. This support occurs, for example, when one tutor relates a problem and the entire group shares having the same kind of experience. Also face-to-face training often adds elements not so readily available in web-based dialogue, such as sudden outbreaks of group laughter when a roomful of tutors and staff learn of their shared experience. Again, one format allows for a more reflective exchange, while the other may allow for a more spontaneous form of communication. Both have their advantages in tutor and mentor training.

Staff of the AEC now use different forms of training in a complementary way. Students are encouraged to reflect on what emerges in a face-to-face session and take it deeper through online reflection, identifying and expanding on whatever seems most personally meaningful. When others pick up on a thread, affinity groups can form around common interests. Conversely, web forum posts are used to develop ideas for face-to-face training. Studying web forum dialogs is a useful way to learn what issues are transferring from training to practice and what issues are most important to tutors and mentors. The author of a particular thought or story can be asked to consider developing a role play or other training activity based on that reflection.

Starting and Facilitating a Dialog Forum

Starting a dialog forum in a learning center is a very simple process. All that is really needed are some posting guidelines and an account. Commercial software and other free or rented hosting sites are available, but the AEC uses Google Groups because it is free and convenient. A learning center can adopt and alter posting guidelines to suit its needs.

At the AEC, all student staff members, regardless of role, learn web dialoging as a mandatory part of their staff development. This mandate is needed to ensure full participation. Staff members are required to post in the first week of employment to introduce themselves to the group, required to post at least twice per month thereafter throughout the semester, and encouraged to post as often as they like. Staff members can post on any topic they choose, provided it is related to their work in the Center. Posts must be at least one well-developed paragraph in length. Longer posts are encouraged and are generally provided.

Each center's staff development needs are different, and administrators should take into account their own goals, programs, and methodologies. Nevertheless, experience suggests that the following ideas be considered when planning a web forum as part of training:

- Set posting deadlines (e.g., end of the month, specific date in month).

- Consider using staggered deadlines (one post every 2 weeks rather than two at the end of each month). Spacing out the posts results in better quality of reflection and more opportunity to build on existing threads.

- Assign a staff member to issue reminders when deadlines are approaching and to track who has submitted posts by the deadline.

- Require an additional post from staff who post late, to serve as a reminder for those who tend to put it off and forget.

- Make sure staff usernames are recognizable, to help build community among staff. Avoid use of nicknames.

- When a new discussion thread is started, be sure the thread is titled clearly enough for readers to browse topics.

- Consider tagging posts or creating categories of posts (e.g., chemistry tutoring, new-student mentoring) for easier browsing.

- Monitor posts frequently.

- Consider how to use posted ideas in face-to-face training; conversely, develop questions to pose in face-to-face training that can be answered via web forum.

- Comment within threads when helpful but resist the urge to comment too often.

Conclusion

The web forum is an excellent training tool. It permits a depth of reflective thought and commentary that is often missing from face-to-face discussions, can be accessed by staff at their own convenience, allows latitude among staff when choosing how to focus their reflections, and provides an excellent means of assessing and strengthening all training areas. A web forum is easy to launch and maintain and creates an archive of information through which individual and organizational growth can be traced. For learning centers seeking to build community, bring depth to their staff's reflections on practice, and create convenient opportunities or additional training, a web forum can be an excellent training program component.

References

Dow, M. J. (2008). Implications of social presence for online learning: A case study of MLS students. *Journal of Education for Library and Information Science, 49*, 231–242.

Freire, P. (1970/2000). *Pedagogy of the oppressed* (30th anniversary ed., M. Bergman Ramos, Trans.). New York, NY: Continuum.

Gilbert, P. K., & Dabbagh, N. (2005). How to structure online discussions for meaningful discourse. *British Journal of Educational Technology, 36*, 5–18. doi:10.1111/j.1467-8535.2005.00434.x

Hrastinski, S. (2008). Asynchronous and synchronous e-learning. *Educause Quarterly, 31*(4), 51–55.

Tiene, D. (2000). Online discussions: A survey of advantages and disadvantages compared to face-to-face discussions. *Journal of Educational Multimedia and Hypermedia, 9*, 369–382.

Vygotsky, L. S. (1978). *Mind in society: The development of higher psychological processes.* Cambridge, MA: Harvard University Press.

Wang, Q., & Woo, H. L. (2006). Comparing asynchronous online discussion and face-to-face discussions in a classroom setting. *British Journal of Education Technology, 38*, 272–286. doi:10.111/j.1467-8535.2006.00621.x

The Tutor Revolution Will Not Be Televised; It Will Be Podcast

Todd S. Phillips

The extensive use of technology makes it essential that tutor and mentor trainers utilize current technologies to disseminate to their staff both pertinent information and the training philosophy that underlies it. Today's students enjoy the rapid dissemination of digital technology and have spent their entire lives using computers and other toys and tools of the digital age (Prensky, 2001a, p. 1); there is no return to using tactics of the past for training now.

As Boylan (2002) pointed out, "training [is] one of the most important variables contributing to success of any component of developmental education . . . the outcomes of tutoring programs [are] enhanced when an emphasis on tutor training [is] present" (p. 46). Hence, the effectiveness of tutoring is improved with training. Along with face-to-face training and instruction, learning assistance professionals must meet the students in their digital comfort zone and provide today's peer tutors and mentors with quality instruction in various forms of digital media. One effective tool to add to one's digital staff training repertoire is the audio or video podcast.

A podcast is audio or video content that is always available on the Internet for download via subscription and can be automatically delivered to a computer or Moving Picture Experts Group Layer-3 Audio (mp3) player (Geoghegan & Klass, 2005, p. 220). A podcast is a perfect medium for tutor and mentor trainers; it allows recipients the ability to listen to disseminated information when and where they want and reflect on the content in a meaningful way. This flexibility in delivery allows the listener some control in receiving and digesting the information while the podcaster still maintains control of quality and specific content that is shared with student staff and other stakeholders for mindful consideration.

Producing Podcasts

Podcasting requires only three basic elements: the podcast itself, which is usually an mp3 file; the Really Simple Syndication (RSS) feed, which allows syndication, or web publication, of content; and a podcatcher, such as iTunes® (Apple Inc., 2011). According to Mallery (2007), there are four basic ways to get started podcasting immediately. The first is as easy as plugging a microphone into a computer's microphone input. The second alternative is to use a USB microphone that provides better sound quality. The third option is an audio interface that allows the user to plug in high-quality microphones for optimal sound quality. The fourth alternative is a portable mp3 recorder, which offers the freedom to record anywhere (Mallery, 2007). All four of these options will work, so the podcaster's purpose and budget can direct the option to use. It should also be kept in mind that video podcasts can be recorded using digital video and disseminated in much the same way as other recordings.

After recording, podcasts should be published through syndication so stakeholders can receive the information. Geoghagn and Klass (2005) have explained that RSS is written in Extensible Markup Language (XML), which is a technical way of saying the feed is simply a raw page of code stored on the Internet so podcatchers can read it. There are stand-alone programs and automatic RSS creators available, so skill in reading or writing code is not a necessity for podcasters. The information technology department of the trainer's institution may have its own source for this process. Learning assistance professionals should not be intimidated by the technology; if they can record their thoughts, they can get their content to the web.

The last piece of the podcast puzzle is the podcatcher, slang for podcast aggregator. A podcatcher is software used to manage or catch podcast subscriptions and automatically download new episodes (Geoghegan & Klass, 2005, p. 19). Weekly training tips or audio content will be sent automatically to those who subscribe to the learning center's podcast, making podcasts an efficient way to disseminate pertinent training information or thoughts about the center's program. There are several podcast aggregators available. One of the most popular free options on the market today is iTunes® (Apple Inc., 2011).

Tutor and mentor trainers are advised to cast what is important to their program and staff specifically. Podcasters should be creative and mindful to choose a variety of formats. A good way to start a podcast is with a musical introduction, daily quote, or tutoring tip, followed by training topics or program information. The podcast can end with a parting thought or musical fadeout. Podcasters should educate themselves on copyright law and educational fair-use policy when utilizing music. It is appropriate to use pod-safe music, available on free music sites designed for podcasting (Mevio, n.d.). There are a variety of applications available for editing audio and video; applications allow one to add musical introductions and fadeouts and audio effects, as well as to cut, paste, rearrange, and organize content. Audacity® (n.d.) is a very popular open-source program that can be downloaded to a Windows® or Apple® computer free of charge. Audacity® is a robust program for audio that is fairly straightforward and user friendly. After viewing the free tutorials available online (Van Orden, n.d.), tutor and mentor trainers should take the next step: utilizing the essential pieces of Audacity® effectively to create professional-sounding podcasts.

Understanding the three elements of podcasting will enable tutor and mentor trainees to start creating positive gains for academic support centers and tutoring and mentoring programs through effective dissemination of training information. Trainers should think about the many uses of podcasts for learning centers. What is the purpose, and who will be podcasting this information? Will it be a solo effort in which information is passed along for training, or will podcasts be utilized to enhance the skills of others to create a collaborative talk radio format? If others will be simultaneously involved in recording podcasts, it is beneficial to use an audio interface to utilize multiple microphones. This will improve sound quality and make editing the audio easier.

Regardless of format, solo or collaborative, podcast developers should remember that "content is king" (Callan, 2006, p. 1). In order to engage stakeholders so that they continue to listen to podcasts, it is important for podcast developers to create them with good information and essential content. The decision of what content to podcast is completely up to the trainee's needs and desire. There is no external oversight; podcasts are truly individual.

Learning center staff should subscribe to syndicated podcasts that have been published to the web. Digital natives (Prensky, 2001a, 2001b)—students who have never lived in a world without digital technology—will listen to the information on a computer or mp3 player at their convenience. Syndication ensures that tutoring and mentoring staff receives training messages. After syndication, more training opportunities are available for tutors and mentors, due to the availability and timeliness of fingertip accessibility of all syndicated podcasts containing pertinent and useful information.

Using Podcasts in Training

Podcasting also creates other exciting possibilities. As Clyde and Delohery (2005) have explained, technology offers tools that can foster thoughtful and widespread collaboration. By having recipients provide feedback to training podcasts on a discussion board in a course management system such as Moodle® or Blackboard®, the podcaster not only creates the culture for tutors and mentors to provide feedback and respond to training content, but also promotes the general perception that student staff contribute and share in the responsibility of training and learning. Teaching tutors and mentors the value of participating with quality feedback reinforces the value of learning communities and collaborative learning (Clyde & Delohery, 2005, pp. 70–71).

Responding to podcasts is an important piece of training that allows experienced staff to give their perspective on training topics while allowing new staff members to generate questions and discuss challenges they are experiencing. The trainer can respond to feedback from tutors and mentors when questions arise and thus close the training loop by providing feedback solutions to challenges.

Even before formal training starts, podcasting is an outstanding way to educate potential tutors and mentors, newly hired staff, and other stakeholders of the mission, values, and goals of the learning center's programs. During training, podcasting then becomes a technological tool to improve training in multiple delivery modes and enhance face-to-face training. Podcasts reinforce training topics, systematically disseminate information, and provide scheduled and just-in-time training to tutors, mentors, and other staff.

Podcasting does not end when the trainer provides the information; podcasting can be utilized as a collaborative training tool for tutors and mentors. Student staff can create their own podcasts on training topics to provide student perspectives on specific information and tutoring pedagogy. Tutors organized into small groups can create, organize, and record 3- to 5-minute public service announcements for tutor training information as it applies to the College Reading and Learning Association (CRLA, 2011b) guidelines and the tutors' own experiences. Tutors and mentors can also create training scenarios relaying how they incorporate goal setting and study strategies into sessions, specifically utilize the tutoring cycle, or model for new student staff the skills of asking leading questions, listening actively, and paraphrasing.

Podcasting can also be used as a sort of cyber-shadowing to showcase strategies so that novice tutors and mentors can hear—and see, if video—how experienced student staff members use the best and most promising practices set up by the certification program. It would be a good idea to have tutors and tutees sign releases when planning to record actual tutoring sessions, but trainees can also showcase the same skills through scenario role plays.

The wealth of information in CRLA's International Tutoring Training Program Certification (ITTPC; CRLA, 2011b) and International Mentor Training Program Certification (IMTPC; CRLA, 2011a) guidelines can easily be broken down into its elements and podcasts developed to disseminate the information. Providing training topic podcasts reinforces the information provided during face-to-face interaction and keeps it readily available for staff. One requirement to obtain CRLA ITTPC Level I certification is to cover 8 of the 14 training topics. Podcasting the information required can ensure that tutors have continuing access to all the information discussed in training. Level II and III certification information can be similarly developed and podcast.

To make it easy for searchers to identify and find training topics, trainers should be specific when titling podcasts. Keeping podcasts short, specific, and focused will make them more useful by creating short bursts of information. Smaller, modular training allows tutors to reflect on specific topic areas and can enhance feedback and categorical discussion.

Directors and coordinators of centers often send updates to tutors and mentors through email, discussion boards, or written letters. They should consider podcasting for this purpose— a medium always available for, and often preferred by, the digital native. Tutors and mentors should be invited to respond on a discussion board or via email to guarantee that they have the information.

Trainers need to step out of their digital comfort zone and utilize the technology that staff and students have already embraced. Trainers should accept their status as "Immigrants into a new Digital world" and should "look to their own creativity, their Digital Native students, their sympathetic administrators and other sources to help communicate the still-valuable knowledge and wisdom in that world's new language" (Prensky, 2001b, p. 7).

There is no secret to effective podcasting; trainers just need to get started, have fun, and take risks. Podcasting is a center's conduit for the future of ongoing staff development and enhanced academic support.

References

Apple Inc. (2011). *What is iTunes?* Retrieved from http://www.apple.com/itunes/what-is/

Audacity. (n.d.). *The free, cross-platform sound editor.* Retrieved from http://audacity.sourceforge.net/

Boylan, H. R. (2002). *What works in remediation: Research-based best practices in developmental education.* Boone, NC: National Center for Developmental Education.

Callan, D. (2006). *Content is king.* Retrieved from http://www.akamarketing.com/content-is-king.html

Clyde, W., & Delohery, A. (2005). *Using technology in teaching.* New Haven, CT: Yale University Press.

College Reading and Learning Association. (2011a). *IMTPC certification requirements.* Retrieved from http://www.crla.net/imtpc/certification_requirements.htm

College Reading and Learning Association. (2011b). *ITTPC certification requirements.* Retrieved from http://www.crla.net/ittpc/certification_requirements.htm

Goeghegan, M. W., & Klass, D. (2005). *Podcast solutions: The complete guide to podcasting.* Berkeley, CA: Apress.

Mallery, S. (2007). *An introduction to podcasting equipment.* Retrieved from http://www.bhphoto-video.com/find/newsLetter/pro_audio_podcasting_jan2007.jsp

Mevio. (n.d.). *Music alley from Mevio.* Retrieved from http://www.musicalley.com/

Prensky, M. (2001a). Digital natives, digital immigrants. *On the Horizon, 9*(5), 1. doi:10.1108/10748120110424816

Prensky, M. (2001b). Digital natives, digital immigrants, Part II: Do they really *think* differently? *On the Horizon, 9*(6), 1–9. doi:10.1108/10748120110424843

Van Orden, J. (n.d.). *How to podcast.* Retrieved from http://www.how-to-podcast-tutorial.com/17-audacity-tutorial.htm

Virtual Environments: Have You Met My Avatar?

Thomas C. Stewart

The hallway looks much like any college campus hallway around the world. At the end of the hall sits the classroom used for training tutors and mentors. Andrew, heading to his first training session of the semester, is dressed casually in jeans, sneakers, and a t-shirt with the college logo. When he enters, Andrew sees a large, carpeted training room. Dr. James, the new assistant director of tutoring and mentoring programs on campus, is standing behind the podium. Andrew doesn't know Dr. James well yet, so he decides to find out more about her. To do so, he clicks on her face with his mouse, and a small window appears, listing her contact information and department. A small window? What's going on here? Welcome to the new world of tutor and mentor training.

The classroom described above is not an actual room but a virtual space created online specifically for training sessions. Avatars of the participants are created by the participants themselves as portraits shared with other members of the community. The platform used to create the virtual classroom allows participants to share information with each other. This virtual environment can be used to enhance and supplement tutor and mentor training.

Web 2.0 and Tutor Training

The newest generation of Internet applications, often referred to as Web 2.0, offers a new way of enhancing synchronous online tutor and mentor training (and subsequently actual tutoring and mentoring) in ways that even a decade ago would have seemed pure science fiction (Banks, 2008; Okin, 2005). Today there is an established range of online tutoring and mentoring programs (Dvorak, 2004; Packard, 2003; Sanchez & Harris, 1996). If a student's sole contact with a college or university is through online courses, it seems only appropriate that tutoring and mentoring programs be available online as well. And it follows that, if delivery of tutoring and mentoring is online, at least some of the training should be performed online.

By using a program specifically dedicated to this purpose, a tutor and mentor training community—and later a related center—can be set up securely on an institution's server and will be accessible only to students, staff, and faculty who have access privileges. Furthermore, these offerings can be embedded in Blackboard® and other platforms and specifically tailored to individual needs in setting up an online tutoring and mentoring community in which a student, using his or her avatar, can visually enter an online training room—something that will greatly enhance the experience.

Challenges and Benefits

Trainers interested in adding social networking approaches to existing tutor and mentor training programs may be concerned about security. Identity theft is a broad concern that has gained increased attention over the years (Britt, 2009; Caeton, 2007; Marshall & Tompsett, 2005). When adding a social networking component, there is no need to collect an abundance of personal data. To increase network security, student information can be kept separate from course information. A bigger concern is allowing participants to control who has access to data even within their group (Couros, 2008).

For example, it is possible to create a follow-up group using an existing platform such as Facebook. The downside is that this format may unintentionally lead to *too much* sharing. Those who already use Facebook as a personal website may feel uncomfortable letting supervisors and fellow tutors and mentors see too much of their private lives—photos with family members and friends, personal musings, and the like. Using a platform such as *Second Life*, in which participants create their own avatars, can also cause potentially uncomfortable blurring between personal and professional aspects of participants' lives. Students may either not feel comfortable enough to sign up at all or unintentionally give out or receive too much personal information that is unrelated to their work as tutors or mentors. Part of making a virtual environment successful, then, is to allow the social networking to take place in a closed, secure environment where participants feel comfortable about who else has information about them and what that information is.

One of the biggest benefits of online training is flexibility. Effectively developed and designed training can be delivered to tutors and mentors with widely varying schedules. Any program coordinator who has struggled to find a suitable meeting time that catches all tutors and mentors at the same time certainly can recognize the value of this option. Such courses can be synchronous— live online meetings—or asynchronous—tutors and mentors joining online at various times. In most cases, particularly in programs certified through College Reading and Learning Association (CRLA) International Mentor Training Program Certification (IMTPC; CRLA, 2011a) and International Tutor Training Program Certification (ITTPC; CRLA, 2011b), online meetings will be used to supplement existing training sessions. Adding a social networking component to this approach opens a new dimension that promises to offer that much more of a sense of belonging to tutors and mentors, further helping them identify with the program.

One of the biggest challenges for colleges and universities trying to incorporate social media is that there are two key pieces to the puzzle: the institution's technology and the social platform itself. How do trainers tie them together? With the onset of open web services, this is becoming easier to do as long as the institution's technology supports open architecture. If institutional systems do support open architecture, then it is possible to start right away. If not, the institution can change the system so that it will incorporate open architecture or invest in proprietary architecture that can be adapted to the system. In the long run, though, the open-architecture approach is recommended because it allows more flexibility.

Trainers must know the programs well enough to be able to provide detailed instructions to tutors and mentors as well as to anticipate questions about how things work, making a "train-the-trainer" session vitally important. Nothing will derail the social networking element more quickly than a design that is too complex for the casual, infrequent user to navigate. If tutors and mentors are asked to revisit the social networking component 3 weeks after the initial meeting, it is important to have a user interface that is easy to use and can be navigated intuitively.

Virtual Environments: Getting Started

As noted earlier, there are numerous models for applying a social network element to tutor and mentor training offerings. Both blended and online-online offerings can be considered.

BLENDED OFFERINGS

The blended model, combining an existing onsite course or workshop with a follow-up piece using social networking and 3D virtual space, offers a chance to get into the area of social networking with the safety net of a modality with which the trainer and students are already familiar (face-to-face). Some key questions need to be addressed first:

- Do we have the IT support, both hardware and software, to do this? What is the overhead?

- How will we train staff facilitators to use this? How will we support tutor and mentor questions?

- How often will we interact with tutors and mentors?

- How much user training will we build into our existing training (e.g., how to navigate the virtual space, create an avatar)?

- How will we manage security?

These questions definitely need to be addressed at the outset. Without the hardware and software, it will not be possible to run this type of training successfully. Virtual environments require a tactical investment in both short- and long-term benefits.

A help line (often but not always managed by the platform provider) as well as a Frequently Asked Questions (FAQs) page should be in place before training begins. The trainers must be fluent with the technology as well. One of the best ways to avoid a lot of back-end confusion among tutors and mentors is to have trainers who are able to teach the platform clearly and effectively.

Security is always a concern because a single breach can have a costly long-term impact. One solution is to collect no more information than needed. Are Social Security numbers or home telephone numbers really needed? It is critical to build in security protocols on the front end, and make sure staff members are well aware of them.

ONLINE-ONLY OFFERINGS

While the blended model may be appropriate for getting started, going all-in for a 100% online training program with a social networking element can be successful, too. Before diving in, however, several additional questions must be addressed beyond those posed for blended models:

- Who will be responsible for maintaining the virtual space?

- Will it be synchronous or asynchronous? If synchronous, how will the schedule be determined?

- Will tutor and mentor participation be mandatory? How will it be encouraged or rewarded? If required, how will it be enforced?

If training is offered 100% online, a dedicated staff must be in place to deal with it, including a point person. For a single course, that could be one person. A more complex offering may require a team of people with specific responsibilities. Furthermore, if CRLA ITTPC or IMTPC certification is an issue, certain guidelines must be followed regarding type of training delivery. A key question is whether to offer synchronous sessions with live online meetings using VirtualU, Elluminate Live, or another platform, or whether to choose an asynchronous approach by which participants can view prepared materials at their convenience. The live meetings have some major advantages in terms of the issue of bonding and identity. They make for a more complete experience but are much more labor intensive. Training sessions can be recorded with nearly all software platforms, meaning even asynchronous offerings can provide an enriched multimedia experience.

Testing the Waters

Is virtual training worth trying? Is it appropriate for the organization's objectives? Should it be avoided altogether? These are questions each program must decide based on its own needs, but educational institutions historically have had to adapt to survive in new eras. Furthermore, they have had to go where students are—whether physically, socially, or psychologically—in order to serve those students most effectively. Social networking has become an important part of many students' lives. Students and others now spend far more time on the Internet than watching TV (Sachoff, 2008). Making tutor and mentor training a part of that time spent is one more way of making such training relevant to the student experience.

References

Banks, A. (2008). *On the way to the web: The secret history of the Internet and its founders.* Berkeley, CA: Apress.

Britt, P. (2009). Identity thieves hit a new low. *Information Today, 26*(2), 43–44. Retrieved from http://www.infotoday.com/it/feb09/Britt.shtml

Caeton, D. A. (2007). The cultural phenomenon of identity theft and the domestication of the World Wide Web. *Bulletin of Science, Technology, & Society, 27*(1), 11–23. doi:10.1177/0270467606297624

College Reading and Learning Association. (2011a). *IMTPC certification requirements.* Retrieved from http://www.crla.net/imtpc/certification_requirements.htm

College Reading and Learning Association. (2011b). *ITTPC certification requirements.* Retrieved from http://www.crla.net/ittpc/certification_requirements.htm

Couros, A. (2008). Safety and social networking. *Technology & Learning, 2*(7), 20–22.

Dvorak, J. (2004). Managing tutoring aspects of the learning assistance center. *Research for Educational Reform, 9*(4), 39–51.

Marshall, A. M., & Tompsett, B. C. (2005). Identity theft in an online world. *Computer Law & Security Report, 21*(2), 128–137. doi:10.1016/j.clsr.2005.02.004

Okin, J. A. (2005). *The Internet revolution: The not-for-dummies guide to the history, technology, and use of the Internet.* Winter Harbor, ME: Ironbound Press.

Packard, B. W. (2003). Web-based mentoring: Challenging traditional models to increase women's access. *Mentoring & Tutoring: Partnership in Learning, 11*(1), 53–65. doi:10.1080/1361126032000054808

Sachoff, M. (2008, February 19). Internet outpacing TV for time spent [Online newsgroup posting]. Retrieved from http://www.webpronews.com/topnews/2008/02/19/internet-outpacing-tv-for-time-spent

Sanchez, B., & Harris, J. (1996). Online mentoring: A success story. *Learning and Leading With Technology, 23*, 57–60.

Interactive Tasks: Engaging Peer Educators as Trainers

Nathalie M. Vega-Rhodes

In a learning center, tutors and mentors come from a variety of backgrounds. Some may have experience tutoring or working with a diverse range of students, while others bring expertise from a content area or life experience. As tutors and mentors progress to *advanced* and then *master* levels of College Reading and Learning Association (CRLA) training in programs certified by International Mentor Training Program Certification (IMTPC; CRLA 2011a) and International Tutor Training Program Certification (ITTPC; CRLA 2011b), they gain valuable insights. Everything that they have learned on the job and from academic coursework can be beneficial to less experienced student staff as well as those just beginning their training. Master tutors and mentors can play an extremely helpful role in assisting new staff in their growth and improving skills. Further, these master tutors and mentors benefit from their responsibility and contributions to improve the center.

There are several projects in which master-level student staff can participate that will benefit themselves as well as the center. They can assist with and lead training, facilitate workshops, handle caseloads, and update publications and training manuals.

Assisting With and Leading Training

Probably the most interesting way that a master tutor or mentor can get involved is to assist with training of other tutors and mentors, or to lead some aspect of the training. Professional staff can invite each master staff member to lead a different segment of training. The most beneficial services such experienced staff members provide may be helping with role playing and leading discussions about how to handle difficult situations. It is beneficial for new staff to learn how experienced tutors and mentors handle various situations as well as to hear several different views of the same subject from the master staff.

If a master tutor or mentor is particularly skilled with demonstrating a certain topic (for example, communicating with introverted student clients or welcoming international students), the individual can lead that section of training. These tutors and mentors may also have ideas on new activities to facilitate training. In addition to providing a learning experience for new and old student staff alike, staff-led training sessions also liven up the training program with fresh perspectives and provide opportunities for staff discussion.

Facilitating Training

Another way master tutors and mentors can be involved in the work of the learning center at a higher level is to lead workshops for other student staff. These workshops could consist of professional development topics or content tutoring areas. Master tutors and mentors create workshops and lead them according to specifications provided by supervisors. Topics may include dealing with negativity, conflict management, or—for master tutors in training—leadership. Additionally, if there are particularly challenging concepts or several ways to explain a topic (e.g., word problems in mathematics), a workshop on the topic would benefit both the facilitator and the center's student staff.

Handling Caseloads

Master tutors and mentors who carry a caseload of new tutors can greatly expand the efficiency of the learning center. Each master staff member can be paired with one or more new student staff members (and even those who have been with the center for more than a semester) to assist with any problems that may arise. Each master tutor or master mentor can work with up to five lower-level student staff members, touching base with each individually once a week. Topics to discuss include meeting the requirements for CRLA ITTPC or IMTPC certification, coping with problems on the job, dealing with difficult situations, and developing ideas for providing more intensive or extensive training.

Updating Publications and Training Manuals

Finally, more advanced tutors and mentors can be assigned to update learning center publications, especially those intended for student readers. These publications may include an ongoing column in the campus newspaper, campus-wide marketing brochures, and especially tutor and mentor training manuals. Although the trainer and program director may wish to retain final editing rights, student staff with insights into what works and what needs to be edited out of the training materials can make excellent suggestions for relevance and focus in these important documents.

By utilizing master tutors' and mentors' skills and insights, learning centers can benefit tremendously. Advanced-level student staff members develop an appreciation of their importance to the center. Further, master tutors and mentors are able to expand their own learning in addition to assisting newer employees. New staff members feel as if there is always someone to listen to what they have to say and to give advice if the supervisor is unavailable at the moment. New tutors and mentors have an opportunity to learn from those who have been in their shoes and who have succeeded. Additionally, program publications are regularly updated by those in a position to know what works.

References

College Reading and Learning Association. (2011a). *IMTPC certification requirements*. Retrieved from http://www.crla.net/imtpc/certification_requirements.htm

College Reading and Learning Association. (2011b). *ITTPC certification requirements*. Retrieved from http://www.crla.net/imtpc/certification_requirements.htm

Role-Playing Activities in Tutor and Mentor Training

Amanda L. F. Weyant

Several learning theories suggest that learning is a process of moving through stages. Theorists describe these stages differently, but many agree that students learn best when they are actively involved in their own learning. One such theorist is Kolb, whose Theory of Experiential Learning describes a four-stage process of feeling, watching, thinking, and doing. Kolb's (1984) theory emphasizes the "central role that experience plays in the learning process" (p.20) as students move through involving themselves "fully, openly and without bias" in the concrete experimentation stage, reflecting on their experiences in the reflective observation stage, and creating "concepts that integrate their observations into logically sound theories" in the abstract conceptualization stage (p. 30). The fourth stage of Kolb's (1984) theory is active experimentation, where learners "must be able to use these theories to make decisions and solve problems" (p. 30).

Learning is a Transforming Experience

To encourage learners to engage in active experimentation, educators have developed various active learning techniques that can be used in any educational setting, including tutor and mentor training. Active learning asks "students to participate in constructing their own knowledge through discussion, role-play, simulation, problem-based learning, and other methods" (Powner & Allendoerfer, 2008, p. 75). These techniques are "uniquely capable" of appealing to "students with a variety of learning styles" and help "turn students into mentally engaged participants" in their own learning (Powner & Allendoerfer, 2008, p. 77). Advocates of active learning have found that "students retain 10% of what they read, 26% of what they hear, 30% of what they see, 50% of what they see and hear, 70% of what they say, and 90% of what they say as they do something" (Powner & Allendoerfer, 2008, p. 77).

To Kolb (1984), learning is "the process whereby knowledge is created through the transformation of experience. Knowledge results from the combination of grasping and transforming experience" (p. 41). Knowledge can be grasped by concrete experience and abstract conceptualization, and experience is transformed through reflective observation and active experimentation. An educator's purpose is often to help students unlearn, that is, to dispose of or modify less productive knowledge and either integrate or substitute new knowledge (Kolb, 1984).

Trainers of new tutors and mentors can utilize Kolb's model of learning by devising experiential training activities. Trainers often use workbooks, textbooks, DVDs, or lectures to convey important information about working with students, and certainly these modes of training are useful. A well-planned role-playing activity lets trainees do something new (active experimentation), see and observe (concrete experience), watch (reflective observation), and then think (abstract conceptualization).

Thus role playing, an active learning technique, gives trainers another avenue for instructing new tutors and mentors while also providing the opportunity for trainers to assess and observe tutors and mentors. Unlike watching a video or observing other tutors or mentors, an active learning exercise is intended to "encourage students to both 'say' and 'say as they do something,'" which is likely to increase their learning (Powner & Allendoerfer, 2008, p. 77).

To assist new peer tutors and mentors in effectively retaining and applying the information learned throughout Level I International Tutor Training Program Certification (ITTPC) training (CRLA, 2011), this module outlines an exercise that presents tutors and mentors with scenarios like those they will encounter while working with students. For maximum effect, role-play activity is best completed at the conclusion of Level I training after trainees understand the basics of tutoring or mentoring. Earlier Level I training sessions provide the principles and touchstones that trainees need in the reflective observation and abstract conceptualization modes of the experiential learning process. This exercise is also designed to present new tutors and mentors with role-playing scenarios that are specific to their college or university—unlike role-playing activities in textbooks—so that tutors and mentors are prepared to deal with students at their own institution. This module describes how the tutor or mentor trainer can create and implement a role-playing activity unique to his or her own college or university student population.

Preparing for the Role-Play Activity

The first step in providing an appropriate role-play activity is to gather information about the student population or students likely to request the services of tutors and mentors. Institutional research offices can be helpful in gathering information for this activity, and experienced tutors or mentors can also offer their insights into the student population. This information will help create characters to use in role-playing scenarios. Questions to consider include the following:

- What types of diversity exist within the student population?

- What are the age range and average age of the student population?

- Are the students who use the services coming for specific issues or courses?

- Is the campus residential or commuter?

- Are there recurring situations among the students typically served, like finals-week frustration over certain content areas or stress among first-year students as they approach their first midterm examinations?

Using the information about the student population gathered from faculty, staff, and students themselves, it is possible to create profiles of students reflecting those at the institution who may use tutoring or mentoring services. These profiles can then be named and developed to include as much detail as possible about the student's personality and situation. Profiles can be written to vary from beginning to intermediate and then advanced content, including more difficult concepts for tutors and mentors to tackle as they become more comfortable with the activity.

The beginning-level profiles should include the basics of a tutoring session or mentor meeting to introduce students to the typical flow of a session. Intermediate-level profiles can include students who need additional tutoring beyond the content area, such as help with learning strategies in a variety of courses, or students who need more guidance than a typical mentoring session provides. Advanced-level profiles involve students in distress, whether over an assignment or a nonacademic situation. In developing several profiles for each category, varying gender, age, and personal characteristics can be used to acknowledge students' diverse social identities.

A beginning-level profile might feature "Marco," a college student of traditional age who needs help understanding one concept. An intermediate-level profile named "Sarah" might focus on a returning adult student who struggles to balance her difficult course load, her children's needs, and the emotions from a recent divorce. She comes to a peer mentor for advice about time management but is unable to concentrate because she and her ex-husband are fighting over custody of their children. "Lisa," the student discussed in an advanced-level profile, comes to a peer tutor for assistance in preparing for her final exam but grows so frustrated with the material that she throws her textbook and starts crying.

The next step in preparing for interactive training is to meet with the Level III tutors and mentors to explain the purpose of the activity and gather useful feedback. Experienced tutors and mentors can provide insights about what they found to be daunting in their early tutoring or mentoring experiences. Giving tutors and mentors the opportunity to practice their student profiles with each other and to ask questions or seek clarification before working with the Level I trainees will encourage the development of more authentic profiles. Trainers should use sensitivity when assigning scenarios to experienced tutors or mentors. Individuals who have been involved in traumatic situations should not be asked to relive those situations unless they are comfortable doing so.

The trainer then matches Level III tutors or mentors with those in Level I training. The trainer can pair them based on personal style, discipline specialty, or shared experiences. Additionally, several different pairings of Level III tutors and mentors with trainees can be made, to give trainees a varied experience during the activity. The trainer should work with Level III student staff before the activity to prepare content for discussion during the mock tutoring or mentoring sections. Level III tutors could plan discipline-related questions from textbooks, like sample math or chemistry questions, while Level III mentors could develop situations like roommate conflict, disagreement with parents, or uncertain academic goals.

Building Skill Through Role-Play Activity

When trainees have completed all of the reading, discussion, and other requirements of Level I training, they are ready for the role-playing exercise. It is important for skill building to start with beginning-level scenarios. Trainees need to be comfortable with the basics of tutoring or mentoring before they are able to tackle the more complicated issues associated with working with students. Training can move to intermediate and advanced scenarios as trainees feel comfortable and are considered ready to progress.

To role play the tutoring or mentoring situation, Level I trainees should be instructed to act as they would when waiting for an appointment to arrive. Because the goal of the training exercise is to give new trainees as much hands-on experience as possible, it is helpful to prepare mock schedules and ask office staff to participate as they would for a real situation. This activity attempts to replicate the culture of the tutoring center or mentoring program as much as possible. From a distance the trainer can observe the scenarios being acted out without interrupting the session.

After the completion of each scenario, the trainer brings the entire group together to discuss what they have seen and heard. Trainees should summarize their mock session and their reactions to it while the Level 3 tutors or mentors offer comments and suggestions. As trainees feel comfortable they can move on to intermediate and advanced-level profiles, continuing the activity until they and the trainer are confident in their tutoring or mentoring skills.

A variant of this approach to training through role-playing exercises is to have trainees play the student role first, while experienced tutors and mentors demonstrate their expertise in their usual role of tutor or mentor. Both groups of student staff thus share in the experiential learning session, and new staff learn also from the debriefing that follows, to which they contribute their observations, concerns, and questions. After all Level I trainees have experienced the student role, they can practice the role of the tutor or mentor. Upon completion of this exercise, trainees should feel more prepared to tutor or mentor students and more confident in utilizing their tutoring or mentoring skills with students.

A role-playing activity consistent with Kolb's (1984) Theory of Experiential Learning is designed to give trainees a chance to retain and apply the knowledge they gained during Level I training. The activity also gives the trainer an opportunity to work with trainees on areas that need improvement before trainees work with students. In addition, it will also help tutors and mentors bond with others in their training class and with Level III tutors and mentors. At the University of Akron Wayne College where this approach to role-play activity was developed, Level I tutors often return to the Level III tutors to ask questions or seek advice later in the semester because they are more familiar with those tutors. These tutors also point to this activity as the most helpful part of Level I training.

References

College Reading and Learning Association. (2011). *ITTPC certification requirements*. Retrieved from http://www.crla.net/ittpc/certification_requirements.htm

Kolb, D. A. (1984). *Experiential learning: Experience as the source of learning and development*. Englewood Cliffs, NJ: Prentice-Hall.

Powner, L., & Allendoerfer, M. (2008). Evaluating hypotheses about active learning. *International Studies Perspective, 9*(1), 75–89. doi:10.1111/j.1528-3585.2007.00317.x

Effectively Onboarding New Staff

Kathryn Van Wagoner

A management idea that has developed recently in the corporate world is that of *onboarding* new employees. The term refers to the approach used to help new employees to "get on board" in the new organization. What is new about this type of employee orientation is that it includes "introducing new members to the culture and to the accepted practices of the organization" (Herman, 2009, p. 1). Effective onboarding minimizes the time it takes for the new employee to become a productive member of the team.

The cultural orientation of onboarding shares an important principle with most tutoring and mentoring centers: reliance on peer relationships. A peer tutor can establish rapport with a tutee in a way a professor is less likely to accomplish. This rapport facilitates more open communication and a greater willingness from the tutee to accept the advice of the tutor. Developing peer relationships between new and experienced student employees is an effective method for onboarding new tutors or mentors into a learning center. This training activity is a good way to help new student staff feel welcome and comfortable in their new position, even as it provides them information they need to be effective as peer tutors and mentors.

A long-standing tutor training topic in programs certified by the College Reading and Learning Association (CRLA, 2011) International Tutor Training Program Certification (ITTPC) is known as Tutoring Dos and Don'ts, based on MacDonald's Basic Dos and Don'ts (2000). The name itself implies a list of things a tutor should and should not do and is often presented as a written or oral list. As an alternative to spending training time simply reading from a list, Advice for the New Guy (AFNG) or Advice for the New Gal (also AFNG) was developed.

Advice for the New Guy or Gal

At Utah Valley University, AFNG occurs during the fall tutor training conference held prior to the start of the semester. It is a casual session, as compared to the breakout sessions held earlier in the day. The new tutors are seated across the front of the room and face the experienced tutors. Every experienced tutor shares one piece of advice with the new tutors. By the time they are done, the tutors have covered all the major dos and don'ts. The group usually includes about 30 tutors, of whom 6-10 are new.

The interaction is enjoyable for a training supervisor to observe. Advice ranges from "Smile" to "Try to tutor a whole shift without a pencil," which leads nicely into a discussion on allowing the student client to maintain ownership of his or her own work. What is interesting about the no-pencil idea is that it originated with a tutor who worked in the center over 5 years ago, and her advice has been handed down through the ranks. The advice that experienced tutors give about what to do or what to avoid doing is often related to an issue with which they themselves have struggled. For example, one tutor who had experienced some consequences regarding confidentiality thereafter gave advice about the importance of maintaining confidentiality.

The trainer may feel the urge to editorialize or elaborate on a tutor's piece of advice. To preserve the peer interaction, it is advisable for the trainer to keep quiet at the time and take notes of ideas to be saved and contributed at the end of the AFNG activity. Before the exercise is over, one of the tutors may think to offer that idea, precluding the trainer from having to provide it.

At Utah Valley, the session provides many opportunities for laughter. As the new tutors learn some important advice on doing the work of their new job, they also experience the organizational culture of their new workplace.

Reflection and Assessment

This exercise lends itself well to the "What? So What? Now What?" reflection model described by Ender and Newton (2000). After the activity, new tutors write journal entries that permit the trainer to assess how well they can articulate and internalize the advice from experienced student staff. Trainees reflect upon the following questions: *What* experiences did you expect to have as a tutor? Did you find any major differences between your expectations and the information you gained from the experienced tutors? *So what* do these differences mean to you? Do you feel any anxiety over what is expected of you as a tutor? *Now what* are you going to do to remember and apply the advice you have received?

A new tutor commented, "One of the most important tips to me as a new tutor was that I don't have to know everything & it is ok to tell students that." Another new tutor summed up the experience well, showing that, at least for him, the exercise achieved its objective:

> I thought it was very useful. You can't really know about all those little things that are hard or necessary in a job until you've been doing it for awhile. Because there were lots of [experienced tutors] sharing at the same time, they kind of reminded each other of the things that they worry about and think about as they do their job each day. Listening to that was helpful to get me thinking correctly for the job, and it gave me little ideas about how to best help people and perform my job well.

Experienced tutors are also asked to write a reflective journal entry on the exercise. One very experienced tutor has captured well the essence of the activity:

> I like this activity because it reminds me of my special tutoring skills right before the semester begins. Sometimes the other tutors have great advice that I haven't heard before or even just things I needed to be reminded of. I like feeling as if I have some secret. It also seems to me [as if] after we've given the advice, [the new student staff] now have all our secrets and become part of the tutoring cohort. They are no longer the "newbies" because they have all our secrets so they know just as much as we do.

Student staff can be asked to submit their journal entries in notebooks, by email, or in a shared blog space for tutors. Lists of recommended actions, forbidden actions, and puzzling points to ponder may be posted in the fall or regularly through the academic year for review at any time.

References

College Reading and Learning Association. (2011). *ITTPC certification requirements.* Retrieved from http://www.crla.net/ittpc/certification_requirements.htm

Ender, S., & Newton, F. (2000). *Students helping students: A guide for peer educators on college campuses.* San Francisco, CA: Jossey Bass.

Herman, A. E. (2009). *Onboarding new employees: An opportunity to build long-term productivity and retention.* Wayne, PA: Kenexa Research Institute. Retrieved from http://www.kenexa.com/getattachment/385cbc05-19f9-4fbb-bc36-c5512ade7132/OnboardingNew-Employees-An-Opportunity-to-Build-.aspx

MacDonald, R. B. (2000). *The master tutor: A guidebook for more effective tutoring* (2nd ed.). Williamsville, NY: Cambridge Stratford Study Skills Institute.

Tutors Mentoring Tutors

G. Mason Tudor

In high-functioning tutoring programs, the tutors become a team, warm and welcoming to all clients, so much so that clients often feel a sense of inclusion. Some clients even bring food, the universal currency of appreciation. When the team becomes so close that new student staff cannot be integrated into the tutoring team, a stressful struggle is likely to ensue. The supervisor must take action in order to limit any adverse effects upon the program.

In a group brainstorming session, a senior tutor on the staff of one institution's learning center suggested a mentoring program to help new tutors to be accepted by and integrated into a well-established team. Because tutors value both being trained and being helpful, the experienced tutors can share training with new tutors in a different role, the role of helper. Mentoring and tutoring often overlap, so this progression seemed natural and obvious.

Tutors Need Mentors

Because many programs train throughout the semester rather than attempt to provide all training before tutors begin their work, tutors are often faced with situations requiring expertise beyond their training and experience, which can reduce tutors' confidence and, as a result, their efficiency as peer educators. In addition, although the tutoring supervisor is available as a resource for the tutors during normal working hours, the tutoring center may be staffed until late at night and on the weekends. A mentoring program that incorporates peer training can offer on-demand assistance with work-related issues. Consequently, a mentoring program by and for the tutors incorporates two immediate outcomes: speedier responses to problematic tutoring situations and continuous training utilizing veteran tutors as training resources.

Creating an environment in which tutors feel empowered and included is also an important aspect of any tutor training program. According to the research of Harris, Moritzen, Robitschek, Imhoff, and Lynch (2001), when employees feel connected to the program in a genuine way, there are fewer problems; empowering and including tutors may then be expected to reduce problems such as those normally associated with the employment of undergraduate students. Using the stress-strain-outcome model developed by Myung-Yong and Harrison (1998) in their study of social workers, supervisors can predict, in the absence of an intervention, that the poorly compensated staff upon which tutoring programs depend for a majority of their workforce can be expected to experience low levels of motivation and work commitment with high levels of absenteeism and burnout. By offering experienced tutors a connection to the success and growth of the program, the supervisor can help them develop confidence in tutoring and a passion for teaching and learning.

Developing the Program on One Campus

The unifying goal of Western Kentucky Community and Technical College's Academic Support Center (i.e., the program implementing the tutor mentor program) is to supply each student with the resources and confidence to become an independent learner, which is made possible through the tutors' knowledge, friendliness, and attentiveness to each client. Because of this central aspect of the Center's mission, phase one of the tutor mentoring program was to establish clear goals related to student success through increased tutor effectiveness. Further, in order to accomplish these goals, the Center's staff needed to integrate both a sense of purposeful training and a direct contribution to the program by student staff. The four goals of the mentoring program were to increase new tutor access to training resources, create a more cooperative and collaborative approach to training new tutors, develop an atmosphere of warm acceptance of new staff, and increase the quality of tutoring, which in turn should increase student success.

The tutor mentoring program was implemented in a spring semester. Before any new staff members were hired, many of the veteran tutors were informed that they would have mentees. New tutors were informed that a part of their training would be to complete a set of requisite skills under the tutelage of their mentor.

In the initial stage of the process, new tutors were assigned to veteran tutors who served as mentors and resources. Novice tutors were expected to complete a set of requisite skills under the guidance and expertise of their individual mentors and in some cases with the assistance of other mentor-tutors. The checklist of requirements contains skills identified by the supervisor and veteran tutors as crucial to the tutor's first days and weeks as a peer educator. (See Appendix for a sample checklist.) An introduction to the program was disseminated to new tutors at the beginning of the semester in a training session. This introduction included a brief purpose statement, a description, and a statement of goals and requirements for the first and second semesters of the program. In addition to skills work, the mentor-tutor and mentee-tutor were also assigned discussion topics and given a meeting schedule with the supervisor.

As the mentoring program for new tutors was developed with a varied group of students, some adjustments became necessary. These features are offered as advisory for individuals seeking to create a similar program on other campuses:

- For efficiency, mentor and mentee should be scheduled as a team.

- Mentor and mentee should exchange contact (email, phone) information.

- Mentors need to demonstrate an understanding of every task on the checklist before working with their mentees.

- Scheduled meetings between mentor and mentee should be regular and frequent; attendance should be consistent and required.

- Mentor, mentee, and supervisor should meet weekly.

- Mentors' observation of mentees' tutoring sessions should occur frequently.

- The skills checklist should be updated at the beginning and end of each new tutor's shift.

- New tutors should indicate on the checklist a brief description of how the criterion was met for each skill.

- The skills checklist should be relevant to the culture of the institution and the tutoring program.

Also, training time and staffing should be budgeted to create a checklist initially and to update it at the end of each term.

Benefits of Tutor Mentoring

Since the adoption of mentoring by experienced tutors, the new tutors were integrated into the tutoring team by the middle of their first semester. By the end of the semester, tutors had begun discussing strategies for integrating newly hired tutors for the next term. This progressive attitude and culture were in sharp contrast to the former, generally negative perspective in which the veteran tutors waited for or forced new tutors to prove themselves before conditionally accepting them onto the team.

Individual tutors have commented that the program has worked very well; furthermore, clients and stakeholders have noticed much more cohesiveness among tutors and continuity in the tutoring occurring within the center. One tremendous benefit in a more consistent tutoring program is a decrease in the turnover rate of the tutoring staff; moreover, because of the mentoring program, tutors now receive better training and demonstrate better learning and effectiveness. With these unexpected outcomes the program has been able to focus on creating new programs and can assume that the tutoring team is capable of more and more tasks usually reserved for full-time professionals. The most poignant example of this extension in tutoring duties is the development of study strategies: the tutors now research and then train one another in study strategy areas to utilize these strategies on demand in our walk-in tutoring center.

Another unanticipated outcome has been a different atmosphere among the tutoring center's clientele. Because the Center has a policy on self-regulated learning roughly translated as, "We don't do your homework; we help you learn how to do it yourself," the program has often encountered resistant students who do not understand or appreciate this approach. In the first semester of tutor mentoring, student referrals showed a new attitude. This shift is evident in the logging system: the number of sessions in which a tutor documented a problem with the students' expectations decreased from approximately 17% of sessions in the semester before implementation of tutor mentoring to fewer than 5% of sessions in the first semester of implementation. One of the regular clients encouraged a friend to seek help in the center but warned, "Don't go in there trying to get your homework done for you. . . They help you more with *understanding* the class. Then homework is easy and the quizzes and tests weren't as tough." The program's consistency of message and approach has thus changed the client culture and the expectations of potential clients. Documented cases of clients seeking homework answers decreased from approximately 10% of clients in the semester before implementation to fewer than 5% after implementation. Though unexpected, this outcome is important because the mission of the Academic Support Center is to create more independent and resourceful learners.

At the end of the pilot term, individual interviews were conducted with both tutors who were involved and tutors who were not involved in the mentor program. After only one semester, many of the tutors were already articulate about the program and nearly as knowledgeable as the designers of the program. In each interview, in response to questions about the purposes, benefits, problems, and potential improvements, tutors tended to respond with very similar terms and concepts. For instance, more than one tutor labeled the team a "family." Of the tutors interviewed, each reported positively upon the increased and strengthened "team" culture within the center. One tutor in his first and final semester of employment remarked, "That's why I hate to leave... This is my other family." The experienced tutors smiled as they spoke about increased team building, better team bonding, and feeling connected to the people they work with (coworkers and clients), the tutoring program, and the college. New tutors commented on the "peer" or egalitarian nature of their relationship with the veteran tutors. This team atmosphere seemed to contribute to a decrease in work-related stress noted by a few veteran tutors, one of whom commented, "We function better . . . [like] a family."

Tutors also reported a perceived increase in confidence. Veteran tutors observed that they were more comfortable in leadership roles, while new tutors confided they had much less anxiety than they would have expected. They were also more comfortable with having some freedom to make mistakes because mentors were like "a safety net," helping new tutors avoid feeling "adrift." New tutors truly enjoyed having multiple resources and felt no hesitation in asking questions of any of the veteran tutors by the end of the first 2 weeks. Veteran tutors also believed that assisting a new tutor made them better at their job.

Student success rates improved as well, with the course pass rate going from an average of about 65% before implementation of tutor mentoring to 70% following implementation. One tutor's most positive and introspective observation was that this program has increased the quality of tutoring. Veteran tutors reflected that they believed the number of repeat clients increased this semester and noticed fewer complaints about tutoring quality, competence, and policy. New tutors believed that they received much more training than they would have received without the mentoring program, and veteran tutors many times commented of the new staff, "They are better tutors than I was."

References

Harris, J. I., Moritzen, S. K., Robitschek, C., Imhoff, A., & Lynch, J. L. A. (2001). The comparative contributions of congruence and social support in career outcomes. *The Career Development Quarterly, 49,* 314–323.

Myung-Yong, U., & Harrison, D. F. (1998). Role stressors, burnout, mediators, and job satisfaction: A stress-strain-outcome model and an empirical test. *Social Work Research, 22,* 100–115.

Appendix

TUTOR MENTORING PROGRAM SKILLS CHECKLIST

Skill	Date Training Completed	Date Example Shown	Date Observed
Greet client			
Keep paper log			
Explore learning preferences			
Use textbook in session			
Explain a concept appropriately			
Guide with strategy			
Redirect a question			
Demonstrate study strategies	*Use spaces below for each type*	*Use spaces below for each type*	*Use spaces below for each type*
1			
2			
3			
Use a major learning "style"	*Use spaces below for each type*	*Use spaces below for each type*	*Use spaces below for each type*
1. Social			
2. Physical			
3. Aural			
Summarize during session			
Make appointments			
Enter digital log			

General Training Topics

Introduction

Although the training modules in this handbook encompass a rich range of topics and trainings, all share a common structure. Authors present first the theoretical or philosophical rationale for their training, then describe the training activity, and conclude with methods of assessing how well the peer tutors or mentors have learned from training. Appropriate assessment of learning is a critical part of the training session. Assessing merely tutors' and mentors' satisfaction with sessions and asking for their suggestions for improving sessions in the future is not sufficient; trainers must determine whether the training accomplished its objectives. Of course, both training activities and learning outcomes must be consistent with the theoretical or philosophical rationale for the training session.

Authors of these modules provide an array of assessment methods. Some embed assessment into every phase of training, so that the learning that tutors and mentors demonstrate guides the forward movement of the training activity. Other authors offer summative assessments at the end of the training session or measure knowledge before and after training. Tutors' and mentors' learning will ultimately be demonstrated in their work with student clients, but so will any lapses in learning. Measuring trainee learning against the learning outcomes anticipated for each training session permits trainers to (a) manage the training program by outcomes, (b) provide the best service they can to student clients, (c) document their tutors' and mentors' developing skills and expertise, and (d) demonstrate the quality of their training program in self-assessment to prepare for program review and institutional accreditation review.

The training topics of Chapter 3 are equally useful for peer tutors and peer mentors. Requirements of the College Reading and Learning Association (CRLA) International Mentor Training Program Certification (IMTPC) specify that the first 10 hours of an IMTPC-certified training program for mentors may be satisfied by International Tutor Training Program Certification (ITTPC) training for peer tutors (CRLA, 2011a, 2011b). The modules of Chapter 3 serve the same dual duty, because the topics they discuss—communication and relationships, rights and responsibilities, resources, student populations, and learning—should be part of the training of any student staff. Topics specific to tutor training can be found in Chapter 4. Mentor training topics are offered in Chapter 5.

During development of this handbook, some reviewers in our stringent peer review process observed that they could not endorse every module in this chapter. However, each of the 40 modules surviving that process had the confidence of a plurality of the reviewers. Because of the variety of options available here, readers should utilize for training the activities that are both compatible with the mission of their program and consonant with their theoretical or philosophical perspective.

Note that CRLA is making available some copyright-free, web-based handouts and other, copyrighted resource materials at www.crla.net/handbook/. Readers should check that site from time to time to see what new resources have been provided by authors of these Chapter 3 training modules.

REFERENCES

College Reading and Learning Association. (2011a). *IMTPC certification requirements*. Retrieved from http://www.crla.net/imtpc/certification_requirements.htm

College Reading and Learning Association. (2011b). *ITTPC certification requirements*. Retrieved from http://www.crla.net/ittpc/certification_requirements.htm

(A) COMMUNICATION AND RELATIONSHIPS

The Woo-Hoo Welcome: Creating Rapport With Students

 ### M. E. McWilliams

An important goal for tutor and mentor training is that tutors and mentors consistently establish responsive, supportive sessions for students. This attitude of enthusiasm, encouragement, and empathy for the student is the *woo-hoo welcome*. The tutors' and mentors' level of effort toward this objective in large part controls the success of the session. They can engage the student by fostering a "concerned human interaction" (Jarvis, 2002, p. 29), or they can estrange the student by coming across as "cold and uncaring" (Ryan & Grolnick, 1986, p. 550).

The rapport between tutor or mentor and student is a critical foundation for learning. Maslow's (1943) Hierarchy of Needs affirms that the fulfillment of basic psychological needs of the student must occur before the student is able to process the higher-order thinking required of college curricula. The Woo-Hoo Welcome Workshop focuses the majority of the training on how tutors and mentors can significantly influence Maslow's stages two through four: safety and security, love and belonging, and self-esteem. Good interpersonal skills can establish the trust, friendship, community, and self-worth that a client experiences at the learning center. Only then can students reach the point of self-actualization at stage five and begin to recognize their full potential to think critically.

Those who contend that these needs are not sequential as Maslow (1943) suggested would surely still concede that learning is inhibited when students are under duress if these basic needs are not met, and that most students approaching the learning center for the first time may be experiencing frustration, anxiety, and insecurity due to deficiencies in these areas. The information regarding one's studies is then muddled with emotional messages concurrently entering the brain (Illeris, 1999). A successful rapport with students then depends upon a Gestalt approach to learning—one that is holistic (Rogers, 1969) and addresses the affective processing of the student so that attention to cognition can follow.

Training Activity

The Woo-Hoo Welcome Workshop is an interactive training experience to build rapport with students at the learning center. The workshop has two parts: a game called Drawing in the Dark that develops empathy for the student who is distressed, and conversation regarding specific strategies for alleviating distress so that learning can occur. The materials necessary for this 1-hour training exercise include a space where participants can sit comfortably, a large dry-erase board, dry-erase markers, and two blindfolds.

PART 1: DRAWING IN THE DARK

The trainer divides the room of tutors or mentors into two teams. The trainer tells two trainees, one from each team, to step forward to a dry-erase board and announces that they are going to play Pictionary, the game in which their team members race to guess what is being drawn. A random audience member draws from a short stack of cards with words for what would ordinarily be easy-to-draw objects (e.g., cat, dog, horse, fireman, football player, cheerleader, truck, and boat). The artists are poised to draw when the trainer suddenly announces that she or he has forgotten something—and blindfolds each one. The trainer can expect giggles, as the trainees at the board are unsuccessful at drawing the intended object. The game can be played repetitively, as it is those who draw who will best understand the point to be made.

The trainer should ask those who participated as artists to explain how they felt while drawing in the dark, without the benefit of seeing the board. Artists will likely offer adjectives such as *confused, frustrated, lost*. The trainer then asks the tutors and mentors how this experience might parallel the mindset of many of our students when first coming to the center.

The trainer can underscore that many students feel stupid, humiliated, and maybe even hopeless upon that first visit. Whatever they have been trying to learn has made them feel as if they are in the dark. Naturally, first-time visitors assume that the subject is easy for the tutor or mentor, heightening feelings of intimidation and confirming their worst fear: they don't belong at college. They lack the very attributes identified by Maslow (1943) as necessary for self-actualization. This exercise illustrates that if the tutor and mentor are to establish rapport with the student, the tutor and mentor must empathize with the student.

PART II: CREATING A TRUSTING RELATIONSHIP

Tutors and mentors must be equipped with specific strategies for creating a communicative, trusting relationship that meets the student's need for security, belonging, and self-esteem. The trainer asks questions and guides the conversation to elicit some of the thoughts that follow in each section.

Space

What about the physical tutoring and mentoring space of the learning center would make the student feel comfortable? The space in which learning occurs "not only influences but also is a part of the learning" (Illeris, 1999, p. 97). Side-by-side seating is best for individual tutoring, and circles are best for groups. Materials should be readily available, and markers and erasers should be in good working order. Students also appreciate being able to snack and drink if they are to relax and engage (Hunley & Schaller, 2009). Cell phones should be off.

Greeting

What about the way a student is greeted would make the student feel welcomed? Eye contact is a sign of authenticity that can lessen the student's doubts about the tutor or mentor. Tutors and mentors should also use the student's name when meeting and frequently thereafter; however, nothing sets a student more at ease than a genuine smile. The trainer can show the tutors or mentors an enjoyable website on which visitors are asked to "spot a fake smile" (BBC Science, n.d.). The trainer will emphasize that, fake or not, smiles should be ubiquitous at the learning center. No tutor or mentor should be too occupied to give a proper greeting. Even the tutor at a demanding walk-in table can greet by saying, "Someone will be with you in just a minute."

Control

How can students know their learning is the focus of the session? Although the domain, such as math or writing, will often lend itself to a particular mode of conversation (Willingham, 2005), the tutor or mentor should seek opportunities to let the client *drive*, that is, let the client choose how the information will be discussed. Options for delivery include learning styles (auditory, visual, kinesthetic; Willingham, 2005) and multiple intelligences (spatial, kinesthetic, naturalistic, musical, mathematical, interpersonal, intrapersonal, and linguistic; Gardner, 1983). These options are best used to generate ideas for the tutor or mentor to suggest to students, not to label students and thereby restrict their learning (Claxton, 2009; Stahl, 2002). The overarching purpose is to keep the situation centered on the learner.

Respect

What can the tutor and mentor do to show respect while the student speaks? As one author wrote, "the trouble with listening for many of us is that while we're supposedly doing it, we're actually busy composing what we're going to say next" (Goldsmith, 2007, p. 148). Active listening means that the tutor or mentor is able to comment on what the student has said and ask appropriate questions. If tutors or mentors in a session hear their own voice more than the student's, they are not listening but lecturing. Tutoring and mentoring should be dialogues, not monologues.

Body Language

How might the tutor's or mentor's body language affect rapport with the student? The impact of a message is about 55% facial (Mehrabian & Ferris, 1967). If the tutor or mentor says to the student, "Tell me more," while looking at the clock, then the student will believe that the tutor or mentor is uninterested. Rapport with the student is greatly affected by the gestures, postures, and facial expressions of the tutor or mentor. To communicate interest, one should slightly lean in, nod the head in encouragement, and maintain eye contact. When shaking hands, the tutor or mentor should avoid a *vise grip*, which communicates dominance, or the *limp fish*, which suggests a lack of confidence. The grip should be firm.

Verbal Language

What might the tutor or mentor say that would inadvertently indicate dominance over the student? Rapport is built upon equality between tutor or mentor and student. When mentors or tutors present themselves as superior, they disrupt the safe environment in which a student can expose shortcomings. The student may become unresponsive when overshadowed by the tutor's *greatness*: "I'm in advanced calculus right now, so algebra is baby work to me." The tutor's or mentor's humility often has a surprising effect: "The more you [the tutor or mentor] subsume your desire to shine . . . the more you will shine in the listener's eyes" (Goldsmith, 2007, p. 156).

Challenging Clients

What student behaviors make establishing rapport most difficult? Students who challenge rapport include those who are unresponsive, dominating, talkative, angry, or hurried. Like old, stinky cheese left to rot in the refrigerator, these problems will just get *stinkier* until the tutor or mentor addresses them. The trick is to address the problem while maintaining rapport, a technique that trainers can call *cutting the cheese*:

- Confront the student alone to avoid the ripple effect of negative emotions in a public venue.

- Avoid a tongue-lashing that would only hurt or inflame the student, mindful that "some thoughts are best left unsaid" (Fisher & Ury, 1983, p. 37).

- Use your grandma voice, speaking calmly and politely.

- Use the sandwich method: Start and end with a positive statement that affirms an adaptive behavior. Between those two statements, give the directive for correcting the maladaptive behavior. This way the negative statement is buffered a bit. Avoid connecting any of those statements with the word *but*: "It's great the way you come to meet with me every week. We could also get a lot more done if your phone were off."

- Smile and say "thank you." If the problem persists, the tutor or mentor should be the broken record and repeat the directive verbatim.

Assessment

Following this training session, tutors and mentors should be able to recognize the need for rapport with the student and identify specific strategies to achieve the woo-hoo welcome. Assessment of these learning outcomes occurs first on a formative level at the close of the workshop when participants select one description from among four ranked statements to describe their ability to create welcoming environments for their clients. This self-analysis provides the baseline data required for the tutor and mentor to recognize the need to improve interpersonal communication.

Several weeks later, trainers should observe tutors and mentors for communication skills as they work with their students. Trainers may consider using a standardized rubric with a corresponding Likert-type scale for multiple skills, including communication. Concurrently, trainers can circulate surveys to clients for additional assessment of these skills, including rapport strategies. On the survey, students can identify appropriate statements about their tutors or mentors on a Likert-type scale.

Observations and surveys are returned to tutors and mentors for their review, followed by joint review as necessary. The trainer should continue to coach trainees in specific skills and strategies for improving their rapport with students.

References

BBC Science. (n.d.). *Spot the fake smile.* Retrieved from http://www.bbc.co.uk/science/humanbody/mind/surveys/smiles/

Claxton, G. (2009, February 13). *What's the point of school?* Retrieved from http://www.dystalk.com/talks/49-whats-the-point-of-school

Fisher, R., & Ury, W. (1983). *Getting to yes: Negotiating agreement without giving in.* New York, NY: Penguin.

Gardner, H. (1983). *Frames of mind: The theory of multiple intelligences.* Orlando, FL: Harcourt.

Goldsmith, M. (2007). *What got you here won't get you there: How successful people become even more successful.* New York, NY: Hyperion.

Hunley, S., & Schaller, M. (2009). Assessment: The key to creating spaces that promote learning. *Educause, 44,* 26–34.

Illeris, K. (1999). *How we learn.* New York, NY: Routledge.

Jarvis, P. (2002). Teaching styles and teaching methods. In P. Jarvis (Ed.), *The theory and practice of teaching* (pp. 22–30). London, United Kingdom: Kogan Page.

Maslow, A. (1943). A theory of human motivation. *Psychological Review, 50,* 370–396.

Mehrabian, A., & Ferris, S. (1967). Inference of attitudes from nonverbal communication in two channels. *Journal of Consulting Psychology, 31,* 248–252.

Rogers, C. (1969). *Freedom to learn: A view of what education might become.* Columbus, OH: Charles Merrill.

Ryan, R. M., & Grolnick, W. S. (1986). Origins and pawns in the classroom: Self-report and projective assessments in individual differences in children's perceptions. *Journal of Personality and Social Psychology, 50,* 550–558.

Stahl, S. A. (2002). Different strokes for different folks? In L. Abbeduto (Ed.), *Taking sides: Clashing on controversial issues in educational psychology* (pp. 98–107). Guilford, CT: McGraw-Hill.

Willingham, D. (2005, Summer). Do visual, auditory, and kinesthetic learners need visual, auditory, and kinesthetic instruction? *American Educator.* Retrieved from http://www.aft.org/newspubs/periodicals/ae/summer2005/willingham.cfm

Creating Rapport With Neurolinguistic Programming

Sara Weertz

Building or creating rapport is an integral part of the tutoring cycle (MacDonald, 2000) and an essential ingredient for successful tutoring or mentoring, because to communicate effectively, tutors and mentors must understand the power of rapport. Without a personal connection to the tutor or mentor, there is little likelihood a struggling student will discuss difficulties, ask and answer questions, or attempt to respond to suggestions, let alone return for additional visits. Building rapport, therefore, is a necessity for dynamic communications.

Communications experts have described the process of building rapport as the ability to align or connect with someone in order to develop trust and understanding (Boothman, 2002; Gerson & Gerson, 2006; Losier, 2009). Instant rapport is the spontaneous or natural connection people feel when they are immediately in synchronization, which is called *rapport by chance* (Boothman, 2002). Tutors and mentors, however, cannot expect to connect instantly with every student. When situations are devoid of instant rapport, tutors and mentors must rely on *rapport by design* (Boothman, 2002).

Psychologists and communications experts, particularly those involved in behavioral theory and more specifically neurolinguistic programming, support an interpersonal communication model focusing on creating rapport (Brooks, 1989; Sandoval & Adams, 2001). Through education and awareness of verbal and nonverbal cues, tutors and mentors can learn to recognize communication styles and understand the mechanics of rapport. More importantly, by using neurolinguistic programming they can learn to build rapport with each student they assist. To paraphrase Sandoval and Adams (2001), neurolinguistic programming (NLP) is based on three concepts:

- The senses—taste, touch, smell, sight, and sound—establish human behavior (*neuro*).

- People communicate with language, both verbal and nonverbal (*linguistic*).

- Each person organizes ideas in a specific manner (*programming*).

The theory supporting NLP is that people think differently and therefore process information differently. Individuals rely on their senses as intake measures and coding systems, with one preferred sense dominating the others; and when perceptions and experiences are shared, they are often transmitted using a dominant or preferred sensory modality (Sandoval & Adams, 2001). Humans use their senses to communicate; as individuals, however, they tend to lean on one sense more than the others (Brooks, 1989; Losier, 2009).

In the context of a tutoring or mentoring session, when the peer assistant and student have instant rapport, it is probable they are communicating using the same preferred sensory modality. On the flip side, when the peer assistant and student clearly do not have rapport, more than likely the two have clashing dominant sensory modalities. In this case, it is the responsibility of the tutor or mentor to build rapport with the student. Building rapport can be accomplished using NLP or what Brooks (1989) referred to as *rapport-technology*, which is gauging the preferred communication style by watching for and listening to the student's verbal and nonverbal cues.

Each communication style (visual, auditory, kinesthetic, and digital) has specific cues. When tutors or mentors recognize the dominant style in action, they then can match or mirror that style. Losier (2009) called this process "calibrating" and referred to it as "the art of paying attention and responding to what you've noticed" (p. 4), heeding body cues, eye cues, and language cues and intentionally adjusting communication style to that of the student. The success of tutors and mentors is closely tied to their ability to calibrate and thus build rapport. After calibration, the student is more inclined to open up and subsequently respond. If peer assistant and student fail to achieve rapport, the tutor or mentor may make assumptions and assertions or, worse, jump to conclusions as to what students are thinking or why they are struggling. Moreover, not paying attention leads to misunderstandings, causing students to leave the tutoring or mentoring session feeling annoyed and frustrated.

The most obvious of the verbal and nonverbal cues is language, because one's choice of words is intimately connected to one's thoughts (Brooks, 1989). Language cues in four sensory modes are charted in the Appendix.

Training Activity

The purpose of this training activity is to introduce tutors and mentors to NLP theory and the practice of building rapport. Objectives are to (a) define rapport, (b) recognize instant rapport, (c) develop modeling skills for creating and maintaining rapport, and (d) understand how rapport aids productive tutor and mentor communications.

Required equipment includes access to computers and the Internet for all participants. While the practical application and modeling of NLP is best accomplished in groups so trainees can witness a variety of communication styles and practice the techniques with peers, the activity can be a solo assignment with private journaling. In a group setting, the entire workshop can be completed in an hour. As an individual assignment, trainees can read Losier's (2009) book, complete the self-assessment, and write journal entries documenting their use of the new interpersonal communications skills. In a group setting, the training requires a room with adequate chairs and tables as well as a stage area that allows various pairs (e.g., auditory communicator and digital communicator) to practice in view of the other trainees.

The trainer starts the workshop with an enrolling question such as, "Who has had difficulty connecting with certain students?" To bridge prior knowledge to new knowledge, trainees discuss "difficult students" and the associated lack of communication.

Losier's (2009, n.d.) self-assessment questionnaire can be taken by trainees online and scored automatically. It will provide each trainee's dominant sensory modes in order of preference. When trainees understand their own preferred sensory modes, they will more easily recognize other sensory modes and thus calibrate their communication with that of their students. The trainer should emphasize that no one sensory mode is better than the others. A person's sensory mode bears no relation to the type of person he or she is but merely indicates how the person tends to relate to others (Brooks, 1989; Losier 2009).

Using the chart of typical linguistic indicators for the four sensory modes (Appendix), the trainer should guide trainees to identify characteristics of each sensory mode. For example, auditory communicators tend to use language associated with sound.

Finally, the trainer facilitates an exercise allowing trainees to practice matching or mirroring sensory modalities. The trainer should design several role-play scenarios and let participants develop their own scripts. For example, one scenario may be a student who says he is doing everything he is supposed to do but cannot pass the course exams. Ideally, each trainee should have an opportunity to play the student role and utilize the trainee's preferred sensory mode, and also play the role of tutor or mentor to practice calibrating communication style based on cues from the trainee playing the role of student.

Training ends with a description of rapport, a review of the four communication styles along with associated cues and characteristics from each style, and a discussion of how this new information may improve tutors' and mentors' interpersonal communication. The focus should primarily be on interpersonal communication within tutoring and mentoring sessions, but trainers and trainees may want to draw conclusions to other real-world settings in which NLP concepts are useful.

For trainers seeking an alternate activity, Gerson and Gerson (2006) pinpointed some techniques to help build rapport and connect with others using "similar words, language patterns, and jargon" (p. 120). The brief role plays are ideal but neither essential nor sufficient to meet the training objectives. Trainers should instead view rapport building as a skill set and seek to provide continuous feedback and improvement when observing and evaluating the practical application of these strategies.

Assessment

The trainer's objectives are to spotlight instant rapport, examine the underlying dynamic when two people lack rapport, describe the four sensory modalities and associated cues, give trainees an opportunity to determine their primary communication style, and offer practice for modeling or mirroring other styles. If the group is small enough, trainers can assess trainees' learning by questioning at the end of the training session. Personal assessment is a built-in self-assessment if trainees demonstrate an understanding of their preferred sensory mode. The training activity's role-play exercise provides another opportunity for trainees to demonstrate that they can observe and respond to others' linguistic cues to modify their own communications.

When trainees understand their own style and recognize how they signal that style to others, they can also learn to adjust or calibrate their communication with students. Likewise, trainers can assess calibration skills by observing tutoring or mentoring sessions. Trainees encountering difficult communications with a student may be urged to review the tutoring or mentoring session and reflect on how to recalibrate communication for the next session. Reflections may be private (in a journal) or shared (e.g., by weblog).

References

Boothman, N. (2002). *How to connect in business in 90 seconds or less.* New York, NY: Workman.

Brooks, M. (1989). *Instant rapport.* New York, NY: Warner Books.

Gerson, R. F., & Gerson, R. G. (2006). *Positive performance improvement: A new paradigm for optimizing your workforce.* Mountain View, CA: Davies-Black.

Losier, M. J. (n.d.). *Law of connection online assessment and communication styles and worksheets.* Retrieved from http://www.lawofconnectionbook.com

Losier, M. J. (2009). *Law of connection: The science of using NLP to create ideal personal and professional relationships.* New York, NY: Wellness Central.

MacDonald, R. B. (2000). *The master tutor: A guidebook for more effective tutoring* (2nd ed.). Williamsville, NY: Cambridge Stratford.

Sandoval, V. A., & Adams, S. H. (2001). Subtle skills for building rapport: Using neuro-linguistic programming in the interview room. *The FBI Law Enforcement Bulletin, 70*(8), 1–9. Retrieved from http://www2.fbi.gov/publications/leb/2001/august2001/aug01p1.htm

Appendix

TYPICAL LINGUISTIC INDICATORS OF FOUR SENSORY MODES

	VISUAL	AUDITORY	KINESTHETIC	DIGITAL
Common Features	Likes pictures Memorizes by creating visuals Bores easily without plans Is punctual Likes "big picture"	Remembers what is heard Learns by listening Tells stories well Hums or talks to self when working	Often speaks slowly Learns by doing Feels the way through issues Senses when something is right or wrong	Memorizes steps Detail oriented Learns by mentally working things out Needs time to process info Logical
Language Cues	Focus Imagine Look/See Observe Visualize Illustrate Clear/Clearly/Clarity Picture Bright Appear Dull/Hazy View/Scan Enlighten Show	Resonate Harmony Repeat Tune in Buzz Discuss Ringing Listen/Sound Noisy Whisper Tune Earshot Clicking Babble	Feel Firm Together Relationship Touch Connect Press Catch Hard/Soft Complete Numb Stumble Strike Grasp/Handle	Perceive Consider Detail Know Describe Figure out Process Logical/Rational Conceive Change Sequence Think/Thought Decide Understand
Common Expressions	I see what you mean. That's not clear. Don't keep me in the dark. Can you clarify? It's fuzzy to me.	Tell me more. I hear you loud and clear. That rings a bell. It was music to my ears. It was all double talk.	Let's touch on this. Get comfortable. Walk me through this. It just rubs me the wrong way. I get the point.	Without a doubt. Word for word. Describe in detail. Figure it out. Make sense of it Pay attention to. . . I know what you mean.
Common Greetings	How good to see you. You're looking great. I've been looking forward to this. See you later. I'll look for you. See you soon.	I'm glad you called to chat. So good to talk to you. I called to tell you. I'll talk to you soon. Call later.	I love it when you call. I'm happy to hear from you. Let's catch up. It feels good to connect again. I'm excited to talk to you.	Hello. Hey. This is John. Bye now. Yes. . .

Note. Chart developed using material from *Law of connection: The science of using NLP to create ideal personal and professional relationships,* New York, NY: Wellness Central, by M. J. Losier, 2009, pp. 24–61. Copyright 2009 by Wellness Central.

Positive and Supportive Communication

◾ Diana Calhoun Bell

Communicating effectively during a tutoring or mentoring session is the cornerstone of success-ful interactions between peer educators and the students with whom they work. Gibb's Com-munication Model, originated by communication scholar Gibb (1961, 1964, 1970), allows peer educators to provide supportive rather than destructive communication as they work within the paradigm of inquiry-based pedagogy. Inquiry-based pedagogy focuses on the student rather than the tutor or mentor. Questions provide feedback to let the student actively participate in the tutor-ing or mentoring process and ultimately become more active learners.

Gibb's Communication Model is based on six dimensions of communication (see Figure 1), in which destructive communicative patterns serve as a negative force and supportive communicative patterns serve as a positive force.

The key in this model is for tutors and mentors to train themselves away from destructive patterns of communication and toward supportive patterns. For example, using the language of destruction, a writing tutor might say: "Look at this sentence. Your grammar is wrong. You connected these two sentences with a comma, making a comma splice error." The problem with this destructive language of evaluation is twofold. First, the tutor makes a judgment about the student's product by bluntly using *your*, implying that the error is within the writer rather than in the sentence itself and creating a value judgment against the student rather than within the writing. Second, indicating that the grammar is *wrong* is destructive because it does not help determine why the student used a comma there and quashes the student's inclination to respond.

The supportive counterpart to this destructive language pattern would be descriptive communi-cation. The key to encouraging inquiry is to separate the student from the problem, thus opening up the door to dialogue. A writing tutor may say, "I see a comma error in this sentence, but we can talk about how to correct it easily. See these two main clauses connected with just a comma? That's the issue. Why did you decide to use this form of punctuation? I can think of several legitimate reasons why a comma was used instead of a period—and you may not even need a period here, depending on what you are trying to say." Here, the tutor points out that the problem resides in the text, not in the person; assures the student that the problem can be solved; and tries to find the problem's source. The tutor focuses on solving the problem *with* the student rather than *for* the student.

The second dimension of supportive communication to discuss is language that controls as opposed to language that assists. The tutor's or mentor's role is to assist rather than control the stu-dent's learning. If a student has an incorrect answer to a problem based on insufficient knowledge

Destructive Patterns (Negative Force)	Supportive Patterns (Positive Force)
Evaluate	Describe
Control	Assist
Manipulate	Facilitate
Superior	Equal
Certain	Possible
Indifference	Empathy

FIGURE 1   Gibb's Communication Model. Adapted from analysis presented in "Defensive Communication" by J. R. Gibb, 1961, *Journal of Communication, 11,* 141–148.

of trigonometry, the math tutor's goal is to help the student understand the basic function needed to solve the problem. The tutor who uses a controlling pattern of language might say, "The problem is that the tangent of pi over 4 is 1. It is important for you to memorize that in order to work the problems effectively." In this example, ownership over the problem has shifted to the tutor, who controls the knowledge base and the answers to questions. This creates a situation in which the student can become reliant upon the knowledge of the tutor. A math tutor using the more positive assistive pattern of communication may say something like, "There are several ways of solving this problem. We can break down tangent into sine over cosine and refer back to definitions in your book to come to our conclusion. Should we start by looking at the definitions and then work our way through the problem step by step?" Here, the tutor lets the student retain ownership of his or her thinking and problem-solving. The tutor shows the student where to find resources to help solve this problem *and future problems* while working by steps to enable the student to solve the problem.

The third dimension of communication important to Gibb's model is the idea of manipulation compared with facilitation. This dimension is closely related to the idea of control and assistive language but is subtly different. Tutors and mentors manipulate when they try to influence the direction the session takes rather than facilitate the direction that students want to take. For example, a manipulative tutor might go into a session on classical conditioning with a preconceived idea about what the student needs to know based on past sessions with other psychology students who fail to understand a specific process. Therefore, at the beginning of the session, without ascertaining the student's needs, the manipulative tutor might say, "So, let's get started—what is presented first, a conditioned stimulus or an unconditioned stimulus?" This manipulative approach makes assumptions about the students' knowledge base and then manipulates the student into progressing in a particular order with a particular agenda during the session. By contrast, using facilitative communication, the tutor would set the agenda by asking the student questions about what he or she already understands about classical conditioning, perhaps by asking questions of definition, such as, "At this point, can you say in your own words what an unconditioned stimulus is?" Only after achieving clarity about each of the four major terms would tutor and student discuss how the entire learning theory works. This strategy ensures that the student controls the pace and content of the session. Also, rather than asking a general question like, "What do you want to start on," or "Tell me what you know," the facilitative tutor asks more specific open-ended questions. Asking very broad questions generally just wastes time because few people have the knowledge or confidence to generate effective questions about what they do not know.

The next dimension of Gibb's (1961) model is the idea of superiority as opposed to equality. When using communication of superiority, tutors and mentors dominate ideas; in equality they serve as peers who stimulate thought. An example of the language of superiority might be drawn from a political science session in which the tutor says, "So, in class, you talked about the PC movement, and what you are saying is that forcing people to use politically correct terminology creates resentment. I remember when I used to think like that, too. After we cover all of what the movement entails, I'm sure you will understand the whole issue." Here, the tutor tries to be supportive by responding back to the student about what the student just said and using personal experience to connect with the student; however, by using the language of superiority the tutor implies a higher state of enlightenment from a position of more complete and detailed understanding. This pose of superiority is destructive to inquiry because the student may now be unwilling to continue to advocate the other side of the argument and may feel inferior to the tutor. Using the language of equality instead, the tutor may say, "So in class you talked about the PC movement, and you are saying that forcing people to use politically correct terminology creates resentment. Can you tell me what ideas you will use to support your position? Then I can give you some of the opposing viewpoints and you can refute them. That way, you will be prepared for either multiple-choice or essay questions." Notice here that the tutor begins the same way, by rephrasing the students' position, but then encourages the student to support an opinion. This leaves room for the tutor to assert the opposing side without making the student feel uncomfortable or inferior.

The fifth dimension of Gibb's (1961) Communication Model is perhaps the most profound. It upholds the supportive language pattern of possibility rather than the destructive pattern of certainty. Tutors and mentors need to foster ideas of what may be rather than to close off ideas by being certain of outcomes. In a tutoring session on criminal justice, the tutor says, "You didn't mean to say that our justice system always makes fair and ethical decisions, right? I can assure you that the professor will count that wrong on the test." Here, both the student and tutor may feel satisfied with the session: the tutor demonstrates certainty about the instructor's expectations, and the student, whose ultimate goal is a good grade, takes this advice without question. The tutor, in this case, assures the student that he or she knows the answer, and, by doing so, encourages what Freire (1970/2000) called the banking model of education—depositing information in students' heads so that they can make withdrawals at a later date. Instead, the tutor should guide the consideration of possibilities and encourage student understanding and critical thinking. An example of the language of possibility may be, "You just made an interesting comment about the judicial system that is different from the way it is presented in the text. First, let's consider the implication of the word 'always.' How does that word impact the meaning of your statement? Then let's think of ways you might provide your answer in an essay question format so that you can show the instructor that you understand the implications of your position." Here, the tutor does not force a certain answer onto a student who may very well have important contributions to make but instead thinks of possibilities, of ways to help the student effectively communicate ideas and learning and inspire inquiry and critical thinking.

Finally, the sixth dimension of the Gibb's (1961) Communication Model focuses on the language of indifference compared to that of empathy. Tutors and mentors working with multiple students a day can feel drained, yet it is important that they come to each session with renewed energy and enthusiasm for the student and the questions students bring. If students come to them with excuses after performing poorly on a test, tutors and mentors may unintentionally show indifference by saying something like, "Dr. Gradelow typically asks questions that she didn't cover in class. To get a better grade next time, you need to pay more attention to what we cover here and study the questions at the end of the chapter more carefully." Now, while this may be true, the student can read this as indifference to his or her plight. Instead, if tutors and mentors use the language of empathy, students know their emotions are understood and can move on. An empathic tutor may say, "I don't blame you for being upset and frustrated about your test grade. Now that you know the way Dr. Gradelow creates her exams, how do you think we can better prepare for the next exam?" This language of empathy acknowledges to the student that the tutor understands this kind of frustration and knows how to think ahead, using that testing experience as a learning experience.

Training Activity

The goal of the activity is to recognize the difference between destructive and supportive language and to implement supportive language into interaction with students. The trainer needs a room with an AV screen, computer, and projector. Trainees will need paper or small whiteboards and markers.

The trainer begins by introducing trainees to Gibb's (1961) model through PowerPoint® slides (Bell, 2011) or other visual means, using and dramatizing specific language examples of each of the dimensions. Then the trainees are divided into six groups; each group works on one of the dimensions of Gibb's model. The trainer should either prepare destructive language examples for the trainees to manipulate or have trainees come up with their own examples. Trainee tutors and mentors may be surprisingly forthcoming about the destructive language they have used or experienced in the past. The trainer should have trainees revise the destructive language of these examples into supportive language.

Assessment

Assessment is built into the small-group activity. As each group presents its destructive and supportive language examples to the larger group, the trainer should invite other groups to listen carefully and find ways to be even more supportive of student learning through inquiry. Further assessment can be conducted through observations of tutors and mentors as they work with students and through self-reflection activities with tutors or mentors after training.

References

Bell, D. C. (2011). *Positive and supportive communication.* Retrieved from http://www.crla.net/handbook/ch3/bell

Freire, P. (1970/2000). *Pedagogy of the oppressed* (30th anniversary ed., M. Bergman Ramos, Trans.). New York, NY: Continuum.

Gibb, J. R. (1961). Defensive communication. *Journal of Communication, 11,* 141–148.

Gibb, J. R. (1964). Climate for trust formation. In L. Bradford, J. Gibb, & K. Benne (Eds.), *T-group theory and laboratory method* (pp. 279–309). New York, NY: Wiley.

Gibb, J. R. (1970). Sensitivity training as a medium for personal growth and improved interpersonal relationships. *Interpersonal Development, 1,* 6–31.

Communicating Across Cultures

Anita H. Ens

In interactive tutoring and mentoring relationships, communication requires making many assumptions about others; however, when barriers in the learning process occur, tutors can examine the relationship between culture and communication to address difficulties. Social learning theory provides a helpful framework to analyze the constructs of culture and communication, particularly as it relates to discourse communities (Gee, 2000) or communities of practice. Members of a community of practice develop their identity through their interactions and knowledge construction (Lave & Wenger, 1996). For tutors and mentors who cannot possibly know all potential clients' cultures, it is useful to be able to view themselves as working together with the student client in a given discourse community, or academic discipline, and learning that language together. Ethnic, religious, athletic, or other cultures may offer analogies or points of intersection for them, but the reference point in the tutoring or mentoring session becomes the academic community of practice in which joint attention brings a pair together in the negotiations that further learning (Plumb, 2005).

It is important to keep in mind that not all students will view acculturation to the academic norms as desirable, possibly seeing acculturation as a loss of important, unique qualities in a process of assimilation (Stieg, 2001). Others may not realize how becoming more knowledgeable and accepted in one community may require losses in others (Murray & Kouritzin, 1997). By talking about academic practices as norms in college and university education and pointing out what behaviors are expected in such a way that tutees and mentees retain the choice to change, tutors and mentors can respect difference rather than assume that learning the dominant discourse will be desirable. Tutors and mentors who model understanding of various viewpoints and who acknowledge the existence of power in structures and relationships (Banks, 2001) will be more likely to see their student clients as people with knowledge and strengths rather than as needy and ill-informed individuals requiring improvement (Lum, 2006).

Another useful approach to improving cross-cultural tutoring and mentoring is to consider communication as a construct. Human communication is both verbal and nonverbal and has been represented in a basic model, originally mathematical (Shannon, 1948) or in literary criticism (Jayne, 1970), but subsequently developed in psychology (e.g., Bavelas & Chovil, 2000), sociology, and business. Based on this model, the message carries the sender's idea and is shaped by choice of words, gestures, tone, and what is not said. How the message is received is affected by the recipient's prior experiences with the sender; "noise" as the message is relayed; the receiver's familiarity with the words and language; and a host of other factors such as state of being (e.g., hungry, therefore distracted), prior experiences of similar messages, and general background knowledge. Even in its simplified form, communication runs more than one way; the model acknowledges this by including a feedback loop established by the "uh huhs," nods, smiles, raised eyebrows, glazed eyes, fidgeting, or other cues from the listener.

While moment-to-moment interactions often occur subconsciously, when difficulties in communication arise between tutor and tutee or mentor and mentee, it can be helpful to use the speaker-listener model to examine and potentially address its communication aspects consciously. For example, attending to the facial expression of the listener, a tutor may say, "You look confused. Is there something here that doesn't make sense?" The tutee may respond, "No, I'm just thinking," or "Yeah, could you repeat what you said about exponential growth?" Specific communication behaviors that facilitate learning can also uncover and address problems as they arise. These include probing, paraphrasing, clarifying, reflecting, interpreting, and questioning (Duffey & Hodges, 2003) as well as validating feelings (MacDonald, 2000) and making cultural comparisons. A tutor may say, for example, "I know in some cultures students are encouraged to learn by listening rather than speaking" (McGroarty, 1993). Checking for verbal or nonverbal response, the tutor may continue, "Here we are quite direct. And for me to figure out what's going to work best, it will help if we have more of a conversation than a lesson. You can ask questions or explain things to me. If we each speak freely, it will be easier for me to know where you have strong understanding."

A tutor may also point out associated gains in the discourse community such as comfort in participating in class discussions and showing an understanding of academic cultural expectations (e.g., by challenging ideas appropriately). The examples illustrate how inextricably communication and culture are intertwined and offer rich possibility for discussion.

Training Activity

A room with chairs grouped around tables and chalkboard, interactive board, or flip charts is needed. An AV screen, DVD player, and LCD projector are also required. This training session will take an hour. Learning objectives for the tutors and mentors in training are to (a) become aware of culture as nuanced and layered, (b) explain basic interpersonal communication through a model and become aware of assumptions, and (c) equip themselves with ways of examining and developing intercultural communication in a tutoring or mentoring context.

The trainer should introduce the concept of culture by writing "What is your culture?" on the board and asking trainees to discuss in groups of two or three. The question is deliberately broad. By allowing trainees to articulate their thoughts on culture by defining it in a group activity before presenting definitions from the field, trainers start with what trainees know and model the negotiation of ideas in mutual knowledge construction. The varied responses give an excellent example of how individual perspective directs interpretation. Although discussion may elicit arguments about which version of culture is more influential in tutoring and mentoring scenarios, the point to emphasize is that because culture forms the framework for both idea expression and interpretation, it is sometimes difficult to identify underlying beliefs and assumptions (Taylor, 1994). In addition, "students' intersecting worlds may at times create conflicts between academic goals and other aspects of students' lives" (Higbee et al., 2004, p. 63). Mentors' and tutors' awareness of their own starting points as well as ability to draw out and empathically listen to tutees' perspectives will help to move the learning forward (MacDonald, 2000). Using the discourse community approach can provide parameters for a potentially inflammatory, divisive, or overwhelming topic.

Trainers should have trainees share ideas as a whole group and should collect them on the board, valuing the variety of interpretations that surface or problematizing the concept if trainees provide homogenous responses. In training sessions, trainees have said, "I don't really come from a culture; I'm just Canadian." When probed to explain what that means, trainees who identify as generically Canadian may say it means being polite, apologetic, kind, and liking hockey and Tim Hortons.

Other participants may associate with that description but notice differences, too, arising from particular experiences within that greater societal affiliation. For example, defining experiences may involve religious, gender, first-family, or other factors. One tutor described the culture she came from as restricting; the privileging and dominance of men in her first family outlined clearly what her place was and defined her life in terms of whose knowledge was valued (men's) and what her role was (subservience). This type of cultural understanding crosses ethnic lines and becomes a definition based on gender or power. Frequently tutors describe their culture along ethnic, national, or linguistic lines and report blending. For example, "My mom was Jamaican, and my dad was part Irish and part Scottish, so I'm not sure what that makes me." Less frequently students also acknowledge complexity when considering their culture from perspectives of intersection: national, ethnic, racial, class, familial, and schooling.

Building on the discussion, the trainer should use definitions from the field to challenge assumptions and to make connections to campus culture:

> Giroux (1997) has described culture as the dynamic interplay between the experiences of people and the social structure at large; it is the individual perceptions of one's societal situation. Wang (2001) described culture as one's identification with the shared social construction or "sameness" that is shared with others. (Lum, 2006, p. 113)

Both definitions work well with the notions of communities of practice.

MacDonald (2000) in his chapter on intercultural tutoring first defined culture as "a set of socially transmitted behavior patterns, beliefs, values, creative works and processes, institutions, and so forth," (p. 97) and then indicated how it can influence communication: "culture is the framework any individual brings to any communication" (p. 99). The speaker-listener model offers a micro view much affected by the macroculture, such as the weight given to gestures over words (Triandis, 2000). However, it is misleading to think that a solitary culture forms the framework, providing "ever-present lenses that color all our social perceptions" (Hong, Benet-Martinez, Chiu, & Morris, 2003, p. 453). Individuals may choose from their various internalized cultural constructs to interpret and act in given situations (Zaidman & Holmes, 2009).

After this introductory discussion about cultures, the trainer should provide the communication model (Figure 1) inductively by drawing a simple diagram on the board and soliciting input on how messages are transmitted and received. The trainer should discuss "noise" (Shannon, 1948) and possibilities for differences in interpretation of messages. Most trainees will be familiar with the concepts, and the exercise may be done quickly as it reinforces earlier discussion. The final activity brings in voices of students from various cultures.

One way to deepen tutors' and mentors' understanding of the cultural schemata that students bring to learning tasks is to show a video in which cultural approaches to academic tasks are made explicit. Education, learning, and knowledge are viewed differently in different cultures (Merriam, Caffarella, & Baumgartner, 2007; Triandis, 2000; Zhang, 2009) and affected by value orientations such as Western individualism and Eastern collectivism. Clips from *Writing Across Borders*

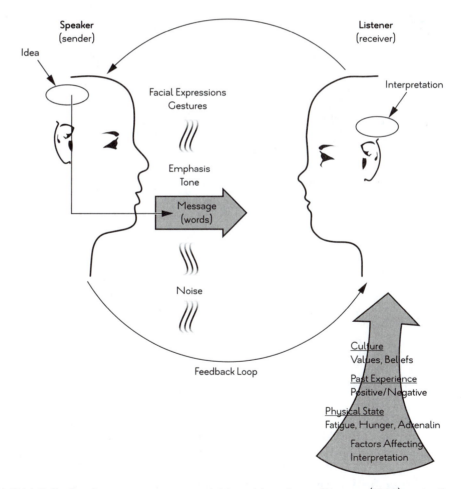

FIGURE 1   A communication model based loosely on Shannon (1948) and influenced by a model of intention and effect (Mediation Services, 1996, p. 12).

(Robertson, 2005) can catalyze rich discussion. Although this DVD's interviews focus on writing, trainers can help tutors and mentors draw parallels to their own discipline's discourse patterns or knowledge systems in view of other cultural frameworks, again using the notion of discourse communities.

After viewing the DVD, the trainer should encourage trainees to share their reactions, asking them to extrapolate how culture may also affect the one-to-one interaction of their work and habits of thought in different disciplines. The trainer can close by reminding trainees (or having them remind each other) how asking questions, paraphrasing, listening, and other tutor and mentor behaviors can serve to deepen cross-cultural understanding.

Assessment

To assess whether trainees understand culture as complex and nuanced, the trainer should ask again the initial question (What is your culture?) and let trainees acknowledge the impossibility of answering the question simply. To assess trainees' understanding of the basic communication model, the trainer can ask them to explain, draw, or describe it. To assess trainees' knowledge of cultural understanding in the practice of tutoring and mentoring, the trainer can provide brief scenarios and ask trainees to describe how to develop cross-cultural understanding.

References

Banks, J. A. (2001). Citizenship education and diversity: Implications for teacher education. *Journal of Teacher Education, 52*(1), 5–16. doi:10.1177/0022487101052001002

Bavelas, J. B., & Chovil, C. (2000). Visible acts of meaning: An integrated message model of language in face-to-face dialogue. *Journal of Language and Social Psychology, 19,* 163–194. doi:10.1177/0261927X00019002001

Duffey, T., & Hodges, R. (2003). Establishing a helping relationship: Facilitating non-verbal and verbal communication. In S. Deese-Roberts (Ed.), *College Reading and Learning Association tutor training handbook* (rev. ed., pp. 65–80). Hastings, NE: College Reading and Learning Association.

Gee, J. P. (2000). Discourse and sociocultural studies in reading. In M. L. Kamil, P. B. Mosenthal, P. D. Pearson, & R. Barr (Eds.), *Handbook of reading research* (Vol. III, pp. 195–207). Mahwah, NJ: Erlbaum.

Higbee, J. L., Miksch, K. L., Jehangir, R. R., Lundell, D. B., Bruch, P. L., & Jiang, F. (2004). Assessing our commitment to providing a multicultural learning experience. *Journal of College Reading and Learning, 35*(2), 61–74.

Hong, Y-Y., Benet-Martinez, V., Chui, C-Y., & Morris, M. W. (2003). Boundaries of cultural influence: Construct activation as a mechanism for cultural differences in social perception. *Journal of Cross-Cultural Psychology, 34,* 453–464. doi:10.1177/0022022103254201

Jayne, E. (1970). *I. A. Richards: Theory of metaphor, theory as metaphoric variation* (Unpublished doctoral dissertation). The State University of New York, Buffalo, NY. Chapter 1 retrieved from http://www.edwardjayne.com/critical/Richards.pdf

Lave, J., & Wenger, E. (1996). Practice, person, social world. In H. Daniels (Ed.), *An introduction to Vygotsky* (pp. 143–150). London, United Kingdom: Routledge.

Lum, L. (2006). Internationally-educated health professionals: A distance education multiple cultures model. *Education & Training, 48*(2/3), 112–126. doi:10.1108/00400910610651755

MacDonald, R. B. (2000). *The master tutor: A guidebook for more effective tutoring* (2nd ed.). Williamsville, NY: Cambridge Stratford Study Skills Institute.

McGroarty, M. (1993). Cross-cultural issues in adult ESL literacy classrooms. *ERIC Digest.* Washington, DC: National Clearinghouse on Literacy Education. Retrieved from http://eric.ed.gov/PDFS/ED358751.pdf

Mediation Services. (1996). *Interpersonal conflict resolution training manual.* Winnipeg, Canada: Author.

Merriam, S. B., Caffarella, R. S., & Baumgartner, L. M. (2007). *Learning in adulthood: A comprehensive guide* (3rd ed.). San Francisco, CA: Jossey-Bass.

Murray, G., & Kouritzin, S. (1997). Re-thinking second language instruction, autonomy, and technology: A manifesto. *System, 25,* 186–196. doi:10.1016/S0346-251X(97)00007-9

Plumb, D. (2005). Cultural learning. In *International encyclopedia of adult education* (pp. 173- 176). New York, NY: Palgrave-Macmillan.

Robertson, W. (Writer & Director). (2005). *Writing across borders.* [DVD]. Corvallis, OR: Oregon State University Center for Writing and Learning and Writing Intensive Curriculum Program. Retrieved from http://cwl.oregonstate.edu/wab

Shannon, C. E. (1948). A mathematical theory of communication. *The Bell System Technical Journal, 27,* 379–423, 623–656. Retrieved from http://cm.bell-labs.com/cm/ms/what/shannonday/shannon1948.pdf

Stieg, E. J. (Ed.). (2001). *Fields of vision: Readings about culture, race, and ethnicity.* Toronto, Canada: Pearson Canada.

Taylor, E. W. (1994). Intercultural competency: A transformative learning process. *Adult Education Quarterly, 44,* 154–174. doi:10.1177/074171369404400303

Triandis, H. (2000). Culture and conflict. *International Journal of Psychology, 35,* 145–152. doi:10.1080/002075900399448

Zaidman, N., & Holmes, P. (2009). Business communication as cultural text. *International Journal of Intercultural Relations, 33,* 535–549. doi:10.1016/j.ijintrel.2009.06.002

Zhang, Q. (2009). Perceived teacher credibility and student learning: Development of a multicultural model. *Western Journal of Communication, 73,* 326–347. doi:10.1080/1057031090308207

Effective Cross–Cultural Communication

 Linda T. Barr

Every day students from other cultures walk into learning centers to engage in a primal act of human experience: asking for help. Compounding the stress behind this dynamic is the need to express the nature of the help required in a second language and in a manner that will be understood by the receiver of the request. The tutor or mentor, in turn, must interpret the message given and respond appropriately. Both parties need to be adept communicators to make this interaction successful. Student competence in communicative skills may vary, so it is highly desirable to provide tutors and mentors with strategies for effective cross-cultural communication.

The objectives of this training module are to acquaint tutors and mentors with collectivist cultural norms, define some specific communication variants, and suggest strategies for effectively communicating with people from other cultures. Collectivist norms were selected because a large percentage of students from other cultures belong to collectivist societies. Although cultural norms are not the same for any two cultures and may in fact vary between subcultures, collectivist cultures share a perspective that is often at odds with the individualist norms prevalent in North America. Successful interaction between individualists and collectivists requires sensitivity and accommodation, but the value of these attributes can be generalized and used effectively across socioeconomic, regional, age, and gender boundaries as well.

Effective communication results from both parties' making fewer misperceptions (Gudykunst & Kim, 2003) and more accurate contextual presuppositions (Reynolds, 2000). Knowledge about cultural differences cannot be inferred, so some direct instruction regarding possible sources of misunderstanding is advisable. Communication is a symbolic activity, according to Gudykunst and Kim (2003), so to provide tutors and mentors with visual materials outlining the differences between collectivist and individualist cultures, a PowerPoint® or other visual presentation should be created. Slides outlining and illustrating individualistic cultural imperatives give tutors and mentors visual points of comparison, so those should be included in the presentation as well. Works such as *Communicating With Strangers* by Gudykunst and Kim (2003) provide ample material on cultural differences, but trainers may use other sources if they choose. Trainers should arrange to upload PowerPoint® presentations to their tutor and mentor training website or to the institution's website for future reference.

Training Activity

This training session will require about 90 minutes. The trainer begins with a brief introduction to the topic and a prepared 20-minute PowerPoint® presentation.

PREPARED PRESENTATION

Trainers should prepare slides on fundamental differences between collectivistic and individualistic cultures. Slides should also explain communication differences and possible sources of communication conflict between individualistic and collectivistic cultures.

Individualistic vs. Collectivistic Values

Individualistic cultures value individuality and direct speech. In other words, individualists like to point out their differences, claim uniqueness, look each other in the eye, and come straight to the point. Individualistic cultures prize personal achievement and consider self-actualization a fundamental right. Collectivistic cultures, on the other hand, prize group harmony and interdependent achievement. The values of collectivistic cultures are different from those of individualistic cultures. Collectivists emphasize group goals over those of the individual. The focus is on fitting in with the group and conforming to group values rather than reshaping the group to suit the individual and demanding that the group heed the individual's will. In collectivistic cultures, individuals identify strongly with the group; that is, the individual gains both identity and self-image through membership in the group. Following traditions is important, rather than always seeking something new. Speech is often less direct, which may create communication challenges when interacting with members of individualist cultures (Gudykunst & Kim, 2003).

In collectivistic cultures, communication is more likely to be understood as highly contextualized: words are no more important than tone, pauses, and body language. Knowledge of cultural expectations and dictates makes words unnecessary at times. Meaning is imbedded in physical cues and unstated messages. Speakers may expect the listener to know the intended meaning and may talk around the point. There may be less openness and more use of silence in conversation than in individualistic cultures. A good example of imbedded cues is illustrated by the Japanese approach to writing position papers. Rather than stating and proving a position, in Japanese culture students paint pictures with words to lead the reader to the point, which may be unstated (Fox, 1996).

These differences in cultural values and communication styles put individualists at odds with many world cultures. Unfortunately, individualists may be so conditioned to view their behaviors as "normal" that they ascribe negative motives to behaviors that do not match their cultural values and communication style.

Communicating Across Cultures

The presentation should also include information about *face*, which is the public image that individuals seek to project (Jabs, 2005), *proxemics*, which is the way individuals use space (Gudykunst & Kim, 2003), and *power distance*, or the social distance between people of unequal rank (Littlemore, 2003). Useful strategies for cross-cultural communication are provided by Gudykunst and Kim (2003). One should not make assumptions about people, particularly when those individuals do not share the same contextual communication cues. One should not assume that one understands or has been understood, because the interpretation of meaning based on body language as well as vocabulary can vary greatly between cultures (Jenkins, 1997). One should avoid criticizing in any way a student's country of origin, customs, culture, or religion. If students appear confused, differences between educational practices in students' home countries and in the tutor's or mentor's country should be explained in a nonjudgmental manner. One should show sensitivity to cultural dictates regarding gender and age, respect students' right not to disclose personal information, and be prepared for students in culture shock to exhibit some animosity toward mainstream North American culture (Kang & Dutton, 1994).

GUEST SPEAKER

In addition to the prepared presentation, the presence of a representative of the predominant nonnative culture(s) or a person who is familiar and comfortable with intercultural communication, such as an English as a Second Language instructor, provides added depth to discussions. If possible, the trainer should find and schedule such a participant to attend training.

PROBLEM SCENARIOS

After the PowerPoint® presentation has been shown and questions answered, and after any comments by a guest speaker, trainees should be divided into four groups. To become more aware of potentially different interpretations of communication events, each group is asked to discuss a common learning center occurrence that is open to interpretation (Kang & Dutton, 1994). Groups can all discuss the same scenario or work with different scenarios. After 20 minutes of discussion, a representative from each group should present strategies for resolving potential conflict in that group's scenario, as well as affective cues that will make the student feel at ease. These presentations may take about 30 minutes.

- Scenario Example 1. A non-native speaker of English comes for help with a paper but appears to be academically unprepared to complete the assignment. The student expresses frustration when asked to review grammar and insists that she or he needs an A on the paper and in the course to get into a particular program. The student expresses concern about parental reaction to a poor grade. (Topics to consider: face, social position, gender)

- Scenario Example 2. A student has questions about the text but is unable to articulate them sufficiently for the tutor to understand the request. (Topics to consider: face, social position, gender, student's progression of language courses)

- Scenario Example 3. A student asks for help with math but appears to have difficulty with the math symbols in the text and in the homework assignment. (Topic to consider: consistency of math symbols in other cultures)

- Scenario Example 4. A student presents for review a completed assignment that does not address the parameters of the instructor's directions. The student insists that this is how such an assignment would be done in his or her country. (Topics to consider: conflicting academic customs among countries and cultural connections to different educational traditions)

ROLE PLAY

After the discussion, a DVD or role-playing session featuring two brief (2–3-minute) simulated interactions between tutors or mentors and students from other cultures should be presented to help tutors and mentors form a schema for effective performance in such circumstances and to boost their cultural competence. These interactions should highlight low- and high-context communication, with one illustrating direct speech and the other presenting a student who needs to be drawn out and cultivated before disclosing the kind of help needed (Lakoff & Tannen, 1984). Observation of interactions between communicators from different cultures, even when those interactions are simulated, will help tutors and mentors recognize nonverbal behaviors indicating cultural conflict and help them develop appropriate responses (Kang & Dutton, 1994, p. 4). Finally, tutors and mentors are asked to assess their cultural competence through discussion and written reflection.

Assessment

After trainees have viewed the DVD or role play, the trainer can ask tutors and mentors to assess their current intercultural communication skills as well as new strategies that they will use in sessions with students from other cultures. Trainees may answer (yes, no, or not sure) statements like these: I am a successful intercultural communicator. I am comfortable speaking with people who know little English. I can tell when I have communicated effectively. I am comfortable with silences in conversations. I am aware of the issues surrounding face and power distance. I am able to shift from a businesslike stance to a more people-oriented approach in tutoring sessions. I am attuned to students' body language.

Essay-style assessment questions may be asked, such as, "How will you adapt future tutoring sessions to reflect what you know about intercultural communication?" Answers to these questions permit both trainer and trainees to assess learning from the training session.

About 10 minutes should be allowed for completion of the assessments, after which trainees can be asked to share insights with the group. Because trainees may not have had sufficient time to discover all appropriate adaptations, presenters should be ready to suggest any strategies that tutors and mentors need for successful interactions.

To conclude the session, the trainer can ask the group to identify two or three points that were demonstrated in the training session and that they will continue to use in tutoring and mentoring sessions. The trainer should collect the self-assessments, review them for quality of learning to determine whether group review or individual coaching may be necessary, and retain them for trainees' files.

References

Fox, H. (1996, March). *Never the twain shall meet: International students writing for a U.S. university audience*. Paper presented at the Annual Meeting of the Conference of College Composition and Communication, Milwaukee, WI. Retrieved from http://www.eric.ed.gov/PDFS/ED400540.pdf

Gudykunst, W. B., & Kim, Y. Y. (2003). *Communicating with strangers: An approach to intercultural communication*. New York, NY: McGraw-Hill.

Jabs, L. (2005). Collectivism and conflict: Conflict response styles in Karamoja, Uganda. *The International Journal of Conflict Management, 16*, 354–378.

Jenkins, S. (1997). *Cultural and pragmatic miscues: A case study of international teaching assistant and academic faculty miscommunications*. Cincinnati, OH: University of Cincinnati, Division of Teacher Education.

Kang, H. W., & Dutton, B. (1994, February). Becoming multicultural: Helping students develop intercultural competence. Paper presented at the annual meeting of the National Association for Multicultural Education, Detroit, MI.

Lakoff, R. T., & Tannen, D. (1984). Conversational strategy and metastrategy in a pragmatic theory: The example of *Scenes from a Marriage*. *Semiotica, 49*, 323–346. Retrieved from https://www9.georgetown.edu/faculty/tannend/pdfs/conversational_strategy_and_metastrategy_in_pragmatic_theory.pdf

Littlemore, J. (2003). The effect of cultural background on metaphor interpretation. *Metaphor and Symbol, 18*, 273–288.

Reynolds, K. M. (2000). *ESL learners' and tutors' expectations of conversational participation, roles, and responsibility*. New Haven, CT: Southern Connecticut State University. Retrieved from http://www.eric.ed.gov/PDFS/ED447696.pdf

Practicing Nonverbal Communication Skills and Referrals

 Mark F. Daddona

As college students bring a greater number and increased severity of mental health issues to campus (Bishop, 2006; Erdur-Baker, Aberson, Barrow, & Draper, 2006; Gallagher, 2008; Kitzrow, 2003; Wolgast et al., 2005) and more students use medication (Schwartz, 2006), more student clients are likely to bring psychological issues into the working relationship with peer tutors and mentors. Students may want an opportunity to discuss some of their pressing issues before starting their tutoring or mentoring session.

In the role of peer educator, the student staff member is trained to listen to, guide, and offer suggestions to other students in a supportive way through the use of reflective communication skills; words are spoken to reflect, paraphrase, question, and summarize what the individual is sharing (Waitley, 2010; Weiten, Lloyd, Dunn, & Hammer, 2009). Reflective communication ensures the sender that the receiver accurately hears what is said and is both present and focused on the sender. Nonverbal communication should also be practiced, because it can support the intent of the dialogue by congruence between words and actions.

Students often need someone with whom to express frustration, distress, sadness, and other emotions. An understanding peer who may have experienced similar issues in his or her college career may be helpful to students; however, caution must be taken to avoid shifting into a counselor role. When a situation appears to require expertise in counseling or psychology, the effective peer educator should be trained to discuss student issues with a supervisor, and the supervisor can make an appropriate referral.

Training Activity

The purpose of this activity is for peer tutors or mentors to learn and practice effective nonverbal communication skills to enhance verbal interactions, understand the difference between peer and counselor roles, and learn about counseling and other psychological services available on campus in order to make appropriate referrals as needed. No specific room set-up is needed other than furniture that can be rearranged. Training and activities can be completed in approximately 90 minutes, but additional time permits more practice.

NONVERBAL COMMUNICATION SKILLS

The trainer begins by asking participants to define nonverbal communication and to list some examples. Nonverbal communication, communicating without actually speaking, is also referred to as actions as distinct from speech (Mehrabian, 1972) and "messages expressed by nonlinguistic means" (Adler, Proctor, & Towne, 2005, p. 211). It is described as "the transmission of meaning from one person to another through means of symbols other than words" (Weiten et al., 2009, p. 208). Nonverbal communication is an effective method of communicating by using body language, physical contact, proximity, silence, or paralanguage.

To develop an understanding of the various categories of nonverbal communication, trainees work in groups of three or four and select one of the following individual categories. After reading the brief description, each trainee demonstrates the technique while the other group members attempt to identify which of the techniques is being modeled. The activity continues until all nonverbal communication categories have been demonstrated.

Body Language

Body language consists of *facial expressions, posture,* and *use of gestures*. Facial expressions include maintaining eye contact that shows interest and concern; raising eyebrows to display surprise;

frowning to indicate disapproval, worrying, or thinking; and smiling to indicate approval or happiness. A dropped jaw can show shock or disbelief. Nodding can signify agreement, while a horizontal nod indicates disapproval or disagreement. Facial expressions may contradict verbal expressions and indicate the real message (Key, 1975).

Posture also communicates. Leaning in with open arms shows interest and concern. Leaning back with crossed arms can suggest lack of interest or not wanting to get too close to a discussion, situation, or individual. Use of gestures (using arms, legs, feet, hands) can display excitement, interest, and enthusiasm (Waitley, 2010) as well as anger and other emotions.

Physical Contact

A light touch on the shoulder, hand, or arm can be appropriate. Both males and females should avoid meeting with students in a private, closed location to avoid possible misunderstanding of the touch. Comfort with touch depends on the age, gender, cultural background, and personality of individuals.

Proximity

The physical proximity of tutor or mentor to student should let the student feel at ease. Sitting too close can feel like an invasion of personal space, which Adler et al. (2005) described as an invisible bubble carried wherever one goes. Sitting too far away can suggest a lack of interest. As with physical contact, a comfortable personal distance between individuals varies by culture; however, two to four feet is generally acceptable.

Silence

Many people are uncomfortable with silence and feel they must respond to gaps in discussion, leaving little time for the sender or receiver to think and process information. Silence can be thought of as no words, but it can communicate comfort, companionship, or support (Key, 1975). Silence can indicate that the listener simply cares enough to stay present. It can let both parties reflect on a previously sent or received message and form a response.

Paralanguage

Paralanguage, *how* something is spoken, includes vocal cues such as volume, speed, pitch, tone, overall quality of speech (Waitley, 2010; Weiten et al., 2009) and pause length (Adler et al., 2005); these cues can change the meanings of words. Paralanguage also includes extra-speech sounds (Key, 1975) such as *uh huh*, *um*, and *hmm* to convey approval or doubt, as well as hissing, shushing, whistling, and imitation sounds.

PEER EDUCATOR ROLE VERSUS PROFESSIONAL COUNSELOR ROLE

When peer educators practice good verbal and nonverbal communication skills, they can receive more information than they expect. Although open communication is part of the peer educator role, students who continue to share serious personal issues can put undue stress on the peer educator as the need becomes evident for referral to a trained and licensed professional. Peer educators must consult with supervisors about students with concerns beyond their training. Supervisors determine if a specific referral to the counseling center is needed and, if so, who will talk with the student to make the referral. This decision will be based on institutional policy.

Prior to the training session, the facilitator should visit the counseling center to gather print materials and obtain information about office hours, types of services, limit on number of sessions per student, and any counseling fees. Some centers offer drop-in counseling for emergencies, while others require students to make appointments for all services. Peer educators need knowledge of procedures in order to provide accurate information to lessen students' fears of attending their first counseling session. Whenever possible, the informational portion of the training should be presented by staff of the counseling center.

ROLE-PLAY TRAINING ACTIVITY

To put into practice what trainees have just learned about nonverbal communication and making good referrals, trainees work in triads and rotate through three roles: *peer educator*, *student*, and *process observer*. Each trainee in the student role is given a slip of paper with a role that he or she will act out. The trainee in this role does not share this information with other members of the triad. Trainers may include their own topics or adjust topics provided here to reflect typical concerns at their institution. Following are sample roles the student may play:

- I am angry with my parents because they will not send me any more money next semester, and I'll have to get a part-time job.

- I failed a few midterms, and I don't know how to tell my parents.

- I'm really having trouble with one professor. He (or she) doesn't like me, and yesterday I was embarrassed in front of the class.

- I just feel so sad and tired all the time. I don't have the energy to make it to class. When I try to study, I just stare at the same page for 30 minutes.

- My parents are really pushing me to major in biology because they want me to go to medical school. I would really like to be an artist. My drawings are pretty good. I don't know how I am going to bring up this subject with them.

- I am so stressed out with school, family problems, and my work schedule that sometimes I get these really bad chest pains and feel as if I can't even breathe. There is nothing I can take off my plate, and I feel trapped.

- I found my roommate's graded paper on the desk. The grade was an A. When I looked more closely, I saw that it was *my* paper, retyped with my roommate's identification. Should I pretend I never saw this, to keep the peace between us?

- I'm going home next weekend and can't focus on anything because I'm finally going to break up with the person I went with through high school. I met someone else here. I am so worried about this conversation that I failed a big test the other day.

Category	Points 1–limited 2–developing 3–proficient	Comments and Example (should support assigned points)
Body Language: Facial Expressions	1 2 3	
Body Language: Posture	1 2 3	
Body Language: Use of Gestures	1 2 3	
Physical Contact	1 2 3	
Proximity	1 2 3	
Silence	1 2 3	
Paralanguage: volume, speed, pitch, tone, speech quality	1 2 3	
Congruence between verbal and nonverbal communication	1 2 3	
Peer Educator: **Process Observer:**		**Overall Comments:**

FIGURE 1 Process observer feedback form.

As trainees begin to role play their issues, they should be creative and dramatize their roles. The peer educators respond with appropriate verbal and nonverbal interpersonal skills but will especially practice their nonverbal skills. Process observers take notes on a feedback form (see Figure 1, developed by the module author) and provide feedback to peer educators as to their effective use of nonverbal communication. The student also provides informal feedback with an emphasis on how he or she felt during the role play.

Assessment

As a result of this training, student staff members should know how to respond effectively to issues in a peer educator relationship by identifying and using appropriate nonverbal communication skills. Feedback and assessment of their nonverbal communication skills will be provided by scores and comments on the process observer feedback form.

The role-play activity also permits assessment of peer educators' understanding of their role versus the role of a professional counselor. The trainer can circulate during the role-play activity to observe for appropriate language and nonverbal communication, and student and observer members of each triad can look for evidence that the peer educator demonstrates understanding of role limitations.

Finally, the role-play activity lets the facilitator gauge peer educators' understanding of when to discuss student issues with their supervisor. Student staff will demonstrate their knowledge of the name, location, and available services of the campus counseling center. They will also demonstrate that they know how to obtain an initial counseling appointment on their campus. By closely observing the role play and following up with writing assignments, trainers will know that their peer tutors and mentors are ready to meet with students in distress as concerned peers, without becoming counselors.

References

Adler, R. B, Proctor, R. F., & Towne, N. (2005). *Looking out/looking in* (11th ed.). Belmont, CA: Thomson Wadsworth.

Bishop, J. B. (2006). College and university counseling centers: Questions in search of answers. *Journal of College Counseling, 9,* 6–19.

Erdur-Baker, O., Aberson, C. L., Barrow, J. C., & Draper, M. R. (2006). Nature and severity of college students' psychological concerns: A comparison of clinical and nonclinical national samples. *Professional Psychology: Research and Practice, 37,* 317–323. doi:10.1037/0735-7028.37.3.317

Gallagher, R. P. (2008). *National survey of counseling center directors 2008.* Alexandria, VA: International Association of Counseling Services. Retrieved from http://www.education.pitt.edu/survey/nsccd/

Key, M. R. (1975). *Paralanguage and kinesics (nonverbal communication).* Metuchen, NJ: Scarecrow Press.

Kitzrow, M. A. (2003). The mental health needs of today's college students: Challenges and recommendations. *NASPA Journal, 41*(1), 167–181.

Mehrabian, A. (1972). *Nonverbal communication.* Chicago, IL: Aldine-Atherton.

Schwartz, A. J. (2006). Are college students more disturbed today? Stability in the acuity and qualitative character of psychopathology of college counseling center clients: 1992–1993 through 2001–2002. *Journal of American College Health, 54,* 327–337. doi:10.3200/JACH.54.6.327–337

Waitley, D. (2010). *Psychology of success.* New York, NY: McGraw-Hill.

Weiten, W., Lloyd, M. A., Dunn, D. S., & Hammer, E. Y. (2009). *Psychology applied to modern life: Adjustment in the 21st century* (9th ed.). Belmont, CA: Wadsworth Cengage.

Wolgast, B. M., Rader, J., Roche, D., Thompson, C. P., von Zuben, F. C., & Goldberg, A. (2005). Investigation of clinically significant change by severity level in college counseling center clients. *Journal of College Counseling, 8*(2), 140–152.

Active Listening Training for Multimodal Learners

Anne Vermont Shearer

Listening to students think aloud is an important part of tutors' and mentors' work. Peer tutors and mentors who employ active listening skills encourage students to talk more during sessions (Ivey & Ivey, 2007). Active listening has many benefits for student learning. Patient, active listeners can assist students who have social, communication, or learning problems because they give students the time they may need to think and construct ideas (Ivey & Ivey, 2007). Tutors and mentors who use active listening in sessions can also convey their concern and empathy for students' needs, thus making each session together a more positive experience (McNaughton, Hamlin, McCarthy, Head-Reeves, & Schreiner, 2007). Properly teaching peer tutors and mentors to use active listening skills improves their communication skills, which can assist the tutors and mentors to be better learners themselves (McNaughton et al., 2007).

Active listening skills encompass both verbal and nonverbal communication skills. There are three verbal active listening skills to incorporate into the training program: paraphrasing, encouraging, and summarizing (Ivey & Ivey, 2007). *Paraphrasing* is rewording the student's words into the tutor's or mentor's own words. Paraphrasing helps students hear their thoughts expressed by another and gives them an opportunity to process and reflect. *Encouraging* uses short phrases or words such as "uh huh," "okay," and "yeah" to show that the tutor or mentor is following along. These words and phrases demonstrate to the talker that the tutor or mentor is actually listening and paying attention. *Summarizing* is similar to paraphrasing except that it is used to recap whole conversations and highlight important concepts or ideas the student may have said. Summarizing speech, just like summarizing written text, requires practice.

While verbal active listening skills require considerable concentration and patience to practice, nonverbal listening skills are much more commonly used in everyday conversation and may be more familiar to tutors and mentors. Nonverbal active listening cues encompass the full range of nonverbal communication: looking directly at the other person, making eye contact, using voice quality and tone to indicate warmth and interest, and having open body language (Ivey & Ivey, 2007). All of these cues show interest in and attention to the conversation without expressing that interest verbally. *Verbal quality* and *tone* should be practiced with another person until they are warm, welcoming, and nonjudgmental so the speaker does not feel threatened. *Open body language* is sitting with arms and legs relaxed and uncrossed, sitting up or leaning in, with the body and face toward the speaker. Body language should reflect that the listener is participating in the conversation. While nonverbal active listening skills can be acquired and understood quickly, they require constant awareness to develop automaticity and expertise.

The following activity to train tutors and mentors in active listening skills is structured on a theory of cyclical learning: better learning and retention may come from following a teaching cycle (Garcia-Ros, Perez, & Talaya, 2008). The cycle is composed of explaining, modeling, practicing, and assessing the skills taught. Trainees receive a verbal explanation, a visual explanation, and a kinesthetic explanation. Additionally, the trainer should develop a handout or e-learning resource of the skills, including both prescriptions and proscriptions on using verbal and nonverbal active listening cues.

Training Activity

The objective of this training is for tutors or mentors to learn and demonstrate the ability to use both verbal and nonverbal active listening cues in tutoring or mentoring sessions. The trainer will provide supplemental materials and instruction on active listening skills, in addition to opportunities for tutors and mentors to practice the skills with feedback provided by the trainer.

The time required for this active listening training activity is at least 30 minutes. Trainees will need writing materials, and the room should be arranged with furniture and equipment for viewing the trainer, viewing video clips, and participating in practice sessions in groups of two. The trainer should prepare at least two role-playing scenarios or utilize scenarios A and B provided in the Appendix.

The trainer should also prepare video clips demonstrating poor use of active listening cues. Useful YouTube.com clips include Good Listening Skills (CIPD Publishing, 2008) and Dilbert: Good Morning and Bad Listening Video (Adams, 2008). Because media are often removed from or added to the Internet, the trainer should look several times a year for new video clips to use. Using new media will also keep training sessions interesting for tutors or mentors who participate in training for several years. As an alternative to presenting video clips, experienced tutors or mentors could demonstrate good and poor use of active listening cues.

The trainer should begin by introducing the importance of using active listening skills during a tutoring or mentoring session. The trainees' attention can be captured by showing them a video clip demonstrating poor use of active listening cues followed by a clip demonstrating proper use of active listening cues. Next, the trainer should outline both verbal and nonverbal active listening cues, define those strategies, and analyze how and when to use the skills during a session. What happens if cues are overused or too intrusive? What happens when the timing is a little off?

After verbal and nonverbal active listening skills have been sufficiently explained and demonstrated, the trainer should provide the role-playing scenarios. When trainees have had time to read and review the role-playing scenarios, they should be given a few minutes to act out the scenarios, switching roles after 10 minutes. While the tutors or mentors practice their active listening skills in the role plays, the trainer observes each group around the room, serving as a consultant, providing feedback, and responding to questions and concerns.

To conclude the exercise, the trainer leads a quick wrap-up discussion, making certain that difficulties and concerns of the dyads are shared with the group as a whole. The tutors or mentors will be given a few minutes to complete an assessment of their learning at the end of the training session.

Assessment

Assessment occurs during the training. Tutors or mentors will be able to demonstrate their understanding of both verbal and nonverbal active listening cues during the dyadic scenarios, share their understanding with their partners, and respond to the trainer's critique. The trainer knows the level of expertise needed in the learning center and can provide both positive feedback and constructive criticism during the practice sessions.

A sample assessment for administration at the end of the training session is provided here. Trainees may be assessed in their knowledge of both verbal active listening skills and nonverbal active listening skills.

VERBAL LISTENING SKILLS ASSESSMENT

1. Paraphrase the following statement: "I'm tired all the time. I'm tired of homework, I'm tired of studying, I'm tired of going to class, I'm tired of going to practice. I don't want to do this much work. I thought college would have more partying and intellectual discussions about socialism at the coffee shop."

2. Summarize the above statement. (The summary will be different from the paraphrase.)

3. What are three encouragers you can use to demonstrate that you are paying attention to your student?

NONVERBAL LISTENING SKILLS ASSESSMENT

1. Describe open body language.
2. Describe the importance of verbal quality and tone to an understanding of a speaker's meaning.

A third assessment opportunity occurs later, preferably within 3 weeks, when the trainer or supervisor observes trainees during their tutoring or mentoring sessions and provides written and oral comments about their use of active listening strategies. The trainer should note specific active listening cues the tutors or mentors use and communicate whether the cues were used appropriately. Allowing 3 weeks after the training session before this assessment gives trainees some time to practice and improve all of their tutoring and mentoring skills, yet trainees will not have developed inappropriate listening habits and will therefore be able to respond quickly to constructive criticism.

References

Adams, S. (Producer). (2008). *Dilbert: Good morning and bad listener* [Video file]. Retrieved from http://www.youtube.com/watch?v=xAp9n3yBjyo

CIPD Publishing (Producer). (2008). *Good listening skills* [Video file]. Retrieved from http://www.youtube.com/watch?v=-pY_7q7ZP5o

Ivey, A., & Ivey, M. (2007). *Intentional interviewing and counseling: Facilitating client development in a multicultural society* (6th ed.). Belmont, CA: Thomson Higher Education.

Garcia-Ros, R., Perez, F., & Talaya, I. (2008). New university students' instructional preferences and how these relate to learning styles and motivational strategies. *Electronic Journal of Research in Educational Psychology, 6*, 547–570. Retrieved from http://www.investigacion-psicopedagogica.org/revista/articulos/16/english/Art_16_230.pdf

McNaughton, D., Hamlin, D., McCarthy, J., Head-Reeves, D., & Schreiner, M. (2007). Teaching an active listening strategy to preservice education professionals. *Topics in Early Childhood Special Education, 27*, 223–231. doi:10.1177/0271121407311241

Appendix

SAMPLE ROLE-PLAYING SCENARIOS

Role-Playing Scenario A

Student role: You are here to discuss your writing performance. Instructors frequently indicate on your papers that your ideas are poorly organized. When you sit down to write a paper, you just jump in. Quite often you are confused by assignments and struggle to figure out what instructors want. You do not like your writing instructor because her speech is strongly accented.

Tutor or mentor role: The student is here to work on improving organization in writing assignments. This is the first time you have met with this student. Remember to practice your listening skills.

Role-Playing Scenario B

Student role: You are here to discuss your time management skills. You have a planner but look at it only once a week. You are frequently late to class. Sometimes you schedule two activities for the same time or completely miss an appointment. You turn in most of your assignments late. You work about 30 hours a week and live at home with your parents.

Tutor or mentor role: The student is here to talk about time management strategies. This is the first time you have met with this student. Remember to practice your listening skills.

Active Listening in Different Contexts

Richard George Johnson

Tutors and mentors are familiar with listening in social contexts, but they generally lack formal training in fundamental components of listening for diagnostic and instructive purposes. This lack of formal training in these useful tutoring skills makes training for instructional listening both important and difficult. While the advanced skill of listening for understanding is often encouraged and developed in their role as students, trainers realize that peer tutors and mentors also need to listen for diagnostic purposes and that such a skill is even more complex than merely listening for understanding. Listening in three different contexts can be discussed in training: listening for socializing, listening for understanding, and listening for diagnostic purposes. These three listening objectives are interrelated but in some ways very different.

Social listening is the listening that people do in their casual social environments. This is the context in which peer tutors and mentors have the most experience. The consequences of success and failure in social listening are rarely significant, yet general success helps us in our day-to-day activities. Judging from the near-universal inclusion of a chapter devoted to the subject of listening in textbooks on effective learning, it seems that most educators would agree that listening for understanding is a separate skill that needs to be honed beyond students' usual social listening habits. Pauk and Owens (2008) outlined 10 keys to effective listening in academic settings. These encompass many of the recommendations found in textbooks on effective learning, for example, "find areas of interest"; "judge content, not delivery"; "hold your fire"; "listen for ideas"; "be a flexible note taker"; "work at listening"; "resist distractions"; "exercise your mind"; "keep your mind open"; "thought is faster than speech—use it" (Pauk & Owens, 2008, pp. 330–334). These are useful skills, and tutors and mentors should look for opportunities to discuss them with tutees and mentees who need them.

Listening for diagnostic purposes is another kind of listening and requires a different kind of advice and instruction. As an illustration, consider Pauk's and Owen's (2008) fourth key to effective listening, to "listen for ideas." Pauk's point is that the poor listener listens for facts while the good listener at the college level listens for central themes. That a poor listener listens for facts does not mean that facts are inconsequential, but in an academic setting central themes lead to better understanding. For the tutor or mentor attempting to discern a student's difficulty, however, errant facts may be just as revealing as general impressions and general understanding. It is important to reiterate that diagnostic listening is a separate, more advanced skill, and training should include attention devoted to mastery of this skill.

Lochhead and Whimbey (1987) advocated a process of problem solving called Thinking Aloud Pair Problem Solving (TAPPS) that is relevant to tutoring and mentoring situations. In TAPPS, students work in pairs, with one student assigned to talk through the problem as the other listens and attempts to clarify what is being said. Lockhead and Whimbey claimed that the TAPPS process leads to greater learning by both parties. In effect, the process separates the activities of listening and explaining while giving both partners the opportunity to focus on each. Similarly, tutors and mentors should encourage students to explain the problem and then should repeat back their own understanding of the student's concern, to the student's satisfaction.

A tutor or mentor actively engaged in clarifying a student client's concern or problem can easily overcommit effort to listening for understanding. So how do peer assistants listen for understanding and simultaneously for diagnosing? Medical treatment texts and automotive repair manuals typically have something in common that may be useful in the learning center context: a flowchart. A flowchart developed in advance by student or program staff can become a useful diagnostic aid. Most tutors and mentors eventually develop an informal mental process for analyzing what they hear, but a formalized flowchart provides the benefits of experience to tutors and mentors just beginning their training, offers a diagnostic tool of considerable power, and ensures more consistent service to students. Armed with a formal flowchart like the one provided in the Appendix, tutors and mentors can separate listening for understanding from listening for diagnosing.

A flowchart, ideally developed by a team of tutors or mentors for a specific concern or subject, helps diminish the temptation for inexperienced tutors or mentors to project their own previous difficulties with academic concerns onto the student. Although empathy is useful to a degree, it can potentially hinder making an accurate assessment of the student's concerns. Asking questions is a useful way to avoid projecting, although questions themselves will take form based on the tutor's or mentor's past experiences. The discussion process that takes place in a tutoring or mentoring session is one of gradual understanding and exploring (Chaffee, 2000); student staff should be trained to utilize this gradualness to diagnose problems beyond their own experience.

Training Activity

In order to encourage the development of a formalized diagnostic listening protocol, the following training activity is suggested. Depending on the length and number of video clips or scenarios, this training activity may take 1 to 2 hours.

Preparation for this activity requires planning and the cooperation of students seeking tutoring or mentoring. The trainer needs to prepare a series of videos or actual sessions with students so that tutors and mentors in training can observe and discuss the interactions and communications they hear. If videotapes of sessions are routinely made to monitor the work of tutors and mentors in the learning center, those tapes can be used. This assumes, of course, that the trainer has already taken precautions to respect the privacy and dignity of students whose sessions are taped, sought permission of these students to record their interactions for assessment purposes, and ensured that trainees will maintain confidentiality of what they hear and see in training. Tapes chosen for this training should include instances of student clients' exhibiting general misunderstanding of the material as well as misplaced confidence in "wrong" answers. Trainees will watch the video and discuss what the student is trying to communicate to the tutor or mentor.

For purposes of this training or for general assessment purposes, students being tutored or mentored should also complete a brief questionnaire asking what concerns brought them to the learning center and what seem to be the primary difficulties. The students' answers to these questions will be shared at the end of the training activity and compared to trainees' perceptions.

The trainer begins the training activity by asking tutors or mentors to define active listening and distinguish it from passive listening. Trainees may already have encountered these concepts in coursework and certainly have experienced them. They should identify times in their lives when they are actively listening. In which of the three contexts—social, educational, diagnostic—do trainees find themselves most actively engaged as listeners? They may listen actively in other contexts; thus they already possess the general ability to do so, as opposed to identifying others doing the same.

After offering the three listening contexts articulated earlier (social, educational, and diagnostic), the trainer should ask if the trainees' instances included all three. If not, has someone had an experience of active or passive listening in the role of speaker or listener in one of the contexts not yet discussed? The trainer should clarify that diagnostic listening is the skill to be learned and practiced in this session.

The trainer then shows a video clip of a tutoring or mentoring session. As they watch the video, trainees should look for instances of listening diagnostically and opportunities for doing so. How is the tutor or mentor in the taped session demonstrating active listening in this diagnostic context? What are the successful questions or approaches? That is, what questions or approaches seem to elicit good diagnostic information? A prepared handout structured for trainees to take notes on their observations would be helpful. After the video clip, trainees discuss their findings and attempt to resolve confusions, disagreements, and inconsistencies.

Finally, the trainer should note that the trainees themselves have been listening diagnostically while viewing the clip. What concern do they think the student is bringing to the session? What did the student say was the primary difficulty? Did the tutor or mentor in the taped session come to the same conclusion they (the trainees) did? After their findings have been discussed, the trainer shares the description of the difficulty provided by the student who was taped, from the brief question-naire provided following the taped session. Did the trainees hear the same concern that the student intended to express? When possible, the trainer should invite the student client from the video to the training and utilize the TAPPS technique to confirm the student's genuine concern in the session.

The trainer repeats the process with additional clips and discussion. Are the same kinds of questions and approaches useful for each of the students in the taped sessions? Are some approaches more productive than others? Trainees should listen carefully for evidence of the taped tutor's or mentor's diagnostic listening skills while they are at the same time practicing their own. Are there some questions or approaches that never seem productive and always miss the mark? Trainees should continue to take notes on more and less productive diagnostic listening strategies.

Trainers should then provide the diagnostic flowchart they have prepared (as in the Appendix) and ask if this would have been helpful to them and to the tutors or mentors taped in the sessions. Does this flowchart need to be fine-tuned or updated to make it relevant to the kinds of sessions the trainees will have with students and to the kinds of reporting the trainees will make on their sessions? Trainees should then discuss the strengths of beginning a tutoring session with such a tool.

Assessment

After the training session, trainees' learning can be assessed in any of the following ways:

- Trainees can later be asked to demonstrate their listening skills by correctly identifying the concern of a student in an additional video clip.

- Trainees can list more and less productive diagnostic listening approaches, as evidenced by their close observations of the video clips or their own subsequent experience as tutors or mentors.

- Trainees' own sessions with students can be taped over the course of a semester and analyzed for evidence of good diagnostic listening strategies.

- Trainees individually or together can develop their own diagnostic flowchart for a particular course or concern, utilizing what they know of effective and productive diagnostic techniques.

- Student clients served by the center can be asked to assess the extent to which their tutor or mentor seemed to understand their concern and knew what to do.

Any of these five measures assesses the trainees' understanding of the fundamental components of listening for diagnostic and instructive purposes.

References

Chaffee, J. (2000). *Thinking critically* (6th ed.). Boston, MA: Houghton Mifflin.

Lochhead, J., & Whimbey, A. (1987). Teaching analytical reasoning through thinking aloud pair problem solving. In J. E. Stice (Ed.), *New directions for teaching and learning: 30. Teaching thinking through problem solving* (pp. 73–92). San Francisco, CA: Jossey-Bass. doi:10.1002/tl.37219873007

Pauk, W., & Owens, R. (2008). *How to study in college* (9th ed.). Boston, MA: Houghton Mifflin.

Appendix

SAMPLE FLOWCHART - SCIENCE AND MATHEMATICS

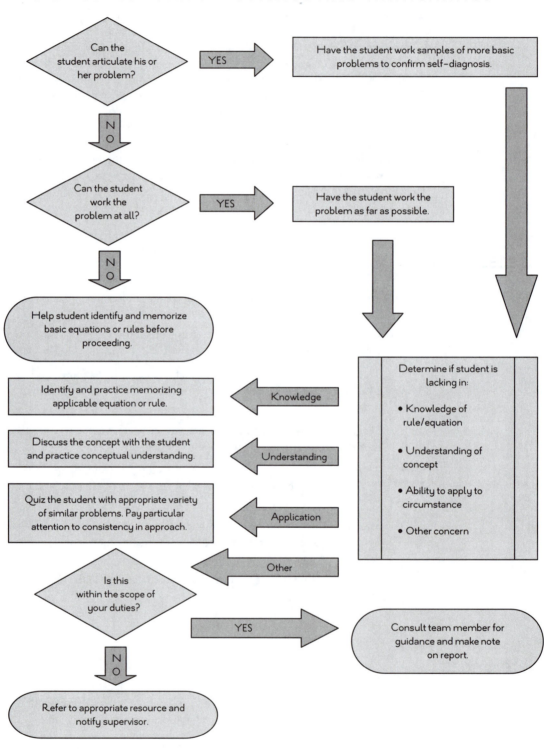

Politeness Theory and Effective Tutoring and Mentoring

Diana Calhoun Bell, Holly Arnold Laue, and Rebekah Haddock

Cogie (2001) used the analogy of improvised dance to explain the dynamics and tensions between a tutor and a student performing collaborative work during a tutoring session. Within the "collaborative dance," tension can stem from the seemingly contradictory roles that the tutor must play, talking confidently and professionally about subject content but at the same time collaborative and egalitarian, "asked on the one hand to restrain their authority so as to focus on the student while on the other to assert it so as to aid in student understanding" (p. 38). Caught between these two expectations, tutors and mentors must situate themselves and somehow find a way to work with students to learn content material and academic strategies, yet manage to do so with minimal imposition upon the students with whom they collaborate.

Politeness helps. Politeness can be understood as a "discursive conversational contract" that depends heavily on tacit understandings of the terms and conditions of that contract (Murphy, 1999, p. 233). The dominant perspective on linguistic politeness is Brown and Levinson's (1987) model, based on Goffman's (1967) study of social interaction. The notion of *face* was derived from Goffman's research and the common expression of "losing face." The concept is defined as "an image of self, delineated in terms of approved social attributes" (p. 5). Goffman explained that in social interactions people "perform" in a certain way to present their self-image and give a certain impression of themselves to other people. There is a mutual understanding between two people in conversation that they both acknowledge, consciously or unconsciously, the vulnerability of face and thus try to maintain each other's face accordingly. As Brown and Levinson (1987) pointed out, "face is something that is emotionally invested and that can be lost, maintained, or enhanced and must be constantly attended to in interaction" (p. 61).

Although there is a mutual interest for both people in a conversation to maintain each other's face, some actions may threaten face (Brown & Levinson, 1987). Both positive and negative politeness strategies maintain the hearer's face in conversation. Positive politeness is used by the speaker to acknowledge and support the hearer's desire for approval and to be accepted. Brown and Levinson listed 15 strategies of positive politeness such as noticing and attending to the wants of the other person; exaggerating interest, approval or sympathy (I *absolutely love* those shoes!); seeking agreement (That movie was sad, *wasn't it?*); using humor and joking, especially in self-deprecation; using the inclusive "we" (*We* should get some lunch.); showing optimism (*You won't mind* if I borrow this pen. *I'm sure* you'll all show up for the meeting on time.), to paraphrase a few of their strategies. The following dialogue illustrates positive politeness:

DAVE: When you come over Friday, I can show you the videos of our last vacation.

SUE: Oh, I *really look forward* to seeing them. It's *so wonderful* when *we* get to spend time like that with our families. *I'll bring the popcorn!*

Here, Sue demonstrates positive politeness in a variety of ways. First, she demonstrates and perhaps even exaggerates interest by saying that she *really looks forward* to the show. She shows optimism about spending time with family and she uses the inclusive *we*, demonstrating that both she and Dave have common interests and likes. Finally, she uses humor and joking to further indicate that she understands Dave's desire to show her the video and that she agrees it would be a good way to spend the evening. Sue attends to Dave's positive face by noticing and approving of Dave's desire to show her his family videos.

On the other hand, negative politeness attends to the hearer's negative face. A speaker attends to a hearer's "want to have his freedom of action unhindered" (Brown & Levinson, 1987, p. 129) by minimizing imposition of the speaker onto the hearer. Brown and Levinson list 10 strategies for negative politeness, including being conventionally indirect, hedging (*I think, maybe,* you should put it on the table.), showing pessimism (*I know you're busy, but if you have a little time later,* could you read over this paper?), minimizing imposition (I *just want* to ask you if I can borrow one sheet of paper.), questioning (What do you think?), using modals (You *may want* to think about that some more.), and apologizing (*I'm sorry to bother you*, but may I ask a question?). A good example of the use of negative politeness can be seen in this unlikely exchange between Dave and Sue:

DAVE: I'm thinking of giving up my job in sales and training to become an astronaut!

SUE: You know, Dave, *I think* you would need to have *some kind of* scientific qualifications and aeronautical experience, but your background is in retail, so I'm *just not sure* you ought to do that. You *may* want to check this idea out before you give up your job. *What do you think?*

In this exchange several examples of negative politeness are at work. Sue does not want to impose her potentially hurtful suggestions on her friend Dave and therefore mitigates what could be a crushing response to his dream of becoming an astronaut by softening her comments and being conventionally indirect. Dave's confession is a face-threatening act and, sensitive to preserving Dave's face, Sue engages in negative politeness strategies. First, she implies that his idea is a bad one by hedging: *I think* you would need to have *some kind* of qualification, which Dave does not have. She then uses a minimizer (*just*), a hedge (*not sure*), and a modal (*may*) in order to avoid issuing a direct suggestion. Finally, she hands over the ultimate decision to Dave, underscored by the fact that Sue asks Dave what he thinks about this idea.

Sue has tried to be considerate of Dave's face but has also voiced her concern that she thinks his idea is not a good one. Sue successfully avoids imposing her will or suggestions on him. Whatever Dave decides to do (and it will probably be to keep his day job), the illusion is maintained between the two friends that it was Dave's own sensible idea not to proceed with his astronaut plan. As per the Brown and Levinson (1987) model, Dave's negative face is saved by Sue's use of negative politeness.

Learning center conversations, like other kinds of conversations, are face-threatening situations mediated through politeness. At least two types of face threats occur in this context. First, by visiting the center, students leave themselves vulnerable to imposition by allowing tutors to help determine the direction of their writing projects or mentors to help them navigate the choice of a major. In addition, students leave themselves open to criticism of their work and, by extension, their academic competence, which characterizes this situation as a face-threatening act for students.

Investigating tutoring and mentoring sessions through the lens of politeness theory sheds light on the way in which tutors or mentors and students build rapport; whether it is a one-time drop-in visit or a semester-long series of sessions, they negotiate the roles they play in this peer education setting through communicative patterns (Bell, Arnold, & Haddock, 2009, in which article many of the ideas presented here were earlier offered by the authors). The ways in which participants use politeness in their interaction can help or hinder the work that gets accomplished. If tutors and mentors mediate the dialogue with too much politeness, whether positive or negative, the session can be compromised (Bell & Youmans, 2006; Bell, Arnold, & Haddock, 2009).

However, negative politeness is an important communicative tool within peer sessions. When tutors and mentors appropriately use negative politeness, they can help students understand two important tenets of the peer education model: first, that students themselves are ultimately responsible for the end result of the session, and second, that the goal of the session is to engage students in learning and study strategies that help them become more independent learners. Through negative politeness, tutors and mentors can emphasize the magnitude of the student's role in this collaboration and minimize the student's dependence on the tutor or mentor to accomplish educational goals.

Likewise, positive politeness is a crucial component of rapport-building communication. Laughter, inclusive language, and praise all facilitate a bond that helps establish a positive learning environment. The session becomes less of a face-threatening act when trust has been established; tutors and mentors trust that the students will contribute and participate fully in the session and in their own learning goals, and students trust that tutors and mentors have students' best interests at heart as they challenge students to think critically. Thus politeness, whether positive or negative, helps the parties shape their relationship and helps mediate the contradictions that often occur in peer education settings.

Understanding politeness theory and communicative patterns that employ politeness strategies can impact the ways in which learning center professionals think about, train, and prepare peer tutors and mentors, but it is also important for tutors and mentors to consider their own function within the educational dynamic of a session—to begin looking at how they may impact the effectiveness of the session. Politeness theory provides a means to that end. Incorporating politeness theory in tutor and mentor training helps peer educators think more carefully about what they say and how what they say is perceived by others.

Training Activity

The goal of the activity is to understand politeness theory and its implication in tutoring and mentoring sessions. In order to complete the activity, trainers need only one room with an AV screen, computer, and projector. Trainees will need paper or small whiteboards and markers.

First, the trainer introduces trainees to the politeness theory model through PowerPoint® or other visual means, using specific examples of each type of politeness. Then trainees are divided into small groups; each group works on one type of politeness. Trainers should either have specific language examples ready for the tutors and mentors to manipulate or have them come up with their own examples. Finally, trainees should discuss the implications of each of the types of politeness and how it may help or hinder a session.

One way to introduce politeness theory is through videotaping actual tutoring or mentoring sessions, or recording mock sessions between two volunteers. When trainees can see and hear sessions from a third-party perspective, they can more readily engage in meaningful dialogue about the session, especially the learning strategies and communicative patterns of both effective and ineffective moments that occur during the course of a given session. Watching these sessions together and discussing them as a group creates a nonthreatening and positive group dynamic and develops technique while also creating a way for the group to solve problems together.

Another way to incorporate politeness theory into a training session is to provide authentic tutoring dialogue, short examples of language in use as taken from actual tutoring sessions that were either observed or recorded. After the trainer introduces politeness theory in general, dialogue boxes help trainees focus on specific moments of politeness within tutoring or mentoring sessions. Trainees can identify types of politeness within the dialogue boxes and then discuss their effectiveness. If the group members find a particular statement to be ineffective, they can work together to rewrite the dialogue box to demonstrate a more useful communication strategy. Whichever training tool is used, politeness theory is a valuable means of encouraging tutors and mentors to focus inwardly so that they can better understand their own responsibility for creating rapport and providing feedback to the students with whom they work.

Assessment

To demonstrate their understanding of politeness theory and its application to the peer session, each group presents its analysis to the larger group. Further assessment can be conducted by the trainer through direct observation of tutoring or mentoring sessions and self-reflection assignments.

References

Bell, D. C., Arnold, H., & Haddock, R. (2009). Linguistic politeness and peer tutoring. *The Learning Assistance Review, 14,* 37–54.

Bell, D. C., & Youmans, M. (2006). Politeness and praise: Rhetorical issues in ELL writing center conferences. *The Writing Center Journal, 26*(2), 31–47.

Brown, P., & Levinson, S. C. (1987). *Politeness: Some universals in language use.* Cambridge, United Kingdom: Cambridge University Press.

Cogie, J. (2001). Peer tutoring: Keeping the contradiction productive. In J. Nelson & K. Evertz (Eds.), *The politics of writing centers* (pp. 37–49). Portsmouth, NH: Boynton/Cook.

Goffman, E. (1967). *Interaction ritual.* New York, NY: Pantheon.

Murphy, S. W. (1999). *Politeness and self-presentation in writing center discourse* (Unpublished doctoral dissertation). Texas A & M, College Station, TX.

What Everyone Needs to Know About Sex: Gendered Communication Styles

Robin Redmon Wright

The goal of this training session is to help tutors and mentors recognize that men and women may approach tutoring and mentoring with differing objectives, perceptions, and expectations that are deeply rooted in socially constructed gender norms. Although these are generalizations and certainly do not apply to everyone, studies have shown that differences between prevalent male and female communication styles may significantly impact tutoring and mentoring outcomes (Tannen, 1990; Wright, 2007). It should be noted that these are generalizations based on Tannen's (1990) socio-linguistics research, are not true of all individuals, and are not meant to reinforce stereotypes.

Sociolinguists Tannen (1990) and Gee (1996) have shown that males and females tend to exhibit different communication styles. According to Tannen (1990), men in Western cultures have been acculturated to see the world as hierarchical and to position themselves in conversations as either one-up or one-down. Women, on the other hand, are often taught to think of communication as establishing community and sharing information. Although the implications of such studies are vast and quite troubling for critical feminist scholars and educators, gender-related differences in communication styles in a range of teaching-learning relationships are well documented. So, too, are the possible negative student outcomes when tutors, mentors, and instructors are unaware of and fail to adjust for those differences.

Smith-Jentsch, Scielzo, Yarbrough, and Rosopa (2008) found that females were more effective mentors in electronic peer-mentoring relationships because "male mentors were simply unaware of their relative ineffectiveness" (p. 203) in online chat sessions. Female mentors were more conscious of the possibility for misinterpretation and were more focused on interactive dialogue—and, thus, on creating an online community. Rester and Edwards (2007) explored the effect of gender on student perceptions of instructor "immediacy," which they defined as "a cluster of behaviors used by a communicator with the intent of enhancing feelings of closeness" (p. 35). They found that these practices, while having positive effects on learning, are often perceived as offensive, even as sexual harassment, when the instructor is male (p. 35). Moreover, Sosik and Godshalk (2005) found that women mentors are often perceived by mentees—particularly male mentees—as having less value than male mentors. Obviously, gender matters.

Gee (1996) suggested that the development of such sexist perceptions originates with the very language and discourses used, and that such perceptions are so pervasive as to be almost universally accepted, despite consistent evidence to the contrary. Indeed, Tannen (1990) found that sexist perceptions are embedded not only in everyday language but also in resultant differences in communication styles. She posited that understanding the different ways men and women engage in dialogue is essential for effective cross-gender communication.

These studies are supported by recent studies in neuroscience. Lauter (2008) found that sex hormones affect the fetal brain in a variety of ways and foster permanent brain activity patterns that are significantly gendered. Later in life, these brain "types" affect the way men and women communicate. Male and female brains, according to Lauter, become hardwired for different styles of communicating with and relating to others. With so much evidence that men and women respond differently to human interactions, it is clear that "tutor trainers must set aside training sessions to talk about gender communication issues" (Wright, 2007, p. 73).

Understanding common stylistic differences between genders can help tutors and mentors communicate more effectively. As one study shows (Wright, 2007), male students often feel that seeking academic help positions them as "less than" (p. 68) or one-down in the academic social hierarchy; therefore, they may approach tutoring or mentoring sessions defensively, seeking to gain status during the interaction. Conversely, women may seek help even when they do not need it. Women "are not only comfortable seeking help, but feel honor-bound to seek it, accept it, and display gratitude in exchange" (Tannen, 1990, p. 65). These contrasting ways of interacting in the world require peer tutors and mentors to practice different approaches based on their own gender as well as the gender of the client.

Men often approach a tutoring appointment by negotiating for status—as individuals in a hierarchical social order (Tannen, 1990). When a tutor or mentor offers information, the fact that he or she has the information and the student does not sends a metamessage of superiority. The tutor or mentor is automatically one-up on the hierarchical ladder. Males are often comfortable in the role of giving help but not in receiving it. Publicly men tend to engage in what Tannen (1990) called "report talk" (p. 77). They may use talk to claim attention in a crowd; talk becomes a tool for gaining status. Tannen noted that although women are often accused of being more talkative than men, studies consistently provide evidence to the contrary when it comes to public speaking. Men talk more at work, in classrooms, and in social settings. They view such situations as venues for competitions of knowledge and skill. They "claim center stage" (p. 77).

Women, on the other hand, may engage the world as individuals in a network of connections where conversations are negotiations for closeness (Tannen, 1990). Women tend to engage in "*rapport* talk" (p. 77). Rather than seeing conversation as a competition, women tend to see conversation as a way of connecting with people and sharing experiences. This sort of rapport talk may embarrass men who view public conversations from a completely different perspective. Women tend to talk more in private conversations and in intimate settings, and they emphasize "similarities and matching experiences" (p. 77) rather than status.

Training Activity

This training activity focuses on differences between men's and women's conversational styles as described by Tannen (1990). Tutor and mentor trainers should assign the first four chapters of Tannen's book, *You Just Don't Understand: Women and Men in Conversation*, before the training session on gender and communication; this text is a quick and valuable read.

The activity requires about 1 hour and should take place in a room with movable chairs. If possible, AV equipment with computer and LCD projector should be used. Costume pieces may be used if desired.

PRESENTATION

The trainer should develop a presentation that bullets the main points in the assigned chapters as well as additional information from brain research (as in Appendix A) to make training sessions fun and respectful. Carefully selected humorous photographs or graphic illustrations added to the presentation slides often help the group feel comfortable. Copyright issues prevent reproduction of such additions here, but fair use allows for each trainer's creative input. Costuming willing tutors and filming reenactments of tutoring sessions is another good idea. With the summary of gender differences should be included several slides with suggestions for dealing with those differences in tutoring or mentoring sessions, such as those listed here.

Tutors and mentors should remember that male students may view the world as hierarchical and could feel the need to assert independence and maintain status. Suggestions for working with male students who indicate this need may include the following:

- Consider beginning a session with a male student by asking him about himself. Ask him to enlighten you on an interest he expresses about which you are less informed.

- Avoid one-up phrases ("Do it this way"; "I'll show you"). Instead offer multiple-choice questions ("Would you think it's this, or this?") followed by an inquiry expressing interest ("Why?").

- Try to understand and affirm an aspect of his reasoning, even when his solution is wrong.

- Look for ways to allow male students to maintain status. Do not position them as one-down.

Tutors and mentors should keep in mind that female students often seek connection and intimacy, according to research. Suggestions on slides may include the following:

- Begin with a "get to know you" question just as you do with male students, but share comments on similarities rather than ask for information.

- Use phrases like, "I enjoy that, too!" and "I never liked working these problems either."

- Briefly share personal experiences concerning the subject, instructor-student interactions, or mutual interests.

- Look for ways to connect. Allow occasional *brief* tangential conversations.

These and other bulleted suggestions, along with the reading assignment, will help guide thinking during the role-playing activity.

ROLE-PLAY ACTIVITY

Role-play cards should be prepared in advance (Appendix B). Depending on who is attending the training, the cards should set up a typical scenario between tutor or mentor and client. The key is that tutors or mentors playing the roles will play a gender not their own. Gendered "costumes" may be provided by the trainer for added effect and to remind trainees of the communication role they will play. These can be elaborate or simple (i.e., actual full costumes or simple hats). The day after Halloween is a great day to stock up on treasures for role play.

After the PowerPoint® presentation and discussion of examples from trainees' experiences, the trainer chooses three teams, each with two members—one male, one female—and hands out role-play cards. Teams may want to step out of the room to get into "costume" and character. Meanwhile with the remaining group the trainer continues to discuss the ideas presented in the PowerPoint®. When the costumed teams return, they take 5 minutes each to enact the role play assigned to them. The last 10 minutes should be used to allow the whole group to discuss their observations.

Assessment

To build assessment into the activity, trainers should note responses and level of engagement with the session. Trainers should also assess participants' grasp of the importance of communication in the tutoring or mentoring relationship and the impact of gender on communication styles. A worksheet can be provided at the end of the session if trainers feel the need for further assessment. Continuing assessment should be done in the next training session by asking tutors and mentors to give examples of how they used the techniques learned.

References

Gee, J. P. (1996). *Social linguistics and literacies: Ideology in discourses* (2nd ed.). London, United Kingdom: Taylor & Francis.

Lauter, J. L. (2008). *How is your brain like a zebra? A new human neurotypology.* Bloomington, IN: Xlibris.

Rester, C. H., & Edwards, R. (2007). Effects of sex and setting on students' interpreting of teachers' excessive use of immediacy. *Communication Education, 56*(1), 34–55.

Smith-Jentsch, K. A., Scielzo, S. A., Yarbrough, C. S., & Rosopa, P. J. (2008). A comparison of face-to-face and electronic peer-mentoring: Interactions with mentor gender. *Journal of Vocational Behavior, 72,* 193–206.

Sosik, J. J., & Godshalk, V. M. (2005). Examining gender similarity and mentor's supervisory status in mentoring relationships. *Mentoring and Tutoring, 13*(1), 39–52.

Tannen, D. (1990). *You just don't understand: Women and men in conversation.* New York, NY: William Morrow.

Wright, R. R. (2007). Real men don't ask for directions: Male student attitudes toward peer tutoring. In J. L. Higbee et al. (Eds.), *Best practices in college reading and learning* (pp. 47–62). Eldorado, KS: College Reading and Learning Association. Reprinted from *Journal of College Reading and Learning, 34*(1), 61–75.

Appendix A

● ● ● ● ● EXAMPLE SLIDES OF BRAIN RESEARCH INFORMATION FOR INTRODUCTORY TRAINING LECTURE

Are We Really the Same?

Traditional brain research (Lauter, 2008) says no.

- The female brain processes both language and feelings at the same time far more efficiently than the male brain.
- Male and female brains are hard-wired differently: the male for doing—one thing at a time—and the female for talking and doing.

Lauter, J. L. (2008). *How is your brain like a zebra?* A new human neurotypology. Bloomington, IN: Xlibris.

Location, Location, Location

- Language Mechanics — Men: Left hemisphere front and back
  Women: Left hemisphere front

- Vocabulary — Men: Left hemisphere front and back
  Women: Left and right hemispheres front and back

- Visual-spatial perception — Men: Right hemisphere
  Women: Right and left hemispheres

- Emotion — Men: Right hemisphere
  Women: Right and left hemispheres

Lauter, J. L. (2008). *How is your brain like a zebra?* A new human neurotypology. Bloomington, IN: Xlibris.

Biology or Culture? Both.

- Sociocultural influences are everywhere—from the dolls and trucks of childhood to fashion magazines and reality shows in current pop culture.
- Brain chemistry, brain connections, and hormones are different in males and females.

Generally Speaking

According to sociolinguist Deborah Tannen (1990)

- Men engage the world as individuals in a hierarchical social order in which they are either one-up or one-down in every conversation.
- Women engage the world as individuals in a network of connections in which conversations are negotiations for closeness.

Tannen, D. (1990). *You just don't understand: Women and men in conversation.* New York, NY: William Morrow.

Report Talk vs. Rapport Talk

Deborah Tannen (1990) called the differences between men and women's communicative tendencies report talk (men) vs. rapport talk (women). Men, in social and classroom situations, will often speak more than women; they want to report their knowledge. Women in the same situations will often seek intimacy and connection; they want to establish rapport. Whereas men tend to "hold court" or draw attention to themselves, women want to make everyone feel that they have equal status.

Tannen, D. (1990). *You just don't understand: Women and men in conversation.* New York, NY: William Morrow.

Intimacy vs. Independence

- For men, independence is key; many men establish status by telling others what to do. Being told what to do connotes lower status.
- For women, intimacy is more important than status. Sharing information builds intimacy.

Tutoring: *The client has a problem; the tutor tries to address it, but. . . .*

- Women expect their problems to be answered with matching troubles—intimacy and connection.
- Men want to preserve independence and avoid feeling put down—they resist the lower status they perceive in the act of asking for help.

Why Won't Men Ask for Directions?

- When a tutor offers information, the fact that he or she has the information and the client doesn't sends a metamessage of superiority. The tutor is one-up on the hierarchical ladder.
- Finding their own way is essential for a high percentage of male clients.

Why will women sometimes ask for help even when they don't need it?

- Having information, skill or expertise is not the primary measure of power for most women. Rather, they feel their power is enhanced if they can help someone. They focus on connection rather than independence and self-reliance and feel stronger when part of a community.

Appendix B

EXAMPLE CARDS FOR ROLE PLAY

The role-play requires that a female tutor trainee play the "male" role and that a male tutor trainee play the "female" role.

Male Tutor; Female Tutee

- Help the math-phobic tutee understand how to use factoring to solve the quadratic equation $x^2 - 3x - 10 = 0$.
- Explain the cultural significance of ESPN (or another pastime popular with the men in the group) and its importance to the development of lasting romantic relationships.

- Help the student learn the definitions of 3 or 4 of the following: blitz, quarterback sneak, illegal formation, Hail Mary play, bump and run, hurry-up offense, offensive pass interference, and hook-and-ladder play.

Female Tutor; Male Tutee

- Help the tutee understand the need for accurate comma placement (or use of semicolons or appropriate citation style). The student thinks of punctuation as confetti to be sprinkled liberally in writing. Encourage him to come up with examples for each comma rule.

- Describe a variety of bargain-shopping strategies, including the need for—as well as techniques for development of—an affordable, high-quality, yet expansive shoe wardrobe (or another pastime popular with female tutors).

- The tutee has been asked to interpret a poem for a sophomore literature survey course. (An appropriate piece—for example, a poem by feminist poet Marge Piercy—should be attached to the card.) The tutee is resistant.

Conflict Resolution for the Pre-Professional

Melissa Thomas

Conflict is an inevitable part of every person's life (McKay, Davis, & Fanning, 1995), but the stakes are high when conflict arises in the working environment. Ury's (2000) research about conflict revealed a "third side" (p. 4) and how it is in the best interest of the two parties and the community to resolve disputes. Ury (2000) called this a "triple win" (p. 17).

For many tutors and mentors, learning center employment is their first experience working in an office environment in close conjunction with other pre-professional employees. This training is based upon the work of Ury (2000) and others who believe that a workforce that can resolve its conflicts is a healthy workforce, leading to a productive work environment. This training utilizes self-reflection, as each person's conflict resolution style is his or her own and is best identified by the individual. The training also utilizes collaborative learning as a tool to build cohesion among a team of employees (Wlodkowski, 1999).

Training Activity

Approximately 1 hour is required for the instruction, activity, and assessment. One room with movable chairs, five easel pads or five sheets of butcher paper, masking tape, copies of handouts for all participants, and markers for each of the five stations are needed. After tutors and mentors have completed this training they will be able to (a) identify different conflict resolution styles, including their own; (b) understand the three sides to conflict—people, process, and problem; and (c) be able to evaluate whether to have a "difficult conversation" or not.

First, the trainer draws a circle on the board with the word *conflict* in it and asks trainees to brainstorm conflict issues in regard to tutoring or mentoring while the trainer mind-maps their ideas on the board. Figure 1 provides an example. The trainer erases the board when finished.

Then on each piece of butcher paper (spread equidistant around the room) the trainer writes one of the conflict resolution styles: accommodating, collaborating, avoiding, compromising, or competing (adapted from Blake & Mouton, 1970). Trainees physically move to the word that best reflects their own personal conflict resolution style, with no definition of the style provided by the trainer or participants. Trainees need to define the term for themselves, as a group. Later an official definition and analysis of each style will be provided, and at that time trainees will be permitted to move to a different group.

F I G U R E 1   Conflict mindmap. This sample conflict map shows some of the issues that trainees may have with the students they tutor or mentor, the faculty they support, and their fellow tutors or mentors.

Conflict Resolution Style	Description	Advantage	Disadvantage
Accommodating	Putting someone else's needs ahead of your own	Lets the other person know you value the relationship	Can build potential resentment
Collaborating	Working long and hard to find a workable solution	Provides a long-term solution	Takes time, and all parties must be vested
Avoiding	Choosing to value the relationship more than the conflict	May preserve safety (such as physical safety, job security)	Never addresses the problem, which may grow or fester
Compromising	Finding the most obvious quick solution	Quick and to the point.	May not be a lasting solution
Competing	Acting on principle, not relationships	Useful when something important is on the line—values or ethics	Could destroy relationships

FIGURE 2 Conflict resolution styles. This chart defines each conflict resolution style and speaks to the pros and cons of each style.

The trainer instructs trainees in their newly formed groups to write on their sheet of paper all the words that come to mind in regard to their conflict management style. Using a visual aid based on Figure 2, the trainer reviews with trainees each style and the advantages and disadvantages of each. It is important not to devalue any one style but rather to talk about circumstances in which each style could be useful in life.

The trainer then draws for trainees the conflict triangle (Beer & Stief, 1997; Furlong, 2005) as seen in Figure 3, and discusses with trainees the observation that people in conflict can easily see the problem yet overlook the importance of the process and the people.

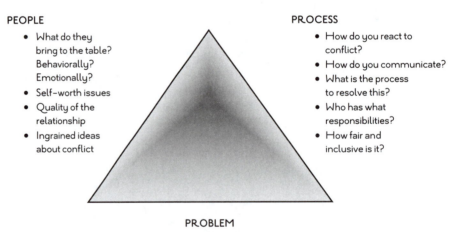

PEOPLE
- What do they bring to the table? Behaviorally? Emotionally?
- Self-worth issues
- Quality of the relationship
- Ingrained ideas about conflict

PROCESS
- How do you react to conflict?
- How do you communicate?
- What is the process to resolve this?
- Who has what responsibilities?
- How fair and inclusive is it?

PROBLEM
- What is the tangible part of the conflict?
- What result is wanted?
- What facts are at issue?
- What position is everyone taking?

FIGURE 3 Conflict Triangle (adapted from Beer & Stief, 1997, and Furlong, 2005). All three sides of the conflict need to be seen and appreciated for conflict to be resolved. This diagram illustrates those three sides.

The trainer should tie the problem, people, and process conversation into the next discussion by presenting trainees with a handout about difficult conversations (Appendix, adapted from Stone, Patton, Heen, & Fisher, 2000), which outlines the three parts of a difficult conversation: (a) the "what happened?" conversation (problem); (b) the feelings conversation (people); and (c) the identity conversation (process). The trainer leads trainees through the three steps and then asks them to reflect on a difficult conversation in which they have wanted to engage. Then trainees reflect on what they want to get out of that conversation and whether the conversation is even worth having.

To end the training session, the trainer once again draws a circle on the board with the word *conflict* in it. The trainees brainstorm again about conflict issues in regard to tutoring and mentoring. The trainer reflects with the trainees on how much more they are able to add to the mindmap after the training.

Assessment

Trainees should now have a better understanding of the five conflict resolution styles and the complex nature of conflict. They should also have evaluated a difficult conversation to see if they would want to have that conversation or not. The final self-assessment activity is Head, Heart, Hand (Wlodkowski, 1999). Trainees are randomly assigned a task, whether *head* (identify something they will continue to think about because of the training), *heart* (identify a feeling that emerged as a result of the training), or *hand* (identify a desired action that they will now take which was stimulated by the training). The trainer can cut out cards in the shape of heads, hearts, and hands to use for this final closing activity. Trainees can write upon the head, heart, or hand cards and then keep them or post them in their common or private workspace (a workroom or office space) so that they keep this training ever present before them.

References

Beer, J. E., & Stief, E. (1997). *The mediator's handbook* (3rd ed.). Gabriola Island, Canada: New Society.

Blake, R. R., & Mouton, J. S. (1970). The fifth achievement. *Journal of Applied Behavioral Science,* 6(4), 413–426. doi:10.1177/002188637000600403

Furlong, G. T. (2005). *The conflict resolution toolbox: Models & maps for analyzing, diagnosing, and resolving conflict.* Mississauga, Canada: John Wiley & Sons.

McKay, M., Davis, M., & Fanning, P. (1995). *How to communicate* (2nd ed.). New York, NY: MJF Books.

Stone, D., Patton, B., Heen, S., & Fisher, R. (2000). *Difficult conversations: How to discuss what matters most.* New York, NY: Penguin.

Ury, W. L. (2000). *The third side.* New York, NY: Penguin.

Wlodkowski, R. J. (1999). *Enhancing adult motivation to learn: A comprehensive guide for teaching all adults.* San Francisco, CA: Jossey-Bass.

Appendix

DIFFICULT CONVERSATIONS HANDOUT

(Adapted from Stone, Patton, Heen, & Fisher, 2000, *Difficult conversations: How to discuss what matters most.* New York, NY: Penguin.)

Preparing to have a difficult conversation requires some inner reflection beforehand. (You may decide you do not even want to have the conversation.) It also requires that you address the three faces of a difficult conversation, based on the three sides on the conflict triangle (problem, process, and people).

1. The "What Happened?" Conversation (PROBLEM)
    a. This conversation is about substance.
    b. Who said what? Who did what? Who intended what? What did you each contribute to the PROBLEM?
        i. Understand each other's stories (not just your own).
        ii. Sort out contributions.
        iii. Disentangle intent and impact.

2. The Feelings Conversation (PEOPLE)
    a. The second conversation involves the feelings each person is grappling with.
    b. What should you do with the feelings? Should you tell others how you feel? And what about their feelings? What if they become angry or start to cry?
    c. Just because you list the feelings doesn't mean you have to bring them up in the conversation.
    d. Also, always use "I" statements, not "you" statements. It is easier to use "you" statements because you are reacting to what the other person has done, but this is an important moment to reflect inward about how this makes you feel.
        i. My feelings.
        ii. Their feelings.

3. The Identity Conversation (PROCESS)
    a. This is the conversation you have with yourself, about yourself.
    b. What does this all say about me? Am I a good person? Lovable? Competent? How do I want this to proceed to keep my identity intact? How do I feel about conflict? How do they feel about themselves and conflict? How can we keep their identity intact?
        i. My self-image.
        ii. Their self-image.

Once you have looked at all three conversations, then you can decide if you want to go through with the conversation and what your purpose will be.

4. Choosing My Purposes

    You need to enter the conversation with a clear purpose and one that you can actually control. You cannot enter the conversation with the intent to change or persuade the other person. Only he or she can decide to change or be persuaded.

    a. Learning: Listen first to understand, then to be understood.
    b. Expression: You are an unparalleled expert on you.
    c. Problem-solving: You take the lead.

The "What Happened" Conversation	My problem:
	Their problem:
The Feelings Conversation	**My feelings:** How do I feel about this situation? Which feelings make sense to share? **Their feelings:** What may they be feeling?
The Identity Conversation	**My self-image:** What do I fear this situation says about me? What's true about this? What's not? **Their self-image:** What may the situation say about them that would be upsetting to them?
Choosing My Purposes	**My purpose for having this conversation:** What do I hope to accomplish in this conversation? Circle the purposes that are: 1. In your control, and 2. Helpful to you.
Opening Line	Consider how you may want to begin the conversation.

Conflict Resolution

Howard Y. Masuda and Reyna I. Torres

Conflict, according to Taylor (2003), "can be understood as a process of expressing dissatisfaction, disagreement, or unmet expectations with another person" (p. 526). Therefore, when tutors or mentors work with students, the possibility of conflict exists due to differences in expectations, wants, needs, beliefs, values, or interests. Students may become angry, for instance, if they expect tutors to provide direct answers to questions on course assignments or rewrite essays for them. If the student expresses anger, an untrained tutor or mentor may feel threatened and react defensively with anger or with excuses leading to further escalation rather than a resolution of the situation, because "conflict affects how you think, behave, and feel" (Masters & Albright, 2002, p. 69).

Conflict resolution guidelines can be extracted from research on conflict resolution (Barsky, 2000; Bodine, Crawford, & Schrumpf, 2002; Masters & Albright, 2002; National Association for Community Mediation, 1999; Raffel, 2008; Taylor, 2003) and customer service (Leland & Bailey, 1995; Martin, 1993; Morgan, 1989). However, regardless of the theoretical framework, basic communication skills are a core component of resolving conflicts. According to Hocker and Wilmont (as cited in Taylor, 2003, p. 531), "communication behavior can create conflict, reflect conflict, and act as a means of productive or destructive resolution of conflict."

In just 2 hours, peer tutors or mentors can accomplish and be assessed on conflict resolution training. This training module has two objectives, to define *conflict*, and to describe and demonstrate understanding and use of the guidelines when working with angry students.

Training Activity

This 2-hour training session requires a room equipped with tables and chairs and a whiteboard, chalkboard, or flip chart. A set of mirrors is suggested. To prepare, the trainer should create sample typical tutoring or mentoring scenarios involving angry students, for use as role plays (as in Appendix A), and should also prepare a handout with listed guidelines as in the summary handout (Appendix B), and become familiar with the guidelines. The following paragraphs describe the objectives of this training activity and how to meet them.

OBJECTIVE 1

The first objective of this training activity is for trainees to define conflict. The trainer should ask the trainees to describe situations in which students may get angry during sessions and what the students may say. Sample scenarios are available in Appendix A. In groups, the tutors or mentors will take a situation and write a role-play script to perform and discuss.

OBJECTIVE 2

The second objective of this training activity is for trainees to describe and demonstrate understanding and use of guidelines for dealing with angry students. When people are upset, they generally want two basic things: they want to express their feelings, and then they want their problem solved (Leland & Bailey, 1995). They also want, among other things, "to be taken seriously," "to be treated with respect," to get immediate action," "to clear up the problem so it never happens again," and "to be listened to" (Morgan, 1989, p. 36). How does a tutor or mentor accomplish all of this? The following guidelines provide a foundation of skills and techniques to use; however, no single technique will work with every upset person and in every situation. The trainer should have trainees stand with a partner and try out the guidelines described in the following script.

Body Posture

Be on the same physical level as the other person; that is, if the person is standing, stand up. A person standing over a seated person has a position of power over the other person. Stand straight with arms at your sides; crossing your arms suggests defensiveness, closed-mindedness, or unwillingness to listen. Touch your index fingers to your thumbs to prevent making fists, which suggests hostility. Keep your hands to yourself; placing your hand on the person's shoulder could be perceived as patronizing or showing authority rather than a sign of concern, resulting in an aggressive physical response (e.g., slapping away your hand). Squarely face the person at a comfortable distance; don't crowd or stand too far way. Leland and Bailey (1995) suggested standing two to four feet apart. How close is two feet? How far apart is four feet? Ask trainees to take a ruler and measure the distance and describe what distance feels comfortable.

Eye Contact

Maintain comfortable eye contact. Eye contact signals interest, receptiveness, and attention. Look away occasionally to avoid the impression of staring, which can be perceived as hostile. Facial expressions should indicate caring. Avoid the inappropriate smile, smirk, scowl, or rolling of the eyes. The key elements of facial expressions are the shape of the eyes and mouth and the slant of the eyebrows.

Trainees should demonstrate these facial expressions, using the mirrors to view their own expressions. Stock photographs of facial expressions are available online at Fotosearch (2011). Search Google Images for specific facial expressions.

Mental Preparation

Focus on mental preparation. Take deep breaths to relax, and breathe while listening and responding. Instructions for deep breathing exercises are available online (Weil, 2011).

Use positive self-statements, such as, "Stay calm and listen carefully—I can handle this," to help you cope with the stressful situation. The Mayo Clinic (Mayo Foundation for Medical Education and Research, 2010) provides examples of positive self-talk.

Keep in mind that you cannot control the behavior of others, but you can control your own behavior. According to Martin (1993), "difficult people are merely expressing a need, although they are choosing an inappropriate and impolite way to communicate this need" (p. 75).

Listening Behavior

Listen carefully to identify the facts and the person's concerns and needs. Listen to the tone of voice and observe body language as clues to the person's emotions. What are the facial expressions, body language, and tone of voice of someone who is angry? Disappointed? Frustrated? Be empathetic and try to see the situation as the other person sees it. Separate your feelings about the other person—disapproval, contempt, indifference—and his or her actions—obnoxious, rude, sarcastic—from what the person is saying because these feelings can distract you from the issue and possible resolutions.

Show that you are listening by occasionally nodding your head up and down. Continually nodding your head may convey impatience. Say "uh-huh," and maintain eye contact. Regardless of your own feelings, avoid sighing, which suggests annoyance or impatience.

Be patient and respectful. Let the person talk without interrupting to respond or ask questions. If the person is angry, do not take the anger personally and react defensively. Making excuses ("No one told me"), blaming someone else ("Don't blame me, I didn't do it!"), or arguing about who is right or wrong, ("You're wrong! It's your own fault, you should have . . .") will escalate the situation. Do not tell a person to "calm down" because this implies insensitivity to the person's feelings and may agitate the person further. Whenever you are tempted to say an inappropriate remark, use Raffel's (2008) strategy and imagine taking a huge clothespin and pinning your lips together.

If the person curses, calmly say, "I understand you're upset. I really want to resolve this. I'm having trouble focusing on the problem because of the language I am hearing. Could you please not use that kind of language?" If the cursing continues, repeat and substitute the last sentence with, "Would you please stop." If the person does not stop, call your supervisor ("Please excuse me. I will have to call my supervisor to assist you"). If the person shows definite signs of becoming hostile or violent (e.g., clenched fists, tight lips, agitated tone of voice, tense body posture, flared nostrils, red face, wide-open eyes), get help from your supervisor. Do not make threats to call campus police unless you are going to follow through. If your supervisor is not available and the student becomes extremely hostile, walk away from the situation and get help. Develop a plan for this situation.

Replying

Speak in a calm, firm, confident voice that has an even tone. When nervous and excited, we may speak too quickly and loudly.

Apologize for the situation ("I am sorry about this") but not for your behavior, actions, or words unless you were at fault. In this case, take responsibility for your actions ("I'm really sorry that I made a mistake. I will do the best I can to . . ." or "I apologize for . . . and making you upset"). Apologizing does not automatically mean you are guilty of something; it just means that you are sorry the person has had a bad experience. Acknowledge the person's feelings ("I can see how you would be angry [frustrated, annoyed, disappointed]. I would be angry [frustrated, annoyed, disappointed], too."

State your desire to resolve the situation ("I can see you are upset. I am willing to listen, so please tell me what happened"). Ask questions if you have not identified or are unclear about the problem or issue ("I'm not sure I understand what you mean"). Repeat the person's concerns to show your understanding ("Let me see if I understand . . ."). If the person is having difficulty expressing his or her thoughts, do not finish the person's sentence or say, "What you are trying to say is. . . ." These actions imply the person is not capable of speaking for himself or herself.

Propose available and feasible options or solutions and briefly explain their value or benefit to the person. State what you can, not what you cannot do (which people don't want to hear), based upon your authority and program policies and procedures. Saying, "I can . . ." and adding, "Would you like to . . . ?" gives the person a choice in the matter. If the person is not agreeable, invite the person to participate in the resolution of the problem by asking, "What do you think would be a fair way to resolve this?" If the request is unreasonable, calmly re-offer the available options, starting the sentence with the person's name ("Dana, if we are going to resolve this situation, we are going to have to cooperate with each other. This is what I can do") (Morgan, 1989, p. 42). If the person's request is reasonable and can be accommodated, fulfill the request. If you do not have the authority to grant the request, find a supervisor who can, saying, "Please excuse me. I'd like to check with my supervisor about this."

Closing

If a settlement is reached and the situation is resolved, summarize what actions you and the other person will take. Apologize again, and thank the person for bringing the problem to your attention.

Trainers should consider creating and using incident reports. Tutors or mentors can write down the context of the incidents (who was involved, what happened, what caused the incident, what was said and done) and their answers to the following questions: What could I have done and said to prevent this in the first place? What did I do and say that helped to calm and resolve the situation? What did I do and say that escalated the situation? What did I learn from this situation that I can apply in the future? These incident reports can be shared and discussed at tutor or mentor meetings.

Assessment

To assess the effectiveness of this training, the trainer should have trainees demonstrate their competence in each of the two areas of training in the summary handout, defining conflict and demonstrating guidelines for dealing with conflict (see Appendix B). Groups should be instructed to incorporate into their role plays the guidelines regarding body posture, eye contact, mental preparation, listening behavior, replying, and closing. Individual trainees should be able to identify as appropriate or inappropriate the behaviors demonstrated by other trainees or by the trainer.

References

Barsky, A. E. (2000). *Conflict resolution for the helping professions.* Belmont, CA: Brooks/Cole.

Bodine, R. J., Crawford, K. C., & Schrumpf, F. (2002). *Creating the peaceable school: A comprehensive program for teaching conflict resolution* (2nd ed.). Champaign, IL: Research Press.

Fotosearch. (2011). *Facial expression stock photos and images.* Retrieved from http://www.fotosearch.com/photos-images/facial-expression.html

Leland, K., & Bailey, K. (1995). *Customer service for dummies.* Foster City, CA: IDG Books Worldwide.

Martin, W. B. (1993). *Quality customer service.* Menlo Park, CA: Crisp.

Masters, M. F., & Albright, R. R. (2002). *The complete guide to conflict resolution in the workplace.* New York, NY: AMACON.

Mayo Foundation for Medical Education and Research. (2010). *Positive thinking: Reduce stress, enjoy life more.* Retrieved from http://www.mayoclinic.com/health/positive-thinking/SR00009

Morgan, R. L. (1989). *Calming upset customers: Staying effective during unpleasant situations.* Menlo Park, CA: Crisp.

National Association for Community Mediation. (1999). *Face-to-face: A presenter's manual on conflict resolution and communication skills* (2nd ed.). Washington, DC: Author.

Raffel, L. (2008). *I hate conflict! Seven steps to resolving differences with anyone in your life.* New York, NY: McGraw-Hill.

Taylor, S. L. (2003). Conflict resolution. In S. R. Komives, D. B. Woodward, Jr., & Associates (Eds.), *Student services: A handbook for the profession* (4th ed., pp. 525–538). San Francisco, CA: Jossey-Bass.

Weil, A. (2011). *Three breathing exercises.* Retrieved from http://www.drweil.com/drw/u/ART00521/three-breathing-exercises.html

Appendix A

SAMPLE SCENARIOS

Scenario 1

The student is resistant to doing his own work and says angrily, "Why do you keep asking me to do the problems? If I knew how, I wouldn't be here, would I? Just give me the answers! It's your job!"

Scenario 2

The last few questions are giving you trouble and you have to refer to the student's textbook. Impatient, the student says angrily, "Why are you wasting my time? Why can't you solve these problems? Why did they hire you?"

Scenario 3

The student throws down his test with a D grade in front of you and says angrily, "What you told me last week was all wrong. I got a D because of you! It's all your fault!"

Appendix B

SUMMARY HANDOUT ON CONFLICT RESOLUTION

Objective 1

Define conflict.

Objective 2

Describe and demonstrate understanding and use of the guidelines for dealing with angry students.

Motivation of Upset Individuals

1. According to Leland and Bailey, what two things do upset people want?
2. According to Morgan, what are five additional things upset people want?

Body Posture

1. Be on the same physical level. Why?
2. Stand up straight. How do you position your arms and hands?
3. Squarely face person at comfortable distance. What is the suggested distance?
4. Keep hands to self. Why?
5. Maintain comfortable eye contact. What does eye contact signal? How might staring be perceived?

Mental Preparation

1. Take deep breaths. Why?
2. Use positive self-statements. Give an example of a positive self-statement for dealing with angry situations.

Listening Behavior

1. Listen carefully. What are six things to listen for and observe to identify?
2. Separate how you feel from what the person is saying. How might they be different?
3. Show you are listening. What are two ways to convey you are listening?
4. Be patient and respectful. What is the effect of being defensive or argumentative? What is the effect of telling a person to calm down? What would you say if the person uses profanity?

Replying

1. Speak in a calm voice. Describe voices that are not calm.
2. Apologize for the situation. Does apologizing mean you are at fault? Give an example of an appropriate apology.
3. Acknowledge the person's feelings. Give an example of an acknowledgement of feelings.
4. State that you want to resolve the situation. Give an example of what you might say.
5. Ask questions. Give an example of what you might ask.
6. Repeat the person's concerns. Give an example of how you might express the student's concern. What is wrong with saying, "What you are trying to say is. . . ."?
7. Propose options or solutions. Give an example of what you might say. What would you say if the person does not accept your options or solutions? What would you say if the person makes an unreasonable demand? What would you say if you do not have the authority to grant the request?

Closing

1. Summarize actions to be taken. Give an example of what you might say.
2. Apologize and thank the person. Give an example of what you might say.

Using Probing Questions

 Rebecca Daly Cofer

It is the job of tutors and mentors to guide students through the unfamiliar practice of learning center work, to provide questions that lead students to empowerment and knowledge. As North (1982) put it, students visit the learning center "looking for help. Often, they don't know what kind of help is available, practicable, or sensible" (p. 434). Student clients may at first be nervous, anxious, or self-conscious, but they quickly become participants in the session if guided by the tutor's or mentor's probing questions.

Probing questions are questions that seek more detail. Here are adaptations of sample probing questions from Straker (n.d.): What exactly did you mean when you said the test was hard? Could you tell me more about the issues you had with the test? What, specifically, will you do next week to prepare for your next quiz in this class? How do you know that the information you provided on the test is true? How does this test compare to the previous test you took for this math course? How will you begin to prepare for the upcoming quiz in biology?

In training student staff to utilize probing questions during sessions with students, the training coordinator teaches tutors and mentors to lead and guide sessions and not just supply answers to students' questions. This particular training on using probing questions in tutoring and mentoring sessions should (a) empower both the tutors or mentors and the students during their sessions, (b) give tutors and mentors a way to guide sessions, (c) define and provide examples of types of probing questions, and (d) provide scenarios for tutors and mentors to practice probing questions.

By providing training on probing questions, tutor and mentor coordinators can equip student staff with practical approaches for dealing with uninformed tutees and mentees. This training teaches tutors and mentors to use open-ended and engaging questions to allow for open dialogue. A good tutor or mentor listens to students and allows them opportunities to voice their own ideas in a safe environment; probing questions can open the door to conversation.

Training Activity

This training activity is designed to be both informative and interactive. Rather than providing only a lecture or PowerPoint® training session on probing questions, the tutor or mentor coordinator needs to engage student staff with activities and real-life scenarios to prepare them for their work with students. Providing different types of learning activities in each training session acknowledges the many learning styles of tutors and mentors as well as the diversity of styles of the students with whom they will work, modeling for student staff the benefits of accommodating a variety of learning styles in a session. The tutor or mentor coordinator needs to train student staff in the same way that tutors and mentors work with their students—interactively and directly.

The probing questions training session requires one room with a projector and online computer access, movable chairs for the final activity, and a whiteboard or chalkboard to record answers to the written activity sheet about turning nonprobing questions into probing questions. The training takes approximately 1 hour.

PREPARATIONS

In preparation for this training session, the trainer should prepare some sample questions on a sheet for the tutors or mentors to transform into probing questions. As a guide to the trainer, in the list provided here, the first, nonprobing question is followed by a probing question in italics; the trainees, however, will see on their worksheets only the nonprobing questions, which they will transform into probing questions. The trainer will compare their responses to the probing questions here or to Straker's (n.d.) examples:

- Did you do your homework from our last session? *What problems, specifically, did you encounter in your assignments since our last session?*

- Are your classes going well? *Could you tell me about your courses and update me on how each course is going this week?*

- How many classes did you miss this week? *How do you plan to handle the classes you missed this week?*

- Are you ready for the exam on Thursday? *What changes have you made in your preparation for this second exam, coming up on Thursday?*

- Do you have any questions about the work we did during our last session? *During the last session, we covered your in-class lecture notes on the Civil War; what parts of the material were hard to make sense of later?*

- Do you like math? *How have your feelings about math been changing in the past couple of weeks?*

- Did you pay your semester tuition and fees? *What concerns do you have about tuition and fee payments for this semester?*

- Do you like that your parents are involved in your college education? *In your judgment, what role should your parents play in your college life?*

- Did you apply for scholarships for school? *How do you see yourself paying for college?*

- How many finals do you have? *How will you prepare this week for each of your finals?*

A FILM CLIP

Beginning the entire training session with a film clip not only provides an enjoyable and interesting opening for the training but also gives real examples of probing questions, foreshadowing the game with which trainees will conclude the session. The trainer shows a clip from *Rosencrantz and Guildenstern are Dead* (Azenberg, Brandman, & Stoppard, 1990). This brief movie clip has two actors playing a game of tennis with words, so to speak, hitting back and forth with questions rather than a tennis ball. The trainer asks participants to note how the actors use questions to answer questions, which is good practice for the tutors and mentors.

A LECTURE

The second section of the training offers a more traditional mode, lecture and listening, to convey the definition of and rationale for using probing questions in sessions with students. Following this brief lecture, the trainer provides nonprobing questions gathered from tutoring or mentoring sessions in the learning center and has trainees turn these questions into more useful probing questions. Using examples gives staff needed practice and also builds their confidence. People learn well in groups when they are asked to collaborate, so much of this training, including the question transformation activity, consists of group work. As Cox (2002) argued, collaborative learning for students provides "an opportunity for members of [the] group to be teachers *and* learners in a safe and supportive group" (p. 4).

After showing the clip and discussing what the actors were doing by using the questions they employed in this volley of words, the trainer explains the definition of a probing question and some techniques for asking these types of questions. Probing questions seek more than simple yes-or-no answers. The trainer addresses the types of probing questions that should not be asked because of confidentiality or professionalism, such as questions regarding personal information or information about a disability. Because tutors and mentors may be working with students with disabilities, this explanation of confidentiality is extremely important. For instance, a tutor should never ask a student struggling in English, "Do you have a learning disability? How does it affect your writing?"

At this point the trainer should respond to the common assertion that answering a question with a question is rude and can explain the rationale behind asking probing questions. As North (1982) articulated in the context of writing center work, "the best tutorials are those [that] lead/encourage/prompt the writer to engage in or reflect on composing" (p. 435). Tutors and mentors need to know that success in the tutoring or mentoring session may not always result in immediate improvements in grades, as learning center staff work with students to change learning behaviors (p. 436).

The trainer also explores the relevance of having student clients verbally explore their ideas rather than simply answer yes-or-no questions. Clark (1984) argued, "you simply have to let [the student] fumble around and more or less talk to [himself/herself]" (p. 239). The trainer can demonstrate the validity of this position by asking one of the trainees some yes-or-no questions about a recent positive experience, then follow with an open-ended question that provides encouragement for real communication and expression about this meaningful event.

Because many people seem to learn best with specifics and examples, the trainer should provide the examples of closed-ended questions for trainees to rewrite in small groups or individually. As Flage (2004) discussed in his introduction to *The Art of Questioning*, "critical thinking [and questioning] is a practical enterprise" (p. xi), so probing questions should be practiced. The open-ended or probing questions can then be shared with the entire group and written on the board so trainees can copy them onto their worksheets. The closed-ended question, "Did you bring your completed assignment for today's session?" could become a probing question, "What specific assignment did you bring to work on today?"

A GAME

The final section of the training is a game in which trainees answer questions with questions. This exercise also provides an assessment of trainee understanding, so trainers will know if any further explanation is needed. This game, beyond providing practice with the probing questions and an assessment of trainee skills, also allows for an enjoyable and relaxing way to conclude the training.

All sit in a circle and ask probing questions around the circle to the next person. The coordinator begins the circle, and then the next person in the circle needs to answer with a probing question, as in the film clip. This continues until someone in the circle cannot ask a question or makes a mistake by failing to ask a probing question. Individuals disqualified from the game in this way still participate by listening for nonprobing questions from others. Play continues for a specified number of minutes or until the last person in the circle wins the game.

Assessment

Assessing the trainees' learning means evaluating to what extent the session has been useful to the trainees in their work with students. Observation of tutoring and mentoring sessions provides the best long-term assessment of communication training. In the short term, however, another list of nonprobing questions can be provided for trainees to transform into probing questions: Did you get the reading done since our last session? Is math class going well? Did you pass that test? All set for next week's test? Any questions left over from our last session? Do you like history? Did you complete the Free Application for Federal Student Aid (FAFSA)? Are you meeting with your professors regularly? Did you apply for scholarships for school? Are you managing your time okay?

References

Azenberg, E., & Brandman, M. (Producers), & Stoppard, T. (Director). (1990). *Rosencrantz and Guildenstern are dead* [Motion picture]. USA: Walt Disney Video.

Clark, B. L. (1984). Tutoring, within limits. *College Composition and Communication, 35,* 238–240.

Cox, M. D. (2002). The role of community in learning: Making connections for your classroom and campus, your students and colleagues. In G. S. Wheeler (Ed), *Teaching and learning in college: A resource for educators* (4th ed., pp. 1–38). Elyria, OH: Info-Tec.

Flage, D. E. (2004). The art of questioning: An introduction to critical thinking. Upper Saddle River, NJ: Pearson/Prentice Hall.

North, S. M. (1982). Training tutors to talk about writing. *College Composition and Communication, 33,* 434–441.

Straker, D. (n.d.). *Techniques: Questioning.* Retrieved from http://www.changingminds.org/techniques/questioning/questioning.htm

Codependency in Education: Training Tutors and Mentors Not to Rescue

Karin E. Winnard

The concept of codependency or disempowering behavior was developed in the early 1980s to explain addictive behavior in the field of substance abuse. Such books as *Codependent No More* (Beattie, 1987), *When Society Becomes an Addict* (Schaef, 1987), and *Another Chance: Hope and Health for the Alcoholic Family* (Wegscheider-Cruse, 1989) discussed behaviors that are exhibited when people believe their happiness or value is based upon controlling another person or situation. For purposes of this module, codependency is seen as having four characteristics: (a) one feels the need to take care of, rescue, fix, or control another person or situation; (b) one values the needs or goals of another person more than one's own needs or goals; (c) one's self-worth depends on the need to be needed; and (d) the behavior becomes a pattern and continues despite negative consequences (Beattie, 1987; Wegsheider-Cruse, 1989; Winnard, 1991).

Codependency occurs in tutoring situations in which students' expectations of what tutors will do (e.g., work with them to solve their homework problems, proofread a paper) may not be aligned with what tutors are directed to do (e.g., work on example or practice problems, assist students to develop proofreading skills). The same can be true within the peer mentoring relationship when mentors believe their responsibility is to take care of the student's problem rather than assist the student to figure out what action to take and then to develop the confidence to take the next step. There is a danger that instead of empowering students to develop independent learning and living skills, many tutorial and mentoring programs perpetuate codependency by relying on the "quick fix": they train tutors and mentors to give answers rather than assist students to develop and practice skills necessary to discover answers (Winnard, 1991).

It is recommended that tutors and mentors be trained to recognize their own codependent behaviors, shift their frames of reference, and set boundaries in order to alter their responses to unhealthy situations (Winnard, 1991). When tutors and mentors make these changes in their own lives, they can identify these patterns more easily in sessions with their student clients and respond in a manner that is empowering, productive, and supportive. The following activity aims to train tutors and mentors to accomplish this goal by requiring them to learn about codependency as it relates to their own lives and then to address it effectively in actual tutoring and mentoring situations.

Training Activity

This activity takes approximately 1.5 hours regardless of how many people are being trained. A list of the four characteristics of codependency can be posted at the front of the room for easy reference. Handouts with several assessment scenarios are needed (see Assessment section), with pertinent multiple-choice or short-answer questions. Prior to this exercise, trainers are advised to refer to an article on codependency and tutoring (Winnard, 1991) to prepare.

UNDERSTANDING CODEPENDENCY OF TUTORS AND MENTORS

The first task of the training activity is to provide the participants with two or three written scenarios that will be performed and discussed during the actual training. After reading each scenario, trainees will be required to provide responses to either short-answer or multiple-choice questions as to how they would manage each scenario. These written responses are to be collected by the trainer and matched with the post-assessment activity (see Assessment section of this module). After this initial task is completed, the trainees are then to read the list of characteristics of codependent service providers that is posted in the room and work individually to provide five characteristics or observable behaviors of codependent tutors or mentors. Trainees are to be given a maximum of 3 minutes to create their independent lists. Trainees then present and discuss as a group and collectively identify the top 10 behaviors. Time needed for discussion depends on the facilitator's assessment of trainees' understanding of the definition and characteristics of codependency. Possible responses for each component are provided here.

One Feels the Need to Take Care of, Rescue, Fix, or Control Another Person or Situation

A tutor gives answers to tutees without using any of the center's agreed-upon "best" tutoring practices. A tutor shares copies of the center's textbooks with unprepared tutees who own the textbook but do not bring it to sessions. A mentor extends scheduled session times because student clients need more help.

One Values the Needs and Goals of Another Person More Than One's Own Needs and Goals

A tutor waits to meet with the supervisor, who is 30 minutes late for the meeting, and as a result will now be late to class. A tutor breaks program policy by tutoring students when not scheduled to work. A mentor agrees to work extra shifts despite needing the extra time to study.

One's Self-Worth Depends on the Need to be Needed

A tutor measures tutoring effectiveness by the grades tutees obtain on exams. A mentor enjoys providing extra, over-the-top help to student clients and to the program director, thereby feeding the mentor's craving to be needed. A tutor is devastated to learn that she or he is not the most requested or most popular tutor.

The Behavior Becomes a Pattern and Continues Despite Negative Consequences

A tutor continues to accept extra shifts despite falling behind in class. A mentor comes to work sick. A tutor is criticized by roommates for hosting emergency tutoring sessions in their residence. A mentor is available 24/7 even though paid only when meeting with student clients at the center.

When trainees have a concrete understanding of codependency in the context of learning assistance and mentoring, the trainer gives them an opportunity first to demonstrate codependent tutoring or mentoring behaviors through role playing and then to explore behaviors to discourage codependency.

ROLE PLAYS FOR UNDERSTANDING CODEPENDENCY IN THE TUTORING AND MENTORING PROCESS

Two volunteers are selected for each role play. One plays the codependent tutor or mentor while the other plays the student client. Both are given the situation or title of the scenario and then have less than 5 minutes' time to act out the scenario, demonstrating no more than three observable codependent behaviors. The more exaggerated the tutors' or mentors' behaviors, the clearer the lesson becomes. Suggested role plays include the following:

- The mentee calls the mentor at 11:00 p.m. (Program policy states that mentors' phone and email information is confidential and is not to be distributed to the institution's students, faculty, or staff.)

- A mentee is 15 minutes late to a small-group session. The mentor starts the session over.

- The tutee brings the textbook but does not bring notes from the reading. The tutee says she or he left the notes at home. Luckily, the tutor took this class from the same instructor and remembers *everything* from the class.

- The tutee attributes improved grades to the tutor rather than to the tutee's skill development and hard work.

As the volunteers play their roles, observers identify and write down the codependent behaviors for a brief discussion that follows. After all of the role plays have been performed, the trainer works with the trainees to brainstorm strategies that will transform these codependent and disempowering behaviors into empowering actions. For example, the discussion may address the importance of working with only the materials tutees bring to the tutorial session in order to encourage tutees to be fully prepared for each session. Similarly, the trainer will encourage mentors not to come to work when they are ill, to ensure that student staff take care of their own needs before those of their supervisor or student clients. Finally, tutors may explore ways to assess their tutees' increased level of understanding by measuring their students' progress in their sessions together, instead of using the grades their tutees achieve on exams.

ACTIVITY FOR PREVENTING CODEPENDENCY OF TUTEES AND MENTEES

Once trainees see ways that codependency is exhibited by tutors and mentors, they can then practice identifying behaviors exhibited by codependent student clients. Trainers can conduct the previous exercise again, this time instructing trainees to work individually for no more than 3 minutes to provide 10 observable behaviors of codependent tutees or mentees. Participants work together to create a final list of 10 observable characteristics. The recommended discussion time for each characteristic depends once again upon the trainer's assessment of trainees' understanding of codependency. Some examples for each component are provided here.

One Feels the Need to Take Care of, Rescue, Fix, or Control Another Person or Situation

The tutee begins to cry or yell because she or he wants the tutor to proofread a three-page paper that is due in an hour. A mentee asks the mentor to work with him or her privately (for money) during the center's hours of operation. The tutee tells the tutor that without at least a B in the course the tutee will be "thrown out of school."

One Values the Needs and Goals of Another Person More Than One's Own Needs and Goals

Two tutees are in the same class and in the same tutoring session; the codependent tutee asks no questions, thinking the other student's questions are more important. The mentee is late to a third session with the mentor and, fearful of suspension of program privileges, begs the mentor not to follow program policy by notifying the director.

One's Self-Worth Depends on the Need to be Needed

The tutee unnecessarily comes to tutoring twice a week because she or he knows the tutors are paid only when they have a scheduled appointment. The mentee continues to play the role of victim in his or her roommate situation, so that the mentor-in-training can practice developing active listening and counseling skills with this student.

The Behavior Becomes a Pattern and Continues Despite Negative Consequences

The mentee wants to work exclusively with one mentor and repeatedly skips class to attend the sessions rather than asking the mentor to adjust his or her availability. The tutee continues to be unprepared for sessions even though center policy will now restrict his or her use of the center's services.

Assessment

The role-play exercise at the end of this training session permits participants to demonstrate how much they know about how codependency can manifest itself in tutoring or mentoring and what strategies participants have developed to transform these situations into empowered and productive experiences. Based upon the trainer's assessment of the tutors' or mentors' comprehension, future training sessions may be developed.

One week after the training session and after the participants have had an opportunity to apply what they learned to actual tutorial or mentoring sessions, trainees are given the same scenarios as before training. Trainees are asked to respond to the same short-answer or multiple-choice questions.

It is critical that tutor and mentor training continue to encourage student staff to share their experiences of applying effective strategies to avoid or dissolve codependent situations in their sessions with student clients. Supervisors and trainers may wish to bring current examples and possible solutions to future trainings for the tutors and mentors to role play, discuss, and consequently incorporate into their existing frames of reference.

References

Beattie, M. (1987). *Codependent no more*. New York, NY: Harper/Hazeldon.

Schaef, A. W. (1987). *When society becomes an addict*. San Francisco, CA: Harper & Row.

Wegscheider-Cruse, S. (1989). *Another chance: Hope and health for the alcoholic family* (2nd ed.). Palo Alto, CA: Science & Behavior Books.

Winnard, K. E. (1991). Codependency: Teaching tutors not to rescue. *Journal of College Reading and Learning, 24*(1), 32–39.

Ⓑ RIGHTS AND RESPONSIBILITIES

Confidentiality for Tutors and Mentors

▨ Randy E. Dale

In August 1974, the United States Congress passed 20 U.S.C. 1232g, formally named the Family Educational Rights and Privacy Act and also referred to as the Buckley Amendment but best known throughout the education world simply by its acronym, FERPA (Groves & Groves, 1981). Groves and Groves explained that the purpose of FERPA was "to protect the privacy of student records from unauthorized inspection" (1981, p. 336). FERPA applies to institutions of higher education that receive federal funds for certain programs (Dinger, 2001). Based on the legal doctrines of respondeat superior and vicarious liability (Garner, 1999), the postsecondary institution is liable for the conduct of its tutors and mentors when acting in the course and scope of their employment; therefore, ensuring FERPA compliance by tutors and mentors is important.

The purposes of this training module include (a) familiarizing mentors and tutors with FERPA, its specific provisions, and how those provisions affect the work of tutors and mentors; (b) demonstrating some of the pitfalls by which FERPA provisions might unexpectedly snare a tutor or mentor; and (c) providing student staff with a clear understanding of how they can conduct themselves without causing the institution to run afoul of FERPA provisions.

Training Activity

The trainer will need a room with movable chairs, an AV screen and LCD projector (if a Power-Point® presentation is utilized), copies of case studies, markers, and a whiteboard or flip chart with easel. One hour is required for this session.

The trainer may want to begin the session with a short get-acquainted exercise of the facilitator's choice. This activity should be completed in about 5 minutes. There are many good resources for locating such an exercise, such as *40 Ice Breakers and Other Warm-ups* (n.d.). For an exhaustive list of such games, the terms "ice breaker games" or "get-acquainted games" can be entered into a search engine.

To introduce the subject of the session, the trainer can deliver a short presentation covering FERPA's history, recent amendments, and highlights. The facilitator may choose to provide some information from recent court decisions or legislative amendments that would be interesting to the participants. For example, when FERPA was in its infancy, ingenious but mostly unsuccessful plaintiffs' attorneys attempted to litigate a plethora of perceived FERPA violations. In *Owasso ISD et al. v. Falvo et al.* (2002), a FERPA violation was alleged when an elementary school teacher had her students grade each other's quizzes, a common practice known as peer grading. In *Doe and Curto v. Anonymous Unnamed School Employees and Officials of Cornell University et al.* (2004), a FERPA violation was one of many allegations brought by plaintiff Curto after being expelled by Cornell University's College of Veterinary Medicine. After failing an exam, Curto recruited a former faculty member to review the exam. In the course of performing the evaluation, the reviewer learned from a veterinary school official, in an alleged FERPA violation, that Curto was also failing anatomy. In 2003, in another interesting postsecondary case, a FERPA violation was alleged when the editor of the Portland State University campus newspaper became embroiled in a contest of wills with the school's administration. With all the intrigue of a John Grisham novel, the facts of this case involved discovering wrongfully discarded student records, a quasi-extortion attempt by the editor, and the school's padlocking the door to the newspaper's offices (*Desyllas v. Bernstine et al.*, 2003).

In 2002, the United States Supreme Court spoke on the subject, essentially halting the plaintiffs' claims. In the landmark decision of *Gonzaga University et al. v. Doe* (2002), the court ruled that individuals have no cause of action rights under the plain reading of FERPA. Although the statute provides for monetary penalties for schools that routinely violate the statute's mandates, none of those penalties involves the creation of a personal cause of action on behalf of the aggrieved students or parents. As a result of *Gonzaga*, which continues to be the guiding precedent, there have been no further attempts by individuals to hold a school liable for damages under FERPA. Even though there is no personal cause of action for a FERPA violation, the institution is still liable for punishment in the form of monetary penalties levied by the Department of Education. Additional information is available online from the National Association of Colleges and Employers (2010).

For the purposes of this training, the tutors and mentors need to know that educational records are defined by FERPA as records that directly relate to a student and that are maintained by an educational agency or institution or by a party acting for the agency or institution (Van Dusen, 2004). The statute separates this information into two categories: directory information and non-directory information. Prior written consent of the student is required for the release of non-directory information but not for the release of directory information, which includes name, address, phone number and email address, dates of attendance, degrees awarded, enrollment status, and the student's major or minor field of study. Non-directory information is the more personal, private information such as social security number, race, ethnicity, nationality, gender, grades, and transcripts.

FERPA remained relatively unchanged for 20 years. Then in 2008, partly due to the tragic shooting deaths of 30 Virginia Tech students by a fellow student, Seung Hui Cho (Hauser & O'Connor, 2007; Lipka, 2008), the Department of Education determined that some changes were necessary. Amendments to FERPA were promulgated and adopted and became effective in early 2009. The change most pertinent to the work of mentors and tutors has to do with revealing information about a student's mental health condition. At Virginia Tech, faculty members and students were disturbed by Cho's bizarre behavior and wanted to notify his parents but believed that doing so would violate FERPA (Carter, 2009; Lipka, 2008). In fact, FERPA has always allowed institutions to share information about a student if there existed a "health or safety" emergency, but the statute also required a strict construction of the term emergency (Bernstein, 2008). What the amendment does is to "strip away this condition that the definition of emergency must be narrow and emphasizes that schools may use this health-or-safety exception as long as there is an articulable and significant threat to the student or other individuals," (Bernstein, 2008, p. 102). LeRoy S. Rooker, director of the Family Policy Compliance Office of the Department of Education, said, "We wanted to strike that balance between privacy and safety and certainly emphasize that safety on a campus is paramount," (Lipka, 2008, p. A18). In elaborating, Rooker said that as long as a university can articulate what the emergency is, the Department of Education will not second-guess the school's decision. If a mentor or tutor witnesses a student's behavior as bizarre, and the tutor believes that the student is in danger of harming himself or another, the tutor now has the freedom to advise his or her immediate supervisor of the situation, provided the tutor can articulate the observed behavior and perceived threat.

The oral presentation of this training session concludes with an explanation to the trainees of how the requirements of FERPA and confidentiality affect their work as mentors and tutors. Because mentors and tutors are employees of the institution, the institution will be held liable for any FERPA violation committed by the mentor or tutor. Time should be allowed for the participants to ask questions during or after the presentation. This portion of the training session should take approximately 15 minutes.

An interactive discussion activity follows the presentation and puts FERPA rules in context. Two case studies are provided for discussion (see Appendix A), but they can be adapted to fit circumstances at the trainer's institution. The trainer should contact the dean of students or vice president of student affairs for FERPA-related incidents particular to the institution. At this point, the facilitator may choose one of two possible avenues, and the choice depends primarily on the size of the participating group. For either direction, the activity should take approximately 30 minutes.

For a small group of trainees, each case study is read by a volunteer. When a volunteer reads the first scenario, the group then discusses whether FERPA is applicable to the situation, and, if so, whether it has been violated. The facilitator will simply facilitate and attempt to draw trainees into thinking through and discussing the situation and FERPA's relevance. The facilitator's other role is to record all main points and good ideas on the whiteboard or flip chart and insure that the discussion covers the essential points. After approximately 15 minutes, the second scenario is read by a volunteer, repeating the process. Facilitators never want productive discussion to be discouraged but should keep an eye on the clock. For additional information or to have easy access to a valuable resource, tutors and mentors should read Van Dusen's (2004) overview.

As an alternative exercise, a group of 16 or more trainees should be divided into two or more groups. Volunteers should be solicited from each group to read the case studies. After about 10 minutes for discussion of each scenario, the groups together should discuss and record good ideas and main points as each group reports on its case study. At least 5 minutes at the end of this activity should be reserved for cross-group discussion of any issues that may have surfaced during the discussion.

Assessment

The purposes of this training are to inform peer mentors and tutors about FERPA and to raise awareness about how school personnel must work within the parameters of the FERPA regulations. A short and easy, 10-question written quiz can be administered to the trainees to assess their knowledge at the completion of the training period. The quiz provided in Appendix B is designed to be completed in a few minutes. When all trainees have completed the quiz, reviewing the questions as a group can serve as a fulcrum for a final discussion period.

Trainees should also be advised to consult their immediate supervisor on any FERPA-related issues. If necessary, the supervisor can consult the institution's general counsel or compliance officer.

References

Bernstein, E. (2008, December 9). Education Department reworks privacy regulations. *The Wall Street Journal*. Retrieved from http://online.wsj.com/article/SB122878222728889843.html?mod=googlenews_wsj

Carter, D. (2009, January 12). Updated privacy law addresses student safety. *E-school News*. Retrieved from http://www.eschoolnews.com/2009/01/12/updated-privacy-law-addresses-student-safety/

Desyllas v. Bernstine et al., 351 F. 3rd 934 (9th Circ. 2004).

Dinger, D. R. (2001). Johnny saw my test score, so I'm suing my teacher: Falvo vs. Owasso Independent School District, peer grading, and a student's right to privacy under the Family Educational Rights and Privacy Act. *Journal of Law & Education, 30*, 575–627.

Doe & Curto v. Anonymous Unnamed School Employees and Officials of Cornell University College of Veterinary Medicine et al., 87 F. 3rd 788 (2nd Circ. 2004).

Family Educational Rights and Privacy Act of 1974, 20 U.S.C. 1232g, 34 CFR § 99.

40 ice breakers and other warm-ups. (n.d.). Retrieved from http://www.training-games.com/pdf/40FreeIceBreakers.pdf

Garner, B. A. (Ed.). (1999). *Black's law dictionary* (7th ed.). St. Paul, MN: West.

Gonzaga University et al. v. Doe, 536 U. S. 273; 122 S. Ct. 2268; 153 L. Ed. 2d 309 (2002).

Groves, S. L., & Groves, D. L. (1981). Professional discretion and personal liability of teachers in relation to grades and records. *Education, 101*, 335–340.

Hauser, C., & O'Connor, A. (2007, April 16). Virginia Tech shooting leaves 33 dead. *The New York Times*. Retrieved from http://www.nytimes.com/2007/04/16/us/16cnd-shooting.html

Lipka, S. (2008, December 19). Education department gives colleges new flexibility on student privacy law. *Chronicle of Higher Education, 55*(17), A18.

Owasso ISD et al. v. Falvo et al., 534 U. S. 426; 122 S. Ct. 934; 151 L. Ed. 2d 896 (2002).

National Association of Colleges and Employers. (2010). *FERPA primer: The basics and beyond.* Bethlehem, PA: Author. Retrieved from http://www.naceweb.org/public/ferpa0808.htm

Van Dusen, W. R. (2004). *FERPA: Basic guidelines for faculty and staff—a simple step-by-step approach for compliance.* Retrieved from http://www.nacada.ksu.edu/Resources/FERPA-Overview.htm

Appendix A

CASE STUDIES FOR GROUP TRAINING

Case Study 1

Jennifer is a senior biology major looking forward to attending medical school next year. In an effort to earn extra money, she serves as a tutor in the biology department. One of her assigned students is Aaron, the star quarterback of the football team. At their regularly scheduled tutoring session the first week of October, Aaron seems crestfallen and shares with Jennifer that he is now academically ineligible to play football, since he scored 47% on the only test in biology. Jennifer sympathizes with him, and then they work on biology matters for the remainder of the session.

Later that week, Jennifer and several of her sorority sisters visit the River Pub to enjoy happy hour. After a couple of drinks, the conversation turns to the upcoming football game against their school's rival. At some point in the conversation, Jennifer, who is indifferent about football but wants to take part in the conversation, blurts out, "Well, we're going to lose because Aaron made a 47 on his biology exam and is now academically ineligible to play!" Neither the news of Aaron's ineligibility nor the reason for it had been released by the athletic department to the press.

In this instance, has there been a FERPA violation? Please discuss.

Case Study 2

Juanita is a senior biology major looking forward to attending medical school next year. In an effort to earn extra money, she serves as a tutor in the biology department. One of her assigned students is Ali, the star quarterback of the football team. At their regularly scheduled tutoring session the first week of October, Ali seems crestfallen and shares with Juanita that he has a minor injury that will keep him out the upcoming game. Juanita sympathizes with him, and then they work on biology matters for the remainder of the session.

Later that week, Juanita and several of her sorority sisters are at the River Pub enjoying happy hour. After a couple of drinks, the conversation turns to the upcoming football game against their school's rival. At some point in the conversation, Juanita, who is indifferent about football but wants to take part in the conversation, blurts out, "Well, we're going to lose because Ali is hurt and is not going to play!" Neither the news of Ali's injury nor his playing status for the game has been released by the athletic department to the press.

In this instance, has there been a FERPA violation? Please discuss.

Appendix B

FERPA KNOWLEDGE ASSESSMENT QUIZ

True or False:

_____ 1. As a mentor or tutor, I do not have to follow the rules and regulations of FERPA.

_____ 2. If I do violate the rules and regulations of FERPA, the offended student can hold me liable in a court of law.

_____ 3. If I suspect that a student whom I tutor or mentor is suffering from severe mental pressures, I will run afoul of FERPA if I advise my supervisor of my suspicions.

_____ **4.** The university could be penalized monetarily by the Department of Education if I release a student's private, non-directory information in violation of the provisions of FERPA.

_____ **5.** Because of FERPA, I must be diligent not to violate its rules or regulations, regardless of my social setting.

FERPA designates two categories of student information: directory and non-directory. Please place a D or an N in the space to identify the information type.

_____ **6.** Name

_____ **7.** Social Security Number

_____ **8.** Grades, Grade Reports, or GPA

_____ **9.** Address

_____ **10.** Race

Answers: 1. F;   2. F;   3. F;   4. T;   5. T;   6. D;   7. N;   8. N;   9. D;   10. N

Learning Center Emergency Preparation

Michael Ruwe

Comprehensive emergency planning is not only prudent for learning centers, but it is also part of the "Standards and Guidelines" set forth by the Council for the Advancement of Standards in Higher Education (CAS, 2009): "[Learning Assistance Programs] must ensure that staff members are knowledgeable about and trained in emergency procedures, crisis response, and prevention efforts" (p. 289). For the purpose of this training module, an emergency is defined as any occasion that necessitates an urgent need for action to maintain a safe environment for learning center students and staff. The intention of this training module is to provide learning center administrators with both a guide for developing an emergency preparation plan and a guide for training tutors and mentors in emergency preparation.

Learning occurs when it is fostered in a safe and welcoming environment. For this reason, a learning center should strive to provide such an environment. Although *every* emergency scenario cannot be anticipated, careful planning may help to address or even prevent an emergency situation. Tutor and mentor trainers might easily overlook emergency preparation; however, learning centers are physical and communal locations that demand unique emergency preparation. Because some learning services are provided outside the learning center, learning center personnel must create comprehensive plans. Trainers must also be role models of preparation for their tutors and mentors, just as tutors and mentors should be role models of preparation for their student clients.

Five questions may guide development of a comprehensive emergency plan. From the answers to these questions, learning center personnel should create an emergency plan that is posted in the applicable places, including the learning center lobby, handbook, webpage, and all tutoring and mentoring rooms.

First, how well prepared for emergencies is the center? Federal and state regulations may govern how to respond to an emergency situation; however, because staff members have not usually trained intensively in these regulations, they should consult with the experts at campus police, the office of the dean of students, the counseling center, and the environmental health and safety office. All of the units can offer advice on how to craft emergency plans for the center. The coordinator and a university police officer together should conduct a "walk through" of the center. From these observations, campus experts can suggest elements of the center's detailed emergency plan based on the unique physical characteristics of the center.

Second, what is the institution's role? Faculty and staff of higher education institutions do have a responsibility to provide, within reason, a safe learning environment for their students. As Davies (2008) observed, "The notion of 'threat assessment teams' seems foreign to institutions of higher learning. But something like them is necessary to evaluate a wide range of possible incidents: storms, toxic spills, or leaks, pandemics, and, yes, active shooters" (p. 14). Given the tragic occurrences in recent years at postsecondary institutions, administrators must take into consideration threatening situations of both natural and human origins.

Third, is the center responsible for tutors and mentors? The learning center coordinators are responsible for all aspects of tutor and mentor training, including emergency preparation; therefore the coordinator needs to make tutors and mentors aware of possible emergency situations and train student staff how to identify, respond to, and if possible prevent threatening situations.

Fourth, are student staff responsible for student clients? Tutors and mentors are not legally responsible for the lives and safety of their student clients; however, student staff are employees of and therefore representatives of the institution. Therefore, even though tutoring or mentoring may be promoted and implemented as a "peer" relationship, in a time of crisis the student client will probably expect guidance from the tutor or mentor. For that reason, student staff should be trained to respond appropriately.

Finally, how can student staff be prepared for a threatening situation? The origins of natural disasters may be explained in a scientific, factual manner; however, the origins of a human disaster, such as an active shooter on campus, are much more difficult to comprehend. Consequently, there is a need for tutors and mentors to discuss these issues in an environment in which they feel safe to express their thoughts: "Education can and should play a significant role in helping society respond to these events by fostering imagination through critical inquiry" (Jenkins, 2007, p. 366). Every opportunity for students to engage in critical thinking and intellectual enquiry should be recognized and utilized.

To gather information useful for maximizing learning center safety, utilization of sources outside the center may be helpful. With the assistance of their respective campus or local police departments, many postsecondary institutions already have some type of training in place. In addition, there are several commercial products available. These campus and local training options may include videos, PowerPoint® slides, and presentations with titles such as "Emergency Management," "Active Shooter," and "Shots Fired on Campus." Learning center administrators must decide if outside sources will be helpful for their training procedures and, if so, which sources will be appropriate.

One such source that may be applicable is the active-shooter response booklet produced by the U.S. Department of Homeland Security (2008). This booklet includes topics such as how to respond when an active shooter is in the vicinity and how to train staff for an active-shooter situation.

Training Activity

At least 1 hour should be allowed for this training activity. If available, a room in the learning center is appropriate for the discussion. Before this activity, trainees should explore the learning center to assess the emergency preparedness of the space. After trainees complete this task and are seated in the room, they discuss each of the following nine questions. Answers can be given orally; however, having each trainee write a response is also an effective way to engage them in the discussion. Answers will vary depending on the unique circumstances of each learning center.

- If the fire alarm goes off, what should you do?

- Where is the nearest fire extinguisher?

- What would you do if a student client faints or is suddenly injured?

- Where is the nearest first-aid kit, and what does it contain?

- If a tornado, hurricane, or other natural disaster is forecast as imminent, what should you do?

- If a student client's behavior leads you to believe he or she may be a threat to self or others, what should you do?

- What kinds of student client behavior would prompt you to alert your coordinator or another appropriate campus administrator?

- Look around this room and notice its physical characteristics. If a shelter-in-place or lockdown order is given by the appropriate campus administrator, what should you do?

- How would your answers to the above questions change if you are in the learning center during a period of time when no center administrators are present?

Assessment

A worksheet of the same nine questions can be created and then distributed a week after the training activity to assess trainees' understanding of departmental policy and practices. Alternatively, at each of the next few staff meetings, the trainer should ask three of the nine questions. Trainees with incomplete understanding should be required to review the training manual until they demonstrate understanding of the emergency preparation plan.

References

Council for the Advancement of Standards in Higher Education. (2009). *CAS professional standards for higher education* (7th ed.). Washington, DC: Author.

Davies, G. K. (2008). Connecting the dots: Lessons from the Virginia Tech shootings. *Change, 40*(1), 8–15. doi:10.3200/CHNG.40.1.8-15

Jenkins, T. (2007). Rethinking the unimaginable: The need for teacher education in peace education. *Harvard Educational Review, 77,* 366–369.

U.S. Department of Homeland Security. (2008). *Active shooter: How to respond.* Retrieved from http://www.dhs.gov/xlibrary/assets/active_shooter_booklet.pdf

Medical Situations Awareness

 ## Howard Y. Masuda and Reyna I. Torres

Given the number of students who use or work in learning and tutoring centers, the likelihood of occurrence of a medical situation can be high. In fact, a study conducted by Fisher, Ray, Savett, Milliron, and Koenig (2006) of 145 U.S. colleges and universities with emergency medical systems reported that the average call volume required 568 responses (range: 315–820) per year. Common minor injuries such as simple cuts are expected and are often treated without much concern. On the other hand, less frequently occurring medical situations such as nosebleeds, fainting, seizures, choking, stroke, and heart attack occur unexpectedly in the workplace and are more frightening to bystanders. Tutor or mentor training sessions do not typically include information and contingencies for handling these situations. However, if the student staff are presented with this knowledge, the likelihood is greater that they will stay calm, feel empowered, remain at the scene, call medical personnel, and, if they so choose, assist the victim when unexpected medical situations such as these do occur.

This training activity is only an introduction to medical situations that may occur and not a substitute for professional medical advice, emergency treatment, or a formal first aid or cardiopulmonary resuscitation (CPR) training course. The intent of this training is for student and professional staff to realize the importance of first aid and CPR training and to understand the importance of formal training (such as that provided by American National Red Cross courses) to prepare themselves for emergency situations that may occur at work or home. Trainers and supervisors, in consultation with the institution, may decide to omit portions of this module (e.g., choking, strokes, and heart attacks) based upon concerns for personal injury liability.

In 2 hours of training, peer tutors or mentors can accomplish and be assessed on the following eight objectives:

- State seven reasons why witnesses to a serious accident may not take action.

- Explain the state or province's Good Samaritan laws and discuss the decision to act.

- Explain and demonstrate how to get permission to treat an apparent victim.

- Explain and demonstrate how to Check, Call, Care.

- Explain and demonstrate how to check the A(irway), B(reathing), and C(irculation).

- Explain and demonstrate how to place a person in the recovery position.

- View and discuss demonstrations of first aid for nosebleeds, fainting, seizures, choking, strokes, and heart attacks.

- Get formal first aid training.

Training Activity

This 2-hour session requires a room equipped with tables and chairs that can be moved to create a 9' × 9' floor area for demonstrations and practice. Also needed is a white board, chalkboard or flip chart.

Trainers in the United States must prepare by becoming certified in standard first aid with CPR and Automated External Defibrillator (AED) for Adults through the American Red Cross (2010); review the appropriate sections in *First Aid/CPR/AED for Schools and Community* (American National Red Cross, 2006) to identify key points to present in training; check online for the state's Good Samaritan law or its equivalent; and check with the campus public safety office about campus protocol for reporting injuries and illnesses. A health educator, nurse, or physician from the campus health center may be available to conduct the training or serve as an advisor or resource person for this training. The public safety office and athletic program may also have personnel trained and certified in first aid and CPR. First aid handouts are available from the Mayo Foundation for Medical Education Research (2010) and the Epilepsy Foundation of America (2010). Some demonstrations will require a clean blanket to lie on and a box of inexpensive vinyl (not latex) gloves. A CPR mannequin may be available from the campus health center.

OBJECTIVE 1: OFFER REASONS FOR DECIDING NOT TO ACT

If faced with a serious automobile accident with injured, bloody victims, why may a passerby hang back? Why might untrained tutors and mentors hesitate to help? The American National Red Cross (2006) lists seven possible reasons: "the presence of other people," "being unsure of the . . . person's condition," "the type of injury or illness," "fear of catching a disease," "fear of doing something wrong," "fear of being sued," and "being unsure of when to call 9-1-1" (pp. 3–6). After discussion of these points, peer tutors or mentors will likely conclude that the decision to act is their decision alone.

OBJECTIVE 2: EXPLAIN GOOD SAMARITAN LAWS

Trainees should read the Good Samaritan law of the state or province and discuss under what conditions, if any, the law applies to the tutors or mentors if they decide to act. Trainees should be reminded that there is no liability for calling the local emergency number.

OBJECTIVE 3: EXPLAIN AND DEMONSTRATE GETTING PERMISSION TO TREAT

Before care is given, the person must give consent. First, responsiveness is determined by asking, "May I help?" or "Are you okay?" (Carline, Lentz, & MacDonald, 2004). If there is no response, the person is tapped on the shoulder and the query repeated. The American National Red Cross recommends informing the victim "who you are, how much training you have, what you think is wrong, and what you plan to do" (2006, p. 9). A conscious person can then decide whether to give consent. If consent is refused, no care should be given other than to call the local emergency number. If the person is unconscious or unable to respond, permission to provide care is implied.

OBJECTIVE 4: EXPLAIN AND DEMONSTRATE *CHECK, CALL, CARE*

The first step is to *check* the scene and the person before approaching to see (a) if the area is safe from hazards, (b) what may have happened, and (c) what may be wrong with the person. For purposes of this training and the activities that follow, the assumption will be made that a neck or back injury is not suspected and the scene is safe. In these situations, the person is not to be moved, and the head, neck, and back are to be kept perfectly still to prevent further injury. The next step is to *call* the campus emergency number or follow procedures for reporting campus injuries and illness. The third step is to *care* for the person by doing the following: (a) check for a medical identification bracelet or necklace for information on medical conditions and allergies, (b) monitor breathing and consciousness, (c) help the person rest in most comfortable position, (d) prevent chilling or overheating, (e) reassure the person, and (f) give needed specific care (American National Red Cross, 2006, pp. 16–19).

OBJECTIVE 5: EXPLAIN AND DEMONSTRATE CHECKING FOR THE ABCS

The ABCs are A (Airway), B (Breathing), and C (Circulation) (American National Red Cross, 2006). The MedlinePlus Medical Encyclopedia (2011) illustrates the process of opening the airway and checking breathing. The American National Red Cross (2006) and New York Hospital Queens

(2010) illustrate how to check for a pulse. To prevent any confusion, note that the American Red Cross and the American Heart Association differ on the meaning of the letter C in the acronym A-B-C. The American Red Cross uses C for "circulation," and A-B-C represents the vital signs (Airway, Breathing, Circulation). The American Heart Association uses C for "Chest compressions" and A-B-C represents the CPR sequence (Airway, Breathing, Chest compressions). After years of studies, the American Heart Association recommended in 2010 to change the sequence of steps from A-B-C (Airway, Breathing, Chest compressions) to C-B-A to so that rescuers would initiate chest compressions sooner.

OBJECTIVE 6: EXPLAIN AND DEMONSTRATE THE RECOVERY POSITION

If it is necessary to leave the person alone or the person begins to vomit, the individual needs to be moved into the recovery position. The British Red Cross (2009) provides a video with directions for moving someone into the recovery position.

OBJECTIVE 7: VIEW AND DISCUSS DEMONSTRATIONS OF FIRST AID FOR NOSEBLEEDS, FAINTING, SEIZURES, CHOKING, STROKES, AND HEART ATTACKS

Trainees should know that, although medical situations do not occur frequently, being aware of what to do can help prevent panic and helplessness when they do occur. They should also be reminded that although they are not expected to be doctors or nurses and may not yet have completed a course in first aid, they can take some measures to assist the victim. First aid handouts should be distributed. The trainer should demonstrate and explain how to treat for nosebleeds, fainting, seizures, choking, strokes, and heart attacks. Before considering omitting the demonstration and discussion on choking and heart attack (more accurately, cardiac arrest), trainers should consider the findings and recommendations of the American Heart Association (2010). According to the American Heart Association's *CPR Fact Sheet* (2011), less than one-third of victims who experience cardiac arrest outside of a hospital setting receive any bystander CPR. Those victims that do not receive bystander CPR have a less than 8% survival rate. Unless CPR and defibrillation are administered within minutes of collapse, few attempts to resuscitate the victim are successful. However, if effective bystander CPR is administered immediately after sudden cardiac arrest, the victim's chances of survival are doubled or tripled. Chest compressions are emphasized for both trained and untrained rescuers. If a bystander is not trained in CPR, the bystander should provide Hands-Only (compression only) CPR for the adult who suddenly collapses (American Heart Association, 2010). In a life-threatening situation, administering compression-only CPR before emergency medical personnel arrive may be the difference between life and death.

OBJECTIVE 8: GET FORMAL FIRST AID TRAINING

Awareness training is not a substitute for formal first aid training. If first aid courses are not offered free of charge to peer tutors and mentors by the department or institution as a requirement or benefit of their employment, the trainer should strongly recommend that student staff enroll in first aid courses such as Standard First Aid with CPR/AED for Adults (American National Red Cross, 2006).

Assessment

To assess the effectiveness of this training, the tutors or mentors will be required to reflect upon and correctly answer questions and demonstrate the skills presented in the training. Sample questions are available in the Appendix. For the final objective, the tutors or mentors will need to access the Internet to find information on local training options for first aid and CPR and present documentation when they have completed formal training.

References

American Heart Association. (2010). *Highlights of the 2010 American Heart Association Guidelines for CPR and ECC.* Dallas, TX: Author.

American Heart Association. (2011). *CPR statistics.* Retrieved from http://www.heart.org/HEARTORG/CPRAndECC/WhatisCPR/CPRFactsandStats/CPR-Statistics_UCM_307542_Article.jsp

American National Red Cross. (2006). *First aid/CPR/AED for schools and community* (3rd ed.). Yardley, PA: StayWell.

American Red Cross (2010). *Preparing and getting trained.* Retrieved from http://www.redcross.org/

British Red Cross (2009). *First aid—how to put someone into the recovery position.* Retrieved from http://www.youtube.com/watch?v=uCDa-AhrjHo

Carline, J. D., Lentz, M. J., & MacDonald, S. C. (2004). *Mountaineering first aid: A guide to accident responses and first aid care* (5th ed.). Seattle, WA: Mountaineers Books.

Epilepsy Foundation of America. (2010). *First aid for seizures.* Retrieved from http://www.epilepsyfoundation.org/about/firstaid/

Fisher, J., Ray, A., Savett, S., Milliron, M., & Koenig, G. (2006). Collegiate-based emergency medical services (EMS): A survey of EMS systems on college campuses. *Prehospital & Disaster Medicine, 21*(2), 91–96.

Mayo Foundation for Medical Education and Research. (2010). *First aid.* Retrieved from http://www.mayoclinic.com/health/FirstAidIndex/FirstAidIndex

MedlinePlus Medical Encyclopedia. (2011). *CPR-Adult-Series.* Retrieved from http://www.nlm.nih.gov/medlineplus/ency/presentations/100219_1.htm

New York Hospital Queens. (2010). *Check pulse.* Retrieved from http://www.nyhq.org/Check_Pulse

Appendix

ASSESSMENT QUESTIONS FOR MEDICAL SITUATIONS AWARENESS TRAINING

Objective 1. Offer Reasons for Deciding Not to Act

- If you came across a car accident with injured, bloody victims, state whether you would act or stand back, and give reasons for your choice.

- From the presentation, list seven reasons why someone witnessing a serious accident might not act.

- Based upon what has been presented, would you change your decision to act or not act? Why or why not?

Objective 2: Explain Good Samaritan Laws

- Summarize the Good Samaritan laws of this state or province.

- How might the law affect your decision to act when witness to a serious accident?

Objective 3: Explain and Demonstrate Getting Permission to Treat

- What would you say and do to check for responsiveness?

- What would you say and do if there is no response?

- If the person refuses to give consent, what would you do?

- If the person is unconscious or unable to respond, what would you do?

Objective 4: Explain and Demonstrate Check, Call, Care

- What three things do you look for when checking the scene and the person?
- What campus emergency telephone number do you call?
- What five things do you do to provide care?

Objective 5: Explain and Demonstrate Checking for the ABCs

- Explain and demonstrate how to position the head properly to open the A(irway).
- What is the danger in opening the airway as described if a neck or back injury is suspected?
- Explain and demonstrate how to check for B(reathing).
- How much time should you spend checking for breathing?
- Explain and demonstrate how to check for C(irculation).
- What is the difference between the American Red Cross and the American Heart Association's use of the acronym A–B–C?
- Why has the American Heart Association changed the order of the acronym from A–B–C to C–A–B?

Objective 6: Explain and Demonstrate the Recovery Position

- How should the arms be positioned?
- How should the legs be positioned?
- What areas of the body should be supported when turning the body?

Objective 7: View and Discuss Demonstrations of First Aid for Nosebleeds, Fainting, Seizures, Choking, Strokes, and Heart Attacks

- How can nosebleeds be stopped?
- What should be done if an individual faints?
- What should be done if an individual has a seizure?

Note: The following three items will be omitted if not covered in the training.

- How should you help someone who is choking?
- How should you help someone who is apparently suffering a stroke?
- What should be done for an individual who is apparently suffering a heart attack?

Objective 8: Get Formal First Aid Training

- When and where is first aid training available locally?
- What does first aid training cost in time and fees?
- What kinds of emergency training certifications are available locally?

Reaching a Consensus on Ethics

Eric Dunker

Professionals and paraprofessionals in higher education must maintain high standards of ethical behavior that uphold the integrity of the institution and all its stakeholders. Due to diverse individual world views and backgrounds, it can be difficult to get a group of individuals to agree on a set of guiding principles to govern their work. However, agreement can be facilitated through focused training and group interaction on the subject of ethics.

The Council for the Advancement of Standards in Higher Education (CAS) Standards and Guidelines for Learning Assistance Programs (2009) provided an entire section devoted to self-assessment of a program's ethics. The CAS standards made the learning program director responsible for orienting staff members to relevant ethical standards and statements of practice. CAS also developed a Statement of Shared Ethical Principles (CAS, 2006) in part from the College Reading and Learning Association (CRLA; 2003) guidelines for professional ethics. All of these—CAS Standards for Learning Assistance Programs, CAS Statement of Shared Ethical Principles, and CRLA Guidelines for Professional Ethics—can give learning center staff an ethical framework for developing a shared set of principles or guidelines for their center. Copies of these ethical guidelines can be printed and shared with student staff, or staff can be assigned to access and review the statements prior to the training session.

The first goal for this training activity is to facilitate the development of a working definition of ethics and ethical frameworks among the tutoring or mentoring staff. The second goal is to facilitate discussion among group members about possible ethical situations in a learning center environment, including issues such as confidentiality and diversity. The third goal is to develop a working set of learning center ethical standards as agreed upon by tutors or mentors and their supervisors using group interaction and mutual understanding. By the end of this training session, peer tutors or mentors should be able to define and understand multiple lenses in relation to the concept of ethics, demonstrate awareness of individual ethics and the complexity of group ethics, and articulate a working code of ethics for the learning center as agreed upon by tutors or mentors and supervisors.

Training Activity

The ethics workshop is a training activity involving an individual ranking of 10 actions. Trainers can devise their own ethical situations; the worksheet provided in the Appendix serves as a sample or guide for devising a worksheet customized for the student staff, institution, and campus setting. The ethical scenarios are intentionally broad in nature to allow for differences in individual interpretation.

Trainees will first rank-order the actions from most ethical to least ethical while working alone. In only a few minutes all trainees will have completed this task. The trainer will then divide the trainees into groups of three or four and attempt to come to group consensus on a rank order of the same 10 actions, in 10–15 minutes. As with most ethical discussions, the difficulty for the group will probably be to reconcile diverse individual perceptions of the sample situations. Members of each group will need to discuss and negotiate toward consensus.

This activity works best with at least two groups of three or four individuals and will therefore work well for any number of trainees greater than six. The entire ethics training session will require 1–2 hours, with the ethics order-ranking activity requiring the first 20 minutes.

After groups have reached consensus, a member of each group reports that group's most ethical and least ethical situation. The groups then discuss why it was easy to do this task individually but difficult to accomplish it as a group. The facilitator should engage in discussion with the trainees about the factors that led to differences in individual interpretation of the ethical scenarios.

The facilitator can focus on the two or three scenarios that had the greatest difference in rank order between groups. This will allow trainees to reflect on how others made meaning of the activity.

Next, trainees should be provided with a general overview of ethics and the multiple working definitions and lenses it can take. Because learning centers seek to achieve particular student learning and development outcomes and view individuals as always in the process of changing, it is useful for tutors and mentors to understand various theories of human development, including theories of the development of ethical values. Kohlberg's theory of moral development (Kohlberg & Wasserman, 1980) is a useful perspective because it presumes that morality is learned developmentally as understanding increases. As an alternative to or in addition to Kohlberg's theory, Gilligan's (1982) theory attempted to explain the development of ethics in women's decision making.

Kohlberg's theory, summarized by Kohlberg and Wasserman (1980), posited that at the early, preconventional level, individuals make moral decisions in a *punishment and obedience orientation*: direct consequences of an action determine right and wrong, so the right action is one that is not punished. In the *instrumental-relativist orientation*, moral decisions are made pragmatically, based on equal exchange, in a system of mutual backscratching. At the next level of development, the conventional level, the *interpersonal concordance orientation* defines good behavior as whatever pleases others and gains their approval. In the *law-and-order orientation*, actions are based on upholding the system and obeying the rules of society; what is important is showing respect for authority and maintaining the social order for its own sake. According to Kohlberg, few individuals develop beyond the conventional level of moral reasoning to the post-conventional level, the *social contract or legalistic orientation*, in which right action is determined by standards that have been agreed upon by society, but at this point of development awareness is growing that rules can be reevaluated and changed. In the *universal ethical principle orientation*, self-chosen ethical principles, including justice, equality, and respect for human dignity, guide behavior.

In addition to Kohlberg's theory, trainees should learn about principle-, case-, and virtues-based approaches to ethics (Lampkin & Gibson, 1999). Rules are the main source of authority for principle-based ethical systems—rules to act on and provide guidance. Case-based ethical systems focus on analyzing a situation. The guiding rules emerge from the facts of the case; that is, it would not be appropriate to take principles and impose them on a case without thinking about or knowing the circumstances or elements of the situation. Virtues-based ethical systems consider the consequences and long-term impact of moral action. They focus on the impact of action on the community and thus have more to do with shaping ethical character than establishing behavioral norms. Issues of character such as personal honesty, trustworthiness, and integrity are paramount with this approach.

Trainees should discuss how their difficulty coming to group consensus may derive from decisions based on different ethical bases. Within their groups, did trainees demonstrate all three kinds of ethical decision making, based on principles (rules), cases (contexts), and virtues (consequences)?

Trainees should then discuss key ethical issues that arise in tutoring and mentoring sessions. Participants should be able to come up with multiple examples in their small groups, such as dependency, confidentiality, plagiarism, and punctuality.

When each group has a list, the group as a whole can develop a code of ethics upon which all staff members can agree. The trainer should facilitate discussion around the various factors that contribute to personal ethics such as religion, laws, ethnicity and culture, sex and gender, professional identity, ability and disability, political persuasion, education, global experience, age and experience, geographic habitats, and family background. When a comprehensive list has been developed, it can be displayed on the center's website and in a creative poster (created by a professional or student staff members).

Assessment

Contributions of each trainee to the shared ethical statement can be assessed as measures of understanding. In later staff meetings, during individual evaluations, and through surveys of tutees and mentees, the trainer can assess the progress of the group and of individual trainees in living up to the ethical standards agreed upon in this training session.

References

College Reading and Learning Association. (2003). *College Reading and Learning Association guidelines for professional ethics.* Retrieved from http://www.crla.net/about/ethics_statement.htm

Council for the Advancement of Standards in Higher Education. (2009). Standards and guidelines for learning assistance programs. In Council for the Advancement of Standards in Higher Education, *CAS professional standards for higher education* (7th ed., pp. 286–293). Washington, DC: Author.

Council for the Advancement of Standards in Higher Education. (2006). *CAS statement of shared ethical principles.* Retrieved from http://www.cas.edu/index.php/resources/ethical-statements/

Gilligan, C. (1982). *In a different voice: Psychological theory and women's development.* Cambridge, MA: Harvard University Press.

Kohlberg, L., & Wasserman, E. R. (1980). Moral stages and moralization: The cognitive-developmental approach and the practicing counselor: An opportunity for counselors to rethink their roles. *Personnel & Guidance Journal, 58,* 559–576.

Lampkin, P. M., & Gibson, E. M. (1999). *Mountains and passes: Traversing the landscape of ethics and student affairs administration.* Washington, DC: National Association of Student Personnel Administrators.

McKelfresh, D. (2011). *Ethics workshop.* Unpublished document. Fort Collins, CO: Colorado State University, Student Affairs in Higher Education Graduate Program.

Appendix

RANKING ETHICAL ACTIONS

In the first column below, rank the statements from 1 (most ethical) to 10 (least ethical). Assign each rank only once. Wait for instructions before moving to the second column, which requires group consensus to complete.

		Using a fake ID to enter a bar when below legal age to enter
		Downloading copyrighted music from the Internet without paying
		Texting during a meeting or class session after the speaker asked for electronic devices to be turned off
		Looking at someone else's homework for help during a group tutoring session
		Lying or not responding to an officer who asks for more information
		Playing a joke on a friend that unintentionally results in a slight injury to the friend
		Arriving 15 minutes late to a meeting with a student while always arriving early to meetings with the supervisor
		Leaving a negative, anonymous phone message about a former friend who is a final candidate for a job
		In a tutoring or mentoring session, giving an answer to a student who is struggling without making sure the student understands the concept, because you are in a hurry
		Making a promise during an interview, and then breaking that promise a year later due to extenuating circumstances

Note. Adapted with permission from *Ethics Workshop* by D. McKelfresh, 2011, unpublished document, Colorado State University Student Affairs in Higher Education Program.

Applying Ethical Principles to Tutoring and Mentoring Scenarios

Mark S. May

Tutoring and mentoring college students is a challenging job, especially for student employees who may have little relevant work experience. In addition to training peer tutors and mentors to provide exceptional support for their fellow students, learning centers need to ensure that employees fully understand and follow workplace policies, achieve the highest possible professional standards, and think critically about ethical matters.

First, to help avoid tutor or mentor misconduct, the center should provide all employees with copies of college or university policies on topics such as sexual harassment; the Americans With Disabilities Act (ADA, 1990; ADAAA, 2008); the Family Educational Rights and Privacy Act (FERPA, 1974); drug use policies; appearance standards; and attendance (punctuality) policies. Explaining workplace rules helps inexperienced workers avoid simple mistakes.

Second, tutors and mentors need to understand that they must act professionally. Professional standards help them avoid, recognize, or resolve ethically sticky situations.

Third, because tutors and mentors play many roles (e.g., teacher, confidant, friend, advisor, teaching assistant), these student employees and volunteers face complex and sometimes conflicting ethical responsibilities to clients, the center, faculty, and staff. Ethical codes for tutoring and mentoring (as for any profession) are abstract, so tutors and mentors have to understand ethical theories and apply these theories wisely to the real-world situations they face. The College Reading and Learning Association (CRLA, 2003) has written its own guidelines for professional practice. CRLA also supports the Association for the Tutoring Profession's (ATP) Code of Ethics (n.d.), which provides 10 principles to guide tutors' work.

Norton (2009) offered a list of ethical scenarios that is useful for helping students to think critically about ethically complex situations. In one scenario tutor and tutee have been working together for over an hour when the client asks to continue working together after the center has closed. The best-interest principle from the tutoring code of ethics indicates that tutors should be "committed to acting in the best interest of the tutees as specified by the employing organization or institute" (ATP, n.d., p. 1). It may well be in the best interest of the client for the tutor to continue working with the student, so a tutor might conclude that following the code of ethics entails working after hours. Working after hours, however, may not ultimately serve the best interest of the student, and tutors may disagree as to how "best interest" should be specified by the employer.

An understanding of the basic insights of some of the major ethical theories will help student employees to interpret the ethical standards and think critically when standards collide. The training session must give tutors and mentors the opportunity to think critically about ethics and discuss their perspectives with others. The design of this workshop is based upon the psychological theory of constructivism (Fosnot, 1996). Trainees are provided with insights into prominent ethical theories and asked to engage actively in a discussion about case studies. Trainees' understanding of both theory and practice will grow as they learn about the strengths and weaknesses of the ethical theories. In keeping with constructivism, it is the tutors' and mentors' task to build upon the basic framework that the trainer provides.

The trainer who leads this workshop acts as a facilitator and may wish to access additional information about ethics available online. A faculty member from the philosophy department could be invited to facilitate this workshop; however, an academic background in ethics is not a prerequisite for leading this workshop. Wrestling with the issues of this workshop will make the trainer more credible as an ethically-engaged leader and supervisor with whom trainees can communicate their ethical dilemmas.

This workshop draws upon insights from four ethical perspectives. Virtue ethics is represented by Aristotle, social contract theory by Hobbes, deontological theory by Kant, and consequentialism by Bentham.

Ideas attributed to Aristotle (Barnes, trans., 1984) provided an example of virtue ethics. According to his theory, the virtuous (excellent) person has basic physical and psychological needs met, experiences the proper emotions on the right occasions, and uses reason to choose the right action (a mean between two extremes). Rashness, Aristotle argued, is an example of an excess of an emotion and therefore a vice. The person who dives off a cruise ship in a storm to save a person who fell overboard is acting rashly. The deficiency of this emotion is cowardice; one who sees that someone fell overboard but freezes up is cowardly. Bravery is the properly experienced emotion, and the moderate course of action in this example might be to sound an alarm and throw life jackets overboard. The Golden Mean varies with circumstances and capabilities; therefore, wise actions taken by a person trained in water rescue techniques may differ from those taken by an inexperienced swimmer.

Thomas Hobbes (1651/1968), a 17th-century social contract theorist, asked his readers to consider what it would be like to live in the state of nature, the hypothetical state before the existence of government and other human conventions. In this state, Hobbes argued, there are no ethical rules or laws, so people would be selfish brutes, acting without regard for the welfare of others. The strong would naturally take advantage of the weak, but even the strong need protection. The strongest person in this state is still vulnerable when asleep. In their need for protection, people are all essentially equal. To secure rights, people enter into a social contract (i.e., reach an agreement with others) to protect rights to life, liberty, and property. It is thus in everyone's mutual interest to establish rules, judge when they are violated, and enforce them.

Deontological theory gives priority to the concept of duty. Immanuel Kant (Friedrich, trans., 1949), a philosopher of the 18th century, believed that people must do their duty no matter the consequences, like knights of old. He held that just as the physical universe is governed by physical laws, so too the moral universe contains moral laws that humankind must obey. These laws are universal; they apply to everyone. The determining factor in deciding whether an act is right or wrong is one's intention, a person's will to act in accordance with or contrary to moral law, not the consequences of the action. Anyone stealing from the rich to give to the poor has broken a prohibition against stealing even if the rich do not miss the money and the poor benefit greatly. One way to test whether a proposed principle is a moral law is to see if the principle can be applied universally without contradiction. For example, to see if "lying is permissible" is a moral law, one asks what would happen if everyone lied. If everyone lied, Kant argued, no one would trust anyone anymore. This creates a logical contradiction, and thus lying is not moral.

Jeremy Bentham (1789/1973), an 18th-century legal scholar, proposed a consequentialist ethical theory arguing that only the outcome of an action, not the intention, determines whether the action is good or not. Bentham argued that there is a supreme moral principle—the Principle of Utility—that determines the moral worth of an action by weighing the benefits of an action versus its costs (Burns & Hart, 1996). In 1863, John Stuart Mill (1966), building upon Bentham's work, described an ethical theory he called utilitarianism. In Mill's view, the action that produces the greatest amount of good for the greatest number of people is most moral. People should try to maximize the happiness of everyone, now and in the future. A person trying to decide whether to save someone from drowning should consider all consequences of the action. One assumes that the pain involved for a competent rescuer would be minimal and the happiness resulting from saving a drowning victim would be great, but what if the drowning victim were planning to carry out horrible acts if rescued? Or what if the victim were a scientist on the verge of a cure for cancer and could be rescued only by sacrifice of the rescuer's life?

Applying these theories to an example involving tutoring is useful. Suppose a final-semester senior needs to pass one basic math course in order to graduate but failed the course before. The client is a brilliant musician who assumes that knowing algebra will serve no purpose in a career as a recording artist. A passing grade is possible if the client correctly answers some extra-credit questions. The client asks the tutor to look over her extra credit work "just to see if I have the right answers." On the assignment sheet, the professor has specified that students do their own work on the extra-credit questions.

In this case, Aristotle would have valued compassion toward others, midway between lack of empathy and its excess. Although the tutor could easily perform the requested action, the tutor is not choosing excellence by telling the client the answers. The compassionate tutor could refer the client to the professor, review similar problems with the client, or teach the student how to check answers by plugging them back into the equation.

Hobbes would probably have argued that by registering for classes college students agree to abide by rules that are intended to protect all students and maintain the value of the degrees they seek. Although this assignment is for extra credit, a tutor who answers the student's question and indicates right and wrong answers implicitly breaks the social contract.

For Kant, providing the client with information would clearly violate one's duty. The client is asking the tutor to cheat, and Kant would have argued that one should never cheat. Cheating is not a moral imperative which everyone should do; therefore it is wrong.

The case is complicated when considered in the light of utilitarianism. Giving the client a bit of information would help her earn a degree and bring her and others a good deal of happiness through her music; however, providing this kind of help could backfire by encouraging the client to take unethical shortcuts, negatively impacting the client and others. The action could also negatively impact the tutor or the center if the instructor finds out the work is not the student's own.

Training Activity

This workshop requires 2 hours. The trainer should select a room arranged for discussion. Round tables that seat six to eight participants are preferred. The facilitator may wish to print or project the CRLA and ATP codes of ethics and tutor ethics scenarios. A laptop, online access, and projection equipment may also be necessary to show clips from films or YouTube segments. Whiteboards and tablets can be used if the facilitator wishes small groups to record their analyses and report out to the entire group.

The trainer begins the training activity by asking participants to read the ATP code of ethics aloud, each reading one of the 10 principles. After each principle is read, someone other than the reader explains the principle or offers a hypothetical situation in which a tutor or mentor acts professionally or does not. This part of the activity may require 30 minutes.

The trainer then explains how professional standards differ from ethical theories and outlines the basic insights into ethical theories provided by Aristotle, Hobbes, Kant, and Bentham or Mill. Differences among the theories can be illustrated with academic examples. This section of the activity may require 20 minutes.

If desired, the trainer can show movie clips that illustrate ethical quandaries. Rosenstand's (2000) textbook provides many summaries of film segments useful for illustrating contrasts among ethical theories. The trainer invites participants to analyze the situations in these films using one or more of the theories presented, working individually or in small groups.

Cases from tutor ethics scenarios (Norton, 2010) can be read and discussed in small groups, one case per group. Each group should apply all four theories and decide which best clarifies the best action to take. Are participants in agreement? What should a tutor or mentor do in each case? Why? The trainer moves from group to group, listening and asking questions where necessary to clarify thinking. This part of the training activity requires 30 minutes.

Each small group should then lead the whole-group discussion on one case. The facilitator's role is to foster interaction among groups and attempt to elicit the reasons why the groups' responses differ. This activity may require 30 minutes.

The trainer ends by asking the entire group what they learned about ethics from the workshop that they can apply to their work as tutors or mentors. What additional information is needed? How will the staff operate the center ethically? This activity may require 15 minutes.

Assessment

In accordance with constructivist theory, the assessment process for this training activity occurs throughout the workshop as the facilitator interacts with the tutors or mentors. The last segment of the workshop, however, provides the facilitator with the opportunity to judge whether trainees have understood ethical theories and internalized ethical standards. From this exercise, the facilitator should be better able to predict whether the tutors or mentors are likely to behave ethically as employees and colleagues in the learning center.

References

ADA Amendments Act of 2008 (ADAAA), 42 U.S.C., § 12101-103, 12111-114, 12201, 12205a; 29 U.S.C., § 705.

Americans With Disabilities Act of 1990, 42 U.S.C., § 12101.

Association for the Tutoring Profession. (n.d.). *Code of ethics.* Retrieved from http://www.crla.net/ittpc/code_of_ethics.htm and http://www.myatp.org/ethics.htm

Barnes, J. (Ed.). (trans. 1984). *The complete works of Aristotle.* Princeton, NJ: Princeton University Press.

Bentham, J. (1789/1973). *Principles of morals and legislation.* New York, NY: Anchor Books.

Burns, J. H., & Hart, H. L. A. (Eds.). (1996). *The collected works of Jeremy Bentham.* New York, NY: Oxford University Press.

College Reading and Learning Association. (2003). *College Reading and Learning Association guidelines for professional ethics.* Retrieved from http://www.crla.net/about/ethics_statement.htm

Family Educational Rights and Privacy Act of 1974, 20 U.S.C. 1232g, 34 CFR § 99.

Fosnot, C. T. (1996). Constructivism: A psychological theory of learning. In C. T. Fosnot (Ed.), *Constructivism: Theory, perspectives, and practice* (pp. 8–33). New York, NY: Teachers College Press.

Friedrich, C. J. (Ed.). (trans. 1949). *The philosophy of Kant: Immanuel Kant's moral and political writings.* New York, NY: Random House.

Hobbes, T. (1651/1968). *Leviathan.* New York, NY: Penguin.

Mill, J. S. (1966). *John Stuart Mill: A selection of his works.* New York, NY: St. Martin's Press.

Norton, J. (2009, March 17). *Re: Training scenarios* [Electronic mailing list message]. Retrieved from archives of the LRNASST listserv at http://128.227.74.150/cgi-bin/wa?A2=ind0903c&L=lrnasst-l&T=0&O=A&F=&S=&P=760

Rosenstand, N. (2000). *The moral of the story: An introduction to ethics* (3rd ed.). Mountain View, CA: Mayfield.

Quaker Values and Learning Center Ethics

Carol E. O'Hara

Many educational institutions stress character- or values-based education as a means of helping students understand the importance and value of each person as an individual while being open to a wide spectrum of diverse attitudes and cultural perspectives. As a private, four-year, Christian, liberal arts college, Friends University has a history grounded in the Quaker heritage and belief system that originated in the middle of the seventeenth century (Holmes, 2007). Integral to the Quaker belief system are its social testimonies of peace, integrity, simplicity, equality and community (Cooper, 2001, p. 200). These ethical values can be implemented in any institution of higher learning. But should colleges and universities be providing moral and character education?

In the keynote address for the first Australian National Forum on Values Education, Hill (2004) explained the timeliness and significance of values study and character education in educational institutions. Although values education continues to be a complex and controversial challenge, Hill emphasized the importance of a clear understanding of values, which are "the priorities individuals and societies attach to certain beliefs, experiences, and objects, in deciding how they shall live and what they shall treasure" (p. 4). Should tutors and mentors encourage students to speak of their "experiences" and reflect on what it would be like to live by these values? According to Hersh and Schneider (2005), every college or university and its faculty and staff have a distinct obligation to prepare "morally astute individuals who will positively contribute to the communities in which they participate" (p. 10). It is imperative that faculty and staff model high standards and strong ethical values in the work that they do.

It is also important for student staff to foster relationships with their student clients that effectively and outwardly communicate these high standards of ethical behavior. Student tutors and mentors should be active participants in exploring values, analyzing and role playing situations that reflect the significance of these values as they relate to their work in the learning center, and modeling high standards. The more that student staff are involved in building the character and values of student clients by helping them learn to be honest and ethical, the greater the benefit for them (Medway, 1991). Modeling these values and ethical standards in a positive way is the best example that tutors and mentors can give to others. Modeling ethical behavior is simply an investment in the future for all of us.

Training Activity

The purpose of this training activity is to help student tutors and mentors to recognize and understand basic core values and beliefs. Student tutors and mentors will become aware of how these values and beliefs can be applied to the learning center environment. Even though the majority of college students live in non-Quaker belief systems, the Quaker core values of peace, integrity, simplicity, equality, and community can be meaningful to students with a variety of differing cultural and religious backgrounds. Trainees will be able to incorporate these values and principles successfully into future tutoring and mentoring situations after collaborating and modeling together in this activity. Alternatively, trainers can create a similar activity based on the core values of their own college or university.

This training activity can take 40–50 minutes depending on the detail that trainees provide. Each group will create a scenario to highlight a specific value in the learning center context. Because these values represent some universal core beliefs, debate of specific religious and cultural ideologies is not the intention.

Each small group of four or five participants should be provided with a brief description of one of the values. After addressing their specific value, each group discusses each of the questions posed for that value in the Values Handout (Appendix). One person in each group serves as a recorder to list important aspects of the value examined and how it can be applied to a tutoring or mentoring relationship with students. For example, students can discuss the meaning of the term *integrity* and why it is regarded as such an important virtue, recognizing that a person with integrity is said to be honest, sincere, and trustworthy.

Each group of trainees should create a scenario to highlight the value being discussed. Trainees playing the roles of tutor and student can demonstrate the value as discussed in each group. A sample scenario may have a freshman come to the center to attend a study session for an upcoming biology exam. When the study session begins, the student shows a copy of what he or she believes to be the midterm biology exam to the tutor and four other students in the group.

Each group should also develop questions relevant to the circumstances and the value being represented. Questions for the sample scenario mentioned earlier might include these: How can a tutor uphold the campus honor code and show integrity in handling this situation with the student? How could the ramifications of this situation jeopardize the other group members? How could the tutor encourage the freshman with the exam to do the right thing? How does the tutor's model of honesty and integrity help others, too?

When the groups have had time to review their value and prepare their scenarios, they should rejoin the whole group, present the group scenarios, and discuss the questions they have devised. The questions posed in the Values Handout (the Appendix) are valuable to this large group discussion.

The trainer should solicit ideas from all trainees in the group. What did each group learn about the value in relation to their tutoring or mentoring? A list can be made on the board, overhead, or learning center blogspace of some ways that the center could be more sensitive to these values when working with student clients.

Assessment

Competence will be demonstrated in journal reflections or blog entries, questionnaire evaluations, and mock tutoring sessions. To assess learning, each trainee will document when and how he or she used the values and beliefs before the next training opportunity, by either posting on the online discussion board or by making notations on session reports.

A form for evaluation (in survey or questionnaire format) provides an assessment chart with each value posted; this allows peer tutors and mentors the opportunity to analyze how they may have made a difference in a student's thinking. They can contemplate how the student felt after leaving the session and whether or not the student had an understanding of the value presented. Questions could include the following: Which value was the easiest to implement during a tutoring session? Did implementing the value cause you to plan ahead of time what you intended to do? When applying these values activities in a tutoring or mentoring situation, what surprised you?

References

Adams, M., Bell, L. A., & Griffin, P. (2007). *Teaching for diversity and social justice* (2nd ed.). New York, NY: Routledge, Taylor & Francis Group.

Chickering, A. W. (1969). *Education and identity.* San Francisco, CA: Jossey-Bass.

Chickering, A. W., & Reisser, L. (1993). *Education and identity* (2nd ed.). San Francisco, CA: Jossey-Bass.

Cooper, W. A. (2001). *A living faith: An historical and comparative study of Quaker beliefs* (2nd ed.). Richmond, IN: Friends United Press.

Hersh, R. H., & Schneider, C. G. (2005, Summer/Fall). Fostering personal and social responsibility on college and university campuses. *Liberal Education, 91*(3), 6–13.

Hill, B. V. (2004, April). *Values education in schools: Issues and challenges.* Keynote address for National Forum on Values Education, Melbourne, Australia. Retrieved from http://www .curriculum.edu.au/verve/_resources/ve_acsa_paper.pdf

Holmes, E. (2007). Friends University. In J. W. Oliver, Jr., C. L. Cherry, & C. Cherry (Eds.), *Founded by Friends: The Quaker heritage of fifteen American colleges and universities* (pp. 223–239). Lanham, MD: Scarecrow Press.

Macy, H. (2008, October 1). Picky about principles. *Northwest Yearly Meeting of Friends* [newsletter]. Retrieved from http://nwfriends.org/picky-about-principles/

Medway, F. J. (1991). A social psychological analysis of peer tutoring. *Journal of Developmental Education, 15*(1), 20–32.

Appendix

VALUES HANDOUT

The purpose of this handout is not to impose a specific religious ideology on peer mentors and tutors; rather, the following descriptions of Quaker values are provided as a framework for conversations about ethical behavior in tutoring and mentoring contexts. For each value, questions to guide this conversation are provided in italics.

Integrity

This value parallels one of Chickering's (1969; Chickering & Reisser, 1993) seven vectors of college student development. As George Fox, one of the founders of the Religious Society of Friends, asserted, it is important for all people to "possess what they profess" (Macy, 2008, para. 1), to live a life consistent with their beliefs. To have integrity is to be honest and to have consistently high standards. A commitment to integrity or authenticity should shape every aspect of our lives. *How can we as mentors show integrity in how we work and how we interact with our students? How can we encourage integrity among the students that we help? What are the marks of integrity in exploring and tutoring in our subject matter? How should we treat students who seem to lack honesty or integrity? How can we help others realize the "cost" to being dishonest—the cost to all of us as individuals, to institutions, and the cost in terms of the perceived value of the degrees our institutions bestow?*

Simplicity

This means that we become good stewards of all that we have, and that we become sensitive to the needs of others. The life of simplicity is the focused, disciplined life in which we do not take on more than we can reasonably handle. *At times our students' lives are overly stressed, scattered, and hectic. How can we recognize students who are not living a life of simplicity? How can we honor and nurture simplicity among ourselves, our colleagues, and our students? How can we help students prioritize what is important and eliminate what causes clutter in their lives?*

High Regard for All

Everyone should be held in high regard, regardless of their status, class, gender, education, ethnicity, or other distinction. Peer tutors and mentors need to be concerned for the worth, dignity, and equality of each person in the process of building a community of learners. *In what ways are we tempted to dismiss or neglect the value of others—student clients, instructors, and others? How can we nurture the potential that we may see in other students? In what ways can we hold and convey our high regard for our students in our tutoring or mentoring? In what ways might we imagine a broader range of possibilities for a person's significance and contribution beyond how we see him or her in our setting?*

Peace and Justice

Quakers seek "peace as an inner spiritual state" (Cooper, 2001, p. 137). Social justice is an important goal of higher education (Adams, Bell, & Griffin, 2007). *How can we ensure equitable learning experiences for all students who seek services in the learning center?*

Education "Civil and Useful"

Tutors and mentors can contribute to facilitating students' learning related to how to be citizens and to participate effectively in their culture. *When we look to the future of the learning center, what kind of "civil" and useful programs would be helpful for our students? What do we do now that is relevant, and what could we strengthen or make better?*

Learning as a Community

When we recognize that each individual can apprehend truth, we can establish an environment of respect, careful listening, and collaboration. We can set a welcoming tone in the learning center, and a spirit of welcome can guide our approach to student learning. *How do we welcome others coming into our center? What are some ways we can help ourselves and our students become thoughtful inquirers and deeply listening learners? How have we established an environment of respect, patient teamwork, and collaboration? Give specific examples.*

Using Case Studies for Tutor and Mentor Training on Plagiarism

Anne Vermont Shearer

Plagiarism—passing off someone else's work as one's own—may seem to be a black-and-white issue. While it can be easy to define, plagiarism is neither clear nor obvious when it occurs in students' lives. Purchasing an essay from an online source and submitting it as one's own is clearly plagiarism. Stealing paragraphs from a reference for one's paper is easily identified as plagiarism. At what point, though, does asking a classmate for information, seeking advice about a paper, or working together on a project become cheating?

A useful theoretical framework for designing a training activity on plagiarism is Kohlberg's (1963) theory of moral development. According to Kohlberg, moral development progresses in stages oriented successively toward obedience and punishment, self-interest, interpersonal accord and conformity, authority and social-order maintenance, social contract, and universal ethical principles. While any student could be at any stage of moral development, the trainer would benefit from paying special attention to the stages of individualism and exchange, good personal relationships, and maintaining the social contract.

Additionally, it is important for the trainer to be informed by cultural standards on cheating, as cultural views on phenomena such as group work and collaboration vary. A combined understanding of moral development and various cultures and expectations represented on campus, including standard academic culture, will help the trainer shape a strong experience for peer tutors or mentors to share. By the end of the training activity, through the use of case studies and discussion led by the trainer, student staff should be able to explain, identify, and educate their peers on plagiarism.

Training Activity

Before this activity, the trainer should prepare copies of case studies or problematic scenarios for use in the session. Three case studies are provided in the Appendix, but the trainer may prefer to draft others more appropriate for the particular campus situation and to write questions that reflect the institution's standards for handling plagiarism. Case studies should reflect situations tutors and mentors are likely to encounter at that institution.

It is also advisable to gather and to print out (or have ready to show on screen) definitions of plagiarism from the American Psychological Association (2009), the Modern Language Association (2009), a peer institution, and one's own campus. Another valuable source of information on how the institution handles plagiarism is the campus teaching center or senior academic administrator's office, which may provide resources to faculty who must confront students suspected or known to have plagiarized. While using various definitions of plagiarism will help the peer tutors and mentors understand the complexity of plagiarism, during training particular emphasis should be placed on the institution's policy.

This session will require 30–60 minutes, depending on the number of groups reporting on their work. The training room should be adaptable to full-group and small-group work.

The training session begins with definitions of plagiarism, making sure all participants can give clear examples of what constitutes this form of theft. After reviewing the institution's policies about plagiarism and cheating and the consequences for students caught plagiarizing, the trainer should divide participants into small groups and give them one or more of the case studies to read and discuss.

After the students have a short discussion about the case studies in their small groups, the trainer should bring the tutors or mentors back together as a large group and review the cases together. During the large group discussion, the trainer should make sure that all important aspects of the cases are brought up and that trainees not only know but also can demonstrate how to handle them. The trainer should emphasize the use of institutionally-appropriate or assertive language and give trainees opportunities to act out (or role play) the use of that language when confronting a peer about suspected plagiarism. Additionally, the trainer needs to make sure that the solutions and actions agreed upon by the participants are consistent with the philosophy and guidelines of the institution's statements on student rights and responsibilities.

Trainers can easily expand this activity by adding more educational components, such as an explanation of moral development. Experienced student staff might be assigned to create a short activity using Kohlberg's theory to introduce the idea of responding to moral lapses appropriately for the level of moral development attained by the individual.

On the other hand, if trainers have limited time, they can shorten training by offering one case study for all trainees to discuss together. If training is adjusted for time considerations or other reasons, the learning objective and assessment should be adjusted to reflect the change.

Assessment

Trainers should expect responses on the assessment of the training to show that trainees have fulfilled the learning objectives: student staff should be able to explain, identify, and educate their peers on plagiarism. The following questions can be used for assessing the training on plagiarism. They can be altered from short-answer form to fill-in-the-blank, multiple-choice, or oral explanation form:

- What is the institution's policy on plagiarism?

- How should someone on this staff confront a student about suspected plagiarism? (The answer should include being respectful yet assertive in communication and also educating the student about plagiarism.)

- What should a student staff member do if confronting a student client about plagiarism seems dangerous, counterproductive, or destructive to the peer relationship? (This answer depends on learning center policies, but student staff should generally bring difficult situations to their supervisor for guidance.)

- What are the consequences for a student caught plagiarizing?

- What are the learning center's policies about plagiarizing, both for student staff and for student clients?

Additional readings may be provided for student staff whose understanding is revealed by assessment to need more support. The Purdue Online Writing Lab (n.d.) provides useful readings on this topic.

References

American Psychological Association. (2009). *Publication manual of the American Psychological Association* (6th ed.). Washington, DC: Author.

Kohlberg, L. (1963). Moral development and identification. *Child psychology: The 62nd yearbook of the National Society for the Study of Education, Part 1* (pp. 277–332). Chicago, IL: National Society for the Study of Education. Retrieved from http://psycnet.apa.org/psycinfo/2009-06337-008

Modern Language Association. (2009). *MLA handbook for writers of research papers* (7th ed). New York, NY: Author.

The Purdue Online Writing Lab (OWL). (n.d.). *Preventing plagiarism*. Retrieved from http://owl.english.purdue.edu/owl/section/3/33/

Appendix

THREE CASE STUDIES FOR TRAINER USE

Case Study 1: Biology Lab

Kate attends every biology class lecture. She takes notes, reads the book, and occasionally visits the tutor for the course. Students are expected to come prepared to the weekly lab, so Kate carefully writes her pre-lab reports and even starts her post-lab reports before lab so she can know what to expect during the experiment. One week, Kate is not getting the data she thinks she should be getting. After reviewing her process and double-checking her actions, she still cannot find the answer to her problem. Kate turns to her classmate and asks what he got for his results. His answer makes sense to Kate, so she substitutes his numbers in her results, as she does not have time to run her experiment again before the lab is over. Later Kate's lab report is returned with red X's by her data. Kate is puzzled about why she got her figures wrong.

What went wrong with Kate's experiment? Can you identify any elements of plagiarism? What could Kate have done differently?

Case Study 2: Essay Exam

Jorge has been given a final essay exam 3 weeks before it is due but waits until 3 days before the paper is due to start gathering information and writing. Jorge is worried because he has earned only 78% of the points in this course and wants a final grade of 80%. Jorge's college developed an honor pledge, a copy of which must be attached to every paper or essay exam. The pledge states, "I have neither given nor received any unauthorized aid on this assignment." Fretting about his grade, Jorge takes his exam answers to the learning center to receive last-minute assistance with writing style. During the appointment, Jorge explains the assignment. The tutor then informs Jorge that she cannot help him with the paper because the professor has not authorized writing tutors to assist on the assignment.

Why would the tutor require permission from the professor? How can the tutor help Jorge without violating the honor pledge?

Case Study 3: A New Writing Style

Myra, a writing tutor, had been working with Simon twice a week for 3 weeks. A big paper is coming up for Simon and is due in the next week. Simon brings in a draft, and Myra sees that the clarity and technical accuracy of Simon's writing has improved greatly since the previous week. At first Myra is pleased with and proud of Simon's accomplishment. The more she reads, though, the more concerned she gets. Certain phrases do not sound like Simon's voice or style. Myra thinks that parts of the paper have been plagiarized.

How can Myra talk to Simon about his suspected plagiarism? How should she confront Simon assertively without his becoming defensive? After Myra has identified with Simon that he has plagiarized, how can she help him learn more about plagiarism so he will not plagiarize again?

Ⓒ RESOURCES

Thinking Critically About the Internet as a Tutoring and Mentoring Resource

 Nancy F. Mills

Because most of today's college students have grown up with access to computers, the Internet, and social networking technology, they are conversant with the technology. Conversant, however, does not necessarily mean critically analytical. Just as students need to learn to think analytically about what they hear and read, they have to learn to be critical and analytical about online resources. In a study of 6,300 students at 63 participating institutions (Katz, 2007), the Educational Testing Service tried to assess students' critical thinking about technology. The assessment found that of the participating students, 52% could judge the objectivity of a site, 65% could gauge the authority, and 72% could recognize timeliness, but only 49% recognized sites that met all three criteria. Even fewer were able to conduct and narrow an online search efficiently

Indeed, the need for a critical stance is increasing, given Web 2.0's emphasis on user-generated and -edited materials. Students need tools to help them sort the high-quality pages from the problem pages. According to de Kunder (n.d.), in July 2011 there were over 19 billion indexed pages on Google, Bing, Yahoo and Ask. Blogs and wikis, for example, allow many more individuals of undetermined credentials to post information that superficially may look just as legitimate as and more appealing than more scholarly work. There are indeed wikis, Creative Commons, and other academic-supported sites that allow broader participation with some academic monitoring. Easy access for those wishing to disseminate their work combined with students' easy access to a range of information may conflict with professors' beliefs about what constitutes quality and reliability. Furthermore, the complexity of an academic discipline may or may not be reflected on a particular site. Tutors and mentors, therefore, may be accustomed to turning to web resources for information but carry an extra responsibility when doing so with their student clients. Tutors and mentors need to ensure that the information on the site is relevant, accurate, timely, and likely to enhance students' learning, not confound it.

Because St. Cloud State University's tutoring program is founded on commitment to active learning (Bonwell & Eison, 1991), meaningful learning (Stalheim-Smith, 1998), and student demonstration of understanding, one tutor training session of the program requires tutors to do web evaluation and contribute to the tutor community's knowledge and resource base. The training session is highly participatory, incorporating brief instructional periods, face-to-face and electronic interaction, tutor use of the Internet, evaluative checklists, pre- and post-session assessment, and communication with faculty.

Upon completion of this training session, tutors and mentors should be able to explain and use criteria for evaluating both general websites and sites in their particular tutoring field or mentoring focus. Trainees will have examined sample sites provided by the trainer and will have applied criteria to identify good and poor examples of sites in their fields. If possible, trainees will post and share links to useful sites and share information about those sites with the faculty in their subject areas. The learning center will add any newly identified sites to its bank of useful sites for staff reference and post them on the tutoring and mentoring site used by the center for online training and communication.

Training Activity

The 1-hour training session is conducted in a computer lab equipped with a projector. The trainees are seated at computers, either individually or in pairs with another peer educator in the same subject discipline. Much of the content for the instructional portion, including a PowerPoint® presentation with embedded links, can be stored and shared on a Desire to Learn (D2L®) or similar teaching platform such as Blackboard®. Tutors and mentors in the training session can then have the PowerPoint® open on their own computers while the session proceeds. Being able to access the presentation on their lab computers allows the participants to follow along more easily and have live links to the demonstration sites used, thus enhancing active participation in the process. An alternative would be to provide the links to the trainees in a handout.

The trainer prepares for the session by gathering up-to-date information on the scope, scale, and utility of web-based resources. The trainer contacts faculty teaching courses for which there is tutorial support, asking them for preferences concerning web resources and for exemplary sites they recommend. This initial step serves to engage faculty with the tutoring and mentoring program in the role of resource guides and to provide the trainer with current information about faculty preferences. At the author's campus, some faculty members have reported that the request led to lively departmental discussions about the use of the web and characteristics of high-quality sites within their field of study.

Before the training session, the trainer should also identify sites that demonstrate pitfalls involved in web use. For example, one site (Gray, 1996) reports on the size of the Internet but has not been updated for at least 10 years, making it woefully outdated. Other sites may be updated daily. Some sites provide teaser information and initially seem useful but later ask for credit card information before permitting access to the rest of the information students need. Each semester these links need to be tested and updated as URLs change and sites are removed or updated. Because of these changes, even the information provided here should be viewed as a general guide and rechecked regularly.

Before the training session, trainers should access a third body of information: sites that guide users to critical evaluation of online resources. There are a number of useful websites concerning evaluating material on the Internet. Many college and university libraries provide information on their websites. Such sites are easily located by a simple search, starting with the campus library and then expanding to the Internet. Since links and sites change so frequently, the trainer should verify that links work prior to a training session. At the time of this writing, University of California at Berkeley's library (2011) and Johns Hopkins University's library (2010) are examples of informative sites on using the web.

Prior to the training session, tutors complete a five-question assessment concerning the general criteria used to evaluate websites, indicators of high-quality or problematic sites, discipline-based or learned-society sites, and professor preferences:

- List four indications of a high-quality website in your area of tutoring.

- List three "red flags" or warning signs that suggest you would want to avoid using a site.

- What helpful websites are provided by professional societies in your field?

- What are two useful websites in your field?

- What web resources have been recommended or are preferred by the professors for whom you tutor?

At the end of the session, trainees will return to these questions and answer them again with new knowledge from the training.

The training session begins with a brief, interactive PowerPoint® presentation covering basic considerations in evaluating sources of all kinds and electronic sources in particular. A good place to begin is the de Kunder (n.d.) site, which is updated daily with an estimate of the number of web pages indexed by the major search engines. For teaching general web evaluation, trainers can present domains, types of URLs, authors' identity and credentials, publisher, accuracy, relevance, ease of use, substance (as opposed to "flash"), and timeliness. The quality of Wikipedia pages varies widely, so this exercise provides an opportunity to discuss what qualities may increase confidence in a particular Wikipedia page. If trainees have the PowerPoint® open on their computers, they can follow the live links illustrating the criteria for evaluation. Trainers can offer basic suggestions concerning textbook resources, library databases, free textbook sources, and learned society postings before looking at other materials.

The presentation should also cover the specific disciplines for which the learning center provides tutoring. Learned societies may have sites that offer links to glossaries, research, and lessons in their particular fields. In their specific disciplines, tutors can learn to consider disciplinary approach, appropriate sources, and level of complexity of the material accessed. After working through the criteria and examining examples of good and poor sites, the trainer gives tutors and mentors paper and electronic copies of an evaluation checklist covering the aspects of web analysis discussed in the presentation.

During the remainder of the training session, tutors and mentors work individually or in pairs to search the Internet for their own resources. Trainees then use the checklist to assess the sites they have identified. When they locate what they believe to be a good example—a site that may be useful to them in tutoring or mentoring other students—they post that site on the discussion board. Trainees may also be instructed to send a link to the site to a faculty member for additional feedback. Sites that are considered useful can later be posted by the trainer to a links section on the tutoring or learning center home page for others to use.

Assessment

In addition to administering the five-question, post-session assessment and comparing answers to those on the pre-assessment, trainers can assess trainees' learning by the quality of the sites they contribute to the resource bank for the tutoring community on campus. The outcomes of this training session are that the tutors use websites as resources, can articulate to students the characteristics of high-quality websites, and actively participate in the construction of a resource list of high-quality sites. Over time, other faculty and tutors can recommend additions and deletions, tracking the development of materials in the ever-changing online world.

References

Bonwell, C., & Eison, J. (1991). *Active learning: Creating excitement in the classroom.* Washington, DC: ASHE-ERIC Higher Education Reports. Retrieved from http://www.oid.ucla.edu/about/units/tatp/old/lounge/pedagogy/downloads/active-learning-eric.pdf

de Kunder, M. (n.d.). *The size of the World Wide Web.* Retrieved from http://www.worldwidewebsize.com/

Gray, M. (1996). *Web growth summary.* Retrieved from http://www.mit.edu/people/mkgray/net

Johns Hopkins University Library. (2010). *Evaluating information found on the Internet.* Retrieved from http://guides.library.jhu.edu/evaluatinginformation

Katz, I. R. (2007). ETS research finds college students fall short in demonstrating ICT literacy: National Policy Council to create national standards. *College and Research Library News, 68*(1), 1–5. Retrieved from http://www.hawaii.edu/lilo/summer10/pubs/info_lit_ets_jan_2007.pdf

Stalheim-Smith, A. (1998). *Focusing on active, meaningful learning* (IDEA Paper 34). Manhattan, KS: IDEA Center, Kansas State University.

University of California Berkeley Library. (2011). *Evaluating web pages: Techniques to apply and questions to ask.* Retrieved from http://www.lib.berkeley.edu/TeachingLib/Guides/Internet/Evaluate.html

Identifying and Using Campus Resources

Pamela Czapla

Because tutors and mentors often develop rapport with students who attend multiple sessions, they become aware of issues with which their students are dealing. For this reason training should contain a unit on the resources of the institution. The unit should reveal the value of suggesting these resources to their students. This training should also serve as a reminder for peer tutors and mentors to refer students when issues arise beyond their training or qualifications.

Role play provides one avenue for conveying this lesson. Johnson and Johnson (2004) note that role play brings "patterns of behavior and their consequences into focus by allowing students to (a) concretely experience the situation, (b) identify effective and ineffective behavior, (c) gain insight into their own behaviors, and (d) practice the skills required to manage similar situations constructively" (p. 171). Thus, after playing out scenarios in practice carefully supervised and supported by the trainer, trainees should better understand the value of mentioning campus resources to their students and be more effective when doing so.

Training Activity

This activity suggests campus resources that could be mentioned during such a lesson and concludes with a role-play activity. The list of campus resources provided in this module is suggestive, not exhaustive. A more complete list should be provided by the trainer on the training website or in a training handbook. Obviously the list would vary with the institution.

CAMPUS RESOURCES

A large campus map or virtual map should be displayed for locating each of the resources. A list of the resources to be mentioned should also be displayed in alphabetical, geographical, or hierarchical order. Each tutor or mentor trainee can be given a card of information about one resource and read the information when called upon. Alternatively, trainees can work together at monitors to pull up websites of the resources and summarize information for other trainees. This part of the activity can take 15–30 minutes.

Academic Advising

Tutors and mentors probably have their own ideas about how to develop a plan of study and choose academic courses. They should be reminded, however, to send the student to an advisor for the latest on academic requirements. Advisors can also be helpful in redirecting students who run into difficulties with finances, illness, family situations, or other life events.

Arts

Art resources should be discussed not only as opportunities for viewing pleasure and stimulation of thought but also as venues for personal expression. The arts supplement general education courses and provide venues for student employment. Campuses may feature art galleries and museums. There is usually at least one auditorium or theater for professional and student performances. Tickets are often available to students at reduced prices, and admission may even be free of charge at institutions where charges are folded into an activity fee.

Career Centers

Career centers provide information about internships, jobs, and career opportunities for many academic majors. Center workshops convey the latest strategies for interviews and résumé writing.

Job fairs offer opportunities to meet potential employers and gain experience in job searching. Tutors and mentors should advise their students to start using these services as early as possible in their academic careers.

Clubs and Organizations

Students may be unaware of the value of joining a club or student organization. Tutors and mentors should attest to the value of clubs and organizations not only as a social outlet but also as a means of professional networking. In addition, involvement in student organizations offers experience in leadership, human relations, fundraising, and event management. Some colleges and universities provide websites listing all clubs and organizations so students can see at a glance the range of possibilities: academic, social, honors, ethnic, cultural, interest, political, religious, service, government, sports, and more.

Counseling

When tutors and mentors observe signs of distress, they should encourage students to talk to an advisor or counselor. If services are provided free of charge, tutors and mentors should make this clear, because students may hesitate to get help if they think a fee is charged.

Faculty Office Hours

Tutors and mentors should remind students that their services are a supplement to and not a substitute for faculty office hours. Tutors and mentors should encourage students to talk with their instructors and professors about matters such as grade concerns and group project problems. The long-term value of developing relationships with faculty, especially faculty in the student's major, should be emphasized.

Health Centers

When tutors and mentors observe signs of health problems, they should encourage students to get help. Health services are generally available to address minor health concerns and make referrals to community resources as necessary. Hotlines for mental and physical crises may be available. Health care insurance and basic medications and inoculations may be included in student fees.

Learning Centers

Learning centers may also be called success centers or tutorial services. The student should be informed about separate centers providing services for students in particular courses (e.g., math, writing) and with particular qualifications (e.g., honors, student athletes, TRIO programs).

Library Services

Tutors and mentors should make sure their students are aware of the range of library resources. In addition to the online catalog and books, libraries provide electronic media such as digital cameras, printers, scanners, laptops, and DVDs. Library web-based resources include dictionaries, citation rules, and databases of resources available around the world. Students should also be encouraged to visit the reference desk for expert help with resources and citations.

Police Services and Campus Safety Offices

Students may mention that they have observed drug or alcohol violations or had property stolen. Tutors and mentors can suggest police services and provide information on how to contact them. Such offices may serve as the central location for lost items like keys, coats, or rings. The campus safety office may also be a source of parking and parade permits.

Policies

Campus policies regarding students' rights and responsibilities usually govern issues such as copyright, plagiarism, sexual harassment, withdrawal from courses, and classroom behavior. These policies should guide tutors and mentors through troublesome situations. Institutional policies should be presented to students in a positive light, that is, as ways to resolve problems and insure fairness. Procedures for updating and changing institutional policies can also be discussed.

Recreational Facilities

Tutors and mentors should impress on students the importance of balancing study with recreation. Outlets may include student recreation centers, athletic fields, equipment rental, walking trails, swimming pools, golf courses, tennis courts, sports clubs, intermural teams, and running clubs.

Resident Assistants (RAs)

If a student mentions problems with a roommate or others in a campus residence hall, the tutor or mentor can remind the student to discuss the situation with the RA. RAs may be helpful in arranging a room change or negotiating problems, discussing roommate agreements and contracts, and promoting citizenship in the hall.

Study Abroad and International Offices

Tutors and mentors may suggest studying abroad to enhance the student's academic experience. International offices can clarify the expenses and necessary arrangements. The possibilities are enhanced by agreements the institution has made with institutions in other countries.

ROLE-PLAY ACTIVITY

Winnard and Hazard (2007a, 2007b) provided role plays appropriate for tutors or mentors to share information about campus resources. Two sample scenarios are provided in the Appendix. This part of the activity can take 20–45 minutes depending on how much time the trainer wants to devote to this lesson.

Two volunteers can be requested to illustrate the application of the role play to one-on-one tutorial sessions. More volunteers can participate in role plays to illustrate the application of the concept for group peer sessions of four to six tutees or mentees. When volunteers are given a scenario, a few minutes should be allowed for the volunteers to conjecture how they might enact the role play. Ordinarily not too much advance preparation should be necessary; the role play should be spontaneous rather than heavily scripted. About 5 minutes should be allowed to enact each scenario. After the scenario is enacted, the trainer invites participants to discuss individual reactions to the scenario and the quality of advice provided.

As a variation, the trainer can arrange those who are not playing roles into groups. The groups can be given 3–5 minutes to discuss their reactions. Each small group then reports to the whole group. The discussion should incorporate a critique of how the scenario was handled as well as suggestions for other ways to handle the student's concern.

Assessment

There are at least three ways that trainees can be assessed. First, the discussion section of training should provide an opportunity for the trainer to observe and correct misunderstandings. Second, a subsequent quiz or test may include a short-answer question describing a scenario and asking how it should be handled. Finally, real-time observations of actual tutoring or mentoring sessions can provide authentic assessment opportunities. Observers can note whether trainees mention campus resources when appropriate. After an observed session, the trainer can remind the tutor or mentor of the relevance of campus resources to the situation encountered when working with the student or commend the trainee for appropriately sharing information about campus resources.

References

Johnson, D. W., & Johnson, R. T. (2004). *Assessing students in groups: Promoting group responsibility and individual accountability.* Thousand Oaks, CA: Corwin.

Winnard, K. E., & Hazard, L. (2007a). *The first-year revue.* San Jose, CA: Wizard Education Products.

Winnard, K. E., & Hazard, L. (2007b). *The tutor revue.* San Jose, CA: Wizard Education Products.

Appendix

SCENARIOS FOR ROLE PLAYING

Several role-play scenarios offered by Winnard and Hazard (2007a, 2007b) provide opportunities to prepare tutors and mentors for situations in which it would be appropriate to mention campus resources. The following are examples paraphrased from the originals:

Role Play 1

Student role: The tutee—a good student who is usually prepared for the session—comes to a Monday session tired, unprepared, and disheveled. The tutee's roommate made a mess of their residence hall room over the weekend with a party that involved smoke and alcohol. The tutee, returning to campus from a weekend away, was distressed by the smells and stayed up late cleaning the room. (This scenario is adapted from *The Tutor Revue*, Act V, Scene 4.)

Tutor or mentor role: The tutor is encouraged to explore the depths of this roommate problem and remind the tutee of the role of the RA and any relationship training available through campus counseling services. The tutee's responses to questions about the kind of smells in the room could indicate appropriateness of referral to the hall director or public safety office to ensure that the tutee is not charged with violations of campus policy, state statutes regarding tobacco products on campus, or federal drug laws.

Role Play 2

Student role: A commuter student struggling to balance the demands of family, school, and work has been 5 minutes late for mentoring sessions several times. (This scenario is adapted from *The First-Year Revue*, Act VI, Scene 4.)

Tutor or mentor role: The mentor is encouraged to discuss campus resources that help students with time management, provide places to study on campus, and offer tutorial services. If the student rushes to campus late and leaves early because of a sense of alienation from campus, this is also an opportunity to discuss clubs and organizations on campus. If the student's time and finances are constrained by off-campus employment, the mentor is asked to discuss resources available for finding work on campus. If the difficulty has been finding a parking place, the mentor could discuss campus parking resources and possible upgrades to the student's parking permit. Alternatively, if the student uses public transportation, the mentor may suggest using resources for better routes or connection times. Or does the student's wristwatch need to be realigned to the clock in the mentor services program?

Making Informed Referrals

 ## Suzanne Ponicsan

Peer tutors and mentors want to share their knowledge and help their fellow students succeed academically. Such sessions may run without incident. However, students may bring to the session some issues that require referrals to other services and resources. For example, there may be tutees who become so frustrated with their lack of academic progress that their tutors cannot redirect sessions to the topic at hand. Tutors and mentors must be able to recognize the problem and make good decisions about what to do. Thus, it is important that tutors and mentors know not only what services and resources are available for students but also how to make the best referrals to the extent that institutional and learning center policy permit referral by student employees.

Decision-making skills and values are important to human resource development and shared problem solving in the learning center. They also aid in matching students with appropriate services in order to meet their fullest potential. Owens and Valesky (2007) wrote on rationality in decision making; in the Modern era, Western thought began to apply science to social concerns, developing "human engineering" approaches to maximize efficiency (p. 300). Scientific decision-making models include those of Drucker (1954) and Simon (1987). Drucker (1954) listed and discussed five specific steps to take when confronted with a dilemma: define the problem; analyze the problem; develop alternative solutions; decide on the best solution; and convert decisions into effective actions. Drucker's model as applied to problems confronted in a learning center may look like this:

Step 1. Define the problem: What is the student's main concern or difficulty?

Step 2. Analyze the problem: Why is this problem a concern? What caused the problem?

Step 3. Develop alternative solutions: What types of available services could be offered to help the student?

Step 4. Decide on the best solution: Of the choices, which may work best for the student?

Step 5. Act effectively: Refer the student to an option and encourage the student to consider its benefits.

As Simon (1987) observed, specific and thoughtful decision-making steps like Drucker's (1954) are appropriate for "well-structured, deliberative, and qualitative" decision making (p. 57), but sometimes decisions must be made quickly, with no time for a process of formal logic. Managers must be able to "analyze problems systematically" and "respond to situations rapidly, a skill that requires the cultivation of intuition and judgment over many years of experience and training" (p. 63). Training and experience, then, can equip tutors and mentors with the speedy judgment, intuition, and controlled emotion they need to make important decisions.

McGregor's (2006) management theory, though first presented in 1960, is still studied today and is useful for tutors and mentors and their trainers to consider. McGregor identified the prevailing management culture as Theory X, which posits that workers require motivation, resist change, and do not want to work. McGregor's Theory Y posits that workers are motivated to perform their jobs well in order to meet the organization's objectives. A student-centered learning center operating on Theory Y will anticipate and foster students' attempts to gain control over their academic work and to perform with competence and skill.

Decision-making models assume that deciders have a responsibility or right to make decisions; however, as Kelley (2003) noted, some problems cannot be solved by peer assistants. Such problems may be similar to those suggested by Kelley (2003): referrals to professionals in other services may be necessary if client students use time inappropriately, resist communication, become depressed or anxious, act abusively toward the tutor or mentor, show signs of substance abuse, or demonstrate dramatic behavior changes. Thus, student staff should be reminded to discuss problem situations with their supervisor to determine the best course of action.

Training Activity

There are three learning objectives for this training activity: trainees should (a) learn about decision-making processes and theories on which they are based, (b) be aware of and empowered to decide which situations require outside assistance, and (c) identify appropriate resources for students. Trainees first focus on the topic of decision making. They are shown various decision-making models following those discussed above (see Appendix A for examples) and then create their own model for tutoring or mentoring purposes. For the second topic, referral skills, trainees discuss the various services or resources that are offered at their institution and create a list that describes when those services might be recommended. Finally, trainees create and act out mock tutoring or mentoring sessions for various situations.

The training activity should be held in one room that is large enough to accommodate all tutoring or mentoring staff. Tables and chairs should be arranged in a circle around the room with another small table and two chairs placed in the center.

Poster board, paper (white or colored), scissors, tape, and markers (or other writing utensils) should be provided. A dry-erase board or electronic presentation board should be available. The only equipment required is a projector and screen to view a PowerPoint® presentation; however, a video recorder may be necessary if role-playing sessions are to be recorded. Print and online materials should be provided for the resource search section. A set of situation cards should be created for the role-play activity, with a different concern or problem on each card. These should be the situations or concerns for which the trainer intends to prepare student staff to respond (see Appendix for examples). Depending on the size of the group, 1 or 2 hours should be allotted for this activity.

The trainer can offer a PowerPoint® presentation or otherwise highlight various models of decision making, such as those mentioned earlier. Tutors and mentors may discuss the similarities and differences among these models and any others they may have learned previously. This introduction to the topic and short presentation requires about 15 minutes.

In pairs or small groups, trainees can then create their own decision-making models for the situations they are likely to encounter and the culture of their learning center. They may use the writing and drawing materials provided and whatever other materials they have with them. There are no requirements to this activity other than to be creative and illustrate their model as clearly as possible. About 15 minutes should be allowed for this creative activity.

To determine the best course of action for their students to take, trainees should determine what campus services may be most appropriate for students with various concerns. To create a list of all available resources, trainees should return to the large group to review materials available online and in print, such as department lists, directories, charts of campus administrative units, maps, and other indicators of the rich and various resources that may be available to students at their academic institution. These resources include online self-help programs, counseling services, career and academic advisors, mentoring resources, health services, financial aid, the registrar, libraries, and other providers of information and assistance on campus. A list can probably be generated by the large group in less than 10 minutes.

Trainees can then be asked to work individually to list when these services and resources should be recommended. If campus services provide this kind of information on their websites, then access to web resources makes this task easy for trainees. Taking turns around the circle, trainees read their lists aloud. As responses are shared, a master list should be compiled and displayed on the whiteboard. This portion of the training activity may take about 15 minutes.

Trainees pair up for the final activity. Each pair randomly draws one of the situations from the set of prepared cards. If trainees have thought of concerns not included on the cards, the trainer can very quickly add cards for those concerns to the stack. Based on the selected situation, each pair will create their own mock tutoring or mentoring session (no more than 5 minutes long) in which the individual in the role of tutor or mentor decides whether the situation should be dealt with in that session or referred. The individual in the role of tutor or mentor should be encouraged to use the decision-making model he or she created. After each pair's presentation, tutors or mentors engage in a discussion as to the effectiveness of their decision and service referral. If possible, role plays should continue with a draw of fresh situation cards so that both members of the pair play both roles. This part of the training activity requires about 30 minutes.

Assessment

To ensure that the learning objectives of this activity have been met, assessment is built into all activities. Trainers will be able to assess trainees' knowledge of problem-solving models by the quality of the models they produce in the first activity. Trainees' contributions to discussion as the group creates a resource list should also be noted. It is especially easy to note trainees' critical thinking and behavior in the collaborative role-play activity toward the end of the training session.

It is equally important, however, to assess the effectiveness of this training activity by observing whether real-life tutees and mentees take advantage of any referrals by peer tutors and mentors. In order to assess whether referrals made by student staff are effective, trainees should be in regular communication with their supervisor regarding potential concerns, and referral slips should be available for tutors and mentors to direct student clients to recommended services. Assessment is complicated by the fact that, due to confidentiality rules, a student client referred to another department may choose not to inform student or professional staff of the learning center as to the appropriateness and usefulness of the referral, or even whether the student acted on the referral. Also some offices to which students are referred may not be permitted to reveal a student's contact with an office. However, peer tutors and mentors may inquire of student clients about the effectiveness of the referral.

Trainees may also be assessed on their continuing knowledge of campus programs and services. They should also expect to update their decision-making models as further training increases their knowledge of the institution's resources and policies.

References

Drucker, P. F. (1954). *The practice of management.* New York, NY: Harper & Row.

Kelley, P. (2003). Referral skills. In S. Deese-Roberts (Ed.), *College Reading and Learning Association tutor training handbook* (rev. ed., pp. 129–131). Hastings, NE: College Reading and Learning Association.

McGregor, D. M. (2006). *The human side of enterprise* (Annotated ed.). New York, NY: McGraw-Hill.

Owens, R. G., & Valesky, T. C. (2007). *Organizational behavior in education: Adaptive leadership and school reform* (9th ed.). Boston, MA: Pearson Education.

Simon, H. A. (1987, February). Making management decisions: The role of intuition and emotion. *The Academy of Management Executive, 1*(1), 57–64. doi:10.5465/AME.1987.4275905

Appendix

SAMPLE SITUATION CARDS

Life Problems

Sarah, a 20-year-old mother of two, needed assistance with writing. During the session, all Sarah could focus on was her problems: her mom was very ill, she was laid off from her job and was not being considered for other jobs, and her current grade in the class was a D. The tutor/mentor tried unsuccessfully multiple times to redirect the session to her writing; however, Sarah refused to change the topic and focus on the session at hand.

Uncooperative Client

Jessica, a psychology student, reluctantly came to the center for writing assistance—only at the prompting of the Dean of Students. She asked to work directly with a certain tutor only. The session started well; a topic and outline were developed for the assignment. However, when asked to write a thesis statement, Jessica suddenly flushed and stated she could not do it. When encouraged, Jessica growled angry words at the tutor and nearly hit the tutor with a textbook.

Student Complaint About Faculty

Jacob visited the center for assistance with math. He was upset because he had been doing very well on his homework assignments but failed his tests. He complained to the tutor that the professor was purposefully acting mean because the professor would not explain why Jacob had not done well on the tests. Jacob, quite discouraged, would not leave the topic and continued to make negative remarks about the professor.

Distraught Student

During a session to work on basic computer skills, first-term undergraduate Herbert complained that a school official asked him to leave the computer classroom because class had ended early and his professor had left for the night. (Students were not allowed in the room unsupervised.) Using inappropriate language, Herbert described how he had paid a large tuition bill and was therefore entitled to remain in the classroom to study during the remainder of his scheduled class time.

Financial Distractions

Sue, 50 years of age, needed math assistance. However, throughout the session, she regularly interjected with comments on how expensive tuition is and how badly she needed a job to cover the expenses. The tutor continually attempted to redirect Sue to math examples in the textbooks, but Sue could not focus; finding a resolution to her financial dilemma was currently more important, and she wanted the tutor to help her with that as well as with her math problems.

Practice Does Not Make Perfect

Jack, a student mentor, attempted to assist Janel with her basic math class. Both were becoming increasingly frustrated; Janel continually transposed numbers, and no matter how many times Janel practiced or Jack repeated concepts, Janel did not understand the material. Jack did not understand why Janel could not grasp the basic concepts, and both were feeling as if the sessions were a waste of time.

ⓓ STUDENT POPULATIONS

The Power of the Testimony: Motivating Reluctant Students

▣ M. E. McWilliams

The first step in motivating reluctant students at learning centers is to identify exactly what the tutors and mentors wish these students to do. In many instances, the overarching objective boils down to changing a student's goal from getting good grades quickly and effortlessly to learning deeply and fully. Certainly not all students have such superficial learning goals; however, this training module will address the need for many students to make their goals more realistic and appropriate. According to goal orientation theory, the student's goal determines the effort expended on studying (Ames, 1992). Therefore, if the student's goal is to get good grades to earn the reward of peers' admiration or to avoid the loss of parents' funding, then the student will study superficially, scanning notes quickly, glancing at the book, memorizing, and guessing. However, if the student's goal is really to learn, then the student will study slowly and deeply as marked by rereading, reviewing errors, and seeking assistance (Schunk, Pintrich, & Meece, 2007). This student will likely earn a high grade point average (GPA) plus have the value-added experience of truly acquiring knowledge.

To motivate students successfully to change their learning objectives, tutors and mentors will need to influence students in two ways. First, they will need to convince students to believe that they can master the material. As suggested by self-efficacy theory, students must first believe in their own ability to do a task before they will attempt the task (Bandura, 1997). Second, tutors and mentors will need to convince students to value their learning. Research on expectancy-value theory supported that students study with persistence and commitment when they both expect to master the material *and* find the material valuable (Wigfield & Eccles, 2000). Such an approach to motivation avoids incentives like rewards (also known as carrots), such as extra points on a test. This approach also avoids incentives that involve fear of punishment (also known as sticks), such as frequent reminders that students may fail a course. Both of these motivation strategies are apt to lead to shallow, temporary results. However, learning for the sake of learning—an intrinsic approach to motivation—produces deep, lasting results.

Many student clients working with tutors and mentors lack a model for learning intrinsically. As many as one in six freshmen may be first-generation students (Capriccioso, 2006) who lack role models for academic success. The following training activity prepares tutors and mentors to inspire students with models of appropriate and effective learning behaviors.

Training Activity

This *testimony workshop* trains tutors and mentors to share their personal testimonies of learning with students. By sharing their stories of struggle and joy as students, tutors and mentors may be able to inspire students to engage in their own learning. The workshop begins with an overview of the topic, including the theories discussed previously: goal orientation, self-efficacy, and expectancy-value theory. In this way, tutors and mentors better understand the nature of reluctant students and the role of tutors and mentors in changing their attitudes about learning.

The remainder of the workshop focuses on developing personal testimonies as a strategy for changing those attitudes. This workshop should arm the tutors and mentors with an array of testimonies (both their own and those of their colleagues) that can then be articulated at opportune moments during their sessions with students. In turn, these testimonies will likely increase students' self-efficacy and value for the subjects they study.

The only items necessary for this 1-hour training exercise are chairs and perhaps a bell or whistle. For the following interactive portion of the workshop, the trainer asks that the participants divide into groups or pairs and then calls out prompts for 5-minute discussions. The trainer floats from each group to the next to hear as much conversation as possible. The trainer calls time with a bell or whistle and then calls out, "Time to testify!" Students self-select to stand up and offer their personal testimonies. The trainer then moves to the next topic, and the pattern is repeated.

TESTIFY TO THE CAPABILITY

The trainer asks participants to share stories with each other regarding any previous experience in which they initially lacked confidence to learn a certain subject. Tutors and mentors may confess to once believing that their brains maintained fixed, unchangeable deficiencies preventing them from mastering certain subjects, such as an inability to do math (Dweck, 2006). Some tutors and mentors may divulge that their ACT or SAT scores once led them to confirm a lack of ability in given subjects. Tutors and mentors should identify what happened to change their minds about their capabilities. What happened so that now they can say with assurance that there is no bad-math gene? What experience gave them evidence that the brain is not fixed and unchangeable but actually grows new neural connections that become deep grooves as one studies?

Tutors and mentors may note that they did not necessarily rise to the top of their most challenging classes. Certainly some people process certain information faster and better than others because of certain "genetic aptitudes," but "experience, training and personal effort" allow most students to be proficient at their tasks (Dweck, 2006, p. 5). When students understand that many law school graduates and even college professors have achieved academic success in spite of low SAT and ACT scores (Brown, 2009), they must recognize that personal effort is a greater predictor of capability than an entrance exam. With testimonials to similar academic beginnings, tutors and mentors can provide the evidence to motivate students to believe in their own capabilities.

TESTIFY TO THE PERSISTENCE

The trainer asks participants to share stories with each other regarding any previous experience in which their struggle to learn something nearly made them give up. Tutors and mentors may recall suffering a disappointing grade. Perhaps they thought of dropping the course or even dropping out of school but then decided to stay on. They learned that failure is sometimes necessary in learning and renewed their commitment to the course. As a consequence, they developed "failure tolerance" (Clifford, Kim, & McDonald, 1988, p. 19), a trait common to all great athletes. Michael Jordan missed 9,000 shots and lost almost 300 games; he was trusted to take the winning shot but failed 26 times (Nike, 2010), yet he kept stepping back onto the court. Learning demands painful persistence even for great geniuses. Aristotle said, "One can name all kinds of great men who were not very gifted. They acquired greatness, became 'geniuses'. . . [with the] diligent seriousness of a craftsman" (De Botton, 2001, p. 226). If trainees testify to their own persistence through the struggles of learning, they will serve as coping models for students (Schunk et al., 2007), prompting students to consider, "If they can do it, we can too!"

TESTIFY TO THE PASSION

The trainer asks participants to share the passion they hold for the subjects they tutor or mentor. Tutors and mentors may be able to motivate students to learn and not just memorize by testifying to a passion for the subject. Dewey (1916) noted that one can learn all the parts of the flower but regrettably overlook the wonder of the flower as a whole. Tutors and mentors should attempt to recall some experience in which the wonder and delight for the subject suddenly became clear. That experience should be shared with students, because such enthusiasm for learning is contagious. The best teachers "make the students love the material as much as they do" (Solomon & Solomon, 1993, p. 113), as do the best tutors and mentors. In turn, students are likely to model the study habits of tutors and mentors who love to learn (Haberman, 2004, p. 52). Research on social learning theory has supported such an assertion (Bandura, 1977). For example, the ongoing personal relationships that tutors and mentors have with students provide an opportunity for the students to observe carefully their tutors and mentors. If students observe that the behavior of the tutors and mentors that leads to a deep understanding of the material also yields a certain measure of delight, then they are likely to imitate that behavior. Students may begin to reference the study behavior of tutors and mentors as a guide to action.

TESTIFY TO THE CONNECTION

In the fourth testimonial, the trainer asks participants to share the connections they see between the subjects they tutor and mentor and their personal lives. Tutors and mentors can talk about how these subjects relate to their hobbies, majors, and general routine. Perhaps a little geometry helped to build that stand for the Wii game. Or maybe that political science course influenced a vote. Did learning to write an effective argument in Rhetoric and Expression help to win the last debate with a roommate? The tutors and mentors should be encouraged to share these real-world applications and associations with students and then ask that students also reflect on the same kinds of connections. Until students see relationships between their personal worlds and the subjects they study, the process of learning is nothing more than the "mere superficial amassing of information" (Dewey, 1916, p. 209): "It might as well be about Mars . . . unless it fructifies in the individual's own life" (Dewey, 1916, p. 342). Tutors and mentors should *bring the topic to earth* for students. Such recognition of "relatedness" increases the student's "commitment, effort, high-quality performance" (Ryan & Deci, 2000, p. 76).

Students may be most motivated intrinsically when they recognize the value of what they learn. When they see that the information can be used to benefit them or when the information connects to something of interest to them, they read more attentively and listen more carefully. Students may then "determine" to study as opposed to feeling forced to study. This moment of "self-determinism" (Ryan & Deci, 2000, p. 68) forms the foundation for intrinsic motivation.

CONCLUDING REMARKS

After ample time has been spent testifying to the topics of capability, persistence, passion, and connectedness, the trainer directs tutors and mentors to articulate these same experiences to students during their sessions. All great marketers know the value of testimonials to inspire an audience; however, instead of soap, sports drinks, or cars, tutors and mentors sell learning. Tutors and mentors can learn how to motivate reluctant students to want to learn, without resorting to carrots or sticks, prizes or reprisals.

Assessment

Following this training session, tutors and mentors should be able to recognize the need for motivating students and to identify testimonials as a technique for achieving that outcome. Assessment of these learning outcomes occurs first on a formative level at the close of the workshop when participants select one description from among four ranked statements to describe their abilities to engage students in the learning process. This self-analysis provides the baseline data required for tutors and mentors to recognize the need to improve motivation skills.

Several weeks later, trainers should observe tutors and mentors for their motivation skills as they work with students. Trainers can use a standardized rubric with a corresponding Likert-type scale for multiple skills, including motivation. Concurrently, trainers can circulate surveys to students for additional assessment of these skills, including motivation strategies. On the survey, students can identify appropriate statements about their tutors or mentors, with statements corresponding to a Likert-type scale.

Observations and anonymous survey results should be returned to tutors and mentors for their review, followed by joint review with the trainer as necessary. On the basis of the trainer's observations and students' surveys, trainers should coach peer tutors and mentors in specific skills and strategies for improving their abilities to inspire students to engage fully in their learning.

References

Ames, C. (1992). Classrooms: Goals, structures, and student motivation. *Journal of Educational Psychology, 84*, 261–271. doi:10.1037/0022-0663.84.3.261

Bandura, A. (1977). *Social learning theory.* New York, NY: General Learning Press.

Bandura, A. (1997). *Self-efficacy: The exercise of control.* New York, NY: W. H. Freeman.

Brown, T. (2009, March). *Bridging EOP's past to the present and future: Challenges, opportunities, responsibilities.* Keynote address to the 40th anniversary EOP conference, Sacramento, CA. Retrieved from http://webcache.googleusercontent.com/search?q=cache:3oOVGm MFTBgJ:webapps2.csus.edu/saseep/eop40th/presentations/Tom_Brown_EOP_40th_ Keynote_Powerpoint.ppt+tom+brown+underprepared+urtecho+700+SAT&cd=2&hl= en&ct=clnk&gl=us

Clifford, M. M., Kim, A., & McDonald, B. A. (1988). Responses to failure as influenced by task attribution, outcome attribution, and failure tolerance. *Journal of Experimental Education, 57*, 19–37. Retrieved from http://www.jstor.org/pss/20151751

Capriccioso, R. (2006, January 26). Aiding first-generation students. *Inside Higher Education.* Retrieved from http://www.insidehighered.com/news/2006/01/26/freshmen

De Botton, A. (2001). *The consolations of philosophy.* New York, NY: Vintage Books.

Dewey, J. (1916). *Democracy and education: An introduction to the philosophy of education.* New York, NY: Macmillan.

Dweck, C. S. (2006). *Mindset: The new psychology of success.* New York, NY: Random House.

Nike. (2010, October 10). *Michael Jordan "failure" Nike commercial* [Video file]. Retrieved from http://www.youtube.com/watch?v=45mMioJ5szc

Haberman, M. (2004). Can star teachers create learning communities? *Educational Leadership, 61*(8), 52–56.

Ryan, R. M., & Deci, E. L. (2000). Self-determination theory and the facilitation of intrinsic motivation, social development, and well-being. *American Psychologist, 55*, 68–78. doi:10.1037/0003-066X.55.1.68

Schunk, D. H., Pintrich, P. R., & Meece, J. L. (2007). *Motivation in education: Theory, research, and applications.* Upper Saddle River, NJ: Prentice Hall.

Solomon, R., & Solomon, J. (1993). *Up the university: Re-creating higher education in America.* Boston, MA: Addison Wesley.

Wigfield, A., & Eccles, J. S. (2000). Expectancy-value theory of achievement motivation. *Contemporary Educational Psychology, 25*, 68–81. doi:10.1006/ceps.1999.1015

Preparing to Work With Student Athletes

Thomas C. Stewart

Who is the student athlete? While one common stereotype of the college student athlete is of a privileged and even pampered student on the receiving end of scholarships and adulation, the reality is often quite different. Many student athletes in the National Collegiate Athletic Association (NCAA), especially those in lower-profile sports, toil away at their avocation in relative obscurity, often with smaller crowds than they saw in high school, for little more than the love of the sport. Regardless of whether they are top basketball stars who find themselves highlighted on ESPN's *SportsCenter* or Division II bowlers rolling strikes for a handful of fans, student athletes face unique challenges and pressures (Fletcher, Benshoff, & Richburg, 2003). The uniqueness of student athletes' experiences warrants dedicated training for the tutors and mentors with whom they work. How can these challenges be addressed, and how can training prepare tutors and mentors for this? The first step is to identify the challenges, and part of the training session gets tutors and mentors involved in this identification process.

Generally student athletes "will benefit from intense integration of support services and life-skills development programs to help balance the demands of their academic responsibilities and participation in athletics" (Storch & Olson, 2009, p. 75). Tutoring and mentoring certainly play a key role in this dynamic. Overall, student athletes have a positive view of the balance they must maintain between athletics and academics (Potuto & O'Hanlon, 2007; Simons, Rheenen, & Covington, 1999) and tend to be motivated to succeed academically even if satisfactory academic progress is tied to being qualified to compete (Woodruff & Schallert, 2008). However, Woodruff and Schallert (2008) found that student athletes also tend to feel that they miss out on some elements of the student experience because of the time they spend on athletics. Because time management is one of the biggest challenges for all students, the fact that student athletes have less free time than many students makes their development of effective time management skills all the more important. That is where effective tutoring and mentoring can come into the picture. Because tutoring, in particular, is planned time for studying with the assistance of a trained tutor—as opposed to just a study hall, whether supervised or unsupervised—tutoring, along with an effective mentoring program, can be especially helpful for student athletes striving to meet their academic goals.

The unique nature of the student athletes' experience may be foreign to many who have not had that experience. In addition to other concerns, many student athletes, in particular males, identify with the athletic aspect of their experience more than the student aspect because they see athletics as valued externally (Killeya-Jones, 2005). If what student athletes are struggling with academically is not seen as important to their view of themselves, they have a harder time putting in the effort to overcome that obstacle. In addition, student athletes often have to overcome negative perceptions among some faculty and students as well as the public at large that they are less qualified academically than other students (Umbach, Palmer, Kuh, & Hannah, 2006).

Clearly, student athletes represent a population that has special needs based on the unique nature of their experience at college (Carodine, Almond, & Gratto, 2001; Potuto & O'Hanlon, 2007; Storch & Olson, 2009; Umbach et al., 2006). It is also clear that involvement in athletics and the identity it creates for student athletes can be very helpful in their academic success (Curry & Weiss, 1989; Murphy, Petitpas, & Brewer, 1996). Integrating services is important. Also, because the experience of student athletes is different, tutor and mentor training should dedicate some special attention to the needs of student athletes, just as to working with students with learning disabilities, students with different language backgrounds, or other populations with unique needs.

Although the academic failure of any student is an unfortunate occurrence, the academic failure of a high-profile student athlete can garner a disproportionate amount of attention and can have serious consequences for that student athlete's eligibility to participate in athletic competition. The tutoring and mentoring program can play a role in avoiding either kind of failure. Furthermore, bringing in representatives from athletics can break down the artificial but often very powerful psychological barrier between academics and athletics on campus, and new relationships can be created to improve services for student athletes even further.

Training Activity

This training exercise focuses specifically on helping tutors and mentors understand how best to work with student athletes. For this activity, a standard classroom that includes a computer, projector, and screen would be suitable. Also a separate table is recommended for the panel of experts in the second training session.

Who should be on this panel of experts? Some consideration should be given to this question. There are elements besides availability that should be taken into account. The objectives are for tutors and mentors to become familiar with rules and regulations that apply to student athletes and familiar with the role of athletics on their own campus and to become more aware of some of the unique challenges faced by student athletes and methods for addressing them. The primary consideration is who can provide the best, most accurate information to tutors and mentors. A secondary consideration is who would build bridges between academics and athletics.

Choosing the right panel of guest speakers is a key to the effectiveness of the exercise. Some suggestions that would fit the bill for both the primary and secondary considerations listed previously would be a panel that includes a student athlete; a coach, coach's assistant, or athletic trainer; and a representative from the athletics department, such as the athletic director or NCAA compliance officer. A tutor or mentor who is also a student athlete would be a good addition to the panel. It is always helpful to have one more person available as a contact if some assistance is needed with a student—athlete or otherwise.

This activity spans two sessions. Approximately 20 minutes is needed at the end of one training session to do the set up, and an entire hour-long session is needed to complete the activity.

SESSION ONE

The trainer can introduce the topic of college sports and solicit from tutors and mentors some of the stereotypes of student athletes. This discussion can be enhanced by a visual presentation using both positive and negative images of athletes. A simple web search will yield numerous photos and headlines relating to positive and negative achievement by student athletes. The trainer should consider contrasting headlines of championships and awards with cheating scandals and other negative headlines such as at Florida State University in 2007 (Kaczor, 2007). The contrasting headlines can be added to the presentation and displayed to the tutors and mentors. Besides complementing the topic, this is a helpful way of getting tutors and mentors to think of any preconceptions they may have, based on the images presented and modified by the student athletes they know.

The trainer should divide tutors and mentors into groups and assign them to develop questions for the panel of experts attending the next week and report back to the larger group. From these lists of questions, the group as a whole can select 10 or fewer primary questions (e.g., What are some key regulations affecting student athletes? What is a typical in-season training schedule?). These will be forwarded to the panel of experts in advance. This is an important courtesy for outside guests. The goal is not to throw a panelist off balance or to put someone in an uncomfortable position; instead, speakers appreciate a chance to prepare and present the most accurate possible responses.

SESSION TWO

In this session, the objective is to provide tutors and mentors with expert answers to the questions they generated in the previous session. This time, the panel of experts will attend and respond to the primary questions, with time for ancillary questions. The panel has had a chance to prepare in advance. The questions could be offered visually again as a reminder to each attendee, to facilitate an open discussion on each item led by the panel of experts' responses.

At the conclusion, as a way of wrapping up the session and reaffirming new perspectives, the visual presentation of positive and negative impressions of student athletes could be repeated, this time accompanied by a new discussion including the panel of experts' input on the impression of college athletics.

Assessment

As with any activity, there must be some element of assessment both to ensure that tutors and mentors understood the content they learned in the training session and to reinforce that learning. To these ends, tutors and mentors will complete the following assessment at the conclusion of the activity: write down two academic regulations that apply to student athletes; and write down a unique academic challenge faced by student athletes and how tutoring or mentoring can help. This assessment can be done at the end of Session Two. Alternatively, if there is not too much time between training sessions, the assessment could be completed at the beginning of a later training session.

References

Carodine, K., Almond, K. F., & Gratto, K. K. (2001). College student athlete success both in and out of the classroom. In M. F. Howard-Hamilton & S. K. Watt (Eds.), *Student services for athletes*. San Francisco, CA: Jossey-Bass.

Curry, T. J., & Weiss, O. (1989). Sport identity and motivation for sport participation: A comparison between American college athletes and Austrian student sport club members. *Sociology of Sport Journal, 6*, 257–268.

Fletcher, T. B., Benshoff, J. M., & Richburg, M. J. (2003). A systems approach to understanding and counseling college student athletes. *Journal of College Counseling, 6*(10), 35–45.

Kaczor, B. (2007, September 26). Nearly 2 dozen Florida State athletes accused of cheating. *USA Today*. Retrieved from www.usatoday.com/sports/college/2007-09-26-floridast-cheating_N.htm

Killeya-Jones, L. A. (2005). Identity structure, role discrepancy, and psychological adjustment in male college student athletes. *Journal of Sport Behavior, 2*, 167–185.

Murphy, G. M., Petitpas, A. J., & Brewer, B. W. (1996). Identity foreclosure, athletic identity, and career maturity in intercollegiate athletes. *The Sport Psychologist, 10*, 239–246.

Potuto, J. R., & O'Hanlon, J. (2007). National study of student athletes regarding their experiences as college students. *College Student Journal, 41*, 947–966.

Simons, H. D., Rheenen, D. V., & Covington, M. B. (1999). Academic motivation and the student athlete. *Journal of College Student Development, 40*(2), 151–161.

Storch, J., & Olson, M. (2009). Student services and student athletes in community colleges. *New Directions for Community Colleges, 147*, 75–84. doi:10.1002/cc.379

Umbach, P. D., Palmer, M. D., Kuh, G. D., & Hannah, S. J. (2006). Intercollegiate athletes and effective educational practices: Winning combination or losing effort? *Research in Higher Education, 47*, 709–733. doi:10.1007/s11162-006-9012-9

Woodruff, A. L., & Schallert, D. L. (2008). Studying to play and playing to study: Nine college student-athletes' motivational sense of self. *Contemporary Educational Psychology, 33*(1), 34–57. doi:10.1016/j.cedpsych.2007.04.001

Using Scouting Reports to Teach Student Athletes Notetaking Skills

Penny Turrentine

During the course of their sports careers, student athletes develop a number of skills that can be successfully transferred to the classroom. Coaches instruct student athletes in acuity, which is a keen awareness of the behaviors of their competitors. In football, defensive linemen watch the eyes of the opposing quarterback to predict to whom the quarterback will pass. Linebackers can anticipate the receiver of an upcoming pass by observing which of the possible receivers adjust his glove before the ball is snapped to the quarterback. Studying film of rival teams often reveals who the quarterback's favorite receivers are. Coaches have women's basketball players study films and various scouting reports to learn their opponents' behaviors. They watch how players on the other team will respond to an aggressive offense; they learn in which direction opposing players are most comfortable maneuvering. With their keen awareness developed, athletes can force opponents out of their comfort zone. They can use this strategy to help defeat their rivals. Similar attention to scouting reports occurs in most sports, with the sole purpose of contributing to athletic success.

When pointed out, an athlete's scouting skill can transfer to the classroom and contribute to academic success. Tutors and mentors can guide student athletes to recognize that preparations for a game also provide a basis for better notetaking in the classroom. By observing visual or auditory clues, student athletes can predict what the instructor considers to be vital information or simply extraneous information shared during class time. As Gaston-Gayles (2004) wrote, "The ability to transfer skills from the athletic domain can make a significant difference in how student athletes approach academics" (p. 82).

An *academic scouting report* can help student athletes determine what should be included in their class notes. The tutor's or mentor's role is to familiarize student athletes with useful verbal and nonverbal cues that come from their instructor, such as describing the information as critically important or stepping toward students during lecture. Not only will this conscious awareness allow student athletes to take more effective notes, it will also increase their attentiveness and confidence.

This training activity is based on aspects of schema theory as developed by Anderson (1977). Anderson's theory incorporates the organization of knowledge from an elaborate network of abstract mental structures. The process is particularly applicable to the work that peer tutors and mentors do with student athletes: first teaching general knowledge and broad concepts, then building upon knowledge (schemata) and making connections between ideas, keying in and utilizing prior knowledge as may be necessary for gaining new knowledge, changing schemata as new information is acquired, and organizing information in a meaningful way.

Training Activity

One method for training tutors is to show videos of instructors teaching class. Videos can be uploaded to YouTube or other popular online formats. It is advisable to film two or three instructors from different disciplines. There are two benefits to be gained from involving more than one instructor in this process. First, the content of the presentation is likely to differ according to the discipline. Also, involving instructors in tutor training can encourage faculty support of the learning assistance program.

Before the training session, trainers should also create copies of a scouting report similar to the one provided in the Appendix. Tutors and mentors will use the scouting report in their training and then will need copies to give to the student athletes with whom they work.

In training, tutors and mentors are provided with an opportunity to review the Scouting Report form prior to viewing the videos and are provided a form for each video to be viewed. Trainees are required to fill out individual scouting reports while watching each of the videos. After using the scouting report to observe instances of cuing behaviors made by the instructor on the video (i.e., writing on the board, changing his or her voice volume, using words such as, "experts agree," etc.), tutors and mentors gather in groups to discuss their reports. Each group compiles a group scouting report, and finally the groups compare notes to share their observations. Based on the cues observed on this video, what would a student need to know on the test over this material?

Assessment

The final discussion with the group at large will afford the tutor and mentor trainer an opportunity to assess the degree to which trainees have grasped the concept of the scouting report. Another opportunity for assessment occurs when tutors and mentors apply what they have learned in sessions with student athletes. Tutors or mentors meet with client student athletes and observe videos together. As they watch the video lecture, the student athlete fills out scouting report forms for each video. After the video lecture, tutor or mentor and student athlete discuss their observations and agree on what they would need to know to do well on an examination over the lecture material. Based on the tutor's or mentor's evaluation, they watch the video once again to look for the instructor's cues, or they watch another video together. The student athlete is then instructed to do a scouting report on each of his or her classes that week and to bring the scouting reports to a follow-up session.

The trainer can assess the learning of the tutor or mentor in part by the quality of the training report completed by the student athlete. Assessment is somewhat more difficult when the student athlete returns with scouting reports from his or her own academic courses, unless the trainer has detailed knowledge of the content of the lectures and relevant test questions.

The process described will also lend itself to implementation in a workshop setting or in a learning strategies class. If tutors or mentors instruct student athletes in the use of scouting reports in a workshop or class session rather than individual tutorials, then the trainer can assess trainee learning by sitting in on the workshop or class as the tutors and mentors demonstrate how to scout out potential classroom exam questions.

References

Anderson, R. C. (1977). The notion of schemata and the educational enterprise: General discussion of the conference. In R. C. Anderson, R. J. Spiro, & W. E. Montague (Eds.), *Schooling and the acquisition of knowledge* (pp. 415–431). Hillsdale, NJ: Lawrence Erlbaum. Retrieved from http://www.sil.org/lingualinks/literacy/implementaliteracyprogram/schematheoryoflearning.htm

Gaston-Gayles, J. L. (2004). Examining academic and athletic motivation among student athletes at a Division I university. *Journal of College Student Development, 45*(1), 75–83.

Appendix

THE SCOUTING REPORT

Athletes are always observing, anticipating: "How does my opponent move? How does she react? Where is he looking? What is her footwork?" In nanoseconds, sharp athletes read their opponents' movements and react accordingly. They "got game," if they do that quickly and cleanly.

You can "get game" in the classroom, too, by employing some of the same strategies you use on the court or on the field and transferring them to the classroom. Whom are you scouting this time?

Your instructors, of course. They may not be as fast as your opponents in competition, but they have moves worth watching.

Following is a list of cues that student athletes should use as a guide for taking good, useful notes:

- The instructor writes something on the board. Always include such items in your notes.

- The instructor says something will be on a test or would make a good exam question.

- The instructor talks about some point that is controversial or some contrasting ideas using words like, "Some people argue that . . . while others think that. . . ."

- The instructor talks about some point or issue about which there is widespread agreement, using words like, "Experts agree. . . ."

- The instructor repeats a point using words like, "again" or "as I said before, . . ."

- The instructor indicates that something he or she is about to say is very important: "Here's the key," or "What's significant is. . . ."

- The instructor uses words indicating absolutes: always, never, none, all, everyone.

- The instructor itemizes key points through reviewing: in conclusion, in summary, "So, to sum up. . . ."

- The instructor uses gestures that could indicate the importance of a point: pointing, waving arms, tapping, or the like.

- The instructor changes his or her movement: the seated instructor stands up; the instructor is leaning and then walks; the instructor stops pacing.

- The instructor demonstrates facial expressions that may indicate he or she is making an important point: grimacing, raising eyebrows, staring intently.

- The volume of the instructor's voice changes.

- The instructor's tempo of delivery changes.

- There is an obvious pause in the instructor's delivery, a loaded silence.

- Other noticeable cues.

Developing Deaf Awareness

Katherine A. Firkins and Aileen M. Rolon

Even though institutions offer tutoring and mentoring sessions to a diverse student population in a variety of subjects, students who are deaf and hard of hearing are often not given the same learning opportunities as their hearing peers when they work with tutors or mentors. A workshop on Deaf Awareness is an essential component of a learning center training program to enhance the skills and cultural knowledge of the tutors and mentors. Recognizing the need to provide deaf and hard-of-hearing students equal access to tutoring and mentoring services and reduce communication barriers promotes a healthy learning environment for academic success.

Training Activity

As deaf and hard-of-hearing students follow their educational paths, it is essential for peer tutors and mentors to understand their needs and accommodations. Tutors and mentors in training need to develop awareness of the following topics: the differences among deaf, hard-of-hearing, and late-deafened individuals; the manual and oral communication systems; some differences between American Sign Language and English; the challenges deaf and hard-of-hearing students face in English; and the support services for deaf and hard-of-hearing students.

Learning center trainers should provide a two-part training workshop on deaf awareness to tutors and mentors who work with deaf and hard-of-hearing students. For the first part of the workshop, trainers need to provide a lecture on the topics mentioned above and use the activity in Appendix A. For the second part, trainers should show *Through Deaf Eyes* (Garey & Hott, 2007), a PBS documentary that provides an overview of the lives of deaf and hard-of-hearing individuals, and have an open discussion with tutors and mentors about the documentary using the PBS discussion guide that is available for download from its website.

DIFFERENCES AMONG DEAF, HARD-OF-HEARING AND LATE-DEAFENED INDIVIDUALS

Trainers should explain to tutors and mentors the differences designated by the terms deaf, hard-of-hearing, and late-deafened and enjoin trainees not to assume that all individuals with hearing loss prefer to be identified as hearing impaired, individuals with hearing impairments, or disabled. By definition, an individual with mild to moderate degree of hearing loss is described as hard of hearing, whereas an individual with moderate to severe loss is deaf (Moore & Levitan, 2003, p. 310). A late-deafened individual is one who becomes deaf as a teenager or adult and "has perspectives and challenges that are markedly different from [individuals] who have been deaf most or all of their lives" (p. 310).

Even though the degree of hearing loss is commonly used to classify an individual as deaf, hard-of-hearing, or late-deafened, identification is influenced by the individual's cultural affiliation, upbringing, and personal preference. Some individuals who are audiologically deaf prefer to identify themselves as hard-of-hearing as "they're caught between both Hearing and Deaf communities—wanting to remain in the Hearing community, but having difficulty coping with hearing loss" (Moore & Levitan, 2003, p. 313). Conversely, some individuals who are classified as hard-of-hearing label themselves as deaf due to their cultural affiliation with the deaf community (p. 313).

MANUAL AND ORAL COMMUNICATION SYSTEMS

It is important for tutors and mentors to recognize manualism and oralism as two different communication approaches for individuals with hearing loss. Manual communication is defined as using sign language to convey meaning through various hand shapes, positions, and movements; body movements; gestures; and facial expressions. Sign language methods widely used among deaf individuals in the United States are American Sign Language (ASL), Manually Coded English (MCE), and Contact Sign. ASL is a natural language that does not follow the structure of English. MCE, on the other hand, is a methodical language that uses English-based signs to emphasize different aspects of the linguistic features of English that are not found in ASL, such as prefixes (e.g., un- and re-), suffixes (e.g., -ness and -ment), participles (e.g., -ing), particles (e.g., *an* and *the*), and verbal past tense (e.g., -ed) (Moore & Levitan, 2003, p. 71). Contact Sign is a model of contact (connection) between ASL and English and is frequently referred to as Pidgin Sign English (Lane, Hoffmeister, & Bahan, 1996, p. 64).

Oral communication is described as speaking and lipreading instead of signing. Tutors and mentors need to understand that "a person who is hard-of-hearing . . . or late-deafened will generally have much clearer speech than one who is born deaf or early-deafened" (Moore & Levitan, 2003, p. 210). Trainees should recognize that deaf and hard-of-hearing individuals have different ways of understanding speech. Some individuals use their residual hearing along with assistive devices (e.g., hearing aids and cochlear implants), some use visual supplements (e.g., lipreading, facial expressions, and gestures), and some use both. Tutors and mentors should not assume that deaf individuals have a "magical" ability to read lips (p. 191). Deaf individuals on average lipread only 30% of the words in a spoken sentence, and perhaps more if the context of the conversation is known (Communications Services for the Deaf of Minnesota, 2009).

Tutors and mentors should learn that not all deaf and hard-of-hearing individuals are fluent in both signing and speaking. Some are sign language users, some are oral, and some are both. It is imperative for tutors and mentors to know each deaf or hard-of-hearing student's preference of communicating in the tutoring or mentoring session, whether it may be using sign language or speaking. Tutors and mentors should not be surprised or alarmed if the student feels more comfortable texting or using pen and paper rather than signing or speaking.

STRUGGLES WITH ENGLISH

Tutors and mentors should be taught that not all deaf and hard-of-hearing students are fluent in written English, and therefore some may need additional assistance with its grammatical structure. Deaf and hard-of-hearing individuals do not have the same advantages as their hearing counterparts in terms of learning English because its "written form involves the representation of sounds they may never have heard" (Schein & Stewart, 1995, p. 293). The median literacy level of an 18-year-old deaf or hard-of-hearing individual is the same as that of a 9- or 10-year-old hearing student at the fourth- or fifth-grade level (Toscano, McKee, & Lepoutre, 2002).

Deaf and hard-of-hearing individuals who struggle with English may produce writings that are similar to those of students who are learning English as a second language, portraying patterns of misuse in participles and infinitives, pluralizations, subject-verb agreement, adjective-noun and noun-adjective confusion, active and passive voice, and more (Schein & Stewart, 1995, p. 152). In addition, deaf and hard-of-hearing individuals may confuse the linguistic features of ASL and English and use the structure of ASL in their writings.

Tutors and mentors who work with deaf and hard-of-hearing students on their English skills need to be cognizant that ASL is a separate language from English and is not in any way a broken, mimed, or gestural form of English. ASL is a visual spoken language, whereas English is a written and auditory spoken language (Communication Services for the Deaf of Minnesota, 2009). Linguistic features of ASL and English differ: "Since the role of each sign in the sentence is revealed in the modified sign itself, ASL, like many spoken languages such as Russian, does not have to restrict word order, as English does, in order to indicate roles" (Lane et al., 1996, pp. 81–82). Examples of sentence constructions that are used to convey meaning in ASL include Subject-Verb-Object sentences (e.g., I-GIVE-IT), Subject-Object-Verb sentences (e.g., MAN BOOK READ for "the man reads the book"), and Object-Subject-Verb sentences (e.g., CAR DOG JUMP-ON-IT for "the dog jumped on the car") (Schein & Stewart, 1995, p. 56).

Even if tutors and mentors do not know ASL, they should recognize the linguistic issues and challenges that deaf and hard-of-hearing students face in their writings and use the most appropriate techniques and resources in the sessions. Trainers should suggest techniques that apply to students who struggle with English and recommend resources that focus on literacy issues, such as books by Paul (1998) and McAnnally, Rose, and Quigley (1999).

SUPPORT SERVICES FOR DEAF AND HARD-OF-HEARING STUDENTS

Tutors and mentors need to be aware of interpreting, captioning, and notetaking as the most commonly used support services that enable deaf and hard-of-hearing students to have equal communication access in the educational setting. Interpreting services are popular among deaf and hard-of-hearing students who use ASL as their primary language. An interpreter accommodates the student's preference of the sign language method and translates spoken English into ASL, English-based signs, or contact signs.

TypeWell and Realtime are two different types of captioning services that are commonly used among hard-of-hearing students and late-deafened adults who are not fluent in sign language. A TypeWell captionist types the most important information provided in the professor's lecture, whereas a Communication Access Realtime Translation (CART) captionist types the professor's lecture verbatim. Both TypeWell and CART captioning transcriptions are viewed from a computer screen and are obtained as notes for future reference. Notetaking is the simplest form of captioning; a notetaker handwrites the lecture in the format of notes in class.

It is significant for tutors and mentors to know that deaf and hard-of-hearing students may not have an interpreter or captionist with them to facilitate communication in the learning center. An interpreter or captionist is usually guaranteed to be provided (by disability services) for class sessions but may not be available for tutoring or mentoring sessions. Tutors and mentors should have a pen and paper ready or access to a computer (e.g., Instant Messenger or Word document program) to allow written dialogue to occur and the session to take place.

Tutors and mentors need to find ways to provide support for deaf and hard-of-hearing students. At the same time, they should not pity or express sympathy for deaf and hard-of-hearing individuals or view them as less intelligent or lesser beings in any way. Instead, tutors and mentors should treat deaf and hard-of-hearing individuals with respect and accept their differences: "Deaf people don't want to know that they will be treated decently only if they can seem like hearing people (lipreading, learning speech, using only English), they want to know that they will be treated decently because they are human with all the rights to life that any other human has" (Batson & Bergman, 1985, p. 316). A sense of belonging is a human necessity, and deaf and hard-of-hearing students merely want equal opportunities to succeed.

Assessment

Trainers should use the Deaf Awareness Test for Tutors and Mentors (Appendix B) as a pre- and posttest assessment tool to measure the learning process. After the two-part workshop, tutors and mentors should be able to identify misconceptions and facts of deaf and hard-of-hearing individuals, the effects of hearing loss, the educational and communication needs and linguistic issues of deaf and hard-of-hearing individuals, and the best tutoring and mentoring practices for deaf and hard-of-hearing students. Further training on deaf awareness is necessary if a tutor or mentor does not provide satisfactory responses on the posttest.

References

Batson, T., & Bergman, E. (1985). *Angels and outcasts: An anthology of deaf characters in literature* (3rd ed.). Washington, DC: Gallaudet University Press.

Communications Services for the Deaf of Minnesota. (2009). *What do you know about deaf culture?* Retrieved from Minnesota Coalition for Battered Women website: http://www.mcbw.org/files/u1/deafculture.pdf

Garey, D., & Hott, L. R. (Producers). (2007). *Through deaf eyes* [DVD]. Washington, DC: WETA. Discussion guide retrieved from http://www.pbs.org/weta/throughdeafeyes/resources/guide.html

Lane, H., Hoffmeister, R., & Bahan, B. (1996). *A journey into the deaf-world.* San Diego, CA: Dawn-SignPress.

McAnally, P. L., Rose, S., & Quigley, S. P. (1999). *Reading practices with deaf learners.* Austin, TX: PRO-ED.

Moore, M. S., & Levitan, L. (2003). *For hearing people only* (3rd ed.). New York, NY: Deaf Life Press.

Paul, P. V. (1998). *Literacy and deafness: The development of reading, writing, and literate thought.* Needham Heights, MA: Allyn & Bacon.

Schein, J. D., & Stewart, D. A. (1995). *Language in motion: Exploring the nature of sign.* Washington, DC: Gallaudet University Press.

Toscano, R. M., McKee, B., & Lepoutre, D. (2002). Success with academic English: Reflections of deaf college students. *American Annals of the Deaf, 147*(1), 5–23.

Appendix A

DEAF AWARENESS TUTOR TRAINING WORKSHOP ACTIVITY

Below are statements by three students who have different types of hearing losses by definition. Read the first portion aloud to the tutors and mentors and ask them to identify the student as deaf, hard-of-hearing, or late-deafened. After they have selected the student's identification, read the second portion to help the tutors and mentors understand how culture, not definition, influences a deaf or hard-of-hearing individual's self-identification.

STUDENT #1 - KEN
I have a moderate to severe hearing loss, and I have a cochlear implant and use speech as my primary mode of communication even though I can sign fairly well.
Based on definition this student is DEAF.
I prefer to identify myself as hard-of-hearing instead of deaf. I am more comfortable speaking and lipreading instead of signing, and I use a captionist in my classes. I am rarely involved in the deaf community and enjoy being with my hearing peers.

STUDENT #2 - FATIMA
I have a mild to moderate hearing loss, and I use American Sign Language as my primary mode of communication even though I use hearing aids and can speak fairly well.
Based on definition this student is HARD-OF-HEARING.
I prefer to identify myself as deaf instead of hard-of-hearing. I am heavily involved in the deaf community and went to a residential school for the deaf. I am more comfortable signing instead of speaking, and I use an interpreter in my classes. I am completely deaf when I take off my hearing aids and depend on sign language for full communication access.

STUDENT #3 - MARCOS
I recently lost my hearing when I had an accident during my first year of college. I don't know sign language, but I would like to learn someday.
Based on definition this student is LATE-DEAFENED.
I prefer to identify myself as hard of hearing because I can follow a conversation or class lecture most of the time without using an interpreter or captionist. If I have missed some information, I ask my professor questions using a pen and paper.

Appendix B

DEAF AWARENESS TEST FOR TUTORS AND MENTORS

Provide a short answer for each question to demonstrate your understanding of the characteristics, needs, and accommodations of deaf and hard-of-hearing individuals.

1. How do meanings of the terms deaf, hard-of-hearing, and late-deafened differ?

2. How do manual and oral communication systems differ?

3. What are the most commonly used support services that enable deaf and hard-of-hearing students to have equal communication access in the educational setting?

4. Why do some deaf and hard-of-hearing students need additional assistance with their English skills?

5. Why shouldn't tutors and mentors express pity or sympathy for deaf and hard-of-hearing individuals?

Tutoring and Mentoring Students With Disabilities

 Jane E. Varakin

The number of students with disabilities pursuing postsecondary education continues to increase. According to Lederman (2005), it is estimated that one third of students with disabilities have taken postsecondary courses within 2 years of graduating from high school. In recent years, from 10% to more than 11% of all undergraduate students reported having a disability (Berkner & Choy, 2008; Horn, Nevill, & Griffin, 2006). Students with disabilities are protected by Section 504 of the Rehabilitation Act of 1973 and the Americans with Disabilities Act (ADA) as Amended (2008), which ensure equal and appropriate access to the curriculum and educational environment. In the postsecondary educational setting, the student with a disability is responsible for self-identification and for providing the supporting evaluative documentation that speaks to the nature and functional limitations of the disability and how the disability specifically impacts learning. The level of support that students with disabilities require varies individually; however, factors such as level of preparedness, self-advocacy skills, type and severity of disability, and willingness to request reasonable academic accommodations and learning support are some of the factors that influence the success of a student with a disability in the postsecondary education setting (Office of Disability Employment Policy, 2002).

For tutors and mentors to be able to provide services for students with disabilities effectively, they must understand that the student with a disability is a person first, with her or his own unique personality, talents, cultural background, beliefs, and educational values, who has met the admission criteria for study at the postsecondary institution. It is also helpful to recognize that while there are several models explaining disability (see Evans, 2008, for a review), some may be more useful in a tutoring or mentoring context than others. For example, the medical model's focus is on pathology and diagnosis. If a tutor's attitude toward disability is based solely on the medical model, the tutor may have difficulty accepting the idea that students with disabilities can meet all criteria for admission to college. On the other hand, the social constructivist model and the social justice perspective each propose that social norms and societal barriers, not individual pathology, create disability. If a tutor's orientation toward disability is based on these perspectives, the tutor is mindful that a tutee's learning environment may not always be fully accessible. Furthermore, tutors who have a social justice orientation believe their tutees are unique, multifaceted individuals who are capable of learning.

Categorization of disability may unfortunately perpetuate false stereotypes, disregard other aspects of identity, and fail to focus on strengths and assets (Smart, 2001). Moreover, simulation exercises intended to allow people without disabilities to feel empathy and gain insight into the disability experience may have a negative impact and actually increase prejudice and discrimination (Smart, 2001). By exercising caution with the categorization, definition, and interpretation of disability, trainers of tutors and mentors can provide a better foundation for conceptualizing ranges of disability.

Smart (2001) has provided some basic disability terms and definitions that tutor and mentor trainers may find useful:

- *Disability* is the presence of a physical, intellectual, cognitive, or psychiatric condition that impairs functioning.

- *Congenital disabilities* are present at or around birth.

- *Acquired disabilities* occur after birth at some point during the lifespan.

- *Physical disabilities* include mobility impairments, neurologic impairments, musculoskeletal conditions, sensory loss, and health disorders.

- *Intellectual disabilities* include mental retardation, Down syndrome, and autism spectrum disorders.

- *Cognitive disabilities* include impaired perception, memory, information processing, reasoning, sensory discrimination, and attention.

- *Psychiatric disabilities* include mental illness and chemical and substance abuse.

Other terms used to describe disability include hidden or visible disability, or indicate the degree of disability as mild, moderate, or severe.

Disability also has specific clinical, legal, cultural, and personal definitions, depending on the context (Smart, 2001). Students with disabilities in college may be receiving academic accommodations based on the legal definition of disability in Section 504 of the Rehabilitation Act of 1973 or the ADA. The student disability services office may also provide tutors and mentors with general clinical information about a particular disability. Students with disabilities, if they disclose, are likely to offer their personal or cultural definition of disability; however, it is known that college students with disabilities often have difficulties with self-advocacy skills (Vogel, Fresko, & Wertheim, 2007) and also may have legitimate reasons for choosing not to disclose. The main reason students with disabilities may be hesitant to disclose is risk; they are uncertain about the stereotypes others might hold, how others might react, and ultimately, how they themselves will be treated (Alexandrin, Schreiber, & Henry, 2008).

Interaction strain is a term for the discomfort, tension, and ambiguity a person without a disability may feel when interacting with a person with a disability, symptoms of which may be shorter duration of interaction, less physical and eye contact, and avoidance of personal topics during conversation (Smart, 2001). Training of peer tutors and mentors should attempt to reduce interaction strain and increase knowledge about disability issues.

Training Activity

This training session consists of a series of three experiences and activities totaling around 3 hours. The sessions should be held in a private location, and participants should be reminded of their responsibility to preserve confidentiality of disclosures.

INTERVIEWING STUDENTS WITH DISABILITIES

The trainer invites two or three students with disabilities to the training session. These students should be willing to speak informally and openly about their personal experiences in college as they relate to having a disability. Tutors and mentors are asked to come prepared with a list of questions to ask these students. Such questions could include these: How do you feel about asking for help? What stereotypes and prejudices do you encounter as a student with a disability? When and to whom do you disclose your disability and why? In what ways can tutors and mentors be better prepared to assist students with disabilities? How can we reduce interaction strain with people who are different from ourselves?

This activity is based on the contact theory, which posits that prejudice and discrimination toward people with disabilities will decrease when people without disabilities are encouraged to interact with people with disabilities. Conditions need to be met to ensure a positive outcome: contact assumes relationships of equal social status, contact occurs under voluntary conditions, contact facilitates viewing the persons with disabilities as individuals, and both parties have the same goal (Smart, 2001).

PERSONAL EXPERIENCES AND KNOWLEDGE OF PEOPLE WITH DISABILITIES

According to the Kraus, Stoddard, and Gilmartin (1996), about one in five people in the U.S. has a disability. The odds are good that tutors and mentors in training personally know someone who has a disability. The trainer invites trainees to think of someone they know well who has a disability but not to choose someone whom others would know. Trainees should identify this individual only by relationship (e.g., as a friend or relative) or by a pseudonym. Trainees write responses to the following questions: How does this person respond to his or her disability? How has disability influenced this person's life in the areas of social relationships, work, school, or family? What resources does this person use to enhance his or her functioning? Most of the hour is needed for open discussion.

ASSISTIVE TECHNOLOGY AND UNIVERSAL DESIGN

Major advances in assistive technology have occurred over the last 10 years, some of which were specifically designed to help people with disabilities, and others of which were developed to make various activities of daily living and work tasks more efficient for everyone. Universal design is a relatively new concept that aims to create environments that are easy and effective for all people to use. In higher education, universal design not only applies to the physical inclusivity of the classroom and campus environment but also to instruction itself. Universal instructional design (UID) incorporates flexible teaching and diversity in the measurement of learning and the various forms learning is demonstrated. UID creates a learning experience for all students while accounting for learning differences (Johnson & Fox, 2003).

This activity focuses on both the exploration of assistive technology commonly used by people with disabilities in the college environment and the evaluation of the accessibility of campus spaces that are frequently used for tutoring and mentoring. If possible, disability services staff and the accessibility coordinator should help facilitate this activity to explore assistive technology and meeting spaces that are frequently used on campus. Some suggestions of assistive technology to explore include text-to-speech programs, speech recognition programs, screen-reading software, text telephones, and automatic door openers. Examples of campus spaces to evaluate by universal design principles as related to tutoring and mentoring students with disabilities could include the library, student union, learning center, empty classrooms, and study lounges.

The group travels to the various areas where assistive technology and campus spaces can be explored. Large training groups can be divided into two or three smaller groups, but all reconvene at a common location to problem-solve and discuss together UID considerations in tutoring and mentoring. Just as posting class notes online benefits all students and not just those with hearing disabilities, changes in learning center practice could remove barriers and enable more students. What barriers to learning have been erected by the procedures and practices of the learning center? How would removal of these barriers welcome all to tutoring and mentoring and encourage learning?

Assessment

There are several important learning outcomes for tutors and mentors who work with students with disabilities. Peer tutors and mentors will demonstrate confidence when working with students with disabilities, become more comfortable discussing disability directly with students who do have a disability, and take into consideration the accessibility of the practices and of the space used for tutoring and mentoring to be inclusive for all students, including those with disabilities. Furthermore, tutors and mentors will understand that students with disabilities are people first and will have a diverse range of responses to their disability and college experience. Tutors and mentors will be able to refer students with disabilities successfully to relevant support services on campus when necessary. Because tutors or mentors may not always be aware they are working with a student with a disability, and their supervisors may not be able to disclose such information, assessing these learning outcomes will be done informally.

At the end of this training session, tutors and mentors should be encouraged to discuss or write out specific instances in which they have felt either challenged or successful when working with students with disabilities. The learning outcomes should be framed as direct questions to the tutors and mentors at the conclusion of the session.

References

Alexandrin, J. R., Schreiber, I. L., & Henry, E. (2008). Why not disclose? In J. L. Higbee & E. Goff (Eds.), *Pedagogy and student services for institutional transformation: Implementing universal design in higher education* (pp. 377–392). Minneapolis, MN: University of Minnesota. Retrieved from http://www.cehd.umn.edu/passit/docs/PASS-IT-Book.pdf

Americans With Disabilities Act of 1990, as Amended, 42 U.S.C. 12101 *et seq.* (2008).

Berkner, L., & Choy, S. (2008). *Descriptive summary of 2003–04 beginning postsecondary students: Three years later* (NCES 2008-174). U.S. Department of Education. Washington DC: National Center for Education Statistics. Retrieved from http://nces.ed.gov/pubs2008/2008174.pdf

Evans, N. J. (2008). Theoretical foundations of universal instructional design. In J. L. Higbee & E. Goff (Eds.), *Pedagogy and student services for institutional transformation: Implementing universal design in higher education* (pp. 11–23). Minneapolis, MN: University of Minnesota. Retrieved from http://www.cehd.umn.edu/passit/docs/PASS-IT-Book.pdf

Horn, L., Nevill, S., & Griffin, J. (2006). *Profile of undergraduates in U.S. postsecondary education institutions: 2003–04 with a special analysis of community college students.* Washington, DC: U.S. Department of Education, National Center for Education Statistics, Institute of Education Sciences. Retrieved from http://nces.ed.gov/pubsearch/pubsinfo.asp?pubid=2006184

Johnson, D. M., & Fox, J. A. (2003). Creating curb cuts in the classroom. In J. L. Higbee (Ed.), *Curriculum transformation and disability: Implementing universal design in higher education* (pp. 7–22). Minneapolis, MN: University of Minnesota. Retrieved from http://www.cehd.umn.edu/crdeul/books-ctad.html

Kraus, L., Stoddard, S., & Gilmartin, D. (1996). *Chartbook on disability in the United States, 1996.* Washington, DC: U.S. National Institute on Disability & Rehabilitation Research.

Lederman, D. (2005, July 29). College and the disabled student. *Inside Higher Ed.* Retrieved from http://www.insidehighered.com/news/2005/07/29/disabled

Office of Disability Employment Policy. (2002). *Communicating with and about people with disabilities.* Retrieved from http://www.dol.gov/odep/pubs/fact/comucate.htm

Rehabilitation Act of 1973, Section 504 as amended, 29 U.S.C 794 *et seq.* (1973).

Smart, J. (2001). *Disability, society, and the individual.* Gaithersburg, MD: Aspen.

Vogel, G., Fresko, B., & Wertheim, C. (2007). Peer tutoring for college students with learning disabilities: Perceptions of tutors and tutees. *Journal of Learning Disabilities, 40,* 485–493. doi:10.1177/00222194070400060101

Adult Students

Suzanne Ponicsan

Tutors and mentors should be trained to understand the varying experiences of older adult learners and develop competence in providing a supportive atmosphere. However, readers must first understand the difference between traditional and nontraditional adult students. According to the National Center for Education Statistics (Choy, 2002) and using their terminology, traditional students earned a high school diploma and enrolled in college immediately after high school, rely on their parents financially, and work part-time if at all. By contrast, nontraditional students have delayed entry into college for a year or more. They tend to enroll less than full time, may work 35 hours a week or more, are often financially independent, and may have children (Choy, 2002). Additionally, the skills they need for success in higher education (e.g., reading, computer, writing, time management, and critical thinking) need to be exercised and more fully developed (Byrd & MacDonald, 2005; Norman Davies Group, 2005). This training module begins with a brief summary of adult learning theories followed by an interactive training activity and methods of assessment.

Merriam and Brockett (1997) wrote that "an understanding of adults and how they learn is vital to successful adult education practice" (p. 129), and the term *andragogy* refers to "a way of thinking about working with adult learners" (p. 135) that contrasts with *pedagogy*, teaching children. In *The Adult Learner* (Knowles, Holton, & Swanson, 2005), Knowles, who had significant influence with this theory, described six main principles about adult learning:

- Adult learners need to know the reasoning behind their learning.

- Adult learners need to take responsibility for their own learning.

- Adult learners bring a diverse array of experience to their classes.

- Adult learners need to learn material they can apply to their lives.

- Adult learners "are life centered (or task centered or problem centered)" (p. 67).

- Adult learners are more responsive to intrinsic motivators.

Andragogy is also referred to as self-directed learning. This is "how individuals go about the process of learning on their own and what attributes can be associated with learners who are self-directed" (Caffarella & Merriam, 2000, p. 57). Caffarella and Merriam provided examples of how instructors might apply self-directed learning by permitting students to "write their own learning objectives, choose how they will learn the material, and evaluate what they have learned" (p. 58). Tutoring and mentoring sessions, too, can support adult, self-directed learning; tutors and mentors allow their student clients to identify the areas in which they need assistance and to direct their own session. By asking open-ended questions, tutors and mentors also help students evaluate their own understanding.

Another theory of adult learning useful for trainers of peer tutors and mentors is transformational learning. This theory, developed by Mezirow (2000), claims that growth and learning are magnified when individuals make meaning of their learning experience. Mezirow wrote that adult learning needs to include "contextual understanding, critical reflection on assumptions, and validating meaning by assessing reasons" (p. 3) in order to justify what we believe to be true. In other words, it "is about change—dramatic, fundamental changes in the way individuals see themselves and the world in which they live" (Caffarella & Merriam, 2000, p. 58). As quoted in Merriam and Brockett (1997), Clark explained that transformational learning

> produces more far-reaching changes in the learners than does learning in general, and . . . these changes have a significant impact on the learner's subsequent experiences. In short, transformational learning *shapes* people; they are different afterward in ways both they and others can recognize. (p. 142)

The main seeds of transformational learning are critical thinking and analysis or self-reflection. McGonigal (2005) listed numerous examples of how to implement such learning in class: provide conflicting viewpoints of a topic, use critical questioning techniques, allow students to talk through their thinking, and have them evaluate a situation and then justify their position. These techniques may be easily applied to tutoring and mentoring sessions as well.

Another adult learning theory useful for tutors and mentors is Vygotsky's (1978) Zone of Proximal Development. This "zone" falls between what the learner can do alone and what the learner cannot do; it emcompasses what the learner can do with assistance. Based on Vygotsky's theory, adult learners can be challenged beyond their current abilities within their zone of proximal development with a peer tutor or mentor providing critical support of learning. Tutors may ask tutees to explain what they know about a given topic—even if tutees feel their knowledge is incomplete—and then help them expand that knowledge by providing explanations and examples. Mentors may ask student clients to explain an instructor's purpose for a particular assignment or the design of a test, and then expand their understanding with faculty perspectives on instructional motives.

Finally, theories of instruction are also an important component to the learning process. These theories "attempt to relate specific events comprising instruction to learning processes and learning outcomes, drawing upon knowledge generated by learning research and theory" (Gagné & Dick, 1983, p. 264). Gagné and Dick (1983) referred to the Gagné-Briggs theory, which describes nine events, both internal and external, that lead to learning: (a) gaining students' attention, (b) informing them of the learning objective, (c) stimulating recall of the prerequisites, (d) presenting the stimulus material, (e) providing "learning guidance" (p. 266), (f) eliciting the performance, (g) providing feedback, (h) assessing the performance, and (i) enhancing retention and transfer of learning.

These nine events directly relate not just to classroom learning but also to tutoring and mentoring sessions. At the beginning of each session, tutors and mentors first ensure that students are comfortable and then set goals for the session and review content from previous sessions. During the sessions, tutors and mentors instruct or guide the student, allowing time for the student to practice using the new ideas, and then provide feedback on their progress. Tutors and mentors should encourage their student clients to be more active by letting them speak and solve or identify problems. By the end of a session, students should have met the goal and demonstrated mastery of the concept for their independent course work.

Training Activity

Through discussion and lecture with PowerPoint®, tutors and mentors will learn the various adult learning theories that explain how the adult learner learns, along with common barriers to adult learning. After being given various adult learner scenarios, trainees will identify possible tutoring or mentoring options for the learners along with a plan of action for working with them. Results will then be shared and discussed. Depending on the number of participants, 1–2 hours should be allotted for this training activity. Time approximations may be modified as necessary.

A whiteboard or large display surface should be available as well as pencil and paper for the trainees. The only equipment necessary is an AV screen and computer to show a PowerPoint® presentation.

The training activity should be held in one room that is large enough to accommodate all tutoring or mentoring staff. No particular arrangement of tables and chairs is necessary, although participants may find it helpful to have chairs arranged in a circle around the room so they can see and hear each other.

Trainees will first be introduced to the major adult learning theories mentioned earlier in this training module. Showing a PowerPoint® presentation that provides this information and providing corresponding handouts would be helpful. Afterwards, trainees should be asked to identify various characteristics (or barriers) they have noticed in tutoring adult learners; this will provide actual examples of the differences between traditional and nontraditional students. For example, some may comment on adults intimidated by the idea of returning to school at an older age; their lack of current skills (e.g., using the computer, reading comprehension, mathematics skills); and the difficulties associated with studying, working, and caring for a family, including elderly parents. Most responses may be drawn from the experience of seasoned members of the staff. The presentation and discussion will require 15–30 minutes.

The trainer will then project on the screen or draw three or more stick figures (representing student clients) on the display board with a short, unique story underneath for each. (See Appendix for examples.) Trainees, individually or in small groups, will need to identify all possible tutoring or mentoring options available. For example, if a student is unable to visit during the tutoring lab's hours due to work or family commitments, then online tutoring or telephone sessions may be the best option. Other options may include in-house tutoring or counseling. This activity is based upon Gagné-Briggs' nine events, in which learning is enhanced if the student client and peer tutor or mentor develop learning objectives (Gagné & Dick, 1983). The time required for this segment of the training is approximately 15 minutes.

When trainees have established these options, they must devise a plan of action for each situation, including short-term and long-term goals. Short-term goals would be beneficial for students who understand the material relatively well but may be "stuck" on one or two areas. In this case, occasional visits as necessary may work best for the student. However, if a student regularly struggles with course material, ongoing use of the learning center's services may be required throughout the length of the course. This activity incorporates the basic theories of Knowles (andragogy), Mezirow (transformational learning), and Gagné-Briggs' nine events; peer tutors and mentors work with the student clients to establish together a direction for their learning and develop meaningful learning experiences. The time required for this segment of the training is approximately 15 minutes.

At the end of the session, trainees will share their plans and engage in a group discussion. Discussion should center on the effectiveness and appropriateness of the plans, how they relate to the theories of adult learning, and what was the most important concept they have learned from this activity. The time required for this segment of the training is approximately 15 minutes.

Tutors and mentors need to understand that adult students they work with come from a variety of backgrounds and that each has unique needs; thus, there is no one correct way to tutor every student. Although encouraging students to utilize various resources offered by the institution is helpful, tutors and mentors must also be creative in how they can best assist the student. Understanding the theories of Knowles, Mezirow, Vygotsky, and Gagné and applying their knowledge of adult learners to sessions will greatly benefit the trainees as they will better understand adult learners' needs and barriers—particularly those of nontraditional adult students. Further, the training activities will better equip trainees to help students achieve their goal of a college education.

Assessment

Assessment for this activity is based on the sharing of plans and group discussion. However, close monitoring of the trainees by their supervisor will also determine the extent of their knowledge as they apply these theories to their tutoring and mentoring practice.

References

Byrd, K. L., & MacDonald, G. (2005). Defining college readiness from the inside out: First-generation college student perspectives. *Community College Review, 33*(1), 22–39. doi:10.1177/009155210503300102

Caffarella, R., & Merriam, S. B. (2000). Linking the individual learner to the context of adult learning. In A. L. Wilson & S. B. Hayes (Eds.), *Handbook of adult and continuing education* (pp. 55–70). San Francisco, CA: Jossey-Bass.

Choy, S. (2002, August). *Findings from the condition of education 2002: Nontraditional undergraduates.* Retrieved from http://nces.ed.gov/programs/coe/analysis/2002a-sa01.asp

Gagné, R. M., & Dick, W. (1983). Instructional psychology. *Annual Review of Psychology, 34,* 261–295. doi:10.1146/annurev.ps.34.020183.001401

Knowles, M., Holton, E., & Swanson, R. A. (2005). *The adult learner: The definitive classic in adult education and human resource development* (6th ed.). Burlington, MA: Elsevier.

McGonigal, K. (2005, Spring). Teaching for transformation: From learning theory to teaching strategies. *Speaking of Teaching, 14*(2), 1–4.

Merriam, S. B., & Brockett, R. G. (1997). *The profession and practice of adult education: An introduction.* San Francisco, CA: Jossey-Bass.

Mezirow, J. (2000). Learning to think like an adult: Core concepts of transformation theory. In J. Mezirow (Ed.), *Learning as transformation: Critical perspectives on a theory in progress* (pp. 3–33). San Francisco, CA: Jossey-Bass.

Norman Davies Group. (2005). *Making the decision to return to college.* Retrieved from http://www.adultstudentcenter.com/articles/feature_nov05.html

Vygotsky, L. S. (1978). *Mind and society: The development of higher psychological processes.* Cambridge, MA: Harvard University Press.

Appendix

SAMPLE TUTORING SCENARIOS FOR OLDER STUDENTS

Scenario 1

John is a 43-year-old who spent most of his career in the construction industry. Since the economy's downturn, he has been laid off and forced to seek new employment elsewhere. Because the health field seemed promising, he decided to seek a bachelor's degree in the health studies program. However, if the decision to enroll was difficult, the courses are even more difficult. His previous career did not require the use of computers, and most of his current academic work (e.g., essays, presentations) requires the use of various electronic tools. He is not currently employed and is the single parent of a 6-year-old boy.

Scenario 2

Sara, a 52-year-old Latina, earned an associate's degree in criminal justice at a local community college. The institution did not have a bachelor's program in the field, so she transferred to a private institution. The expectations in course work were much higher at the private school, and she struggled academically. Sara has cerebral palsy; her lips cannot move well, so her speech is difficult to understand, and her fingers are gnarled and stiff, making notetaking and keyboarding difficult. She also works a full-time job at a local hospital.

Scenario 3

Sierra is a single mother of one boy, age 12, who is receiving treatment for bipolar disorder. She works full time at a law office and attends college part time in the legal studies program. Her most recent schooling was high school—20 years ago. She has not written a research paper in years and feels overwhelmed with all the writing, researching, and studying she is required to complete each week.

Andragogy: Tutoring and Mentoring Adult Learners

Leah Allen Jones

Adult learners are commonly defined as those who label themselves as adults and participate in educational activities to increase skills or knowledge (Merriam & Brockett, 1996). The National Center for Education Statistics reported that 6.8 million adult learners age 25 and older enrolled in higher education in 2007 (U.S. Department of Education, 2008), and the number of students in this age group is expected to increase (Lumina Foundation, 2009). One study by Silva, Calahan, and Lacireno-Paquet (1998) reported that adults experience psychological, social, and economic challenges to participation and persistence in higher education. Tutors and mentors can be especially helpful to adult students as they overcome these challenges.

Adult learners are reported to share some common characteristics. First, because stereotypes and cultural ideas may propagate the myth that adults cannot think or learn as well as younger students, tutors and mentors of adults must know that even adults over age 60 are capable of learning (Bjorklund & Bee, 2008; Merriam & Caffarella, 1999). In addition, according to Knowles, Holten, and Swanson (2005), adults want to direct themselves, define themselves, and learn through experiences. They also want to learn information immediately relevant to their lives. Moreover, they are used to working collaboratively in employment. Because it may have been a long time since they were in a structured learning environment, they may lack study skills and feel some anxiety about being in a college setting. However, an adult learner may demonstrate some of these concerns but not others. Therefore, although these characteristics are commonly shared by adult learners, effective tutors and mentors will interact with adults as individuals, seeking to understand their individual experience.

Effective practices for tutoring and mentoring adults build on positive characteristics of adult learners (Knowles & Associates, 1984). First, successful tutors and mentors encourage self-direction by helping adults evaluate learning needs (Knowles et al., 2005). For example, a tutor or mentor can ask adults what they understand already or use pretests to help adults determine their learning needs. In addition, effective tutors and mentors help learners set goals and give frequent and positive feedback. Also, to help adult students maintain motivation, tutors and mentors can help them see the immediate relevance of what they are learning. A tutor or mentor can demonstrate the relevance of course material by helping adult students connect what they are learning to problems they are currently facing.

Successful tutors and mentors use experiences as the foundation of learning, both by helping adults relate new information to past experiences and by creating new learning experiences. For example, tutors and mentors can provide time for adults to reflect on prior knowledge about a situation or task and give real-life examples to support theories. In addition, collaborative and active learning strategies are just as effective with adults as with younger learners (Knowles et al., 2005). For example, adult students can learn well by teaching each other in small groups. In other words, adult students may function best when actively engaged in doing things rather than being told about things.

Although these strategies typically work for adult learners, effective tutors and mentors accommodate learning differences rather than interact with adults as a homogeneous group (Knowles et al., 2005). Since effective study strategies are essential for college success, mentors can help adults discover their learning preferences, and tutors can help adult learners develop a repertoire of effective learning strategies.

The following activity is structured to model various techniques effective in teaching adult learners. Tutors and mentors will not only learn the information better through active engagement but also see examples of effective practices for their own use.

Training Activity

By the end of the session on adult learning, tutors and mentors will be able to identify adult learners, identify characteristics of adult learners and best practices for tutoring and mentoring adults, and design activities for adults. Two different activities in the training session serve as assessment of these skills. The following materials and resources will be needed: handouts and self-assessment worksheets, index cards for each participant, large sheets of paper or poster board for each group, and movable chairs and tables to allow group work. This workshop activity models adult learning and teaching techniques for participants and requires approximately 90 minutes.

The trainer begins by asking participants how they identify an adult learner. Answers are discussed together, and the group creates a shared definition of adult learners.

The trainer asks participants to write on one side of a note card one challenge they have in tutoring or mentoring adults. Trainees are asked to exchange cards with someone in the workshop and discuss both challenges.

Distributing the handout, "Tutoring and Mentoring the Adult Learner" (the Appendix to this module), the trainer briefly describes andragogy (as distinguished from pedagogy) and asks participants to evaluate to what extent their experiences as learners reflect the characteristics of many adult learners. Trainees discuss with the trainer their ideas for designing interactive, collaborative learning activities in a variety of tutor subject areas and mentor settings.

A group activity follows: Trainees write on the other side of the note card one activity that they currently use or a new activity they could use in their work with adult learners. Next participants share their activity with the people at their tables. Then each group at a table writes on a large sheet of paper or poster board these activities and other activities the group develops together. The small groups share their ideas with the entire group, and all discuss them.

Assessment

The trainer distributes a self-assessment worksheet and allows time for participants to complete it. The self-assessment may ask these three questions: How will you know when you are working with an adult learner? What are three activities you can employ to help adult learners be self-directed and maintain motivation to reach their goals? In your work as a tutor or mentor, how can you help adults deal effectively with a new situation or learn new information?

Time should be allowed at the end of the session for questions and answers. Trainees should refer to the questions on the note cards from the beginning of the session to see if their questions and challenges have been addressed.

As workshop participants present their groups' ideas for working with adult learners, the trainer can gauge and guide their responses to be consistent with andragogic theories. Briefly overviewing trainees' self-assessments before the end of the workshop will allow trainers to gauge participants' understanding and provide explanation where necessary in the question-and-answer session or in individual discussions with tutors and mentors.

References

Bjorklund, B. R., & Bee, H. L. (2008). *The journey of adulthood.* Upper Saddle River, NJ: Prentice Hall.

Knowles, M. S., & Associates. (1984). *Andragogy in action.* San Francisco, CA: Jossey-Bass.

Knowles, M. S., Holton, E. F., & Swanson, R. A. (2005). *The adult learner: The definitive classic in adult education and human resource development.* Burlington, MA: Elsevier.

Lumina Foundation. (2009). No more kid stuff: Colleges and universities take a mature approach to serving adult students. *Focus*, Fall 2009. Retrieved from http://www.luminafoundation.org/publications/focus_archive/Focus_Fall_2009.pdf

Merriam, S. B., & Brockett, R. G. (1996). *The profession and practice of adult education.* San Francisco, CA: Jossey-Bass.

Merriam, S. B., & Caffarella, R. S. (1999). *Learning in adulthood: A comprehensive guide.* San Francisco, CA: Jossey-Bass.

Silva, T., Calahan, M., & Lacireno-Paquet, N. (1998). *Adult education participation decisions and barriers: Reviews of conceptual frameworks and empirical studies* (National Center for Education Statistics Working Paper No. 98-10). Washington, DC: U.S. Department of Education, National Center for Education Statistics. Retrieved from http:/nces.ed.gov/pubs98/9810.pdf

U.S. Department of Education, National Center for Education Statistics. (2008, October). Table 191: Total fall enrollment in degree-granting institutions by level of enrollment, sex, age, and attendance status of student: 2007. *Digest of Education Statistics.* Retrieved from http://nces.ed.gov/programs/digest/d08/tables/dt08_191.asp

Appendix

TUTORING AND MENTORING THE ADULT LEARNER

Based on Knowles, Holton, and Swanson's (2005) Theory of Andragogy

Common Characteristics of Adult Learners

- Adults are as capable of learning as younger students.
- Adults want to direct their learning and experiences.
- Adults define themselves and learn through experiences.
- Adults are motivated to learn information immediately relevant to their lives.
- Adults may prefer collaborative activities.
- Adults do better at application–based rather than memorization–based assessment.
- Adults have individual differences.
- Adults are often nervous about succeeding in college.
- Adults may lack effective learning strategies and study skills.

Best Practices for Tutoring and Mentoring Adults

- Remind adult students that they are as capable of learning as younger students.
- Let adult students set goals and direct the session.
- Instead of telling, listen and help connect current learning to previous experiences.
- Encourage adult students by pointing out real successes as they are achieved.
- Use collaborative and interactive learning activities.
- Turn assignments into tasks and activities.
- Listen for unique learning skills and preferences.
- Work with adult students to develop the learning strategies that are effective for their courses, tests, and assignments.

Scaffolding Understandings of Students Identifying as LGBTQ

Annemarie Mulkey

Because LGBTQ identity is often unseen, particular obstacles and issues surrounding LBGTQ individuals' academic success are often overlooked. Tutors and mentors need not only to acknowledge the LGBTQ student population but also to become aware of the challenges LGBTQ students experience. Because of the potential physically and emotionally negative ramifications of being LGBTQ or being seen as LGBTQ, D'Emilio (1992) argued that "speaking about gay oppression involves not only addressing injustice in the abstract but also acknowledging the emotional toll it levies on particular individuals and the institutions of which they are a part" (p. 151). This training module will help tutors and mentors (a) recognize heterosexist practices and understand the effects such practices may have on individuals who identify as lesbian, gay, bisexual, transgender, or queer (LGBTQ); (b) become familiar with common LGBTQ terminology; (c) become aware of the stressors placed on individuals who identify as LGBTQ and how they can affect them academically; and (d) apply new knowledge and feel confident in their ability to support LGBTQ students effectively.

Understanding one's own heterosexist prejudices is a necessary starting point for supporting LGBTQ students: "The more aware we are of our own biases and their impact on our behavior, the easier it is to ensure that our personal beliefs don't undermine our efforts to support LGBT students" (Gay, Lesbian, and Straight Education Network [GLSEN], 2009, p. 7). GLSEN suggested that learning "to use LGBTQ-related terminology accurately and respectfully" is an easy beginning to supporting and understanding LGBTQ peoples (p. 8). Terminology helps build foundational knowledge essential to effective and sensitive tutor or mentor relationships. However, it is necessary to go beyond building a foundation of knowledge. If tutors and mentors merely receive knowledge (e.g., handouts or instruction) without practice, they have what Ball and Lardner (1999) called "teacher as technician" constructs of knowledge about students; because these constructs are neither applied nor practiced, they are therefore insufficient scaffolds for tutors and mentors who work with students (p. 417). Instead Ball and Lardner called for higher efficacy in the teacher's ability to teach a particular population of students and in believing their students are able to be successful. It is therefore necessary for tutors and mentors to feel confident in their ability to communicate with LGBTQ students and to ensure that LGBTQ students, like any other population of students, are not marginalized and are able to succeed and contribute to the college or university and to academia as a whole.

Training Activity

This training activity requires 1 hour. A room with movable chairs is needed. This room must be established as a safe space, a location in which participants have agreed to be respectful of diverse peoples and beliefs. Additionally, the trainer should provide a working list of LGBTQ resources on campus.

HETEROSEXISM QUESTIONNAIRE

The trainer should first have trainees take the Heterosexual Questionnaire (Rochlin, 2005). The Heterosexual Questionnaire, which inverts some of the common misconceptions and prejudices about LGBTQ individuals, helps tutors and mentors evaluate how they view and talk about heterosexuality and individuals who identify as LGBTQ.

Through open dialogue, trainees should be invited to share and discuss some of their responses to the questionnaire. The trainer should explain that, as absurd as the inventory is, it accurately represents the kinds of questions regarding sexuality and gender identity that LGBTQ individuals frequently face. Some discussion questions for consideration may include these: What was your gut reaction to these questions? Why do you think you reacted in this way? Were these questions difficult to answer? Why or why not? How would you respond to someone who asks you this question in earnest? What can you do in the future if you hear similar questions being asked about someone's sexual identity or orientation?

LGBTQ TERMINOLOGY

Trainees should review a glossary of LGBTQ terminology as a means of accessing knowledge about LGBTQ issues and identities. The glossary presented in the Appendix is adapted with permission from Advocates for Youth (2005).

The trainer should remind trainees that when talking to or about LGBTQ individuals it is always important to know or ask and respect how each individual self-identifies. The definitions in this glossary should serve only as a starting point for understanding because meanings and identifications shift with each LGBTQ individual. The LGBTQ community, like any other community, is diverse and encompasses many different identities.

CAMPUS AND COMMUNITY RESOURCES

A prepared list of LGBTQ campus and community resources should be provided to trainees. Tutors and mentors should be encouraged to add other resources with which they are familiar. Such resources may include LGBTQ clubs, diversity centers, campus allies, support groups, or specific events.

SCENARIOS FOR ROLE PLAY

Trainees can be divided into pairs or small groups for working with the scenarios provided here. Each group can focus on one scenario, assigned to or selected by the group. Trainees should read the scenario and explain how they would respond. Then they can collaboratively discuss the strengths and possible weaknesses of the tutor's or mentor's sensitivity and understanding of LGBTQ issues and peoples. Tutors and mentors should be encouraged to think about and use the terms learned from the glossary (Appendix) when responding. Trainees should pay attention to how each of these scenarios could influence or impact the student's academic performance.

- Jean has to write a personal narrative for her first-year composition class. She has never before written about being lesbian but now wants to write about her coming out. She is afraid that if she writes about her experience she will receive a bad grade from her professor, who has never mentioned any LGBTQ issues in class.

- Ricki, who has recently started crossdressing, frequently comes to the tutoring center for help with algebra. Some of the other tutors are startled by Ricki's appearance. They make remarks to you and act uncomfortable.

- Jake's roommate, Marcus, is gay. Jake expresses to you his concern that Marcus will hit on him and do "gay stuff" around him. What steps can you take to help Jake avoid anxiety and homophobic stereotypes?

- Adrian is bisexual and tells you that his gay friends have really been bothering him lately. They won't stop trying to convince him that he is just confused and indecisive. They dismiss his defense of his sexuality. The "good humored" hostility he receives from both gay and straight friends makes him feel out of place and misunderstood.

- Luke is taking a persuasive writing class and comes to you for tutoring. In his paper, Luke makes many generalizations and homophobic statements about gays. He also mentions anger and frustration about having to learn about "those queers." Overall his paper lacks a solid argument and critical thinking. How do you assist Luke, who is already hostile?

- Alex recently broke up with her girlfriend. She hints at being very depressed and mentions missing class regularly.

- Gabriella recently came out to her parents. Last night they told her that they will no longer help her pay for school or any of her expenses. She is panicked and distraught because she may have to drop out of school to get a second job.

- Alonso, who identifies as gay, is assigned a group project. He has experienced anxiety and reluctance to participate in the group because of how much the group members discuss their personal lives. He fears telling the group he is gay and is in a relationship, but he also fears lying. He struggles with the prospect of having his life go unacknowledged or devalued, especially in a group in which it seems to matter so much.

- You are active within the queer community and are eager to share your involvement with your peers.

Assessment

Because tutors or mentors may be the only support some LGBTQ students encounter, an awareness of and willingness to understand students' sexual identity is essential and can support their academic success. The trainer can lead trainees in a Think-Pair-Share (Lyman, 1981) exercise in which they present one way they will serve as allies for students who identify as LGBTQ. A second assessment activity is to have tutors and mentors share one way that LGBTQ students make the college or university a better institution.

As trainees work through their roles in the scenarios of the training activity, they are also demonstrating their understanding of the terms and concepts presented in training. The facilitator should therefore use these role plays as another assessment.

References

Advocates for Youth. (2005). Glossary. In *Creating safe space for GLBTQ youth: A toolkit*. Washington, DC: Author. Retrieved from http://www.advocatesforyouth.org/publications/607-glossary

Ball, A., & Lardner, T. (1999). Dispositions toward language: Teacher constructs of knowledge and the Ann Arbor Black English case. In L. Ede (Ed.), *On writing research: The Braddock essays, 1975–1998* (pp. 413–428). Boston, MA: St. Martin's.

D'Emilio, J. (1992). *Making trouble: Essays on gay history, politics, and the university*. New York, NY: Routledge.

Gay, Lesbian, Straight Education Network. (2009). *The safe space kit: Guide to being an ally to LGBT students*. New York, NY: Author.

Lyman, F. T. (1981). The responsive classroom discussion: The inclusion of all students. In A. S. Anderson (Ed.), *Mainstreaming digest* (pp. 109–113). College Park, MD: University of Maryland Press.

Rochlin, M. (2005). Heterosexual questionnaire. *Creating safe space for GLBTQ youth: A toolkit*. Washington, DC: Advocates for Youth. Retrieved from http://www.advocatesforyouth.org/for-professionals/lesson-plans-professionals/223?task=view

Appendix

GLOSSARY OF LGBTQ TERMINOLOGY

Adapted from Advocates for Youth, *Creating safe space for GLBTQ youth: A toolkit,* Washington, DC, copyright 2005 by Advocates for Youth, and used with permission.

Ally—a person or organization that actively helps another with a specific issue; here, one who openly supports and affirms the rights and dignity of GLBTQ people.

Bi—slang term for people with a bisexual orientation and who self-identify as bisexual.

Coming out—from "coming out of the closet," the process of becoming aware of and open about one's sexual orientation or gender identity.

Gay—men who feel romantic, emotional, and sexual attraction to other men; a term used to proclaim self-acceptance and self-affirmation.

Gender identity—an individual's innermost sense of self as male or female, as lying somewhere between these two genders, or as lying somewhere outside gender lines altogether.

Heterosexism—the assumption that everyone is heterosexual (or should be) and that heterosexuality is the only "normal," right, and moral way to be and that, therefore, anyone of a different sexual orientation is "abnormal," wrong, and immoral.

Homophobia—fear or intolerance of LGBTQ people, a feeling that is not limited to particular cultures or to heterosexual individuals.

Identity—what, how, and who one perceives oneself to be; a multifaceted self-concept that evolves throughout life.

In the closet—the intentional concealment of an individual's own gender identity or sexual orientation, usually due to fear of discrimination and/or violence. (Being in the closet can cause isolation and psychological pain.)

Lesbian—a woman who feels romantically, emotionally, and sexually attracted to other women; a descriptive and socially acceptable label that homosexual women often prefer because it offers an identity separate from that of homosexual men.

Lifestyle—the way individuals live their lives, such as an urban or a rural lifestyle, an artistic lifestyle, an entrepreneurial lifestyle, a hedonistic lifestyle; not appropriately used to denote sexual orientation. (Just as there is no heterosexual lifestyle, there is no homosexual or gay lifestyle. The phrase *homosexual lifestyle* is often used by anti-gay groups to imply that sexual orientation is a matter of choice rather than of identity.)

Oppression—prolonged cruel or unjust treatment, sometimes unconscious, sometimes covert; constant state of denying to others fair and equal treatment or fair and equal opportunities.

Passing—successfully assuming a gender role and gender expression different from the one to which they were born or which they were assigned at birth; also may refer to closeted gay, lesbian, or bisexual people passing as straight. (Please note that in some cultures, passing refers to successfully assuming a different racial, ethnic, or cultural identity.)

Privilege—special rights, advantages, or immunity granted to, or assumed by, certain groups and considered by them as their right; for example, in the U.S., privilege accrues mostly to affluent people, Whites, heterosexual people, and most of all to affluent, White, heterosexual males.

Queer—formerly an exclusively derogatory term for all GLBT people; now proudly used by some as an umbrella term for the entire GLBTQ community; also used by those who see their own gender identity, sexual identity, and/or sexual orientation as not fitting the widely recognized pattern of straight, gay or lesbian, bisexual, transgender, or questioning.

Sexual orientation—a feeling of attraction to others, based on biological sex and gender expression, over which individuals have no choice and different from sexual behavior. Romantic, sexual, and emotional attraction to others, categorized by the sex of the person to whom one is attracted, such as heterosexual (attracted to the other sex), homosexual (attracted to the same sex), or bisexual (attracted to individuals irrespective of their sex).

Sexual reassignment surgery—surgical procedures that modify one's primary and/or secondary sex characteristics; formerly called a "sex change operation," a phrase now considered by many to be offensive.

Transgender—an umbrella term for all who feel that they are outside the boundaries of biological sex and culturally determined gender expression.

Transsexual—an individual who does not self-identify with her/his biological sex; one who identifies physically, psychologically, and emotionally as of a different sex from that one was born or assigned to at birth; one who may choose to alter the body to reconcile gender identity and biological sex or physical appearance.

Graduate Students: Defining Need and Providing Appropriate Assistance

Melissa Thomas

This training module provides a brief introduction to research on graduate students and their needs and what that means for university personnel trying to assist them. When tutors or mentors have completed this training they will be able to (a) understand graduate student needs; (b) define the graduate student learning environment and expectations; and (c) realize they have the potential to assist these students with their transition to graduate studies, which is very similar to the transition that undergraduates experience their freshman year.

The demographics of the graduate student population have shifted dramatically to include more diverse and less traditional students than in the past (Brus, 2006). This means more women, ethnic minorities, and international students, plus more students seeking disability accommodations and more students who are older in age and responsible for both minor and adult dependents (Brus, 2006). Although these less traditional students may come to graduate school with a rusty set of study skills (Peters, 1992), there is a current trend toward acknowledging that all graduate students could benefit from learning assistance services.

Onwuegbuzie, Slate, and Schwartz (2001) emphasized that graduate students need study skills assistance, specifically to overcome passive reading and lackluster note taking. It is possible that those from whom graduate students seek help feel unqualified or underprepared to assist them properly. The training session offered here utilizes collaborative learning and investigational skills to build confidence of undergraduate tutors and mentors in their ability to assist graduate students (Wlodkowski, 1999).

Training Activity

A classroom with movable chairs is needed. The trainer will need to gather sample syllabi from graduate courses on campus from across the disciplines. The trainer will also need to provide poster paper.

First, the trainer should have the tutors and mentors self-assess their confidence level in working with a graduate student who comes seeking assistance. Trainees should rate themselves on a scale of 1 to 10, with 1 being *low level of confidence* and 10 being a *supreme level of confidence*. Reflect on how those with higher levels of confidence may have reasons to be more confident, such as having worked with graduate students before, being graduate students themselves, having experienced graduate level coursework or expectations, and so on.

Trainees should then gather in small groups of three or four, possibly by discipline. Each discipline-specific group looks at a graduate course syllabus in their discipline (i.e., science students look at a graduate chemistry course syllabus, and humanities students look at an English course syllabus); this will make their discussions more relevant. If this is not possible (for instance, if all trainees are writing tutors who work with students across disciplines), trainees should work on the syllabus they have a greater need to understand.

Based on their own experiences and the syllabus in front of them, each group should brainstorm on their poster paper the differences between undergraduate and graduate learning environments and expectations. Each group elects a spokesperson to share the group's findings with the training group. Then trainees return to the larger group to discuss why graduate courses are structured differently from undergraduate courses. What pedagogical reasons would there be, for

Graduate Faculty Expectation	Graduate Student Need
Reading lengthy articles	Sophisticated time management tools
Reading dense materials	Reading comprehension instruction
Speaking up in seminar course	Confidence in themselves as professionals

FIGURE 1   *Translating expectations to needs. This chart demonstrates the beginning of a list of graduate student expectations by their professors and translates those into the study and life skills needed by the student to master the expectation.*

instance, to focus on journal articles? Why structure a graduate course around shared learning, as in a seminar-style class?

Then trainees should create a general list of professors' expectations of graduate students demonstrated in the syllabi trainees have reviewed. Next they translate each of those expectations into a need, as seen in Figure 1.

Finally, the trainees divide back into groups. Each group takes one graduate student need and generates ideas on how they can help a student who comes to them with that particular need. How can they address these needs subtly if the student comes to them with a narrow request (e.g., reviewing a paper) but is obviously exhibiting a poor study habit? If time permits, trainees should role play these scenarios.

Assessment

Tutors and mentors should understand the difference between graduate and undergraduate student learning environments and their respective needs. Trainees should be able to reflect on ways that they can assist students with their transition to the graduate learning environment. As a sample assessment, the matching quiz provided in Figure 2 can be modified to reflect the graduate learning environment on any campus. For example, using a secondary source such as a textbook is typical of an undergraduate experience, whereas reading primary sources such as research journal articles is more typical of a graduate experience. The latter requires critical reading skills like those the peer tutors and mentors have presumably been trained to teach.

At the end of the session, trainees should once again rate themselves on a scale of 1 to 10, with 1 being *low level of confidence* and 10 being a *supreme level of confidence* to assess whether they feel more confident to assist a graduate student who needs help with coursework or overall success in graduate school. If any individual still demonstrates lack of confidence, the trainer should ask what training that tutor or mentor would need in order to develop more confidence.

UNDERGRADUATE	GRADUATE	STUDY SKILL NEEDED
Preparation		
Textbook	Studying bit by bit	Critical reading skills
Detailed notes	Seminar	Weekly review sessions
Cramming	Big picture notes mixed with reading notes	Confidence to participate
Lecture	Journal articles	Discussion-based notetaking skills
Assignments		
Group presentations	Practical applications of knowledge	Back dating assignment
Testing base-level memorization	Socratic method to test if readings are done	Confidence in becoming a professional
Daily quizzes	Semester-spanning paper	Analysis on advanced level with critical thinking
Final exam	Solo presentations of research	Comprehensive notes to rely on when called upon
Writing		
One-shot paper	Several sweeps for revising and editing	Understanding that sources and citing are complex
Source notes kept in memory	Informed conclusion with recommendations	Ideas for what each sweep should accomplish
Generic conclusion	Bibliographic software used to manage sources	Approaching paper in phases: outlining, writing, revising, and editing
One sweep for editing	Longer paper written across the term	Mindmap sources to connect

FIGURE 2 Matching quiz. Trainer's instructions: Please match the undergraduate experience that corresponds with the graduate experience and the study skill needed.

References

Brus, C. P. (2006). Seeking balance in graduate school: A realistic expectation or a dangerous dilemma? In M. J. Guentzel & B. E. Nesheim (Eds.), *Supporting graduate and professional students: The role of student affairs. New Directions for Student Services, 115*, 31–45. doi:10.1002/ss.214

Onwuegbuzie, A. J, Slate, J. R., & Schwartz, R. A. (2001). Role of study skills in graduate-level educational research courses. *Journal of Educational Research, 94*, 238–246. doi:10.1080/00220670109598757

Peters, R. L. (1992). *Getting what you came for: The smart student's guide to earning a master's or Ph.D.* New York, NY: Farrar, Straus, & Giroux.

Wlodkowski, R. J. (1999). *Enhancing adult motivation to learn: A comprehensive guide for teaching all adults.* San Francisco, CA: Jossey-Bass.

Ⓔ Learning

Executive Functions and Self-Regulated Learning

 Anna Z. Crockett

The activities included in this module are based on findings in neuroscience, cognitive science, and education that have identified the pivotal components of Executive Functions (EF) (Fischer & Daley, 2007; Lyon & Krasnegor, 1996) and Self-Regulated Learning (SRL) (Vohs & Baumeister, 2004; Zimmerman, 2007), which impact success across the spectrum of life experiences. These seminal publications and a multitude of later works, several of which are included in this module's references, indicate a consensus among researchers and practitioners that EF and SRL encompass skills that can be developed and taught. Thus, understanding the interrelated processes and concepts and knowing how to apply that knowledge in their work with students are essential training areas for mentors and tutors. Activities and supporting materials are designed to meet this training need.

It comes as no surprise to educators that research has confirmed a myriad of influences on academic performance, including the significant impact of thoughts, feelings, and behaviors and their relationship to intelligence (Dweck, 1986; Gardner, 1999; Goleman, 1995; Immordino-Yang & Damasio, 2008; Sternberg, 1985). Among these determining influences are cognitive skills (e.g., analyzing the task, goal setting, prioritizing, planning, memorizing, sustaining attention, inhibiting distractions and impulses, selecting and shifting strategies, using coping strategies and resources) and personal attributes (e.g., responsibility, initiative, tenacity, resilience) (Gardner & Moran, 2007). For this reason, integrating learning strategies with self-awareness and self-regulation skills and providing instruction, practice, and feedback in these areas is as critical in mentoring and tutoring settings as in the classroom.

The concept of SRL is grounded in a number of well-established perspectives that include constructivist (Piaget, 1972, 1990); social or observational (Bandura, 1986; Vygotsky, 1980); attribution (Weiner, 1974); motivation (Brooks, 2008; Dweck, 1986); and operant (Skinner, 1953) theory. Noteworthy is Pintrich's (1995) description of SRL as the regulation of three aspects of learning—behavior, motivation or affect, and cognition—because these are also components of EF, a term first used by neuroscientists and educational psychologists in the 1980s. Improved technology (e.g., functional magnetic resonance imaging and positron emission topography scanning) has allowed much more advanced study of brain processes, which in turn has increased understanding of factors that influence learning.

Although the theoretical framework for EF is not new, the term has been frequently used since a seminal publication by Lyon and Krasnegor (1996). Many definitions have been presented, but especially succinct is Brown's (2005) description of EF as "the management system of the brain" (p. xiii), that is, the wide range of central control processes used to direct conscious thoughts, emotions, and behavior. Gioia, Isquith, Guy, Kenworthy, and Barton (2002) described EF as "supervisory and self-regulatory functions that organize and direct cognitive activity, emotional response, and overt behavior" (p. 121). There is considerable overlap between EF and the SRL processes listed previously. Both terms are often used interchangeably with metacognition, which also encompasses monitoring and evaluation processes (Brown, 1987).

Several research findings are of special significance for tutor and mentor trainers. Increasing demands on college students require coordination, integration, and synthesis of complex EF processes. EF develops by a trajectory on which the highest-level processes are not fully developed until the early- to mid-20s for the average individual and later for those with developmental delays such as Attention Deficit Hyperactivity Disorder (ADHD; Fischer, Rose, & Rose, 2007). Development can be accelerated by use of explicit instruction, modeling, graphic organizers, guided practice, meaningful feedback, and gradual withdrawal of support (Fischer & Daley, 2007; McCloskey, 2007). Knowledge of theories about motivation, behavior, learning, beliefs about successes and failures, and the structure and function of the brain provides a foundation that contributes to the effectiveness of instructional programs, including mentoring and tutoring. Embedding EF and SRL in these programs can help students develop a repertoire of learning and regulating strategies. Such strategies (i.e., knowing why, when, and how to use particular approaches, as well as the importance of effective, sustained effort) are useful in students' academic, personal, and later professional lives.

Training Activity

The four training activities presented here require 30 minutes, 30 minutes, 1 hour, and 30–45 minutes, respectively, for a total of 2.5–2.75 hours. In preparation, the trainer should prepare sufficient copies of the Self-Assessment of Executive Functions handout (see Appendix), four sheets of Post-It® paper, and markers. Round tables best accommodate small groups of mentors or tutors for activities and discussion.

SELF-ASSESSMENT OF EXECUTIVE FUNCTIONS

Trainers should allow approximately 10 minutes for mentors or tutors to complete the self-assessment (see Appendix) and another 20 minutes for discussion. Questions to prompt follow-up discussion include the following: What did you learn from this exercise? What surprised you? How could having your tutees or mentees complete this exercise be useful in your work as a mentor or tutor? What might be your approach if there were a discrepancy between the student's responses and his or her grades?

If preferred, trainees could complete the self-assessment and consider the discussion questions before the training session begins. Alternatively, trainees can be asked to complete the self-assessment from the perspective of their mentees or tutees and discuss their own perspectives and the likely views of these students.

CONTROLLING INFLUENCES

Four sheets of large Post-It® paper and markers are needed for the Controlling Influences activity, which requires approximately 30 minutes. The trainer should prepare a large Post-It® for each of the four controlling influences on student success: attitudes and beliefs, emotions, behaviors, and external factors. As the four sheets are passed among the groups, participants add their observations and experiences of successful and unsuccessful students in each of the respective areas in response to the question, "What have you observed to be the differences between ways that successful and unsuccessful students deal with these controlling influences?" Each sheet is posted on a wall by the last group to add its entries. When all four sheets are posted, participants walk around to read them and then return to their group tables. The trainer leads a discussion about the conclusions that participants reached from the exercise, and how the information may relate to their work as mentors or tutors. Conclusions can be noted in a chart as in Figure 1.

	SUCCESSFUL	UNSUCCESSFUL
Attitudes and Beliefs		
Emotions		
Behaviors		
External Factors		

FIGURE 1 Controlling influences.

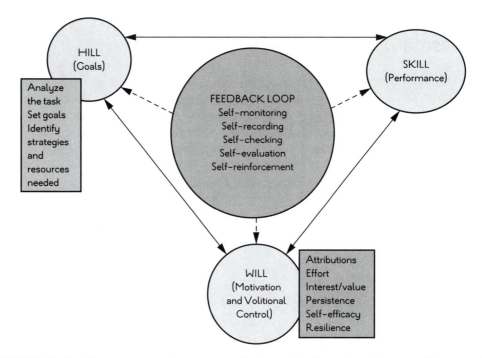

FIGURE 2 Executive control processes and phases of self-regulated learning. Shown are the interrelationships of Hill, Skill, and Will to each other (solid arrows) and to the Feedback Loop (dashed arrows). The combination of terms *hill*, *skill*, and *will* is borrowed from research in human resources (see Pomeroy, 2004) and psychology (Gardner, 2007). Figure developed by Anna Crockett for Miller Academic Center, Virginia Military Institute, 2009.

HILL, SKILL, AND WILL: COMPONENTS OF EF PROCESSES AND SRL

After the groundwork has been laid with the self-assessment of EF and controlling influences activities, the training director provides an overview of EF processes and SRL, using a PowerPoint® presentation (Crockett, 2009). Key ideas of the PowerPoint® are incorporated into the flow chart of Figure 2, EF Control Processes and Phases of SRL, which presents the interactions of hill (goal or challenge), skill (performance or competence), and will (motivation and volitional control) and constant feedback. The phrase "hill, skill, and will" has been used in human resources (Pomeroy, 2004) and psychology (Gardner & Moran, 2007). This section of the training activity requires approximately 1 hour.

MENTORING RUBRIC

The mentoring rubric (Crockett, 2007) incorporates components of effective mentoring relationships and well-developed EF. Two sets of descriptions set the ideal standard in the areas of building the relationship, developing learning skills, and developing life skills. One set of standards in each category applies to mentors or tutors and another to their mentees or tutees. In effect, the rubric details responsibilities and developmental objectives for both partners in the mentoring or tutoring relationship.

Mentors and tutors can complete the rubric on a hypothetical basis early in their training, anticipating the level at which they expect to achieve the standard. Alternatively, they can complete the rubric at a later point as a self-assessment of their level of success in each component. Whenever the assessment is completed, pairs or small groups can share observations and possible applications of the rubric exercise to mentoring or tutoring meetings. Trainers should allow 30 to 45 minutes for completion of the rubric and discussion of the scorings.

Assessment

The purpose of this training is for peer tutors and mentors to understand EF and SRL and to utilize their understanding in tutoring and mentoring sessions. Assessment of trainees' learning can be accomplished by a variety of written activities. Trainees may be required to reflect on the most important points learned and share in their online journal any remaining questions or concerns. Trainees may be required to draw the hill, will, skill model and illustrate with examples. Individually or in small groups, trainees may report how the concepts of EF and SRL can guide their mentoring and tutoring. They may describe how their idea of the tutor's or mentor's role has changed as a result of working through the mentoring rubric.

References

Bandura, A. (1986). *Social foundations of thought and action: A social cognitive theory.* Englewood Cliffs, NJ: Prentice-Hall.

Brooks, R. B. (2008, November). *Creating nurturing classroom environments: Fostering hope and resilience.* Paper presented at the 21st Conference of Learning and the Brain, Cambridge, MA.

Brown, A. L. (1987). Metacognition, executive control, self-regulation, and other more mysterious mechanisms. In F. E. Weinert & R. H. Kluwe (Eds.), *Metacognition, motivation, and understanding* (pp. 65–116). Hillsdale, NJ: Lawrence Erlbaum.

Brown, T. E. (2005). *Attention deficit disorder: The unfocused mind in children and adults.* New Haven, CT: Yale University Press.

Crockett, A. Z. (2007). *Mentoring rubric.* Retrieved from http://www.vmi.edu/show.aspx?tid=30507&id=4294970234 and http://www.crla.net/handbook/ch3/Crockett

Crockett, A. Z. (2009). *Hill, skill, and will.* Retrieved from http://www.vmi.edu/show.aspx?tid=30507&id=4294970234 and http://www.crla.net/handbook/ch3/Crockett

Dweck, C. S. (1986). Motivational processes affecting learning. *American Psychologist, 41,* 1040–1048. doi:10.1037/0003-066X.41.10.1040

Fischer, K. W., & Daley, S. G. (2007). Connecting cognitive science and neuroscience to education: Potentials and pitfalls in inferring executive processes. In L. Meltzer (Ed.), *Executive function in education from theory to practice* (pp. 55–70). New York, NY: Guilford Press.

Fischer, K. W., Rose, L. T., & Rose, S. P. (2007). Growth cycles of mind and brain: Analyzing developmental pathways of learning disorders. In K. W. Fischer, J. H. Bernstein, & M. H. Immordino-Yang (Eds.), *Mind, brain, and education in reading disorders* (pp. 101–132). New York, NY: Cambridge University Press.

Gardner, H. (1999). *Intelligence reframed: Multiple intelligences for the 21st century.* New York, NY: Basic Books.

Gardner, H., & Moran, S. (2007). "Hill, skill, and will": Executive function from a multiple-intelligences perspective. In L. Meltzer (Ed.), *Executive function in education from theory to practice* (pp. 55–70). New York, NY: Guilford Press.

Gioia, G. A., Isquith, P. K., Guy, S. C., Kenworthy, L., & Barton, R. (2002). Profiles of everyday executive function in acquired and developmental disorders. *Child Neuropsychology, 8*(2), 121–137. doi:10.1076/chin.8.2.121.8727

Goleman, D. (1995). *Emotional intelligence: Why it can matter more than IQ.* New York, NY: Bantam Books.

Immordino-Yang, M. H., & Damasio, A. (2008). We feel, therefore we learn: The relevance of affective and social neuroscience to education. In K. W. Fischer & M. H. Immordino-Yang (Eds.), *The Jossey-Bass reader on the brain and learning* (pp. 3–10). San Francisco, CA: Jossey-Bass.

Lyon, G., & Krasnegor, N. (Eds.). (1996). *Attention, memory, and executive function.* Baltimore, MD: Brooks.

McCloskey, G. (2007, November). *Self regulation executive functions: Definitions, observed behaviors, and potential interventions.* Paper presented at the 18th Conference on Learning and the Brain, Cambridge, MA.

Piaget, J. (1972). *The psychology of the child.* New York, NY: Basic Books.

Piaget, J. (1990). *The child's conception of the world.* New York, NY: Littlefield Adams.

Pintrich, P. R. (1995). Understanding self-regulated learning. In P. R. Pintrich (Ed.), *New directions for teaching and learning, 63,* 3–12. San Francisco, CA: Jossey-Bass.

Pomeroy, A. (2004). Successful outsourcing. *HR Magazine, 49*(6). Retrieved from http://findarticles.com/p/articles/mi_m3495/is_6_49/ai_n6076878/

Skinner, B. F. (1953). *Science and human behavior.* New York, NY: Macmillan.

Sternberg, R. J. (1985). *Beyond IQ: A triarchic theory of human intelligence.* New York, NY: Cambridge University Press.

Vohs, K. D., & Baumeister, R. F. (2004). Understanding self-regulation. In R. F. Baumeister & K. D. Vohs (Eds.), *Handbook of self-regulation: Research, theory and applications* (pp. 1–9). New York, NY: Guilford Press.

Vygotsky, L. S. (1980). *Mind in society: The development of higher psychological processes.* Cambridge, MA: Harvard University Press.

Weiner, B. (1974). *Achievement motivation and attribution theory.* Morristown, NJ: General Learning Press.

Zimmerman, B. J. (2007). Developing self-fulfilling cycles of academic regulation: An analysis of exemplary instructional models. In D. H. Schunk & B. Zimmerman (Eds.), *Self-regulated learning: From teaching to self-reflective practice* (pp. 1–19). New York, NY: Guilford Press.

Appendix

SELF-ASSESSMENT OF EXECUTIVE FUNCTION PROCESSES FOR LIFE AND LEARNING SUCCESS

RATE YOUR PROFICIENCY IN THE AREAS BELOW:	POOR	FAIR	GOOD	EXCELLENT
Section I: HILL* (goals/tasks)				
1. Set short-term and long-term goals (study sessions, daily, weekly, monthly)				
2. Analyze task requirements (project, term paper, test preparation, etc.)				
Section II: SKILL* (performance)				
Life Skills				
1. Attend/Concentrate (during class and study sessions)				
2. Plan (strategies and timelines for completing tasks)				
3. Organize (tasks and materials, planner, To Do lists, notebooks, etc.)				
4. Prioritize (ensure completion of highest priority tasks)				
5. Change strategies, as needed				

(Continued)

Rate your proficiency in the areas below:	Poor	Fair	Good	Excellent
6. Manage stress (diet, exercise, time)				
7. Solve problems (identify, evaluate, and choose options)				
Learning Skills				
1. Space review (short, frequent study vs. longer, less-frequent study				
2. Take notes (in class)				
3. Read assigned texts (identify, record, and learn important ideas)				
4. Prepare for exams (rework homework/quizzes, create notecards, outlines, charts)				
5. Take exams (follow directions, budget time, show work, check answers)				
Section III: WILL* (volitional control, motivation, and resource management)				
Motivation/Beliefs				
1. Believe in my ability to accomplish a chosen or assigned task.				
2. Believe that success is generally based more on effort and skills than on fixed ability.				
3. Believe that obstacles, errors, and frustration are a normal and valuable part of the learning process rather than indicators of low aptitude.				
Volitional Control (the will to take and maintain action)				
1. Make the effort (invest physical and mental energy)				
2. Persist (work through obstacles)				
3. Be resilient (rebound after setbacks)				
Resource management				
1. Use resources (e.g., instructors, tutoring, Writing Center)				
2. Control environment (study time and location)				
Section IV: SELF-REGULATION (umbrella term for Hill, Skill, and Will)*				
1. Self-monitor (pay attention to thoughts, feelings, and actions while working on a task)				
2. Self-check (identify and correct errors of thought and action)				
3. Self-evaluate (evaluate effectiveness of strategies used to complete a task				
4. Self-reinforce (reward oneself for accomplishments)				
5. Self-record (keep logs or journals to record time and effectiveness of activities related to tasks)				

*The combination of terms *hill*, *skill*, and *will* appears in research in human resources (Pomeroy, 2004) and psychology (Gardner & Moran, 2007). A version of the self-assessment instrument was developed by Crockett for Miller Academic Center, Virginia Military Institute, 2009.

Self-Regulated Learning: A Scenarios Approach to Training

Janice B. Heerspink and Thea J. Brophy

According to Sellers, Dochen, and Hodges (2011), self-regulation is "our effort to monitor and regulate our own behaviors, cognitions (thinking), and emotions, . . . that is, our ability to manipulate ourselves to reach specific goals" (p. 185). As not-yet-experts, peer tutors and mentors can guide students to become self-regulated learners by using a framework to think about learning (Bransford, Brown, & Cocking, 2000). Figure 1, a visual model of learning based on the work of DuBois (1985), will provide tutors and mentors with a tool to conduct their own self-analyses so they in turn can help others.

Performance in an academic setting is evaluated through tests, quizzes, papers, course presentations, and class discussions. Students often think about performance as their primary goal. They may need to learn to develop performance strategies, such as planning their time in a test, writing effective essay answers, or taking multiple-choice tests strategically, but a self-regulated student must attend to other areas of learning first.

Acquisition is acquiring or gaining the knowledge needed to perform; acquisition is primarily accomplished through active reading and through effective listening and leads to note-taking. Tutors and mentors can help students develop active approaches to reading, such as SQ4R (survey, question, read, recite, record, review; Pauk & Owens, 2008), and apply them where appropriate. Students must evaluate different types of textbook reading required for each course. They must learn to see how chapters are laid out, turn headings into questions, read to answer the questions, and learn to create charts, graphs, and diagrams as appropriate. Students may need to take notes from reading, depending on the task. Tutors and mentors should teach, model and practice these active strategies with students.

Peer tutors and mentors can guide students in creating complete and effective lecture notes for each course and teach active strategies such as the Cornell method (Pauk & Owens, 2008) or a similar split-page note-taking system requiring review and analysis of lecture notes. Tutors and mentors can also urge students to compare notes regularly with classmates for accuracy and completeness. Particularly helpful is asking students to demonstrate their understanding by explaining their notes as if the students were their own professor.

Tutors and mentors teach, model, and practice *retention* strategies so that students will learn to engage actively with their textbooks and their notes in order to retain what they need for successful performance in declarative or procedural knowledge learning. Retention requires regular and active review; simply re-reading notes or the textbook is not active learning. Appropriate retention strategies for declarative knowledge are based on the type of information being learned and could include drawing concept maps, writing outlines of the main ideas, making and using flashcards, and explaining aloud to oneself or to others. For procedural or problem-solving

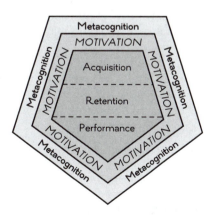

FIGURE 1   Model of the learning process. Adapted by J. B. Heerspink and R. E. Stegeman from DuBois (1985).

courses, understanding concepts and practicing repeatedly are essential. Tutors and mentors can ask students at each meeting what they have done in the past week to retain the knowledge they have acquired; before the end of the session, they can ask what students will do to retain new knowledge in the week ahead. Tutors and mentors may give advice on alternative strategies, how to test their retained knowledge, and how to pace the use of these strategies over time to avoid the pitfalls of cramming.

Acquisition, retention, and performance assume *motivation*. In the learning process model (Figure 1), motivation surrounds acquisition-retention-performance because without motivation students will not take the time and effort to engage actively in acquisition and retention. Students may think that motivation is something people either have or do not have. They may also think that motivation is related to something outside themselves—the professor, the material, or the tutor or mentor; however, students are responsible for their own actions (VanderStoep & Pintrich, 2008). Others can help to inspire, but intrinsic motivation is based on factors other than the inspiration of others. Self-directed learners have a belief that they can succeed, and they use positive self-talk about that belief, avoiding negative self-talk. VanderStoep and Pintrich (2008) described the importance to students of setting goals, small and large, to reach their desires.

It is critical that students learn to set priorities to meet these goals. Every student has goals in varied categories: social, spiritual, and physical, in addition to academic. The self-directed learner will learn to balance all of these in order to keep the most important goals in mind when other opportunities abound. To accomplish their priorities, students must manage their time, which is really managing themselves. Students are not *only* academic beings, but academic goals need to be a primary focus in order to succeed in college. To maintain motivation and self-management, students also need to manage their concentration. If a student has a learning disability such as attention deficit hyperactivity disorder (ADHD), medication may be required to facilitate concentration. All students must find the times and places to study that work effectively for their learning.

In addition to working with students on acquisition, retention, and motivation, tutors and mentors work with students in the area of *performance*, such as guiding students to write effective essay tests or showing them how to take multiple-choice tests strategically. Tutors and mentors match performance strategies to the needs of each task and each student client.

In the learning model (Figure 1), m*etacognition* surrounds all of these factors. Cognition refers to thinking or knowing; metacognition, in simple terms, is understanding one's own thinking and learning—getting above one's thinking and learning to understand what is working well and what is not, and monitoring and controlling one's learning (Bransford, Brown, & Cocking, 2000). Effective students are aware of whether they understand what they read and can evaluate whether their notes are complete or not. They recognize whether or not they are retaining material. Effective students also know whether their goals and priorities are clear. In addition, they know whether they employ productive essay and multiple-choice test strategies. In other words, effective students are metacognitively aware of where change is needed in any aspect of learning, and they know how to correct problem areas. All of this presumes knowing multiple active strategies, learning to use them, and applying them for effective learning and the student's desired outcome, successful performance.

Although tutors and mentors may not be involved in every area of the model with every student, student sessions will be improved if the student leaders have the model in mind. It will be a useful guide for leading students to become self-directed learners. If tutors and mentors deal only with immediate concerns and problems, they are giving students fish; if they help students understand a model of learning and apply it to their own academic work, they will be teaching students to fish, that is, they will guide them to self-regulation.

Training Activity

The objective of this training activity is that tutors and mentors understand the model of learning and how each of its parts can be applied for a student to regulate his or her own learning. Through this understanding, tutors and mentors will lead students to develop an awareness of what they need to do or change (regulate) for effective learning to take place. The entire training activity requires approximately 1 hour.

The trainer begins by providing a handout of the model of learning to each trainee and also projecting it onto a screen. The trainer explains the parts of the model with active input from trainees. Student tutors and mentors already have knowledge about these topics; the model will help them to realize their knowledge and will provide a framework for thinking about their learning.

The trainer can then break participants into small groups or pairs; if practical, trainees may be divided by the subject they tutor or the focus of their mentor assignment. The trainer provides scenarios of student concerns often seen in the learning center, with each "student" having a need in a different aspect of college learning. Using the model of learning, trainees identify the areas of need and devise strategies for the student to try. Small groups report their findings to the whole group. (In addition to scenarios, comic strips can be an effective means of helping trainees identify student issues to address, but they are not included here due to copyright issues.) Scenarios such as these can be presented:

- Sarita states that she studied for hours for a history test, "more than she has ever studied before," yet she scored only 54%.

- Jack does his math homework and can usually do the problems unassisted; when taking tests, however, he never scores above 65%.

- Carrie states that she reads and re-reads the summary pages of the psychology textbook, yet she cannot answer the "picky" multiple-choice questions on tests and has now failed her second test.

- Matt is concerned about getting his paper completed by the deadline a week away. He has had the assignment for 6 weeks but has not started it yet.

- Kristin says that she "knew everything in her notes" for the political science test, but she got a D, and the professor indicated that she needed to include more details.

- Frederico believes that there are so many facts to learn in the history course that it is impossible to memorize everything.

- Brianne is frustrated with her geography text, professor, and exams because the course is "just a liberal arts requirement." She has not yet chosen a major.

Assessment

To demonstrate their understanding of the learning model and concepts presented in training, tutors and mentors should be asked to identify the learning needs of students successfully through one or more of the following assessments created by the trainer: (a) three-person role-play conversations, with one person doing the assessment; (b) comic strips featuring learning problems or academic concerns; (c) videos that show students who have learning needs; (d) short, printed excerpts of students' stories; and (e) a quiz requiring trainees to identify students' learning issues.

Discussion should follow, to reinforce the importance of tutoring or mentoring beyond surface concerns. The ultimate goal of the training session is to help each student client to become self-analytical in order to self-regulate learning.

References

Bransford, J. D., Brown, A. L., & Cocking, R. R. (Eds.). (2000). *How people learn: Brain, mind, experience, and school.* Washington, DC: National Academic Press.

DuBois, N. F. (1985, March). *A cognitive information processing model of studying.* Paper presented at the 9thAnnual Conference of the National Association for Developmental Education, St. Louis, MO.

Pauk, W., & Owens, R. J. (2008). *How to study in college* (9th ed.). Boston, MA: Houghton Mifflin.

Sellers, D., Dochen, C. W., & Hodges, R. (2011). *Academic transformation: The road to college success* (2nd ed.). Boston, MA: Pearson.

VanderStoep, S. W., & Pintrich, P. R. (2008). *Learning to learn: The skill and will of college success* (2nd ed.). Upper Saddle River, NJ: Pearson Prentice Hall.

The Self-Regulated Learning Workshop as a Training Tool

Mark F. Daddona

Self-regulated learning involves moving beyond study skills and strategies toward specific approaches that include awareness, planning, monitoring, and reflection. Metacognition is a major component of self-regulated learning, and the terms at times are used interchangeably. However, metacognition is the process of monitoring progress as one learns and making changes and adapting strategies when one is not doing well; both processes occur at the same time (Winn & Snyder, 1996).

College students typically lack expertise in regulating their learning because they have not been taught principles of metacognition and self-regulated learning. In college, students often continue to employ study habits learned in high school, with only moderate success. Although many students engage in cognitive strategies to help them understand their learning (rehearsal, time management, elaboration), those who employ metacognitive strategies and behaviors to help them plan learning (goal setting, monitoring, self-efficacy, allocation of study time) are more aware of what they know and what they do not know and are able to make changes to their learning in order to be more successful. Therefore, there is a need to teach metacognitive skills and strategies explicitly to college students (Nietfeld, Cao, & Osborne, 2005; Peverly, Brobst, Graham, & Shaw, 2003; Veenman, Van Hout-Walters, & Afflerbach, 2006).

When students regulate their own learning, they set goals for upgrading knowledge, deliberate about which strategies they will select, and monitor the cumulative effects of their engagement (Butler & Winne, 1995). Peverly et al. (2003) discovered that increased self-regulation is correlated with improved test scores. In addition, they found that taking notes in class helped students become aware of what they do and do not know. Success using self-regulated learning strategies was also found with regularly-admitted students as compared to developmental students (Ley & Young, 1998) and students of nontraditional age (Justice & Dornan, 2001).

College instructors can develop course materials in ways that encourage self-regulated learning. In addition, learning center faculty and staff can contribute to students' understanding and strategies needed to self-regulate. However, peer mentors and tutors can also play an active role in this process while working closely with students on course assignments. The tutoring or mentoring session is the optimal place to move beyond reviewing, practicing, and explaining course content. It provides an opportunity for students to learn how to change behaviors and monitor their learning. This learning transition can be accomplished by introducing tutors and mentors to concepts of self-regulated learning and working through assignments using the Self-Regulated Learning Worksheet (see Appendix).

Training Activity

For this activity, trainees need a room that lets them work in pairs for part of the session. The module can be completed in approximately 90 minutes. If additional time is available, trainees can further practice the material. The purpose of this activity is for trainees to understand self-regulated learning definitions, components, and concepts; apply self-regulated learning techniques to their own courses; and assist students in applying self-regulated learning to their courses.

The trainer should first introduce the definitions of self-regulated learning and metacognition in a short lecture segment. The following components of self-regulated learning should be discussed: *goal orientation, strategy use, time management,* and *motivation.* These additional components may be unfamiliar to trainees. *Allocation of study time* is determining how much time is needed for a specific task or assignment. *Calibration of comprehension* is a match between self-perception of understanding and external performance measures. When self-rating of comprehension is consistent with actual test performance, comprehension is well calibrated. Poor calibration occurs when there is a mismatch between self-ratings and actual comprehension performance (Zabrucky & Agler, 2008). *Self-efficacy* is belief about one's ability to perform a specific behavior (Weiten, Lloyd, Dunn, & Hammer, 2009). *Monitoring* and *regulating* strategies are used to monitor learning when it takes place and determine when a new approach or technique must be considered.

The trainer should then draw trainees' attention to critical differences between *novice learners* and *expert learners* (Ertmer & Newby, 1996). Students often come to college as novice learners and continue as novices until they experience academic difficulty. Novice learners often do not stop to evaluate how they understand course material; therefore, they do not revise their work during the process of learning. They do not delve deeply into their work, as their goal is simply to get it finished. They seldom make connections or see the relevance of their studies to their own lives. When reading a textbook chapter, novice learners consider the assignment completed when the chapter is read, although they may remember very little of what they read.

By contrast, expert learners know how to regulate their learning. They know when they need to stop and check for errors in their work and are aware when they are not comprehending. They know when it is time to redirect their efforts and often have a large pool of strategies from which to select a new approach. They are motivated and view their learning as valuable, interesting, and useful. When reading a chapter in a text, expert learners will reread sections, write down possible questions, and take notes while trying to put material in their own words.

The third section of this training is teaching the four phases of self-regulated learning (Ertmer & Newby, 1996; Halter, n.d.), while trainees complete the corresponding section of the Self-Regulated Learning Worksheet (see Appendix). Trainees select a specific assignment from among their own academic courses and respond to the questions. After each section is complete, a few trainees are asked to share how they responded to each item.

In the *awareness* phase, students define their learning goal and think about what they already know about the topic. They consider task requirements, determine their available resources, and gather information from the instructor as to how assignments will be evaluated. In this phase trainees should also do a self-check on their anxiety level and ask themselves why they are at that level. Trainees complete Awareness items 1–6.

The *planning* stage comes next. To ensure that students plan sufficient time to complete the task, they estimate how long the assignment is expected to take and schedule blocks of study time. They also make a list of tasks in an effort to break larger assignments down into smaller components. Trainees then complete Planning items 7–9.

At the *monitoring* phase, students ask, how do I know that I know it? Throughout the process students question themselves and provide their own feedback. They monitor their time and, when the work gets difficult, keep their motivation high and even remind themselves why they are in college. Trainees are asked to complete Monitoring items 10–11.

The *reflection* phase comes last. Upon completion of an assignment or test, students should not simply move to the next task at hand. It is important to reflect on their learning process as they determine which strategies were productive and which were not. When an assignment or test has been graded, students should decide what action to take. All instructor comments and feedback should be carefully reviewed and considered. Trainees must wait until the completed assignment is graded prior to completing Reflection items 12–13.

After the worksheet is completed individually, trainees talk through their charts in pairs or small groups and provide reflections and insights to each other. A few minutes at a later training session can be used to share completed Reflection comments from the worksheet.

The fourth section of the training activity is a pair interview. Trainees ask one another the following questions to gain an understanding of each other's studying and learning approach:

- How do you prepare for exams? How do you know when you have studied enough?

- What strategies have you utilized to monitor your own learning? Were those strategies successful? Explain.

- Were you ever taught specific strategies to evaluate or modify your learning as needed? Can you give an example?

- What do you do to help remember and understand what you read?

- Do you usually go into an exam feeling well prepared? Why or why not?

- After you take an exam, do you usually have a sense of how you did on the exam? Does your sense of how well you did match the grade you received?

- Do you adjust your studying behaviors after you have taken an exam? Why or why not?

Trainees help one another determine if they are novice or expert learners and if they believe they are practicing components of self-regulated learning. If time permits, participants share their responses with the larger group.

After this training session, when trainee tutors and mentors are working with student clients who appear ready to further explore their learning, they may introduce the self-regulated learning phases and worksheet, guiding students through completing the worksheet for longer-term assignments such as research papers, major exams, and in-class presentations. During subsequent sessions, tutors and mentors can help students monitor their progress and complete the reflection process after assignments have been graded and returned. Over time students will become more comfortable completing the chart as they incorporate self-regulated learning concepts into more of their assignments.

Assessment

When trainers are confident that student staff are prepared to apply self-regulated learning to tutoring and mentoring, they can encourage students to begin introducing these concepts into sessions. This may be easier to accomplish in mentor sessions, because students being tutored may be eager to begin sessions with content work. Both tutors and mentors may begin by sharing the model of self-regulated learning components and the terms *novice* and *expert learners*. Over several sessions, they ask the pair-interview questions to encourage students to begin thinking about their own learning. As a second measure that peer tutors and mentors are competent to guide their student clients to self-regulated learning, trainees can be surveyed to determine whether they experience greater self-awareness of their current self-regulated learning as a result of the pair interviews, and student clients may be surveyed about their knowledge, confidence, and satisfaction.

Copies of the self-regulated learning chart can be made available in the learning center, and a downloadable version can be posted on the center's website. An indirect measure of success will be the number of copies of the chart taken by students wanting to use them for future assignments and the number of hits on the chart's web page.

References

Butler, D. L., & Winne, P. H. (1995). Feedback and self-regulated learning: A theoretical synthesis. *Review of Educational Research, 65,* 245–281. doi:10.2307/1170684

Ertmer, P. A., & Newby, T. J. (1996). The expert learner: Strategic, self-regulated, and reflective. *Instructional Science, 24,* 1–24. doi:10.1007/BF00156001

Halter, J. (n.d.). Metacognition. In *The encyclopedia of educational technology.* San Diego, CA: San Diego State University Department of Educational Technology.

Justice, E. M., & Dornan, T. M. (2001). Metacognitive differences between traditional-age and nontraditional-age college students. *Adult Education Quarterly, 51,* 236–249. doi:10.1177/07417130122087269

Ley, K., & Young, D. B. (1998). Self-regulation behaviors in underprepared (developmental) and regular admission college students. *Contemporary Educational Psychology, 23,* 42–64. doi:10.1006/ceps.1997.0956

Nietfeld, J. L., Cao, L., & Osborne, J. W. (2005). Metacognitive monitoring accuracy and student performance in the postsecondary classroom. *Journal of Experimental Education, 74,* 7–28.

Peverly, S. T., Brobst, K. E., Graham, M., & Shaw, R. (2003). College adults are not good at self-regulation: A study on the relationship of self-regulation, note taking, and test taking. *Journal of Educational Psychology, 95,* 335–346. doi:10.1037/0022-0663.95.2.335

Veenman, M. V. J., Van Hout-Walters, H. A. M., & Afflerbach, P. (2006). Metacognition and learning: Conceptual and methodological considerations. *Metacognition and Learning, 1,* 3–14. doi:10.1007/s11409-006-6893-0

Weiten, W., Lloyd, M. A., Dunn, D. S., & Hammer, E. Y. (2009). Psychology applied to modern life: Adjustment in the 21st century (9th ed.). Belmont, CA: Wadsworth Cengage Learning.

Winn, W., & Snyder, D. (1996). Cognitive perspectives in psychology. In D. H. Jonassen (Ed.), *Handbook of research for educational communications and technology* (pp. 112–142). New York, NY: Simon & Schuster Macmillan.

Zabrucky, K. M., & Agler, L. L. (2008). Metacognition and learning. In N. J. Salkind (Ed.), *Encyclopedia of Educational Psychology* (pp. 673–676). Los Angeles, CA: Sage.

Appendix

Self-Regulated Learning Worksheet

Name : Pat Brown   Course : PSYC 1101

Assignment : Final Examination   Due Date : December 10th

<table>
<tr><td rowspan="3">AWARENESS</td><td>

1. Why am I here?

I would like to be successful in college for me and to make my family proud of me.

</td><td>

2. What are my goals for assignment/project?

To earn a high "B" on my final exam which I think will give me an "A" in the course.

</td></tr>
<tr><td>

3. What do I already know?

- Material from first 8 chapters fairly well
- Scientific method
- Psychological theories
- Personality
- Some of the Psychological Disorders

</td><td>

4. Anxiety Level Check:

Not too bad right now because it seems so far away, but I usually get more nervous as exams get closer. I think I might like to major in psychology so I really want this class to be one of my highest grades this semester.

</td></tr>
<tr><td>

5. What resources are available to me?

- Textbook
- Class notes
- Instructor website materials
- Practice questions on textbook website
- Tutoring center
- Residence hall study group

</td><td>

6. How will I be evaluated?

- Final includes everything we covered over entire semester
- Mostly multiple-choice questions
- Several short-answer questions

</td></tr>
<tr><td rowspan="2">PLANNING</td><td>

7. How much time do I need? Block out calendar.

I need to begin studying at least 3 weeks before the exam due to the amount of material. I will write study times my calendar beginning with five 1-hour study blocks for the first 2 weeks and then five 2-hour study blocks the week before the exam.

</td><td>

8. What strategies should I use?

- Reviewing class notes
- Rereading major topics in textbook
- Practice tests
- Schedule an appointment with a tutor
- Rehearsal with note cards while studying aloud

</td></tr>
<tr><td colspan="2">

9. List of steps:

    a. Organize notebook and class notes. Fill in gaps in notes, if needed.
    b. Reread difficult portions of textbook.
    c. Prepare note cards.
    d. Review material with notes and note cards.
    e. Take online practice exams from textbook website.

    f. Attend a review session with study group in residence hall. Try it once and see if it works for me.
    g. Schedule appointment in tutoring center with psychology tutor to review topics that may be giving me difficulty.
    h. Focus remaining study time on topics I still do not fully understand.

</td></tr>
<tr><td>MONITORING</td><td>

10. Monitoring checkpoints dates:

11/25   11/30   12/5   12/8

</td><td>

11. What do I need to change now?

12/5 – I need to spend more time on the more difficult topics that we recently covered in class, will see if a tutor is available 12/8 – there are still terms I'm having trouble with, and I seem to be running out of time.

</td></tr>
<tr><td>REFLECTION</td><td>

12. What worked and didn't work? What should I do differently next time?

Studying seemed to go well, but I was surprised that I didn't have enough study time when I got to the end. I should have started sooner. I also did better on the short-answer questions than the multiple-choice. I'm not sure why.

</td><td>

13. Grade for assignment/project:

I received a grade of 85% on the final exam and a grade of "A-" for the course.

</td></tr>
</table>

Self-Regulated Learning: Rewards and Consequences

Patricia Fullmer

The use of self-regulatory behaviors by students has been correlated to increased academic achievement and improvement in grades (Bembenutty, 2007; Jakubowski & Dembo, 2002). The self-regulation strategies of increased self-efficacy and setting of goals have been significantly related to academic achievement and success (Ley & Young, 1998). High-achieving and self-regulating college students have been found to set detailed learning goals, use a variety of study strategies, monitor themselves often, and adapt their efforts, goals, and strategies in a more systematic manner than low-achieving college students (Ruban & Reis, 2006). Self-regulated learners are able to manage their behavior and environment and are more successful in college.

Self-regulated learning consists of knowledge, beliefs, and skills that can be learned. The components of self-regulation include self-efficacy, awareness of acquired knowledge, knowledge of study and learning strategies and how to use the strategies, and the ability to retrieve knowledge at will. The setting of goals, self-monitoring capabilities, and the ability to adapt and modify one's strategies and plans are also important parts of self-regulation (Winne, 1995). In a review of research on science education and self-regulation, Schraw, Crippen, and Hartley (2006) found evidence to support the importance of metacognition as a component of self-regulation and the significance of self-efficacy (confidence in ability to accomplish a task). Self-efficacy was also found by Zimmerman (2000) to be a substantive influence on self-regulation.

Vockell (2001) found that a self-regulated learner approaches a learning task in a certain way: first analyzing the task and determining the requirements of the task; second, setting detailed goals and choosing strategies; third, monitoring achievement of goals; fourth, modifying strategies; and, fifth, marshalling the motivation to remain on task.

Zimmerman (1998, 2002) proposed a cyclical model of self-regulation that included forethought, performance control, and self-reflection. Forethought consists of planning, developing goals, and choosing strategies. Performance control entails monitoring one's behavior to assess progress and encouraging oneself. Self-reflection includes reviewing the effectiveness of one's strategies and modifying goals and strategies to improve effectiveness.

Training Activity

Tutors and mentors should not only know self-regulatory behaviors and strategies and when and how to use such behaviors and strategies but also how to share this valuable information with their tutees and mentees. By the end of the training session, trainees will be able to define self-regulation, identify cognitive and study strategies, and recognize task behaviors of high-achieving, self-regulating students. Tutors and mentors will also be able to describe the phases of the cycle of self-regulation. The activity requires a flip chart, markers, rewards and consequences handouts, a computer, LCD projector, and a wall or screen if using PowerPoint® or Prezi®. The time required is about 1 hour.

The facilitator begins by explaining that the topic is self-regulation and that a significant self-regulatory behavior is the ability to give oneself rewards and consequences. An important component of self-regulation is the ability to reward oneself for successfully completing a task and to give oneself consequences when one does not successfully complete a task. The first training activity helps tutors and mentors gain an understanding of using self-rewards and consequences to self-regulate behavior.

Each trainee receives a handout on rewards and consequences and determines his or her own personal rewards and consequences. The handout is a simple chart in two columns, *Rewards I can give myself* and *Consequences I can give myself*. Trainees are given time to list how they can reward themselves for a job well done and what consequences they can give themselves for not doing the job. Participants are then requested to volunteer to share their lists.

The facilitator asks trainees to share how they go beyond rewards and consequences. How do they regulate, monitor, and manage themselves to get done all that they accomplish academically? Suggestions are written on flip chart paper and posted on the wall.

The trainer then presents key scholarly research on self-regulation, including several definitions, how researchers have explored the topic, the task behaviors that scholars have associated with self-regulated learners, and the Cyclical Model of Self-Regulated Learning (Zimmerman, Bonner, & Kovach, 1996). A PowerPoint® or Prezi® presentation prepared well in advance can be used for this training and updated for future sessions. The reference list for this training module provides information useful for the presentation, including a PowerPoint® presentation (Fullmer, 2011) that is available for use. Trainees in small groups next brainstorm and record on flip chart paper the self-regulation strategies they think most likely to lead to academic success or those from which their student clients could most benefit. The flip charts are posted on the walls, and a reporter from each group shares its ideas with the larger group.

The members of each small group choose one strategy to demonstrate in a scenario they design. The trainee acting in the role of tutor or mentor demonstrates how to present and support the chosen self-regulating strategy to a tutee or mentee. At the end of each demonstration, the whole group is given time to comment and ask questions.

Participants may also find a listing of self-regulation strategies helpful. The trainer can list such strategies as organizing information (outlining, summarizing, highlighting, diagramming, concept mapping, using index cards); goal setting; time management; notetaking, rehearsing, and memorizing (mnemonic devices, sample questions, mental images, repetition, overlearning, saying notes aloud); behavioral strategies (monitoring, evaluating progress, rewarding and giving consequences); and environmental strategies (seeking information from libraries, the Internet, textbooks, past tests, notes; eliminating distractions in the physical study setting; seeking assistance).

Assessment

The trainer can assess trainees' understanding of the concepts of self-regulated learning presented in this training by evaluating the merits of the rewards and consequences they list on the handout and present in small group on a flip chart. Trainees' implementation of this knowledge can be assessed by the quality of the role play they present for the other trainees.

Peer tutors and mentors may also demonstrate their understanding of self-regulated learning by describing in writing how they will utilize this knowledge in their work with one or more student clients. Assessments could be completed at the very end of the training session, sent to the trainer by email within 2 days of training, or shared with the rest of the staff via a web dialog forum.

References

Bembenutty, H. (2007). Self-regulation of learning and academic delay of gratification: Gender and ethnic differences among college students. *Journal of Advanced Academics, 18,* 586–616.

Fullmer, P. (2011). *Self-regulated learning: Students take charge of their own learning.* Retrieved from http://www.crla.net/handbook/ch3/fullmer

Jakubowski, T., & Dembo, M. (2002, April). *Social cognitive factors associated with the academic self-regulation of undergraduate college students in a learning and study strategies course.* Paper presented at the annual meeting of the American Educational Research Association, New Orleans, LA.

Ley, K., & Young, D. (1998). Self-regulation behaviors in underprepared (developmental) and regular admission college students. *Contemporary Educational Psychology, 23,* 42–64. doi:10.1006/ceps.1997.0956

Ruban, L., & Reis, S. M. (2006). Patterns of self-regulatory strategy use among low-achieving and high-achieving university students. *Roeper Review, 28,* 148–156. doi:10.1080/02783190609554354

Schraw, G., Crippen, K. J., & Hartley, K. (2006). Promoting self-regulation in science education: Metacognition as part of a broader perspective on learning. *Research in Science Education, 36,* 111–139. doi:10.1007/s11165-005-3917-8

Vockell, E. L. (2001). Self-regulation of learning. In E. L. Vockell (Ed.), *Educational psychology: A practical approach* (Online ed., Chapter 7). Retrieved from http://education.calumet.purdue.du/vockell/edPsybook/Edpsy7/edpsy7_self.htm

Winne, P. H. (1995). Inherent details in self-regulated learning. *Educational Psychologist, 30*(4), 173–187. doi:10.1207/s15326985ep3004_2

Zimmerman, B. J. (1998). Developing self-fulfilling cycles of academic regulation: An analysis of exemplary instructional models. In D. H. Schunk & B. J. Zimmerman (Eds.), *Self-regulated learning: From teaching to self-reflective practice* (pp. 1–19). New York, NY: Guilford Press.

Zimmerman, B. J. (2000). Self-efficacy: An essential motive to learn. *Contemporary Educational Psychology, 25,* 82–91. doi:10.1006/ceps.1999.1016

Zimmerman, B. J. (2002). Becoming a self-regulated learner. *Theory Into Practice, 41*(2), 65–70. doi:10.1207/s15430421tip4102_2

Zimmerman, B. J., Bonner, S., & Kovach, R. (1996). *Developing self-regulated learners: Beyond achievement to self-efficacy.* Washington, DC: American Psychological Association.

Use Chess to Illustrate Differences Between Novice and Expert Learners

Kathleen Speed

This training module examines three types of knowledge: declarative, procedural, and meta-cognitive. It also focuses on self-regulated learners, who are expert learners who know how to use and practice the different types of knowledge. The expert versus novice paradigm is one way to help students understand the concept of self-regulated learning. What types of knowledge does an expert learner use? What makes an expert learner different from a novice learner? Assisting students to find answers to these questions and become self-regulated learners is a fundamental component of training for peer tutors and mentors.

Sellers, Dochen, and Hodges (2011) argued that it is important for students to understand how they acquire knowledge and specifically how students acquire declarative, procedural and conditional knowledge. *Declarative* knowledge is "specific information about something" (p. 43). In the academic setting, declarative knowledge comes in the form of facts, such as terminology and dates, and concepts, such as theories and models. Techniques that students use to learn declarative knowledge include creating terminology notecards, timelines, compare-and-contrast charts, and mnemonics. *Procedural* knowledge is "knowing how to do something" (p. 45). In the academic setting, procedural knowledge may be learning how to solve math, chemistry, and physics problems or learning how to write code in computer science or haiku in a literature course. Allowing enough time and providing opportunities for practice are essential components, because both help students learn the required procedures. Last, *conditional* knowledge is "knowing when and why to use a particular strategy" based on understanding the task and themselves (p. 48). In the academic setting, conditional knowledge comes in the form of planning, monitoring, and evaluating choices and behaviors. Determining the most appropriate study strategy for the cognitive demands of the subject matter, creating a study schedule that takes into account the declarative and procedural knowledge of the subject matter, and evaluating prior behavior and changing that behavior if needed are all important applications of conditional knowledge. (For additional explanations of these terms, see Anderson & Krathwohl, 2001.)

Expert learners would seem to be conversant with all three kinds of knowledge. Weinstein and Stone (1993) explained that expert learners "know more, their knowledge is better organized and integrated, they have better strategies and methods for getting to their knowledge, using it, applying it, and integrating it, and they have different motivations" (p. 32) than novice learners. Generally expert learners know their strengths and weaknesses as learners. Experts are purposeful in their approach when learning something. When they understand the cognitive demands of a task, they choose the appropriate strategy and method to help them learn it. Experts use their prior knowledge to help them make meaning, and they monitor their comprehension. Additionally, they are aware of their motivation, thus the term "self-regulated" (Weinstein & Stone, 1993). In other words, expert learners are strategic in their approach to learning.

Novice learners, on the other hand, may not know much about a particular subject. A novice may use the same learning strategy (e.g., memorizing) over and over even when that strategy does not appear to work. The novice learner, when confronted with difficult tasks, may skip them or give up quickly. Even after a poor grade, the novice learner does not change the behavior or approach (Sellers, Dochen, & Hodges, 2005).

Training Activity

The game of chess has sometimes been used to explain the theory of self-regulated learning, typically by means of pictures of a chess board inserted into a textbook. Peer tutors and mentors have a greater appreciation for the paradigm when they can actually experience the concepts in person by playing or attempting to play a game of chess. It is important for tutors and mentors to show students that it is possible to transition from novice to expert learning. Playing chess is an enjoyable way to illustrate for tutors and mentors the differences between expert and novice learners as well as highlight the different types of knowledge required for different tasks.

The learning objectives for the trainees in this training session are to describe differences between novice and expert learners and to identify declarative, procedural, and metacognitive knowledge needed to be successful in a given course. For this activity a table, two chairs, and a chess board are needed. Approximately 20 minutes are required for demonstration and discussion.

The trainer first asks for two volunteers who have little or no familiarity with chess to sit in the two chairs. Selection of volunteer participants is important. The authentic response of these first two volunteers is integral to the success of this activity. As a result, the trainer must select participants who are true chess novices. When seeking the novice volunteers, the trainer can select (a) two experienced tutors, (b) one experienced tutor and one new tutor, or (c) two new tutors. Because this activity results in authentic reactions on behalf of the novice (confusion, frustration, feeling clueless, and laughter), trainers concerned about any potential embarrassment of a new trainee should choose a more experienced staff member, provided that staff member is truly a chess novice. When the volunteers have been selected, the trainer asks the rest of the participants to gather around the table, to remain quiet, and to refrain from answering questions or giving advice. It is important to let the two players do what they think is correct.

The trainer asks the two players to set up the board together, identifying the chess pieces by their official names as they do so. The facilitator should pay attention to the names given by the players. The trainer does not correct the players but makes a mental note of their accuracy at this point in the activity.

After the novices have set up the board (correctly or incorrectly), the trainer asks one of them to make the first move in order to start the game, and then asks the player who makes the first move why that player got to make the first move. The novice chess players play for 3 to 5 minutes, or long enough for each player to make multiple moves.

After each player makes the first move, the trainer asks: Why did you move that piece? During the course of the game, the trainer asks questions like these: Why are you moving that piece? Are you sure that piece can move that way? How are you feeling? How are you interacting with your opponent? What is your strategy? How many moves are you thinking ahead? As the novices play and answer the questions, the trainer makes notes of their answers for the discussion to follow.

After these two players have had an opportunity to demonstrate their skill, the trainer stops the game. The novices are thanked for playing and asked to stand with the rest of the group.

Now the trainer asks for two more volunteers. This time two players should be chosen who are very familiar with how to play chess. As the new players set up the board, they should identify the chess pieces by their official names.

After the experienced players have set up the board, one of them makes the first move in order to start the game. After each player makes the first move, the trainer asks about the play: Why did you move that piece? Is that a typical move for you? During the course of the game, the trainer asks the same questions that were asked of the first pair of players. As the new volunteers play and answer the questions, the trainer makes notes of their answers for the discussion to follow.

When the experienced players have each made enough moves to demonstrate their skill level, they should be thanked for volunteering. All the participants then return to their seats.

The trainer next will discuss with trainees the differences between expert and novice chess players. How did they answer the questions differently? The trainer's observations and notes can be used to foster discussion. Participants should identify the declarative and procedural knowledge required to play. They can also discuss how metacognitive knowledge is used.

Finally, trainees discuss how this analogy applies to course content. What declarative, procedural, and metacognitive knowledge is required of expert learners in the participant's content area? The group should brainstorm ways to assist students to become confident, sophisticated, knowledgeable, self-regulated learners.

Assessment

Trainees' oral responses during discussion are one way that trainers can assess their learning. Trainees can also be asked to demonstrate their learning in writing, by listing differences between novice and expert players of chess and between novice and expert college learners. Trainees can demonstrate their understanding of declarative, procedural, and metacognitive knowledge by listing how students might use the different types of knowledge for success in a particular course chosen by the trainer, or the choice of course may be left to the trainees themselves.

References

Anderson, L. W., & Krathwohl, D. R. (Eds.) (2001). *A taxonomy for learning, teaching and assessing: A revision of Bloom's taxonomy of educational objectives*. New York, NY: Longman.

Sellers, D., Dochen, C. W., & Hodges, R. W. (2005). *Academic transformation: The road to college success*. Upper Saddle River, NJ: Pearson Education.

Sellers, D., Dochen, C. W., & Hodges, R. W. (2011). *Academic transformation: The road to college success* (2nd ed.). Boston, MA: Pearson.

Weinstein, C. E., & Stone, G. V. M. (1993). Broadening our conception of general education: The self-regulated learner. In N. Raisman (Ed.), *Directing general education outcomes* (pp. 31–39). San Francisco, CA: Jossey-Bass.

Learning, Tutoring, and Mentoring Styles

Cindy Walker

Tutors and mentors play an important role in helping their student clients improve their learning process by increasing their awareness of how they learn. Understanding learning styles allows tutors and mentors to guide their student clients more strategically and effectively into active learning. According to Fink (2003), active learning is defined as "significant learning" requiring "some kind of change in the learner. No change, no learning. And significant learning requires that there be some kind of lasting change that is important in terms of the learner's life" (p. 3).

In this training session, tutors and mentors will engage in deep learning by actively examining, discussing, and applying ideas and strategies related to learning styles throughout the training activity. Learning styles are the way individuals prefer to learn and incorporate learning into their schemata of knowledge. By learning in a variety of ways, trainees will internalize and model experiential and deep learning. They will learn through kinesthetic means (online assessment and role-play activities), auditory means (discussion), and visual means (handouts). This training is designed to encourage tutors and mentors to change and adapt their tutoring style to the learners with whom they meet.

Training Activity

There are three learning objectives for this training session. Trainees should identify and understand their personal learning styles, recognize the learning styles of student clients, and develop strategies to adapt their tutoring or mentoring to various learning styles. The trainer needs to provide index cards, pens, scenario cards, handouts derived from the appendices of this module, and computers with Internet access. Use of a document image projector is optional.

The training session consists of nine different components, which can be accomplished in a single, 2.5-hour session or in two sessions of 2 hours each, depending on how much time the trainer gives to components one, four, five, and eight. (Trainers can increase the time for these activities as deemed appropriate).

COMPONENT ONE

The tutors and mentors first complete at least one learning styles inventory (see Appendix A). This component can be completed prior to the training session to save time. By interacting with learning styles assessment tools, trainees will engage in experiential learning and be able to make stronger connections to the theoretical and practical aspects of learning styles theory. Additionally, it is important that the tutors and mentors understand their own learning preferences so that they can analyze how these preferences may impact the strategies they use in sessions with students. Without training, tutors and mentors may have a tendency to teach others using their preferred learning style; however, when trainees become more aware of other learning styles, they can adapt to their student clients' learning preferences more easily.

Trainees should complete one or more learning styles assessments. The trainer should choose the appropriate assessments for trainees' area of study from the resources listed in the reference section (see Appendix A).

COMPONENT TWO

After completing the learning styles assessment, trainees complete a brief reflection and response activity individually, the Learning Styles Assessment Reflections of Appendix B. Responding to the reflection questions gives the tutors and mentors an opportunity to process their results and integrate this new information more deeply in their personal and tutoring or mentoring schemas. If trainees complete the learning styles assessment prior to the training session, they can also respond to the individual reflection questions in advance.

COMPONENT THREE

After completing the individual reflection questions, trainees should return to the large group to discuss the Group Discussion Questions of Appendix B. Trainees discuss their conclusions with the other trainees.

COMPONENT FOUR

Trainees should then divide into five separate groups. Each group receives a handout developed by the trainers, based on materials listed in Appendix A, on one of five learning style theories or frameworks. One group receives a handout on Kolb (Atherton, 2009). The second group receives information on Dunn (International Learning Styles Network, 2008). The third group receives a handout on DVC, the Diablo Valley College learning style inventory (Jester & Miller, 2000), the fourth group a handout on VARK (Fleming, 2006), and the fifth group a handout on Felder (Felder, n.d.; Felder & Soloman, n.d.). Group members become knowledgeable by reading the handout and discussing the information among themselves. Each group should spend 15 minutes learning their assigned learning theory.

COMPONENT FIVE

After 15 minutes, members of each group will meet in a new group consisting of one person from each learning theory group. Each person in the new group should teach the others about the theory their original group learned.

COMPONENT SIX

As a whole group, the trainer and trainees should discuss the differences, strengths, and limitations of the various learning styles theories and frameworks. Also, the group should evaluate which learning styles assessment would work best for various student populations (e.g., English language learners, first-year students, returning students, vocational education students, general education students, students in the sciences) by considering factors such as language skill, types of studying tasks, subject areas, and educational background of the students taking the assessment.

COMPONENT SEVEN

As a large group, trainees should also discuss the various ways that their learning styles impact their own tutoring or mentoring styles. They should be encouraged to brainstorm strategies they can use to adapt their tutoring or mentoring to various learning styles and ways that they can help students learn to adapt to various teaching styles. The trainer might explain that although it is important to teach to various learning styles, it is also important to help students learn how to adapt to different teaching styles. Students rarely have control over the type of teaching style they encounter, so they need to learn how to use their learning styles to adapt to various teaching styles. For example, a student who learns through reading and writing can adapt to lecture-based instruction by taking detailed notes of the lecture and reading through the notes later.

COMPONENT EIGHT

Trainees should be paired up and each pair given a learning style scenario (see Appendix C). Together each pair should analyze the scenario and practice role playing the situation as they apply what they have learned about learning styles theories and tutoring or mentoring strategies. Some scenario examples are provided in Appendix C, but it is recommended that trainers adapt these to the circumstances of their student clientele.

COMPONENT NINE

Trainee pairs demonstrate their role-play scenario to the group. The trainer should debrief each role play with additional ideas and discussion from the group.

Assessment

There are three learning objectives for this training session: trainees should identify and understand their personal learning style, recognize the learning styles of students, and develop strategies to adapt their tutoring or mentoring to various learning styles. It can be determined if trainees have met the first two objectives by asking them to identify and describe their own learning styles and assessing their knowledge of learning styles in the discussion and role-play activities. Assessment of trainees' ability to adapt their tutoring or mentoring to students with different learning styles can be evaluated both in the role-play activity and in the follow-up discussion.

A pre- and post-training assessment can also be administered by giving trainees a survey with the following questions: What are the most common learning style frameworks and theories? What are your learning styles? Describe at least one tutoring or mentoring strategy that is effective for each learning style.

References

Atherton, J. S. (2009, November 4). *Experiential learning cycle*. Retrieved from http://www.learningandteaching.info/learning/experience.htm

Felder, R. M. (n.d.). *Index of learning styles*. Retrieved from http://www4.ncsu.edu/unity/lockers/users/f/felder/public/ILSpage.html

Felder, R. M., & Soloman, B. A. (n.d.). *Learning styles and strategies*. Retrieved from http://www4.ncsu.edu/unity/lockers/users/f/felder/public/ILSdir/styles.htm

Fink, L. D. (2003). *What is significant learning?* Retrieved from http://www.wcu.edu/WebFiles/PDFs/facultycenter_SignificantLearning.pdf

Fleming, N. (2006). *The VARK questionnaire*. Retrieved from www.vark-learn.com/english/page.asp?p=questionnaire

Fleming, N., & Baume, D. (2006). Learning styles again: VARKing up the right tree! *Educational Developments, 7*(4), 4–7.

International Learning Styles Network. (2008). *About learning styles*. Retrieved from http://www.learningstyles.net/index.php?option=com_content&task=view&id=20&Itemid=70&lang=en

Jester, C., & Miller, S. (2000). *DVC online: Introduction to the DVC Learning Style Survey for College*. Retrieved from http://www.metamath.com/lsweb/dvclearn.htm

Appendix A

LEARNING STYLE RESOURCES FOR TUTOR AND MENTOR TRAINERS

Websites for Learning Styles Assessments

Felder Index of Learning Styles: http://www.engr.ncsu.edu/learningstyles/ilsweb.html

VARK Learning Styles Questionnaire: www.vark–learn.com/english/page.asp?p=questionnaire

DVC Learning Styles Inventory: http://www.metamath.com/multiple/multiple_choice_questions.html

Kolb's Learning Styles Inventory (must be purchased): http://www.learningfromexperience.com/assessment-tools/#LSI

Resources for Handout on Kolb

Atherton, J. S. (2009, November 4). *Experiential learning cycle*. Retrieved from http://www.learningandteaching.info/learning/experience.htm

Resources for Handout on Dunn

International Learning Styles Network. (2008). *About learning styles*. Retrieved from http://www.learningstyles.net/index.php?option=com_content&task=view&id=20&Itemid=70&lang=en

Resources for Handout on DVC, the Diablo Valley College Learning Style Inventory

Jester, C., & Miller, S. (2000). *DVC online: Introduction to the DVC Learning Style Survey for College*. Retrieved from http://www.metamath.com/lsweb/dvclearn.htm

Resources for Handout on VARK

Fleming, N., & Baume, D. (2006). Learning styles again: VARKing up the right tree! *Educational Developments, 7*(4), 4–7.

Resources for Handout on Felder

Felder, R. M., & Soloman, B. A. (n.d.). *Learning styles and strategies*. Retrieved from http://www4.ncsu.edu/unity/lockers/users/f/felder/public/ILSdir/styles.htm

Appendix B

LEARNING STYLES ASSESSMENT REFLECTIONS

After completing your learning styles assessment(s), please answer the following questions about yourself.

1. What is your most dominant learning style? What is your secondary learning style?
2. Do your learning styles change based on what you are learning? If so, how?
3. In what ways do your current learning behaviors confirm or negate your assessment results?

Have a group discussion about the following questions.

1. How do your learning styles preferences influence your learning strategies?
2. How do your learning styles preferences emerge in your approach to tutoring and mentoring?
3. What characteristics or behaviors do students exhibit that reflect each learning style?

Appendix C

LEARNING STYLES SCENARIOS

Scenario 1

James comes to get help for his upcoming test. He is frustrated that the instructor assigns reading in the textbook but does not discuss the text in class. James says he does not understand the material from the textbook. He also struggles with reading the text and is easily distracted while reading; however, James remembers the information the instructor discussed during class. He studies for the test by trying to read the textbook out loud, but he doesn't know which parts to focus on.

Scenario 2

Angela is studying for a midterm and needs help understanding a difficult concept. She has read the material many times and listened to her instructor lecture on the material, but she still doesn't understand it. She says that she is having difficulty understanding the material because it doesn't seem relevant or connected to the rest of the course. While you are talking with Angela, she seems unsettled. She keeps asking you to just help her "get" the concept and doesn't want seem to want the details.

Scenario 3

Ming is frustrated with her course and is struggling to stay motivated. She is concerned that she will not be prepared for the upcoming quiz because the teacher only lectures in class, and she has difficulty paying attention. Her lecture notes are filled with doodles and pictures. She is not sure what to focus on when studying or how to stay motivated in class. She likes the textbook and understands much of the information in it but doesn't see the connection to the lecture. She thinks that the problem is the instructor's teaching style, because she is doing well in her other courses.

Learning Styles: Contrasting Models

Preston C. VanLoon

Learning style theory suggests that a person's ability to learn is less a matter of intelligence and more a matter of utilizing one's preferred way of learning. According to Jensen (1997), 98% of all new learning comes through the senses. In a study of brain development, Sprenger (2002) argued that because all information is received through the senses, people have a dominant sensory pathway and develop a preference for using a specific sense in the learning process. Therefore, listening to lectures may not be the best way for most students to learn. Dias and Sousa (1997) reported that 20% of students are auditory learners while the remaining 80% are visual or kinesthetic learners.

In the past 30 years, several approaches to learning styles have been offered to educators. Dunn, Dunn, and Price (1979) presented a learning style model consisting of five dimensions composed of 21 different instructional and environmental elements that affect an individual's learning preference. Kolb (1984) argued that learning occurs from an experiential perspective, which is represented by his Experiential Learning Style Model. Felder and Silverman (1988) created the *Index of Learning Styles* to identify a preferred learning modality from one of four dimensions. James and Galbraith (1985) suggested that learning occurs through the use of seven perceptual modes or pathways identified as Perceptual Learning Styles. One of the more commonly used approaches to sensory learning is the VARK model; in their research, Fleming and Mills (1992) found that students have particular learning preferences or a dominant learning style in one of four categories: visual, auditory, reading and writing, and kinesthetic (VARK).

Dunn, Beaudry, and Klavas (1989) urged educators to provide responsive instruction to the learning styles of diverse student populations. Tutors and mentors frequently encounter students whose learning styles and experiences may be very different from their own. Therefore, as they acquire a basic knowledge of learning style theory and understand how people learn, tutors and mentors can more effectively assist student clients.

In this training session, tutors and mentors will develop a better understanding of their dominant learning styles and learn how to help assess the learning preferences for another person using the VARK model. As tutors and mentors reflect on their learning modalities and identify strategies that have been effective in helping themselves learn, they are better able to select appropriate learning activities that are consistent with each of the learning preferences in the VARK model and use them with potential clients when providing tutoring services. By the end of the training session, trainees will be able to describe their preferred learning styles, name and describe each of the four learning styles in the VARK model, identify strategies that can be used with student clients appropriate for each of the VARK learning styles, and compare and contrast the VARK learning style approach with another model.

Training Activity

Approximately 1 hour is needed for this training activity. Flip chart paper, markers, handouts (see Appendix), and trainee access to the Internet are needed.

The trainer begins by asking trainees to think of a time when they learned something exceedingly well. Trainees should reflect for 2 minutes on the method they as learners used in the learning activity or the presenter's instructional strategies. As participants consider their learning experiences, they should write a few sentences describing the process they used to master this new learning—whether visual, auditory, reading and writing, or kinesthetic—or a combination of approaches.

When trainees have finished writing their reflection sentences, they should group themselves into pairs and discuss with their partner what instructional activities took place that enabled them to learn something well. After about 5 minutes, the whole group can be called back together to share with one another what they learned about their partner's learning experience and the effectiveness of methods used by the presenter.

As trainees share with the whole group, the trainer lists on flip chart paper the various instructional and learning strategies that were described in the pair discussions. Strategies listed can be written on four different pieces of flip chart paper, each with a different heading: visual, auditory, reading and writing, and kinesthetic. The trainer may want to mention that this is one way that learning approaches have been categorized.

Members of the whole group then make observations from the lists of instructional and learning activities on the four pieces of paper and identify strategies that have helped them to learn in the past. The trainer should point out that not everyone learns in the same way and that each has learning preferences that make learning more efficient and effective.

After the discussion, trainees access the VARK link (www.vark-learn.com) on their computers and complete the VARK questionnaire (Fleming, 2006) to see if their learning experience is consistent with their preferred learning styles. About 10 minutes will be needed to complete the questions and receive the results. After all trainees have completed the VARK questionnaire, they should share with the group their results and explain whether or not they agree with these results based on their previous learning experiences.

When tutors and mentors have shared their preferences with the group, the trainer leads a discussion with the group asking about experiences when the trainees may have learned something well using an approach different from their preferred or dominant learning style. The preferred or dominant style is not the only way one learns. Learning is a complex process and often occurs when the learner is using a modality different from what is preferred because of the situation and type of instructional approaches employed. It is appropriate also to emphasize that students need to take responsibility for themselves as learners, using multiple strategies to enhance effective learning. Because tutors' or mentors' learning preferences may be different from those of the student clients with whom they work, it is helpful to find out before beginning an instructional session how the student learns and to identify and use tutoring and mentoring strategies that will enhance the student client's learning.

The trainer then moves trainees into small groups of three to four with others who have the same learning style to list different strategies that can be used to tutor someone with that learning preference. After 5 minutes, each group shares its list with the whole group.

The trainer concludes by asking trainees to complete and share with the group their responses to the following "ticket out the door" (Lowman, 1984): "Something I learned today about myself as a learner is _____. Strategies I can use with someone who learns visually are _____, auditorily are _____, through reading and writing are _____, and kinesthetically are _____."

For further learning, the trainer instructs trainees to select and research one of the learning style models described above (i.e., Kolb, 1984; Felder & Silverman, 1988; Dunn et al., 1979; or James & Galbraith, 1985) and on the Learning Styles handout (Appendix). Trainees should create a Venn diagram that compares and contrasts the VARK learning style approach with the model of their choice.

Assessment

Trainees can be assessed on each of the training activity's objectives. That is, trainees will be able to describe their preferred learning styles, name and describe each of the four learning styles in the VARK model, identify strategies appropriate for each of the VARK learning styles they may encounter in their work with student clients, and compare and contrast the VARK learning style approach with another model. As trainees carry out their work with clients, the trainer can continue to assess the tutors' or mentors' understanding by occasionally observing and discussing with them the instructional strategies they are using to accommodate the learning styles of their student clients.

References

Dias, P., & Sousa, P. (1997). Understanding navigation and disorientation in hypermedia learning environments. *Journal of Educational Multimedia and Hypermedia, 6,* 173–185.

Dunn, R., Beaudry, J. S., & Klavas, A. (1989). Survey of research on learning styles. *Educational Leadership, 46*(6), 50–58.

Dunn, R., Dunn, K., & Price, G. (1979). Identifying individual learning styles. In *Student learning styles: Diagnosing and prescribing programs* (pp. 39–54). Reston, VA: National Association of Secondary School Principals.

Felder, R. M., & Silverman, L. K. (1988). Learning and teaching styles in engineering education. *Engineering Education, 78,* 674–681.

Fleming, N. D. (2006). *VARK: A guide to learning styles.* Retrieved from http://www.vark-learn. com

Fleming, N. D., & Mills, C. (1992). Not another inventory, rather a catalyst for reflection. *To Improve the Academy, 11,* 137–147.

James, W. B., & Galbraith, M. W. (1985). Perceptual learning styles: Implications and techniques for the practitioner. *Lifelong Learning, 3*(2), 20–23.

Jensen, E. (1997). *Completing the puzzle: The brain-compatible approach to learning.* Del Mar, CA: Turning Point.

Kolb, D. (1984). *Experiential learning: Experience as the source of learning and development.* Englewood Cliffs, NJ: Prentice-Hall.

Lowman, J. (1984). *Mastering techniques of teaching.* San Francisco, CA: Jossey-Bass.

Sprenger, M. (2002). *Becoming a wiz at brain-based teaching.* Thousand Oaks, CA: Corwin Press.

Appendix

LEARNING STYLES HANDOUT

Instructional and Environmental Learning Style Model (Dunn, Dunn, & Price, 1979)

This model consists of five dimensions (emotional, environmental, physiological, psychological, and sociological) with 21 subcategories that consider the instructional and environmental learning preferences of students.

Experiential Learning Style Model (Kolb, 1984)

Experiential Learning Theory is based on six premises: Learning is primarily (a) a process, (b) involving relearning and building on prior knowledge, (c) driven by the resolution of conflicts, differences, and disagreements, (d) involving the total person's adapting to the world, (e) resulting from interacting with one's environment, and (f) involving creation of new knowledge.

Four-Dimensional Learning Style Model (Felder & Silverman, 1988)

This learning style model assumes that learners process and receive information primarily through one of four dimensions: Sensing/Intuiting, Visual/Verbal, Active/Reflective, and Sequential/Global.

Perceptual Learning Style Model (James & Galbraith, 1985)

Perceptual learning styles focus on the different pathways used by learners to absorb information through the senses. These pathways include print, aural, interactive (verbalizing with others), visual, haptic (touch), kinesthetic (bodily movement), and olfactory (taste and smell).

VARK Model (Fleming & Mills, 1992)

This model suggests that students have learning preferences or a dominant learning style in one of four categories: visual, aural or auditory, reading and writing, and kinesthetic (VARK).

Tutor Training Topics

Introduction

The modules of this chapter convey their authors' best ideas for training tutors. Each module presents the theoretical or philosophical rationale for the training, followed by a description of the training activity and the assessment method recommended. Readers should check the www.crla.net/handbook/ page from time to time for additional updated resources provided for Chapter 4. Although the modules included in this chapter were intended by their authors primarily to guide the training of peer tutors, trainers may also explore these topics with peer mentors (College Reading and Learning Association [CRLA], 2011a).

The certification requirements of CRLA's International Tutor Training Program Certification (ITTPC) include training in these topics:

- "Basic tutoring guidelines and/or Tutoring dos and/or Tutoring don'ts"
- "Techniques for successfully beginning and ending a tutor session"
- "Setting goals and/or Planning"
- "Study skills"
- "Critical thinking skills"
- "Compliance with the . . . philosophy of the tutor program . . ."
- "Modeling problem solving." (CRLA, 2011b, p. 1)

These topics are explored in the training modules of this chapter, organized under three general headings.

The first group of modules in Chapter 4 centers around the tutoring session itself: developing a shared philosophy, learning the program's unique dos and don'ts, beginning and ending sessions, and setting goals for sessions. The first section also includes modules on training for particular kinds of tutoring sessions—online and embedded—and for especially difficult sessions.

The next modules in this chapter offer training ideas for strategic tutoring, strategic learning, and tutoring across the curriculum, including reading, critical thinking, taking lecture notes, and preparing for exams. These 10 modules demonstrate that tutors should teach students strategic approaches to use in their studies. These modules also demonstrate that tutoring itself must be strategic and student centered; unlike some other forms of peer academic support, tutoring sessions develop from the student client's needs and understanding and are not predetermined by lesson plans.

The last modules of Chapter 4 offer strategies for training tutors in specific content areas, grouped by subject area. This section of the chapter begins with three training ideas for tutoring writing, followed by topics for tutors of literature, foreign languages, history, and music, and concluding with two training ideas for tutoring mathematics and one for chemistry. Certainly only a fraction of the academic curriculum is represented, and each topic deserves a book of its own, but readers will find intriguing tutor training ideas in these 10 subject-tutoring modules.

REFERENCES

College Reading and Learning Association. (2011a). *IMTPC certification requirements*. Retrieved from http://www.crla.net/imtpc/certification_requirements.htm

College Reading and Learning Association. (2011b). *ITTPC certification requirements*. Retrieved from http://www.crla.net/ittpc/certification_requirements.htm

Ⓐ Tutoring Sessions

Getting Hands On With Learning Center Philosophy

 Ali Mageehon

Tutors are often provided with the mission or philosophy statement of the learning center in which they work. Trainers may provide this statement in a handbook or some other written form. Some learning centers post the mission statement in the center so that the nature or philosophy of the work in tutoring sessions is clear to both learners and tutors. Although some missions are reviewed annually in a process engaging all tutors, many mission statements are constructed by administrators without tutor involvement. Moreover, in the absence of discussion or instruction, tutors can fail to reflect on the center's mission. Thus the mission statement becomes meaningless to most tutors—a part of the culture of higher education in which tutors are not invited to participate.

This training activity encourages tutor participation in reflecting on the mission statement and understanding the philosophy of a learning center. The activity also supports engaging and reflective learning techniques that will assist tutors in working with their own students. The objectives for this training activity are to help tutors explain the mission or philosophy statement for a learning center, synthesize their understanding of the mission or philosophy statement using their preferred learning modalities, and develop new strategies for working with students through exploring their own learning approach as they consider the mission or philosophy statement.

The conceptual framework for this training activity is grounded in Mezirow's (1991, 1998) work on reflective learning. Other researchers have also examined the use of art as a means to help adult learners reflect on their experiences (Aprill & Townsell, 2007; Dirkx, 1997; Lawrence, 2005). Art can bring about a deeper understanding of abstract material, because it allows the adult learner to make concrete something that may not have immediate tangible meaning. In addition, "adults will eagerly engage in learning and growing and will participate when meaningful opportunities and conditions are presented" (McDaniel & Thorn, 1997, pp. 67–68). This training also relies on collaborative learning (Goodsell, Maher, Tinto, Smith, & MacGregor, 1992) and tutors' exploration of a potentially different modality for learning, presenting material in visual form (Silver, Strong, & Perini, 2000).

Tutors come into their jobs in the learning center at various stages of adult development. Some may be accustomed to asking questions, relating their experiences to larger social contexts, and engaging in discussions during training about philosophical issues of tutoring. Others may be content to accept at face value the philosophy or mission put in front of them. This training is designed for tutors to move toward a more reflective approach in their practice as it relates to integrating the mission statement and philosophy with their own knowledge and values to create authentic ownership.

Mezirow's theory of transformative learning supports such engagement with the philosophy of tutoring. Mezirow (1991) suggested that part of the process of changing or developing new perspectives on meaning involves

> the process of becoming critically aware of how and why our assumptions have come to constrain the way we perceive, understand, and feel about our world; changing these structures of habitual expectation to make possible a more inclusive, discriminating, and integrating perspective; and, finally, making choices or otherwise acting upon these new understandings. (p. 167)

By engaging in this hands-on training activity, tutors will have a chance to view their own assumptions about the mission or philosophy statement, making it visually real. This, in turn, provides an opportunity for the trainer and tutors to engage in discussion about what assumptions may be present in the mission statement as well as the tutors' interpretation of the mission or philosophy statement. The training facilitator may also encourage tutors to reflect on their process of interpretation to build links in their work with students as part of a transformative learning process.

The training also relies on collaborative learning: tutors will work toward a communal understanding of the mission or philosophy of the learning center. Through the collaborative process, different views may become apparent, requiring the tutors to work toward a consensus about what the mission statement means and how it influences the work they do as tutors.

Training Activity

The activity can be conducted within a 1-hour training session. Before the session, the trainer should provide tutors with a copy of the learning center mission or philosophy statement as well as the institution's mission statement. Tutors should be on the lookout for where either mission statement is posted: in the learning center, on the institution's website, in the institution's catalog, and elsewhere.

The first step in the training activity is to discuss tutors' reactions to and impressions of the mission statement and guiding philosophy of the learning center. This is a good opportunity for the trainer to discuss briefly the research and theoretical grounding for the philosophy statement so that tutors come to understand the statement broadly. It may be important at this point also to discuss the rationale behind how the mission statement or philosophy statement was written and discuss the larger context of the mission statement of the learning center within the institutional mission, because many tutors may be unfamiliar with the significance of the mission statement of an institution as a whole. Trainers should encourage tutors to discuss their own search for the mission statement around the institution and whether the learning center mission statement seems to be highly valued.

Tutors are then asked to work together in groups. In a learning center that offers tutoring in various subject areas, it is a good idea to ask tutors to work in diverse groups rather than subject-area groups. Each group is provided with a poster board, magazines, glue, markers and other art materials. The tutors work together to create an intention poster that represents their interpretation of the philosophy or mission statement for the center. Tutors may be encouraged at this stage to discuss in their groups whether they intend to use other approaches in interpreting the mission statement (e.g., a song, rap, or skit) to supplement their poster.

In explaining the activity, the trainer may want to take the opportunity to discuss learning styles with the tutors. This is a good training in which to embed looking at learning style inventories and discussing how information is processed, asking the tutors to reflect on tutoring sessions as either tutor or student and assess how different strategies (e.g., concept mapping, discussion) can best support student motivation and engagement. Although this activity is primarily focused on a visual representation of the mission statement, tutors may also be encouraged to make use of other modalities (e.g., writing a rap about the mission statement to be performed at the end of the session).

The trainer can encourage groups to discuss their interpretations of the mission statement or philosophy statement as they work on their posters. Students may come up with variations on themes like the learning center as a place for growth or development, learning, dialogue and discussion, or other themes depending on the mission statement and the tutors' perceptions of the purpose of the learning center. When tutors present the intention posters, the trainer will want to discuss each poster with the groups to gain a full understanding of the ways in which the mission statement was interpreted as well as discussing with the groups what such an interpretation may mean for engaging with learners.

A variation on the training session is to have tutors create individual intention posters. Posters can be displayed around the center or used as text in discussing with the center director (or other tutors) each tutor's individual approach to tutoring, as part of continued training. Discussing the tutor's vision behind the intention board can open up discussions about tutoring philosophy and approach.

The posters can be useful in discussing the learning center mission and philosophy, as well as in helping tutors begin to understand how to fit their tutoring approach to the mission and philosophy of the center. This activity may also open up opportunities for the trainer or other learning center leaders to reflect on the mission statement and how it may be adjusted or revised for a better fit with the perceived values of the learning center and its personnel.

Assessment

Assessment of tutor learning can be conducted informally through group discussion of the tutors' intentions and interpretations and formally through trainer evaluation of the intention posters. The outcome from the training should be a clearer understanding of the center mission, and this foundational understanding can then be discussed in subsequent trainings and session evaluations with individual tutors. The posters are artifacts that can be revisited throughout the semester. Tutors may be invited to complete a second poster at the end of the year, either individually or as a group, for purposes of additional reflection.

The posters can also be displayed throughout the learning center for discussion with students. Tutors may use the posters as a starting point for discussion with new students to clarify the purpose and role of the tutoring center. The posters can be useful during orientation sessions or tours of the learning center as well, to help explain the role of the tutoring center to new students.

References

Aprill, A., & Townsell, R. (2007). The arts as an occasion for collective adult learning as authentic community development. *New Directions for Adult and Continuing Education, 116,* 51–63. doi:10.1002/ace.276

Dirkx, J. (1997). Nurturing soul in adult learning. *New Directions for Adult and Continuing Education, 74,* 79–88. doi:10.1002/ace.7409

Goodsell, A., Maher, M., Tinto, V., Smith, B. L., & MacGregor, J. (1992). *Collaborative learning: A sourcebook for higher education.* University Park, PA: National Center on Postsecondary Teaching, Learning and Assessment.

Lawrence, R. L. (2005). Knowledge construction as contested terrain: Adult learning through artistic expression. *New Directions for Adult and Continuing Education, 107,* 3–11. doi:10.1002/ace.184

McDaniel, N., & Thorn, G. (1997). *Learning audiences: Adult arts participation and the learning consciousness.* Washington, DC: John F. Kennedy Center for the Performing Arts, Association of Performing Arts Presenters.

Mezirow, J. (1991). *Transformative dimensions of adult learning.* San Francisco, CA: Jossey-Bass.

Mezirow, J. (1998). On critical reflection. *Adult Education Quarterly, 48,* 185–198. doi:10.1177/074171369804800305

Silver, H., Strong, P., & Perini, M. (2000). *So each may learn: Integrating learning styles and multiple intelligences.* Alexandria, VA: Association for Supervision and Curriculum Development.

Tutoring Dos and Don'ts

Linda Stedje-Larsen and Roberta T. Schotka

A review of tutoring websites and printed materials from tutor training programs certified by International Tutor Training Program Certification (ITTPC) of the College Reading and Learning Association (CRLA, 2011) reveals that although there is no universal list of appropriate or inappropriate tutoring behaviors and practices, most programs include a component of training that addresses *basic dos and don'ts* of tutoring. These components tend to reflect the characteristics of individual programs as they relate to an institution's mission, strategic initiatives, and philosophy and offer an overview of both the training and the tutor's role in program delivery. As may be expected, these components also tend to be practical and realistic. For example, "Do help tutees earn As in all courses" establishes a goal that is neither realistic nor attainable; however, "Do help the tutee develop a stronger understanding of course content and the skills required for success in the course" is a more attainable goal.

The authors have noted similarities in how certified tutoring programs present tutoring dos and don'ts, which are typically created to clarify expectations in nine general categories: (a) job readiness; (b) professionalism, courtesy, and basic ethics of working as a tutor; (c) preparing for the tutorial session; (d) role modeling; (e) verbal and nonverbal communication; (f) adhering to institutional and tutorial center policies and procedures; (g) facilitating student-centered, active learning; (h) demonstrating empathy rather than sympathy; and (i) skillful session management. The inclusion of such directives in training programs, particularly when organized around specific functional and theoretical categories, provides a snapshot of the role of tutors in a particular learning center. The snapshot displays the responsibilities and limitations of tutors and the expectations of tutees.

Falchikov (2001) observed that tutor training should provide a balance among the technical, educational, social, structural, and affective aspects of service delivery. Deliberately incorporating information about basic expectations and techniques early in a training program gives tutors not only a clear picture of the technical standards of their jobs but also an encapsulation of other key aspects of effective tutoring in the program.

There are a number of ways to incorporate tutoring dos and don'ts into a training program. They can be used to introduce the basic requirements for satisfactory job performance, to overview subsequent in-depth training sessions, or to review what tutors have learned.

In addition to helping tutors gain essential knowledge about tutoring, a training session on tutoring dos and don'ts can also serve as a team-building exercise; all the trainees may be new and need to learn about each other as well as the program, or new trainees may need to be incorporated into the social group already formed by experienced tutors. Presenting basic dos and don'ts is also a way of insuring immediate learning of a few key points, each of which can be elaborated during subsequent training activities. A training session on the basics of tutoring can also serve as a reminder and an assessment of what tutors have learned in their training sessions about effective tutoring. By engaging tutors in the collaborative, learner-centered, hands-on activities characteristic of dos and don'ts training, trainers are not only teaching tutors requisite information but also modeling for them the active learning that is a key behavior for successful tutoring practice.

Finally, training tutors in the basic dos and don'ts of the job provides an opportunity for trainers to model adult learning theory, or andragogy, which in turn provides an effective approach to tutoring (Lipsky, 2011). Setting a climate conducive to learning, involving learners in planning the session, deciding on objectives for the session, and helping students understand their own learning needs as well as helping them carry out their learning plans are all elements of the andragogical process (Wood, 1996). This process allows the trainer to present the basic dos and don'ts in a way that offers practical information while taking into consideration the needs of the tutee, the skills of the tutor, the constraints of the program, and parameters of the service. Doing so in an engaging, process-oriented way models the approach tutors themselves should take.

Training Activity

The following activity is adapted from Silberman's (1998, p. 75) training handbook and requires about 1 hour of training time. On the board or somewhere visible in the room should be posted either the nine general categories of dos and don'ts or more job-specific categories such as confidentiality, ethics, tracking hours, limitations, and communication. Silberman suggested beginning with an anecdote, fictional story, cartoon, or graphic to focus attention on the topic. For example, what should the tutor do when a student comes in for help the night before an exam and asks the tutor what is going to be on the test? Cartoon options may include *Shoe* comics (Cassatt & Brookins, 2009, 2010).

To create synergy, as suggested by Silberman (1998), the trainer divides the trainees into two groups, giving one group a sheet of paper labeled "Dos of Tutoring" and the other, "Don'ts of Tutoring." Each group should designate a recorder and a reporter. Participants list what they think would be appropriate or inappropriate behaviors for tutors in either the nine general categories or more job-specific categories listed on the board (e.g., confidentiality, ethics, basic responsibilities, limitations, relationships), which can guide their responses. Back in the whole group, reporters share the decisions of their group. The trainer should record the responses on the board, reorganizing and regrouping them where necessary to fit into the selected categories.

Another technique would be for the group to create categories to synthesize the various groups' suggestions, for example, "Check In and Check Out" (for procedures for recording work hours), "Check Your Role" (for the basic role of a tutor), and "Check Your Limitations" (for what tutors must not do). Discussion can continue with scenarios or role-plays scripted by the trainer.

As an additional or alternate activity, the trainer can take the role of a new student who is asking what to expect from a tutor. Group members take the role of staff members of the tutoring program and offer one of the items from a prepared list of dos and don'ts in response to the trainer-as-student's inquiry. The trainer can follow up with questions to foster learning. For example, the student may ask, "How can a tutor help me with my history course?" A trainee may reply, "Tutors can help you understand readings you have completed." Follow-up from the student may be, "But what if I haven't had a chance to do the readings?" This gives the opportunity to review or check for understanding of a "do" of tutoring: "I can work with you on assigned texts when you have read them. Let's reschedule." (This scenario is appropriate for training tutors who do not serve as reading buddies or other collaborative reading assistants.)

We have gathered other ways to address the dos and don'ts of tutoring from materials of CRLA ITTPC-certified programs and offer the following ideas with the permission of their authors, who submitted program materials for certification review:

- The tutoring program of Thomas College in Waterville, Maine, first introduces dos and don'ts and then instructs tutors to keep journals with regular entries on what did and did not work well in actual tutoring situations. A group discussion of the tutors' entries follows in a later session.

- The tutor training program of the University of Houston-Victoria in Victoria, Texas, uses a combination of lecture and small- or large-group discussion. The trainer prepares questions in advance based on the program's list of dos and don'ts and the program's frequently asked questions (FAQs) to facilitate discussion. Returning, experienced tutors sometimes lead this session under the guidance of the tutorial program coordinator and director and conduct a roundtable to encourage greater participation by trainees.

- In addition to creating a PowerPoint® presentation about dos and don'ts, staff of the tutoring center at Ohio State University at Newark and Central Ohio Technical College in Newark, Ohio, make their session interactive and engage tutors in critical thinking skills by asking directed questions that require trainees to apply the specific points to tutoring scenarios.

As with any topic addressed in tutor training, the dos and don'ts can be revisited several times to model effective tutoring strategies.

Assessment

The tutoring dos and don'ts session can serve as an overview of a tutoring program, at beginning or end of training, so that session assessment can become part of the formative or summative evaluation of the program. When tutors have begun tutoring or at least have shadowed experienced tutors (or at the conclusion of training), trainees can collaborate in small groups to develop a list of specific dos and don'ts based on the content of the training, under each of the nine main categories presented earlier in this module. Tutors can develop a list or chart to compare and contrast dos and don'ts. The purpose is to engage trainees in thinking about what they have learned and applying that to some type of rubric that includes the broad categories that are most applicable to the program. At the conclusion of the activity, the small groups merge into the larger group to share their ideas and discuss key points, creating a master list of specific dos and don'ts to be included in their training manual.

Trainers can also assess trainees' learning by having tutors write scenarios of horrendous tutoring sessions in which tutors violate many dos and don'ts. Tutors may present these scenarios as handouts or short videos to be discussed in small groups.

Trainers may decide to host mock talk shows in which participating tutors grapple with and take sides on issues in a scenario. For example, the host (trainer) may state that tutors should do all they can to help students do their homework. Tutors can demonstrate their understanding of their program's dos and don'ts in their roles as show participants. Some game show formats allow audience members to participate in demonstrating their understanding or in assessing the knowledge of game participants.

For a variety of training formats, trainees can respond on index cards to prompts asking what they learned or what new ideas they acquired from beginning to end of the session. Their responses can be used to design a review for the next training session (Davis, 2001, p. 135).

References

Cassatt, C., & Brookins, G. (2009, July 10). Dating do's and don'ts. *Shoe*. GoComics. Retrieved from http://www.gocomics.com/shoe/2009/07/10

Cassatt, C., & Brookins, G. (2010, September 8). Relationships do's and don'ts. *Shoe*. GoComics. Retrieved from http://www.gocomics.com/shoe/2010/09/08/

College Reading and Learning Association. (2011). *Current certified tutor training programs*. Retrieved from http://www.crla.net/ittpc/current_certifications.htm

Davis, B. (2001). *Tools for teaching*. San Francisco, CA: Jossey-Bass.

Falchikov, N. (2001). *Learning together: Peer tutoring in higher education*. London, United Kingdom: Routledge-Falmer.

Lipsky, S. A. (2011). *A training guide for college tutors and peer educators*. Boston, MA: Pearson.

Silberman, M. (1998). *Active training: A handbook of techniques, designs, case examples, and tips*. San Francisco, CA: Jossey-Bass.

Wood, D. (1996). Andragogy: Appreciating the characteristics of the adult learner. In T. Gier & K. Hancock (Eds.), *College Reading and Learning Association tutor training handbook* (pp. 22–27). Anchorage, AK: College Reading and Learning Association.

Beginning and Ending Tutoring Sessions: A Customer-Service Approach

Suzanne Ponicsan

The key to any business is its employees' excellent customer service skills (Sykes, 2011). Academic support centers, too, should be warm and welcoming. Many students may voluntarily solicit the services of a tutor, but there are others who are reluctant. The latter students may be required by faculty to attend tutoring sessions, or they may be afraid to see a tutor for fear of seeming unintelligent. Therefore it is essential that tutors display high-quality customer service skills. These skills are especially critical at the beginning and end of a tutoring session. At the beginning of a session, the student assesses the tutor's competence and personality. First impressions are important because they can determine the success or failure of the session.

This training module begins with a discussion on why the beginning and end of tutoring sessions are important and highlights some key customer service skills. An interactive training activity is then outlined and focuses on two areas: key customer service skills and role-play scenarios to put customer service skills and general tutoring techniques into practice. The module concludes with methods of assessing trainees' customer service skills.

The importance of customer service skills should be brought into perspective with a true story. One day a tutor was sitting at her desk in the tutoring lab calmly working on a project. The tutoring lab was open, but there were no scheduled appointments until the next hour. Suddenly a student came storming into the tutoring lab, walked abruptly to the circular table at the far side of the lab, and slammed her books down on the table. For a moment, the tutor was stunned; the student had not said a word, and she seemed to place all of her focus on arranging her books into neat piles without glancing up from her task.

After a moment's thought to collect herself, the tutor stood up and cheerfully greeted the obviously distraught student. The student glanced up and said a brusque hello, then resumed her task. The tutor, aware that the student was quite uncomfortable, introduced herself, welcomed the student to the tutoring lab, and asked if she could help at all. The student finally stopped what she was doing and responded that she needed help with a class and should have sought help sooner, but she was too afraid to come into the tutoring lab. In fact, that was the reason for her abrupt entrance; she admitted that she had to force herself to come in or it would not have happened. After tutor and student chatted about her concerns and discussed how the tutors could work with her, the student became calmer and looked around the room. The student scheduled an appointment for a tutoring session and left apparently more confident and as if relieved of a heavy burden.

The trainer may want to share this story with tutoring staff and reflect that this scenario ended positively because the tutor used customer service skills effectively. She welcomed the student, introduced herself, and inquired about the student's needs. Ignoring or snubbing the student would have confirmed the student's fear of seeking help, and she might have spread the word on campus about her negative experience.

The Institute for Management Excellence (2007) provided a list of excellent customer service skills that can easily be applied to tutoring situations. The Institute suggested welcoming customers (or tutees) in a friendly manner (standing up, shaking hands, and so forth) and providing a name for a personalized touch. Other advice included getting to know the tutees and their situation and then discussing with them how the tutoring program can meet their needs. Tutors should ask questions to clarify the tutee's concerns and determine whether the recommended plan of action is likely to help them, treat clients with respect, and above all be patient with and empathetic to their needs and concerns. As the Institute for Management Excellence suggested, "Remember that the customer called because they have a problem they need solved. The customer is often stressed and seeking help from an expert. You are that expert" (2007, para. 25). If other students walk in while tutors are busy, tutors can either inform the more recent visitors that they will be with them soon or politely excuse themselves from the current session to assist the visitors. The key is to make sure the tutees feel welcomed and appreciated. Then, at the end of a visit, tutors should thank tutees for visiting and ask if there is anything else that can be done to help them.

The same courtesy must be extended in telephone and virtual tutoring sessions. Telecommunications Services at Southern Illinois University Carbondale (n. d.) noted that answering the telephone is a "human moment" that provides "the opportunity to create relationships for the future of your department, college or the university" (p. 2). Telecommunications Services recommended the following: answer the phone by the third ring; be completely focused on the call at hand; answer with a polite, confident, and friendly tone; appropriately greet the caller using a standardized greeting; be prepared for the call (e.g., have writing utensils ready and ask for the caller's name if none is given right away); and "treat the caller with respect" (Southern Illinois University Carbondale, p. 2). In virtual tutoring sessions, similar courtesies must be extended. Rein (2009) emphasized the importance of building rapport in online sessions: "Because in writing our voices can more easily be perceived as stoic, authoritative, or harsh, developing a friendly cyber-voice is crucial" (para. 3). Whether assisting students over the phone or online, tutors must be mindful of their voice and avoid any potential for comments to be misinterpreted. Overall, the Institute for Management Excellence (2007) suggested that staff can "make someone's day much better just by being helpful" (para. 26).

There are two learning objectives for this training activity. First, tutors should understand the importance of having solid customer service skills. Second, tutors should be able to apply the various skills to the beginning and end of their tutoring sessions.

Training Activity

This activity focuses on turning negative scenarios into positive scenarios. Tutors will reflect on their own experiences related to customer service and what could have turned them into positive experiences. The training activity will then focus on negative tutoring session beginnings and endings. Trainers should allow approximately 60–90 minutes (depending on the size of the group) for the training session. Approximate time frames may be modified as necessary.

No audiovisual equipment is necessary for the training session, although a video recorder is useful for recording role-playing sessions. A whiteboard or large display surface should be provided in order to write the tutors' thoughts collectively, and each tutor should have pencil and paper for jotting ideas individually. Handouts offering negative introductions and concluding sessions should be prepared. Trainers can use or modify the sample negative introductions and conclusions in the Appendix to create these handouts.

The training activity should be held in one room that is large enough to accommodate all tutoring staff. Tables and chairs should be provided, but no particular arrangement of tables and chairs is necessary.

The trainer begins the session by asking tutors to consider and share any negative customer service incidents they have experienced. Then tutors should be asked to describe any positive experiences. Tutors can draw on experiences from retail stores, educational institutions, medical centers, and help desks, for example. The characteristics of these positive and negative experiences should be identified and displayed on the board. Trainer and tutors should agree on a set of customer service behaviors required when working in the learning center. This section of the activity requires approximately 15 minutes.

Next, tutor trainers should refer tutors to the handout on negative session narratives (see Appendix). In groups of two or more (preferably matching each new tutor with an experienced tutor), trainees should identify the *don'ts* of the narratives and how they can be changed into *dos*. All groups may then share and discuss their changes. This section of the activity requires approximately 15 minutes.

Then tutors create and act out their own tutoring scenarios. Remaining in small groups (either the same as the previous activity or in different groups for a different perspective), each group will come up with its own positive or negative scenario. Finally, each group acts out its scenario. Time required is approximately 2 minutes per group.

Finally, bringing all groups together, the trainer should discuss with trainees each smaller group's response to the role-playing scenario. The trainer can ask questions to facilitate the discussion. What worked in the scenario? What did not work in the scenario? What improvements, if any, could have been made to make the dramatized beginnings and endings even better? The time required for discussion is approximately 30 minutes.

Assessment

By the end of the training session, tutors should understand the importance of having solid customer service skills. To assess tutors' understanding, the trainer can ask for written or oral responses to a question about the consequences of poor customer service skills.

Also, tutors should be able to apply the various skills to the beginning and end of their tutoring sessions. The trainer's assessment of tutor skill in this area is built into discussion of the handout situations and the quality of each group's scenario. However, regular or ongoing assessment of tutors' customer service skills can also be made. If tutees are asked to evaluate their tutors' customer service skills, tutees' responses may help determine whether the students' experiences have been positive or negative. Trainers may also observe tutoring sessions to determine whether tutors are demonstrating the customer service skills the group has determined are necessary.

References

Institute for Management Excellence. (2007). *Good customer service tips.* Retrieved from http://www.itstime.com/print/jun2007p.htm

Rein, J. M. (2009, September). Do you understand? A practical guide to synchronous online tutoring. *Writing Lab Newsletter, 34*(1), 14. Retrieved from http://www.writinglabnewsletter.org/archives/v34/34.1.pdf

Southern Illinois University Carbondale. (n.d.). *Telephone etiquette: Customer service begins here.* Retrieved from http://telecom.it.siu.edu/index.php/etiquette.html

Sykes, E. (2011). *Customer satisfaction secrets: Six secrets of outstanding customer retention.* Retrieved from http://www.thesykesgrp.com/CustomerServiceSatisfaction01.htm

Appendix

NEGATIVE INTRODUCTIONS AND CONCLUSIONS

Introductions

- Jim, one of the learning center's tutors, sits at a desk reading when a student walks into the tutoring lab. Jim glances up briefly and says, "Hi there! Go ahead and have a seat; I'll be with you in just a sec," before resuming his reading.

- Sarah, a student at the institution, wanders by the tutoring lab and stops to read some information from the board outside. Shreya, already working with a tutee, notices this but does not acknowledge Sarah's presence or offer assistance and instead continues the session.
- Juan comes to the tutoring lab at the request of his writing instructor. The tutor, Jonah, greets Juan with a smile and asks how he can help. Juan explains that he needs someone to proofread his paper for him. Jonah's smile fades, and he informs Juan he cannot help and that Juan needs to go elsewhere for assistance.

Conclusions

- Maria is working with a student who has a 30-minute appointment. At the 30-minute mark, Maria abruptly informs the student the session is over and that she has to do something else—even though the student has additional questions.
- Nathan, a math tutor, has worked for the past hour with a frustrated student who could not grasp even the basic rules of the order of operations. Finally Nathan tells the student to go home, spend time working on more problems, and return next week. Nathan's parting comment is, "If you don't get it by then, you never will."

Beginning and Ending a Tutoring Session: Incorporating Active Learning Strategies

Maija M. Braaten

Successfully beginning and ending tutoring sessions is both important and fundamental (MacDonald, 2000). Tutors need to be instructed in how to open and close a session effectively. The training session in this module utilizes principles of Gardner's (1999) multiple intelligences theory (Multiple Intelligences) and Bloom's (Anderson & Krathwohl, 2001) revised taxonomy of educational objectives (Bloom's Taxonomy) as conceptual frameworks. Training is active through the tutors' creation of their own original role plays incorporating the fundamentals discussed in the brief opening lecture or PowerPoint® presentation (Braaten, 2009). Several of the Multiple Intelligences are utilized through structured and interactive learning activities. Structuring the training in this manner moves the tutors through the revised levels of Bloom's Taxonomy, including Remember, Understand, Apply, Analyze, Evaluate, and Create (Anderson & Krathwohl, 2001).

The tutors work collaboratively in pairs to create and perform the role plays. Through the process of creating the role plays, tutors will have the opportunity to use several learning intelligences and will demonstrate all levels of Bloom's revised taxonomy. The process of writing and acting out the role plays involves Interpersonal, Linguistic, and Kinesthetic intelligences (Gardner, 1999). Utilizing a multimodal approach to learning during this training activity increases the retention of the information for the tutors in the training group and stimulates more thinking than a strictly lecture-based format might. This multimodal approach also emphasizes the importance of providing a strong beginning and ending of a tutoring session through the focused activity and practice of delivery.

Learning objectives for the tutors in training are (a) to understand the key components of an effective beginning and ending of a tutoring session; (b) to understand the importance and significance of effectively beginning and ending a tutoring session; (c) to demonstrate this understanding and application through creating role plays of their own original scenarios; and (d) to develop understanding and demonstrate analysis of the material by discussing and critiquing the role plays. Both trainer and tutors will be able to engage in the assessment process because of the format of the training. The tutors' involvement with the critiques empowers them by providing an opportunity to demonstrate their mastery of the material. Engaging in an open discussion of the strengths and areas for improvement of the role plays actively involves the tutors in the training and allows them to showcase their critical analysis skills. The trainer will comment on and direct the discussion as appropriate to provide focus and ensure that understanding and analysis of the principles of the training content are demonstrated.

Training Activity

One classroom or conference room with movable chairs and desks, LCD projector and laptop, an AV screen or a large whiteboard that can be used as a screen, copies of the PowerPoint® presentation and tutoring paperwork (e.g., tutor/student contract, time cards, notes sheets), and some extra pens are required for this training activity. Tutors will have paper and should have pens with them to take notes and to write their role plays. Trainers should plan approximately 60–90 minutes for the training, depending on the size of the group and duration of discussions and critiques.

The trainer gives a presentation on beginning and ending a tutoring session that includes a rationale of the importance of the topic and the dos and don'ts of these components of the tutoring session. The presentation is approximately 15 minutes long. A sample presentation is provided by the author (Braaten, 2009). This PowerPoint® presentation is available for trainers to use as a way to deliver the information and concepts discussed in this training.

Tutors are paired with each other. One tutor is assigned the role of tutor and the other the role of tutee. Half of the pairs are assigned to create and act out a brief scenario of an effective beginning, and the other half must create a scenario for ending a tutoring session. The trainer should allow 10–15 minutes for the tutors to create and practice their role plays.

The trainer first asks for volunteers for pairs to present their role play to the group. If not enough volunteers come forward, the trainer calls on pairs to present. Each role play lasts 2–3 minutes.

After each dramatization, the trainer facilitates discussion with the training participants. The tutors comment on and critique the role plays using criteria derived from the trainer's earlier presentation, and the trainer adds positive feedback and constructive criticism as appropriate.

Assessment

Assessment is integrated throughout this training activity: both tutors and trainer can assess trainees' skill by analyzing trainees' scenarios and role plays. The assessment instrument for this performance-based demonstration of tutor knowledge is the list of key components of effective beginnings and endings of a tutoring session as presented in the lecture or PowerPoint® presentation.

Ongoing assessment of tutors' skill will also be evaluated by the trainer during observations of tutoring sessions. The trainer should continue to monitor for employment of the key components in real tutoring sessions.

References

Anderson, L. W., & Krathwohl, D. R. (Eds.). (2001). *A taxonomy for learning, teaching, and assessing: A revision of Bloom's taxonomy of educational objectives.* New York, NY: Addison, Wesley, Longman.

Braaten, M. (2009). *PowerPoint on beginning and ending a tutoring session* [PowerPoint slides]. Retrieved from http://www.montevallo.edu/SSS/tutor_e_resources.shtm

Gardner, H. E. (1999). *Intelligence reframed: Multiple intelligences for the 21st century.* New York, NY: Basic Books.

MacDonald, R. B. (2000). *The master tutor: A guidebook for more effective tutoring* (2nd ed.). Williamsville, NY: Cambridge Stratford Study Skills Institute.

Clarifying Goals for a Tutoring Session

 ## Mark S. May and Jacqueline Harris

Tutoring sessions are most effective when both the tutor and client work toward accomplishing the same set of goals. When a tutor and client meet for the first time, it is important to clarify the purpose of the session, talk about the roles of the tutor and client, establish a few goals for the session, and work toward helping students to develop longer-range goals. According to Schermerhorn, Hunt, and Osborn (2003), goal setting is "the process of developing, negotiating, and formalizing targets or objectives that a person is responsible for accomplishing" (p. 163). Goals that are challenging and specific (not vague) are likely to improve performance. Additionally, the client needs to be given feedback about progress toward meeting the goals. The client must be able, self-efficacious, and committed to achieving the goals (Schermerhorn et al., 2003). Tutors can help clients by analyzing their strengths and weaknesses, setting specific goals for the session, and suggesting some intermediate and longer-range goals.

This training session is intended to help tutors understand the process of setting goals in a tutoring session. Beginning tutors typically answer questions, provide information, or demonstrate problem-solving techniques. Tutors can improve their sessions by analyzing strengths and weaknesses, establishing session goals, and helping clients to define broad goals, rather than simply resolving the short-term problems that brought clients to the center. When tutors establish goals, both the tutors and the center will be better able to assess the tutors' impact on student learning. The tutor and clients may already be familiar with goal setting because many first-year-experience textbooks describe the process (e.g., Ellis, 2011, pp. 67–68). This training session helps tutors to recognize the importance of setting goals and teaches them how to begin helping clients to formulate measurable and achievable educational goals in tutoring sessions.

Some clients come to tutoring sessions because a parent, advisor, coach, or instructor asked them to take action to get off academic probation. Clients in this situation may not be motivated to meet with tutors. In addition to meeting their other responsibilities, tutors will have to persuade these clients that the services of the center will be beneficial. Some clients may be overwhelmed by upcoming tests or projects and demand immediate action. Goal setting may be introduced at different times or to a different extent depending upon the circumstances, but it is a critical part of every tutoring session. Talking about goals often provides the tutor with the opportunity to help clients determine what they really want, no matter the circumstances.

To begin, tutors need to understand a little about the diagnostic process. Before starting the tutoring session, the tutor has five responsibilities:

- Seek all relevant sources of information. The client should be instructed to bring lecture notes, past course tests, time management tools, textbook, syllabus, and other relevant course materials to the first meeting. The center may give tutors access to assessments, academic history, test scores, and other relevant information.

- Talk with the client about the tutor's role.

- Talk with the client about the client's role.

- Ask some probing questions about the client's perception of the problem or area to improve.

- Agree upon some preliminary goals for the session by asking what the client wishes to accomplish in the session and negotiating appropriate outcomes.

The tutor also has four additional responsibilities:

- Observe the client while working. Ask questions about what the client is thinking and doing to learn the material.

- Make use of diagnostic checklists. There are many good checklists available on study habits, solving math problems, and reading habits (see, for example, Van Blerkom, 2012).

- Offer encouragement.

- Identify strengths as well as weaknesses.

After the tutor has analyzed one or more of the main reasons why a client is having difficulties, the tutor can tactfully share his or her observations or conjectures with the client. This discussion can provide an opportunity for setting longer-term goals.

By asking broad questions about the student's immediate needs at the start of the session, the tutor can get an idea of the scope of tutoring the client may have in mind. In order to get the session started with a focus on goals, here are some suggested conversation openers for setting short-term goals:

- What would you like to accomplish in the next 45 minutes?

- What are your biggest concerns in this course?

- When we have finished today, what do you want to have learned?

The answers will vary. The tutor's job is to help shape the client's responses into productive goals.

Productive goals are clear and measurable. Here are two examples of client goals that are not clear: "I want to understand the chapter better," or "I want to pass the course." The tutor can help the client to clarify goals and apply a specific study strategy that matches the diagnosis. For example, a better goal statement may be, "I want to learn how to use a study-reading method to review the key points of Chapter 10." For someone who wants to "pass the course," the tutor can ask some follow-up questions about what the client needs to do or understand to accomplish that broad goal or ask how the tutoring session can help the client to reach the goal of passing the course. What is preventing the client from achieving the goal? A better goal statement in this situation may be, "I want to learn how to take notes more effectively so I can pass the course, because test questions come primarily from lectures." Using a counseling approach, as suggested by Casazza and Silverman (1996, pp. 115–117), may be useful in helping the tutor ensure that the goals established are the client's, not the tutor's.

Long-term goals are more difficult to establish. They may need to be broken down into mid-range goals. For example, if a client asks for help writing an essay, the tutor may need to investigate the student's use of elements of the writing process, such as brainstorming, choosing a topic, narrowing down a topic, generating ideas, organizing an essay, and using correct grammar. The long-term goal may be to learn how to write a coherent, grammatically-correct five-paragraph essay, but achieving that goal may require focusing on establishing and accomplishing many shorter-range goals.

How can a tutor tell if the goals for the session have been met? Obviously, tutors want to know if their efforts have been successful. One simple suggestion is to try this exercise. As soon as goals have been set, the tutor can ask, "On a scale of 1-10, how far along are you to reaching this goal?" This simple exercise sets the stage for the end of the session, when the tutor can ask the same question again. It gives both tutor and student the opportunity to provide each other with immediate feedback and positive reinforcement. It also helps define short- and longer-term goals for the client and establishes a possible framework for the next session.

Training Activity

This workshop will help tutors learn how to set goals with clients and use the goals effectively in tutoring sessions. This session requires a comfortable room that is suitable for group discussion. Butcher paper, pens, tables, and movable chairs should be provided. The trainer should prepare and provide copies of a handout that defines the tutoring process in terms of the center's needs and provides examples of suitable discipline-specific session goals and long-term goals. The trainer should also provide evaluation forms as described later in this module. The training session requires about 60 minutes.

ICEBREAKER

The tutors will find partners and introduce themselves. Each tutor states three personal goals for the semester, two of which have been accomplished and one yet to be accomplished, but without telling each other which goals have already been accomplished. Each partner guesses which two goals have been achieved and which one is still in progress.

The trainer will give the tutors an evaluation form. The first part has a section with the heading, "Before the Workshop" and asks the question, "On a scale of 1–10, how well do you understand the process of setting goals?" This icebreaker session may require 7–10 minutes.

ESTABLISHING WORKSHOP GOALS

The trainer will provide a statement of goals for the training session and ask the tutors to state whether they think the goals are clear, measurable, and valuable. Some background on goal setting as discussed previously in this training module can be presented. Tutors should be given a handout that defines the tutoring process and provides examples of suitable session goals and long-term goals. Veteran tutors and others can be invited to share their goal-setting experiences in tutoring sessions. This section of training may require 10 minutes.

WRITING GOALS

Tutors are divided into groups and go to stations equipped with butcher paper and markers. They are instructed to draw three vertical lines on the paper to form four columns. On the paper tutors will write goals that are too broad, unclear, or not measurable in the first column. In the second column they will list questions they could ask clients to help the clients make these goal statements more appropriate. In the third column they will write the new goals. In the fourth column, they will describe how they will know if these goals have been met. The tutors' examples can be discussed as a group of the whole. This part of the session may require 15 minutes.

ROLE PLAY

The tutors then match up in pairs and take turns playing the roles of tutor and client at both the beginning and end of a tutoring session. The goal of the exercise is to practice asking appropriate questions that will help the client take responsibility for developing clear, measurable goals. After the role play, the tutors should discuss what they learned about asking questions. If one pair of tutors is particularly good at the process, they should demonstrate the process while the entire group watches. This part of the session may require 15 minutes.

Assessment

After this exercise is over, tutors complete their evaluation forms. This part of the session may require about 10 minutes.

Trainees have already answered the question under the "before the workshop" heading. The form should have another heading labeled "after the workshop" in which the following questions appear: On a 1-10 scale, how well do you understand the overall process of setting goals? How well do you think that you are able to write goals that are clear and measurable? How good are your skills at asking questions that will help clients to formulate appropriate goals? How important to a tutoring session is setting goals? A comment question can also be asked: What additional information would you like to learn regarding this topic? Responses may be discussed with the tutors at the end of this training session or used to create or improve future workshops.

The trainer should follow up with the tutors a few weeks later and review their tutoring session evaluation forms. Tutors should talk with their trainer about specific clients, how the tutors diagnosed strengths and weaknesses, what short- and longer-term academic goals were established, and how the tutors evaluated the effectiveness of those tutoring sessions. Tutors may also conduct peer observations to mentor one another.

References

Casazza, M. E., & Silverman, S. L. (1996). *Learning assistance and developmental education: A guide for effective practice*. San Francisco, CA: Jossey-Bass.

Ellis, D. (2011). *Becoming a master student* (13th ed.). Boston, MA: Wadsworth.

Schermerhorn, J. R., Hunt, J. G., & Osborn, R. N. (2003). *Organizational behavior* (8th ed.). New York, NY: John Wiley.

Van Blerkom, D. L. (2012). *College study skills: Becoming a strategic learner* (7th ed.). Boston, MA: Wadsworth Cengage Learning.

Monique Idoux

Establishing goals for the tutoring session enables tutors to manage the time for tutoring effectively and efficiently and model for the tutee how best to use the time, resources, and abilities of the tutor. This training module will introduce tutors to a student-centered philosophy of tutoring by which the tutoring sessions are structured around the goals, needs, and ideas of the student. Thus the tutor learns how to guide the student through the tutoring process, enabling the student to gain academic skills and confidence and ensuring that the student is an interdependent, not dependent, learner.

Goals affect performance in four primary ways (Locke & Latham, 2002). First of all, goals are directive; they direct attention and effort toward activities that are relevant to achieving the goal and away from activities that are not relevant to the goal. According to Locke and Latham, this effect is both cognitive and behavioral. In a learning environment, then, students with specific goals may pay more attention to and learn more from the task at hand, such as reading a passage or listening to a lecture. Second, goals are energizing; high goals lead to greater effort than low goals. Third, goals affect persistence, prolonging the effort spent on a task. However, with goals that are difficult to achieve, there could be a trade-off in work between time spent on a task and intensity of effort (Locke & Latham, 2002). For example, a student could work at a higher intensity for a shorter period of time or less intensely for longer time. Fourth, goals affect action indirectly by "leading to the arousal, discovery, and/or use of task-relevant knowledge and strategies" (Locke & Latham, 2002, p. 707). In this sense, action is the result of cognition and motivation.

One of the determinants of whether or not a person will set a goal, attempt a task, and persist at it is self-efficacy (Lemme, 2002). Bandura (1977) suggested four sources of self-efficacy beliefs: past performance, psychological states, vicarious experiences with observed models, and verbal encouragement and persuasion from others. Research on self-efficacy suggests that changes in attitudes toward the self may be related to changes in effort and achievement (Lemme, 2002). These sources of self-efficacy can interact in complex ways, and fluctuations along these four variables will affect motivation, effort, and persistence accordingly (Lemme, 2002). Self-efficacy is defined in relationship to a particular task or goal (Lemme, 2002) and thus has been found to affect choice of goal level; greater self-efficacy is associated with setting higher goals and with higher performance (Phillips & Gully, 1997).

Self-efficacy is also related to goal orientation, a construct that suggests individuals hold either a learning (i.e., mastery) or performance orientation toward tasks. Individuals with a learning orientation have a desire to increase task competence; on the other hand, those with a performance orientation have a desire to do well and be positively evaluated by others (Phillips & Gully, 1997). Individuals with a high learning goal orientation believe that their abilities are malleable; as a result, they approach tasks with the intention of developing their skills and abilities. Conversely, individuals with a high performance goal orientation see their capacities as static and approach tasks with the intention of doing well (Phillips & Gully, 1997). Those who view intelligence as fixed (high performance goal orientation) are likely to have lower self-efficacy than those viewing intelligence as malleable (high learning goal orientation). Phillips and Gully (1997) posited that these orientations are true in a sense because a person with a high performance goal orientation will interpret any mistake or less-than-perfect performance as indicative of failure and lower ability. Those with a higher learning orientation may be more likely to interpret a past experience, even if it is a failure, as something positive from which they can learn. In a learning environment, individuals are likely to make mistakes, and for performance-oriented people, these mistakes are often seen as failures (Phillips & Gully, 1997).

Therefore, setting goals for a tutoring session is useful for two important reasons: tutors can effectively and efficiently manage the time available for tutoring, and students can move toward a learning orientation and enhance their self-efficacy. Goals for this module include training tutors in

(a) determining the student client's needs, (b) establishing goals and organizing the tutoring session accordingly, (c) identifying ways to assess effectiveness of assistance and adjust during the session, and (d) setting goals for the next tutoring session.

Training Activity

This activity can be conducted in a typical classroom with movable desks and chairs that can be rearranged as needed. Role-playing scenarios should be prepared in advance. Length of time needed for instruction, activity, and assessment is approximately 1 hour.

The following steps can be placed on a checklist or flow chart to distribute to tutors. Tutors can keep this list or chart as a reference tool until the steps have become automatic and feel natural, according to the unique personality and strengths of each tutor.

First, tutors should establish a relaxed relationship with the tutee in two ways: by making the student feel welcome, comfortable, and supported; and by asking for the student's name, course of concern, and other background information. Next, tutors determine the exact subject, specific part of the subject, and exact skills the tutee wants to work on. Figure 1 lists sample methods for evaluating the specific nature of a tutee's needs.

TYPE OF PROBLEM	TECHNIQUE TO DETERMINE SPECIFIC NEEDS
Reading	Have the tutee read a passage in the text to determine reading fluency, comfort, and comprehension.
Mathematics	Have the tutee complete basic math problems and discuss math anxieties.
Note taking	Check tutee notes for legibility, organization, and content. Ask the tutee to explain the notes to you.
Language	Ask tutee to explain or interpret facts or points of information.
Test-taking strategies	Administer a short mock-test with a variety of question types, or ask to see tutee's returned exams.
Study habits	Review with tutee the location, hours, and methods of studying.
Class attendance	Check class notes, ask about material covered recently in class, or ask if tutee goes to class.
Time management	Ask if tutee has a schedule for school, work, and personal tasks and if tutee has allowed for studying during free time.

FIGURE 1　Methods for evaluating tutee needs.

After evaluating the tutees' needs, tutors need to work with tutees to establish goals and organize the session accordingly. This will help the tutor prioritize what assistance will be the most useful in the time the student has for tutoring and the time before an assignment is due or an exam is scheduled. For example, a student may bring in a paper for proofreading, but if the paper does not respond to the assignment or lacks clear direction or purpose, the writing tutor must address these issues before reading for spelling or comma errors. Math tutors could begin by focusing on the procedure a student is using to solve a problem, then watching and listening for erroneous logic or incorrect procedures as well as strengths and clear thinking.

The next step is for tutors to learn how to ask questions of students in order to check for understanding and assess effectiveness of assistance. The trainer should teach tutors to avoid closed questions such as "Do you understand now?" or "Does this make sense to you?" that elicit a yes or no answer. A good activity is to place common questions tutors ask in one column on a flip chart or dry-erase board. Examples include: How far along did you get? How do you feel about learning this? How is your understanding of the things we are going over? What questions do you have? What have you studied about these things before? Then, in a corresponding column, tutors can rephrase the questions as if the tutee had trouble understanding what was first asked. Good questions will elicit feedback that can help the tutor adjust tutoring sessions accordingly. For example, if a student needs help citing source material in the proper style format, but this question uncovers that the student does not know how to read a research article effectively, then the tutor should go back to that point (i.e., how to read a research article) and proceed with tutoring.

Finally, the trainer should show tutors how to establish follow-up goals for students by reviewing with clients what they have worked on, indicating the next possible steps students should take, and asking them to return with another assignment or with concerns about another course. If tutors document their tutoring sessions, the goals or suggestions for the next step should be recorded in their documentation and a copy provided to the tutee. For example, if a tutoring session reveals that a student's body paragraphs lack topic sentences, a suggestion for the next step is to write topic sentences based on what was learned in the tutoring session. In the case of the student having difficulty reading research articles, a goal for future sessions would be to apply active reading strategies to the articles; the tutee can annotate, ask questions, make predictions, identify key vocabulary, and mark areas where comprehension broke down. In the next tutoring session, the tutor and tutee can review the tutee's work, building on what the tutee is doing well and providing help in areas where it is still needed.

As the next step in the training activity, the trainer can assign trainees to analyze role-playing scenarios of tutoring sessions. Scenarios can be created in advance based on typical student concerns brought to the tutoring center. After this instruction, pairs of trainees can role-play the scenarios, followed by a brief discussion of what went well and what did not go well. This activity will be concluded with a whole-group discussion of goal-setting strategies to use in each situation.

Assessment

The objective for this training session is that trainees understand how to use goals to structure the tutoring session and engage the student in learning. By the end of the activity, tutors should know how to determine the student's needs, establish goals and organize the tutoring session accordingly, identify ways to assess effectiveness of assistance during the session, and set goals for the next tutoring session.

Assessment is built into the final learning activity. If each trainee can play the role of a tutor who successfully works with a tutee to set goals appropriate for the scenario devised by the trainer, then each trainee will have demonstrated the knowledge and skill taught in this training activity.

References

Bandura, A. (1977). Self-efficacy: Toward a unifying theory of behavioral change. *Psychological Review, 84,* 191–215. doi:10.1037/0033-295X.84.2.191

Lemme, B. H. (2002). *Development in adulthood* (3rd ed.). Boston, MA: Allyn & Bacon.

Locke, E. A., & Latham, G. P. (2002). Building a practically useful theory of goal setting and task motivation: A 35-year odyssey. *American Psychologist, 57,* 705–717. doi:10.1037/0003-066X.57.9.705

Phillips, J. M., & Gully, S. M. (1997). Role of goal orientation, ability, need for achievement, and locus of control in the self-efficacy and goal-setting process. *Journal of Applied Psychology, 82,* 792–802. doi:10.1037/0021-9010.82.5.792

Training for Online Tutoring

▪ Johanna Dvorak and Kevin Roessger

Online tutoring is rapidly expanding among college tutoring centers across the United States. Why should learning centers offer online tutoring in their array of academic support services?

- Many campuses are growing their online course offerings (Allen & Seaman, 2010).

- Online students may be distant from not only academic courses but also academic services (Chi-Sing & Beverly, 2008; Driscoll, 2002).

- Students are often returning adults who need the flexibility of doing coursework during evening and weekend hours (Karber, 2003; Lyons, 2004).

- Students may favor online services because of their age, cultural preferences (Gunawardena & LaPointe, 2007), access to multicultural perspectives (Chi-Sing & Beverly, 2008), and learning styles (Allen, Burrell, Bourhs, & Timmerman, 2007).

- Technology now makes it easier to use audio and video components in online tutoring.

- Experience has shown us that many online students have less academic success working independently and therefore need academic support.

Panther Academic Support Services (PASS) at the University of Wisconsin-Milwaukee is meeting these needs by assigning tutors to provide 2 or more hours weekly of online tutoring, or two online exam reviews per semester, in addition to in-person tutoring. PASS has hired a half-time graduate program assistant to train 100 tutors to use the online tutoring technology; two student clerical assistants provide additional individualized support throughout the fall, spring, and summer semesters.

Social constructivism is one theory underlying face-to-face and online tutoring at PASS. Central to social constructivism is the idea that knowledge is socially constructed (Merriam, Caffarella, & Baumgartner, 2007); therefore, pedagogical activities that focus on communicative learning processes such as cooperation, dialogue, and collaboration are integral to a learner's skill and knowledge development. Vygotsky (1978) argued that learning occurs in a "zone of proximal development" (ZPD), a concept he used to illustrate the difference between learners' current skill and knowledge bases and those that can be achieved with assistance. Bruner (1986) proposed the idea of instructional scaffolding to assist learners working within the ZPD. Supports are provided until specific skills, strategies, and content are comprehended, then removed as students become more confident with the material (Sutton, 1998). The scaffolding paradigm allows educators to act as facilitators of learning rather than lecturers and imparters of knowledge (Sutton, 1998).

Behavioral learning theory can be used to complement a social constructivist approach. By focusing on and reinforcing overt behavior, trainers can ensure that tutors possess requisite skills for practical applications and that programs are effectively reaching predetermined goals. Two specific instructional practices derived from behavioral learning theory are particularly relevant: behavioral objectives and task analyses. Behavioral objectives allow participants to gauge learning progress and quantify socially-constructed knowledge. Facilitators also benefit by having a tool to measure learner success. Task analyses offer program designers a method for breaking down complex tasks into successively more manageable units (Elias & Merriam, 2005), which participants can then learn through instructional scaffolding.

Rather than adopting a singular theoretical approach, we have found that combining elements of social constructivist and behavioral learning theories offers the most effective means to focus on learners, program content, and accountability. This module offers a training activity based on both social constructivist and behavioral learning theories. Information provided here should help administrators plan, implement, and assess a hands-on web-based training sequence.

Training Activity

Rekkedal (1997) has recommended that tutors receive adequate technology training in order to provide online student support effectively. In addition, Wai-Kong (2007) found that training in new technologies yields positive tutor perception and comprehension of online delivery platforms, which may improve tutors' support of students. With this in mind, the first task of the online tutor trainer is to help tutors master the technology by which they will provide that support.

Training can be conducted over a 1-month period across four 1-hour weekly sessions. The overall institutional time investment for program analysis, design, development, implementation, and evaluation will vary according to resource availability and existing technology infrastructure. In our experience, a director and one half-time graduate student with instructional design knowledge can carry out these phases over a 6-month period. Initial design and development stages can be carried out in 2 months. Prior to the first session, a tutor training course site is created within the institution's learning management system (e.g., Blackboard Learn®, Desire2Learn® Learning Environment, Moodle). Trainees are given access to review training-related materials, practice using web conferencing tools, and communicate asynchronously with fellow participants. Trainers are encouraged to use the social constructivist approach of allowing trainees the opportunity to collaborate and discuss shared problems. A designated campus computer lab is used, and trainees are assigned computers.

Four themes are covered in consecutive sessions: (a) introducing the web conferencing platform, (b) utilizing web conferencing tools, (c) integrating interactive whiteboard technology within the web conferencing platform, and (d) fostering student interactivity in online tutoring sessions. In each session, new skills are first introduced and modeled for participants, then tutors are given time to practice and apply these skills in a manner relevant to their subject area. As web conferencing tools are demonstrated on an overhead screen, participants are asked to participate on their own computers, allowing them to experience a student's perspective while simultaneously viewing a tutor's perspective on the overhead screen. Each session incorporates approximately 25% trainer modeling and 75% guided practice. During the latter phase, questions are posed to the group to promote dialogue and build connections between new information and tutors' subject area knowledge.

Job aids and program objectives are distributed at the first session. Electronic copies are made available in the content area of the tutor training course site. Job aids are created for all procedural tasks related to online tutoring, including directions for student participants. For example, if tutors are required to set up their own web conferencing rooms, a job aid is made available listing the step-by-step procedure involved. Each job aid is based on a task analysis of the sequential skill. Job aids are an integral tool of the scaffolding process, inasmuch as they provide initial support that can be gradually faded as trainees develop competency. This decreases demand on support staff during online sessions.

Program objectives are created based on Mager's (1997) three-part model, which focuses on the behavior the learner will exhibit, the conditions under which the behavior will occur, and the criteria used to determine effective performance. Objectives must address not only demonstrable web conferencing skills but also meaningful applications within the context of online tutoring. To accomplish this, a two-tier objective design is used. Thirty first-tier objectives (FTOs) are grouped in four categories representing specific web conferencing competencies: whiteboard tools, audio tools, type-chat tools, and advanced tools. For example, objective 21 in the advanced tools grouping reads, "Given a uniform resource locator (URL), produce its web page using the web tour program feature so all participants can view it." Specific FTOs vary depending upon the web conferencing platform used and tutors' needs. A detailed listing of the authors' FTOs is available online (Dvorak & Roessger, 2011).

Five second-tier objectives (STOs) are also presented. These focus on applied performance expectations—that is, how tutors are to apply new knowledge and skills in real-world online tutoring sessions. Objective one, for example, reads, "Upon completion of online tutor training and demonstrated competency of the 30 specified web conferencing features, tutors will be able to conduct one synchronous tutoring session with students during the semester." STOs will also vary depending upon an online tutoring program's goals. However, PASS recommends that STOs include a tutor's expected number of online sessions and expected response time to students' asynchronous discussion postings. Our STOs are available online for review (Dvorak & Roessger, 2011).

Assessment

Trainers of online tutors should conduct both quantitative and qualitative assessment. Quantitative assessments measure tutor performance on program objectives. Trainees should be given the option to demonstrate competency on FTOs immediately following training in one of three contexts: a scheduled meeting with a program assistant, a recorded web conferencing session conducted on the tutor's own time, or a supervised online session with students. In addition, tutor performance on STOs can be evaluated at semester's end, measured quantitatively, and recorded.

STOs are a valuable tool to assess the effectiveness and impact of a training program on an online tutoring initiative. To reinforce participation, tutors who successfully demonstrate all FTOs and STOs are presented with training completion certificates and pay raises at the start of the following semester. Quantitative assessments of FTOs and STOs are critical to assessing overall tutor competency within the web conferencing platform.

Because all tutoring sessions are recorded in the archives, tutoring coordinators can review them and provide qualitative feedback to the tutor about content of sessions. Just as with in-person observations, trainees may be assessed on their knowledge of the subject matter, their skill at involving student clients in the learning process, and their effective guidance of the tutoring session. Online tutors may be assessed on their preparation for the session, use of polling features, screen sharing, or document exchange to encourage active participation in the session and organization of the session. Trainers can make written comments as they observe the archive and provide valuable feedback to the tutor in a follow-up conference. Tutors can examine their own sessions by reviewing and screen-capturing segments to be placed in the course management system's content site for trainees' use.

Online tutoring presents more communication challenges to tutors and students than face-to-face tutoring, in part because of tutors' unfamiliarity with the technology. As trainees gain confidence through a structured online tutor training program, they are more likely to conduct effective online sessions. Trainers can use both quantitative and qualitative data to assess whether student clients, in turn, benefit by gaining increased access to tutoring services online.

In addition to training sessions, online tutoring support staff must continue to address additional tutor and student inquiries as well as routine technology maintenance. Evaluation completes the training loop so that tutors can improve their practice in subsequent sessions.

References

Allen, M., Burrell, N., Bourhs, J., & Timmerman, E. (2007). Literature of satisfaction. In M. G. Moore (Ed.), *Handbook of distance education* (2nd ed., pp. 149–156). Mahwah, NJ: Lawrence Erlbaum.

Allen, I. E., & Seaman, J. (2010). *Class differences: Online education in the United States, 2010.* Retrieved from http://sloanconsortium.org/publications/survey/class_differences

Bruner, J. (1986). *Actual minds, possible worlds.* Cambridge, MA: Harvard University Press.

Chi-Sing, L., & Beverly, I. (2008). An overview of online education: Attractiveness, benefits, challenges, concerns, and recommendations. *College Student Journal, 42,* 449–458.

Driscoll, M. (2002). *Web-based training: Creating e-learning experiences.* San Francisco, CA: Jossey-Bass/Pfeiffer.

Dvorak, J., & Roessger, K. M. (2011). *FTOs and STOs for an online tutor training program.* Retrieved from http://www.crla.net/handbook/ch4/dvorak-n-roessger

Elias, J. L., & Merriam, S. B. (2005). *Philosophical foundations of adult education* (3rd ed.). Malabar, FL: Krieger.

Gunawardena, C. N., & LaPointe, D. (2007). Cultural dynamics of online learning. In M. G. Moore (Ed.), *Handbook of distance education* (2nd ed., pp. 593–608). Mahwah, NJ: Lawrence Erlbaum.

Karber, D. J. (2003). Comparisons and contrasts in traditional versus on-line teaching in management. *Higher Education in Europe, 26,* 533–536.

Lyons, J. F. (2004). Teaching U.S. history online: Problems and prospects. *The History Teacher, 37,* 447–456. Retrieved from http://www.historycooperative.org/journals/ht/37.4/lyons.html

Mager, R. F. (1997). *Preparing instructional objectives: A critical tool in the development of effective instruction.* Atlanta, GA: Center for Effective Performance.

Merriam, S. B., Caffarella, R. S., & Baumgartner, L. M. (2007). *Learning in adulthood: A comprehensive guide.* San Francisco, CA: Jossey-Bass.

Rekkedal, T. (1997, June). *Training of distance tutors: A case from the NKI Foundation, Norway.* Paper presented at the 18th International Council for Open and Distance Education (ICDE) World Conference, Pennsylvania State University, State College, PA. Retrieved from http://www.nettskolen.nki.no/forskning/32/icde97.htm

Sutton, S. M. (1998). *Advocacy and social scaffolding: A paradigm for motivating underachieving students* (Doctoral dissertation). Available from ProQuest Dissertations & Theses database. (Order No. 9830214)

Vygotsky, L. S. (1978). Mind in society. Cambridge, MA: Harvard University Press.

Wai-Kong, N. (2007). Training of distance education tutors at Wawasan Open University. *The Quarterly Review of Distance Education, 8*(3), 261–268.

Embedded Tutoring

Loren Kleinman, Candice Kaup Scioscia, and Roseann Torsiello

Embedded tutors are peer tutors who work in an academic course with individual students or small groups to increase students' understanding of the course material, in a program that offers additional in-class support to students who may be wary of seeking academic support on their own. "Peer learning is becoming an increasingly important part of many courses" and "students learn a great deal by explaining their ideas to one another" (Boud, Cohen, & Sampson, 2001, p. 3). Embedded tutors can be trained to facilitate classroom learning by helping students build and refine their understanding of the content area—using conversation, questioning, and content-based workshops—as well as navigating the classroom environment in a role between professor and student.

Embedded tutors must be trained for their multiple roles: as liaisons between instructor and students, offering opportunities for small-group work and individual attention; as group leaders working under the guidance of the course instructor; and as observers of individual student work, as in a studio class, to assist where they determine need is greatest. In order to play their roles effectively, embedded tutors must have not only good intuition about which students need assistance and which students will perform adequately on their own but also good training. Embedded tutors must develop interpersonal skills and a sense of conversational nuance. This training sequence is intended to develop the embedded tutor's skills to perform multiple aspects of this important role.

Training Activity

An important aspect of the embedded tutor's role is his or her relationship with the instructor. This relationship is unique to the embedded tutoring program, as embedded tutors have to work alongside faculty members. This training activity aims to help embedded tutors understand their role, including how to communicate effectively with faculty and students to establish a helping relationship in the classroom. The training activity requires 1–2 hours; however, trainers can adapt the activity to their own needs by dividing training into several shorter sessions. No special room or equipment is needed.

ICEBREAKER

The training session begins with a communication icebreaker. Because the tutors will be working closely with both students and faculty, they must learn to listen carefully and respond effectively to multiple expectations in the classroom. The main purpose of the icebreaker is to introduce tutors to one another, reduce tension, promote interaction, and even stir up some laughter.

The trainer can begin by explaining that more than half of communication is nonverbal (55%), with 38% of meaning conveyed by voice quality and only 7% by words themselves (Wills, n.d.). To demonstrate, the trainer divides the group into pairs and gives one person in each pair a card with a simple task to communicate to that person's partner. The cards may offer tasks like closing a door, picking up a book, moving a table, or sitting down. Trainees may communicate with each other through gestures, sounds, or tone of voice, but they may not use identifiable words. The exercise ends when the task has been completed. Trainees will see the effectiveness of wordless communication when all tasks are completed within seconds (Wills, n.d.).

COMMUNICATING IN MULTIPLE ROLES

The next phase of the training introduces tutors to the various roles they will play as embedded tutors. They must be flexible in the assistance they provide to students; they are simultaneously members of the student community and members of the college support staff and therefore need to think consciously and intentionally about how and when to navigate these roles throughout a student session. Embedded tutors must be sensitive not just to the needs of their tutees but also to the teaching style and goals of the course instructor. To foster thinking about these roles, the trainer offers a presentation outlining the following guidelines:

- Although the instructor and the embedded tutor both function as authority figures in the classroom, they are not peers.

- Building and maintaining good relationships with both students and instructor is necessary.

- Relationships with tutees and instructors must be steeped in mutual trust and understanding and built with positive regard between participants. The end result should be a teaching and learning relationship, as well as collaboration.

- Tutors must be confident in their abilities and must be able to display their confidence to the course instructor and students. It has been estimated that it takes the average person fewer than 4 minutes to form a positive or negative impression of another (Heathfield, 2010). Good listening and communication skills help tutors make positive impressions.

- Because only 7% of communication is conveyed in words and the remaining 93% is nonverbal (e.g., body language, posture, tone of voice) or symbolic (e.g., clothes, vehicle) (Heathfield, 2010), humans are always communicating, whether or not they intend to do so.

- Tutoring requires self-awareness and insight. How can patience be developed even in stressful situations? How do emotionally intelligent people monitor their reactions to various situations?

In this phase of the training session, tutors engage in a role-playing activity with learning center staff and experienced embedded tutors. Staff and tutors play the role of various faculty members so the new embedded tutors can begin to think about and apply the ways in which they will navigate particular scenarios. These scenarios include but are not limited to the following:

- The instructor issues an ambiguous assignment (e.g., "Write a paper about any topic of your choosing"), giving students little direction or purpose for the assignment. The tutor is faced with an anxious tutee, unclear as to how to proceed.

- After class, the instructor pulls the tutor aside and asks if he or she worked with a particular student. The tutor has and says so. The instructor then berates the tutor for not having provided appropriate assistance to the student, who just failed a quiz. The student misunderstood both major and minor concepts of the course, and the instructor says the tutor must be incompetent.

- One particular instructor is a favorite with students and tutors because his classroom is a casual and comfortable environment. He invites students to address him by his first name and treats the course as a workshop and discussion roundtable rather than a lecture series. After class one day, he invites the tutor to discuss a student's work and grades over lunch.

Following the role play, tutors complete a reflective exercise in which they write down the answers to the following questions and then upon completion discuss them with the rest of the training group and head trainer:

- Reflecting on the exercise you just completed, think about your communication strengths and weaknesses. Briefly describe your strengths. Briefly describe what you will try to improve.

- List three nonverbal behaviors you would use to demonstrate to your tutees and instructor your good listening and communication skills.

- What instructor characteristics are most challenging for you? What can you do, specifically, to build a relationship with the instructor and manage his or her expectations of you?

Following a discussion of the self-reflection exercise, the training staff and senior tutors engage in the same or similar role-playing exercises to demonstrate various effective techniques for engaging with faculty members and addressing concerns.

GENERAL PROCEDURES

General procedures should also be reviewed. Embedded tutors are reminded that they are not to interrupt or try to lead class; their role is always to facilitate classroom learning. If students appear confused or ask for help, tutors should ask them to restate or paraphrase what the professor has said in order to check for understanding, and then ask questions to prompt new information or clarify what the tutee is saying. If neither the tutor nor the tutee is clear on an assignment's objectives, the tutor should feel comfortable asking the professor for further guidance; the embedded tutor is there not to speak for the instructor but to assist with the learning process. By using these approaches to student learning and classroom participation, an embedded tutor is able to walk the academic terrain between faculty and student, assisting each with his or her classroom needs.

Assessment

To assess whether embedded tutors have been trained successfully, supervisors should carefully attend to trainees' participation and responses to questions during the training session. Tutors' written answers to the reflection questions can also be used to measure their understanding of the responsibilities of the embedded tutor role. Supervisors can utilize several other measures, as well: instructor feedback, center observations, tutor and tutee feedback, and tutee surveys.

The embedded tutor program supervisor is advised to contact the instructor for bi-weekly briefings via email, phone, or in-person visit on the attendance and performance of the embedded tutor. Discussion should also center on how the students and the instructor are utilizing the tutor. In addition to these communications, the supervisor can also encourage each instructor to complete an Embedded Tutor Evaluation Form (Appendix) at the end of service for an assessment of the entire term's work. This form was developed for Berkeley College by Loren Kleinman, one of the authors of this training module, and may be borrowed and adapted for use on other campuses.

The embedded tutor program supervisor should also visit class at least once during the semester and at that time conduct an evaluation of the interaction among tutor, students, and instructor. This observation is not prescheduled or preannounced, and therefore the professor, supervisor, and embedded tutor must all agree before the semester begins that at least one such visit will be made.

The embedded tutor program supervisor should also contact each embedded tutor for bi-weekly briefings electronically or in person. Discussion should cover the entire range of performance issues, including attendance, as well as how the students and the instructor are utilizing the embedded tutor's service.

References

Boud, D., Cohen, R., & Sampson, J. (2001). *Peer learning in higher education: Learning from and with each other*. Sterling, VA: Stylus.

Heathfield, S. (2010). Listen with your eyes: Tips for understanding nonverbal communication. *About.com Guide*. Retrieved from http://humanresources.about.com/od/interpersonal communicatio1/a/nonverbal_com.htm

Wills, M. (n.d.). *Mumblers*. Retrieved from Mike Wills Learning Services, http://www.mwls.co.uk/icebreakers/mumblers.pl

Appendix

● ● ● ● ●   E M B E D D E D   T U T O R   E V A L U A T I O N   F O R M S   F O R   T U T O R S

THE ASC EMBEDDED TUTOR PROGRAM	EXCELLENT	GOOD	FAIR	POOR
How would you rate the embedded tutor experience overall?				
Did the students work well with you?				
Were the students respectful toward you?				
Did the students better understand the subject matter after working with you?				
Was communication between you and the instructor sufficient?				
Did you feel that the instructor, with your help, fostered a positive learning environment?				
Were you able to adapt to students' different learning styles?				

THE ASC EMBEDDED TUTOR PROGRAM	AGREE STRONGLY	AGREE	DISAGREE	DISAGREE STRONGLY
I enjoyed meeting the class.				
Instruction was informative, educational, and worth my classroom time.				
An embedded tutor is a good means for students to learn more about a particular subject.				
The students gained a better understanding of their subject by the end of the quarter.				
I look forward to working as an embedded tutor for the next quarter.				

Dealing With Difficult Tutoring Situations

Wendy L. Wilson

Tutoring is a helping relationship that is based on the interaction of two or more individuals whose goal is to enhance learning. In most situations, the tutor and student are able to establish an effective relationship that enhances learning; at times, however, students' attitudes associated with their own feelings in the learning process can lead to challenging tutoring sessions. These challenges may lead tutors to conclude that certain students are difficult. What tutors are actually experiencing is trouble working with individuals due to differences in personality, expectations, or other variations from the typical tutoring situation (Wessler, Hankin, & Stern, 2001). Tutors may also experience difficulty due to their own negative or self-critical feelings. In general, a breakdown occurs when tutor and student have different expectations about their roles in the session, an imbalance in expectations about participation, or negative feelings associated with anxiety, shame, or low self-efficacy (Norton & McGauley, 1998).

It is helpful for tutor trainers to identify some of the most common situations that may challenge tutors. This module presents an overview of the disruptive styles identified by Maxwell (1997) and Roberts (1994) and a brief definition of each style (Table 1). In the training activity, tutors will have the opportunity to identify appropriate strategies for each style. As a result of participating in this training session, tutors should be able to describe disruptive styles that influence the learning relationship, identify situations that may present difficulties to the interaction between tutor and student, and develop strategies to preserve an effective learning relationship.

Training Activity

The training activity will require at least 50 minutes. The trainer will need to create handouts of Figure 1 and Figure 2. A copy of Figure 2 should be cut into cards to be used during the session. Writing paper should be provided to complete the 1-minute paper. The training should occur in a room that will allow the tutors to move around and act out situations.

ONE-MINUTE PAPER

The trainer should first distribute paper and ask tutors to identify a challenging situation they have experienced in a recent tutoring session. It is helpful to provide an example so that trainees understand the types of situations to consider. The situation could feature a difficult student attitude or disruptive behavior. Tutors should describe the situation in writing, in 1 minute. If this training session is conducted at the beginning of the semester prior to tutoring, tutors should write about a difficult situation they anticipate could occur. The trainer then collects the papers for use later in the training.

PRESENTATION OF TOPIC

The trainer next provides a brief overview of the topic by presenting the seven disruptive styles shown on Figure 1 and describing how the styles may present in a session. The trainer should also discuss the nature of the tutoring transaction; tutors should realize that the difficulty experienced in the session is not completely a result of the student's obstreperousness but rather a result of the interaction of the tutor and the student.

Style of Difficulty	Behavior Characteristic of Difficult Tutoring Situation
Blocking	Students typically withhold or avoid communication. When questioned, they may say, "I don't know," and then remain silent. Blocking students typically have a low tolerance for frustration and become agitated, saying "I'll never get it." They may respond emotionally to frustration or become uncomfortably quiet.
Confusion	Confusion is a variation of blocking; however, instead of withholding communication, students try to focus the content of the session on their own frustration. They say they do not know what the professor wants or where they should start. They may question the value of course content, asking, "Why do we have to know this, anyway?"
Miracle Seeking	Students expect tutors to take control of the tutoring transaction. They believe that their tutors are the solution to their problems; they have unrealistically high expectations for the tutors. Students may flatter tutors or compliment their skill often, and although tutors may feel good about the compliments, tutors may find themselves enabling students and doing too much of the work.
Over-Enthusiasm	This situation is a variation of miracle–seeking, but students want to complete all the work. Students have inflated goals and expect tutors to devote themselves to the cause. Students may request additional tutoring hours beyond limits set by policy, offer to pay for additional sessions, or contact tutors after hours for additional help. Students want tutors to devote extra time and resources to assist them.
Resisting	Students directly or indirectly oppose changing their behaviors. They fail to implement agreed–upon strategies or complete work prior to sessions. Students may directly refute tutors' use of strategies during a session or question tutors' credibility in the subject area. Students may appear confrontational or hostile toward tutors. Tutors may interpret resistance as lack of interest in the course or in college.
Passivity	Students care more about seeking approval, pleasing others, avoiding conflict, and maintaining relationships than about expressing genuine concerns. They may therefore prefer less challenging assignments and courses. Students may not believe that their thoughts and ideas are as important as the tutors'. Students may also be anxious and overly concerned about being critiqued.
Evasion	Students may or may not consciously realize that they are avoiding the content of tutoring sessions by discussing topics unrelated to the tutoring sessions, such as social or current events, and changing the topic of conversation several times throughout sessions. Students who are more aware of their evasion may provide vaguely worded responses or provide several plausible answers without choosing one particular answer, in an attempt to manipulate tutors to provide answers.

FIGURE 1   Methods for evaluating tutee needs.

SCENARIO AND SOLUTION CARDS

Figure 2 provides sample scenario solution cards for each of the seven disruptive styles. The trainer gives each participant (or pairs) either a scenario card or a solution card.

Option 1

The pairs of students with the scenario cards role play the situation depicted on the card. Tutors should improvise appropriately for the characteristics of the style discussed in the presentation of the topic. At the end of the scenario, the students who played the student role will ask the group, "Does anyone have suggestions for this situation?" The individual or pair of trainees holding the solution cards will assess whether their solution card is appropriate for the situation and use the ideas on the card to provide guidance for completing the role-play. The trainer should help tutors evaluate the effectiveness of the solution.

Option 2

If the group is smaller, the trainer can give each of the tutors either a scenario card or one of the solution cards to match that scenario. The tutors should then circulate in the room to identify the best match of solutions to scenarios. Because many of the solutions are related, tutors should be discriminating in order to find the best match. When a pair of trainees has identified their scenario and solution as a good match, they will sit down. Soon all the tutors are seated. Trainees will then be asked to read their scenarios and solutions. Note that for these pairings to work, only one solution per scenario can be distributed.

Scenario	Possible Solutions
Blocking. In the first session, the student indicated, "I'll never get it," was very quiet, and said he didn't even know the questions to ask. In the second session, you began making some progress reviewing previous material, and the student left with some pieces to continue to work on. Now, in the third session, the student has arrived indicating that he tried working on the material but is stuck and will never learn it.	• Begin the session by asking the student questions that you know can be easily answered—open-ended questions that do not have right or wrong answers. • Start with easier material and scaffold your questions to more difficult material. • Provide continual support of and feedback to the student. • Reinforce successes.
Confusion. The student arrives at the tutoring session complaining that she has tried everything but nothing works. She says she studies all the time but is still not getting good grades on the tests and made a D on the last exam. She comments that she is not sure she knows what the professor wants.	• Have the student explain exactly what she is doing when she is studying for the course exams. (She may have been taught ineffective as well as inefficient methods.) If possible, complete an exam analysis with the student and determine the source (text, lecture, other) of the material that was missed on the exam. • Help the student see patterns in the course material. Make concept maps or outlines for the text chapters. Make concept cards that can be used to study course material.
Miracle Seeking. The student arrives at the tutoring session on time. He has a math homework set that is due the next day. He tells the tutor that he is so glad that he learned about his availability because he didn't know what to do before. Now he wants the tutor to work through all the homework problems so he can submit the homework tomorrow.	• Be clear on the goals of the tutoring session and your role as a tutor. • Make sure that the student is holding the pencil as you work together. Indicate that you will provide support, but the student will complete the work. • Suggest a time management workshop or work with the student to create a homework study plan to complete homework before it is due.
Over-Enthusiasm. Two weeks remain in the semester when a student makes an appointment to see you. At the end of the session, he explains that he has failed the last two exams and needs to make an A on the comprehensive final in order to pass the course. The student would like to schedule a 2-hour appointment with you every day for the next two weeks to get caught up on the assignment. He tells you that he must pass this course to move to the next course, and he is already behind. He knows that you can help him pass the course.	• Make sure that the student understands tutoring policies. (How many hours are allowed per week?) • Clarify the goals of the tutoring session. • Create a study plan with the student so he can begin to identify tasks to accomplish outside the tutoring session. • Help the student to set realistic goals for the course. • Refer the student to an advisor to discuss course options and possibly a back-up plan for the next semester.
Resisting. In your first appointment with a new student, you began by having the student explain the struggles she faced in the course. You then suggested several strategies that you could work on during the session, but after each option, she explained that she has already tried it and it does not work. You finally agree on an approach. In the next session, the student comes without implementing the suggested changes and says she just didn't try it.	• Spend some time understanding the student's needs. What are her goals? • Provide time in the session to listen to the student's frustrations. • Empathize with the student. Let her know that you found the material difficult, too. • Show the student how you have implemented changes in similar situations (even your current courses).

FIGURE 2 Scenario and solution cards for group activity.

Scenario	Possible Solutions
Passivity. A student has been seeing you for political science tutoring. It has been difficult to get the student to take a position on issues, and he has typically asked what you thought when you took the course. In today's appointment you plan to review a position paper for the course. The student arrives without the expected draft. He says that you are very good at explaining the material and asks you to talk through the major issues so that he can understand them better. You are frustrated.	• Create a safe environment for the student. He may fear failure and need to know that you will not judge him. • Get the student involved and active as much as possible in the session, perhaps by creating a comparison-and-contrast chart. • Reinforce all activity and successes.
Evasion. You have met with a student a few times, and each session seems to get off track. In each session you start talking about an unrelated topic. At first you thought it would be good to build a relationship with the student. Now you are concerned that you are not accomplishing much. You just met with the student for the 3rd time and have your next appointment scheduled in two days.	• Identify goals for the tutoring session and check progress at the end of the session. • Keep the student active through questioning, content organization strategies, and problem-solving. • Explain your concerns to the student and in a non-judgmental manner ask what his reasons are for seeking tutoring or what he expects from you. • Reflect critically on the sessions. Were your expectations too high or out of alignment with the student's expectations? Are you asking too much of the student or yourself?

FIGURE 2 (continued).

Assessment

The trainer begins assessment by asking trainees to review the 1-minute papers they completed at the beginning of the session. Can they identify in their paper any of the difficult situations or styles discussed in training? It is important to discuss with tutors that the process was not meant to label students or situations but to help tutors identify possible solutions by categorizing disruptive situations into styles. Tutors should use the material provided in the scenario-solution matching exercise to identify possible solutions to the issues they identified in their 1-minute papers.

As an alternative or addition to reviewing their 1-minute papers, trainees who have acquired some tutoring experience can be asked to write reflection papers. In reflection papers, tutors describe a difficult tutoring situation they have experienced, the type of styles exhibited by the student, and how they were able to manage the learning encounter based on information in the training session.

References

Maxwell, M. (1997). *Improving student learning skills: A new edition*. Clearwater, FL: H&H.

Norton, K., & McGauley, G. (1998). *Counselling difficult clients*. Thousand Oaks, CA: Sage.

Roberts, V. C. (1994). *Tutor resource manual: Tutoring students in the community college*. Washington, DC: Office of Special Education and Rehabilitative Services. Retrieved from ERIC database. (ED386838)

Wessler, R., Hankin, S., & Stern, J. (2001). *Succeeding with difficult clients: Applications of cognitive appraisal therapy*. San Diego, CA: Academic Press.

(B) STRATEGIC LEARNING

Using the Structure Matrix to Determine Appropriate Tutor Support

Marcia L. Toms

There is widespread acceptance in the learning center community that tutors should help students to become independent learners (Gattis, 2000; MacDonald, 2000). At times, this ideal or goal can be interpreted as meaning that tutors should give as little support as possible or even place the full burden of responsibility on students (Brooks, 1991). Although minimalist tutoring works for some students, it will not significantly improve the progress of others. Moreover, taking the minimalist approach can leave tutors frustrated, feeling unable to help the student as needed.

To help tutors decide when to allow students to work on their own and when to steer students toward more productive activities, coordinators of North Carolina State University's

TABLE 1 Structure matrix for providing appropriate tutoring support.

LEVEL OF STUDENT SKILL	LESS AUTONOMOUS LEARNER SESSION DIRECTOR: TUTOR	MORE AUTONOMOUS LEARNER SESSION DIRECTOR: STUDENT
Novice Tutor Support: High	Student is having trouble grasping material because of insufficient or inefficient studying. Student is not performing well and probably cannot identify why. Has difficulty grasping basic principles presented in resources and may not retain information from one session to the next. Goals: • Hold student accountable • Encourage self-testing • Check motivation • Check time management • Spend a lot of time in notes and book • Predict and prepare for test questions	Student is able to identify conceptual difficulties but is having difficulty using resources for better understanding. May be studying a lot but not necessarily on important issues. Goals: • Help student use resources to answer questions • Provide multiple opportunities for practice • Predict and prepare for test questions
Expert Tutor Support: Low	Student is able to learn relatively easily from class and resources but may not be persistent or use all resources to their full extent. Overconfidence may cause poor performance on exams. Student probably has experienced previous courses in which minimal studying was effective. Goals: • Hold student accountable • Encourage self-testing • Check motivation • Check time management	Student is able to identify weak areas of content knowledge, is doing well in course, and is able to use resources effectively. May need reassurance; may be achieving beyond course expectations. Goal: • Help with content not easily accessible in classroom lecture, textbooks, or other sources

Note. Adapted with permission from *Put the Pencil Down: Essentials of Tutoring*, by M. Toms, 2010. Copyright 2010 by North Carolina State University.

Undergraduate Tutorial Center (Toms, 2010) developed a *structure matrix*. The matrix juxtaposes two theoretical perspectives: experts versus novices and adult versus child learners. The language in both perspectives can be problematic because clearly one side of each continuum (adult, expert) is more valued than the other (novice, child). For this reason, Table 1 provides an adapted version of the matrix in which the terms child and adult have been replaced with *less autonomous* and *more autonomous* learners, focusing on a key component of Knowles's andragogic adult learning theory (Knowles, Holton, & Swanson, 1998).

Expert learners (a) see features and information not observed by novices; (b) have background knowledge and thorough understanding of how it relates; (c) have developed ways of retrieving information smoothly; and (d) are flexible in their ability to solve problems (National Research Council, 2000). *Novice learners* are those who have not yet developed this knowledge base.

More autonomous learners (a) learn material because they want to apply it, not just to pass the test; (b) see themselves as being responsible for their learning instead of at the mercy of an instructor or subject; (c) bring their "life experience" to the learning situation and value it; (d) see learning as a tool for solving a problem or completing a task; and (e) are motivated by internal factors in addition to external factors. *Less autonomous learners* (a) are motivated by external factors, such as grades; (b) may not take responsibility for their own learning; and (c) may accept information as presented without assessing, questioning, or challenging it (Knowles et al., 1998).

Two important aspects of the structure of a tutoring session are support and direction. *Tutor support* is determined by how frequently the tutor provides support when the tutee is working on specific content. In a highly structured session, the tutor will step in frequently to ask guiding questions, direct the student to a specific resource, or give feedback. When the tutor's support is less frequent and the student can answer many of the questions, the structure is low. *Session direction* is a question of who decides what to work on during the session. In a high-structure session, the tutor will make decisions about how to spend the session or frequently help the student with this decision. In a low-structure session, the student will decide what material to work on and how long to work on it.

In general, expert learners are able to use resources well without much tutor assistance, whereas novice learners need more assistance processing the course material. The following questions can guide how much tutor support a learner needs:

- How much guidance does the student need while working through a problem?

- Is the student able to make connections within the material?

- Is the student able to see patterns?

- Is the student able to use resources to solidify understanding?

If students are closer to experts, they will often be able to understand resources on their own; the tutor often offers support by helping with material beyond what is available in the textbooks and the notes. If students are closer to novices, they may need help using textbooks and notes to answer questions. The tutor may also spend time helping the student see connections in the material.

In general, more autonomous learners will decide what concepts they need to study, whereas less autonomous learners will need more assistance. The following questions can guide how much session direction a learner needs:

- Can the student identify which concepts are important and difficult?

- Can the student gauge his or her understanding of the concepts?

- Can the student study effectively?

If students are more autonomous, they are probably able to identify what they need to work on, and tutors should allow them to direct the session. If students are less autonomous, they may only want help with homework. Tutors should consider providing more session direction, even if students want to direct sessions themselves. For instance, if the student wants to move ahead without understanding fundamental material, the tutor should direct the session back to the core concepts.

Training Activity

This training activity requires about 1 hour. The trainer should prepare handouts of the structure matrix (Table 1) revised to omit the goal statements and scenarios describing situations for each of the four categories. Because there is so much information to present to tutors, the trainer should slowly build the concepts with them. First, the trainer can present each term (novice, expert, more autonomous learner, less autonomous learner) individually and ask tutors to write their own definitions of the terms. During the ensuing discussion, it should be pointed out that each apparent dichotomy is in fact a continuum; that is, a student does not jump from novice to expert in a day, for instance, but moves gradually toward expertise. Terminology should also be discussed; students who are experts in physics are not necessarily experts in chemistry. And can tutors think of anyone they know who is financially and socially dependent on others but with attributes of a more autonomous learner? This discussion helps tutors see that this terminology is only shorthand used for discussing students. The purpose is to determine how to help students, not to label them, and the next discussion should be about the usefulness of the theories to help tutors decide how much help to give and when to give it.

Next, tutors receive copies of a version of the structure matrix (Table 1) rewritten without the goals listed. Tutors divide into four groups, read the description for their section of the matrix, and talk about what the student needs to learn or do in order to succeed in this course, and what the tutor can then do to facilitate success. When the groups report back, the trainer adds additional comments if necessary.

Finally tutors look at scenarios based on the structure matrix. For instance, the scenario for the less autonomous, expert student may show a student who is very capable of doing the work but does not review the notes or book and instead wants the tutor to provide answers. In the scenario for the more autonomous, novice student, the student is unable to understand concepts despite hours of studying. Tutors then discuss each scenario, describing what they think the student needs and what they would do as a tutor.

Assessment

At the end of the session, tutors should be able to articulate definitions of experts, novices, more autonomous learners, and less autonomous learners and identify how these continuums determine the structure they should provide in a session. A mid-semester video project may provide additional assessment of tutor understanding. Trainees record one of their own sessions, watch it, and then write a reflection. In their reflection, tutors respond to the following questions:

- Do you believe this student is a more autonomous or less autonomous learner? Explain.

- Do you believe this student is a novice or expert? Explain.

- Who chose the direction of the session?

- How much support did you, the tutor, give?

- Considering the student's circumstances on the more-to-less-autonomous continuum and novice-to-expert continuum, was the structure you provided appropriate for the student?

After using this matrix, tutors should report great ease adapting their style to their students' needs. They will no longer feel trapped in inaction by the idea of minimalist tutoring.

References

Brooks, J. (1991). Minimalist tutoring: Making the student do all the work. *Writing Lab Newsletter, 15*(6), 1–4.

Gattis, K. (2000). *User's guide to* A look at productive tutoring techniques. Raleigh, NC: North Carolina State University.

Knowles, M. S., Holton, E. F., & Swanson, R. A. (1998). *The adult learner: The definitive classic in adult education and human resource development* (5th ed.). Houston, TX: Gulf.

MacDonald, R. (2000). *The master tutor: A guidebook for more effective tutoring* (2nd ed.). Williamsville, NY: Cambridge Stratford Study Skills Institute.

National Research Council. (2000). *How people learn: Brain, mind, experience, and school* (expanded ed.). Washington, DC: National Academy Press.

Toms, M. (2010). *Put the pencil down: Essentials of tutoring*. Raleigh, NC: North Carolina State University.

Summarizing for Strategic Learning

Nicole Foreman Tong

The ability to summarize is one of the most important skills a college student will use. Summarizing not only demonstrates comprehension of the text but also plays a part in higher-level writing assignments like research papers. In research projects, students are asked to enter into a kind of conversation with their sources; the activity presented here encourages them to do something comparable. In this activity tutors will consider the characteristics and flaws of two multimedia clips as summaries of a film, *Titanic* (Sanchini & Cameron, 1997), before turning their attention to two recent news articles on the same subject. Tutors will use metacognitive techniques to solve problems and write a missing headline before working collaboratively toward a fully realized summary. Finally, tutors will evaluate their work based on the criteria of summary characteristics they devise for the multimedia clips.

The goal of the activity goes beyond the tutor's ability to write a headline or a summary. The goal is for the tutor to help a student learn the self-regulatory and metacognitive strategies that will result in student-developed headlines or summaries. Modeling, questioning, and evaluating are important to this module. Thus, facilitators of this activity should use a scaffolded approach in line with Vygotsky's (1978) theory of proximal development. It is important that tutors be able to relinquish control at the appropriate time in a tutorial; therefore, trainers should allow tutors to develop a summary independently and to self-correct if necessary. This process of self-correction is one of the most important steps in a tutorial, so it should be practiced in this training activity as well.

The activity is a blend of direct instruction and inquiry-based frameworks of learning. Direct instruction, according to Casazza (1993), "provides a natural framework for emphasizing to students that it is their responsibility to bring meaning to the text" (p. 202). This training activity models for tutors the ways in which they will gradually give up control as tutees become able to work independently toward crafting missing headlines and summaries on their own. The problem-solving nature of the activity—to devise a headline for an article that lacks one—leaves room for inquiry-based learning in addition to direct instruction.

Finally, because the activity uses multimedia videos in addition to written text, trainers can appeal to tutors who are likely to engage reading, thinking, and teaching using media literacy. The integration of multiple literacies is a responsibility of 21st-century teachers (Considine, Horton, & Moorman, 2009). However, instructors should be wary of "hypermedia environments" that "allow learners to access, manipulate, or restructure multiple representations of information while receiving little or no scaffolding during learning" (Azevedo & Jacobson, 2008, p. 93). Thus, multimedia clips are used in this activity as a way to develop a set of criteria for a good summary, but printed text is the medium by which tutors will come to understand the metacognitive processes of reading and generating headlines and summaries.

Training Activity

To conduct this training activity, trainers will need a room with a computer or a laptop, a projector and a screen, two highlighters of different colors for each tutor, copies of recent articles pertaining to the RMS Titanic (with and without signposts to aid reading), and copies of the activity provided in the Appendix of this training module.

The trainer begins the activity by asking a question in which a tutor's answer is likely to contain some element of summary. The trainer may ask, perhaps, "What did you do on your last vacation?" or "What did you do yesterday?" Tutors should be encouraged to write their answers in a sentence or two on a sheet of paper. Next, the trainer asks the tutors whether or not they tied their shoes, took a shower, or opened a door the day before or while on that vacation. These examples of the quotidian will illustrate the fact that summary is a skill we use out of logical and practical necessity; their summary narratives left out such details because they were not pertinent.

Trainers should explain to tutors the purposes of the training, the objectives (see Assessment section), and the context for the discussion—the sinking of the RMS Titanic. Trainers will find it helpful to determine who has seen the film *Titanic* (Sanchini & Cameron, 1997), but even tutors who have not seen the movie in its entirety may be familiar with the fact that it is a love story involving characters portrayed by actors Leonardo DiCaprio and Kate Winslet. The activity should begin with the viewing of two YouTube clips from *Titanic*. The first is a 5-second YouTube clip (Gtotheordon, 2007) from Cameron's film in which actor Bruce Ismay says, "This ship can't sink," right before video editors cut to a quickly sinking ship.

The trainer should take a moment to query tutors as to ways in which that clip is a flawed summary of the film. Tutors should get to the fact that although that clip gets at the irony of the actual historical event—the ship sank although it was deemed unsinkable—it does not represent Cameron's directorial interpretation; Ismay's character is a minor player, and the love story central to Cameron's *Titanic* is left out entirely.

The second YouTube clip (Shiman, 2004) is a 30-second reinterpretation of Cameron's (Sanchini & Cameron, 1997) *Titanic* featuring the Starz Network bunnies. The trainer should ask tutors about the flaws in the longer clip. Tutors should note the following: though this clip does hint at the love story between the characters of Rose and Jack and uses direct quotes, it is condensed to such an extent that it loses narrative linearity, and in its humorous approach deviates from Cameron's original dramatic tone.

After using the video clips to lay the foundation for a productive discussion, the trainer should introduce definitions for *metacognition* and *signposts*. Then the trainer can pull up a recent Internet article on the RMS Titanic. A *National Geographic News* article (Roach, 2008) provides an excellent example passage: its signposts include the title, caption, and headings. The trainer can ask tutors to identify the ways in which the author of the article intended to guide a reader's thinking. Tutors should note such features as the article's title, its date of publication, photos and their captions, headings, and formatting deviations such as the use of bold font and italics.

Next, the trainer should lead a discussion with tutors about their own metacognitive practices when reading. Common practices include annotating, highlighting, circling unknown words, and similar strategies. The trainer can ask tutors which signpost is essential to summary writing; their conclusion should be the article's title.

Finally, the trainer can distribute a printer-friendly, signpost-free article having to do with the RMS Titanic (Lorenzi, 2010). The trainer should ask participants to come up with a headline, and provide them with two different colors of highlighters: one color should be used to mark major points and the other color to mark minor details. The tutors should work collaboratively to formulate a summary after deleting minor details. It is helpful, for this reason, to cut and copy the signpost-free article into a word processing program so that tutors are left with only the major points to sift through.

Assessment

The learning objectives of this activity are to activate prior knowledge, to encourage active and strategic reading in tutors, to discuss the workings of the brain as they read (metacognition), and to understand the ways in which they can assist students with critical reading or content literacy needs, in the context of devising summaries and noting reading signposts. A worksheet is provided in the Appendix and should be collected by the trainer at the end of the activity.

It is important that the trainer include in the session an opportunity for tutors to evaluate and self-correct. Doing so will allow tutors to play the role that their tutees play in actual tutorial sessions. If time allows, facilitators can continue the inquiry-based approach by asking tutors what other types of signposts they might include if they were newspaper editors wanting to be sure the article's readers have the visual cues necessary to work toward a written summary.

References

Azevedo, R., & Jacobson, M. J. (2008). Advances in scaffolding learning with hypertext and hypermedia: A summary and critical analysis. *Educational Technology, Research & Development, 56*, 93–100. doi:10.1007/s11423-007-9064-3

Casazza, M. E. (1993). Using a model of direct instruction to teach summary writing in a college reading class. *Journal of Reading, 37*, 202-208. Retrieved from http://www.jstor.org/pss/40033359

Considine, D., Horton, J., & Moorman, G. (2009). Teaching and reaching the millennial generation through media literacy. *Journal of Adolescent & Adult Literacy, 52*, 471–481. doi:10.1598/JAAL.52.6.2

Gtotheordon. (2007). Titanic *in 5 seconds* [Video file]. YouTube. Retrieved from http://www.youtube.com/user/gtotheordon

Lorenzi, R. (2010). Steering error sank Titanic, says author. *Discovery News*. Retrieved from http://news.discovery.com/history/steering-error-sunk-the-titanic-says-author.html?print=true

Roach, J. (2008). Titanic was found during secret Cold War Navy mission. *National Geographic News*. Retrieved from http://news.nationalgeographic.com/news/2008/06/080602-titanic-secret.html

Sanchini, R. (Producer), & Cameron, J. (Director). (1997). *Titanic* [Motion picture]. Los Angeles, CA: 20th Century Fox.

Shiman, J. (Producer & Director). (2004). Titanic *in 30 Seconds* [Motion picture]. Angry Alien Productions. Retrieved from http://www.angryalien.com/0604/titanicbunnies.html

Vygotsky, L. S. (1978). *Mind and society: The development of higher psychological processes*. Cambridge, MA: Harvard University Press.

Appendix

SUMMARY ACTIVITY

Video Clips:

SUMMARY EVALUATION	SUMMARY CHARACTERISTICS	SUMMARY FLAWS
5–Second Clip		
30–Second Clip		

Titanic Article A:

Signposts for reading:

1.   3.   5.
2.   4.   6.

Titanic Article B:

POSSIBLE HEADLINE	Minor Details	Major Points
SUMMARY EVALUATION	Summary Characteristics	Summary Flaws

Reading Assignments

Anita H. Ens

Tutors who know effective reading strategies and can help their tutees to prioritize reading tasks will be better able to facilitate learning. To assist students optimally with reading assignments, tutors should be aware of efficient and effective reading behaviors as they relate to types of reading assignments across academic disciplines. In addition, tutors should be able to model the flexible use of a variety of reading strategies and support tutees as they apply the strategies to their reading assignments. This training session is designed to increase tutors' awareness of factors affecting reading success, teach tutors to recognize different purposes for different reading tasks, and provide both acquaintance with and practice of reading strategies.

Tutors who understand basic processes of reading will also be better able to make moment-to-moment decisions while tutoring. Both cognitive and social models of reading are helpful to understanding reading processes. In an environment of increasingly varied literacies (Franzen, 2005; Street, 1999), including visual and technological literacies (Alvermann & Hagood, 2000), new complexities have arisen to enhance and complicate learning. The sheer volume of media and availability of information add new challenges for reading. These realities make it even more important for students to become adept at selecting and evaluating information, that is, at improving their information literacy (Franzen, 2005). Understanding text or reading as particular to context offers a way of selecting appropriate strategies to address reading assignments (Gee, 2000; Lave & Wenger, 1996; Simpson & Nist, 2000; Street, 1999).

Cognitive models of reading outline the thinking activities of readers who undertake reading tasks. Good readers are more aware of their metacognitive reading strategies, such as recovering from distraction during reading (Wong & Chang, 2001), and use them effectively (Fotovatian & Shokrpour, 2007; Poole, 2005). Students who read strategically have better comprehension and recall than peers who read without strategies (Taraban, Rynearson, & Kerr, 2000). Explicitly teaching cognitive and metacognitive reading strategies can increase students' self efficacy (Schunk & Zimmerman, 1997) and comprehension (Carrell, 1998). Many of the cognitive processes occur simultaneously (Rummelhart, 1994) and not necessarily consciously (Carrell, 1998); therefore, talking with tutees about thought processes connected to reading can help to increase tutees' awareness of their existing thought processes as well as the potential to try different patterns of thought.

Reading strategically involves making a plan and monitoring its effectiveness. This necessitates thinking before, during, and after reading. Cognitive approaches have been helpful to make invisible and often unconscious planning processes explicit. For example, in the strategic tutoring model (Hock, Schumaker, & Deshler, 2001), a learning strategy is defined as "how a person thinks and acts when planning for, completing, and evaluating performance on a learning task" (p. 50). A tutor can establish with a learner how to approach, carry out, and reflect on a reading assignment. The tutor may support the tutee at any point: establishing a purpose; assessing background or prior knowledge; monitoring comprehension; making associations; challenging or adjusting existing schemata; deciding what needs to be remembered and how it will be committed to memory; and determining what needs to be checked, what sources to consult, and what can be skipped.

For some students, executive functioning (Petersen, Lavelle, & Guarino, 2006; Zera & Lucian, 2001) may need to be addressed. With students who consistently forget assignments, manage their time ineffectively, or have difficulties prioritizing steps within a learning task, tutors can assess options for addressing a given behavior and focus on one option. If a student has reading or physical disabilities, the tutor may need to modify strategies to fit an alternate mode of learning. Other modifications may be helpful for tutees learning in English as an additional language. Explicit instruction in task requirements may be helpful, or more conversation regarding the content of a text to address specific vocabulary and language challenges.

From a social constructivist approach, readers construct meaning along with writers, other readers, within a particular discourse context, and from text that was shaped by language carrying particular historical meanings (Gee, 2000). Because knowledge is socially patterned and built and reading is one practice used to build knowledge, reading practices are social acts (Straw, 1990). From the perspective of proponents of New Literacy Studies, multiple literacies "vary with time and place and are embedded in specific cultural practices" (Street, 1999, p. 37). Moreover, literacy can be seen as a set of skills related to particular domains of social life. Viewing reading as a socially situated practice allows tutors and tutees to address task demands and subsequent cognitive and metacognitive actions for particular purposes within the norms of a given discourse community (Gee, 2000; 2001). For example, a biology text and an English novel represent two different discourse communities with their own knowledge, language, values, and structures. Tutor and tutee are thus able to determine how assignments vary in type of text and purpose for reading. Adjusting strategy according to tutees' background knowledge, available time, and other individual factors is considered alongside specific expectations of discipline, course, or professor. Discourse communities are not static, and even norms such as close reading in English (Bialostosky, 2006) are contested and may change over time.

Reading assignments vary across disciplines and from professor to professor (Simpson & Nist, 2000). College reading assignments include reading textbook chapters, journal articles, lab manuals, novels, anthologies, newspaper or magazine articles, brochures, webpages, government or organizational reports, computer programs, blueprints, and so on. Extending the notion of reading to other texts (Franzen, 2005), students may also be asked to read performances, artworks, and video or film. The purpose for reading varies; readers may be expected to do close reading to analyze plot devices in an English course, or read critically to evaluate the events leading to a major historical conflict, or read to learn enormous amounts of detail, for example in anatomy. Student reading may be required for in-class or online discussion, research for an essay, preparation for a lab, multiple-choice exams, or oral presentations. Asking tutors in training to list all the assignments involving reading in their own courses will make this variety evident.

From the outset, a tutor can ensure that a learner is aware of the need to be flexible in reading approach according to the purpose for reading (Falk-Ross, 2002); this purpose will be based on the assignment requirements, what the reader already knows, what skills the reader possesses, how considerate (Armbruster & Anderson, 1984) the text is, and how much time the student has. Tutors can help students develop skills such as establishing purpose; identifying text structure (e.g., compare and contrast, cause and effect); reading text cues (bold font, signal words); and problem solving when comprehension is challenged. The tutor continually facilitates tutee learning by guiding the student to sources rather than giving answers, modeling problem-solving behavior, or selectively teaching content or strategy as necessary (MacDonald, 2000).

When the task is understood and tutees have assessed both prior knowledge and the readability of the text, it is possible to create a plan based on what to read, when, why, and how much (Carrell, 1998; Simpson & Nist, 2000). Strategies before, during, and after reading may be chosen (Falk-Ross, 2002; Taraban, Kerr, & Rynearson; 2004). Reading strategies such as PREP (Preview the reading, Read key paragraphs, Express ideas in writing, and Prepare study cards; Hock, Deshler, & Schumaker, 2000) or SQ3R (Survey, Question, Read, Recite, Review; Robinson, 1946, as cited in Stahl & Henk, 1986) can form frameworks for approaching a variety of reading assignments while modifying the steps to match task demands. Strategies during reading can include identifying themes, using marginalia, highlighting, written or audio notetaking, mapping, diagramming, or outlining. Activities to use after reading may include memory strategies such as summarizing, elaborating, or creating graphic organizers. Generalizing the processes, the tutor can help the tutee to establish reading habits; with every reading assignment, the tutee can be prompted to plan a suitable reading strategy.

Reading and tutoring reading are complex processes. Tutors can be reassured that the relationship with their tutees and their willingness to learn together with tutees is more important than knowing everything. Tutors can be encouraged to keep in mind the overall process of reading in a given social context at a particular time. Tutors' willingness to assess tutees' understanding and use of various strategies, model them, support tutees in their application, and evaluate in an ongoing way will help tutees to become better readers.

Training Activity

This training activity requires a room with movable chairs, optimally grouped around tables. A whiteboard, blackboard, interactive board, or flip charts should be provided. This training session could take one or more hours depending on number and type of activities chosen by the trainer. Learning objectives for the tutors in training are to recognize different purposes for different reading tasks and to practice one of the several reading strategies to which they are introduced. A sample quiz for assessment is included in the Appendix.

The trainer should first introduce the learning objectives of the session. Participants then write down two strengths and two challenges they have when reading for courses.

Trainees can be divided into pairs. Sample texts are offered to partners to read and discuss, to answer three guiding questions: What academic discipline does this text represent? What is the main idea? How is the text structured? During group discussion, the trainer assesses trainees' strengths and challenges and prepares to share them with the group.

As a group, participants discuss the sample texts, highlighting similarities and differences. The trainer then shares information from this introductory activity and expectations and challenges of academic reading in the context of the cognitive and social models of reading.

The trainer models teaching one reading strategy (e.g., marginal notes) to a volunteer playing the role of tutee. Trainees choose a text (e.g., English literature, sociology case study, biology text chapter). Partners discuss a reading strategy and practice teaching it with the text. The group debriefs, discussing factors to be considered when choosing a reading strategy.

Trainers may opt to add a video clip of someone tutoring a reading strategy, debrief trainees after viewing, try the same strategy with a different type of reading assignment, and try a different strategy with the same text. Tutors should discuss how to help tutees become more strategic readers.

Assessment

To assess trainees' learning in this activity, the trainer can administer the assessment quiz provided in the Appendix. The quiz should be modified to match the level of theoretical and practical knowledge provided in training.

Trainees can take the quiz in the last few minutes of the training session or respond to questions by email or to the staff training blog. The trainer should respond to each trainee with comments about his or her answers to quiz questions.

References

Alvermann, D. E., & Hagood, M. C. (2000). Critical media literacy: Research, theory, and the practice in "new times." *Journal of Educational Research, 93,* 193–206. doi:10.1080/00220670009598707

Armbruster, B. B., & Anderson, T. H. (1984). *Producing "considerate" expository text: Or easy reading is damned hard writing* (Reading Education Report No. 46). Cambridge, MA: Bolt, Beranek, & Newman.

Bialostosky, D. (2006). What should college English be? Should college English be close reading? *College English, 69,* 111–116. Retrieved from http://www.jstor.org/stable/25472195

Carrell, P. (1998). Can reading strategies be successfully taught? *The Language Teacher Online, 22*(2). Retrieved from http://jalt-publications.org/old_tlt/files/98/mar/carrell.html

Falk-Ross, F. C. (2002). Toward the new literacy: Changes in college students' reading comprehension strategies following reading/writing projects. *Journal of Adolescent & Adult Literacy, 45,* 278–288.

Fotovatian, S., & Shokrpour, N. (2007). Comparison of the efficiency of reading comprehension strategies on Iranian university students' comprehension. *Journal of College Reading and Learning, 37*(2), 47–63.

Franzen, A. M. (2005). Effective literacy teaching: Concept paper. Paper commissioned for the *Education for All Global Monitoring Report 2006, Literacy for Life.* Retrieved from http://unesdoc.unesco.org/images/0014/001460/146069e.pdf

Gee, J. P. (2000). Discourse and sociocultural studies in reading. In M. L. Kamil, P. B. Mosenthal, P. D. Pearson, & R. Barr (Eds.), *Handbook of reading research* (Vol. 3, pp. 195–207). Mahwah, NJ: Erlbaum.

Gee, J. (2001). Reading as situated language: A sociocognitive perspective. *Journal of Adolescent & Adult Literacy, 44,* 714–725. doi:10.1598/JAAL.44.8.3

Hock, M. F., Deshler, D. D., & Schumaker, J. B. (2000). *Strategic tutoring.* Lawrence, KS: Edge.

Hock, M. F., Schumaker, J. B., & Deshler, D. D. (2001). The case for strategic tutoring. *Educational Leadership, 58*(7). 50–53.

Lave, J., & Wenger, E. (1996). Practice, person, social world. In H. Daniels (Ed.), *An introduction to Vygotsky* (pp. 143–150). London, United Kingdom: Routledge.

MacDonald, R. B. (2000). *The master tutor: A guidebook for more effective tutoring* (2nd ed.). Williamsville, NY: Cambridge Stratford Study Skills Institute.

Petersen, R., Lavelle, E., & Guarino, A. J. (2006). The relationship between college students' executive functioning and study strategies. *Journal of College Reading and Learning, 36*(2), 59–67.

Poole, A. (2005). Gender differences in reading strategy use among ESL college students. *Journal of College Reading and Learning, 36*(1), 7–20.

Rummelhart, D. E. (1994). Toward an interactive model of reading. In R. B. Ruddell, M. R. Ruddell, & H. Singer (Eds.), *Theoretical models and processes of reading* (4th ed., pp. 864–894). Newark, DE: International Reading Association.

Schunk, D. H., & Zimmerman, B. J. (1997). Developing self-efficacious readers and writers: The role of social and self-regulatory processes. In J. T. Guthrie & A. Wigfield, (Eds.), *Reading engagement: Motivating readers through integrated instruction* (pp. 34–50). Newark, DE: International Reading Association.

Simpson, M. L., & Nist, S. L. (2000). An update on strategic learning: It's more than textbook reading strategies. *Journal of Adolescent & Adult Literacy, 43,* 528–541.

Stahl, N. A., & Henk, W. A. (1986). *Tracing the roots of textbook study systems: An extended historical perspective* (College Reading and Learning Assistance Technical Report 86-02). Atlanta, GA: Georgia State University.

Straw, S. B. (1990). The actualization of reading and writing: Public policy and conceptualizations of literacy. In S. P. Norris & L. M. Phillips (Eds.), *Foundations of literacy policy in Canada* (pp. 165–181). Calgary, Canada: Deselig.

Street, B. V. (1999). The meanings of literacy. In D. A. Wagner, R. L. Venezky, & B. V. Street (Eds.), *Literacy: An international handbook* (pp. 34–40). Boulder, CO: Westview Press.

Taraban, R., Kerr, M., & Rynearson, K. (2004). Analytic and pragmatic factors in college students' metacognitive reading strategies. *Reading Psychology, 25,* 67–81. doi:10.1080/02702710490435547

Taraban, R., Rynearson, K., & Kerr, M. (2000). College students' academic performance and self-reports of comprehension strategy use. *Reading Psychology, 21,* 283–308. doi:10.1080/027027100750061930

Wong, M. Y., & Chang, S. C. A. (2001). *Knowledge and use of metacognitive strategies.* Singapore, China: National Institute of Education. Retrieved from http://www.aare.edu.au/01pap/won01419.htm

Zera, D. A., & Lucian, D. G. (2001). Self-organization and learning disabilities: A theoretical perspective for the interpretation and understanding of dysfunction. *Learning Disability Quarterly, 24,* 107–118. Retrieved from http://www.jstor.org/stable/1511067

Appendix

1. What are some examples of different academic reading assignments and their purposes?

    Assignments: textbook chapters, journal articles, lab manuals, novels, anthologies, dramas, film scripts, newspaper or magazine articles, brochures, webpages, government or organization reports, blueprints, performances, artworks, video, film.

    Purposes: analyze for paper, discussion or exam; build foundational knowledge; participate in classroom or online discussion; present orally; inform a paper; prepare for a lab; retain for multiple-choice testing.

2. What factors affect the reading of text?

    Reader factors: understanding of task demands, background content knowledge, motivation, reading ability.

    Text factors: considerateness, readability (vocabulary and syntax), features (font, graphics, use of bold, white space, color).

    Situational factors: assignment due date, concurrent commitments, physical factors (sleep needs, emotional state, resources available).

3. What factors should be considered when choosing a reading strategy?

    Factors affecting reading of text, purpose for reading (task, or assignment demands), type of learner, time available for learning and applying the strategy.

4. How can you support tutees to become more strategic readers?

    Increase tutee awareness of task, self as reader, available reading strategies, importance of flexibility (different strategies for different purposes). Rather than presenting the array of strategies, help tutee to identify the strategies suitable to a particular task. Then generalize underlying processes to other reading assignments (what modifications would be needed; which steps can be consistently followed in planning). Include tutee in decisions by questioning, explaining, modeling, and then prompting, supporting, questioning again.

Critical Thinking Within the Reading Process: Creating Desire and Enhancing Skills

Melissa Thomas

Aretz, Bolen, and Devereux (1997) concluded that critical thinking involves three main components: content knowledge, a positive disposition toward critical thinking, and reflective thinking skills. Although this training module cannot address content knowledge, it does attempt to address the other two components of critical thinking. When tutor and mentor trainers create a positive disposition toward critical thinking and reading in tutors and mentors, they hope that tutors and mentors will transfer that disposition to their students. This expectation is supported by Gillespie and Lerner (2008), who encouraged tutors to talk about reading strategies in order to facilitate their students' metacognition (or an awareness of one's own learning process), especially when the student is challenged by a reading.

The tutors' desire to use reflective thinking skills will be promoted by reading and evaluating the classic text, "Corn-Pone Opinions," by Mark Twain (1923). Additionally, tutors will be taught reflective thinking skills using Ruggiero's (2007) basic skim, reflect, read, and evaluate process layered with McGrath's (2005) critical reading skills and Paul and Elder's (2003) universal intellectual standards. When tutors and mentors have completed this training, they will have an increased desire to think critically, understand and utilize critical reading strategies, and be able to evaluate a reading based on solid reasoning skills.

Training Activity

Approximately 1 hour is required for the instruction, activity, and assessment. One room is needed, with movable chairs and copies of handouts for all participants.

First, the trainer should distribute copies of Twain's "Corn-Pone Opinions," an essay that directly addresses the lack of critical thinking in society. The trainer should either allow time for trainees to read the essay in this session or assign it to be read before the session begins. During the training session, the trainer should lead a discussion about the issues of thought conformity and serious critical thinking, with particular emphasis on the role of tutor or mentor. In what ways do students exhibit "corn-pone" opinions in writing and learning? Why do corn-pone opinions stand for self-approval and conformity? And how can tutors and mentors get students to stop "feeling, and . . . mistake it for thinking" (Twain, 1923, para. 15)?

Then a brief overview of Ruggiero's (2007) reading strategy should be provided:

- Readers should skim the reading in about 5 minutes and look closely at the first and last several paragraphs, plus the headings.

- Readers should reflect on what was skimmed. Is the reader to be informed or persuaded by the author? What is the main idea (from the first and last paragraphs)? Are there any secondary ideas (from the headings)?

- Reading should proceed at a diligent pace. The reader should not mark the reading yet.

- The reader should review what has been read and mark the piece where needed, now that the reader understands what is important.

The trainees then break into groups and reread Twain's piece using critical reading skills. Each group should be assigned one specific note taking or organizing skill, as suggested by McGrath (2005): (a) *underlining* by marking sections with a pen or pencil instead of a highlighter to avoid reading in "auto-highlight" mode; (b) *annotating in the margins* by making small notations in the

Purpose	What is the author's purpose? Is it clearly stated?	Goad or shock people into thinking through a conversationally toned piece. Not clearly stated.
Topic	Is there a well written question? Is the topic unbiased and linked to the purpose?	He believed that individual opinions don't exist or are rare and that we make decisions without thought.
Evidence	Relevant sources? Accurate?	No sources; it is an opinion essay.
Assumptions	Does the author explain or address assumptions?	He assumed that his "black philosopher" (Twain, 1923, para. 3) friend was correct in stating that prosperity = conformity, but he didn't address this.
Point of view	Does author consider alternative reasoning or respond to the "cons"?	No. This is a one-sided piece, which is ironic because he argued that we should not read only one side.
Consequences	What are the implications of the position the author is taking?	To inspire people to get their opinions from other places than just the people they know.

F I G U R E 1   Critical thinking standards. Adapted from R. Paul & L. Elder, 2003, *The miniature guide to critical thinking: Concepts & tools*, Dillon Beach, CA: The Foundation for Critical Thinking, p. 5, and applied to Mark Twain's (1923) essay, "Corn-Pone Opinions."

margin with pen or pencil to draw attention to important points; (c) *"blurbing"* by writing two- to three-word summary statements for each paragraph that can serve as an after-the-fact outline; (d) *paraphrasing* by restating in notes what the author says but in the note taker's own words; or (e) *creating a graphic organizer or mind map*, which helps visual learners to categorize large amounts of information in a chart, matrix, or free-flowing mind map. The groups should then return to discuss as a whole how each strategy worked and how trainees would instruct someone else in using it.

During a final brainstorming session, trainees should use the standards listed by Paul and Elder (2003) in their criteria for evaluating reasoning. If there are questions that are not developed or listed by the students, the trainer should present those questions and distribute the checklist provided in Figure 1.

Assessment

With the basic questions for critical thinking in hand, trainees should practice the process on a short document (possibly a *Wall Street Journal* or *Time Magazine* article). Trainees should model Ruggiero's (2007) process: (a) skim the introduction, conclusion, and key arguments; (b) reflect on personal bias that might shape their reading of the piece; (c) read the material actively and be able to summarize it; and then (d) as a group, evaluate the piece by assessing the purpose, assumptions, and evidence. Alternatively, can be required to use the checklist inspired by Paul and Elder (2003) and provided here as Figure 2.

Purpose	What is the author's purpose? Is it clearly stated?
Topic	Is there a well written question? Is the topic unbiased and linked to the purpose?
Evidence	Relevant sources? Accurate?
Assumptions	Does the author explain or address assumptions?
Point of view	Does author consider alternative reasoning or respond to the "cons"?
Consequences	What are the implications of the position the author is taking?

F I G U R E 2   Critical thinking standards handout. Adapted from R. Paul & L. Elder, 2003, *The miniature guide to critical thinking: Concepts & tools*, Dillon Beach, CA: The Foundation for Critical Thinking, p. 5.

References

Aretz, A. J., Bolen, M. T., & Devereux, K. E. (1997). Critical thinking assessments of college students. *Journal of College Reading and Learning, 28*(1), 12–23.

Gillespie, P., & Lerner, N. (2008). *The Longman guide to peer tutoring.* New York, NY: Pearson Education.

McGrath, J. L. (2005). *Strategies for critical reading: A text with thematic reader.* Upper Saddle River, NJ: Pearson.

Paul, R., & Elder, L. (2003). *The miniature guide to critical thinking: Concepts & tools.* Dillon Beach, CA: The Foundation for Critical Thinking.

Ruggiero, V. R. (2007). *The art of thinking: A guide to critical and creative thought.* New York, NY: Pearson.

Twain, M. (1923). *Corn-pone opinions.* Retrieved from http://dsc.dixie.edu/owl/syllabi/Phil%201120/TwainCornPoneMillOnLiberty.pdf

Taking Lecture Notes

Diane Van Blerkom

Taking good lecture notes is one of the keys to college success. In her review of the literature on taking lecture notes, Armbruster (2009) cited a large number of studies and surveys showing that note taking is a valuable strategy. She indicated that some researchers believed note taking to be a significant factor in student success, and in one study of a human development class note taking was the strongest predictor of students' overall performance in the course. She also indicated that in fall 1998, 83% of faculty used lecture as their primary instructional method (p. 220). Although different formats for presenting information are used in today's classrooms, students are still engaged in note taking as a method of recording course content in their notebooks or on their laptops. To be successful in many college courses, students need to have an accurate and complete set of lecture notes from which to study.

Taking lecture notes can help students in a number of ways. First, taking lecture notes promotes active listening. When students are taking lecture notes, they are actively engaged in the class. They must listen, select the appropriate information, paraphrase it, condense it, and then write it down. This heightened engagement helps students process the information during the lecture often by making connections within the material and between the new material and their prior knowledge.

Next, taking notes provides students with an accurate record of information. Students may not realize how rapidly they forget. Without repetition, students may forget 90% of what they hear 1 month later and up to 80% 2 weeks later (Spitzer, 1939). An experiment can demonstrate this for tutors: the trainer plays a portion of a recorded lecture, has tutors take notes on it, and collects their notes. Two days later, the trainer gives tutors a quiz on that lecture material. Most trainees fail the quiz because they are unable to recall the information. Even though they were paying attention during the lecture and taking notes, they did not have time to store the information in long-term memory. Without their notes, the tutors are unable to review. If tutors are then allowed to check their notes to see if they would have done better had they reviewed, many find the answers to at least some of the quiz questions in their notes.

Finally, taking notes helps students organize lecture information. Students can structure the information in a way that makes sense to them; they can create a system of organization that separates main and supporting points, creating cues for self-testing during review (Van Blerkom, 2012).

Many college students are not skilled note takers. They may write too little information in their notes, believing that they should note only the main points presented in the lecture (or wait for some great piece of information to write down) or may write only what is on the board or screen. Armbruster (2009) noted a number of studies done in the 1980s and 1990s indicating that students recorded only 20% to 40% of the lecture's ideas (p. 225). Even if instructors make PowerPoint® slides available to students, these slides do not contain all of the information presented in the lecture. Students may jot notes on lines next to the slides or in the margin around them; however, there is not enough space to record all of the information the lecturer presents. Instead, they should record the information the lecture presents, in as much detail as possible, using either their notebooks or laptops (perhaps numbering the slides and then using the corresponding numbers to organize their notes).

Tutors are at a disadvantage when working with students who do not have accurate and complete sets of notes. If the information is so sketchy that even the students do not know what their notes mean, tutors who have not sat through the same class will have difficulty helping students see the relationships between the main points and the supporting details.

In many courses, most test questions come from lectures. Without a good set of lecture notes, students will not be able to study adequately for the exam. Peverly et al. (2007) found a strong relationship between note taking—that is, quantity and quality of information in the notes—and test performance. The researchers defined quantity as the number of topics that the student was able to record from the lecture, such as key terms or names. Quality was defined as the level of elaboration of those topics, measured by the completeness and accuracy of the notes.

Tutors can help students evaluate the completeness of their notes during a tutoring session. Tutors working with several students from the same course can compare the quantity and quality of information in multiple sets of notes. Another method of assessing a student's notes is to compare with exam questions. If tutors have access to actual exams (whether brought to the session by students or provided by course instructors), tutors can select a particular lecture topic and compare the information in the student's notes to the information that was needed to answer test questions. This comparison allows both tutor and student to assess the accuracy and completeness of the notes. When the answers to various test questions are missing, the tutor can point to places in the student's notes where more information should have been added. This feedback can help the student learn to take better notes in the future.

How else can tutors help students take better notes? First, tutors should help students learn to take more complete notes. One way to do this is to have students take notes on a short section of text material followed by feedback from the tutor on what was included and what was omitted. Of course, if tutors can attend class lectures with students, comparing notes provides a good measure of quality and quantity.

After students have learned how to determine what is important from what is not, they need to learn to condense the information into notes. I suggest taking notes in meaningful phrases—groups of words that capture the important point made (Van Blerkom, 2012)—rather than full sentences, especially if the lecturer talks quickly. Tutors also should encourage students to write as much as they can during lecture. It is important to note all of the information presented in the lecture because few students can accurately predict what the instructor may think is important. Not only main points but also details are important.

Tutors can also help students learn to organize their lecture notes. Information that is well organized is easier to learn and to recall during an exam (Van Blerkom, 2012). Note-taking formats include outlines and bulleted lists (modified block notes). In either case, though, after noting the topic and date at the top of the page (in notebook or computer file), the note taker writes the heading (first point being discussed) next to the margin and skips to the next line to write the details (anything the lecturer says about that heading) indented underneath. Students should skip a couple of lines before noting the next heading, in case the lecturer refers back to the previous topic and adds information. By organizing information in clusters (headings and details), students can easily review notes for exams, using the headings as prompts for self-testing (Van Blerkom, 2012).

Tutors can also help students learn how to edit their notes. In order to develop accurate and complete sets of notes, most students need to do some editing soon after the lecture, while they can still recall the lecture. By checking their notes against the text, recorded lecture, or another student's notes, students can fill in gaps (missing headings, key words, or details they were unable to record during class); check for accuracy (especially names, dates, and numbers of any kind); improve organization (moving details under the correct headings or rewriting notes to form clusters of information); and add recall words or questions in the margin for later review.

Finally, tutors can help students learn how to review their notes. Many students try to learn the information in their notes by reading over them a few times. Unfortunately, this does not work well for deep learning because students often have only a vague memory of the material and will have difficulty distinguishing closely related details during testing. Three strategies that are more effective include reciting from the headings, reciting the answers to recall questions, and talking about the information with others (Van Blerkom, 2012).

Training Activity

The goal for this activity is to help tutors assess the quality and organization of students' notes, the first step in developing better note taking. (The trainer can devise similar activities to let tutors practice working with students to take complete notes and then to organize, edit, and review them.) For this activity, the trainer will need to prepare some materials:

- Portion of a recorded lecture, or notes to present a lecture about 10 minutes in length

- Projector, screen, and video player of some type (DVD or computer)

- Note paper and writing implements or laptops for tutors

- A copy of the trainer's lecture notes and a projector to show those notes (computer or overhead projector)

The entire training activity can be completed in 1 hour.

The trainer tells the tutors that they will hear a brief lecture and should take notes. After the lecture, the trainer has tutors compare notes with a partner, asking tutors to look at the content of their notes and then at the organization. Then the trainer shows the lecture notes used by the lecturer. Tutors check off each topic included in the lecture notes and then look to see whether details related to those topics are also recorded in their notes.

Tutors rate the quantity of their notes (good—recorded 90–100% of the topics; fair—recorded about 75% of the topics; poor—missed a lot of the topics). Then they rate the quality of the content in similar terms. Finally, they look at the organization of their notes. The trainer asks if the tutors recorded all of the headings that were in the lecturer's notes and if they made the headings visually distinct from the details.

Assessment

Assessment by both trainer and tutors is built into the group activity. The trainer tells the tutors that they need to help their students learn how to improve the content and organization of their notes so that they can improve their test performance. The trainer asks tutors to rewrite their notes from the activity to reflect all of the important content in a useful organizational structure so that they can use it as a model when they work with students. A copy of their rewritten notes submitted to the trainer demonstrates each trainee's understanding of how to evaluate and improve notes.

As an alternative or additional assessment of tutors' understanding, trainees can evaluate each other's lecture notes and suggest improvements. For ongoing assessment, each tutor may be asked to supply to the trainer a copy of a student's notes from before an actual tutoring session and a copy of the edited notes created during the tutoring session.

References

Armbruster, B. (2009). Notetaking from lectures. In R. Flippo & D. Caverly (Eds.), *Handbook of college reading and study strategy research* (2nd ed., pp. 220–248). New York, NY: Routledge.

Peverly, S, T., Ramaswamy, V., Brown, C., Sumowski, J., Alidoost, M., & Garner, J. (2007). What predicts skill in lecture note taking? *Journal of Educational Psychology, 99*, 167–180. doi:10.1037/0022-0663.99.1.167

Spitzer, H. (1939). Studies in retention. *Journal of Educational Psychology, 30*, 641–656. doi:10.1037/h0063404

Van Blerkom, D. (2012). *College study skills: Becoming a strategic learner* (7th ed.). Boston, MA: Cengage Learning.

Preparing for Exams

▪ Monique Idoux

Teaching students how to prepare for exams places them in charge of structuring their study time, using active study strategies to learn and retain material, and monitoring their individual learning and performance. Tutors should be trained to understand types of exam questions (multiple-choice, true-false, short-answer, and essay); identify questions based on Anderson and Krathwohl's (2001) revised structure of Bloom's taxonomy of educational objectives (Bloom's Taxonomy; Bloom, Engelhart, Frost, Hill, & Krathwohl, 1956) to help students encode information at a deeper level; and know the components of a successful study plan and the study habits of effective test-taking. A strategic, focused study plan incorporating active study strategies and understanding material at increasing levels of complexity can help students access and retrieve from memory what they need to know on the day of the test.

Anderson and Krathwohl's (2001) revision of Bloom's Taxonomy proposed a framework that is two-dimensional. The knowledge dimension distinguishes among factual knowledge (knowledge of terminology or specific details); conceptual knowledge (knowledge of classifications, principles, generalizations, or theories); procedural knowledge (knowledge of how to do something); and metacognitive knowledge (self-knowledge or knowledge about cognitive tasks). The cognitive processes dimension has six categories: remembering, understanding, applying, analyzing, evaluating, and creating. Each of the six major categories has at least two specific cognitive processes. Anderson and Krathwohl contended that using their framework to guide the classification of learning objectives (e.g., within a study plan) helps determine what students need to know and do to meet that objective. Do students need to memorize discrete facts, or do students need "some sort of cohesive structure that holds these facts together?" (p. 35). Do students need to be able to classify, differentiate, or both? Although the framework was intended to guide faculty who write test questions and assignments, this knowledge also helps students formulate how learning objectives will be represented in tests and other assessment formats, guiding what students study as well as how they study it. Finally, the framework helps students organize their knowledge and understand the subject matter at a deeper level.

This deep encoding of information is the process of moving the information into long-term memory. Long-term memory storage is permanent and unlimited (Freshwater, 2006), but learners need to practice retrieving from it. Frequent practice helps ensure that the path to the information is easily found (Freshwater, 2006). Teaching students self-regulatory study strategies enables students to create and implement tools that assist in the acquisition, transfer, and access of information. A review of the literature on self-regulatory strategies by Hong, Sas, and Sas (2006) concluded that students benefited from monitoring activities such as analyzing their own test preparation behavior and designing study strategies. Hong et al. concluded that teaching students to use self-regulatory strategies enhances their test-preparation and test-taking skills, which consequently enhances their academic success. Students become active participants in the learning process, which Rachal, Daigle, and Rachal (2007) posited has two elements: students' willingness to use available academic resources such as attending class, completing assignments, and using the library; and students' ability to self-regulate their learning by using study techniques that require the students to generate questions and take notes to improve learning. Rachal et al. believed that such strategies enable the learner to perform higher-level mental operations. However, Weinstein, Husman, and Dierking (2000) observed that developing effective learning strategies is not automatic and, in fact, depends on exposure to effective models and environments that facilitate practice and feedback.

This training session teaches tutors to introduce students to appropriate strategies for understanding types of test questions and devising study plans to prepare for exams. Training specifically addresses four practical skills tutors can teach to tutees: (a) gathering information, (b) types of exam questions, (c) overall study habits, and (d) targeted study for exams. The activity consists of didactic (lecture) training for tutors, followed by role plays for applying learning.

Training Activity

This activity can be conducted in a typical classroom with movable desks and chairs that can be rearranged as needed. Role-playing scenarios (prepared in advance) will also be needed. Length of time for instruction, activity, and assessment is 1.5 hours.

GATHERING INFORMATION

The first step is to teach tutor trainees how to gather information about what the student is doing to prepare for tests and complete class assignments. Trainees should be offered a scenario from the student perspective. The trainer should ask trainees to take the role of a student who is frustrated because he or she is working hard in a course yet still not learning the material. Working in cooperative groups, trainees will brainstorm a list of study habits the student is using and questions for tutors to ask to determine how well the student is employing those habits.

For example, if a student says, "I read my textbook," tutors should inquire beyond the surface meaning of this statement and try to determine how the student is reading. Is the student using active reading and study techniques? Is the student monitoring for comprehension and writing down questions or areas of confusion? What is the student doing to get ready for a test? How does the student read the textbook and take notes? How much time does the student spend (daily, weekly) studying? Where and when does the student read? These questions can establish areas of student accountability and responsibility before a study plan can be implemented. For example, if a student's low performance in the course is due to frequent absences and inadequate study time, these issues must be addressed first before further assistance takes place. The trainer should inform the trainees that teaching a student how to study and how to manage time on tests will do little good if the student seldom attends class. A test preparation plan will be most effective if it builds upon what the student is already doing well.

TYPES OF EXAM QUESTIONS

The trainer then can introduce tutors to types of exam questions and to the revised Bloom's Taxonomy structure (Anderson & Krathwohl, 2001). A worksheet on question types can be prepared in advance and handed out to tutors in training. The worksheet will contain multiple-choice, true-false, short-answer, and essay questions. Each question type will have a definition for the type and an answering strategy.

Many students claim to study for a test without having a full understanding of what studying actually entails. Is rote memorization of information studying? Is reading the textbook studying? Atkinson (1993) defined studying simply as the process students use to learn. As with most processes, Atkinson posited, it is necessary to turn raw material—that is, information—into the product; the product is what a student learns about the information. In this sense, studying helps students manufacture learning. This learning takes place at increasing levels of complexity. At the most basic level is recognition and recall. The next level is translating information, where students put the information into their own words. Next, the student connects information, which could include identifying causes and effects or similarities and differences and identifying parts of a whole or solutions to a problem (Atkinson, 1993). At the application level, the student uses or carries out a procedure in a given situation (Anderson & Krathwohl, 2001). At the next level, the student knows information well enough to analyze it—to break it into parts and examine each part in relation to the others and to the whole. Following analysis is evaluation, the level of thinking at which students "make judgments based on criteria and standards" (Anderson & Krathwohl, p. 31). Finally, students synthesize, putting ideas together to "create new ways to solve a problem or perform a job" (Atkinson, 1993, p. 15). Trainees can develop common questions that tutors ask and practice rephrasing each question as if the tutee had trouble understanding what the tutor first asked.

As a group, tutors can now create a working model of a study plan. A successful study plan has two components: overall study habits that generate raw material for learning, and targeted study for an exam that translates the raw material into student learning.

OVERALL STUDY HABITS

In a sense, students should begin planning and studying for final exams from the first week of the semester by reading assignments, listening during lectures, and taking good classroom notes. Tutors can encourage students to use active reading strategies for reading assignments. Active reading strategies such as SQ3R (Survey, Question, Read, Recite, Review; Robinson, 1962) and PORPE (Predict, Organize, Rehearse, Practice, Evaluate; Simpson, Stahl, & Hayes, 1989) help students build a framework for understanding their reading assignments and provide a mechanism to engage students actively as they generate text-based questions and then read to find answers to those questions (Van Blerkom, Van Blerkom, & Bertsch, 2006). As students recite or rehearse and review important information from the reading, they make the material more personally meaningful and thus more memorable (Van Blerkom et al., 2006). Active reading also provides students with background knowledge and key terms and concepts, which will in turn enhance their understanding of class lectures and their ability to participate in class discussions. Such preparation primes students to be active listeners.

To get the most out of a lecture, students can learn to listen for verbal cues that indicate how lecture material is organized and what information is important to know and remember (McWhorter, 1992). Verbal cues can be organizational, emphatic, or summary. Another positive listening strategy for lectures is to anticipate relationships. Students can ask themselves what point is being made in the lecture, what idea is supported by each element of the lecture, and how the information fits together (McWhorter, 1992). Tutors can also teach students to take notes systematically by preparing note-taking paper in a two- or three-column format, heading notes with topic and date, recording main ideas in the middle column and supporting information in the right column, placing a "to-do" reminder at the end of notes, and summarizing the notes (McWhorter, 1992). These learning strategies can be synthesized into daily and weekly reviews, leading up to a major, pre-exam review.

TARGETED STUDY FOR AN EXAM

To block out an ineffective study pattern or to implement effective study strategies, Van Blerkom (2012) recommended the "Five-Day Study Plan" (p. 268). This plan provides a framework for structuring study and learning activities. *Space Your Study:* First of all, students should count backward 5 days from the date of the exam and use that as a starting point. Students could study 2 hours a day for 5 days, for example, but the point is to encourage students not to do all their studying immediately before the exam. *Divide the Material:* In this next step, students divide the material that will be on the exam. They can make a list of the chapters, lecture topics, and outside readings that will be covered on the test and group all textbook readings and lecture notes around related chapters or concepts. *Study the Oldest Material First:* When students set up their study plan, they should start with the oldest chapter first and give it more preparation and review time. *Plan Active Study Tasks:* Students can make word cards or question cards, create study sheets and self-tests, or study in a group (see Van Blerkom, 2012, p. 264). The trainer can present Van Blerkom's Five-Day Study Plan or allow time in the session for tutors to read from her book and discuss each step.

Assessment

Objectives for the trainees are to understand types of exam questions and the process of deeply encoding information for easier retrieval at the time of the test and to identify the components of a successful study plan and the study habits of effective test taking. Assessment is built into the final learning activities.

ROLE PLAY

Tutors are assigned to work on role-playing scenarios in groups. The trainer (or trainer and experienced tutors on staff) should write these scenarios from typical situations in the learning center.

Each group will develop study plans appropriate to the needs of the students in the scenarios. A wrap-up discussion follows, which permits correction of any misconceptions noted during presentation of the groups' study plans.

REFLECTION PAPER

Tutors in training should be assigned to write self-reflection essays in which they relate the Bloom's Taxonomy levels of thinking and the Five-Day Study Plan to their own study and testing habits. What advice would they now give themselves? How should they adjust and modify current behavior to prepare optimally for exams?

References

Anderson, L. W., & Krathwohl, D. R. (2001). *A taxonomy for learning, teaching and assessing: A revision of Bloom's taxonomy of educational objectives.* New York, NY: Longman.

Atkinson, R. (1993). *Study skills, test taking.* Baton Rouge, LA: Associated Builders and Contractors, Pelican Chapter. Retrieved from http://www.eric.ed.gov/PDFS/ED374284.pdf

Bloom, B. S. (Ed.), Engelhart, M. D., Frost, E. J., Hill, W. H, & Krathwohl, D. R. (1956). *Taxonomy of educational objectives. Handbook I: Cognitive domain.* New York, NY: David McKay.

Freshwater, J. (2006, January). *Mastering academics: College study skills.* Paper presented at the learning and study skills training for the Student Achievement, Academic, and Retention Program, California State University, Bakersfield, CA.

Hong, E., Sas, M., & Sas, J. C. (2006). Test-taking strategies of high and low mathematics achievers. *Journal of Educational Research, 99,* 144–155. doi:10:3200/JOER.99.3.144-155

McWhorter, K. T. (1992). *Study and thinking skills in college.* New York, NY: Harper Collins.

Rachal, K., Daigle, S., & Rachal, W. (2007). Learning problems reported by college students: Are they using learning strategies? *Journal of Instructional Psychology, 34,* 191–199.

Robinson, F. P. (1962). *Effective reading.* New York: NY: Harper.

Simpson, M. L., Stahl, N. A., & Hayes, C. G. (1989). PORPE: A research validation. *Journal of Reading, 33*(1), 22–28.

Van Blerkom, D. L. (2012). *College study skills: Becoming a strategic learner* (7th ed.). Boston, MA: Wadsworth.

Van Blerkom, D. L., Van Blerkom, M. L., & Bertsch, S. (2006). Study strategies and generative learning: What works? *Journal of College Reading and Learning, 37*(1), 7–18.

Weinstein, C. E., Husman, J., & Dierking, D. (2000). Self-regulation interventions with a focus on learning strategies. In M. Boekaerts (Ed.), *Handbook of self-regulation* (pp. 727–747). San Diego, CA: Academic Press.

A Metacognitive Approach to Taking Exams

■ Rick A. Sheets

Metacognitive theory predicts that college learners can expedite their thinking and learning by becoming aware of strategies and consciously implementing and appropriately evaluating them (Flavell, 1976; Rings & Sheets, 1991). Flavell (1976) defined metacognition as "the active monitoring and consequent regulation and orchestration of [thinking and learning activities] in relation to the cognitive objects or data on which they bear, usually in the service of some concrete goal or objective" (p. 232). Heerspink (1989) was intrigued by the idea of applying metacognition to study strategies and presented motivation, acquisition, retention, and performance as four components to effective studying.

Sheets (2004) adapted Heerspink's model to design a metacognitive approach to study strategies for training tutors and made the model available as a website resource. Williams (2009) built on this research to develop rubrics by which tutors and other support staff can assess targeted study strategies. Williams' metacognitive model is coherent with two domains of student learning and development outcomes adopted by the Council for the Advancement of Standards in Higher Education (CAS, 2009) and employed in the CAS standards and guidelines for assessing learning assistance programs, the first (knowledge acquisition, construction, integration, and application) and second (cognitive complexity) domains.

All tutors can benefit from training in a metacognitive model of learning strategies. Many tutors, though academically successful, do not utilize efficient study strategies themselves and need training before they can help others to become more efficient, effective, and independent as learners (Rings & Sheets, 1991). Other tutors may be operating on automatic pilot, that is, choosing strategies at a subconscious level, unaware of how they achieve success (Brown, 1980; Rings & Sheets, 1991). Still others may be effective and efficient learners who know the strategies they employ in learning new information but who nevertheless lack the rich repertoire of techniques needed to help other students select strategies appropriate for their learning needs (Rings & Sheets, 1991; Sheets, 1994). Training tutors in metacognitive approaches to exam strategies provides student staff with questions, discussion points, and strategies to use while tutoring. Such training also lets tutors share and hear others' beliefs and expectations, which permits them to explore others' interpretations of academic tasks, situates learning within the tutor trainees' own experience, and encourages trainees to reason their way toward epistemological maturity (Hofer, 2001). Training in metacognitive strategies also provides tutors with ideas students can use to monitor and assess their learning and exam success and thus make intentional, appropriate changes for future exam situations.

Training Activity

Several techniques, including lecture, pair-share, group discussion, and self-reflection, are combined in the following training session. Training time can range from 1 to 2 hours, depending on the depth and length and choice of activities to be included. This activity requires a room with Internet access and projection equipment, tables, and seating that permits grouping into both dyads and small groups. Resources for the entire session include a link to a website (Sheets, 2004) and to five documents available there: a completed metacognition overview, a blank metacognition overview, a metacognitive strategies handout, a handout on preparing for and taking tests, and the learning log.

The learning outcomes for this training session include the following:

- Tutors will identify the exam strategies they use and those they want to change.

- Tutors will state the strategies and resources they plan to share with students and how they plan to share them.

- Tutors will identify their own comfort level with using the exam strategy information with students as a result of this session and indicate whether more training or individual assistance is needed.

The trainer should take time at the beginning of the session to establish rapport, eye contact, and a trust relationship with the group. After introducing the title and the goals of the training session, the trainer asks tutors to pair up. If there is an odd number of trainees, the trainer also participates. First, tutors will answer questions individually:

- What test-preparation and test-taking strategies do you use?

- Are your strategies time efficient and grade effective?

- Should more strategies be available?

Then tutors exchange ideas with their partners. After a few minutes, the trainer announces when it is time to switch, so each partner has time to share with the other. Trainees then should share their most efficient and effective strategies with the entire group. The trainer or a recorder should make a list of the strategies stated so all can see. The trainer should also respond to the strategies as they are shared and then show how the tutors' own analysis of their test-preparation and test-taking strategies leads to developing strategies to use and share with students. The activity so far requires 10-20 minutes.

The second part of the training activity provides an overview of the metacognitive model (including a definition, description, and exam strategy examples for metacognition) and each of its four components: motivation, acquisition, retention, and performance. Trainees should receive copies of the completed overview handout for the presentation and also the blank version for those who wish to make their own notes of details, examples, or insights. The trainer should discuss each part of the model, adding personal experiences or notes. This section of the training activity requires about 15-20 minutes.

Each trainee then chooses one of the four components (motivation, acquisition, retention, or performance) to focus on for the next activity, in which specific strategies will be examined. The trainees should receive copies of the metacognitive strategy worksheet and divide into groups of two to seven individuals by component chosen. There may be enough individuals in some groups to subdivide into working groups.

Groups should be named (e.g., Motivation, Acquisition, Retention 1, Retention 2, Retention 3, Performance 1, Performance 2) as appropriate. Each group should identify a recorder and a speaker. Then each group selects one or more test-preparation or test-taking strategies from the best-strategies list created earlier in the session. These strategies should be chosen because they are the most critical to share with students and most appropriate to the component of the metacognitive model that group members have chosen to work on. Trainees should work in their groups to identify why they chose these strategies and share how they integrate them into a tutoring session. This task will require about 15 minutes if groups are asked to identify one to three strategies, to 45 minutes if groups are large or if groups are asked to identify three to five of the best strategies.

The trainer should ask each group to report, keeping in mind the limited time remaining in the session. This section of the training requires 10-15 minutes.

For the remainder of the session, it may be wise to have participants remain in groups to save time. Trainees should take a few minutes to identify one new strategy (or a revision of a strategy currently used) that they would like to use themselves to prepare for their own exams. Each trainee writes down the chosen strategy and the particulars of how and when the trainee plans to use it. This section of the training requires about 5 minutes. If there is enough time remaining, it is productive to have tutors share their selected strategies and their reasoning.

Assessment

In the last activity of this training session, tutors identify in the required Learning Log (available as a handout from Sheets, 2004) what they have learned about utilizing the metacognitive model to help students prepare for exams. Writing in the Learning Log may be done individually or in the group setting. If additional time is available, trainees write one or more specific, goal-oriented actions they will take as a result of their new insights and share these with the group.

At this point, the trainer should pass out the test-taking strategies handout, which offers specific strategies for preparing for and taking tests (Sheets, 2004). Please note that trainers and tutors are welcome to download or copy the handout for preparing for and taking tests, provided the provenance is acknowledged and logo and credit remain intact. This section of the training requires 10-20 minutes.

After the training session, the trainer reviews all learning log response sheets. Learning logs containing answers that do not seem thoughtful or reflective should not be accepted; they should be returned to tutors with comments for changes before credit is given for completing the training session.

References

Brown, A. L. (1980). Metacognitive development of reading. In R. J. Spiro, B. C. Bruce, & W. F. Brewer (Eds.), *Theoretical issues in reading comprehension* (pp. 453–481). Hillsdale, NJ: Erlbaum.

Council for the Advancement of Standards in Higher Education (CAS). (2009). *CAS professional standards for higher education* (7th ed.). Washington, DC: Author.

Flavell, J. H. (1976). Metacognitive aspects of problem solving. In L. B. Resnick (Ed.), *The nature of intelligence* (pp. 231–236). Hillsdale, NJ: Erlbaum.

Heerspink, J. (1989, March). *Assessing students' needs in a tutorial setting.* Presentation at the Annual Conference of the National Association for Developmental Education, Cincinnati, OH. Retrieved from http://www.lsche.net/resources/lrnr_asses/assess_slo_metacgntv_rubric/heerspink_89.pdf

Hofer, B. K. (2001). Personal epistemology research: Implications for learning and teaching. *Journal of Educational Psychology Review, 13,* 353–382. doi:10.1023/A:1011965830686

Rings, S., & Sheets, R. A. (1991). Student development and metacognition: Foundations for tutor training. *Journal of Developmental Education, 15*(1), 30–32.

Sheets, R. A. (1994). *The effects of training and experience on adult peer tutors in community colleges* (Doctoral dissertation). Arizona State University, Tempe, AZ. Retrieved from http://www.eric.ed.gov/PDFS/ED474187.pdf

Sheets, R. A. (2004). *Learning your way: A metacognitive approach to study strategies.* Retrieved from http://www.crla.net/handbook/ch4/sheets/

Williams, D. (2009). *Assessing student learning outcomes using metacognitive rubrics and general tutoring SLO measurement document.* Retrieved from http://www.lsche.net/resources/lrnr_asses/assess_slo_metacgntv_rubric.htm

Taking Exams

 Monique Idoux

If students lack experience taking complex tests or have not taken tests in a while (e.g., if they are adult learners returning to school), they may not have developed an effective test-taking approach. Research on the differences in strategy use between high-achieving and low-achieving students indicates that certain strategies can be beneficial to learning, retention, and retrieval of information (Hong, Sas, & Sas, 2006); in contrast, other strategies may not be beneficial and could even lead to lower academic performance (Kitsantas, 2002; Parham, 1997). Bruch, Pearl, and Giordano (1986) compared academically successful students with academically unsuccessful students and found that the high performers had a greater knowledge of test-taking skills and used learning strategies that led to a deep level of encoding.

Chittooran and Miles (2001) posited that the chances for test success improve if learners invest time and effort in developing and employing test-taking strategies. Students will be more likely to do well on tests if they are prepared for them—not just because they know the material, but also because they will feel more confident while they take the test and can put their time and energy into answering test questions instead of worrying (Indiana College Placement and Assessment Center [ICPAC], 1993). The following activity employs cognitive and metacognitive strategies as part of a test-taking plan that peer tutors can teach to students.

Training Activity

This activity can be conducted in a typical classroom with movable desks and chairs that can be re-arranged as needed. Role-playing scenarios (prepared in advance) are also needed. Length of time for instruction, activity, and assessment is 1.5 hours.

The trainer should first introduce tutors to questions they can ask to determine students' test-taking approach. For example, tutors can ask students to describe strategies they use immediately before or while taking tests, how they approach multiple-choice or essay tests, whether they skip questions, and what they do when their minds go blank (Driscoll & Ross, 2006). Based on the information from these questions, tutors need to teach appropriate strategies. Strategies can be divided into test-dependent (Stough, 1993) and test-independent strategies (Scruggs & Lifson, 1985). The trainer should prepare handouts of these strategies and give trainees time to preview them before beginning the role-play scenarios.

TEST-DEPENDENT STRATEGIES

To prepare for essay tests, Gallagher (2002) suggested the A-B-C-D approach: **A**ttack the prompt, **B**rainstorm ideas, **C**hoose the order of your response, and **D**etect errors. This strategy is easy for students to remember and gives them a method for tackling timed writing and essay tests. Attacking the prompt helps students focus on key words in the prompt such as *compare, describe, discuss,* or *explain,* and ensures that students understand what the question is asking before they write. Brainstorming ideas gives students abundant raw material for their essay response and helps them craft a thesis that answers the essay question clearly. Choosing the order of the response encourages students to outline ideas before they begin writing and provides a way to structure their response. Students can look back on this outline to make sure they stay on track. Finally, detecting errors reminds students to edit out mistakes or careless errors at the appropriate place within this abbreviated writing process, but not at the expense of fully developing their ideas and completely answering the essay question.

Several strategies are useful for objective tests. In true-false questions, tutors can advise students to watch for statements that contain qualifiers or absolutes and to check each part of the sentence. "If any part of the sentence is false, the entire sentence is false" (ICPAC, 1993, p. 18). For short-answer, fill-in-the-blank, and matching questions, test takers should read each statement or list carefully and all the way through before answering, and pay attention to grammar cues. For matching tests, test takers should mark answers they know well the first time through and eliminate possibilities as they work through the list (ICPAC, 1993). On multiple-choice questions, test takers should anticipate the answer to the question before reading the options and compare the anticipated answer with the alternatives provided. They should analyze and dismiss incorrect alternatives, which is another way of determining the correct answer by eliminating. All answer choices should be considered; even if a first- or second-answer choice is appealing, test takers should continue to read all options. Finally, they should skip questions to which they do not know the answer immediately (McClain, 1983).

TEST-INDEPENDENT STRATEGIES

Test-independent strategies are test-wiseness techniques, useful regardless of the type of test or its content (Scruggs & Lifson, 1985). For example, time-use strategies help students develop a plan at the start of an exam, such as looking over the entire test to get a sense of what the test is like, determining how many questions are on the test and the difficulty and point value of each, and deciding how much time to spend on each question (Atkinson, 1993). Answering easy questions first boosts confidence, and if time is a factor on the test, students should be encouraged not to dwell on questions and problems that do not have immediate, apparent answers. Test takers can be advised to skip those questions and return to them later (Glenn, 2004). One method for doing this is the "one-check, two-check" strategy: one check for questions if the student is fairly certain of the answer, two checks for questions to which the student does not know the answer. The test taker proceeds through all questions, going back to answer one-check questions first, then two-check questions. This method prevents students from getting stuck on a particular question and encourages them to work strategically through exams. In addition, in the process of going through the entire exam, students may find cues to correct answers (Stough, 1993).

Error-avoidance strategies include reading test directions slowly and carefully, paying attention to key terms and steps in the directions, marking answers carefully, answering all parts of the exam, and checking all answers (Glenn, 2004). To keep a formula or process in mind, test takers should write it in the test margins along with helpful notes, rules, equations, or mnemonic devices (Glenn, 2004).

Deductive reasoning strategies include eliminating answer choices known to be incorrect. Clues in the answer choices that could help students eliminate incorrect answers are absolutes (words such as *always, never, every,* or *none*); grammar clues (mismatches in number or gender between question stem and answer option); the choice "all of the above," or similarities between answer choices (ICPAC, 1993). Using content information from other test questions and answer options can also help students choose the correct answer (Stough, 1993).

Guessing strategies can be employed when the test taker has used the "one-check, two-check" method to identify difficult questions and eliminated incorrect answer choices to increase the odds of choosing the correct answer. In these cases, students may still not find the answer to be obvious. If there is no penalty for incorrect answers, it is time to guess (Stough, 1993).

A helpful after-test strategy involves showing students how to analyze their test performance by examining their returned tests. Tutors can provide a checklist like Figure 1, that classifies test errors with the reason for missing the question, which could be the result of insufficient information, test anxiety, or lack of test knowledge and test-taking skills (Atkinson, 1993).

With data from test analysis, students can determine what they are doing well and what changes they need to make in studying and test taking (Atkinson, 1993). Students then can be encouraged to create positive mental messages, such as, "I didn't get every question right, but I studied hard and am pleased with my grade," or "I know a lot more now than before" (Atkinson, 1993, p. 26).

Test item missed	The information was not in my notes	I studied the wrong information	I carelessly marked a wrong choice	I misread the question or the directions
Number of items missed				

FIGURE 1   After–test analysis of missed test items. For a more complex test–analysis form, see *Study Skills: Test Taking*, by R. Atkinson (1993), p. 27.

Assessment

Objectives for the tutors are to (a) understand the components of test taking and (b) develop a test-taking plan to help tutees. Assessment is built into the final tutor activity. The trainer assigns trainees to work on role-playing scenarios in groups. Each group will develop a test-taking plan appropriate to the student's needs as portrayed in the role-playing scenario. The scenarios can be derived from the statements in the chart above. A wrap-up discussion will follow.

Trainees can also be assigned to write self-reflective papers in which they relate the information learned in this training session to their own test-taking behaviors and discuss necessary adjustments and modifications. The quality of their analyses will indicate to the trainer their understanding of the components of test taking and their skill in developing a plan to improve performance.

References

Atkinson, R. (1993). *Study skills: Test taking.* Washington, DC: National Workplace Literacy Program. Retrieved from http://www.eric.ed.gov/PDFS/ED374284.pdf

Bruch, M., Pearl, L., & Giordano, S. (1986). Differences in the cognitive processes of academically successful and unsuccessful test-anxious students. *Journal of Counseling Psychology, 33,* 217–219.

Chittooran, M. M., & Miles, D. D. (2001, April). *Test-taking skills for multiple choice formats: Implications for school psychologists.* Paper presented at the Annual Conference of the National Association of School Psychologists, Washington, DC. Retrieved from http://www.eric.ed.gov/PDFS/ED455488.pdf

Driscoll, R., & Ross, D. B. (2006, October). *Test anxiety: Age appropriate interventions.* Paper presented at the American Counseling Association Southern Region Leadership Conference, Huntsville, AL. Retrieved from http://www.eric.ed.gov/PDFS/ED493897.pdf

Gallagher, K. (2002, March). *Developing effective writers.* Presentation at the Reading Institute for Academic Preparation, Bakersfield, CA.

Glenn, R. E. (2004). Teach kids test-taking tactics. *Teaching for Excellence, 24,* 1–2.

Hong, E., Sas, M., & Sas, J. C. (2006). Test-taking strategies of high and low mathematics achievers. *Journal of Educational Research, 99,* 144–155.

Indiana College Placement and Assessment Center. (1993). *Better study skills for better grades and real learning.* Bloomington, IN: Author. Retrieved from http://www.eric.ed.gov/PDFS/ED395305.pdf

Kitsantas, A. (2002). Test preparation and performance: A self-regulatory analysis. *Journal of Experimental Education, 70,* 101–113.

McClain, L. (1983). Behavior during examinations: A comparison of "A," "C," and "F" students. *Teaching of Psychology, 10*(2), 69–71.

Parham, S. D. (1997). *The relationships between test-taking strategies and cognitive ability test performance* (Doctoral dissertation). Available from ProQuest Dissertations & Theses database. (Order No. 9713116)

Scruggs, T. E., & Lifson, S. A. (1985). Current conceptions of test-wiseness: Myths and realities. *School Psychology Review, 14,* 339–350.

Stough, L. M. (1993, April). *Research on multiple-choice questions: Implications for strategy instruction.* Paper presented at the Annual Convention of the Council for Exceptional Children, San Antonio, TX. Retrieved from http://www.eric.ed.gov/PDFS/ED366135.pdf

Setting Goals

 Patricia Fullmer

Goals have been found to motivate and direct behavior because individuals make decisions based on their desired goals (Locke & Latham, 1984, 1990). Setting goals clarifies expectations, so that one knows what to do and when to do it, and encourages persistence, because one can determine what effort is needed. Setting goals also increases self-efficacy, the belief that one can accomplish a task (Bandura, 1997; Schunk, 1995; Zimmerman, 2000). If tutors can help students to set realistic goals, this should increase students' persistence, enhance self-efficacy, and boost motivation.

Bandura (1997) and Schunk (1995) reported that short-term goals were more effective because they can be achieved more quickly and produced higher motivation than long-term goals. Long-term goals can be approached by dividing them into steps that form short-term goals. Analyzing long-term goals into steps boosts motivation and makes goals easier to achieve. Schunk (1995) and Locke and Latham (1984, 1990) found that to be effective a goal needs to be specific and measurable so that it is clear and understandable. They also found that a moderately challenging goal, not too easy and not so difficult as to be unachievable, is a very successful motivator. Thus, goals need to be "SMART: Specific, Measurable, Achievable, Realistic, and Timely" (Donahue, n.d., para. 1).

The planning process for setting a goal involves choosing a goal and deciding on strategies to achieve the goal. In addition, self-monitoring and self-reflection are necessary to evaluate progress toward the achievement of the goal and modify the goal and strategies (Schunk, 1995, Zimmerman, 2000). The first step in planning to create goals is to involve all the participants from the very beginning in order to establish commitment to the goal (Schunk, 1995; Locke & Latham, 1990).

After a goal has been chosen, several additional actions need to take place in order for the goal to be effective. Strategies to achieve the goal need to be decided on and implemented, and performance toward the chosen goal needs to be evaluated. This requires self-reflection, a self-evaluation of progress, and adjustment of strategies or goals. An important part of goal setting is formulating an implementation plan. An implementation plan may include *when* (the day and time one plans to get started); *where* (the place where the strategic activity will take place); *what* (which strategies will be used); and *how* (how one will continue in spite of difficulties, how one will resume if disrupted, and how long one will act on the goal). For example, if I decide to spend more time preparing for a course exam, my implementation plan may state that starting 7 days before the exam I will study each evening from 7:00 to 9:00 (when); I will study in a carrel in the library (where); I will write a summary of each textbook chapter and summarize each set of lecture notes (what); and I will meet with a tutor if I get stuck, turn off my cell phone, and defer until 9:00 any chats with friends who drop by my carrel (how).

Training Activity

Materials needed for this training activity include paper, markers, handouts on setting goals, handouts on implementing goal plans, and computer and projector if using PowerPoint®. A PowerPoint® presentation created by the author (Fullmer, 2011) is available for use. Time required is about 1 hour.

After an introduction to the topic, each trainee receives a Setting Goals handout, with lines on which to list his or her own 5-year goals in the categories of family life, social life, spirit and adventure, career, and academics. Looking more closely at the academic goal, trainees then list three academic goals they want to accomplish within the year. Alternatively, this step could be completed before the training session; tutors could be asked to list their five 5-year goals and their three 1-year goals in preparation for the session, and to bring their lists to training.

The facilitator then presents information on the benefits of goals, how to set SMART goals, and how to follow through and accomplish goals. A PowerPoint® presentation is an option.

In small groups, trainees work out implementation plans for each of them to refine and accomplish one academic goal. The trainer should prepare handouts in advance that provide space for turning one academic goal (whichever they most want to accomplish) into a SMART goal. This Implementation Plan handout should also ask these questions:

- What three strategies are you going to use to achieve the goal?

- When are you going to start your strategies?

- Where are you going to start?

- How are you going to continue in spite of difficulties?

All tutors in each small group work on one trainee's academic goal together until they agree on an implementation plan. Then the tutors turn their attention to another trainee's academic goal, turn it into a SMART goal, and devise a plan to implement it.

Assessment

To demonstrate their understanding of SMART goals and their implementation, small groups of tutors then script scenarios and play the roles of tutors assisting tutees to develop goals and implementation plans for the current semester. As each group acts out its scenario, trainer and trainees make note of especially good approaches to take. For assessment purposes, the trainer also notes any misapprehensions to clear up.

If enough time remains in the session, or at a future training session, trainees can devise and print table tents or posters with information about setting SMART goals. In this way trainees demonstrate their understanding to each other and to the trainer. Moreover, the visual displays that they produce not only provide information for student clients but also serve as a reminder for tutors, especially if setting SMART goals is a student learning outcome assessed in the learning center.

References

Bandura, A. (1997). Self-efficacy. *Harvard Mental Health Letter, 13*(9), 4–7.

Donahue, G. (n.d.). *Creating S.M.A.R.T. goals.* Retrieved from http://www.topachievement .com/smart.html

Fullmer, P. (2011). *Goal setting.* Retrieved from http://www.crla.net/handbook/ch4/Fullmer

Locke, E., & Latham, G. (1984). *Goal setting: A motivational technique that works!* Englewood Cliffs, NJ: Prentice Hall.

Locke, E., & Latham, G. (1990). *A theory of goal setting and task performance.* Englewood Cliffs, NJ: Prentice Hall.

Schunk, D. (1995). Inherent details of self-regulated learning include student perceptions. *Educational Psychology, 30,* 213–226. doi:10.1207/s15326985ep3004_7

Zimmerman, B. J. (2000). Self-efficacy: An essential motive to learn. *Contemporary Educational Psychology, 25,* 82–91. doi:10.1006/ceps.1999.1016

Developing Relationships With Faculty

M. E. McWilliams

The overarching objective for students is that they learn to self-regulate. They must be able to motivate themselves, determine study strategies, evaluate their progress, and seek resources. This workshop concerns the last component: the most important resource to the student is the professor. As one faculty member adamantly stated, "The professor is the number one defense against failure" (Pierce, 2004, p. 4). However, despondent students in a tutoring center often confess that they have done absolutely everything to ensure academic success except see the professor. Tutors have a continuing responsibility to encourage student clients to consult regularly with their professors during office hours. The purpose of this workshop is to train tutors to teach students how to establish a beneficial association with professors.

Astin's (1999) student involvement theory suggested that "the greater the student's involvement in college [including interaction with professors], the greater will be the amount of student learning and personal development" (pp. 528–529). Based on longitudinal samples totaling 200,000 students, Astin's research underscored the benefit of active participation in class and regular communication with professors in their offices. When students are involved with faculty in this way, students invest a "physical and psychological energy" into the relationship that engenders commitment, enthusiasm, and vigilance in their studies (Astin, p. 518). In other words, students begin to learn more deeply and fully and to care about their learning.

Training Activity

The training workshop has two parts: a game that develops an understanding of the professor's expectations regarding student behavior and a role-play exercise that develops strategies for initiating a receptive interaction in the professor's office. Tutors and mentors serve as the participants so that they may in turn train other students. The materials necessary for this 1-hour training exercise include a bell, prompt cards, two chairs, a desk, a large stack of papers, a red pen, and a Halloween mask with a scary face.

SURVEY SAYS

The trainer tells the tutors or mentors to divide into two teams, one on each side of the room, and announces that the group will play a game called Survey Says. One player from each team comes forward to face a bell. The trainer explains that the trainees will be reviewing the results of a survey in which professors were asked one question: "What student behavior 'ticks you off' the most?" The trainer says that some of the responses to this survey are listed on a set of cards. Those responses include comments about both in-class behavior and behavior in the professor's office, as one affects the other. A professor's willingness to assist outside of class is often compromised if the student demonstrates ignorance of classroom civility and decorum (Dzubak, 2008).

A trainee chosen at random draws from the stack, and the trainer gives a clue to the response, such as, "This is something that you do with your thumbs." The trainer continues to give clues until a participant rings the bell and gives the correct answer. The trainer then elaborates on that point before moving on to the next card. Teams acquire points for each correct answer. The trainer can conduct this survey with professors on his or her campus or use the top 10 responses from the survey conducted at Stephen F. Austin State University (McWilliams, 2010):

1. Arriving late to class. Professors expressed intense irritation with students who are tardy. Two responses were in all capital letters with multiple exclamation marks: "BE ON TIME!!!"

2. Talking to other students. Chatting, whispering, and passing notes to other classmates is not only rude but also distracting to students who are trying to learn.

3. Allowing cell phones to ring. Professors can often hear even a vibrating phone.

4. Leaving class. Students should use the bathroom and get a drink of water before class.

5. Texting. One professor growled that a student had even texted while conversing with the professor in his office.

6. Not coming to office hours. Many professors surveyed were disgruntled that students wait until so late or never come at all to seek assistance.

7. Asking, "Did we do anything important?" This question, asked by a student who has missed class, was the most irritating question reported. It suggests that the professor likely did nothing of consequence.

8. Not doing the homework. Professors also complained that often the students who do show up for help in their offices present them with a blank sheet of paper. Professors want to see that the student has made an effort.

9. Not reading the syllabus. Professors emphasized the annoyance of being asked a question about office hours or number of tests when that information was available in their syllabi.

10. Not reading the textbook. One professor shared that not only were his students not reading the textbook, but also they were not even bothering to purchase the textbook.

The trainer may include other maladaptive behaviors not listed here, such as eating in class. "When did it become acceptable for students to eat and drink in class as if they were sitting in a cafeteria?" lamented one professor (Benton, 2006, para. 9). The trainer will also want to include sleeping in class; a student with the audacity to put head to desk and sleep during lecture is implying that the course is worthless.

One way to generate desirable behavior in class and to create the involvement to which Astin (1999) referred is for students to sit close to the front where these undesirable behaviors are less likely to happen and students are more likely to engage in the class. Of course, this suggestion is not an option if seating is assigned, and not all students can sit at the front. However, recommending the front seats to students will encourage some to arrive early and secure those seats at the front.

PRETEND PROFESSOR

Fearless inquiry is a hallmark of the motivated, engaged student (Schunk, Pintrich, & Meece, 2007), but most students need training in how to approach that inquiry in a professor's office. More students might utilize office hours if they had some understanding of how to behave when they get there.

For this training activity, new tutors and mentors pretend to be the professor so that they can develop some empathy for how a professor might interpret the student's actions. They will take turns playing the role of the professor by strapping on the daunting Halloween mask and sitting at a desk with a large stack of papers and a red pen, pretending to be grading. Veteran tutors and mentors take turns pretending to be the student initiating a conversation in the professor's office. They will demonstrate the following breeches in protocol: walking into the office when the professor is talking to someone else, walking into the office when the professor is on the phone, entering the office without knocking, addressing the professor as "Miss" or "Mr.," not shaking hands or giving a too-strong or too-soft handshake, not providing a first and last name, asking a professor how to do a problem and not showing any work of their own, and not making eye contact.

For each mistake in protocol, the trainer asks the participant to remove the mask and answer the question, "What just went wrong?" The trainer asks the trainee to elaborate on how these actions might be perceived by the professor and how they might hinder the productivity of the conversation between the two. With each new participant, the trainer begins the scene from the beginning, demonstrating the corrected behavior from previous scenes and then introducing a new error. The trainer concludes the role-play by showing how to make a strong exit with yet another thank you and handshake.

The objective is for the participants to realize that the relationship with a college professor demands more decorum and formality than the relationship with one's high school teacher. The student who knows how to behave properly in a professor's office will likely elicit the enthusiastic support of the professor. Moreover, the student will probably learn that professors often only *seem* scary and intimidating. Many will demonstrate a genuine warmth and concern for the student who is clearly taking appropriate actions related to the course.

Assessment

Following the workshop, tutors should be able to (a) recognize the student's need for developing a relationship with the professor as a critical resource, (b) identify the student behaviors most irksome to professors, and (c) suggest appropriate behaviors for class and office hours. The trainer assesses participants for these goals in the final segment of the workshop, entitled Rewind. The trainer asks participants to reflect on the value of making a good impression on the professor. The trainer then asks participants to recall some of those student behaviors that most bother professors. Finally, the trainer asks the participants to synthesize the advice given in the workshop. The trainer can gauge the level of the participants' understanding by following up their answers with these prompts: "Explain that to me. What are some examples of that? Tell me more." If trainees can explain the lesson to the trainer in their own words, then they are ready to explain the lesson to students in their tutoring sessions.

References

Astin, A. W. (1999). Student involvement: A developmental theory for higher education. *Journal of College Student Development, 40,* 518–529.

Benton, T. H. (2006, April 14). The 7 deadly sins of students. *Chronicle of Higher Education.* Retrieved from http://chronicle.com/article/The-7-Deadly-Sins-of-Students/46719

Dzubak, C. M. (2008, September 15). Classroom decorum: What has happened? *The Facilitating Newsletter,* pp. 1–2, 4. Retrieved from http://www.myatp.org/Newsletters/Sept_08_Web.pdf

McWilliams, M. (2010, April). *Kiss kiss: A call to learning centers to champion faculty-student interaction out of class.* Paper presented at the Bright Ideas Conference of Stephen F. Austin State University, Nacogdoches, TX.

Pierce, M. E. (2004). SI professor is first line of defense. *The Beacon: Notes from the AARC, 5*(1), 4.

Schunk, D. H., Pintrich, P. R., & Meece, J. L. (2007). *Motivation in education: Theory, research, and applications.* Upper Saddle River, NJ: Prentice Hall.

Ⓒ TUTORING SUBJECT AREAS

Tutoring and the Writing Process

 Timothy A. Hopp

Many a student rushes into the writing center to have an essay fixed. The student wants the paper to earn an A grade. An untrained tutor could simply focus on grammar or surface issues and work with the student to clean up the paper. Such a tutorial would ignore the primary goal of writing tutorials, which is to help students to become better writers (Brooks, 1995). Grammar rules and style directives may improve student writing, but becoming a better writer involves learning how to write productively.

Writing is a subject that is difficult to tutor because writing involves more than content. Grammar, rhetorical adaptation, sentence structure, and similar concerns are discrete features of language that can be discussed as content area knowledge. Manner of expression, the construction of arguments, and tone are less amenable to this kind of discussion; language usage is intimately tied up in the identity of the writer, and consequently a writing tutorial has personal and interpersonal dimensions that must be addressed.

The training module presented here is but one step in a larger staircase of teaching tutors how to tutor writing effectively. A key assumption is that a tutor's knowledge expands slowly, in a process of gaining experience and expertise. In a more complete training series, the first increment focuses on the nuts and bolts of tutoring a paper for grammar, which is often what tutors believe they can do best. As a first step, it is easier to scaffold the basic structure of a tutorial: welcoming clients; reading papers aloud; talking with writers about choices that they made; helping students to understand the grammatical principles at work; and asking clients to reflect on what they have learned. A second increment would focus on interpersonal elements of the writing tutorial: establishing a personal but professional relationship and understanding the affective factors at play in a tutorial. To accomplish these early steps, role-playing sessions are a primary method of training.

By the time tutors reach the training session that is described in this module, they have been exposed to these basic principles of a writing tutorial, especially how to tutor textual features and how to interact with clients. For example, by this stage of training a tutor should know how to teach a client to fix a run-on sentence error with sensitivity to a client's manner of expression and should have some skill in getting students to fix errors in textual features.

This module expands a tutor's expertise to addressing the underlying process difficulties that may be the root of the client's errors. Perhaps the reason for the run-on sentence in the paper is that the client does not understand what a complete sentence is or what the valid methods are for joining sentences. The tutorial then can focus on the rule that is directly applicable. Perhaps the client knows the rules of sentence construction but did not recognize the run-on sentence error within the context of the paper, which points to a proofreading problem. In this case, the tutor would instead work through different methods of proofreading a paper, such as reading paragraphs aloud or reading the paper in reverse order, sentence by sentence. This sort of tutorial is more likely to lead to an improvement of a client's writing approach (process) and not just to the improvement of a client's paper (product).

Distinctions between process and product are commonly made in writing tutoring, which is a subfield of composition studies called *writing center theory*. Within this specialty, there are a number of rich sources for training tutors and operating writing tutorials. Gillespie and Lerner (2008) and Ryan (2001) are excellent sources of information about tutoring writing. Harris (1986) and Meyer and Smith (1987) provided many nuts-and-bolts ideas about writing tutorials still relevant today. In addition, the W-Center listserv permits fruitful connections to other writing center professionals, the International Writing Centers Association website (writingcenters.org) has many strong tutorial ideas, and *The Writing Lab Newsletter* is an excellent source of articles by tutors about daily concerns. Concerns are ongoing because writing theory and the practicalities of tutoring writing sometimes conflict.

In an ideal world, tutors would role play every possible problem that a writer might face and develop strategies to help each writer to overcome every problem. In such a world, reviewing papers and discussing strategies for how tutors could have responded to writers would work well; however, there is never enough time to train tutors, and sometimes it is necessary for tutors to learn and then apply conceptual knowledge. For this reason, sample papers are not used in this training activity.

Instead the main focus of this module uses group discussion and reflection. Tutors do not need to know the answer to every question (Reigstad & McAndrew, 1984), but they should use a knowledge base derived in part from asking questions of other tutors. This approach directly connects to the social construction theory of composition, that a community creates knowledge by interaction and agreement (Haynes, 1996). This activity therefore emphasizes collaborative problem solving.

Training Activity

The following activity can be presented within 2 hours and requires minimal resources, such as a handout or PowerPoint® slides. The activity can also be presented with minimal preparation time. After completing this training, tutors will be able to negotiate a fundamental conflict between process and product inherent in writing tutorials and employ one model of the writing process to help a client to become a better writer.

DETERMINING PRIOR KNOWLEDGE

The trainer should ask tutors to describe in a 5-minute quick-write exercise a recent tutorial or role-played tutorial. Tutors should then work in small groups to answer the question, "If you were the client of the tutorial, how would you benefit from the tutorial?" Key concepts from small-group discussion should be shared with the larger group. About 30 minutes may be required for this part of the session.

INTRODUCING NEW KNOWLEDGE

The trainer should briefly present one model of the writing process (see Figure 1) with an emphasis on the recursive nature of writing. In composition studies, as well as writing center studies, there are competing theories about what process writers use to complete writing tasks. For examples of competing theories, see Ryan (2001), Ramage, Bean, and Johnson (2009), and Ede (2001). For purposes of this training session, tutors should think of *process* as a broad classification of the kinds of thinking required at different stages during the creation of a text, such as invention, planning, drafting, and revising. *Invention* activities generally focus on methods of coming up with ideas or being creative (Elbow, 1973; Murray, 1991); some common techniques include freewriting, clustering or webbing, and listing. *Planning* activities generally focus on organization and may include techniques such as outlining. *Drafting* activities typically focus on taking ideas and organizational patterns to generate text; one technique is to work in chunks or modules of a text. *Revising* involves bringing critical faculties to a text in an effort to make the text more effective and correct (Elbow, 1973).

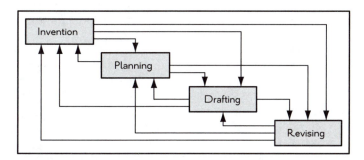

FIGURE 1 Simple model of the writing process.

The most important aspect of process that should be emphasized in this training activity is that the process is recursive. Strong writers jump back and forth among the stages quickly, the stages are not necessarily all present, and they do not always occur in the same order.

SYNTHESIZING NEW KNOWLEDGE

The trainer should ask tutors to work in small groups to brainstorm ideas about how knowledge of the writing process could be used in a tutoring session. Each group should present to all of the tutors the ideas that they devised. The trainer should add to the discussion specific methods of intervening in process, such as freewriting, clustering, outlining, modular drafting, rhetorical analysis, and error journaling. The trainer should also prod tutors to discuss what kinds of learning such techniques foster in clients.

The trainer should then instruct tutors to write a brief (one-paragraph) reflection on the following topic: "How does getting involved in a writer's process move a tutorial away from what most students expect in a writing tutorial?" This section of the training session requires about 1 hour.

Assessment

One of the overall objectives of this module is that tutors be able to negotiate a fundamental conflict between process and product inherent in writing tutorials. By asking tutors to write a reflection after discussion of the recursive nature of writing process, the trainer can quickly gauge whether the tutor has a basic vocabulary for talking about process and whether the tutor understands that improving a paper unfortunately does not necessarily involve improving a client's ability to write. A more important assessment involves later observing tutors to see if they interact only with surface features of a text or attempt to determine the causes of surface errors.

Another objective in this training module is that tutors be able to employ one model of the writing process to help a client to be a better writer. The small-group discussions and presentations can indicate to trainers how well tutors are able to apply the model to situations generally. However, as with the first objective, a more important assessment derives from observing tutors at work to see what techniques they suggest to clients and later asking why they suggested those techniques.

References

Brooks, J. (1995). Minimalist tutoring: Making the student do all the work. In C. Murphy & S. Sherwood (Eds.), *The St. Martin's sourcebook for writing tutors* (pp. 83–87). New York, NY: St. Martin's Press.

Ede, L. (2001). *Work in progress* (5th ed.). New York, NY: Bedford/St. Martin's.

Elbow, P. (1973). Appendix essay. The doubting game and believing game: An analysis of the intellectual enterprise. In P. Elbow, *Writing without teachers* (pp. 147–191). New York, NY: Oxford University Press.

Gillespie, P., & Lerner, N. (2008). *Longman guide to peer tutoring*. Boston, MA: Longman.

Harris, M. (1986). *Teaching one-to-one: The writing conference*. Urbana, IL: National Council of Teachers of English.

Haynes, C. (1996). Social construction. In P. Heiker & P. Vandenberg (Eds.), *Keywords in composition studies* (pp. 221–224). Portsmouth, NH: Boynton/Cook.

Meyer, E., & Smith, L. (1987). *The practical tutor*. New York, NY: Oxford University Press.

Murray, D. (1991). *The craft of revision* (2nd ed.). Fort Worth, TX: Harcourt Brace.

Ramage, J. D., Bean, J. C., & Johnson, J. (2009). *The Allyn & Bacon guide to writing* (5th ed.). New York, NY: Pearson/Longman.

Reigstad, T. J., & McAndrew, D. A. (1984). *Training tutors for writing conferences*. Urbana, IL: ERIC/NCTE. Retrieved from http://www.eric.ed.gov/PDFS/ED240589.pdf

Ryan, L. (2001). *The Bedford guide for writing tutors* (3rd ed.). New York, NY: Bedford/St. Martin's.

Tutoring Writing With Formulas

Suzanne Ponicsan

Writing can be a very challenging subject for tutors because of the many situations they may encounter: the last-minute student, the error-filled paper, the student who can think of nothing to write about, and the student who is an English language learner (ELL). For some of these situations, untrained tutors may not even know where to begin.

The writing process requires a great deal of critical thinking. Writers must choose a thesis, consider the audience, determine how to research information needed, and organize the manuscript. Luckily formulas are available as guidelines to follow. This training module will discuss formula writing as a method to help tutees become more effective writers and demonstrate one way to train tutors to provide appropriate formulas.

Birkenstein and Graff (2008) discussed the assumption of many academics that following a formula for writing is a poor approach: "To say that a mode of writing instruction is formulaic is to charge it with having a 'cookie cutter' quality: the student writer presumably inserts raw material into a mold, and the product automatically comes out, no thought required" (p. 18). Birkenstein and Graff contended that using a formula is no more restrictive than requiring the standard five-paragraph essay (p. 18); in fact, they argued, such eminent composition theorists as David Bartholomae proposed "machine" writing and Irene Clark framed open-ended statements, in both cases to prompt student writers to think more critically. Birkenstein and Graff expanded these earlier formulaic approaches into "they say/I say" argumentation, providing examples like these:

- "Although it is often said that _____, I claim _____."

- "I agree with X that _____, and would add that _____."

- "At this point you will probably object that _____. While it's true that _____, I still maintain _____." (2008, p. 20)

Tutors can be trained to utilize such formulas in their sessions by writing a few fill-in-the-blank questions in the session or having standard questions available (printed or electronic) for students to complete. Completed sentences plot a direction for both the tutoring session and the student's paper.

Another formula tutors can be taught to use with students is the court-case analogy. Broskoske (2007) found that when students have to "prove their case" they are better able to understand the importance of rhetorical conventions. Just as lawyers frame their case, search out evidence, present evidence, and make closing arguments, so students writing papers must define their topic, search for sources, craft the paper, and draw conclusions.

Training Activity

In this training activity, tutors first review the writing process based on the rhetorical triangle (Ramage & Bean, 2000), then learn creative methods to help tutees analyze and understand the process. Finally, tutors participate in a role-playing activity in which they create their own tutoring sessions based on a given topic.

The trainer should prepare handouts with a sample tutor session outline (see the Appendix) and a blank rhetorical triangle. Trainees should know that the rhetorical triangle is used to show how all parts of the writing process connect. The center of the triangle represents the purpose of the writing, while each angle represents the other parts of the writing situation: the writer (top point), subject (bottom left) and the audience or reader (bottom right) (Ramage & Bean, 2000). Copies of mock essays should also be prepared. A PowerPoint® presentation should be created to present key ideas of Broskoske (2007) and of Birkenstein and Graff (2008). An AV screen and computer are necessary to view a PowerPoint® presentation, and a video recorder will be necessary if role-playing sessions are to be recorded. The training activity should be held in a classroom or meeting room large enough to accommodate all tutoring staff. At least one table for role playing should also be available. The training session will require 70–80 minutes.

The trainer should begin the training session by reviewing general writing concepts. Tutors can be given the rhetorical triangle handout and asked to complete it on their own, based on their current knowledge. After reviewing the components, the trainer asks tutors questions about the model, such as which component should be identified first and why, and what purposes the triangle serves. Tutors should then review the sample outline, which can be used as a guide during tutoring sessions. Tutors should be asked about the benefits of using such an outline with their tutees. Responses may include that the outline can serve as a directional tool for new tutors, a resource for tutees, and so forth. Time required is about 15–20 minutes.

Using a PowerPoint® presentation, the trainer then introduces tutors to key ideas of Broskoske (2007) and Birkenstein and Graff (2008) and discusses the step-by-step approach of both formulas: "they say/I say" statements and court case analogies. For each approach, the trainer discusses with tutors the tutoring situations in which it could be most useful and how it may be modified to fit the limited time of a tutoring session. Time required is approximately 25–30 minutes.

Finally, tutors select partners and randomly choose a situation from a bag. Tutoring situations may include the "last-minute" student, ELL student, perfectionist student, and others typical to the learning center's clientele. The pair must then use a mock essay and sample outline and role play their session. After each pair's presentation, the whole group should discuss the approach that was used, its effectiveness, and how the session could have been improved to maximize student learning. Time required is about 30 minutes.

Assessment

Assessment for this session is embedded in the training activity. One measure of individual tutors' understanding of previous training is their facility with the general writing principles under discussion and with the structure and use of the rhetorical triangle. Then, during training in the creative approaches of Broskoske (2007) and of Birkenstein and Graff (2008), the trainer can question tutors to gauge their comprehension of these concepts. The role-play activity constitutes further assessment, a demonstration of tutors' understanding. Finally, as tutors begin to work with students, their sessions can be evaluated for use of helpful writing formulas where appropriate.

References

Birkenstein, C., & Graff, G. (2008). Point of view: In teaching composition, "formulaic" is not a four-letter word. *The Chronicle of Higher Education, 54*(30), A40. Retrieved from http://chronicle.com/article/In-Teaching-Composition/33739

Broskoske, S. L. (2007). Prove your case: A new approach to teaching research papers. *College Teaching, 55*, 31–33. doi:10.3200/CTCH.55.1.31-32

Ramage, J. D., & Bean, J. C. (2000). *The Allyn & Bacon guide to writing* (2nd ed.). Needham Heights, MA: Pearson Education.

Appendix

SAMPLE OUTLINE FOR TUTORS OR TUTEES

1) The Basics

   a) The assignment parameters are _____

       _____

   b) The topic for this paper is _____

       _____

2) The Content

   a) Introduction

      i) The introduction technique being used is (check one)

         ❏ Asking a question

         ❏ Providing statistics

         ❏ Telling a story

         ❏ Other: _____

      ii) The thesis statement (or purpose of the paper) is _____

        _____

      iii) The bridge is _____

        _____

     *The bridge connects the introduction technique to the thesis statement.

   b) Body

      i) Body Paragraph 1

       The first important point is _____

        (a) My first support for this point is _____

        (b) My second support for this point is _____

        (c) My third support for this point is _____

      ii) Body Paragraph 2

       The second important point is _____

        (a) My first support for this point is _____

        (b) My second support for this point is _____

        (c) My third support for this point is _____

      iii) Body Paragraph 3

       The third important point is _____

        (a) My first support for this point is _____

        (b) My second support for this point is _____

        (c) My third support for this point is _____

   c) Conclusion

     The conclusion technique being used is (check two)

       ❏ Summarizing the research and findings

       ❏ Suggesting a course of action

       ❏ Looking to the future

Read Aloud Without Looking: A Strategy for Tutoring English Language Learners

Peggy J. Fish-Oliver

Writing tutors know that a major learning objective is to help students become independent, skilled writers with tools they can use to create their own effective writing. Ultimately, tutors are to work themselves out of a job, so to speak. Tutoring students whose first language is not English is particularly challenging for many writing teachers and tutors. Tutors need to be supportive and encouraging, yet students need to learn how to find and revise their own sentence structure errors such as missing articles, subject-verb disagreement, incorrect prepositions, and mixed constructions, which are some of the most common writing problems of English Language Learners (ELLs).

Non-native speakers of English can read a sentence repeatedly without spotting any problems, even if the tutor reads the sentence aloud as they are both looking at it. However, in my experience, if ELL writers do not look at but only hear a problematic sentence read aloud, they often quickly hear that something does not sound right and usually can revise to correct the problem independently. A tutor may need to lead students to the needed corrections or revisions by means of carefully chosen questions. The point is to let students work to find their own changes. This approach moves students closer and closer to independent revision and correction of sentence errors, the goal of tutoring being to lead students to independent success.

This approach may be successful because tutees who are not native speakers of English generally have stronger speaking, listening, and reading skills than writing skills. Thus, if these ELL writers can hear what they have written, they can draw on their stronger speaking and listening English language skills to improve their writing skills, as demonstrated in the training activity.

Training Activity

There are five objectives for this training module. Tutors should (a) recognize the types of errors ELL writers typically make; (b) learn both the language and cultural barriers ELL writers experience; (c) understand that repeated struggling with writing problems becomes discouraging and even embarrassing for ELL students; (d) recognize that a tutor's confidence in a student's ability to fix problems builds the student's confidence and independence; and (e) learn to use the "read aloud without looking at the writing" strategy to enable students to hear, find, and correct their own errors.

A standard classroom or meeting room with movable chairs and DVD player is suitable for this training activity. Handouts are described; they should be prepared in advance, or online resources may be referenced and utilized instead. Also prepared in advance should be a video with actual tutors and students in a writing center or scripted role players enacting the process.

The time needed for this training is 1-2 hours depending on whether tutors read referenced material (Friedlander, 1984; Gocsik, 2004a, 2004b; Leibowitz, Goodman, Hannon, & Parkerson, 1997; Rodriguez, 2009) as part of the session or independently or with guiding questions before the session as pre-homework.

RECOGNIZING TYPICAL ERRORS OF ENGLISH USAGE

To help ELL students effectively, tutors must be aware of the errors they are most likely to make. Gocsik (2004a) listed 10 of the most common problem areas: using articles; choosing prepositions; using infinitives; confusing parts of speech; achieving agreement between subject and verb, noun and pronoun; choosing proper tenses; avoiding passive voice; learning sentence structure and sentence boundaries; using correct punctuation; and using appropriate idioms. Idiomatic style is a particular concern because instructors and tutors are tempted to exclaim, "We don't say it like that!" instead of explaining grammatical rules (Gocsik, 2004a, para. 14). Mastering this impulse constitutes a major challenge in working with ELL writers.

At the same time, writing centers must welcome these writers and help them be comfortable working with tutors to develop their independent English writing skills. Tutors must empower them to conquer challenges and to begin to write effectively in English. This may be a long, gradual process that involves teaching students the cultural aspects of English writing expectations in academic writing.

The trainer should present these ideas for discussion and provide a handout showing common errors made by ELL students. If possible, the list should be illustrated with actual examples from previous tutoring situations.

LEARN TYPICAL LANGUAGE AND CULTURAL BARRIERS

Tutors must also learn some of the unique needs of ELL student writers and be prepared to work effectively with them. Friedlander (1984) maintained that international students "should not be treated differently from American students" (p. 208); instead, they should be made welcome and comfortable by any tutor available. Yet, depending on their cultural backgrounds, each ELL student brings unique needs and language and composition problems, which must be understood in terms of that student's cultural and native language experiences. According to Friedlander (1984), tutors need awareness of the most common errors such as those listed by Gocsik (2004a), but "must be aware . . . that these errors are indicative of interference from the student's native language. Without training, tutors will find themselves frustrated when dealing with foreign students" (p. 209). Leibowitz et al. (1997) also provided examples of how complex the multilingual context can be. Tutors unintentionally confused ELL students by using words that are easily confused with other words.

Leibowitz et al. (1997) urged that tutors be aware of cultural customs that may interfere with tutoring sessions. Students from various cultures may not speak much or may not make eye contact with tutors, perhaps because they have learned to defer to and give greater respect to a tutor, who is perceived as having higher status or power. Some students may even expect the higher-status tutor to do most of the speaking; in fact, if tutors do not speak more than the tutee, they may be viewed as indifferent and uncaring (Leibowitz et al., 1997). Lack of clear communication about mutual expectations obviously limits conversation, which is the very heart of a tutoring session. These issues of different communication expectations must be taught to tutors so they will be able to make ELL writers as comfortable as possible in the tutoring consultation.

After presenting these ideas to trainees, trainers should invite them to talk about their own experiences learning another language or traveling in locations where English is not the native language. What kinds of English linguistic conventions and American cultural habits reduced their ability to learn the new language and its culture?

AVOIDING EMBARRASSMENT

Having developed such awareness of ELL students' needs that transcend the use of the English language itself, tutors need to understand the discouraging and embarrassing experience of repeatedly making errors and struggling to correct them in an environment that may still feel extremely unfamiliar for a non-native English speaker in college. Although educators generally agree that making mistakes is an important way for students to learn, after too many mistakes and failures, individuals grow discouraged and embarrassed and may begin to give up. Tutors need to be trained to recognize such signs of defeat and to redirect students to find small successes that rebuild confidence. This involves sensitivity to what tutees say and do not say and efforts to focus on strengths their writing does have. Gocsik (2004b) commented that tutors must "remember, first and foremost, not to take anything for granted" (para.1).

The trainer may want to demonstrate briefly some approaches that exacerbate ELL students' embarrassment and others that soothe their discomfiture. Alternatively, the trainer may create some scenarios and invite trainees to play the roles of tutor and ELL tutee to demonstrate these approaches.

DEMONSTRATING CONFIDENCE IN ELL STUDENTS' LEARNING

Tutors may decide to explain to students in tutoring sessions how academic discourse works in the U.S. and Canada compared to the writer's first culture and should be open to learning about the student's academic writing culture. Exploring the differences together, learning from the student writer to expand awareness in future tutoring sessions, can over a period of time help strengthen ELL students' confidence, which in turn builds stronger writing skills. Research has shown that "instructors should design learning experiences and pedagogy that develop and nurture academic self-concept early [in their courses]" (Rodriguez, 2009, p. 534). The same principle applies, even more emphatically, in the relationship between tutor and tutee because a one-on-one learning relationship allows tutors more opportunity to convey directly to an individual student writer both existing strengths and the tutor's confidence that the student can and will continue to learn and develop independent success in college. Thus, a tutor's confidence in a student's ability to begin fixing his or her own problems gradually builds a student's confidence and independence, leading to better and better English writing skills. The more ELL students can find and correct their own mistakes, the more confidence and skills they develop.

If tutors have been assigned to read Rodriguez' (2009) article before attending the session, the trainer can lead a discussion of Rodriguez's conclusions about the relationship between tutoring and confidence. Alternatively, tutors may be invited to share their own academic experiences in which instructors or tutors built or damaged students' confidence.

LEARNING THE LISTENING-WITHOUT-LOOKING STRATEGY

Two videotaped or role-played situations are needed for this activity. The situation in the video or role-playing exercises may be set up as a session that helped a tutee revise for what Purdue OWL (2010) tutors call higher-order concerns (thesis, audience, organization, and development) or as a tutoring session in which the tutee specifically seeks help only with sentence quality and correct English usage. The student in each scenario should have drafted some writing to work on with the tutor, or the trainer can use sample writing pulled from a file, with the ELL student's name occluded. The tutor in each scenario should have the student listen as the tutor reads each sentence. The student should not look at the writing as it is read but should indicate to the tutor whenever reading should stop because the student hears a problem with the text as written. The tutor should use guiding questions to help the student independently figure out how to revise and correct problems.

After watching these two videotaped or role-played situations, tutors and mentors in training should discuss why they think this method works, using what they know about language, culture, and confidence. Trainees may also discuss the types of errors that are most likely to be addressed by this approach. Trainees should then practice this strategy in dyads, making sure each trainee has the chance to play both tutee and tutor roles.

Assessment

Assessment is based on the objectives for the training activity. By quiz or discussion, trainees may be asked to demonstrate that they recognize the types of errors ELL writers typically make, know some of the language and cultural barriers ELL writers experience, understand the discouragement of ELL students who struggle with writing problems, understand that a tutor's confidence in a student's ability to fix problems builds the student's confidence and independence, and know how to use the "read aloud without looking at the writing" strategy to enable students to hear, find, and correct their own errors.

Assessment is also built into the final activity, the role play utilizing the new strategy. A follow-up training session may be held a few weeks later, after tutors have had opportunities to implement the strategy. They may reflect together on how the strategy worked or did not work for them. Does it work with some students but not with others? This could lead to inquiry into how tutors are using the strategy. Are they showing sufficient confidence in the student's ability to hear the errors? Are they using guiding questions to help the student independently figure out how to revise and correct problems or just quickly providing the solution, which does not build student confidence and independence? How could the strategy be improved? A benefit of discussions about this strategy is that they may lead to valuable tutor inquiry into why a strategy that works for one tutor may not work for other tutors and why the same strategy may produce varying results with different ELL writers.

References

Friedlander, A. (1984). Meeting the needs of foreign students. In G. Olson (Ed.), *Writing centers: Theory and administration* (pp. 206–214). Urbana, IL: National Council of Teachers of English.

Gocsik, C. (2004a). Common ESL errors: The top ten list. *English as a second language*. Retrieved from http://www.dartmouth.edu/~writing/materials/tutor/problems/esl.shtml

Gocsik, C. (2004b). Cultural difference and its impact on rhetoric: An overview. *English as a second language*. Retrieved from http://www.dartmouth.edu/~writing/materials/tutor/problems/esl.shtml#overview

Leibowitz, B., Goodman, K., Hannon, P., & Parkerson, A. (1997). The role of a writing centre in increasing access to academic discourse in a multilingual university. *Teaching in Higher Education, 2*(1), 5–19. doi:10.1080/1356251970020101

Purdue OWL. (2010). *Higher order concerns (HOCs) and lower order concerns (LOCs)*. Retrieved from http://owl.english.purdue.edu/owl/resource/690/01/

Rodriguez, C. M. (2009). The impact of academic self-concept, expectations and the choice of learning strategy on academic achievement: The case of business students. *Higher Education Research & Development, 28*, 523–539. doi:10.1080/07294360903146841S

Tutoring Literature: Negotiating a Literature-Response Discourse

Elizabeth J. Threadgill

Discourse mismatch occurs when students' ways of interacting with and responding to texts, classmates, instructors, and the institution conflict with the Discourse of any one text, classmate, instructor, or institutional unit. Gee (2001) described Discourse as integrating "ways of talking, listening, writing, reading, acting, interacting, believing, valuing, and feeling (and using various objects, symbols, images, tools, and technologies) in the service of enacting meaningful socially situated identities and activities" (p. 719). Pransky and Bailey (2002/2003) drew a connection between Gee's Discourse and ideas about culture mismatch. Because cultural values are imbedded in Discourse and affect the way a student interacts with and responds to classroom participants and material, if the home culture—especially the perception of educational achievement and literacy—is significantly different from the school culture, students are at a disadvantage concerning learning expectations (Pransky & Bailey, 2002/2003).

The concerns that students bring to the learning center related to assigned readings in literature (poetry, drama, essays, and prose fiction and nonfiction) may derive from Discourse mismatch. The student's primary Discourse may conflict with literary Discourse in general or with genre-specific Discourses. The Discourses in these specific postsecondary academic studies are complex and can be frustrating to students who are acclimating to the many layers of these Discourses—learning and using language specific to literary studies; acknowledging a different system of values; and learning new processes of reading, listening, and responding. Students studying poetry, for instance, need to be attuned to distinct ways of listening to poetry, particularly hearing line breaks, as well as reading elements on the page that are normally ignored in print texts, such as white space.

At the postsecondary level, instructors often expect students to play various responding roles simultaneously and to value a literary work as serving multiple purposes as art and personal expression but also as an academic text. The New London Group (1996) argued, "To be relevant, learning processes need to recruit, rather than attempt to ignore and erase, the different *subjectivities*—interests, intentions, commitments, and purposes—students bring to learning," and thus "curriculum now needs to mesh with different subjectivities, and with their attendant languages, discourses, and registers, and use these as a resource for learning" (p. 72). Similarly, Pawan and Honeyford (2009) urged instructors to recognize that multiple literacies affect classroom participation and the Discourse of that classroom community.

In response to this need, a more diverse, multimodal, media-literate, and globally connected group of instructors is now immersed in an array of different subjectivities and Discourses. In particular, instructors are becoming more cognizant of the relationship between cultural studies and education (Soetaert, Mottart, & Verdood, 2004). But with the inclusion of these diverse subjectivities and literacies in the classroom comes a necessity that students be able to code-switch among multiple Discourses in class.

The role of the tutor, then, is to orient students in that secondary Discourse specific to their literary studies, encouraging them to practice listening, reading, and responding as influenced by both their primary Discourse and the Discourse within their literature response community. Tutors can do so by negotiating a vocabulary with students that can be used to discuss their responses to literature; additionally, tutors can guide students through close reading processes that require responses in multiple Discourses. This work is similar to what the New London Group (1996) outlined as a flexible metalanguage negotiated by the student and the instructor (or the tutor, in this instance) in order to discuss relationships between texts of various sorts (written, verbal, and visual) and relationships to the students' contexts and cultures.

It is important for tutors to help students acclimate to the classroom and institutional Discourses so that students will feel safer in their learning environment, and so that they may begin to harmonize the Discourses, to build on prior knowledge, and to make stronger connections in their learning. Ideally, trained tutors and their student clients will practice a step-by-step process of careful reading to respond to literature while interacting with the text in their own ways and considering their own value systems alongside those of the academy.

Training Activity

At least 1 hour should be provided for each literary genre in which training is provided. Close-reading training activities can be offered in several different genres every semester.

The materials needed for this training activity are copies of literary excerpts from the genre on which the session will focus. If possible, all participants should have access to a computer from which they can make multimodal responses to the literary works on their screens. Additionally, trainees should have access to copies of any handouts from which the trainer wants to begin. These handouts should be living texts; printed handouts should provide space for participants to make revisions, or on-screen documents (perhaps electronically shared documents) may be offered in a format that allows revision. Revision tools (pens, pencils, paint, computer keyboards, whiteboards) are also necessary.

The trainer begins by introducing a base vocabulary necessary to speak about the responses that tutors and students may have to a literary work. It is useful to point out the language overlap among the different genres. This portion of the training activity should be a discussion to which attention returns throughout the training session.

The trainer should then provide a step-by-step example of the close-reading process for works of a chosen genre such as poetry, fiction, nonfiction, drama, blogging, or screenwriting. After presenting the genre guide to model the tutoring process with a literary text, the trainer should choose a tutor or ask for a volunteer tutor to guide the other trainees (who play the role of students) in practicing this process with a second work of literature. The tutor should be offered a choice from several texts available electronically or on handouts for this purpose. All the trainees should listen carefully to their own and each other's Discourses throughout the practice exercise.

Finally, both experienced and new tutors should negotiate new terms for listening, reading, and responding to literary works. If possible, they should achieve consensus regarding what language is most applicable for responding to these works.

Both the glossary and close reading guide should be negotiated by the immediate community of readers at the institution—literature, composition, and cultural studies instructors and department heads; experienced tutors; students; and learning center staff. A glossary of literary-specific vocabulary can be found in the *Bedford Glossary of Critical and Literary Terms* (Murfin & Ray, 2009), but the institution's own glossary (whether in print, spoken, or multimodal) should consider various applications and nuances that are a part of that institution's literary Discourse community.

After practicing the negotiation of and use of literary genre-specific language and a close-reading process that encourages code switching among multiple Discourses, tutors should be reminded to enact these negotiations with students so that students can create their own living close-reading processes and glossaries.

A 10-step guide for a close reading of poetry is provided in the appendix to this training module to provide students with a way to think about an assigned piece of writing as both an academic text that uses elements of craft to invite a main idea or tone and as a work of art to which students should feel comfortable responding more individually and personally.

Assessment

After participating in this training session, tutors should be able to negotiate meaning for discipline-specific literary language and vocabulary and to use a foundational close-reading sequence to be adjusted in tutoring sessions for individual students. Tutors should also be able to recognize the importance of giving students the tools to explain their responses to literary works so that students may become independent learners who are confident in their ability to participate in an academic Discourse and who understand that their own Discourses are valued in the postsecondary setting.

The tutor trainer should primarily use observation during the close-reading practice to assess tutors' understanding of the process and their ability to guide students in negotiating language and processes to respond to literature. Additionally, the trainer should provide access to a living handout online (e.g., by staff blog or document sharing) so that tutors can continue to revise this resource for both tutors and students. The tutor trainer can approve revisions and assess tutors' understanding over the academic term. Finally, depending on time available for training, the tutor trainer can assess these learning outcomes in additional role plays.

References

Gee, J. P. (2001). Reading as situated language: A sociocognitive perspective. *Journal of Adolescent & Adult Literacy, 44,* 714–725. doi:10.1598/JAAL.44.8.3

Murfin, R., & Ray, S. M. (Eds.). (2009). *The Bedford glossary of critical and literary terms* (3rd ed.). Boston, MA: Bedford/St. Martin's.

New London Group. (1996). A pedagogy of multiliteracies: Designing social futures. *Harvard Educational Review, 66*(1), 60–92.

Pawan, F., & Honeyford, M. A. (2009). Academic literacy. In R. F. Flippo & D. C. Caverly (Eds.), *Handbook of college reading and study strategy research* (2nd ed., pp. 26–46). New York, NY: Routledge.

Pransky, K., & Bailey, F. (2002/2003). To meet your students where they are, first you have to find them: Working with culturally and linguistically diverse at-risk students. *The Reading Teacher, 56,* 370–383. doi:10.1598/RT.56.4.3

Soetaert, R., Mottart, A., & Verdood, I. (2004). Culture and pedagogy in teacher education. *The Review of Education, Pedagogy, & Cultural Studies, 26,* 155–174. doi:10.1080/10714410490480421

Appendix

SAMPLE CLOSE-READING GUIDE FOR POETRY

1. Note the title.

2. Read the poem aloud, pausing at punctuation marks and at the ends of the lines. (Consider when you might change the inflection in your voice if you were reading a piece of prose or speaking to another person as opposed to when your inflection seems to change naturally while reading the poem.) You should let the poem wash over you as a whole during this first reading.

3. Then make a written note of the response you feel in your gut after reading the poem for the first time. Also note the main idea(s) or theme(s) and the general feeling of the poem (the tone).

4. Read the poem again, either aloud or silently.

5. During this second reading, make a written note of any elements of sound that stand out (e.g., alliteration, musical qualities, or discordant harshness).

6. Underline or highlight anything else that stands out, such as images or diction.

7. Finally, during this second reading, look for and note anything that is repeated or out of the ordinary.

8. Afterward make a note of the point of view. Look for and note poetic devices (analogies, metaphors, similes, personification, and symbols). Pay close attention to the words at the beginnings and ends of lines, because their location may be an attempt to draw attention to them. Note any meanings that line breaks may create through separating words and ideas.

9. Read the poem a third time to scan the poem for rhythm and rhyme.

10. At the end of this process, think about the connections between the details and your initial responses.

Tutoring Foreign Languages

Carmen Christopher Caviness

General best practices for tutoring work as well for foreign language learners as they do for tutees in other subject areas. Focusing on task-based learning (Hsiao & Oxford, 2002; Long & Crookes, 1992; Pica, 2005), working collaboratively and in groups (Antón, 1999; Jacob, Rottenberg, Patrick & Wheeler, 1996; Kramsch, 1987; Long & Porter, 1985), and scaffolding tasks (de Guerrero & Villamil, 2000; Donato, 1994; Palincsar, 1986) are a few important examples.

Though tutors may already have strong repertoires, there are several unique strategies that tutors can employ for foreign language learners. Kinesthetic learning (sometimes called "tactile" learning) is a useful strategy in the foreign language classroom (Bates & Dick, 2002; Gullberg, 2008; Gullberg, de Bott, & Volterra, 2008; Gullberg & McCafferty, 2008; Tellier, 2008; Tomlinson & Masuhara, 2009; van Lier, 2007). Researchers have discovered that gestures (a specific form of kinesthetic learning) have a deeper impact on second language learning than vocalics or visual stimuli (Tellier, 2008) and that "gestures are implicated in learning language specifically, not only learning in general" (Gullberg et al., 2008, p. 168).

Kinesthetic learning is learning that "involves both information perception (touching, tasting, smelling) and information processing (moving, relating, doing something active while learning)" (Felder & Silverman, 1988, p. 5). Though kinesthetic learning has been found to be beneficial for second-language learners, it may be underutilized in tutorial sessions. The following activity, designed for a small tutor training class or workshop, can help tutors identify particular strategies for addressing kinesthetic learning and practice engaging students' bodies in language learning. As a result of this module, tutors should understand the importance of kinesthetic learning for students of foreign languages, learn several kinesthetic learning strategies, and utilize kinesthetic learning strategies.

Training Activity

Seating in the classroom should be arranged with two chairs at the front (the tutoring station) and the remaining chairs in a semi-circle around the tutoring station. This activity requires about 1 hour as described but could easily be adapted to a longer training session.

PREPARATION FOR THE TRAINING SESSION

The trainer should find an article about foreign language learning and assign it for trainees to read before the training session. Articles by Oxford and Nyikos (1989) and Oxford (1994) are good choices, as both are meta-analyses of research, are reasonably accessible to new readers of such literature, and provide useful strategies for a variety of learning styles.

The trainer should also find several words in languages not taught at the institution. A quick Web search can provide vocabulary and its pronunciation for languages as diverse as Albanian, Dutch, Portuguese, and Welsh. In step A of the activity, trainees need to learn only two or three words; however, the trainer may choose to select some additional words for step E.

TRAINING SESSION

This activity requires minimal preparation. The foreign language words chosen for the activity may be written on a board, displayed on a screen, or provided on vocabulary cards.

Step A

As the session begins, the trainer teaches the tutors-in-training two or three new words in a foreign language, having the tutors kinesthetically engaged with the words and phrases by gesturing, repeating, and writing them. (As an example, two fingers in the air might represent a bunny, while waving arms might represent a river.) Though tutors may complain that they feel silly, they should be assured that movements associated with the words will help them remember the words later in the activity.

Step B

The trainees should be led in a discussion of theories of language acquisition. The article the trainees read for homework provides a good introduction to the discussion.

Step C

Trainees should then be invited to share how active learning plays a role in their own language acquisition.

Step D

The trainer should ask tutors to generate ideas to engage students in active learning; their ideas may begin with some of the suggestions from the article they read for homework. This brainstorming session could be recorded on chalkboard, dry-erase board, or flip chart.

Step E

Tutors will then role play some of the active listening strategies. An interesting way to dramatize this session is to put different words from different languages into a hat—potentially using extra words already prepared on cards. The tutor of the mock session draws a word from the hat and uses the new tutoring strategies to teach the new word to the tutee.

Step F

The trainer asks tutors to recall the words and phrases they learned at the beginning of the session. Then tutors reflect on which ways they learn best, highlighting differences in learning styles. They may find that some kinesthetic strategies work better with some students than others. This only highlights the necessity for having a strong repertoire of tutoring strategies for different types of learners.

Assessment

To demonstrate the achievement of the module objectives during this training activity, tutors should be asked to recall at least one new foreign language word or phrase, practice several kinesthetic learning strategies, and participate in mock tutoring situations in which they use kinesthetic learning strategies.

After the training session or during the last few minutes of the session, trainees can also be asked to write in an informal journal or weblog. In their entries, trainees should reflect upon the role that active learning plays in their own learning and what strategies seemed to work best for this group of trainees. The journal entry should also include any questions the tutors may have that were not covered during training. These questions may be addressed in the subsequent training session or on the staff weblog.

References

Antón, M. (1999). The discourse of a learner-centered classroom: Sociocultural perspectives on teacher-learner interaction in the second-language classroom. *The Modern Language Journal, 83*, 303–318. doi:10.1111/0026-7902.00024

Bates, E., & Dick, F. (2002). Language, gesture, and the developing brain. *Developmental Psychobiology, 40*, 293–310. doi:10.1002/dev.10034

de Guerrero, M. C. M., & Villamil, O. S. (2000). Activating the ZPD: Mutual scaffolding in L2 peer revision. *The Modern Language Journal, 84*, 51–68. doi:10.1111/0026-7902.00052

Donato, R. (1994). Collective scaffolding in second language learning. In J. P. Lantolf & G. Appel (Eds.), *Vygotskian approaches to second language research* (Vol. Q, pp. 33–56). Norwood, NJ: Ablex.

Felder, R. M., & Silverman, L. K. (1988). Learning and teaching styles in engineering education. *Engineering Education, 78*, 674–681.

Gullberg, M. (2008). Gestures and second language acquisition. In P. Robinson & N. C. Ellis (Eds.), *Handbook of cognitive linguistics and second language acquisition* (pp. 276–305). New York, NY: Routledge.

Gullberg, M., de Bot, K., & Volterra, V. (2008). Gestures and some key issues in the study of language development. *Gesture, 8*(2), 149–179. doi:10.1075/gest.8.2.03gul

Gullberg, M., & McCafferty, S. G. (2008). Introduction to gesture and SLA: Toward an integrated approach. *Studies in Second Language Acquisition, 30*, 133–146. doi:10.1017/S0272263108080285

Hsiao, T.-Y., & Oxford, R. L. (2002). Comparing theories of language learning strategies: A confirmatory factor analysis. *The Modern Language Journal, 86*, 368–383. doi:10.1111/1540-4781.00155

Jacob, E., Rottenberg, L., Patrick, S., & Wheeler, E. (1996). Cooperative learning: Context and opportunities for acquiring academic English. *TESOL Quarterly, 30*, 253–280.

Kramsch, C. J. (1987). Socialization and literacy in a foreign language: Learning through interaction. *Theory Into Practice, 26*, 243–250. doi:10.1080/00405848709543282

Long, M. H., & Crookes, G. (1992). Three approaches to task-based syllabus design. *TESOL Quarterly, 26*, 27–56. doi:10.2307/3587368

Long, M. H., & Porter, P. A. (1985). Group work, interlanguage talk, and second language acquisition. *TESOL Quarterly, 19*, 207–228. doi:10.2307/3586827

Oxford, R. (1994). Language learning strategies: An update. *ERIC Digest.* Retrieved from http://www.eric.ed.gov/PDFS/ED376707.pdf

Oxford, R., & Nyikos, M. (1989). Variables affecting choice of language learning strategies by university students. *Modern Language Journal, 73*, 291–300. doi:10.2307/327003

Palincsar, A. S. (1986). The role of dialogue in providing scaffolded instruction. *Educational Psychologist, 21*(1), 73–98. doi:10.1207/s15326985ep2101&2_5

Pica, T. (2005). Classroom learning, teaching, and research: A task-based perspective. *The Modern Language Journal, 89*, 339–352. doi:10.1111/j.1540-4781.2005.00309.x

Tellier, M. (2008). The effect of gestures on second language memorisation by young children. *Gesture, 8*, 219–235. doi:10.1075/gest.8.2.06tel

Tomlinson, B., & Masuhara, H. (2009). Playing to learn: A review of physical games in second language acquisition. *Simulation Gaming, 40*, 645–668. doi:10.1177/1046878109339969

van Lier, L. (2007). Action-based teaching, autonomy and identity. *Innovation in Language Learning and Teaching, 1*(1), 46–65. doi:10.2167/illt42.0

Tutoring History With PERSIA

Thea J. Brophy and Janice B. Heerspink

Many students leave high school with the impression that learning history involves amassing a large collection of dates, names, and locations but then enter college history courses in which professors typically ask them to explore the relationships and patterns among these individual facts. This disjunction between high school and college expectations can present a challenge for the student whose only study strategy for history courses is memorization. Tutors can help these students begin to recognize, analyze, and understand the relationships and patterns inherent to the study of history.

The most familiar pattern within history is sequence. Though professors expect students to think in terms of the historical "big picture," most lectures and textbooks still present course material in a linear manner, and texts may display time lines. Students learn about events chronologically, so sequence is often fairly simple to establish.

A second pattern of historical thought is the tendency to separate larger concepts into parts, to define types, and to create lists. For example, students may learn about the regions of the British Empire (parts), the variety of government chosen by former British colonies following independence (types), and the prime ministers during the height of British colonial expansion (lists). This pattern can create those large collections of facts that students find intimidating to memorize. The role of the tutor is to help the student process parts, types, and lists using effective strategies beyond simple memorization.

When students are able to recognize the similarities and differences among various parts, types, or elements of a list, they are on their way to mastering yet another pattern important to the study of history: comparison and contrast. Using the above example, students practicing this pattern might identify what the governments of Australia and India have in common and how the two governments differ.

Finally, a student can better understand the relationships among multiple events or phenomena by evaluating cause and effect. How did one event lead to another? What was the inspiration for a particular movement? A classic example of this pattern within the history of Western civilization is the explanation for why the assassination of Austria's Archduke Ferdinand precipitated World War I.

A valuable tool for taking each of these patterns to a level of greater complexity is the acronym PERSIA. (The origins of the acronym are lost; the tool is mentioned in history and other social sciences publications without attribution.) The use of PERSIA helps a student identify the Political, Economic, Religious, Social, Intellectual, and Artistic elements in the patterns previously described. All historical causes and effects fall into at least one of these categories; in fact, most historical relationships call for multiple labels (e.g., socioeconomic causes and religiopolitical dynamics). PERSIA also provides a natural framework for comparing and contrasting and for creating lists or identifying parts or types.

The use of spatial representation is a helpful, practical way both to engage actively with material, analyze a body of text, and organize information into a more comprehensible format. The active learning strategies inherent in spatial representation enable and improve student concentration (Goetz, 1984). Also, students who employ spatial representation are better able to identify gaps in their knowledge as they are faced with a concrete visualization of the relationships among course concepts. The products of spatial representation exercises—charts, maps, diagrams, and lists—can then be used as a tool for review, thus assisting students with exam preparation as well. The practice of organizing material during study time can also lead to more coherent test answers and improved test performance (Heerspink, 1997). This training session will help tutors learn to use spatial representation to illustrate the patterns of thought common in the study of history, providing them with specific tools they can utilize to help tutees engage more deeply with course material.

Training Activity

This training activity can be accomplished within 1 hour, in a typical classroom or staff meeting room. The trainer should provide tutors with a handout that explains the various historical patterns and gives examples of simple spatial representations for each pattern. For example, a simple representation of a sequence might involve placing events in chronological order along a time line like Figure 1.

_/_____/_____/_____/___/_____/

FIGURE 1   Time line.

For representing parts, types, and lists, a visual map like Figure 2 can be a helpful tool.

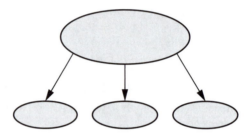

FIGURE 2   Visual map.

Charts (like the sample in Figure 3) are invaluable spatial representations of comparison and contrast relationships.

Characteristics	Greek Empire	Roman Empire

FIGURE 3   Chart.

Finally, cause and effect can be effectively represented through use of a web diagram, like the example in Figure 4.

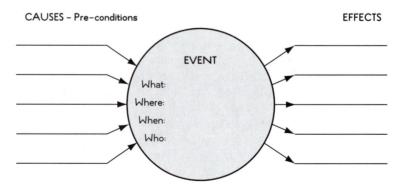

FIGURE 4   Web diagram.

Tutors should give examples of material from history courses fitting into each pattern, or occasions when they helped tutees discover these patterns in tutored courses. The trainer should progress from the simplest pattern (sequence) to the most complex (cause and effect).

For the next part of the activity, the trainer provides tutors with a five-page excerpt from a history textbook. Tutors should be given approximately 5 minutes to skim the text to see how much information they are able to gather. After 5 minutes have elapsed, tutors should discuss how much material they were able to cover, whether they used any note-taking strategies while reading, and the degree to which they expect to retain the information they read. They should also discuss which of the historical patterns they were able to identify within the text excerpt.

Then the trainer should distribute two handouts that demonstrate spatial representations of PERSIA combined with a compare-and-contrast grid (Figure 5) and PERSIA combined with a cause-and-effect pattern (Figure 6). Each tutor should choose one of the two handouts and spend another 5 minutes with the textbook excerpt. At the end of the 5 minutes, group discussion should highlight the benefits of using spatial representation as an active reading strategy. Tutors can brainstorm ways to expand the diagrams provided; find different uses for completed handouts (e.g., exam review, identifying holes in knowledge); and consider other courses for which such spatial representation techniques may be useful.

	SPANISH EXPLORATION/COLONIZATION	ENGLISH EXPLORATION/COLONIZATION
P		
E		
R		
S		
I		
A		

FIGURE 5   Compare and contrast with PERSIA.

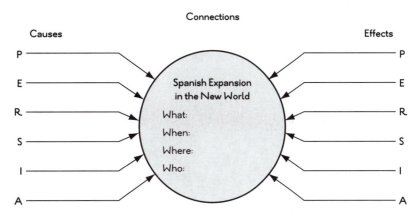

FIGURE 6   Cause and effect with PERSIA.

Assessment

Following this presentation and workshop, tutors should be able to list and explain historical patterns and the use of the acronym PERSIA. Tutors should be able to apply these patterns to new topics such as current events or other disciplines that may contain historical content. Tutors should also be able to give examples of how these concepts will be used in their tutoring. These skills can be assessed during a discussion period at the end of the presentation or by means of a short written exercise, as well as through direct observation of tutoring sessions.

References

Goetz, E. T. (1984). The role of spatial strategies in comprehending and remembering text: A cognitive information-processing analysis. In C. Holley & D. Dansereau (Eds.), *Spatial learning strategies: Techniques, applications, and related issues* (pp. 47–77). Orlando, FL: Academic Press.

Heerspink, J. (1997). *The use of spatial representation in history courses and in courses with historical content*. Unpublished manuscript. Calvin College, Grand Rapids, MI.

Tutoring Music

Michael Ruwe

Music tutors are usually cognizant of the basic musical concepts needed to tutor music on the collegiate level. However, because musical concepts often come naturally to music tutors, it is helpful if they are reminded of the basic steps upon which their knowledge has been built. In addition, learning center administrators may be concerned about their lack of musical background. Concepts such as scaffolding learning, a developed practice process, and active reading may assist both tutors and their trainers to offer music tutoring of high quality.

The goal of this training session is twofold: to help tutors acquire new insights and approaches for tutoring music and to make trainers aware of learning concepts applicable to music tutoring. Music theory, aural skills, and music literature are the three common aspects of typical basic studies music classes. A broad understanding of each of these concepts will assist tutors to become well-versed music tutors.

Music theory can be viewed as a language—with its own set of rules and devices. Without an agreed-upon language of music (music theory), a musician cannot successfully communicate complex ideas with another musician. Though a music tutor may be well versed in music theory, the tutee will most likely be a novice. For this reason, the idea of scaffolding learning—building knowledge on what the tutee already knows—will be integral to the learning process.

Aural skills, also known as ear training skills, have much to do with the practice of listening. Again, this ear training ability may be natural to a tutor but not for the tutee, who may not know what to listen for. The practice of listening critically can be challenging for the tutee: "The listener must possess a fair measure of knowledge and experience in order for the cycle of creation, interpretation (performance), and appreciation of art music to be successfully completed" (Ferris, 1995, p. 21). In other words, learning to listen critically should be a developed practice and also should be connected to previously learned music theory concepts.

Music literature, like other literatures, can be better comprehended if active reading is included in a tutee's study skills. A defined process of reading will assist students in their music literature studies as they read about the history of musical forms and the individuals who added to musical heritage. In addition, because many composers and performers have gained mythical status over the years, it is helpful for the tutor to humanize for the tutee the subjects of music literature study:

> Music history is not an account of dead people in a dull past, but a recounting of the endeavors and accomplishments of persons going about their daily affairs . . . . Moreover, music history is not just the study of the arrangement of symbols on staff paper, but a consideration of all that went into making musical compositions. (Stolba, 1990, p. xv)

Training Activity

The following activities will provide tutors with new ways to discuss information and concepts with their tutees. The section on aural skills requires a piano or keyboard. The section on music literature requires a textbook in music history or music appreciation. Approximately 1 hour is needed for this training session.

MUSIC THEORY

Just as words are composed of letters and sentences are composed of words, music is a language built on basic units: "The letter names and time value names of notes are the alphabet of the 'music language'" (Gordon, 1989, p. 24). For example, a music tutee most likely knows the concept of a

C major scale: C D E F G A B C. A tutor can build on the tutee's knowledge by adding the corresponding scale degree numbers for identification:

C	D	E	F	G	A	B	C
1	2	3	4	5	6	7	8

This added knowledge can help demonstrate harmony, and specifically how to build a major triad. A major triad consists of scale degrees 1, 3, and 5 of a major scale. Referencing this scale, a C major triad is made of the notes C, E, and G.

C	D	E	F	G	A	B	C
1		3		5			

The tutee can be asked to identify the notes of a D or G major triad using the same formula and scale degree numbering system.

AURAL SKILLS

Aural skills demand that a student be able to imagine or recreate a pitch without the aid of an instrument or reference pitch. In other words, according to music theorist Gordon (1989), these skills equal "a cognitive process by which the brain gives meaning to musical sounds" (p. 3).

Almost everyone knows the tune to "Twinkle, Twinkle, Little Star." The trainer can discuss with tutors how students may train their ear by building on what they know and by developing a persistent practice. When the tutor plays an interval of a fifth on the piano, the tutee should sing this interval without the aid of the instrument. Then the tutor can ask the tutee to sing the first few notes of "Twinkle, Twinkle, Little Star." The interval between notes in "Twinkle Twinkle" is a fifth (from note 1 to note 5, or from scale degree 1 to scale degree 5 in the previous segment of training). This practice of singing aids the tutee in interval recognition: "To be able to audiate a melody, a student must be able to sing, because when he engages in tonal audiation, he is actually singing silently" (Gordon, 1989, p. 25). Because the process of listening critically is so demanding, the repeated practice of listening and singing is integral to mastery of aural skills. Other intervals can be presented with their own mnemonic songs, such as intervals of the fourth ("Here Comes the Bride") and the sixth (the first two notes of the old NBC audio logo) and then identified in the student's own choice of iTune selections.

MUSIC LITERATURE

As with any reading assignment, the reader should be actively engaged in the reading and be able to build on previous knowledge. *Scaffolding Reading Experience* (Graves & Graves, 2003) advocates a three-step process for active reading, with activities before, during, and after reading. *Pre-reading activities* should be devised to get readers intrigued and engaged. *Reading activities* are designed to enhance engagement and comprehension. *Post-reading activities* let readers review, consolidate understanding, reflect, and connect this reading with other knowledge.

For this training exercise, the trainer may choose a reading passage typical of those assigned in music courses and preferably taken from the beginning of a chapter. The trainer should make copies for trainees or project the passage to a screen so all may read.

Pre-Reading

Before the tutors begin reading, the trainer should ask an intriguing question that is answered in the passage and have trainees write down the answer if they already know it. The trainer should also invite trainees to share definitions or explanations of esoteric terms that are found in the passage and congratulate trainees who contribute to the group's understanding by sharing their knowledge of the terminology.

Reading

Trainees should turn headings into questions as they read. As they come to information that answers the question, they should highlight or annotate before reading on to the next heading.

Post-Reading

The trainer should invite insights on how the answers to the questions implied by the headings add to understanding of the topic of the chapter. Are there implications for the reader's own life?

Assessment

The two learning objectives for this module are to help tutors to gain new insights and approaches for tutoring music and to make trainers aware of learning concepts applicable to music tutoring. These objectives are accomplished by demonstrating how music theory, aural skills, and music literature can be tutored by scaffolding learning, developing a practice process, and fostering active reading.

As a demonstration of the trainees' mastery of the content of this training activity, each can play the role of tutor and tutee. Alternatively, trainees can describe to each other the approach to take for any of the three basic music concerns covered in this training activity until the trainer is satisfied that all trainees have the knowledge. If desired, a worksheet can be created and then distributed some time after the training activity to assess tutors' retention of these music tutoring concepts.

References

Ferris, J. (1995). *Music: The art of listening.* Tempe, AZ: Brown & Benchmark.

Graves, M. F., & Graves, B. B. (2003). *Scaffolding reading experience: Designs for student success* (2nd ed.). Norwood, MA: Christopher-Gordon.

Gordon, E. E. (1989). *Learning sequences in music: Skill, content, and patterns.* Chicago, IL: GIA Publications.

Stolba, K. M. (1990). *The development of Western music: A history.* Fort Wayne, IN: Wm. C. Brown.

Effective Mathematics Tutoring Strategies

Lorraine Steiner

Individuals have beliefs about the subject of mathematics, beliefs that can be problematic toward the development of mathematics proficiency. This training module describes an educational activity that introduces several tutoring strategies intended to address these beliefs and enhance the development of skilled, confident, and independent learners of mathematics. The activity description is prefaced by a discussion of learners' needs and beliefs with respect to understanding different aspects of mathematics as well as the tutoring strategies that address these aspects.

Learning mathematics involves being able to understand mathematics as a complex subject with interrelated concepts that can be applied in a variety of meaningful situations. In Schoenfeld's (1988) words, "thinking mathematically consists not only of mastering various facts and procedures, but also in understanding connections among them" (p. 164). Kilpatrick, Swafford, and Findell (2001) analyzed successful mathematics learning as a mathematical proficiency consisting of five components: conceptual understanding, procedural fluency, strategic competence, adaptive reasoning, and a productive disposition.

Conceptual understanding is an aspect of understanding mathematics that extends beyond a set of distinct facts, rules, and procedures. It is the comprehension of the nature of mathematics, including mathematical conceptions, operations, and relations (Kilpatrick et al., 2001). Learners can bring to the tutoring session a set of erroneous beliefs about mathematics based on prior academic and social experiences (Muis, 2004). Learners often believe that mathematics is based solely on facts, rules, formulas, and procedures and that mathematics is only about getting the right answer. Learners may also believe that computation is the key rather than derivation, or that the form is more important than the concept. To enhance conceptual understanding in a tutoring session, the math tutor should emphasize the concepts underlying the facts, rules, and procedures.

One tutoring strategy that helps to develop conceptual understanding is to ask learners to explain the problem and to support them in the use of accepted mathematics vocabulary. This encourages learners to reflect on the concept and the process and not to work problems too quickly. Tutors can allow learners to think critically about the problems by asking metacognitive or *why* types of questions, such as, "Why does this work?" and "Why won't it work if we do this?" Metacognitive questions help learners to think about what they are doing and why. Responses to metacognitive questions allow learners to use the mathematical language associated with the concept.

While conceptual understanding is important, procedural fluency and strategic competence are also necessary for successful learning of mathematics. *Procedural fluency* is defined as "skill in carrying out procedures flexibly, accurately, efficiently, and appropriately" (Kilpatrick et al., 2001, p. 116). Learners can have difficulty with procedural fluency if they do not understand that problems can be complex. To aid the learner in developing procedural fluency, the tutor should scaffold instruction by breaking a complex task into smaller parts and guiding the learner through a building process. Initially tutors may need to give direct guidance to the learner on a specific, troublesome task, and then gradually fade the direct prompts, allowing the learner to become more independent.

A belief that mathematical tasks are not complex or interrelated can also stunt the development of strategic competence. *Strategic competence* is defined as "the ability to formulate, represent, and solve mathematical problems" (Kilpatrick et al., 2001, p. 116). A tutor can help tutees develop strategic competence by having learners repeat similar problems. Learners should look for and identify similarities and differences between the problems (Brown & Coles, 2000). Tutors can aid learners in identifying patterns or differences by asking the question, "How do these problems differ?" or "How are they the same?"

Learners of mathematics need to be able to explain or justify mathematical concepts, procedures, or strategies within different contexts. *Adaptive reasoning* is described as the "ability to think logically about the relationships among concepts and situations" (Kilpatrick et al., 2001, p. 116). Learners may not try to think logically about concepts if they believe that the ability to learn mathematics is an innate trait rather than developed, or that mathematics is not useful or relevant. Learners who believe that solving problems consists solely of following a predetermined sequence of steps or of memorizing formulas, rules, or procedures will not be able to translate problems to other contexts or to real-world applications (Muis, 2004). Tutors can illustrate how a mathematical concept can be relevant by defining it within the context of lived experience. It is particularly helpful if the tutor can find an example that is relevant to a learner's specific interests, job, or field of study.

Individuals who believe that mathematics is not useful in daily life or that learning mathematics is an innate trait that they did not acquire are less likely to be successful in understanding mathematics (Guay, Marsh, & Boivin, 2003). A *productive disposition* requires a "habitual inclination to see mathematics as sensible, useful, and worthwhile, coupled with a belief in diligence and one's own efficacy" (Kilpatrick et al., 2001, p. 116). Confidence in learning mathematics has been discussed as one of the most important affective variables influencing motivation and academic performance (Carmichael & Taylor, 2005). The previously mentioned tutoring strategies will all help to build mathematical confidence. For example, tutors can set tasks at the appropriate level, breaking tasks into smaller parts as necessary. Tasks should not be too easy or too difficult so as to avoid undermining confidence and reinforcing feelings of inadequacy. Throughout each tutoring session, tutors should be supportive and at the same time encourage independence. Tutors should not work the problems for their student clients. Tutors can help students view a mathematical concept as useful by applying it to a relevant context that is of interest to the student. Thus tutors can help students develop productive dispositions toward mathematics.

These five aspects of understanding mathematics are not mutually exclusive but rather are interrelated. Becoming better at learning mathematics procedurally and strategically will build self-confidence. Having a better conceptual understanding will help to develop an appreciation for a concept's relevance and usefulness. The following activity allows tutors to learn about the strategies that address these different aspects of understanding mathematics.

Training Activity

The objective of this training session is for tutors to learn strategies that will enhance various aspects of understanding mathematics. In four 1-hour periods, tutors will be introduced to specific tutoring strategies through guided small-group discussions. Trainers can adapt the training activity to a 90-minute session if tutors are already familiar with and skilled in the concepts presented.

PERIOD 1

As an overview, tutors can discuss how mathematics is taught and learned compared to other subjects. For example, getting the right answer is often emphasized in the teaching of mathematics, as are facts, rules, procedures, drill, and practice. Reading the textbook is often not emphasized. Students may also believe that memorization is important in learning mathematics or that mathematics is not useful or relevant.

The group facilitator should then introduce to the tutors the five aspects of mathematics proficiency as described by Kilpatrick et al. (2001). The discussion should focus on conceptual understanding and the tutoring strategy of using questions that spark metacognitive inquiry. After giving examples of metacognitive questions, the group facilitator can ask tutors what metacognitive questions they would typically use in a tutoring session. Examples of such questions may be, "Why did you choose this next step in the process?" "Why is that true?" "How did you reach that conclusion?" and "How would you interpret that answer?"

PERIOD 2

The discussion during this period should focus on procedural and strategic competence. Tutors should understand that development of conceptual understanding will aid procedural fluency. The trainer can model an example, such as the potentially difficult task of solving a quadratic equation. In the tutoring session, the tutor should find the source of the problem. Is it simplifying, factoring, or using the quadratic formula? The tutor can then give direct instruction on the smaller task, gradually fading the direct instruction until the learner is able to return to the larger task of solving the equation. The trainer can also introduce the strategy of finding similarities and differences between problems by comparing examples within a textbook unit and then asking the tutors to do the same.

PERIOD 3

Tutors should be given an explanation of adaptive reasoning and the strategy of applying problems within relevant contexts. The trainer can provide an example, such as exploring the concept of a negative exponent in a decreasing exponential function as it applies to the price of a specific type of car over time. The concept of the negative exponent can be explored, thus justifying why price decreases as time increases. The trainer can have tutors give additional examples that would be relevant to the learner and would encourage logical thinking.

PERIOD 4

The trainer can use this last session as an opportunity to summarize the previous strategies and discuss how these strategies can be used to build mathematical self-confidence and a productive disposition. Tutors should be encouraged to use positive reinforcement and to remind learners that mathematics proficiency is a gradual process that takes time. Finally, tutors should examine their own beliefs about inherent ability. Do they believe most individuals are capable of developing mathematics proficiency, or do they believe individuals are born with the ability to reason mathematically and simply doomed if their math sense is congenitally weak? Tutors should explore together the effectiveness of tutoring in the context of these beliefs.

Assessment

To assess this activity, the trainer should prepare tutoring scenarios for the tutors to role play. As they alternately take the role of tutor and tutee, do they have new insights to share with the group? Each training period should end with performance of key tutoring scenarios to the entire group and sharing of tutors' reflections on what they have learned. The trainer should make note of any concerns and talk with those tutors privately.

In addition, tutors should apply specific tutoring strategies with one or more learners over the course of a semester and look for evidence that the learners are becoming more skilled, confident, and independent. Independent learners will require fewer direct prompts for future tasks. As learners become more confident, they will allow themselves more time to solve problems and be more comfortable in explaining problems using mathematics vocabulary. At the end of the semester, tutors should share their experiences with each other.

References

Brown, L., & Coles, A. (2000). Same/different: A "natural" way of learning mathematics. In T. Nakahara & M. Koyama (Eds.), *Proceedings of the 24th Conference of the International Group for the Psychology of Mathematics Education* (Vol. 2, pp. 113–120). Hiroshima, Japan: Nishiki Print. Retrieved from http://www.eric.ed.gov/PDFS/ED452032.pdf

Carmichael, C., & Taylor, J. A. (2005). Analysis of student beliefs in a tertiary preparatory mathematics course. *International Journal of Mathematical Education in Science & Technology, 36,* 713–719. doi:10.1080/00207390500271065

Guay, F., Marsh, H. W., & Boivin, M. (2003). Academic self-concept and academic achievement: Developmental perspectives on their causal ordering. *Journal of Educational Psychology, 95,* 124–136. doi:10.1037/0022-0663.95.1.124

Kilpatrick, J., Swafford, J., & Findell, B. (Eds.). (2001). *Adding it up: Helping children learn mathematics.* Washington, DC: National Academy Press.

Muis, K. R. (2004). Personal epistemology and mathematics: A critical review and synthesis of research. *Review of Educational Research, 74,* 317–377. doi:10.3102/00346543074003317

Schoenfeld, A. H. (1988). When good teaching leads to bad results: The disasters of "well-taught" mathematics courses. *Educational Psychologist, 23,* 145–166. doi:10.1207/s15326985ep2302_5

Tutoring Mathematics

Nathalie M. Vega-Rhodes

Mathematics tutors should demonstrate a number of critical characteristics: knowledge and mastery of the content being tutored; the ability to communicate this knowledge to others; passion and excitement about the content being tutored; enthusiasm about subject areas and tutoring methods; communication expertise, including responsive listening; motivation to succeed; and patience. Many people believe that the math knowledge a tutor brings to the table is the most important facet of tutoring. Although this knowledge is important, it is definitely not the essential key to a successful tutoring session. In tutoring mathematics, being able to deal effectively with different types of learners and, more to the point, different levels of math anxiety is vital. Also crucial is the ability to build a tutee's confidence with regard to learning math. Indeed, the most difficult task for a tutor is to remember how challenging it was to learn a difficult concept and translate this understanding into the tutoring session.

Because a tutor's role is to assist students in becoming independent learners, it is not the tutor's role to present and teach new material (Janz, 2008). Instead, the tutor supports the instructor's teaching by providing opportunities for students to be more confident and independent. Another difference between the instructor's and tutor's roles is that the tutor can work individually with students and respond to their unique backgrounds, interests, and ways of knowing. For example, some learners may benefit from direct applications of mathematical concepts; if a student learning about addition of negative numbers is familiar with bank accounts, it can be helpful to use the example of being overdrawn on a bank account and writing yet another check. Another student may benefit from seeing a problem written out on the number line. A third could prefer to learn the rules verbatim. In all cases, it is important to consider the student's background knowledge and how this information as well as preferred learning styles could be useful when the student learns a new concept.

Myers (1990) urged that math tutors, like other tutors, have a game plan. First, tutors must figure out where to begin. Does the student know what the difficulty is and where help is needed? Second, tutors must be actively engaged in showing as well as telling student clients what to do. Third, tutors must have students practice the material. Based on this practice, tutors must provide feedback and positive messages.

Why should math tutors provide so much encouragement? According to Schwartz (2006), "The hardest aspect of teaching lower level math is trying to convince students they can succeed" (pp. 50–51). Indeed, students must feel that they are able to accomplish the goals set forth by the instructor.

The training session provided in this module demonstrates to tutors the importance of improving a tutee's confidence in mathematics. Further, this exercise allows tutors to empathize with students while helping them understand concepts in mathematics. By means of this training activity, trainees can anticipate tutees' feelings of frustration.

Training Activity

For this activity, tables and chairs should be arranged so that each group of two tutors shares a table. The trainer should provide paper and pencils at each table. Tutors should be advised to bring the textbooks for their current math courses to the session. The activity will require about 40 minutes.

Tutors are placed in groups of two by class standing or level of coursework already attained, matching each advanced math student with a less advanced student. An alternative approach would be to ask math students from an advanced course to participate as tutors in this training exercise.

The more advanced student of each pair plays the role of a math tutor, and the less advanced student plays the role of the tutee. The tutor will try to teach the tutee a mathematical concept as if the tutee should already be familiar with concepts the tutor knows. The tutor will be speaking above the tutee's level of comprehension.

After the "lesson" has been going on for no more than 10 minutes, the trainer should stop the tutors and have them debrief the tutees individually and then share their comments with the whole group. Because this is the most important part of the activity, discussion should include, at a minimum, what it feels like to be spoken to as an inferior, strategies for adjusting the tutoring session to eliminate demeaning elements, and strategies for letting tutees be active partners in the tutoring session.

During the debrief session, it is most important for the tutees to express their feelings and to try to come up with better alternatives to include students in tutoring. During this discussion, the trainer should capture ideas, strategies, and suggestions on an overhead, whiteboard, or flip chart. Experienced tutors are a valuable resource for this discussion, because they can relate experiences they have had as tutors. All can contribute their experiences with supercilious teachers, tutors, or mentors.

At this point, trainees have had an opportunity to experience the discomfort of insensitive tutoring. The discussion mentioned earlier focused on strategies to eliminate demeaning elements in a tutoring session. The next part of the activity will focus on utilizing more interactive ways to tutor. The tutors should repeat the activity, this time utilizing the strategies discussed. The goal is to model ways for tutors to accommodate the tutees' experience, knowledge, interests, and styles while bringing tutees to the level of understanding expected by the course instructor.

As before, the discussion is the most important part of the activity. Trainees should talk again about their feelings as tutees and the strategies that seemed to produce the best learning and engagement. Trainees should also reflect on and discuss the differences between the two tutoring experiences.

Assessment

An assessment form with the following questions should be prepared in advance and distributed at the end of the activity. Tutors may work in pairs to discuss their answers. After completing the assessment, if time remains, tutors should share their answers to the last question with the whole group.

- Recall specific experiences of stress or fear about math or science. Where were you? How old were you? What were you thinking and feeling? Who else was with you? What did those people say or do?

- Now recall an incident in your experience that gave you positive feelings about math or science.

- Finally, describe how a math tutor should work with a tutee to reduce math anxiety and encourage learning.

References

Janz, A. (2008). *Essentials for successful tutoring*. Lakeland, FL: National Tutoring Association.

Myers, L. (1990). *Becoming an effective tutor*. Los Altos, CA: Crisp.

Schwartz, A. E. (2006). Learning math takes attitude, perseverance, and courage. *Education Digest, 71*(7), 50–54.

Analyzing Text Graphics for Tutoring Chemistry

Barbara Ryan Hausman

Students may expect tutors merely to re-teach concepts introduced in class by their professors. Tutors, however, can facilitate learning of key processes in chemistry rather than just review them. This training module will show tutors how to reinforce their students' higher-level thinking skills when students are reading or deciphering graphic presentations of the text. Tutors can help students analyze their text's charts, diagrams, flow charts, and process webs to develop higher levels of understanding of course material and simultaneously create study guides for exam preparation.

Staff of the Eberly Center for Teaching Excellence at Carnegie Mellon University (n.d.) recognized that students have to construct learning: "To develop mastery, students must acquire component skills, practice integrating them, and know when to apply what they have learned" (para. 4). Tutors, then, need training to support their student clients' learning by helping students gather those skills, integrate them at higher levels of thinking, and use their new patterns of thought to make sense of readings, graphics, lectures, and test questions.

What are the higher levels of thinking needed to make sense of concepts in chemistry? According to Anderson and Krathwohl (2001), Bloom's revised taxonomy has six progressively and increasingly more sophisticated levels of thinking: Remember, Understand, Apply, Analyze, Evaluate, Create. (This contrasts only slightly with the original Bloom's Taxonomy [Bloom, Engelhart, Frost, Hill, & Krathwohl, 1956], which listed the six levels as Knowledge, Comprehension, Application, Analysis, Synthesis, and Evaluation.) By encouraging students to think about graphics in texts at all six levels, tutors can guide students to apply these levels of cognition to understand chemical principles presented in graphic forms.

Training Activity

The purpose of this training activity is to familiarize tutors with the levels of thinking of Bloom's revised taxonomy (Anderson & Krathwohl, 2001) and apply the verbs to create a study guide of questions and answers in chemistry. The trainer should provide copies of Bloom's Taxonomy in print form or project an image so all can see clearly. Tutors will also need Internet access for the Quizlet exercise, printer, cardstock, paper cutter, laminator, hole punch, key rings or round rings, pencils and paper, index cards, and copies of a chemistry text. Trainer and tutors should be seated around a table or at desks formed in a circle. About 1 hour should be allowed for the training session.

INTRODUCTION TO BLOOM'S TAXONOMY AND TAXONOMY CARDS

The trainer can explain Bloom's Taxonomy (Anderson & Krathwohl, 2001) simply and quickly. In the 1950s, cognitive psychologist Benjamin Bloom (Bloom et al., 1956) presented a framework of thinking skills as a stairstep hierarchy of six levels of thinking. The simplest two levels, originally labeled Knowledge and Comprehension and now Remember and Understand, are the easiest thinking tasks, and the levels get increasingly difficult, all the way to Creation. In college chemistry, the highest four levels are most frequently emphasized: Apply, Analyze, Evaluate, and Create, to use the terminology of the Anderson & Krathwohl (2001) version. It is not that the first levels of Remember and Understand should be ignored, but rather in Bloom's classification system they are the lowest levels of thinking upon which the higher constructs are built. The Taxonomy is one way to reach higher-level thinking in chemistry. Tutors who use the levels of thinking in sessions with students can help them independently create meaningful study guide questions. Studying higher-level constructs will prepare students for the kinds of questions they will encounter on college-level chemistry exams.

The trainer should choose one of the two models (Bloom et al., 1956, or Anderson & Krathwohl, 2001) and sets of terminology to present. An Internet search for "Bloom's Taxonomy verbs" provides lists that may be useful for the first part of the training activity, but such resources should be carefully compared to the published taxonomy models for accuracy.

To begin the activity, tutors should create a login with the Quizlet website (Sutherland, 2011). When access to the site is established, tutors should create flashcards from the flashcard menu. To do this, tutors will enter the taxonomy domain names in the "term" field, and the verbs from that category in the "definition" category, numbering each of the six domains in order, beginning with number 1, Knowledge or Remember. For instance, the Analyze flashcard could list the verbs *analyze, classify, compare, contrast, debate, distinguish, examine, outline,* and *relate.* Tutors then will follow the website's instructions for saving and printing their flashcards. After the flashcards are printed on cardstock, the tutors will cut them into cards, laminate them, punch a hole in one corner, and secure them to a round ring or key chain. This will give each tutor a permanent set of taxonomy domains and verbs on a handy key ring, readily available and durable.

One way to practice using the taxonomy key ring during the training session is to look carefully at the diagrams and illustrations of the chemistry text, because they often summarize the main concepts. For example, a topic under study early in the course may be the components of matter. Tutors should find this topic in the text they are using.

The trainer should remind tutors that the taxonomy cards cue certain questions that lead to particular kinds of thinking. The verbs in the Knowledge and Comprehension sectors cue readers to *define* the components of matter, as well as *describe, locate,* and *list* them. Verbs in the Comprehension sector suggest to *explain, relate, paraphrase,* and perhaps *match* similar forms of matter when presented with a picture. Moving on to the next sector on the card ring, tutors will find the word *compare* listed as a verb in the Analysis section; one component of matter can be compared with another, so one possible test question could be to compare elements and compounds and note the differences and similarities. A similar question can be asked with the verb *distinguish,* also from the Analysis category. The question could ask how to distinguish a compound from a mixture.

GUIDED PRACTICE

Verbs from the Analysis section of the taxonomy card ring can be used to formulate short-answer questions or thinking tasks about the illustrations in the text. The trainer can have tutors begin with a diagram from their text, choose one of the verbs from the back of the taxonomy card, and write their own questions. When questions are then shared, it may be noted that not all verbs in the category will fit every diagram. What is important, though, is that reading the diagram and studying it to formulate questions seems to produce an understanding of what the diagram is about. When Analysis-level verbs are used, the level of understanding advances to the Analysis level of the cognitive domain.

The trainer can then hand out index cards and have tutors work in pairs to formulate questions for the textbook diagram from Evaluate and Create levels of thinking. Each question should be written on the index card. The trainer can allow about 5 minutes for tutors to construct and write their questions, then have each pair give their two cards to the pair of tutors working on their right.

Tutors write the answer to each question on the back of the card each has received, working together and using the diagram in the text for help. After 5 minutes, tutors should share questions and answers with one another.

INDEPENDENT PRACTICE

The trainer can then have tutors turn to another page of text that offers an illustration. Tutors can take a few minutes to look at the diagram and then, using each category on the taxonomy card ring and working alone, create 12 questions, two for each domain of the taxonomy, and write them on index cards. This time, tutors also write the answers to their questions on the backs of the cards.

It should by now be apparent that the index cards with questions constitute the beginning of a study guide for the chapter. Students who use all levels of card ring questions for all the illustrations in the chapter will be creating their own study guide to quiz themselves at higher levels of thinking.

CLOSURE

The trainer can invite tutors to discuss the benefits of thinking critically—going beyond simple definitions of terms to a better understanding of the material. Tutors should also examine what they discovered about their own thinking from this exercise.

As a final activity of the training session, tutors should discuss any drawbacks to this method or difficulties they see using it with students who seek assistance in chemistry. Dealing with these concerns early is helpful. Of course, handouts on Bloom's Taxonomy with sources cited should be available for tutors to use with their students. At a later training session, after tutors have had opportunities to utilize this technique with actual students, they could discuss again how the strategy works or needs tweaking.

Assessment

The initial assessment is completed when tutors demonstrate in independent practice their ability to formulate, write, and answer 12 questions using verbs from the taxonomy card ring. If desired, tutors can also be asked to demonstrate their skill in explaining and using the card ring in a role-play exercise in any time remaining in the training session.

References

Anderson, L. W., & Krathwohl, D. R. (Eds.). (2001). *A taxonomy for learning, teaching and assessing: A revision of Bloom's taxonomy of educational objectives* (Complete ed.). New York, NY: Longman.

Bloom, B. S. (Ed.), Engelhart, M. D., Frost, E. J., Hill, W. H, & Krathwohl, D. R. (1956). *Taxonomy of educational objectives. Handbook I: Cognitive domain*. New York, NY: David McKay.

Eberly Center for Teaching Excellence. (n.d.). *Theory and research-based principles of learning*. Retrieved from http://www.cmu.edu/teaching/principles/learning.html

Sutherland, A. (2011). *Quizlet*. Retrieved from http://www.quizlet.com

CHAPTER 5

Mentor Training Topics

Introduction

Peer mentors provide a broad range of services for postsecondary students. Orientation and support programs for first-year students and students in transition as well as federally funded TRiO programs (such as Student Support Services) probably could not survive and function without peer mentors. Jennifer Smith (2011), a past coordinator of the College Reading and Learning Association's (CRLA) International Mentor Training Program Certification (IMTPC), defined peer mentors as "highly trained undergraduates who serve as bridges for academic success and social transition to college life" (p. 2). To serve effectively as "bridges," mentors need relationship training, some ideas for which may be found in the modules of Chapter 3A: General Training Topics, Communication and Relationships.

Other essential mentor training topics of the IMTPC certification requirements (CRLA, 2011) can likewise be found in the modules of Chapter 3 and Chapter 4. These topics include IMTPC training at Level 1 (professional ethics, establishing rapport, questioning and listening skills, preparing to study, campus and community resources and referrals), Level 2 (conflict resolution, cultural awareness), Level 3 (gender issue awareness), and electives (establishing liaisons with faculty, learning styles, goal setting, critical thinking, team building, personal safety, and compliance with privacy laws).

To supplement the 40 training modules for mentors in Chapter 3 and applicable modules in Chapter 4, Chapter 5 offers seven additional modules focused specifically on training peer mentors to provide critical services for their student clients. The first three modules in Chapter 5 provide training in the roles and responsibilities of mentors; these modules may be useful not only for mentor trainers but also for learning assistance professionals exploring the employment of peer mentors to serve student needs at their institutions. The four remaining modules focus on topics of particular concern in mentor training, which may be more or less essential depending on the responsibilities assigned to peer mentors: managing time and setting goals, dealing with difficult mentoring situations, exploring career choices, and sustaining students in crisis.

REFERENCES

College Reading and Learning Association. (2011). *IMTPC certification requirements*. Retrieved from http://www.crla.net/imtpc/certification_requirements.htm

Smith, J. (2011, September). A call to arms for university mentoring program professionals. *CRLA NewsNotes, 35*(3), 2. Retrieved from http://www.crla.net/CRLA_Archives/2011/NN_V35_I3_Sep11.pdf

Mentor Roles and Responsibilities

Lisa M. Johns

Historically, mentoring has had many definitions. Crisp and Cruz (2009) stated that "existing definitions of mentoring offered have been extremely broad" (p. 527). According to Budge (2006), mentoring relationships in postsecondary education traditionally existed between faculty members and students, but definitions are changing as student peers are taking on mentoring roles. Because the possible definitions of peer mentoring are so broad, it is important for peer mentors to be trained in their roles and responsibilities. For the purpose of this training session, peer mentoring in postsecondary institutions is defined as "a nurturing process that fosters the growth and development of the protégé[,] . . . an insightful process in which the wisdom of the mentor is acquired and applied by the protégé" (Shandley, 1989, p. 60).

Postsecondary institutions have implemented peer mentoring programs in part to increase campus connectedness and the engagement of students. Shandley (1989) suggested that a mentor is a "guide or reality checker in introducing the protégé" to campus (p. 60). Cuseo (2010) claimed that "by providing individualized attention and support, peers help students feel they matter at the institution, facilitate academic and social integration, and increase feelings of satisfaction with the institution" (p. 5). Jacobi (1991) compiled fundamental commonalities from a review of the literature that indicated mentoring is usually "focused on achievement" and involves "(a) emotional and psychological support, (b) direct assistance with career and professional development, and (c) role modeling" (p. 513).

To create these fruitful relationships, mentors are trained to adopt a nonjudgmental and authentic interpersonal style. A person-centered communication style helps build mentor-student rapport. Training mentors to adopt a nurturing approach and positive acceptance of the protégé is based on the work of Rogers (1942), the founder of person-centered psychotherapy. In Rogers' therapeutic style, the focus is on the individual and not on the problem. The goal is to assist individuals in learning to solve problems themselves, allowing them to become capable of solving new problems in the future independently (Corey, 2009; Rogers, 1942). Indeed, Jacobi (1991) identified mentoring relationships as "reciprocal" and "personal" although mentors possess more "experience, influence, and achievement" (p. 513).

Training Activity

Mentors in training should be introduced to the roles that mentors assume and the responsibilities mentors undertake. Prior to training, trainers should examine their own mentoring perspective and make preliminary decisions about how typical issues with students will be handled at their institution. Trainers must clearly identify for themselves the breadth and limits of the mentor's role before initiating training. Doing this work in preparation for training—utilizing for guidance both the institution's policies and the program's mission—will steer the direction of the training sessions.

This interactive training activity requires two sessions of 1–1.5 hours each. A room with movable chairs, pen and paper for each trainee, and a whiteboard or large notepad and marker are needed for this activity.

MENTOR ROLES

The first of the two training sessions on mentor roles and responsibilities focuses on the variety of mentoring roles in which trainees engage. Mentors will probably discover that several of the roles fit well with their own communication styles and patterns of interaction.

The trainer should first present an overview of mentoring at the institution. This brief history may include the following: (a) a description of the student needs that led to creation of the mentoring program; (b) a timeline of the program's origins and development; (c) particulars of the program's implementation, whether meeting with students in groups each fall semester and individually in the spring, or matching up for at least a full year, or providing drop-in assistance without assigning students to particular mentors; (d) an explanation of the target populations served by the mentors; (e) a list of daily operational responsibilities (e.g., attending the Freshman Seminar course, setting up the appointment calendar, submitting time sheets); and (f) learning outcomes and accomplishments of previous program years.

The trainer might note that few could reach college without some guidance and mentoring from others. Trainees should reflect on the roles their own mentors have assumed, making individual lists with the pen and paper supplied, and then in group discussion sharing some of their experiences in mentor-protégé relationships.

Cuseo (n.d.) posited some roles that a mentor may play: advocate, cheerleader, coach, confidante, friend or colleague, guide, resource and referral agent, and role model. The trainer can list these roles on the board and invite trainees to plot their own mentors' roles in additional categories. Other roles may be listed as suggested by trainees' experience in mentoring situations.

The trainer should have trainees pair up. Each team of two trainees should choose one role from their lists or draw one by chance, or the trainer may assign a mentoring role to each pair. The members of each team collaborate to create a brief scenario illustrating the characteristics exhibited by a mentor in the chosen role, with one person acting as the mentor and the other as the student. The mentors then take turns role playing their scenarios for the rest of the trainees. At the end of each role play, trainees are encouraged to name the role they believe was portrayed and identify it on the whiteboard. After all teams have participated, a large group discussion is facilitated to brainstorm any roles not yet represented, including those missing from the list provided.

MENTOR RESPONSIBILITIES

The second training session seeks to define the responsibilities of mentors in the program and help create ownership of these responsibilities among the mentors. The trainer begins by facilitating a group brainstorming session to answer the question, "Now that you understand mentoring roles, what kinds of responsibilities do mentors in this program have?" The trainer should write each suggestion on the whiteboard, whether or not it is actually one of the responsibilities for mentors in the program. As a group, the trainees choose the responsibilities they seriously believe will be entrusted to them. Some possible examples are (a) developing welcoming but professional relationships with students and maintaining appropriate boundaries, (b) modeling positive student behavior, and (c) assisting in class by facilitating group activities.

The trainer should then offer any of the following 10 situations that are applicable, or choose examples from campus experience. Scenarios may be printed on handouts or shared on the whiteboard or screen. Trainees should be given a few minutes to think about the first situation before sharing their ideas for the appropriate action to be taken. The trainer plays a critical role in this part of the session by guiding discussion to the roles and responsibilities appropriate at the institution and in the program. Presentation of each subsequent situation should provide some brief thinking time to reflect on the discussion of previous situations as well as on trainees' own experiences.

- The student does not talk when you meet for mentoring. Your questions elicit one-syllable answers. The student always comes to class and to mentoring but just does not participate in discussion. What do you say and do?

- The student appears shy and tells you he or she is very homesick. This is the first time the student has been away from home for an extended period of time. How do you respond?

- One of your students complains about an instructor. The student reports that none of the students likes the instructor and that the instructor talks down to the entire class. What do you say and do?

- During mentor meetings, the student will not stop talking long enough for you to get a word in. What do you say and do?

- A student is obviously not taking class seriously. This student often misses class and rarely turns in homework—and attends mentoring only because it is required for a passing grade. The first test of the semester is scheduled for next week. During the mentoring session, the student assures you his or her study habits are just fine. What do you say and do?

- The parent of one of your mentees telephones, reporting concern about the student's academic performance. The student has mentioned meeting with you for class. The parent says that the student has given permission for you two to speak; how else would the parent have gotten your name and number? What do you say and do?

- A mentee really seems to trust you and discloses personal information at every meeting. One day the student confides that she or he smokes pot at least three times a week. What do you say and do?

- A student is feeling pressure from his or her parents to decide on a major. The student has no idea what to do with his or her life and does not even want to think about it yet. What do you say and do?

- You and your mentees get along really well. They like and trust you, calling you their friend. One particular student that you really enjoy speaking with invites you to a party at his or her house. What do you say and do?

- One of the students that you meet with regularly tells you that he or she is flat broke and has not eaten in 2 days. The student is afraid of having to quit school because of lack of money. What do you say and do?

Working together through these 10 situations should provide peer mentors with information about other resources on campus, the range and limits of their responsibilities, the philosophical approach or tone of the program, and a variety of appropriate actions to take.

Assessment

After completing both sessions, trainees should have a better understanding of possible roles they will assume as mentors and what responsibilities will be theirs to fulfill. The Worksheet of Mentor Responsibilities (see Appendix) may be produced as a handout to use for assessment after the second training session. The trainer can use right and wrong answers to determine which mentors need more training and instruction before beginning their mentoring responsibilities. When returned to the mentors, these worksheets inform mentors of their correct and incorrect responses and can direct them to better understanding of their responsibilities as mentors.

References

Budge, S. (2006). Peer mentoring in postsecondary education: Implications for research and practice. *Journal of College Reading and Learning, 37*(1), 71–85.

Corey, G. (2009). Person-centered therapy. In M. Flemming (Ed.), *Theory and practice of counseling and psychotherapy* (pp. 164–194). Belmont, CA: Thomson Brooks/Cole.

Crisp, G., & Cruz, I. (2009). Mentoring college students: A critical review of the literature between 1990 and 2007. *Research in Higher Education, 50,* 525–545. doi:10.1007/s11162-009-9130-2

Cuseo, J. (2010). Peer leadership: Situation-specific support roles. *E-Source for College Transitions,* 7, 4–5, 8.

Cuseo, J. (n.d.). *The case for faculty and staff mentoring programs for college students.* Retrieved from https://www.campustoolkit.com/pdfs/article_mentoring_program.pdf

Jacobi, M. (1991). Mentoring and undergraduate academic success: A literature review. *Review of Educational Research, 61,* 505–532. doi:10.2307/1170575

Rogers, C. R. (1942). *Counseling and psychotherapy: Newer concepts in practice.* Boston, MA: Houghton Mifflin.

Shandley, T. (1989). The use of mentors for leadership development. *National Association of Student Personnel Administrators Journal, 27*(1), 59–66.

Appendix

WORKSHEET OF MENTOR RESPONSIBILITIES

Responsibility	Yes	No	Depends (on what?)	Referral (to whom?)
Model positive student behavior				
Ensure that students attend class on time				
Facilitate group activities in class				
Create welcoming relationships with students but establish and maintain professional boundaries				
Help students with homework				
Stay after hours to comfort a student who is having problems				
Give a student a ride to the bookstore				
Invite students to a party at his or her residence over the weekend				
Make appropriate campus referrals				
Consult weekly with supervisor regarding student issues				
Lend money to students				
Take a student to see a physician off campus				
Talk to an instructor on the student's behalf regarding a late assignment				
Attend weekly trainings				
Accept students as friends on a social networking service				
Remind students about assignments and exams				
Help students create course schedules for the next semester				
Answer financial aid questions				
Explain how to change a major				
Answer questions about degree plans and required courses				

Establishing Goals for the Mentoring Session

Colleen Rustad–Sampson and Kristine Noll Carnes

Setting goals, determining objectives, and establishing the framework for mentor sessions are tasks essential to successful mentoring experiences. Session guidelines give structure to the program and assist mentors in providing intentional and productive experiences for mentees. This module describes training mentors on how to make the most of the mentoring session by establishing four broad session goals: providing appraisal as well as emotional, informational, and instrumental support (House, 1981). In addition, this module provides sample outlines and progress notes utilized in a College Reading and Learning Association (CRLA, 2011) International Mentor Program Training Certification (IMPTC) Level 2 training curriculum.

The methodology for formulating mentoring session goals presented in this training activity is grounded in House's (1981) categories of social support as well as involvement theory (Astin, 1984) and academic and social integration theory (Tinto, 1975). House (1981) described four main categories of social support: emotional, appraisal, informational, and instrumental. The mentor follows this model by providing demonstrations of concern (emotional support), information relevant to self-evaluation (appraisal support), suggestions or information for solving problems (informational support), and aid in the form of time (instrumental support).

Astin (1984) noted a relationship between student success and student involvement in both the academic and the social aspects of college. Student involvement is therefore an important goal of the mentoring relationship. In each session the mentor should review the student's activities and provide encouragement and suggestions for reaching both academic and social goals.

Tinto developed a Student Integration Model predicting that a student's initial commitment is modified over time as a result of the student's involvement in the campus community. In addition, Thomas (2000) found that students with well-connected networks were more likely to persist in a college environment, particularly if they develop networks with other highly involved and integrated students. Thomas' study showed how important it is to "[help] students develop a portfolio of relations that can provide key resources (academic as well as social) over the freshman year" (p. 609). From these theoretical and practical perspectives, then, peer mentors may be trained to see their purpose as buffering students from the effects of stress by utilizing four categories of social support (emotional, appraisal, informational, and instrumental), increasing student involvement and success as measured through student behavior, and facilitating the emotional process of socialization with a focus on student attitudes, feelings, and self-concept.

This module presents a training activity through which mentors gain understanding of the research that is at the core of the mentoring approach presented in the module. This training demonstrates that, with increased integration and involvement, students become more committed to achieving and maintaining academic and personal success. With the schematic background provided in the training activity, mentors can plan consecutive sessions to integrate and involve mentees in the campus community. Mentoring sessions are guided by these elements as well as the individual student's academic and personal goals.

Training Activity

This training activity requires approximately 1 hour. Before the training session, the trainer should prepare copies of the outlines for first and subsequent mentor sessions and of the Mentor Session Progress Report as handouts (see Appendix).

SETTING GOALS FOR THE FIRST MEETING

Mentors may be uncertain about how to begin a mentoring relationship. Trainers provide guidelines to alleviate doubt and ensure productive sessions. The trainer should share with mentors the program's foundations in the theories of House (1981), Astin (1984), Tinto (1975), and Thomas (2000) and the relationship of these models to the outline designed for an initial meeting:

1. Define the mentoring relationship; discuss expectations, confidentiality, and boundaries.

2. Complete an intake interview to get to know the mentee and begin building a collaborative relationship.

3. Establish a goal for the mentoring relationship.

4. Establish an agenda for the next meeting.

5. Summarize key points and express appreciation for the meeting.

Using a framework for the initial session will ensure that both mentor and mentee clearly understand the relationship as they begin to establish goals. The trainer can model a first session with one mentor in the role of mentee, then invite volunteers to practice the mentor's role for review by the other trainees and the trainer.

SETTING GOALS FOR EACH SUBSEQUENT SESSION

In addition to structuring the initial meeting, mentors will need to set goals for subsequent meetings. Although session goals have to be flexible as other issues or urgent priorities develop during the course of the relationship, planning ahead for meetings can keep sessions productive and meaningful for both mentor and mentee.

During the second meeting, mentor and student develop and formalize a workable goal and realistic action plan. This step is critical to the success of future mentoring sessions. With a written goal and action plan to refer to, the mentor will be able to develop appropriate and progressive goals for each of the subsequent sessions. The mentor and the student will have a general road map to ensure the productivity of each session.

The time commitment for mentor meetings will vary depending on program expectations, and goals for the session may differ if mentor and mentee meet only a few times per semester rather than weekly. Nevertheless, each session can be worthwhile if both participants effectively manage the time they have to accomplish the long-term goal.

The trainer should provide handouts containing the following suggestions, which are designed to keep mentoring sessions on track for achieving established goals:

- Schedule sessions in advance so the next meeting is always on the calendar.

- Review the previous session's progress notes and allow time to prepare for the meeting.

- Start each session with a progress review to focus the session on the student's critical issues.

- Keep appointments and promptly return emails and phone calls.

- Remember that the quality of the session is more important than the amount of time spent together. Do not allow attention to be diverted to other topics during meetings; both partners should focus on the key issues.

- Schedule a follow-up meeting or discussion if necessary.

Trainers should provide an outline for session notes to assist mentors in evaluating progress toward goals and require mentors to reflect on objectives for the following sessions. The trainer can provide copies of the mentor session form (see Appendix) and review this form with mentors, explaining the three phases of a mentor session and use of the form in each phase.

First Phase: Greetings and Establishing Trust

The first phase of the mentoring session supports the emotional function of the mentor relationship: establishing trust, showing concern, and listening to the mentee. The mentor should be ready to greet the mentee pleasantly, positively, and with enthusiasm and be prepared to listen. For the first session, the mentor should be equipped with initial interview questions and should focus on building trust. For the first phase of subsequent sessions, the mentor should be organized with notes from previous sessions and have the session planned as thoroughly as possible. This is an opportune time for the mentor to provide the mentee with the affirmation and feedback that constitute the appraisal element of social support. By reviewing previous notes and reflections on mentee progress, the mentor will prime the mentee to move into the second phase of the session.

Second Phase: Addressing the Present

When past issues have been reviewed, the mentor moves into the present phase. This includes addressing immediate concerns or issues and discussing the session plan with the mentee. The mentor moves into the informational and instrumental part of the session, offering advice, suggestions, and information. During this phase of the session, the mentor should model positive behaviors and demonstrate skills that the mentee may replicate to enhance skills and knowledge.

Third Phase: Planning the Future

The mentor brings closure to the session by appraising the progress made toward goals, providing affirmation, and turning the focus to the future. Planning for the future encourages the behavioral and attitudinal change that will support the mentee in goal attainment. By including the mentee in the planning of future sessions, the mentor maintains the collaborative nature of the mentoring relationship.

To end the training session, the trainer and mentors should review the value of setting clear guidelines and goals for mentoring sessions: providing an emotionally affirming, informational, appraising, and instrumental foundation for productive sessions. Equally important, session guidelines and goals support mentors first embarking on the mentoring experience.

Assessment

At the end of the training session or at the next training meeting, mentors should demonstrate their understanding of the theoretical underpinnings for the organization of mentor sessions. If cued by basic information about the theories of House (1981), Astin (1984), Tinto (1975), and Thomas (2000), can trainees explain how mentoring sessions are structured to support students? Assessment can be made orally, in writing on individual worksheets, or in response to a query on the mentor staff weblog.

After the training provided in this session, mentors should also be able to demonstrate how to use the session report form to structure mentor sessions. For this section of the assessment, pairs of mentors can role play mentor sessions. The trainer should record these practice sessions and review them with the mentors. Stopping the video intermittently, the trainer should engage mentors in reflective conversation about the mentor's approach to leading the session. Mentors should be invited to practice multiple times before their first actual mentor session, until on reviewing the videos each mentor and the trainer agree that the mentor is prepared to lead sessions.

References

Astin, A. (1984). Student involvement: A developmental theory for higher education. *Journal of College Student Personnel, 25,* 297–308.

College Reading and Learning Association. (2011). *IMTPC certification requirements.* Retrieved from http://www.crla.net/imtpc/certification_requirements.htm

House, J. S. (1981). *Work stress and social support.* Reading, MA: Addison-Wesley.

Thomas, S. L. (2000). Ties that bind: A social network approach to understanding student integration and persistence. *Journal of Higher Education, 71,* 591–615. doi:10.2307/2649261

Tinto, V. (1975). Dropout from higher education: A theoretical synthesis of recent research. *Review of Educational Research, 45*(1), 89–125. doi:10.3102/00346543045001089

Appendix

● ● ● ● ● ●   MENTOR SESSION PROGRESS REPORT

Mentee: _____ ID#: _____ Date: _____

Mentor: _____ Type of session: In Person _____ Email _____ Phone _____

What topic or goal was addressed today? (First phase of the session)

_____

_____

How did you assist the student, and what suggestions did you offer? (Second phase of the session)

_____

_____

_____

How did this visit help the student progress toward his or her overall goal(s)? (Third phase of the session)

_____

_____

_____

What are your plans for the next session? (Third phase of the session)

_____

_____

_____

Date of next session: _____ Type of session: IP _____ Em _____ Ph _____

Practicing the Mentor's Role

Ann M. Koefer

Creating a plan of mentoring is an important step in establishing a positive working relationship between peer mentor and student. Just as a ladder has rungs, the plan described in this training module advances communication from introductory prompts to advanced interactions. Mentors must be prepared to assist their students to explore issues of identity and potential, to couple "I know who I am" with "who do I want to become?" Mentoring at this fragile stage can be an exciting and fruitful endeavor and can benefit both the mentor and the mentee. While mentors are helping others, they develop habits of the mind and heart that will increase their own capacity for learning and personal development (Kuh, 2003).

Strong mentoring programs sequence each phase of the annual cycle. The previous year's new mentors cycle back in as experienced mentors who assist in the training of newer mentors, because inexperienced mentors require supervision and support (Freedman & Baker, 1995). Every January, openings for mentoring positions at DeSales University are posted and applicants interviewed. In the spring, new and returning mentors attend the four-session interactive training program described in this training module. In late summer, mentors attend a required college readiness program in which they meet the incoming first-year students they will mentor in the upcoming fall semester. This intensive summer bridge program simulates college life and therefore challenges incoming first-year students socially, academically, and personally. At the end of this program, each mentor is assigned four or five first-year mentees whom they will mentor for the upcoming semester. Starting with the first week of school, mentees are required to see their mentors weekly. In these sessions, mentors model behaviors appropriate to successful college students. The program thus provides both clear guidelines for success in college and sustained social, academic, and personal support—the first two of four actions that institutions should take to enhance student retention and graduation (Tinto, 2004).

Sherk (1999) argued that the best mentoring programs must be both remarkable and noticeable. If exemplary mentoring programs are to be staffed by committed, passionate mentors and staff professionals who love what they do and care about the students they serve, then mentors must be trained in committed passion. Likewise, if the most successful programs are those in which mentors focus on developing trust and friendship with their mentees (Sipe, 1996), then peer mentors must be trained in that focus.

Training Activity

The four workshop sessions described in this training module require a classroom with chalkboard or whiteboard. Copies of the mentor training manual should be readied. Additional materials should be prepared for each session; materials specific to each workshop are explained in the session descriptions below. Each of the four sessions is 90 minutes in length.

SESSION #1: THE LANGUAGE OF MENTORING

In the first workshop session, mentors receive an introduction to the purposes of mentoring. The job description and "dos and don'ts" of mentoring are reviewed, with an emphasis on basic counseling techniques of paraphrasing and summarizing mentees' expressions. Mentors should be trained as paraprofessionals; although undergraduates, they must follow the same rules and regulations as staff employees. Annual raises, training in the Family Educational Rights and Privacy Act

(FERPA) regulations (see National Association of Colleges and Employers, 2010), performance evaluations, and a clear job description are essential to their work performance and professional development. Mentors must also learn to demonstrate their commitment to student success using appropriate communication skills.

Introductory prompts are practiced in this training session with an emphasis on personal, academic, social, and career issues. These prompts allow mentors to employ active listening skills, thus providing the groundwork for meaningful interaction. These well-posed questions also verify understanding, encourage explanation, and move student clients through the stages of communication (Williams, 2000). A few simpler prompts that require only a yes or no answer provide an introductory level of communication necessary to engage students who are hesitant, anxious, or even negative about participating in dialogue. Sample prompts include the following:

- There is so much to learn in getting ready to come to college. I find it best to tackle one thing at a time. How are you coping with it all?

- Eating and sleeping can be really difficult for students as we adjust to college life. Are you eating well on campus? Are you getting enough sleep?

- Homesickness is another thing that can get you down. I finally brought my pillow from home to campus and I felt better. What do you miss from home?

- I make it a rule to know where Financial Aid and the Business Office are; there always seem to be so many questions in those areas. Have you been to those offices yet?

- I would like to introduce you to the Academic Resource Center here on campus. They have helped me with writing papers and getting tutorial help. Want to come along?

- I make it a practice to introduce myself to each of my professors. That way I can approach them for help. What contacts have you had with your professors outside class so far?

- I had never shared a room with anyone before I came to college, so that was new for me. How are you and your roommate working things out?

- My academic advisor is really busy, but I find if I email her and ask if we can meet in advance, she always fits me in. Have you contacted your advisor?

- I never made a résumé in high school, but it is handy to have one here at college for summer jobs, internships, and some courses. Have you put together a résumé yet?

Note that each prompt recognizes a potential difficulty, offers a shared experience, and invites more thinking on the topic. After presenting a list of conversation prompts, the trainer should pair up the mentors and supervise a round of brief mentoring sessions. Each member should have a chance to play the role of mentor and practice giving personal, academic, social, and career prompts.

The end of the first session emphasizes the importance of using prompts throughout the mentoring experience. As mentors get to know their mentees, the prompts will intensify, and the answers from the mentees will change from short, imprecise answers to longer, more detailed responses. The mentor charts these responses on a weekly contact sheet for the staff counselor. Keeping a record of mentee responses is critically important; in the fourth workshop, the mentors learn to use the information tabulated on the weekly contact sheets to evaluate not only the progress of their mentees but also their own performance as staff members.

SESSION #2: CONTENT OF CONTACTS

Mentors must be trained to understand the importance of networking with pertinent campus departments. Dennis (1993) proposed that mentoring programs should provide three areas of service: educational, career, and personal. If the mentoring program utilizes multiple campus services, then mentors should understand the services and their relationship to the mentoring program. Campus mentoring programs interface with the offices of counseling, financial aid, the treasurer or bursar, the academic resource center, and career and academic advising. Peer mentor training should also focus on the issues that are critical to student success. Trainings that focus on improving student performance and addressing students' individual needs are most effective (Mosqueda & Palaich, 1990).

In the second training session, mentors are schooled in the information they need to answer the questions evoked by the prompts practiced in the first session. In the workshop, mentors should pair up and practice making appropriate referrals under the guidance of the trainer. Until they are familiar with all resources, mentors should use the training manual pages on making referrals to individuals and offices on campus. Training manuals may be in either paper or online format and should be designed so that mentors seeking information about specific concerns can tab to those sections. At DeSales University, training manual topics include discussing concerns with faculty, resolving roommate conflicts, choosing a major, college adjustment issues, depression, family relationships, alcohol, and stress management.

SESSION #3: EXECUTION OF CONTACTS

Trainers need to establish a clear plan of communication contacts for mentors. There are many successful ways for mentors to communicate with mentees; viable options include face-to-face, small-group, telephone, texting, email or Facebook, and written communications. For the first 11 weeks of mentoring at DeSales, mentors make two contacts weekly with mentees, one of which must be an individual conversation (rather than a group session). In this third training session, mentors should learn about and role play each of the communication options permitted by the program.

Mentors can be encouraged to include a shared meal in one of their weekly contacts. Dining together not only lets mentors meet face-to-face with mentees and engage in prompted conversation but also gives mentors an opportunity to observe the mentee's eating habits, which may be relevant for program goals. If food is provided at the training session, mentors can practice appropriate dining and speaking etiquette under the direction of the trainer.

SESSION #4: EVALUATION

The final session of the workshop series asks the question, "Is this student functioning well academically, socially, and personally?" At this meeting, mentors are taught how to review the collection of data they will gather from weekly contacts with their mentees. These data include mentee comments and concerns, attendance at mentor meetings, and an overall review of mentee attitude and performance.

In preparation for this workshop session, the trainer should prepare a mock set of weekly contact sheets or an anonymous set from a recent mentor's records. Working through the contact sheets and attendance records, the trainer should draw mentors' attention to the key assessment indicators the program uses. If the program has established particular metacognitive goals or student learning outcomes, in this session mentors should be trained to recognize and note them.

Because of the importance of referring students appropriately to key departments on campus, the mentors should also practice the referral procedure again. If time is short, the trainer simply calls out the concern and mentors respond with the individual or campus office to which they would refer that concern. If time permits, full role-play scenarios should be performed.

Assessment

Each of the workshop sessions contains an assessment opportunity. In the first and second sessions, the trainer observes carefully as mentors practice their prompts and referrals and provides correction as needed. In the third session, the trainer can use the last 20 minutes of the workshop to observe and assess pairs of mentors practicing their prompts and referrals using conversation, tweets, and phone calls. Although mentors work together in the fourth session to formulate an assessment report using mock or anonymous student contact data, the final section of that workshop could incorporate individual testing; the trainer could supply a new set of anonymous data sheets and have mentors construct reports individually.

Has the training as a whole prepared the mentors to serve their students? Have mentors achieved paraprofessional status? Do mentors understand the cycle of service in which they are engaged? To answer these questions, the trainer uses the mentor contact sheets and end-of- semester evaluations completed by each mentee and mentor. The resulting feedback will assist in ascertaining program effectiveness as well as areas in need of improvement. The end-of-semester and end-of-year assessments determine whether Kuh's (2003) "habits of the mind and heart" (p. 24) have been achieved by the peer mentors when trained as paraprofessionals in the education community.

References

Dennis, G. (1993). *Mentoring* (Consumer Guide No. 7). Washington, DC: Office of Educational Research and Improvement. Retrieved from http://www2.ed.gov/pubs/OR/ConsumerGuides/mentor.html

Freedman, M., & Baker, R. W. (1995). *Workplace mentoring for youth: Context, issues, strategies* (Document No. TD/TNC_71.442). Washington, DC: Academy for Educational Development. Retrieved from ERIC database. (ED381670)

Kuh, G. (2003). What we're learning about student engagement from NSSE: Benchmarks for effective educational practices. *Change, 35*(2), 24–32. Retrieved from http://cpr.iub.edu/uploads/Kuh%20(2003)%20What%20We're%20Learning%20About%20Student%20Engagement%20From%20NSSE.pdf

Mosqueda, P. F., & Palaich, R. (1990). *Mentoring young people makes a difference.* Denver, CO: Education Commission of the States. Retrieved from ERIC database. (ED317945)

National Association of Colleges and Employers. (2010). *FERPA primer: The basics and beyond.* Bethlehem, PA: Author. Retrieved from http://www.naceweb.org/public/ferpa0808.htm

Sherk, J. (1999). *Best practices for mentoring programs.* Folsom, CA: EMT Group. Retrieved from http://www.pathwaystocollege.net/PCNLibrary/ViewBiblio.aspx?aid=450

Sipe, C. L. (1996). *Mentoring: A synthesis of P/PV's research: 1988–1995.* Philadelphia, PA: Public/Private Ventures. Retrieved from http://www.ppv.org/ppv/publication.asp?section_id=-1&search_id=0&publication_id=40

Tinto, V. (2004). *Student retention and graduation: Facing the truth, living with the consequences.* Washington, DC: Pell Institute. Retrieved from http://inpathways.net/TintoOccasionalPaperRetention.pdf

Williams, W. (2000). *Developmental counseling.* SHRM Human Resources Development Committee. Retrieved from http://www.luc.edu/hr/pdfs/devcoun.pdf

Time Management and Goal Setting

 Jennifer L. Smith

Equipping students with the knowledge and tools to prioritize their time effectively and set goals is critical to student success, particularly in the first year. Mentors trained to embrace the importance of mastering these skills can model and teach students to implement them in their own lives. The goals of this training activity include (a) defining time management and goal setting, (b) introducing various methods of implementing time management and goal setting, (c) applying time-management and goal-setting skills, and (d) teaching those skills to a mentee.

For incoming students, time management is more than managing time; it is managing all aspects of their newly independent lives: their studies, social interests, and well-being. Time-management and goal-setting training occurs early in the mentoring relationship so that students can be spared unnecessary stress during the semester.

Chickering's Seven Vectors theory of identity development (Chickering, 1969; Chickering & Reisser, 1993) serves as the framework for this training activity. This psychosocial developmental theory envisions students moving through a series of vectors, which have direction and magnitude rather than steps or stages. In order to develop their identity as mature individuals, students learn to develop competence, manage emotions, move through autonomy toward interdependence, develop mature interpersonal relationships, establish identity, develop purpose, and develop integrity (Chickering & Reisser, 1993; Evans, Forney, Guido, Patton, & Renn, 2010).

This training session on time management and goal setting encompasses both vectors of developing competence and managing emotions. Time management and goal setting are essential skills for students to ascertain and successfully apply because few students arrive on campus knowing how to manage their time well or to plan how to meet their goals (Ender & Newton, 2000). Learning time-management and goal-setting skills propels students along the vector of competence development. Learning to identify wants versus needs moves students forward on the vector of emotion management.

Training Activity

For this training, the trainer should create an environment that promotes a sense of community and ease of learning. If possible, the room should be supplied with movable tables and chairs. The training session can be completed in 90 minutes followed by an additional 30-minute session one week later. Materials for this session include sheets of blank paper (enough for each mentor to have two), writing utensils, copies of a personal time survey, and copies of a blank weekly schedule.

After introductions, if necessary, the trainer should set the expectation that mentor trainees will explore ideas about goal setting and time management in addition to applying those skills. This time is set aside just for them and will be an interactive experience, so the trainer will be looking for their questions and responses throughout the training.

SETTING GOALS

Using a variety of delivery methods during training is important to engage learners across learning preferences. The first exercise involves visual and written techniques. Each mentor needs something to write with and a blank sheet of paper for this activity. Mentors should think about their lives and draw a "road map" of their life from high school graduation to 5 years after college graduation. Significant accomplishments and goals along the way should be signposted in pictures or words. After allowing 15 minutes for mentors to complete their drawings, the trainer should instruct mentors to find a partner and explain the personal road map. For goals that have yet to be accomplished, mentors should describe with their partner how they plan to achieve those goals. After 10 minutes of partner discussion, the trainer can debrief the mentor trainees by asking questions of the whole group, such as, "How does this exercise affect your thinking about goals? How did you feel while you were working through this exercise? Does making the road map help you achieve the goals on your road map?" Discussion can explore how using metacognitive skills in assessing progress toward goals leads to managing time to make them happen. This discussion may require about 10 minutes.

In the next section of the training activity, the trainer presents a method of setting goals, for instance the S.M.A.R.T. method (Doran, 1981; Sanft, Jensen, & McMurray, 2008). S.M.A.R.T. is an acronym of the words *specific, measurable, attainable, relevant,* and *time-limited*—all characteristics of effective goals. The mentor trainees can provide an example of a goal and work through the acronym verbally together, meeting all five criteria to turn the original goal into a S.M.A.R.T. goal statement. The trainer can point out that creating a S.M.A.R.T. goal is an easy activity for mentors and mentees to do at the beginning of each semester. This section of training should take about 10 minutes to complete.

MANAGING TIME

The trainer should then transition to examining time management by asking the mentors how they keep track of their time (e.g., using planner, online calendar, cell phone, smartphone) and inviting them to share with the group what method they use. To get an idea of what the mentors do during a given week, the trainer can have each mentor fill out a 1-week personal time survey; this will take about 10 minutes to complete (George Mason University, 1999). Mentors should then be invited to share with each other how much time they set aside for study, work, classes, exercise, sleep, and eating. Did they find any surprises in their use of time? Can they identify areas for improvement of their use of time? This section of the training should take about 5 minutes.

The trainer then should briefly summarize what mentors have experienced during the session by reminding them of the road map activity, the S.M.A.R.T. method for setting goals, and the time survey. Mentors then should have an opportunity to ask questions; giving trainees an opportunity to implement new knowledge is critical.

The session ends with a challenge. Handing out copies of a blank weekly schedule to the mentors, the trainer asks mentor trainees to write down everything that they do (in 1-hour increments) during the next week. At the end of the week, they should color code their activities with different colored highlighters (e.g., using blue for class hours and yellow for study time). The next training session will begin with group review of their schedules.

FOLLOW-UP SESSION

In the follow-up session the next week, discussion of the color-coded time schedules can begin with questions like these: What did this activity show you about how you use your time? Do you have open times in your schedule that you had not been aware of? How will you know if you are dedicating enough time to study? Are these schedules well balanced? Mentors should be invited to discuss how to use what they have learned to balance their schedules and accomplish their goals.

In the remaining time, mentors should discuss how they will utilize their training experience to teach goal setting and time management to their students. Mentors should be provided with blank versions of their training handouts so they can employ the activities with their own mentees.

Assessment

Learning outcomes for this training include mentors' ability to (a) articulate definitions of time management and goal setting, (b) identify multiple ways of implementing time management and goal setting, and (c) demonstrate how they will implement and approach teaching these skills. Formative assessment during the training can be used to shape the training while it is in process. In this training, informal formative assessment occurs any time the trainer checks for understanding or when mentors provide responses to questions regarding content. The trainer can affirm correct answers and guide students from error through provision of more information and facilitation of group discussion.

Summative assessment at the end of the training experience can be implemented during the follow-up meeting. While reviewing mentors' completed schedules and leading mentors through the suggested questions, trainers are completing informal summative assessment. The experience can be formalized by having an observer take notes, treating the session as a focus group session. Notes from the focus group can be used to improve the next training session.

Trainers may also choose to design a pre-training and post-training survey to have a clearer idea of the extent to which the learning outcomes were achieved. Survey questions would be developed from the learning outcomes anticipated. The survey would be administered to mentors before the training begins and after the training session is complete. Differences between scores before and after training measure learning that took place during the session. The trainer can devise a Likert-type scale letting mentors indicate extent of agreement with each survey item. A sample assessment survey for this training appears in the Appendix. Alternatively, trainers can ask mentors before and after training to define time management and goal setting and describe the relationship between these skills and student success. Mentors could provide answers either orally or in writing.

References

Chickering, A.W. (1969). *Education and identity*. San Francisco, CA: Jossey-Bass.

Chickering, A. W., & Reisser, L. (1993). *Education and identity* (2nd ed.). San Francisco, CA: Jossey-Bass.

Doran, G. T. (1981). There's a S.M.A.R.T. way to write management's goals and objectives. *Management Review, 70*(11), 35–36.

Ender, S. C., & Newton, F. B. (2000). *Students helping students: A guide for peer educators on college campuses*. San Francisco, CA: Jossey-Bass.

Evans, N. J., Forney, D. S., Guido, F. M., Patton, L. D., & Renn, K. A. (2010). *Student development in college: Theory, research, and practice* (2nd ed.). San Francisco, CA: Jossey-Bass.

George Mason University. (1999). Time management tips: Personal time survey. In *Academictips. org*. Retrieved from http://www.academictips.org//.html

Sanft, M., Jensen, M., & McMurray, E. (2008). *Peer mentor companion*. Boston, MA: Houghton Mifflin.

Appendix

TIME-MANAGEMENT AND GOAL-SETTING SURVEY

Please indicate your agreement with the following statements using a 1 (strongly agree), 2 (agree), 3 (neither agree nor disagree), 4 (disagree) or 5 (strongly disagree) for each:

1. I can explain to a peer the concept of goal setting.

2. I am able to identify my goals.

3. I can construct a working plan to achieve my goals.

4. I can articulate a relationship between goal setting and student success.

5. I can explain to a peer the concept of time management.

6. I can discern what type of time management system works best for me.

7. I can articulate a relationship between time management and student success.

Dealing With Difficult Mentoring Situations

DeLandra M. Hunter

Peer mentors who learn a framework for understanding difficult situations that may arise during a session will be equipped to prevent the escalation of such situations. The longer negative situations are ignored, the more they impact mentoring relationships (Eby & McManus, 2004). Mentors are key contributors to the mentoring process. Therefore, "mentors should take the lead in restoring relationships" (Johnson & Ridley, 2004, p. 110). Training sessions should (a) define difficult situations, (b) establish how to measure levels of difficulty, (c) discuss the importance of acknowledging difficult situations, and (d) introduce actions to take when addressing difficult situations.

The sessions described in this training module will provide coordinators with training activities based on the six categories of Bloom's Revised Taxonomy, which are remembering, understanding, applying, analyzing, evaluating, and creating (Anderson & Krathwohl, 2001; Krathwohl, 2002). The levels of intellectual behavior that Bloom found to be important in the acquisition of knowledge (Bloom, Engelhart, Furst, Hill, & Krathwohl, 1956) are the same levels of behavior that mentors will use to determine how best to respond to a difficult situation. Bloom's tiered structure complements the three levels of International Mentor Training Program Certification (IMTPC) by the College Reading and Learning Association (2011), because each level builds on the prior level's learning.

After completing the first training session, peer mentors will be able to explain the importance of acknowledging a difficult situation, recognize and interpret a difficult situation with a protégé, and classify a situation's level of difficulty as low or high. These assessment tasks correspond to Bloom's remembering and understanding levels. After completing the second training session, peer mentors will be able to implement appropriate procedures based on a situation's level of difficulty and differentiate responses based on individual circumstances. They will respond to assessment at the application and analysis levels of Bloom's taxonomy. After completing the third training session, based on Bloom's evaluating and creating levels, peer mentors will be able to create, produce, and critique role-play situations depicting and effectively solving difficult situations between a mentor and a protégé, and facilitate role-play situations in future training sessions for new peer mentors.

Training Activity

Three training sessions are described, corresponding to three levels of IMTPC training (College Reading and Learning Association, 2011). They are offered in three consecutive terms or semesters. The first session requires 45–60 minutes and should take place in a room with space and seating for small-group discussions. For this session the trainer should prepare copies of a handout based on the Appendix to this module, adjusting the names and situations as appropriate. The second session also requires 45–60 minutes. Preferably this session should take place in a room with LCD projector and screen, but it can be accomplished in a room with chalkboards or whiteboards and with sufficient space for seating and group activity. Handouts outlining referral procedures should be prepared. These handouts may be added to each mentor's training handbook (if applicable) at the end of the session. Procedures should be clearly outlined for situations of both low and high levels of difficulty. The third session requires more time (60-90 minutes) and a room with video recording equipment and space and seating for whole-group discussion and role-play situations.

SESSION FOR LEVEL 1: REGULAR CERTIFICATION

The first session begins with the trainer's inquiries to the mentors: What kind of difficult mentoring situation do you hope never to encounter with a protégé? What could happen if this situation is not addressed? After discussing a variety of worst-case scenarios and their effects on the mentoring process, the trainer and mentors should list the situations of greatest concern.

Groups of three or four mentors should be formed and allowed time to choose a group reporter. Each group should receive one or two examples of situations (depending on size of group) using the list of examples in the Appendix and any additional situations that may have arisen in the introductory activity. Each group will discuss (a) what makes each situation difficult and (b) what could happen if a mentor does not address this situation with the protégé. Group reporters should share the results of each group's discussion. As necessary, the trainer should discuss, interpret, clarify, and critique the ideas presented and elicit ideas from the other groups as well.

SESSION FOR LEVEL 2: ADVANCED CERTIFICATION

The trainer should begin this session by clarifying for mentors the difference between situations of low-level difficulty and those of high-level difficulty. A situation with a low level of difficulty is one that can be resolved by the mentor, whereas a situation with a high level of difficulty requires support from the mentoring coordinator or another campus resource with the training, skill, and authority to handle such situations. The trainer then explains the procedures for handling situations of low and high levels of difficulty. These procedures are necessarily different for different programs. In some mentoring locations, licensed counselors and other mental health practitioners are available in the center, and mentors should be instructed to take certain concerns directly to these professionals; in other circumstances, counselors are located far across campus and should be accessed through the mentor coordinator. Mentors, too, may be undergraduates or graduate students, capable of different levels and ranges of responsibility. In consultation with relevant service units in other departments, each program must devise procedures that are appropriate for a variety of situations and student clients while giving primacy to safety, security, efficacy, and confidentiality, and trainers should share these procedures with peer mentors in this training session.

In groups of three or four mentors again, the mentors choose a reporter and are given one or two examples of situations (depending on the size of the entire group) using the list of examples in the Appendix, the additional group-generated situations from the first session, and any difficult mentoring situations that may have come to mind since the first session. Each group will decide (a) whether the situation is of a low or high level of difficulty and (b) what steps the mentor should take to rectify the situation. Each group's reporter should present to the entire group the topic and possible solutions. The trainer and other mentors are responsible for providing feedback on the effectiveness of the sub-group's plan so the sub-group can begin working on role-play situations to be completed the following semester in the third session.

SESSION FOR LEVEL 3: MASTER CERTIFICATION

In the third session, mentors re-form their groups from the second session. In this session, the groups create, plan, practice, and implement role-play situations that demonstrate solutions for the difficult mentoring situations they encountered in the second session. The trainer and other mentors observe carefully each group's performance. It is their responsibility to critique and provide feedback to improve the role-play situations so the group can begin working on developing a video recording.

After groups have made adjustments to their role-play situations to accommodate any concerns, they record all of the scenarios. These video recordings are used as podcasts for IMTPC Level 1 and 2 online training sessions. In addition, the mentors create an assessment based on activities of the first session to accompany the use of the videos for online training sessions. At the end of the third session, the mentors upload the video and assessment.

Assessment

At the end of the first training session, mentors should answer these questions individually, in writing: What is a difficult situation? Why should mentors acknowledge a difficult situation? What are some possible outcomes if situations are not addressed? The trainer can ask trainees to write creative public service announcements (PSAs) for a radio broadcast based on their individual responses to these questions. PSAs should be presentable in 30 seconds or less. Trainers can have participants select the best PSA based on criteria established by the trainer.

At the end of the second training session, mentors should answer these questions: What is the difference between low-level and high-level difficult situations? How should a mentor handle a situation of high-level difficulty? How should a mentor handle a situation of low-level difficulty? After answering the questions, trainees can create a "Best Practices for Dealing with Difficult Mentoring Situations" tip sheet. In this document, mentors can list their thoughts on how best to handle situations of low and high levels of difficulty.

By the end of the third training session, mentors will have generated examples of difficult situations and created and facilitated role-play situations for IMTPC Level 1 and 2 podcast training. They will also have helped the trainer critique the effectiveness of mentors' responses in the role-play situations in the first and second sessions. The trainer can observe the mentors at work and assess the knowledge and skill of these mentors by their contributions to discussion. The trainer should also assess mentors' judgment in producing a role-play video that captures both essential difficulties and appropriate solutions.

References

Anderson, L. W., & Krathwohl, D. R. (Eds.). (2001). *A taxonomy for learning, teaching, and assessing: A revision of Bloom's taxonomy of educational objectives.* New York, NY: Addison, Wesley, Longman.

Bloom, B. S. (Ed.), Engelhart, M. D., Furst, E. J., Hill, W. H., & Krathwohl, D. R. (1956). *Taxonomy of educational objectives: The classification of educational goals. Handbook 1: Cognitive domain.* New York, NY: David McKay.

College Reading and Learning Association. (2011). *IMTPC certification requirements.* Retrieved from http://www.crla.net/imtpc/certification_requirements.htm

Eby, L. T., & McManus, S. E. (2004). The protégé's role in negative mentoring experiences. *Journal of Vocational Behavior, 65,* 255–275.

Johnson, W. B., & Ridley, C. R. (2004). *The elements of mentoring.* New York, NY: Palgrave Macmillan.

Krathwohl, D. R. (2002). A revision of Bloom's taxonomy: An overview. *Theory Into Practice, 41,* 212–218. doi:10.1207/s15430421tip4104_2

Appendix

EXAMPLES OF CHALLENGING SITUATIONS MENTORS MAY ENCOUNTER

Example 1

Melanie, your protégé, tells you she is not happy in college. She is having a hard time making friends. She feels lonely, and there is no one she can talk to. She mentions that she has been so depressed she has contemplated suicide.

Example 2

David is having a hard time adjusting to the diverse cultural atmosphere in college. David admits to not knowing how to relate to people of different ethnic groups. He says he cannot really trust people outside his race.

Example 3

Dani reports to you how well she did on her chemistry test yesterday thanks to your advice as a mentor to make note cards from which to study. She found them so helpful that she not only studied from the note cards but used them during the test.

Example 4

Since coming to college, Allen has become more open with his sexuality, as he has met several gay students who can identify with his situation. Recently, Allen told his parents, and they threatened to disown him. They have not spoken to him in over 2 weeks.

Example 5

Marcus tells you that every weekend he gets together with his fraternity brothers and drinks until he cannot remember what happened the previous night. He does not think that he has a problem, because he is just having fun.

Example 6

For the past few weeks your protégé Pat has called you several times to ask you over to socialize in the evening. You know that Pat is attracted to you.

Example 7

During several of your mentoring sessions with your protégé Fante, she has sent text messages to others while you are having a conversation with her.

Example 8

You have gone to a few campus events with your protégé Lauren. Each time you have smelled Lauren's body odor, and other students have talked about her at the events.

Example 9

Hunter complains to you that he cannot understand his professor's speech because his professor is from another country.

Example 10

Right before an exam, Edward feels short of breath and forgets most of the course material he has studied for weeks.

Helping Students Explore Career Choices

Mark F. Daddona

Many students enter college with concerns about choosing a major and matching majors to career options (Gordon, 1995). A national study of first-year students in the U.S. found that 21.6% of students remained undecided about a major and 33.8% changed majors in the first year (Liu, Sharkness, & Pryor, 2008). It has been estimated that 75% of all undergraduates change majors at least once (Gordon, 1995). Not surprisingly, studies of freshman needs have found career and academic concerns to be more important than personal or social needs, both before and after participating in an orientation program (Daddona, 2000; Daddona & Cooper, 2002). Earlier studies (Kramer & Washburn, 1983; Mudd, 1984) discovered that career planning and academic needs were students' most important concerns both before and after orientation.

Having clear career plans or goals can positively impact a student's decision to remain in college (Tinto, 1993). Students reporting job-related career goals have been more likely to persist in college than students without career goals (Hull-Blanks et al., 2005). Certainty about occupational choice, academic achievement, and college readiness, separately and combined, improve the odds that students will attain college degrees and jobs consistent with their occupational choices (ACT, 2009), perhaps because the most important reasons for going to college are a strong career orientation and desire for a better job (Levine & Cureton, 1998; Pryor, Hurtado, Saenz, Santos, & Korn, 2008). Earning more money was a very important reason to go to college for 69% of students surveyed in 2006, up from 50% in 1976 (Pryor et al., 2008).

Not having certainty about a major, however, is appropriate for many first-year students, who must be helped to understand "that initial decisions may be tentative and changing their minds is not only acceptable but often desirable behavior" (Gordon, 1995, p. 63). Therefore, this training activity provides peer mentors with basic skills and tools to support students' career development. Of course, peer mentors cannot replace the professional staff employed in institutional career centers. Mentors can begin the exploration process with students and educate them about the numerous resources available, including the institution's career center.

Training Activity

No specific room set-up is needed. Each of the five training activities can be accomplished in 30 minutes, with additional time required outside the sessions to complete assignments.

ACTIVITY 1: CAREER INTERVIEW WARM-UP

To encourage mentors to begin thinking about their own career development, they practice conducting career exploration interviews with one another. Mentors should be reminded that because they are not career professionals their interviews will always be friendly peer inquiries rather than career assessments.

Students let go of their childhood interests for a variety of reasons, but often because bias and perceived limits constrain their choices. The following questions seek to explore the dreams, values, and skills on which career exploration can be based.

- As a child, what did you want to be when you grew up? How has this ambition changed?

- What are the careers of family members and other significant people in your life?

- What knowledge, skills, and abilities do you have that may be useful in potential careers?

- What majors are you considering? Why these?

Trainees then present brief introductions of their interview partners to the rest of the staff, using any upbeat and affirming information they have learned from the interview.

ACTIVITY 2: A CAREER DECISION-MAKING PROCESS

Students without a strategic approach to selecting a major and career may make decisions with little information about what may fit well with their values and interests, and with limited research about requirements and expectations of the career. One process of making career decisions consists of gathering personal information or knowledge of oneself (traits), then gathering realistic information about the world of work for the careers of interest (factors). This trait and factor approach, which is based on the early work of vocational counselor Frank Parsons (1909/1989), is still fundamental to career counseling (Sharf, 1997).

The trainer should provide each mentor with a copy of the career decision model (Figure 1). Mentors should be given time to start outlining information they already have and what they need to learn to complete the process. They can discover knowledge about themselves from reviewing findings of the career interview activity, thinking about the life they envision for themselves and their families, and considering results of career assessments.

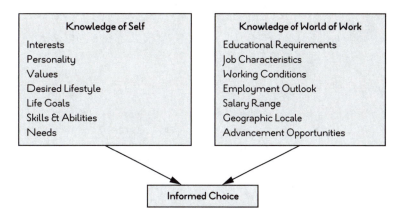

FIGURE 1   Career decision–making process using trait and factor knowledge for informed choice (designed by Daddona based on the work of Parsons (1909/1989) and Sharf (1997).

ACTIVITY 3: WEBSITES FOR EXPLORING KNOWLEDGE OF SELF AND THE WORLD OF WORK

Some of the information needed to make good career decisions can be found on free online websites. Mentors can be assigned to gather information related to their own career exploration from one or more of the following sites and share discoveries at the next training session:

- HumanMetrics Jung Typology Test (similar to Myers-Briggs Type Indicator [MBTI] but developed in Israel and available free of charge at www.humanmetrics.com): After completing this 72-item assessment, students will learn their four-letter personality type, a description of the type, and a list of careers that match their profile well.

- Occupational Outlook Handbook, developed by the U.S. Department of Labor, available free of charge at www.bls.gov/oco: This source features hundreds of jobs, qualifications and required training, employment, job outlook, projection data, earnings, related occupations, and sources of additional information.

- CareerOneStop, another U.S. Department of Labor site, at www.alx.org: This portal links to sites for browsing occupations and exploring green careers, military transitions, disaster recovery services, and salary information.

- Occupational Information Network (O*Net), also provided by the U.S. Department of Labor, at online.onetcenter.org: This site provides detailed descriptions of careers and resources, including information about occupations that are going green.

ACTIVITY 4: CAMPUS CAREER RESOURCES

Depending upon the organizational structure and specific functions of departments at an institution, the location of career information, assessments, and career counseling will vary. When campus career services are offered in a counseling center, mentors should be trained to resolve any negative notions students may have about participating in counseling. Mentor trainers should get to know campus career specialists, become knowledgeable about resources available on the career service website(s), and gather print materials to share with mentors in training. At larger universities each college may have its own career and placement services. In these instances the trainer should provide or help trainees develop an organizational chart of services available at the institution.

For this training activity, trainers should arrange for peer mentors to visit career services as a group for a workshop with a campus career professional. Mentors should then schedule individual meetings to explore their own career decisions with specialists and utilize assessments that may be available on campus. Mentors should share with each other at a future meeting or on their mentor weblog the information from these sessions they think will be useful to other mentors as they coach students to meet with campus career services professionals.

ACTIVITY 5: GATHERING INFORMATION FROM PEOPLE IN CAREERS

Mentors can also gain insights into potential careers by exploring the actual working life of individuals in that career.

- Informational interviews: Mentors schedule an appointment with a professional in the career of interest. Mentors ask questions based on the items listed under Knowledge of World of Work in Figure 1. A tour of the workplace should also be requested.

- Job shadowing: Mentors schedule a partial or full day to shadow an individual in the career of interest. Mentors participate in all activities with the job holder and see what a typical day is like on the job.

- Informal conversations: Mentors should be alert to opportunities to ask people about their work. These conversations can be informal, such as at social functions or while waiting in line. Many people like to talk about their work.

Mentors should discuss the three options, brainstorm possible individuals for each of them to contact, and create a list of questions to ask based on the Knowledge of World of Work section of the career decision model already discussed. Mentors should share with each other at the next training session or on their mentor weblog the information from these experiences that they think will be useful to other mentors as they coach students to explore the world of work.

Assessment

Each of the five career training activities contains its own assessment. Trainers can assess mentors' understanding of conducting a career interview by observing the introductions they give of their interview partners in Activity 1. Do mentors demonstrate the required respect and discretion? To demonstrate their knowledge of the career decision-making process in the model in Activity 2, mentors can report what they already know and what they need to research to complete their model. In Activity 3, trainers can monitor the mentors' reports or weblog entries on their use of career websites as they discuss, in person or in writing, how two of the websites they used furthered their "knowledge of self" or "knowledge of the world of work." If appropriate, mentors can print and submit relevant information from these sites to support their conclusions.

After meeting with a campus career professional in Activity 4, mentors can be asked to report on the deepening or broadening of their own career decision knowledge. Mentors can also report on what they have learned to help them better refer students to the institution's career specialists. Finally, mentors can report on what they have learned about the world of work from their interviews, informal conversations, and job shadowing activities in Activity 5. These reports may be written for the trainer to evaluate or presented to the other mentors in training. Trainers should note that they are evaluating the process of developing informed choice and wise referral skills; assessment should not preference mentors who validate their previous choice of a major and career over those who consider possible alternatives to their earlier choice.

References

ACT. (2009). *The path to career success: High school achievement, certainty of career choice, and college readiness make a difference.* Iowa City, IA: Author. Retrieved from http://www.act.org/research/policymakers/pdf/PathCareerSuccess.pdf

Daddona, M. F. (2000). *The perceived needs of freshmen prior to and after participation in a college orientation program* (Doctoral dissertation). Available from ProQuest Dissertations & Theses database. (Order No. 9984118)

Daddona, M. F., & Cooper, D. L. (2002). Comparison of freshman perceived needs prior to and after participation in an orientation program. *NASPA Journal, 39,* 300–318.

Gordon, V. N. (1995). *The undecided college student: An academic and career advising challenge.* Springfield, IL: C. C. Thomas.

Hull-Blanks, E., Kurpius, S. E. R., Befort, C., Sollenberger, S., Nicpon, M. F., & Huser, L. (2005). Career goals and retention-related factors among college freshmen. *Journal of Career Development, 32*(1), 16–30. doi:10.1177/0894845305277037

Kramer, G. L., & Washburn, R. (1983). The perceived needs of new students. *Journal of College Student Personnel, 24,* 311–319.

Levine, A., & Cureton, J. S. (1998). *When hope and fear collide.* San Francisco, CA: Jossey-Bass.

Liu, A., Sharkness, J., & Pryor, J. H. (2008). *Findings from the 2007 administration of Your First College Year (YFCY): National aggregates.* Los Angeles, CA: University of California-Los Angeles, Higher Education Research Institute. Retrieved from http://www.heri.ucla.edu/PDFS/YFCY_2007_Report05-07-08.pdf

Mudd, M. A. (1984). *Concerns of entering freshmen as perceived by entering freshmen, parents, and faculty at the University of Nebraska at Omaha* (Doctoral dissertation). Available from ProQuest Dissertations & Theses database. (Order No. 8509869)

Parsons, F. (1909/1989). *Choosing a vocation. A reprint of the original 1909 work.* Broken Arrow, OK: National Career Development Association.

Pryor, J. H., Hurtado, S., Saenz, V. B., Santos, J. L., & Korn, W. S. (2008, January). The American freshman, forty-year trends: 1966–2006. *HERI Research Brief,* Higher Education Research Institute at UCLA. Retrieved from http://www.heri.ucla.edu/PDFs/pubs/briefs/40yrTrendsResearchBrief.pdf

Sharf, R. S. (1997). *Applying career development theory to counseling* (2nd ed.). Pacific Grove, CA: Brooks/Cole.

Tinto, V. (1993). *Leaving college: Rethinking the causes and cures of student attrition.* Chicago, IL: University of Chicago Press.

Sustaining Students Through Crisis and Failure

Jennifer E. Bruce

Peer mentoring, by definition, is a "structured and trusting relationship that brings young people together with caring peers who offer guidance, support, and encouragement aimed at developing the competence and character of the mentee" (National Mentoring Partnership, 2005). So many colleges provide this support for students who may be at risk for academic failure that peer mentoring has become "an essential aspect of student life" (Budge, 2006, p. 73). The goal of this training module is to develop peer mentors' questioning skills. Mentors should use thoughtful questions to discover if a student is in crisis, classify the types of crises into referral categories, make appropriate campus referrals, and understand the boundaries of their jobs as peer mentors. Mentors who possess such skills will be better prepared to assist mentored students in moving from crisis to success.

The learning support literature abounds with reports of the benefits of mentoring college students (Brown, David, & McClendon, 1999; Ferrari, 2004; McLean, 2004; Quinn, Muldoon, & Hollingworth, 2002). Benefits for mentees in crisis may include the opportunity to develop close working relationships and discuss personal issues with sympathetic peers (Ferrari, 2004), acquire assistance with academic success strategies that lead to retention (Bruce & Trammell, 2003; Mee-Lee & Bush, 2003), and discover motivation for persistence (Packard, 2003). Mentees benefit, as well: they may improve their self-esteem, gain academic confidence, and learn better self-discipline through continuous guidance and encouragement from their peers (Peer Mentoring, 2011).

Some students who are being mentored may be dealing with various types of difficulties or crises that interfere with their ability to function as students. If unresolved, these difficulties may lead to absence from class, failure to complete assignments, or even academic failure or withdrawal. Mentors with appropriate training can play a major role in coaching students through crisis situations. To accomplish this, mentors' decision-making skills need to include training in the recognition of crises and the special processes involved in referring students quickly and appropriately to additional campus resources. These specialized skills complement other mentoring skills. Strong recognition and referral skills are important qualities that contribute to the success of a competent mentor (National College of Ireland, n.d.) and consequently to the success of mentoring programs as a whole.

Mentoring is usually viewed as one element of a larger support effort, and the existence of a college or university mentoring program presupposes an institutional commitment to retain such students. Retaining students means saving tuition monies. Retaining students also aids in maintaining acceptable retention rates, demonstrates institutional commitment to equal access, and promotes institutional efficiency. When a student is in crisis, peer mentoring can be part of a campus commitment to help all students feel welcome and included, assist the school in maintaining a diverse student population, and increase the likelihood that students who matriculate will also graduate (Budge, 2006; Engstrom & Tinto, 2008; Kuh, Cruce, Shoup, & Kinzie, 2008; Lynn, 2010).

In my experience, most student crises can be categorized into four major types—physical, social, emotional, and academic—although each of these types of crises can have implications for the others. Physical crises include illness, injury, and other physiological impediments that affect students' physical ability to attend class or complete academic work. Social crises include those difficulties that occur primarily outside the classroom environment and may include poor transitioning from high school to college, immature or poorly developed social skills, lack of intercultural understanding and communication skills, difficulties adjusting to roommates, and other problems that are primarily interpersonal in nature. Negative emotional crises are psychological upsets that interfere with students' ability to function, including psychological disabilities such as clinical depression or bipolar disorder. Emotional crises may also result from responses to life problems, including parents' divorce, death of a family member or friend, financial worries, relationship difficulties, perceived stigma related to some aspect of the student's social identity, undiagnosed disability, or even apparently positive transitions and stressors affecting emotional stability. Academic crises, which may result from any of the other types or exist independently, are difficulties that result in and from poor academic progress. Indicators of academic crises may be conditional admission, failed tests, low midterm grades, and academic warning.

Students facing these challenges need support and assistance from their peer mentors. Peer mentors who have developed referral skills can contribute significantly to building success for students by directing them to appropriate campus resources and professionals.

Training Activity

One room with movable chairs is required for this training activity. The room should either provide wall space for hanging posters or be equipped with whiteboards or chalkboards. Handouts should be created from Appendices A–D and copied for the mentors. Four posters labeled physical crises, emotional crises, social crises, and academic crises should be taped to the walls around the training room, or these category titles should be written on the board. Approximately 1 hour is required for the instruction and activity.

The trainer should first introduce mentors to the four kinds of crises that students commonly experience, ask mentors to provide examples of each of the four types, and discuss each. Some examples may consist of two or more types of crises together, such as spending too much time socializing (social crisis) that leads to poor academic performance (academic crisis). The trainer then should divide the large group into smaller groups of three or four mentors each and distribute to trainees the handout, "Examples of Student Crises" (Appendix A). Group members should discuss examples and reach group consensus about the type of crisis each example represents. A scribe from each group writes the examples on the correctly titled poster or whiteboard. Trainer and mentors then discuss results, noting differences among groups or multiple listings.

Mentors should then discuss the handout, "Question Tree" (Appendix B), which provides questions mentors may ask to help them determine the primary type of crisis a student is reporting. In a brief practice session, mentors can offer concerns for other mentors to inquire about and categorize.

The trainer then can discuss with mentors the handout, "Campus Referral Process" (Appendix C), an outline of the steps mentors may use to make appropriate referrals based on the type of crisis the student is experiencing. This handout can be revised by mentor trainers to reflect the types and titles of specific services available at the institution and the policies for referral of students to services. Discussion should include what to do if the crisis is an amalgam of two or more types of crises.

Mentors can return to the large group to brainstorm the parameters of the mentor's job. Together they should determine where the mentor's job ends, using the handout, "A Mentor's Role" (Appendix D). Mentors should add to the handout other limits to their authority and scope as they arise in discussion.

Assessment

To assess mentors' knowledge of their role in responding to students in crisis, the trainer may have each of the small groups select one of the crisis types and develop a brief role-playing scenario. Each scenario should demonstrate how the mentor guides mentees through the campus referral process—which will vary from institution to institution—using the steps outlined in Appendix C. The trainer evaluates these scenarios as they are played out and redirects as necessary. Mentors who constitute the audience should be alert to missed opportunities or overstepped boundaries and question the players about them.

References

Brown, M. C., David, G. L., & McClendon, S. A. (1999). Mentoring graduate students of color: Myths, models, and modes. *Peabody Journal of Education, 74*, 105–119. doi:10.1108/02610150710735471

Bruce, J., & Trammell, J. (2003). Impact of paired tutoring and mentoring. *The Learning Assistance Review, 8*(2), 20–28.

Budge, S. (2006). Peer mentoring in postsecondary education: Implications for research and practice. *Journal of College Reading and Learning, 37*(1), 71–85.

Engstrom, C., & Tinto, V. (2008). Access without support is not opportunity. *Change, 40*(1), 46–50.

Ferrari, J. R. (2004). Mentors in life and at school: Impact on undergraduate protégé perceptions of university mission and values. *Mentoring & Tutoring, 12*, 295–307. doi:10.1080/030910042000275909

Kuh, G. D., Cruce, T. M., Shoup, R., & Kinzie, J. (2008). Unmasking the effects of student engagement on first-year college grades and persistence. *Journal of Higher Education, 79*, 540–563. doi:10.1353/jhe.0.0019

Lynn, C. (2010, September). Student peer mentoring in a hospitality management program. *Techniques*, 52–54.

McLean, M. (2004). Does the curriculum matter in peer mentoring? From mentee to mentor in problem-based learning: A unique case study. *Mentoring & Tutoring, 12*, 173–188. doi: 10.1080/1361126042000239929

Mee-Lee, L., & Bush, T. (2003). Student mentoring in higher education: Hong Kong Baptist University. *Mentoring & Tutoring, 11*, 263–271. doi:10.1080/1361126032000138319

National College of Ireland. (n.d.). *Peer mentor manual*. Retrieved from http://www.ncirl.ie/dynamic/File/Student%20Support%20Publications/Peer%20Mentor%20Manual.pdf

National Mentoring Partnership. (2005). *How to build a successful mentoring program using the element of effective practice*. Retrieved from http://www.mentoring.org/downloads/mentoring_413.pdf

Packard, B. W. (2003). Student training promotes mentoring awareness and action. *Career Development Quarterly, 51*, 335–345.

Peer mentoring. (2011). Pomona, CA: California State Polytechnic University, Pomona. Retrieved from http://dsa.csupomona.edu/ssep/peer.asp

Post, M., Montgomery, J., & Storey, K. (2009). A decision tree for the use of auditory prompting strategies. *Journal of Vocational Rehabilitation, 31*, 51–54. doi:10.3233/JVR-2009-0472

Quinn, F., Muldoon, R., & Hollingworth, A. (2002). Formal academic mentoring: A pilot scheme for first-year science students at a regional university. *Mentoring & Tutoring, 10*, 21–33. doi:10.1080/13611260220133126

Appendix A

LIST OF STUDENT CRISES

1. Academic probation

2. Alcohol abuse

3. Anxiety about school performance

4. Break-up with significant other

5. Death of friend or family member

6. Difficulty making academic work a priority

7. Discrimination

8. Drug use

9. Failing a course

10. Fear of academic failure

11. Fight with friend

12. Financial difficulties

13. Homesickness

14. Illness

15. Inattention in classes

16. Injury

17. Inappropriate classroom behavior

18. Job commitments

19. Lack of motivation to complete academic work

20. Little sense of belonging to the academic community

21. Limited understanding of course material

22. Limited understanding of instructor's directions

23. Low GPA

24. Misplaced priorities

25. Not interested in course material

26. Not making friends

27. Over-commitment; too much to do

28. Poor study strategies

29. Pregnancy

30. Psychiatric disability

31. Roommate difficulties

32. Sadness

33. Shyness

34. Stress

35. Suicidal thoughts

36. Surgery

37. Tardiness to class

38. Target of bullying

39. Time management issues

40. Victim of rape or other violent attack

Appendix B

QUESTION TREE*

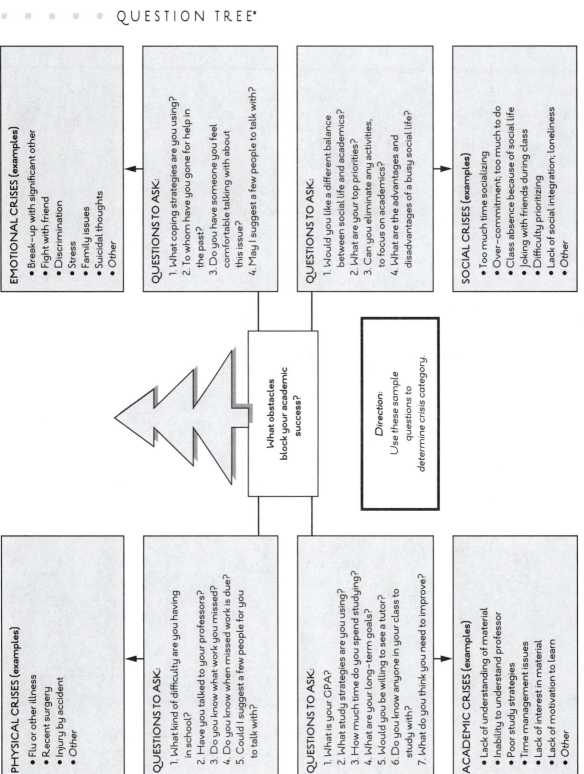

EMOTIONAL CRISES (examples)
- Break-up with significant other
- Fight with friend
- Discrimination
- Stress
- Family issues
- Suicidal thoughts
- *Other*

QUESTIONS TO ASK:
1. What coping strategies are you using?
2. To whom have you gone for help in the past?
3. Do you have someone you feel comfortable talking with about this issue?
4. May I suggest a few people to talk with?

SOCIAL CRISES (examples)
- Too much time socializing
- Over-commitment; too much to do
- Class absence because of social life
- Joking with friends during class
- Difficulty prioritizing
- Lack of social integration; loneliness
- *Other*

QUESTIONS TO ASK:
1. Would you like a different balance between social life and academics?
2. What are your top priorities?
3. Can you eliminate any activities, to focus on academics?
4. What are the advantages and disadvantages of a busy social life?

What obstacles block your academic success?

Direction:
Use these sample questions to determine crisis category.

PHYSICAL CRISES (examples)
- Flu or other illness
- Recent surgery
- Injury by accident
- *Other*

QUESTIONS TO ASK:
1. What kind of difficulty are you having in school?
2. Have you talked to your professors?
3. Do you know what work you missed?
4. Do you know when missed work is due?
5. Could I suggest a few people for you to talk with?

QUESTIONS TO ASK:
1. What is your GPA?
2. What study strategies are you using?
3. How much time do you spend studying?
4. What are your long-term goals?
5. Would you be willing to see a tutor?
6. Do you know anyone in your class to study with?
7. What do you think you need to improve?

ACADEMIC CRISES (examples)
- Lack of understanding of material
- Inability to understand professor
- Poor study strategies
- Time management issues
- Lack of interest in material
- Lack of motivation to learn
- *Other*

*Decision trees or question trees have been used for several decades to teach decision-making skills. They are often used in education, vocational rehabilitation, and cognitive therapy. For example, see Post, M., Montgomery, J., & Storey, K. (2009). A decision tree for the use of auditory prompting strategies. *Journal of Vocational Rehabilitation, 31,* 51–54. doi:10.3233/JVR-2009-0472

Appendix C

● ● ● ● ● SAMPLE CAMPUS REFERRAL PROCESS

Meet with mentee to determine type of crisis

↓

Use question tree model (Appendix B)

↓

Categorize crisis

↓

Make referral based on type of crisis

PHYSICAL CRISIS

Primary Referral:
- Clinical and Health Services

Secondary Referrals:
- Disability Support Office
- Advisor
- Residence Life Office
- Coach/Trainer

EMOTIONAL CRISIS

Primary Referral:
- Counseling Center

Secondary Referrals:
- Advisor
- Roommate or Friends
- Ombudsperson
- Chaplain
- Coach

ACADEMIC CRISIS

Primary Referral:
- Academic Advisor

Secondary Referrals:
- Professors
- Academic Support Center
- Counseling Center
- Disability Support Center
- Peer Mentor
- Coach
- Tutor

SOCIAL CRISIS

Primary Referral:
- Office of Student Life

Secondary Referrals:
- Office of Residence Life
- Orientation Leader
- Resident Assistant
- Advisor
- Friends or Roommate

Appendix D

• • • • • • A MENTOR'S ROLE

A mentor's role IS to establish a comfortable working relationship:

- ❑ Get to know the student.
- ❑ Be open, caring, encouraging, and positive.
- ❑ Respect and value each student as an individual.

A mentor's role IS to help students deal with concerns:

- ❑ Ask questions to determine the student's areas of need.
- ❑ Attend to spoken and unspoken responses
- ❑ Assist the student to identify areas of need.
- ❑ Make on-campus referrals to appropriate support agents and offices.
- ❑ Offer friendly tips, reminders, and support.

A mentor's role is NOT to do this:

- ❑ Be a professional counselor.
- ❑ Solve students' personal problems.
- ❑ Act as an authority figure.
- ❑ Diagnose problems.
- ❑ Judge students' behavior.
- ❑ Scold, criticize, or show disappointment.

After discussion, please complete the following statement: I believe that my primary role as a peer academic mentor is

_____

_____

_____

_____

Introduction

The final chapter in this handbook offers a rich array of topics related to tutor and mentor training support. In brief, these modules provide a short course in creating, funding, institutionalizing, staffing, and evaluating a tutor or mentor program.

Few trainers of peer tutors and mentors have direct educational preparation for their role in the learning center. Trainers generally must shape their own professional development through participating in activities of professional organizations like the College Reading and Learning Association (CRLA) and by reading intentionally in the field. The authors of these Chapter 6 modules address trainers' need for professional advice by providing information from their own experience and pointing the way to other resources. Readers should also check the CRLA website (at www.crla.net/handbook/) for updated resources provided by the authors.

The nine modules are organized in a chronology of program development. Authors of the first three modules explain how to create a program and foster its growth, gather campus support, and seek external funding. The next three modules focus on interviewing and selecting students to staff the program. The final three modules describe how to observe and evaluate student staff, their training, and the program. From evaluation can come the realization that more or different training is needed, and the cycle begins again to reach a higher level of proficiency and expertise.

Designing and Implementing a Holistic Mentor Training Program

Colleen Rustad–Sampson and Kristine Noll Carnes

Postsecondary success and persistence to graduation are dependent on a variety of student, situational, and institutional factors. For this reason, Koehler and Burke (1996) urged college success professionals to address emotional, intellectual, and social dimensions of student development. In addition, Tinto (1998) reported that students' broader involvement with their institution, satisfaction with the college experience, and overall positive perception of the institution correlate with campus involvement. Thus, holistic mentor training must prepare mentors to evaluate strengths and weaknesses in a student's study habits and time management skills, levels of health and wellness, satisfaction with the chosen major or knowledge regarding career options, level of campus involvement and connectedness, and financial resources.

The goal of this module is to provide guidelines for the design and implementation of a mentor training program that meets the holistic needs of mentees. The training concepts presented in this module center in the mentoring model: interpersonal learning is planned, collaborative, and supportive of mentees, and mentees are active and reflective participants in the relationship. Research in educational psychology that draws from self-efficacy and learning-centered models (Bandura, 1986) grounds the pedagogy of holistic mentor training. Utilizing these frameworks, holistic training programs guide mentors to provide to student clients a structured experience that supports these students in persisting to graduation by staying committed to their academic, social, career, and health and wellness goals. This training structure provides mentors with a clear understanding of their roles and helps them address key issues related to college success.

This module will provide information for trainers to begin to prepare peer mentors. It includes general information about mentor training, the core content that should be included in mentor training, and a sample College Reading and Learning Association (CRLA, 2011) International Mentor Training Program Certification (IMTPC) Level 2 training curriculum (see Appendix for the sample training curriculum).

Mentoring Competency Topics for Training

It is important to determine the learning outcomes that connect the mentor program's goals and philosophy to the needs of both mentors and mentees. Questions to ask in the development of a new mentor training program include the following: To whom are we providing mentoring? Why do these students need mentoring? What are the strengths and challenges involved with working with this population? Who are our mentors? What issues must be addressed to prepare mentors for mentoring this target population? What outcomes do we hope to achieve as a result of our mentoring efforts?

When these questions have been answered and the learning outcomes established, mentor training topics can be determined. The following is an overview of the mentoring competency topics described in this module: (a) defining the mentor role, (b) establishing boundaries, (c) building collaborative relationships, (d) developing communication and listening skills, (e) respecting diversity, and (f) making timely and appropriate referrals.

THE ROLE OF THE MENTOR

Defining the role of a mentor during training is crucial in helping mentors understand the parameters of the mentoring relationship and develop realistic expectations about their role. The mentor role includes providing academic assistance (e.g., study and test-taking strategies), assisting with career exploration, encouraging campus engagement, and providing emotional support. Mentors will rely upon their active listening skills to ensure that they understand students' needs and must learn to assess mentee strengths and weaknesses in order to develop appropriate goals. Mentors also need to understand their responsibilities with regard to the Family Educational Rights and Privacy Act, or FERPA (2008). The mentoring role does not include doing a student's homework or editing papers, tutoring in a specific subject, counseling on personal issues, or accepting students' excuses for failing to accomplish tasks.

ESTABLISHING AND MAINTAINING HEALTHY BOUNDARIES

Knapp's relational development model provides information that will assist mentors in developing a mentoring relationship while establishing and maintaining healthy boundaries (Knapp & Vangelisti, 2008). This practical model identifies five stages in the coming-together phase of relationship development (initiation, experimenting, intensifying, integrating, and bonding), and five stages in the coming-apart phase (differentiating, circumscribing, stagnating, avoiding, and terminating).

In order to establish appropriate boundaries while building the mentoring relationship, a mentor must understand and explain the mentor's role to the mentee. The mentor should always model desired behaviors and habits for success while remaining empathic and supportive of the mentee. In addition, creating and following guidelines for mentoring sessions will ensure that goals are achieved while boundaries are maintained. Finally, mentors need to understand procedures for consulting with supervisors and coordinators on a regular basis.

Scenarios are useful small-group activities for mentors learning to establish boundaries and relationships with mentees. The trainer should create scenarios from real or likely situations (e.g., the mentee invites the mentor to a party, tweets late at night about being lonely, or asks the mentor to proofread a research paper) and allow adequate time for mentors to discuss scenarios before acting them out. Mentors might then be asked to brainstorm other issues that may arise, as well as possible solutions. Experienced mentors can provide scenario topics to challenge new mentors, or experienced mentors may role play challenging scenarios to model appropriate behavior for the new mentors' benefit.

BUILDING A COLLABORATIVE RELATIONSHIP

A collaborative relationship is essential to gain mentees' trust and respect. Mentors should listen, ask questions, and summarize what student clients are saying to show understanding of their concerns and strengths. In the first one-on-one meeting with a mentee, a mentor should spend time getting to know the student and working together to articulate the mentee's goals. To support this process, the trainer should provide (or trainer and mentors can work together to create) an initial intake interview with open-ended questions around key target areas for the mentor to utilize in sessions. Questions could include the following:

- On a scale of 1-10 (10 being high), how would you rate your desire to be here on campus? What would make it a 10?

- What do you think or hope your college education will do for you?

- What are your current special interests and activities, and how frequently do you participate in them?

- What activities would you like to learn about or become involved in this year?

- Briefly describe areas of strength (e.g., being good at math) and weakness (e.g., difficulty with English or time management).

- Can you tell me about the people in your life who tend to be on your side or help you feel better when you're down? Who are the people in your life who count on you as a friend or source of support?

- How do you meet new people here?

The guided interview questions will help mentors assess strengths and areas for improvement and then assist students in developing a personalized plan aimed at achieving the stated goals. Trainers should allow time during training for mentors to pair up and practice their interviewing skills with each other.

COMMUNICATION AND LISTENING SKILLS

Effective communication and candid feedback are essential to a successful mentoring relationship. One of the most important aspects of a mentoring relationship is how the mentor provides advice and feedback to the mentee, and how the mentee responds. Mentors should be trained to provide feedback in a positive and constructive manner. To engage in respectful listening, mentors must consider a student's perspective and feelings. As a practice activity, the trainer can divide mentors into small groups and provide each group with a student statement. Mentors should attempt to identify from the statement what the student may be feeling. Mentors can be invited to offer typical but ineffectual responses before finally constructing effective responses that acknowledge and respond to the student's feelings. For example, if a student says, "I hate my biology class and the professor is a jerk," mentors in the small group may identify the feelings behind that statement as frustration and fear. It would be thoughtless and therefore ineffective to respond, "Bio is tough, but don't worry, you'll do fine if you work hard." A more effective response would be, "You seem really concerned about that course. Let's talk about it and see exactly what's troubling you."

As displayed in the example above, training should provide some basic guidelines for effective communication, such as making communication positive; allowing time for mentees to talk without interruption; showing interest in the discussion; paying attention to body language, how things are said, and what is said; asking clarifying questions; and offering examples rather than advice or lectures.

RESPECTING DIVERSITY

Mentors will be more effective at building relationships and supporting mentees as they work toward their goals if they attempt to understand each individual in the context of the individual's circumstances, culture, and heritage. Diversity within mentoring can be defined as any significant personal or cultural difference that has the potential of affecting the development of the mentoring relationship. It is broader than ethnic distinctions.

Completing the Privilege Walk activity (School of Social Welfare, 2009) will help mentors learn to recognize how subtly power and privilege affect individuals' lives. In this guided exercise, mentors listen to statements and follow instructions. Examples of these include, "If your family had health insurance, take one step forward," "If you have visible or invisible disabilities, take one step backward," and "If there have been times in your life when you skipped a meal because there was no food in the house, take one step backward." Upon completion of the activity, mentors reflect upon the complexity of privilege in society and how social identifiers beyond a person's control affect the level of privilege a person experiences. The trainer should be prepared to assist mentors in processing their personal reactions to the Privilege Walk activity and to explore how mentors can use this experience to actualize respect in the mentoring sessions.

MAKING TIMELY AND APPROPRIATE REFERRALS

Trainers should establish relationships with university and community departments, programs, and services and involve these programs in mentor training. The trainer should schedule presentations from these departments either during the initial training or as part of continuing training sessions during the academic term. The following programs and services can provide especially valuable information to mentors: counseling services, disability resources, health center, multicultural student center, tutoring center, and career services. Guest speakers can be invited to present to the mentors, and mentors can follow up by making one or more individual appointments to consult these professionals for their own purposes. In addition, the trainer should develop a role-play activity to practice the process of making appropriate referrals.

An Overview of Mentoring Sessions

Session guidelines give structure to the program and assist mentors in providing an intentional and valuable experience to the mentee. For example, mentors can agree on goals for their first sessions and practice well in advance of their first mentoring session. At least four sessions should be planned out, with the average duration of the mentoring relationship lasting seven sessions. In the first session, mentors should build a collaborative relationship. In the second session, mentors should work with mentees to develop goals and initiate action plans. In the third session and beyond, mentors should assess, offer strategies, and check on progress. At the final session, mentors should revisit goal plans and assess students' experiences.

The Value of Continued Training

The initial orientation and training is only part of a mentoring staff development plan. Mentors need opportunities to reflect on their mentoring skills and to discuss any issues they may be facing in the course of the mentoring relationship. Ongoing training throughout the academic term should further develop mentor knowledge of building collaborative relationships and maintaining boundaries, improving communication and listening skills, working with diverse populations, and making referrals to other programs and services.

References

Bandura, A. (1986). *Social foundations of thought and action: A social cognitive theory*. Englewood Cliffs, NJ: Prentice-Hall.

College Reading and Learning Association. (2011). *IMTPC certification requirements*. Retrieved from http://www.crla.net/imtpc/certification_requirements.htm

Family Educational Rights and Privacy, Final Rule, 34 C.F.R. pt. 99 (2008). Retrieved from http://www.ed.gov/legislation/FedRegister/finrule/2008-4/120908a.pdf

Knapp, M. L., & Vangelisti, A. L. (2008). *Interpersonal communication and human relationships* (6th ed.). Boston, MA: Allyn & Bacon.

Koehler, G., & Burke, A. (1996). *Transforming the treadmill into a staircase: Preparing non-traditional first-generation college attenders for success*. Retrieved from http://www.eric.ed.gov/PDFS/ED414959.pdf

School of Social Welfare. (2009). *The privilege walk*. Albany, NY: State University of New York at Albany. Retrieved from http://www.albany.edu/ssw/efc/pdf/Module%205_1_Privilege%20Walk%20Activity.pdf

Tinto, V. (1998). Colleges as communities: Taking research on student persistence seriously. *The Review of Higher Education, 21*(2), 167–177. doi:10.1353/rhe.1997.0024

Appendix

SAMPLE CRLA IMTPC LEVEL 2 TRAINING PROGRAM AGENDA

Mentor training may be structured into 3 days of instruction and activities.

On the first day of training, topics include the following:

- welcome to mentoring (introductions and an icebreaker), mission, and vision;
- the role of the mentor, and mentoring dos and don'ts;
- policies and procedures, and professional ethics;
- building collaborative relationships and establishing mentoring boundaries;
- communication skills; and
- community resources and campus referrals.

On the second day of training, topics include the following:

- appreciating diversity;
- learning styles and study skills;
- time management and organization;
- choosing a major and exploring careers; and
- setting goals.

On the third day of training, topics include the following:

- balancing school, work, and social life;
- health, wellness, stress, and burnout;
- interactive practice;
- questions and answers; and
- assessment of training learning outcomes.

Institutionalizing Tutor Training

Patricia Fullmer

One of the most powerful ways to improve a learning assistance center is to train the staff. Tutoring programs that have training programs have been shown to help students increase their academic skills, as indicated by first-term and cumulative grade point averages (Boylan, Bliss, & Bonham, 1997). A certification program of the College Reading and Learning Association (CRLA, 2011), the International Tutor Training Program Certification (ITTPC), is the premier guideline for training. In fact, certification by CRLA's ITTPC is recommended in the contextual statement for learning assistance programs by the Council for the Advancement of Standards in Higher Education (CAS, 2009).

At Lincoln University several years ago the reputation of the Learning Resource Center (LRC) among the faculty needed to be improved. Training the tutors and certifying the program both improved services to students and faculty and increased recognition of the LRC in the university community (Fullmer, 2009).

The Process of Change

Implementing training where none existed is not an easy task, but Kotter's (1996) steps in the process of change provided a roadmap. These eight steps helped the LRC navigate through pitfalls and become proactive in addressing resistance toward change.

STEP ONE: ESTABLISH SENSE OF URGENCY

The first step concerns shaping a sense among the constituents that change is necessary. The tutoring laboratories (mandatory group tutoring sessions utilizing review lessons and online tutoring programs) were vital to the academic success of underprepared students but were staffed with professional tutors who had not been trained in the best practices of tutoring. Setting up training was the first action to improve the reputation of the LRC, and discovering CRLA's ITTPC was of great benefit; not only does ITTPC provide an outline for training, but it also provides a means to recognize excellent programs by panel review and certification. Adopting tutor training that met ITTPC certification requirements would improve the reputation of the LRC with the faculty and contribute to the substance of tutor training.

In Step One, the gateway to the change process includes developing a sense that the need for change was urgent. This feeling may emerge from the forces that are at play in an organization over time. Lewin (1997) stated in his field theory that in any situation there is a balancing act between forces against change and forces toward change. When the forces toward change outweigh the forces against change, then change is more likely to take place. Emphasizing the benefits of the change increases the balance of forces toward change. At Lincoln, the newly hired Assistant Director presented the need for training and the benefits of training tutors in order to create enthusiasm and a sense of urgency for change in the LRC. The benefits of training were also presented at every staff and lab meeting to gather support from the staff. With an emphasis on recognition for individual tutors as well as recognition for the LRC that would result when certification was earned, a curriculum was developed for all three levels of training in CRLA's ITTPC (CRLA, 2011).

During this time, the LRC investigated online tutoring programs and decided to proceed with that opportunity. One benefit of an online tutoring program was a valid and reliable pretest and posttest that would not have to be graded by the tutors; another was the structured curriculum designed by experts in the field. Discussion of these benefits encouraged staff to consider the change to online tutoring in the context of increasing effectiveness.

STEP TWO: FORM A POWERFUL GUIDING CONSTITUENCY

In the second step in the process of change, the leader establishes a coalition of staff members to guide the change process and develop a strategic plan. For example, at Utah Valley State College the president established a committee that included senior staff members to provide guidance, but he also established study groups with the faculty and staff to create a dialogue on the change process (Spencer & Winn, 2004/2005). The fact that the LRC at Lincoln University was already established and a process such as that adopted at Utah Valley State was not implemented at Lincoln may have been a factor in the resistance of some faculty toward the LRC, despite efforts to advocate for acceptance and support for the LRC from the faculty.

Each semester the LRC produces a comprehensive report, including statistics concerning improvement from pretest to posttest of all students in the required laboratories for developmental education success course sections. In all semesters students have shown significant improvement in skills from pretest to posttest, supported by a t-test and eta-squared analysis (Fullmer et al., 2010). Support from the highest leadership and faculty groups in the creation of the LRC could have minimized resistance from the faculty concerning the LRC's effectiveness.

STEP THREE: CREATE A VISION

Creating a vision statement congruent with the university's goals keeps the change focused and in alignment with the strategic plan of the institution. The entire LRC staff worked for a semester to write vision and mission statements for the center. The overall goal of the LRC was discussed by all participants at length, and horizons were broadened to national recognition for providing superior assistance with high standards of excellence.

All constituents were invited to participate in vision and mission development, including all students and the entire Lincoln community. This mission incorporated increased collaboration with academic departments, ongoing systematic assessment, and the planned inclusion of best practices.

STEP FOUR: COMMUNICATE THE VISION

Open and transparent communication increases the participation of stakeholders and decreases resistance, a critical concern in the change process. Senge (1990) concluded, "Shared vision is vital for the learning organization because it provides the focus and energy for learning" (p. 206). When all or most stakeholders commit to a shared vision and mission, the group coheres, and resistance to change abates. Including all constituents in the development of a vision and mission and then communicating the vision to the entire community or organization through all means possible solidifies the process of change.

The vision and mission of the LRC are communicated to the Lincoln campus community through postings on bulletin boards, discussions in meetings, and publications of the LRC. Posting reports on the LRC's website demonstrates credibility and transparency, a management priority of Lincoln's president.

STEP FIVE: EMPOWER OTHERS TO ACT ON THE VISION

The fifth step, empowering action, is to remove barriers to change and address any resistance. One of the barriers to training removed at Lincoln was lack of university funds to return the tutors to work early after the summer break for training. The LRC budget was revised, and funds were moved from other parts of the budget to cover the hiring of tutors several days prior to the start of the semester so that training could take place.

In addition, the Assistant Director addressed the faculty of the English, Education, and Mathematics Departments to invite their input to the changes in the LRC. Three English Department professors met with LRC staff to discuss the content of tutoring to be provided, and the LRC accepted the recommendation of the Mathematics Department concerning which online program to purchase.

STEP SIX: PLAN FOR AND CREATE SHORT-TERM WINS

The change process can be lengthy, but showing some progress in the short term encourages everyone to persist. Breaking down a long-term goal into several short-term steps increases motivation because immediate goals can be achieved more quickly, and more opportunities for recognition are available (Bandura, 1997; Schunk, 1995). CRLA's tutor training certification offers three opportunities for recognition, corresponding to the three levels of certification (CRLA, 2011). A ceremony to award certificates at each level proved to be a highly motivating activity for the LRC staff.

Through systematic, semester-by-semester self-evaluation and publication of a report and a newsletter written by the tutors, tutors began to feel recognized for their labors. Seeing their work in writing and determining measures of effectiveness through the differences in student clients' scores between pretest and posttest in the online tutoring program supported feelings of meaning and worth for the tutoring staff. Publishing the report and newsletter online and sharing printed copies with senior administrators and professors increased the standing of the LRC not only with faculty and staff but also with the Board of Trustees, when the president included the LRC report in the materials disseminated at a Board meeting.

STEP SEVEN: CONSOLIDATE IMPROVEMENTS, PRODUCE MORE CHANGE

Consolidating gains, the seventh step, is a time to reflect on the process of the change so far. The establishment of a system of continuous improvement through a semester-by-semester self-evaluation utilizing a SWOT (Strengths, Weaknesses, Opportunities, Threats) analysis and development of an action plan consolidates the continuous improvement of the LRC (Fullmer, 2009; Fullmer et al., 2010; SWOT Analysis II, 2006). The results of this self-analysis are published online and distributed to the Lincoln campus community.

The staff of the LRC creates and publishes a newsletter every semester, detailing important events in the center. All staff contribute articles, student interviews, or photographs to the publication. This newsletter fosters positive feeling about the LRC among the faculty.

STEP EIGHT: INSTITUTIONALIZE NEW APPROACHES

The eighth and final step is to incorporate the vision and strategic plan of the change process into the day-to-day work of the organization. The LRC vision and mission statements are posted in the front office, displayed in each tutoring lab, and published online. These statements guide the work of the center. The vision and mission also appear in the newsletter and the semester report published by the LRC. Not only does the newsletter consolidate gains, but it advertises the services and benefits of the LRC and enhances communication between the LRC and the academic community of the university.

The systematic and continuous self-improvement process conducted each semester, modifying the current student learning outcomes and developing the SWOT analysis and action plan, incorporates the change process into the daily work of the LRC and institutionalizes change. The publication and distribution of the semester report provides recognition for the LRC staff and supports the funding of the LRC.

Lessons Learned

It does take time for changes to be institutionalized, to be worked into the everyday fabric of an organization. Several key practices create real change. Continuously communicating the benefits of the change through all available venues builds support for the change, and including the participants from the very beginning builds success. Including all constituents prior to, during, and after the change process increases ownership and decreases resistance. Participation and open communication of all involved facilitates the change process and helps to minimize resistance.

Removing any obstacles, such as rearranging budgets so tutors can receive training at optimal times, can increase the probability of success. Frequent recognition as short-term goals are attained keeps motivation and enthusiasm high. Incorporating changes into the repertoire of daily work through discussions, announcements, publications, and posters transforms the changes into a new tradition. Conducting self-reflection and a self-evaluation each semester through the development and modification of student learning outcomes and a SWOT analysis and action plan institutionalizes the change process, resulting in systematic and continuous improvement in the LRC. Finally, the publication of effectiveness in online and hard-copy semester reports and newsletters builds a practice of constant self-improvement that is both required by and highly regarded by regional accreditation authorities.

References

Bandura, A. (1997). Self-efficacy. *Harvard Mental Health Letter, 13*(9), 4–7.

Boylan, H., Bliss, L., & Bonham, B. (1997). Program components and their relationship to student performance. *Journal of Developmental Education, 20*(3), 2–9.

College Reading and Learning Association. (2011). *Tutor training certification: (ITTPC) International Tutor Training Program Certification.* Retrieved from http://www.crla.net/ittpc/index.htm

Council for the Advancement of Standards in Higher Education. (2009). *CAS professional standards for higher education* (7th ed.). Washington, DC: Author.

Fullmer, P. (2009). The assessment of a tutoring program to meet CAS standards using a SWOT analysis and action plan. *Journal of College Reading and Learning, 40*(1), 51–76.

Fullmer, P., et al. (2010). *The Learning Resource Center, Lincoln University, Pennsylvania, Fall 2010 Report.* Retrieved from http://www.lincoln.edu/lrc/reportfall2010.pdf

Kotter, J. (1996). *Leading change.* Boston, MA: Harvard Business School.

Lewin, K. (1997). *Resolving conflicts; Field theory in social science.* Washington, DC: American Psychological Association.

Schunk, D. (1995). Inherent details of self-regulated learning include student perceptions. *Educational Psychologist, 30,* 213–216. doi:10.1207/s15326985ep3004_7

Senge, P. (1990). *The fifth discipline: The art and practice of the learning organization.* New York, NY: Currency Doubleday.

Spencer, M., & Winn, B. (2004/2005). Evaluating the success of strategic change against Kotter's eight steps. *Planning for Higher Education, 33*(2), 15–22.

SWOT analysis II: Looking inside for strengths and weaknesses. (2006). Boston, MA: Harvard Business School Press.

External Funding for Tutor and Mentor Programs

Emily Miller Payne

Most postsecondary supplemental programs (e.g., tutoring, mentoring, Supplemental Instruction) compete for resources with other credible and necessary campus services. Program managers who want to try innovative new tutor and mentor training initiatives but have few or no local funds for the initiatives will benefit from learning how to seek external funding, manage a funded project, and evaluate the project for the funder. This article will introduce tutoring and mentoring program managers to strategies for securing external funding for program development and expansion.

Searching for External Funding Sources

Postsecondary programs such as tutor and mentor training have access to different types of funding sources: federal grants, state grants, private foundations, and corporate foundations. No single common online source offers access to all grant announcements, but there are several good online websites where the grant seeker can find out about active requests for proposals (RFPs) and requests for applications (RFAs) as well as preliminary announcements about upcoming competitions for funding.

RFPs for federal grants are listed on the grants.gov website and are typically posted 30-45 days before the application deadline. With tight deadlines between announcement of the competition and application deadlines, it behooves federal grant applicants to subscribe to one or more of the funding subscription services (e.g., Thompson Publishing Group, Inc., or CD Publications) to watch federal legislation for advance notice on proposed funded initiatives. The grants.gov site is searchable by sponsoring entity, such as the Institute for Education Sciences (IES), or by program type, such as Fund for the Improvement of Postsecondary Education (FIPSE). Most federal projects are highly competitive and typically require applicants to collaborate with partners within the applicant institution or with other institutions.

State-funded initiatives are usually announced by the individual state agency responsible for K-12 or postsecondary education, depending on how the state agencies are configured. Applicants should make routine visits to the grants site on the relevant agency's website. As with federal grant funding, applicants need advance awareness to write competitive proposals; therefore, applicants should watch state sites for indications about new funding being debated in state legislatures.

The process for securing private foundation funding may be less complicated in terms of writing the proposal, but finding foundations that support a specific project such as tutor and mentor training may require making calls to the potential funder to explain what the institution proposes to do with the money. The best starting place in a search for private foundation funding may be a website like the Foundation Center (at foundationcenter.org), where an applicant can conduct a free search for foundations by geographic area. To find information about the types of projects that foundations fund requires subscription to a service such as Foundation Directory Online; the applicant institution's grants office may subscribe to such a service. Corporate funding searches are similar to foundation searches in that they require the grant seeker to make a compelling case for supporting a particular proposed project.

The Application Process

Regardless of the type of funding source (federal, state, foundation, or corporate), the applicant should focus on prospective grantors with funding interests that match the institution's proposed plan. The most efficient way to determine grantors' interests is to go to funders' websites and read descriptions of their legislated (federal and state) or philosophical mission and vision and to review projects they have funded in the recent past. The applicant must allow time to make pre-announcement, pre-proposal contact with the grantor to discuss the proposed project.

Successful applications have several characteristics in common: proposals mirror the mission and goals of the grantor, the applicants value the same outcomes as the grantor, the applicant institution meets eligibility for the grant, and the applicant approaches grant seeking from the grantor's perspective. When the applicant has determined that the proposed project is a match in goals and scope, it is time to write the proposal (for federal and state grants) or the detailed letter of inquiry (for foundations and corporate sponsors).

PROPOSALS

If the funding source is a federal or state grant, the applicant should read the RFP or RFA thoroughly several times and construct a proposal guide for internal use to help organize the proposal-writing process. At a minimum, the guide should include the following information: deadline and submission details (electronic or paper-copy submission); proposal length and format (number of pages and required font and line spacing); required sections of the proposal narrative (e.g., statement of need, project design, management plan, description of key personnel, evaluation plan, budget, and statement of impact); maximum points the funder allocates for each section of the proposal; and any supplemental documents that must accompany the application, such as curricula vitae for proposed staff or required authorizations related to lobbying (New & Quick, 2003). If the institution or entity applying for the grant plans to assign proposal sections to members of a writing team, it is helpful to assign those sections and determine an internal timeline with deadlines for each section (Miner & Miner, 2008).

If the applicant seeks public (federal or state) funds, it is important to know the enabling legislation that funds the program in addition to the standard processes involved in managing the project if it is funded. At a minimum, the proposal should tell the funder everything it needs to know about the proposed project, including goals and objectives, specifics about the institution, how the money will be spent, and how the funded project will be evaluated and sustained.

The proposal should follow the organization of the grant announcement with levels of headings that match the RFP or RFA and the same sequence of sections. The needs assessment section should show that the applicant understands the need for the program being proposed (Altschuld & White, 2009). For example, a proposal for a tutor or mentor training program should describe what training currently exists and make a strong case for why additional funding is needed. The goals and objectives section should make clear what work is to be done, who is responsible for doing the work, when it will be done, and how the results of each objective will be evaluated (Bauer, 2007). The project narrative should describe the methodology and activities thoroughly and offer the reader a realistic timeline for project completion. Finally, it is important to conduct an internal review of the proposal draft against the scoring guide published by the funder; the applicant should have several readers who were not on the writing team but are knowledgeable about the proposed program do a mock scoring of the document to assure that the proposal is competitive based on the funder's scoring guidelines.

LETTERS OF INQUIRY

The letter of inquiry to a foundation or corporation is typically a less prescribed document than a proposal written in response to an RFP or RFA. The letter of inquiry should convey similar information to the sections required in a grant proposal (statement of need, description of the proposed project including goals and objectives, key personnel, explanation of the proposed costs, timeline, and an explanation of the evaluation plan). The applicant should already have discussed the general program description and the budget with the funder prior to sending the letter of inquiry. An applicant for foundation or corporate funding should not be deceived by the streamlined application process; most private funding sources require significant pre-proposal work in developing a relationship with the funder to convince it that the program is necessary, viable, and appropriate to the foundation or corporate mission. As with a grant proposal, the applicant should have multiple readers review the draft letter of inquiry to assure that it is clear and complete.

Submitting the Proposal or Letter of Inquiry

When the proposal is prepared for submission, the applicant must be vigilant about following the submission directions. For electronic submissions, the applicant should not wait until the last minute or even the last day to submit. Most institutions have protocols about grant submissions, and typically there is one person in the grants office authorized to press the submit button. These protocols may include an internal institutional deadline, often 2 to 5 working days prior to the funder's deadline, for review by the institution's Sponsored Projects Administration (SPA) office. Usually it is not the role of SPA staff to assess the merits of the proposal or project but instead to ensure that the proposal meets legal and ethical guidelines (e.g., responsible conduct of research) and conforms to any budget restrictions (e.g., negotiated rate for indirect cost recovery, requirements for matching funds or in-kind services) so that the institution is protected from unnecessary liability. The applicant should learn about the protocols at the home institution and follow them. Letters of inquiry typically should follow the same protocol in terms of working with the grants office to submit, but the process is usually less formal. Foundations and corporations are increasingly asking applicants to submit application documents electronically.

Applicants should allow the funding entity time to review the application before contacting personnel there about a decision. Federal and state grants follow a stated timeline to announce results. Foundations and corporations typically publish on their websites their timelines for notification.

Although proposals for external funding require significant time and energy, they can offer programs excellent opportunities to develop new training programs or update existing programs. Good training initiatives need not be constrained by institutional budgets.

References

Altschuld, J. W., & White, J. L. (2009). *The needs assessment kit*. Thousand Oaks, CA: Sage.

Bauer, D. G. (2007). The *"how to" grants manual: Successful grantseeking techniques for obtaining public and private grants* (6th ed.). Westport, CT: Praeger.

Miner, J. T., & Miner, L. E. (2008). *Proposal planning and writing* (4th ed.). Westport, CT: Greenwood Press.

New, C. C., & Quick, J. A. (2003). *How to write a grant proposal*. San Francisco, CA: Jossey-Bass.

Group Interviews: Selecting the Right Staff With the Right Stuff

Lisa N. Putnam Cole and Kimberly K. Kelley

If skillful employees form the framework for effective tutoring and mentoring programs, then judicious employee selection serves as the foundation upon which this framework is built. Group interviews that include authentic activities and purposeful discussion can maximize the predictability of potential employee success and conserve administrative resources.

Group interviewing, a common practice in human resource settings, refers to one of a handful of hiring procedures. In this module, the term refers to situations in which two to five staff members simultaneously screen a group of 6 to 15 candidates using coordinated small- and large-group activities. This iteration of the group interview process was developed by the directors of Illinois State University's Center for Learning Assistance (UCLA) nearly 20 years ago. Refinement began after the first round of interviews concluded at the UCLA and has continued at Heartland Community College (HCC) as one of the directors moved across town to serve as founding coordinator of HCC's tutoring program. This process has been used to hire a variety of part-time academic support personnel (e.g., tutors, Supplemental Instruction leaders, receptionists) with exemplary results.

Guiding Theories and Practices

The group interview process was developed as a possible solution for a specific personnel challenge, and with time it evolved into a functional system. Wheatley (2006) referred to this process as self-organization, which occurs when "we recreate ourselves, not according to some idealized plan, but because the environment demands it. We let go of our old form and figure out how best to organize ourselves in new ways" (p. 24). Over time, this system (i.e., the group interview process) has developed into one that is efficient and responsive as program personnel have made efforts to "look internally" and "experiment to find out what works" (Wheatley, 2006, p. 9). Other aspects of Wheatley's theory that manifest themselves in the group interview process are a focus on relationships, the complementary and inextricable association between individuals and the system in which they are engaged, the social nature of the construction of reality, and the philosophy that the whole is greater than the sum of its parts.

Another theory upon which the group interview process is based is constructivism. This family of learning theories asserts that individuals build meaning by incorporating new knowledge into their existing knowledge base (i.e., their personal context). Although theorists disagree about whether the task is accomplished alone or with others (Merriam & Cafarella, 2001; Silverman & Casazza, 2000), the group interview process provides multiple opportunities for individuals to process information both socially and individually during the small- and large-group activities and their related debriefing sessions.

Behavioral interviewing, a practice that provides a third form of conceptual support for the group interview, is based on the principle that "the most accurate predictor of future performance is past performance in similar situations" (Nancheria, 2008, p. 1). To implement this technique, employers must first identify the skills and behaviors necessary for job success and then develop a set of standard job-related questions requiring candidates to generate examples of situations in which the desired skill set has been utilized (Clifford, 2006; Cohen, 2001; Nancheria, 2008). During the interview, all candidates should be asked the same questions to the greatest extent possible (Clifford, 2006; Nancheria, 2008), and Clifford (2006) suggested the interview be conducted by a team to "minimize any one person's reaction, good or bad" (p. 94). The group interview process takes behavioral interviewing one step beyond simply requiring candidates to share examples of targeted skills by asking them to demonstrate those skills in a simulated situation.

Chickering's (1969) theory, which has come to be known as his Theory of Identity Development (Silverman & Casazza, 2000), is an essential tool for interview personnel attempting to assess potential employees' development. For example, a candidate who seems to have trouble communicating or working in a group may still be working on issues related to the Developing Competence vector and is probably not ready to work with students in a tutoring or mentoring setting. The importance of assessing key aspects of candidates' development cannot be underestimated in the decision-making process.

The Group Interview Deconstructed

Due to space constraints, we are unable to provide examples of interview activities in this module. All materials, including supporting and supplemental documents, are available online (Cole, 2010).

THE IDEAL CANDIDATE

The well-conceived interview plan applies Covey's (1989) maxim to "begin with the end in mind" (p. 95). Interview planners must thoughtfully select activities that allow candidates to demonstrate their aptitude or ability with respect to the targeted qualities and qualifications "rather than against other candidates applying for the same job" (Cohen, 2001, p. 8). The type of position for which candidates are being interviewed will drive decisions about the most effective activity to implement and the criteria against which candidate performance will be evaluated. The Group Interview Feedback Form for Tutor Selection (Appendix) presents desired attributes of potential tutors in order from general to specific, moving from those that are generally desired of all employees (rows 1 and 2) to those that are specific to the position (rows 3, 4, and 5). This form could be adapted quite easily for mentor selection as well by varying qualities and qualifications, particularly in rows 3, 4, and 5, to reflect characteristics that would be observed in an ideal mentor.

OVERVIEW OF A GROUP INTERVIEW

The group interview is the means by which the simulated environment is created. Our version requires approximately 2 hours (with an additional hour required for interview personnel to share feedback about candidate performance) and consists of the following segments: introductory activities (10 min); group activities, including the structured experience (50 min) and the focused discussion (20 min); an information-sharing session (25 min); and concluding activities (15 min). This generic plan may be applied to any type of hiring situation that may arise in an academic support setting by changing the structured experience or by modifying the focused discussion. The concept and the framework of the group interview process are sound and simple, but the process of adaptation requires thoughtful attention to detail that is driven by the desired end and is best engineered by those who will be involved in the selection process.

INTERVIEW PERSONNEL

The facilitator, most likely the program coordinator, is responsible for orchestrating all aspects of the interview including the shrewd delegation of tasks. Before the interview, the facilitator screens applications, invites applicants to interview, plans activities, prepares materials, and trains those who will be assisting throughout the process. The facilitator's responsibilities during the interview include directing events, monitoring time, and troubleshooting. After the interview, this individual presides over the discussion of candidate performance and also communicates with candidates regarding interview outcomes.

The facilitator is aided by two or more assistants, individuals with knowledge of and experience in the position for which the interview is being held. Assistants must attend pre-interview training to become fully acquainted with the assistant role. During the interview, assistants observe candidates, share knowledge and personal experiences, and conduct small-group activities. Assistants' major responsibility after the interview is to provide the facilitator with feedback on each candidate. Assistants must remain mindful of the importance of maintaining strict confidentiality and, as a result, are required to sign statements of confidentiality.

THE STRUCTURED EXPERIENCE

After introductions and other preliminaries take place within the large group, candidates are divided into smaller groups and engaged in our version of what Pfeiffer and Ballew (1988) referred to as *structured experiences*. In a group interview, these experiences may take many forms, such as role plays, simulations, or case studies, which enable interview personnel to observe candidates as they engage in authentic activities. Observations of interview personnel are thus able to "focus on individual behavior" occurring "within a group setting" (Pfeiffer & Ballew, 1988, p. 1). Structured experiences should be intentionally selected and adapted as necessary to highlight the attributes most desired by interview personnel, whether the task be selecting tutors or mentors. The structured experience concludes with a debriefing session, which in some respects is the activity's highlight. By posing a set of prepared questions, the facilitator assists candidates in processing what occurred during the structured experience. The resulting discussion provides interview personnel with a window into candidates' cognitive and metacognitive worlds and a remarkable opportunity to consider their honesty and perceptiveness.

THE FOCUSED DISCUSSION

The focused discussion provides a second opportunity and context in which interview personnel may observe candidates. This admittedly-contrived discussion requires candidates to complete selected sentence stems (e.g., I laugh out loud when I think of . . . . It is easiest for me to learn when . . . . I can't understand students who . . . .) from those presented on a handout, share their responses with the large group, and participate in a second debriefing session. During planning, the facilitator may easily change the content or number of the sentence stems—or even the debriefing questions—to adjust the discussion's focus to address target areas appropriate for tutor or mentor selection. The length of this discussion is easily flexed to adjust for time lost or gained during the structured experience. Though simple and flexible, the focused discussion is also quite revealing. For example, does the candidate contribute relevant information to the discussion or merely irrelevancies as claims for attention? Does the candidate seem engaged with the process (nodding, taking notes) or disengaged (looking at the clock constantly, texting, fidgeting)?

INFORMATION SESSION

The information session is the final major portion of the group interview for candidates, and it is best described as a deliberate exchange of facts, figures, and preferences between interview personnel and candidates in the large group setting. Interview personnel share general information about the program, as well as specific information about the interview schedule and positions. Candidates complete paperwork to inform interview personnel of preferences (e.g., scheduling, work location), qualifications, and other relevant information. Following this session, candidates may ask any remaining questions, and the interview concludes.

AFTER THE INTERVIEW

The facilitator convenes the discussion of candidate performance after lingering candidates have cleared the area. Assistants are reminded of their role, and then discussion commences using the feedback form (Appendix) as a guide and Chickering's (1969) vectors as a back-drop. Assistants share their observations and perceptions about each candidate one at a time, responding to one another before the facilitator expresses his or her thoughts. Soon after this discussion, the facilitator checks references, makes final decisions, and informs candidates of the results.

References

Chickering, A. W. (1969). *Education and identity.* San Francisco, CA: Jossey-Bass.

Clifford, S. (2006). The new science of hiring. *Inc., 26*(8), 90–98.

Cohen, D. S. (2001). *The talent edge: A behavioral approach to hiring, developing, and keeping top performers.* Toronto, ON: John Wiley & Sons.

Cole, L. P. (2010). *Group interview materials.* Retrieved from http://employee.heartland.edu/lcole/groupInterview.html and available at www.crla.net/handbook/ch6/cole-n-kelley

Covey, S. R. (1989). *The seven habits of highly effective people: Restoring the character ethic.* New York, NY: Fireside/Simon & Schuster.

Merriam, S. B., & Cafarella, R. S. (2001). Key theories of learning. In S. B. Merriam, R. S. Caffarella, R. J. Wlodkowski, & P. Cranton (Eds.), *Adult learning: Theories, principles and applications* (pp. 76–85). San Francisco, CA: Jossey-Bass.

Nancheria, A. (2008). Anticipated growth in behavioral interviewing. *T+D, 62*(4), 20.

Pfeiffer, J. W., & Ballew, A. C. (1988). *Using structured experiences in human resource development.* San Diego, CA: University Associates.

Silverman, S. L., & Casazza, M. E. (2000). *Learning and development: Making connections to enhance teaching.* San Francisco, CA: Jossey-Bass.

Wheatley, M. J. (2006). *Leadership and the new science: Discovering order in a chaotic world* (3rd ed.). San Francisco, CA: Berrett-Koehler.

Appendix

GROUP INTERVIEW FEEDBACK FORM FOR TUTOR SELECTION

Candidate qualities and qualifications listed in the left column provide a comprehensive but not exhaustive list of attributes typically exhibited by successful tutors. In columns 2–4, Interview personnel record observations to document their rating of each candidate in each category.

Interview Date and Time: _____   **Interviewer:** _____

Directions: During the interview, record your impressions of each candidate in the appropriate cell and assign a rating for each candidate in each category using the rating scale provided. Be ready to discuss your ratings and the corresponding impressions and observations at the conclusion of the interview.

Rating Scale:	5	4	3	2	1
	Excellent	Good	Acceptable	Poor	Unacceptable

CANDIDATE QUALITIES AND QUALIFICATIONS			
General Impression • Enthusiasm • Sense of humor • Friendliness • Confidence • Engagement with process • Appropriateness of attire	5 4 3 2 1	5 4 3 2 1	5 4 3 2 1
General Qualities, Attitudes and Skills Characteristic of Effective Employees • Leadership • Teamwork • Flexibility • Clarity of and articulateness in speech • Active listening skills	5 4 3 2 1	5 4 3 2 1	5 4 3 2 1
Qualities and Attitudes Characteristic of Effective Tutors • Initiative • Insight • Resourcefulness • Concern for others • Respect for diverse learners • Realistic perception of tutor role	5 4 3 2 1	5 4 3 2 1	5 4 3 2 1
Skills Characteristic of Effective Tutors • Observing keenly • Assisting without revealing answers • Asking questions effectively • Providing honest feedback in a tactful manner	5 4 3 2 1	5 4 3 2 1	5 4 3 2 1
Content Competency • To be completed before or after interview based on application and recommendations	5 4 3 2 1	5 4 3 2 1	5 4 3 2 1

Considerations in the Selection of Tutor Staff

Richard George Johnson

Ask program coordinators to describe their ideal tutor staff candidate and they will likely offer a list of characteristics as varied as the students who use their services. The variety reflects the personality and experience of the coordinator as well as the unique nature of the tutoring program and often the unique character of the institution itself. With this list, there will predictably be several overlapping qualities that diverse coordinators agree upon, but any discussion of hiring practices that begins with seeking appropriate qualities in tutor staff is premature. Selecting the appropriate staff begs the question, "appropriate for what?" "Tutoring" alone is not a sufficient answer.

A comprehensive hiring strategy is needed to identify and ultimately attract the best tutors for a program's needs. One perspective on hiring good tutors may be that programs are always involved in hiring, because every student who comes in contact with the tutoring program is a potential future candidate for a tutoring position. Taking this perspective broadens what may be considered the "hiring process" under consideration. Also, directors cannot make useful decisions about the characteristics desirable in staff until the objectives of the program are identified, including the challenges the staff is working to address and the skills the program wishes to develop in students who participate in the program.

Not Putting the Cart Before the Horse

A typical, albeit brief, list of qualities desirable in an applicant may include mastery of the subject matter, effective communication skills, strong interpersonal skills, previous experience, and punctuality. Essentially this list describes a tutor who knows what he or she is talking about, can talk about it with students in a way that engages them, has some track record of success, and is serious enough to show up for commitments on time.

This list is so general and vague as to apply to nearly any abstract employment position. A typical improvement is to make the list more specific to the job. Research into hiring practices for junior faculty seems to recognize the need for this specificity to achieve desirable employment outcomes (Eddy & Gaston-Gayles, 2008). Given a somewhat similar nature of autonomy in the classroom, tutoring programs may benefit from this objective improvement to the hiring process. To be more specific, then, additional qualities such as knowledge of diagnostic skills and familiarity with general learning theories may be sought. Programs must expand the expectations of suitable qualities of a candidate and can benefit from considering separately which qualities make a good tutor and which make a good employee.

What Directors Really Want and Need

Adult education theory identifies a useful first step of effective teaching to be a needs assessment (Vella, 2002). The idea is that in order to teach a student successfully and develop a plan to do so, the tutor must first understand the student as comprehensively as he or she can. The tutor must identify not only what the student can learn from the tutor but what the tutor and other students can learn from the student. This ability is important because tutors are not fully developed in the learning themselves, and their future practice will incorporate their current experience.

Directors want tutoring staff who exemplify the qualities of good employees, but they should seek much more. The program at Texas A&M University, for example, needs ambassadors. The program requires tutors who, because of who they are and what they bring to the program, enable the director to convince hesitating or hold-out professors to work with the program. The program needs tutors who make it easier for the director to convince the administration to increase the program's funding or, better yet, tutors who convince the administration themselves!

In other institutions' programs, the need may be for tutors interested in marketing and who have the energy, passion, and knowledge to make videos and podcasts about the program. If a program suffers from lack of team unity, the need may be for an event planner who happens to be a good tutor. Program leadership should identify the program's mission and goals, be aware of the program's challenges, and choose student staff who can help meet these challenges. When tutors are hired with basic tutoring skills and interests, most program administrators can help newly hired staff improve and even excel in these basic skills. After all, learning theory and practice specifically in the realm of academic support programs typically fall within the area of expertise of most tutoring program administrators. Therefore, instead of finding a tutor who is interested in marketing, perhaps programs should look for a marketing student who is interested in tutoring. Instead of posting three tutor staff openings, program directors should try looking for one event planner and two videographers, all of whom happen to be interested in tutoring.

Most students are highly successful and talented in some area (Pritchard, 2009). Narrowly defining their program contribution to the act of tutoring, which is admittedly an important aspect of their position, minimizes what they are capable of as assets to the program. To make a cold, impersonal analogy, few would ever consider purchasing a piece of equipment without first knowing what roles the equipment will serve in helping to achieve the program's overall objectives. Considerable time is spent making these decisions, sometimes even more time selecting a major piece of equipment (a new copier, for example) than is invested in identifying the appropriate applicant or in identifying the appropriate objective of hiring in the first place.

What should this candidate to bring to the program? What deficiencies in the program or obstacles can the right person help the program overcome? Potential opportunities are often recognized when they present themselves in an interview, but should program directors not proactively maximize such opportunities through targeted marketing?

Always Hiring

Although tutor trainers may not always be in the process of extending offer letters—a step that reinforces the professionalism of the program—they are always in the process of representing the program to future employees, particularly for programs that are tutoring the very undergraduate students who will in a short time make up the applicant pool. Future applicants are always in the process of interviewing the program; they get a sense of the program by the ads run in the student newspaper, the creativity of the website, the conduct of their personal tutors, and the professionalism of the entire staff. Although the interview process is often viewed as an opportunity for program staff to get to know applicants better and for them to get to know the program better, program staff should realize that applicants begin forming their perspective of the program upon first contact with it. Treating all students as possible future employees has the additional benefit of keeping current staff focused on the professionalism of the program at all times. Every aspect of the program influences the type of student who will ultimately choose to apply to become part of the staff.

There are lessons to be learned from some of the better student organizations on the Student Life side of campus. Student Life departments have long understood the importance and fragility of a student organization's reputation (Kitchener, 1985). Students in organizations are often considered to be representatives of those organizations even when engaged in other activities. Although the general message may not be a revelation for most tutor program directors, the degree to which student organizations take this concept can be surprising but also instructive.

Hiring in response to the urge to fill positions during desperate times can do programs a real disservice. Pressure can come from a professor's too-late request for tutoring support, from an administrator interested only in the numbers, or even from someone who has had a positive experience in the past and is requesting help in a new area. Regardless of the motivation, these desperate hires can be some of the worst, and the damage is not temporary, especially when the hiring timeline does not allow for adequate training. When the program is always in the process of influencing students to seek employment with the program (or not to do so), then exposing students to hastily hired staff can do real harm that extends beyond the current semester. Just as more highly qualified tutors will eventually attract an improved quality of future applicants, so too can poorly qualified or untrained tutors diminish the quality of the future applicant pool.

Conclusion

The purpose of offering these considerations is to make the job of filling staff positions easier and more effective. By the time applicants are in the interview, the process should require merely double-checking all of the qualities that have been prescreened in the applicants. The goal is to hire the best of the best, who will attract well-qualified applicants in the future, for many years to come.

References

Eddy, P. L., & Gaston-Gayles, J. L. (2008). New faculty on the block: Issues of stress and support. *Journal of Human Behavior in the Social Environment, 17*(1), 89–106. doi:10.1080/10911350802168878

Kitchener, K. S. (1985). Ethical principles and ethical decisions in student affairs. *New Directions for Student Services, 1985*(30), 17–29. doi:10.1002/ss.37119853004

Pritchard, G. (2009, July). *All students are talented: Exploiting the strengths potential via a new lens for learning and teaching.* Presented at the HERDSA 32nd International Conference, Darwin, Australia. Abstract retrieved from http://conference.herdsa.org.au/2009/concurrent03. html#2301

Vella, J. (2002). *Learning to listen, learning to teach: the power of dialogue in educating adults.* San Francisco, CA: Jossey-Bass.

Selecting Tutor Staff

 Eric Dunker

Competent, ethical, and creative tutors are the backbone of any learning support center; therefore, a successful center needs to develop a comprehensive staff recruitment and selection plan. Learning center staff members must conceptualize how they can best utilize institutional resources in order to select, train, and mentor the tutors who best represent the center's mission, financial resources, and student clientele. This module suggests a series of brainstorming and mapping activities to assist supervisors in planning to hire a tutoring staff.

Developing a Learning Center Staff Plan

According to Dalton (2003), staff selection strategy should rely on a theoretical framework for human resource management of student employees. Before a learning center supervisor hires any professional or student employees, he or she must be prepared to undertake all of the following supervisory responsibilities:

- Ensuring that the learning center is receiving applications from the best available applicants through innovative recruitment strategies

- Hiring employees who can fulfill the responsibility for which they were hired

- Helping employees master the specific competencies necessary for assigned duties, through focused training and feedback

- Helping employees understand and cope with the culture and requirements of their work environment.

The second bulleted responsibility of learning center supervisors—hiring employees who can fulfill their responsibilities—means in part that those who hire tutors must ensure that candidates are proficient in the subjects they will tutor. The CRLA International Tutor Training Program Certification (ITTPC) guidelines requiring qualifications of a 3.0 GPA and two faculty references support this responsibility (CRLA, 2011). Hiring employees who can fulfill job responsibilities also means that candidates must be willing and able to arrive on time for work, must demonstrate superb communication skills so they can form connections with student clients and with faculty, and should appreciate the tutor's responsibilities and role as a student employee of the college or university.

It is also important for supervisors and staff to develop learning outcomes and program outcomes in advance of any tutor selection process. After the outcomes have been determined, the center's staff can assess the potential of perspective employees to help the program accomplish its goals. The standards for learning assistance programs developed by the Council for the Advancement of Standards in Higher Education (CAS, 2009) are an excellent source of guidelines for competencies and qualities that all learning center staff (including student tutors) should possess.

Utilizing Technology for Marketing and Recruiting

Utilizing information technology can greatly benefit a learning center's recruiting strategy by saving money and creating more effective targeted searches. When a learning center team has determined which academic courses to target for tutoring support and has listed the qualifications of employees to be hired, the top students in each major can be targeted by performing simple queries through the campus administrative database system. If only the best students will suffice as tutors, then the learning center team should recruit aggressively rather than waiting for candidates to come to the learning center and apply.

The campus database of all students in the academic area of interest with a grade point average above 3.0 or 3.50 can be queried and a list of their email addresses obtained. Emails can be sent inviting each student individually to apply for a position as tutor, or a mass email can be sent to all qualified students in the query.

A further query of the database should yield demographics of every area of study. What percentage of students who have above a 3.0 in certain majors are persons of color? What percentage of the overall student body are students of color? These data sets will help the learning center set baselines for a demographically representative peer tutoring staff. Position notices can specify that males and ethnic minorities, for instance, are especially invited to apply.

Position notices can be posted on the student employment website. Notices should be posted on the institution's website if non-students are also sought.

Recruiting Through Campus Collaborators

In addition to utilizing technology to assist with recruiting a staff, the learning center supervisor can also collaborate and meet with academic department chairs, honors program coordinators, and the presidents and faculty advisors of student organizations to let them know that their best and brightest students are favored candidates for tutoring positions. Which faculty members, deans, and vice presidents on campus see the importance of academic support for students? Which individuals have a reputation for collegiality and collaboration? Learning center supervisors must seek out these individuals and begin dialogues about their mission on campus, which of course is ultimately nothing less than academic success for every student at the institution. According to Birnbaum (1988), the most collegial organizations (such as academic departments) place less emphasis on job status and hierarchy and more on common commitments or collective responsibilities. Likeminded, collegial colleagues across campus can help the learning center accomplish its mission.

For instance, if learning center administrators have particular difficulty finding computer science tutors or physics tutors, then the learning center supervisor can meet with the appropriate academic department chairs, let them know about the valuable opportunities available to their students, and ask that candidates be referred to the center. Similarly, if the center is having trouble hiring a peer tutor staff that is demographically representative of the student body, then learning center staff should meet with student organizations whose primary aim is to serve underrepresented students.

The learning center supervisor must also collaborate with the human resources (HR) department to ensure that the center's employment standards are consistent with those approved by HR and that any additional standards created are acceptable to and approved by HR. Student employment policies may differ from policies for other employment groups and may change more often.

Financial Aid and Budgeting

Learning center supervisors must quickly become experts on how the work-study process operates on campus and should therefore meet individually with the financial aid staff members responsible for work-study fund allocation. The financial aid process directly affects the center's recruiting strategy and potential staffing levels. Some questions to take into consideration include the following:

- When is the first day the learning center supervisor can start signing intent-to-hire forms that help put students on the work-study waitlist?

- How can the learning center supervisor best educate students to complete their financial aid forms quickly and correctly?

- Is merit-based work-study available on campus? Could students qualifying for merit-based aid be considered for tutoring positions?

After all options have been explored with financial aid, other options may permit expansion of the tutoring staff without increasing the budget. For instance, a credit-providing, independent study course could be created so students can tutor for credit rather than pay. The academic curriculum committee would provide the process for creating such a course, if this is feasible.

Alternatively, there may be academic departments with funding available to pay for an adjunct faculty member to work at the center to help coordinate the work of the tutors and provide some tutoring. For instance, an adjunct instructor funded to the equivalent of three credit hours might provide 9 or 10 working hours per week at the tutoring center. Graduate students, professional tutors with experience, or adjunct faculty members can be employed as lead tutors for each subject area, with tutoring support by work-study students and volunteers. Such an organization can save money and also create staff stability.

References

Birnbaum, R. (1988). *How colleges work: The cybernetics of academic organization and leadership.* San Francisco, CA: Jossey-Bass.

College Reading and Learning Association. (2011). *ITTPC certification requirements.* Retrieved from http://www.crla.net/ittpc/certification_requirements.htm

Council for the Advancement of Standards in Higher Education. (2009). *CAS professional standards for higher education* (7th ed.). Washington, DC: Author.

Dalton, J. C. (2003). Managing human resources. In S. R. Komives, D. B. Woodard, Jr., et al. (Eds.), *Student services* (pp. 397–419). San Francisco, CA: Jossey-Bass.

Observing and Coaching Tutors

 ## Patricia Fullmer

Managers of tutoring programs rely on committed employees to accomplish the program's goals. The supervisor's responsibility is to motivate, encourage, and communicate effectively in order to enable the workers to perform at their optimum level and in alignment with the program's goals. When the goals of the program are congruent with the career and personal goals of the employee, employees' intrinsic motivation maximizes achievement of the program's goals (Deci & Ryan, 1985; Li, McKeachie, & Kim, 2001).

Supervision of a tutorial program includes not only evaluating and assessing but also providing resources and training to enable the tutors to do their job. Supervisors need to demonstrate excellent interactive skills to communicate effectively with employees, because only through effective communication can the supervisor learn the needs of each tutor, such as the amount of direction, support, and coaching needed to tailor interventions to tutors.

Most employees need opportunities to achieve, to grow professionally and personally, and to be recognized for their work (Deci & Ryan, 1985). The International Tutor Training Program Certification (ITTPC) of the College Reading and Learning Association (CRLA, 2011) provides guidelines for training and also offers opportunities for recognition of the tutors at each of three levels of certification. Employees at different levels of functioning benefit from differing levels of leadership. A new and inexperienced worker may need more direction, while an experienced employee may benefit more from support and delegation (Richer & Vallerand, 1995).

When the style of the supervisor meshes with the needs of the employee, then the program, supervisor, and employee all benefit. Most workers will benefit at times from a coaching supervisory style that emphasizes the sharing of information, provides support during challenges, and nurtures the growth of the worker. Bloom, Castagna, Moir, and Warren (2005) found coaching "[a] proven strategy for increasing productivity and effectiveness . . . [and a] means of providing deliberate support to clarify and achieve goals" (p. 7).

Observing Tutors to Improve Performance

A supervisor provides coaching by offering tutors informative feedback, reflective questioning, and the information needed for each tutor to meet the organization's goals. Observing and giving appropriate feedback is the responsibility of the supervisor, and feedback is more effective if it begins and ends with a positive comment (East Tennessee State University, 2009; National Aeronautics and Space Administration, 2006; Skillpath Seminars, 2007). The feedback provided by a supervisor as coach should be based on attentive observation so that constructive and positive feedback can be provided to the employee. With the aim of conducting an assessment that is as objective as possible, the observation needs to be based on accepted standards of professional behavior. Devising an observation protocol that guides the observation and sharing this protocol with employees reduces employees' anxiety and establishes trust between the supervisor and employees.

A schedule of observations and evaluations shared with the tutor structures the supervisory relationship. In the Learning Resource Center at Lincoln University, the director initially meets with tutors during the first few weeks of hire and discusses the job description, ethics agreement, and confidentiality agreement. The observation protocol is also presented and reviewed. At this point each tutor knows what is expected and what behaviors the supervisor will be assessing. Assessments are constructive tools that can be used by tutors to think critically about their professional skills.

An observation protocol serves as a guideline of behaviors expected of tutors and should be reviewed several times prior to the observation so tutors are clear on what is expected of them. The observation protocol in the Appendix was formulated by a review of positive practices from a wide variety of perspectives (Bandura, 1997; Boylan, 2002; Boylan, Bliss, & Bonham, 1997; Carini, Kuh, &

Klein, 2006; Chickering & Gamson, 1987; Deci & Ryan, 1985; Li et al., 2001; Maslow, 1943; Schunk, 1991, 1995; Skinner & Belmont, 1993). Supervisors may want to work with their most experienced tutors to craft their own observation protocols, uniquely appropriate to their programs and services.

Tutors should be informed of the date and time of any formal observation, which should take place at least once per semester. Informal observations may also be conducted. Supervisors use data from the observations to inform the feedback and supportive comments they provide to tutors. Observations are also opportunities for tutors to reflect on their work and determine what improvements they need to make.

When a tutor and supervisor meet to discuss the results of an observation, reflections on and discussion about the observation should be incorporated into the formal evaluation report. Just as tutors are guided to begin and end each tutoring session on a positive note, supervisors should begin and end evaluation meetings with positive comments. The support and informational feedback provided by formal and informal observations are intended to motivate and guide tutors' professional growth.

Individual SWOT Analysis and Action Plan

Each tutor's self-assessment can take the form of an individual SWOT analysis (Strengths, Weaknesses, Opportunities, and Threats) and an action plan for improvement. SWOT analyses and action plans are generally used at the program level, and many college and university boards of trustees regularly conduct SWOT analyses of the organization. This type of analysis arose from the business sector and has been applied in many other situations (SWOT Analysis II, 2006) and can be adapted for use by individuals seeking to improve their performance.

SWOT self-assessment requests the tutor to discuss his or her strengths, describe areas in need of improvement, discuss opportunities that can be used for improvement, review obstacles to change, and devise an improvement plan. Strengths can compensate for the weaknesses, and opportunities can counteract the threats. These four self-assessments are used to develop the improvement plan.

SWOT analysis meetings between a tutor and supervisor begin with a positive statement by the supervisor about the tutor's work. The topics of the self-assessment are then discussed and the improvement plan reviewed and agreed upon. The supervisor then ends the meeting with a positive comment.

Annual Evaluation

Tutors may be requested to conduct a self-assessment based on several critical job performance areas in preparation for an annual evaluation conference at the end of the year. Topics include proficiency, completion of work, dependability, and relationships with co-workers. Supervisor and tutor review the tutor's strengths, accomplishments, efficiency, punctuality, and reliability. Relationship skills, including teamwork, collaboration with co-workers, and cooperation with the supervisor, are also examined. Achievement of the year's goals and the development of goals for the following year are an important part of planning by the tutor, and requests for training and development are based on the goals indicated. Any special accomplishments are also listed by the tutor and celebrated by both tutor and supervisor.

References

Bandura, A. (1997, March). Self-efficacy. *Harvard Mental Health Letter, 13*(9), pp. 4–6.
Bloom, G., Castagna, C., Moir, E., & Warren, H. (2005). *Blended coaching*. Thousand Oaks, CA: Corwin Press.

Boylan, H. (2002). *What works: Research-based best practices in developmental education.* Boone, NC: Continuous Quality Improvement Network/National Center for Developmental Education.

Boylan, H. R., Bliss, L. B., & Bonham, B. S. (1997). Program components and their relationship to student performance. *Journal of Developmental Education, 20*(3), 2–8.

Carini, R. M., Kuh, G. D., & Klein, S. P. (2006). Student engagement and student learning: Testing the linkages. *Research in Higher Education, 47*(2), 1–32. doi:10.1007/s11162-005-8150-9

Chickering, A. W., & Gamson, Z. F. (1987). The seven principles for good practice in undergraduate education. *AAHE Bulletin, 39*(7), 3–7.

College Reading and Learning Association. (2011). *ITTPC certification requirements.* Retrieved from http://www.crla.net/ittpc/certification_requirements.htm

Deci, E. L., & Ryan, R. M. (1985). *Intrinsic motivation and self-determination in human behavior.* New York, NY: Plenum.

East Tennessee State University. (2009). *Employee performance evaluation procedures guide.* Retrieved from http://www.etsu.edu/humanres/relations/evaluations.aspx

Li, Y., McKeachie, W., & Kim, Y. (2001). College student intrinsic and/or extrinsic motivation and learning. *Learning and Individual Differences, 13,* 252–259.

Maslow, A. H. (1943). A theory of human motivation. *Psychological Review, 50,* 370–396. Retrieved from http://psychclassics.yorku.ca/Maslow/motivation.htm

National Aeronautics and Space Administration. (2006). *Tips for effective performance appraisal sessions.* Retrieved from http://ohcm.gsfc.nasa.gov/sup_info/toolbox/empperf/Tips.htm

Richer, S., & Vallerand, R. (1995). Supervisors' interactional styles and subordinates' intrinsic and extrinsic motivation. *Journal of Social Psychology, 135,* 707–722. doi:10.1080/00224545.1995.9713974

Skillpath Seminars. (2007). *Excelling as a first-time manager or supervisor.* Mission, KS: Author.

Schunk, D. H. (1991). Self-efficacy and academic motivation. *Educational Psychologist, 26,* 207–232. doi:10.1207/s15326985ep2603&4_2

Schunk, D. H. (1995). Inherent details of self-regulated learning include student perceptions. *Educational Psychologist, 30,* 213–216. doi:10.1207/s15326985ep3004_7

Skinner, E. A., & Belmont, M. J. (1993). Motivation in the classroom: Reciprocal effects of teacher behavior and student engagement across the school year. *Journal of Educational Psychology, 85*(4), 571–581. doi:10.1037/0022-0663.85.4.571

SWOT Analysis II: Looking inside for strengths and weaknesses. (2006). Boston, MA: Harvard Business School.

Appendix

OBSERVATION PROTOCOL

Positive Practice	Comment
Greets student by name.	
Begins on a positive note.	
Engages with students, moving around the lab and reviewing work with each student.	
Sets session goals with student.	
Uses appropriate eye contact.	
Smiles appropriately.	
Exhibits positive attitude.	
Exhibits patience.	
Is encouraging and enthusiastic.	
Expresses empathy.	
Uses appropriate questioning.	
Uses wait time.	
Breaks tasks into steps.	
Reinforces student's understanding.	
Asks student to summarize.	
Asks student to explain.	
Corrects student sensitively.	
Responds calmly and quickly to conflict.	
Responds appropriately.	
Summarizes at end of session.	
Previews next session.	
Ends on a positive note.	

Emily Miller Payne

Postsecondary programs that deliver tutoring and mentoring services increasingly require more sophisticated and data-driven evaluation plans to meet the demands of institutional and funding accountability requirements. Those demands exert pressure on program planners to engage in targeted needs assessment, to attend to data that represent the program delivery process, to assess the impact of the program overall, and to report results to stakeholders at various levels. Outcome evaluations play a prominent role in education, especially when funding for education programs is scarce (Chen, 1996; Fitzpatrick, Sanders, & Worthen, 2004; Rossi, Lipsey, & Freeman, 2004; Scriven, 1996) because they monitor whether programs are achieving their goals sufficiently to continue to be funded.

The program outcome evaluation strategies that will be discussed here will help programs measure the impact that effective tutor and mentor training has on tutor and mentor performance and ultimately on their students' academic performance, study behaviors, and academic success (Kirkpatrick, 1994). The intent of this module is to help program managers plan and implement an effective internal evaluation strategy for a tutor or mentor training program.

Needs Assessment

The first step in conducting an outcome evaluation of this nature is for the evaluation team, typically made up of stakeholders who are familiar with the program, to review the needs assessment that program planners conducted initially to guide the development of the tutor or mentor training program (Sonnichsen, 2000). Needs assessment data help the evaluation team learn about the history and origins of the program: What was the initial problem the program was developed to address, how has implementation of the program reduced the problem, and how do the goals and objectives of the program link to the results of the needs assessment?

Because a needs assessment represents the current mandate for the training program, the evaluators should use the data that established the need for the program in developing the evaluation plan (Gupta, 1999). However, if the needs assessment is outdated or if the program has shifted its focus or the personnel it trains, it may be necessary to conduct a new needs assessment prior to developing the evaluation plan. In order to determine the viability of the most recent needs assessment, the evaluators should talk with the staff who conducted the assessment and, if possible, with any stakeholders who participated. In a tutor and mentor training program, stakeholders can be students who receive tutoring and mentoring, faculty who teach the students who partake of the services, and others in the institution with knowledge of the training program. When the evaluators have established the extent of the current need for the program, the next step is to plan the evaluation guided by the needs assessment data.

Program Evaluation Plan

The second step in the process of program assessment is developing the comprehensive program evaluation plan. The evaluation team should develop a concise description of the nature of the program to be evaluated. How do program staff and stakeholders describe the training program? The evaluators should determine what elements or components of the program will be included in the evaluation. If the evaluation covers tutor and mentor training for staff in a comprehensive learning center, the components could be extensive (e.g., how well tutors and mentors were trained to conduct outreach to students, to work with students in the intended settings, to conduct outreach to faculty), but if the evaluation covers one component or service (e.g., tutor training in a specific content area), the focus of the evaluation may be narrower and the evaluation plan less elaborate.

As the evaluation team develops the plan, it will be important to determine what existing data are available. The program probably already collects student satisfaction survey data and may collect feedback data from faculty who refer students to the center. If that is the case, the evaluators should plan to use existing data as much as possible in the evaluation plan. Many tutoring programs use online or one-question exit surveys to gather student feedback; if this survey strategy works, it will be easier and more cost effective for the evaluators to incorporate the existing collection and analysis method into the plan. Most postsecondary programs have access to survey software or online services that make data collection and analysis relatively seamless.

Next evaluators should determine what new data can be collected relatively easily. Tutor and mentor training programs can ultimately touch many people beyond the students with whom tutors and mentors work and the faculty who teach those students; therefore, the evaluator should think broadly when considering what data to collect and from whom. The intent of this module is to inform practitioners about outcome evaluations, but evaluators may also want to think about setting up a plan for an impact evaluation by which the latent effects of good tutor and mentor training might ultimately be measured.

A major task in developing evaluation instruments is determining the key questions to ask for both the formative (process) and summative (product) evaluation. Logically, the program evaluation questions should reflect the needs assessment questions if the needs assessment was done thoroughly and if the questions are current and relevant (Holden, 2008). If the program depends on external funding from a grant or other external source to support the tutor and mentor training, the funding source may require that the evaluation address specific questions related to the effectiveness of operations; if that is the case, the evaluators should address the funder's questions as part of the plan. If the evaluation involves getting feedback from multiple stakeholder groups, it may make sense to develop more than one instrument in order to keep the instrument length manageable and to focus specific questions to the stakeholders who can offer the most relevant input.

A second consideration in developing the questions for assessment instruments is the institutional reporting line of the tutor and mentor training program. Whether the program reports to multiple divisions (e.g., academic affairs and student affairs) or to just one division, the evaluators should inquire about specific information that administrators up the reporting line will require in an evaluation of the program.

When the evaluation team has developed and piloted questions to ask of stakeholders, it is time to consolidate them into one or more instruments. If the evaluation will solicit input from stakeholders with very different connections to the program, such as students and faculty, multiple instruments targeting the specific populations' interests would be in order. The reporting authority may call for answers that are quantitative (such as Likert-scale responses) or qualitative (such as open-ended responses) or a combination of the two. Generally speaking, a combination of quantitative and qualitative questions will offer a more comprehensive picture of the training program, but evaluators should consult with program staff about the specific needs of the funding source and reporting lines.

Data Collection and Analysis

Data for a program evaluation can be gathered through various means, and typically the least complicated strategies are the best. If the tutor and mentor training program currently gathers data using an electronic instrument in an online medium like Blackboard® or other commercially available survey systems such as Survey Monkey™ or MR Interview, and if that system works well, the evaluators should consider staying with what works and is familiar to the stakeholders. If the current data collection system depends on collecting and analyzing hand-written data, staying with the current system is an option to consider; however, the evaluators and the training program manager may want to explore more efficient and less expensive means of collecting and analyzing ongoing data.

If data collection is well planned, evaluation of large amounts of quantitative data can be as simple as downloading from Survey Monkey™ or MR Interview into a statistical program. Data sets that are less complicated or less robust may be a good match for a well-designed spreadsheet available in most comprehensive software programs. Large quantities of qualitative data collected via open-ended questions in an online survey can be analyzed by using a commercially packaged qualitative data management and analysis software package such as HyperRESEARCH™. If the qualitative data are limited to only a few questions with no more than 50 or so respondents, analysis by hand may be more efficient. Many good sources can guide the evaluation team through that sort of analysis (Lichtman, 2010; Punch, 2009). Typically, program evaluation benefits from qualitative data gathered by the evaluator or surrogate in the form of interviews or observations. Interview and observation data tend to be qualitative and robust and will, therefore, require more time and experience in the analysis phase (Punch, 2009).

Evaluation Reports

When the data are collected and analyzed, the evaluation team must determine who is to be the intended audience or audiences to whom the report will be directed. In preparing the evaluation report for a tutor or mentor training program, it may be appropriate to plan, at a minimum, reports with two or three levels of detail: a comprehensive report for the program staff, an overview report for primary stakeholders such as administrators immediately above program staff, and an executive summary of the results for upper administration, students served by the tutoring and mentoring services, and other interested parties (Sonnichsen, 2000). Programs often report the results of a good evaluation via the campus newspaper or the institution's public affairs office, and for those purposes the executive summary is typically sufficient. Program staff should determine in advance how they intend to use the results of the evaluation in order to gain maximum advantage from the reports.

The second factor to consider is whether the funder or institution requires that the evaluation team reports the results on a specific form or in a particular format. If the report is part of a training program's accountability plan with the institution or funder, a prescribed form or format is probably specified. If no form or format is specified, the program staff and the evaluators should discuss what format will best showcase the results.

Evaluation should be a natural part of program planning and administration; this is especially true of training programs that must continually reevaluate effectiveness to remain viable. Ultimately, the completed evaluation will allow all stakeholders in the tutor or mentor training program to understand which processes are working and which require revision. The process and the resulting report can be invaluable as planning tools for the future of the training program.

References

Chen, H. (1996). A comprehensive typology for program evaluation. *Evaluation Practice, 17,* 121–130. doi:10.1016/S0886-1633(96)90017-3

Fitzpatrick, J. L., Sanders, J. R., & Worthen, B. R. (2004). *Program evaluation: Alternative approaches and practical guidelines* (3rd ed.). Boston, MA: Pearson Education.

Gupta, K. (1999). *A practical guide to needs assessment.* San Francisco, CA: Jossey-Bass.

Holden, D. J. (2008). *A practical guide to program evaluation planning: Theory and case examples.* Thousand Oaks, CA: Sage.

Kirkpatrick, D. L. (1994). *Evaluating training programs: The four levels*. San Francisco, CA: Berrett-Koehler.

Lichtman, M. (2010). *Understanding and evaluating qualitative educational research*. Thousand Oaks, CA: Sage.

Punch, K. (2009). *Introduction to research methods in education*. Thousand Oaks, CA: Sage.

Rossi, P. H., Lipsey, M. W., & Freeman, H. E. (2004). *Evaluation: A systematic approach* (7th ed.). Thousand Oaks, CA: Sage.

Scriven, M. (1996). Types of evaluation and types of evaluator. *Evaluation Practice, 17*, 151–161.

Sonnichsen, R. C. (2000). *High impact internal evaluation: A practitioner's guide to evaluating and consulting inside organizations*. Thousand Oaks, CA: Sage.

◼ Jan Norton

Assessment and evaluation are ever present in higher education, especially within the accreditation cycles that institutions routinely face. In addition to demonstrating effectiveness, evaluation can help tutoring programs make decisions about future services. Five guidelines can help tutoring program staffs make a commitment to evaluation and improvement:

- Embed evaluation in the program.
- Refer to respected standards for excellence.
- Incorporate both qualitative and quantitative data.
- Use direct and indirect measures.
- Specify tutor training outcomes.

These basic guidelines encompass many evaluation elements and can be only briefly explored in these pages. Even within this brevity, however, there is one critical caution: evaluation is specific to context. The information that follows may not be fully relevant to every aspect of every program, but the basic principles can be adapted to unique program characteristics.

Embed Evaluation in the Program

To be most effective, a tutoring program's commitment to evaluation and quality should be included in the program's mission or goals statement. Evaluation needs to be an ongoing process with routine collection of usage data and systematic imports of student information. However, embedding evaluation does not mean that every evaluation process needs to occur at every opportunity. Programs can develop cycles of evaluation processes that occur every week or every semester for some measures and annually or every 2 or 3 years for others.

Refer to Respected Standards for Excellence

There are numerous local measures of quality for a tutoring program, many of which may be determined by an institution's funding, mission, priorities, and student profile. Tutor program evaluators should also consider established, nationally and internationally recognized standards for excellence. Comparison to nationally and internationally accepted standards brings a level of validation to a tutoring program, and higher education does traditionally respect external measures of quality.

The Association for the Tutoring Profession (ATP) certifies individuals as tutors and tutor trainers, and the National College Learning Center Association (NCLCA) certifies the people who manage learning centers. Three other organizations take a broader view of standards for excellence in tutoring. The College Reading and Learning Association (CRLA) sets standards of skill and training needed for peer academic support in postsecondary education through International Tutor Training Program Certification (CRLA, 2011b) and International Mentor Training Program Certification (CRLA, 2011a). These standards are used for evaluating training in tutorial programs, academic support programs, retention efforts, and student development programs. The National

Association for Developmental Education (NADE; 2009) sets standards for programs in developmental education and promotes best practices and effective evaluation. All of these certification programs derive historically from standards and guidelines established by the Council for the Advancement of Standards in Higher Education (CAS; 2009). CAS standards for learning assistance programs as well as the CAS general standards require assessment of student learning and development outcomes in 6 domains and 28 dimensions. More information about each of these organizations and certifications can be found on their websites.

Incorporate Both Qualitative and Quantitative Data

The best evaluation plans incorporate a healthy variety of information and processes, including attention to standards and the benefits of both direct and indirect measures of tutoring effectiveness. Part of the overall evaluation picture also includes a combination of qualitative and quantitative data.

Qualitative data are usually sought in order to provide a human voice in evaluation. Most programs can incorporate some focus group discussions and conduct opinion surveys. Focus groups can consist of mixed groups that combine faculty, staff, clients, nonclients, and tutors, or groups of just one category or role. If there are concerns about objectivity, focus groups can be led by someone outside the tutoring program. Surveys are another way to generate qualitative input for evaluation. Some general surveys for evaluation consist of only three or four questions; others are far more extensive. Some opinion surveys are offered to tutoring clients at every session, and others are scheduled for specific times in the semester or at specific levels of service provided.

Client satisfaction surveys are a valuable component of evaluation systems. Clients can rate the overall extent to which they felt assisted as well as more specific elements of the tutoring session, such as the tutor's level of patience or knowledge, effectiveness of the tutor's questions and explanations, and ease of communication. It is important to consider that clients are not trained observers and evaluators; their high ratings of tutor helpfulness may be more related to their sense of immediate gratitude, and low ratings may indicate not reasoned judgment but frustration that the tutor would not share old tests or "grade" homework or any number of other misunderstandings about what a tutor's appropriate role is.

Quantitative evaluation of a tutoring program usually includes data about client demographics and either simple tallies of usage or more complex calculations involving student grades and retention. Demographics consist of client personal information and incoming academic measures; to assure that the tutoring program's data matches the institution's records and to save time in data collection and entry, demographics should be uploaded from the student database if at all possible. Usage data should consist of a minimum of three data points: the number of individual students who receive tutoring, the number of hours those clients spend in tutoring, and the number of each client's visits. A fourth and fifth point are extremely valuable: one identifies the course(s) for which the client received tutoring, and another identifies the nature of the service provided, such as one-on-one tutoring, online assistance, or Supplemental Instruction (SI) session.

A thorough quantitative evaluation process also looks at clients' grades to estimate the impact of tutoring. Grades or other numeric measures allow comparisons between clients and nonclients. One argument sometimes made against comparing client performance to that of nonclients is that clients are typically the more motivated students and thus would normally perform better regardless of any tutoring intervention. However, while no comparison proves or disproves a cause-and-effect relationship, if clients and nonclients have similar overall demographic profiles, similar incoming characteristics, and similar prior grade performances, there is far less reason to assume that student motivation is suddenly a more significant contributor to the improved performance exhibited by clients.

Use Direct and Indirect Measures

Direct measures assess a tutor's or client's ability to perform a particular skill or exhibit a specific behavior, while indirect measures are more of an estimate or interpretation (usually measured via self-report surveys). The outcome statement is what determines whether a measure is direct or indirect. For example, if a tutor training outcome is that the client be able to select the main idea of a paragraph or solve a quadratic equation, then a direct measure of success may be to give the client an equation to solve or to provide a paragraph and ask the client to select the main idea. An indirect measure would be a tutor's judgment or the client's opinion about whether the client could demonstrate the skill. If a desired outcome is satisfaction with services, asking the clients if they are satisfied is a direct measure, and counting the percentage of students who return for another visit is an indirect measure of satisfaction with services. (Of course, return visits may not measure satisfaction at all.) Although direct measures are occasionally difficult to gather, they are often considered more authentic.

One way to measure learning directly is to use miniature pretests and posttest measures, such as the main idea or equation example noted previously. If the client wants assistance with quadratic equations, the tutor can select a sample equation and ask the client to solve it. The pair can then work through any confusions that the client is having, and at the close of the tutorial the client can work another, similar equation to be sure learning has occurred. Course vocabulary, diagrams, process steps, sentence construction, and many other tutor session activities can be assessed in the same way. Although not every tutorial lends itself to such specific, direct measures of relatively isolated skills, these pre- and post-tutoring assessments can be components of an overall evaluation plan.

Specify Tutor Training Outcomes

A tutor training outcome is basically a goal: a statement of what is hoped will happen as a result of the training. For every tutor training topic, there is an underlying expectation for specific tutor behaviors. An outcome may be a change of attitude or confidence; it can also be the performance of a particular skill at a specified level of competence. For example, when tutor training includes a discussion of core job duties, tutors are clearly expected to adhere conscientiously to those duties. Training about ethics should result in tutors' knowing when and how to help clients without crossing the line into too much involvement in the clients' assignments and learning. Training tutors about reducing test anxiety is beneficial for the tutors but is also usually intended to help tutors be more effective in reducing their clients' test anxiety. Training about campus resources presumes that tutors would then know about the services for themselves and be able to refer other students appropriately.

The necessary counterpart to any outcome is a way (or several ways and occasions) to determine whether the outcome was reached. For example, if a tutor training session focuses on tutors' understanding of thinking skills using Bloom's Taxonomy (Anderson & Krathwohl, 2001), a pretest before training and a posttest afterward—whether immediately at the close of training or delayed for a week or more—can provide a measure of the tutors' learning and training effectiveness. More important may be an evaluation of the tutors' use of the information rather than merely their understanding of it for themselves; perhaps direct observation of tutors before and after training would provide a means to evaluate training effectiveness, or tutors could write brief summaries of sessions, explicitly noting how they incorporated knowledge from a recent training.

Establishing an evaluation rubric for training outcomes and tutor behaviors can be challenging. Some training outcomes are clearly measurable; for example, tutor patience may be defined and evaluated in part as a function of wait time between questions, or training about critical thinking may focus on the percentage of open-ended versus yes-or-no questions posed by the tutor. Other training topics require more subtle assessment; many will need to be evaluated using tutor, client, or observer ratings and comments. For example, a tutor training about campus resources and referral would be difficult to evaluate using observations of tutoring sessions because resource referrals will not be necessary or appropriate in all tutoring sessions. For that training topic, assessment before and after the training or a system of tutor session summaries would be a more effective evaluation method. In any case, when evaluation is embedded in the program not every evaluation process needs to occur at every opportunity. Evaluating tutor training effectiveness can occur in a number of ways with the likely result that multiple measures will all point to the same general conclusion.

For all five of the previously stated guidelines help is available. Hiring a consultant or arranging peer reviews is an excellent evaluation option. Other resources include websites, publications, coursework, faculty partners, offices of institutional research, and professional organizations. As more evaluation research about tutoring is conducted and published, evaluation processes may become more consistent across programs and institutions, thus providing a clearer base of performance measures and expectations that programs can use as benchmarks for excellence.

References

Anderson, L. W., & Krathwohl, D. R. (Eds.). (2001). *A taxonomy for learning, teaching and assessing: A revision of Bloom's taxonomy of educational objectives* (Complete ed.). New York, NY: Longman.

Council for the Advancement of Standards in Higher Education. (2009). *CAS professional standards for higher education* (7th ed.). Washington, DC: Author.

College Reading and Learning Association. (2011a). *International Mentor Training Program Certification: About IMTPC.* Retrieved from http://www.crla.net/imtpc/about.htm

College Reading and Learning Association. (2011b). *International Tutor Training Program Certification: About ITTPC.* Retrieved from http://www.crla.net/ittpc/about_ittpc.htm

National Association for Developmental Education. (2009). *NADE Certification Council: Mission statement.* Retrieved from http://www.nadecertification.net/index.asp

About the Contributors

Taylor W. Acee is assistant professor in the Department of Curriculum and Instruction at Texas State University-San Marcos. Taylor earned his Ph.D. in educational psychology from the University of Texas at Austin. His research is focused on strategic and self-regulated learning, achievement motivation, and college student achievement and retention.

Linda T. Barr is an English as a Second Language instructor and the Learning Center Coordinator for the Harrisburg Campus of Central Pennsylvania's Community College (HACC). She received a B.A. in English from Ursinus College and an M.Ed, in Teaching English to Speakers of Other Languages (TESOL) from Shenandoah University. Current research includes successful academic interventions with emphasis on intercultural and interpersonal communication.

Diana Calhoun Bell, Associate Professor of Rhetoric and Composition at the University of Alabama in Huntsville, has served as Writing Center Director, Writing Program Administrator, and Executive Director of the Student Success Center. Diana edited the *Journal of College Reading and Learning* of the College Reading and Learning Association and co-authored *Toward Deprivatized Pedagogy* (Hampton Press).

Maija M. Braaten, M.Ed., is Coordinator of Instruction for ASPIRE/Student Support Services at the University of Montevallo (Montevallo, AL), with primary interests in learning assistance, tutoring management, First Year Experience, academic advising, and retention.

Thea J. Brophy is an Academic Counselor at Calvin College in Grand Rapids, MI. She also supervises the peer tutoring program at Calvin College. Her undergraduate and graduate work both focused on history.

Jennifer E. Bruce, Ph.D., Virginia Commonwealth University, is the Director of Instruction and an Associate Professor of Education at Randolph-Macon College. Her research interests are in the areas of mentoring at-risk college students and the growth of centers for teaching and learning.

Kristine Noll Carnes (M.A., Curriculum and Instruction, New Mexico State University, and M.Ed., Higher and Postsecondary Education, Arizona State University) currently teaches in the Humboldt Unified School District, Prescott Valley, AZ. She has taught in New Mexico and Arizona and served as Coordinator for the Academic Success Coaching Program at Arizona State University.

Martha E. Casazza is the Vice President for Academic Affairs at The Adler School of Professional Psychology (Chicago, IL). She has co-authored three books: *Learning Assistance and Developmental Education: A Guide for Effective Practice* (1996), *Learning and Development* (2000), and *Access, Opportunity and Success: Keeping the Promise of Higher Education* (2006).

Carmen Christopher Caviness, Director of the Learning Center and English faculty at Meredith College, has a master's degree from North Carolina State University and is a Ph.D. candidate at Old Dominion University. Her work appears in *Issues in Writing* and *The Writing Lab Newsletter*; her primary research interests include the rhetorics of material bodies.

Daniel A. Clark is a graduate student in the Department of Educational Psychology at The University of Texas at Austin. His research is focused on motivational self-beliefs, perceptual disfluency, and test-enhanced learning.

Rebecca Daly Cofer currently serves as an Academic Support Counselor and Study Abroad Coordinator at Abraham Baldwin Agricultural College in Tifton, GA. Rebecca previously worked in the TECHniques Center at Texas Tech University as an academic counselor and the program's tutor coordinator. She has her B.A. and M.A. from Virginia Polytechnic Institute and State University (Virginia Tech).

Lisa N. Putnam Cole has an M.S.Ed. in Reading from Northern Illinois University and certification from the Kellogg Institute. She co-edited the *NADE Self-Evaluation Guides* (2nd edition). Lisa is faculty in Reading and founding coordinator of Heartland Community College's tutoring program in Normal, IL. She acknowledges Julia Visor (now deceased) and Janice Neuleib in the development of the group interview process.

Ellyn K. Couillard (M.S. in College Counseling and Student Development, St. Cloud State University, MN; B.A. in Sociology, The University of Georgia) is a TRiO Student Support Services Counselor at Mercer University in Macon, GA. She has experience working with diverse populations of students from varied types of institutions.

Lisa Cradit is Director of Academic Support Services at Texas Lutheran University. She received a B.A. in English from Texas A&M University-Commerce and an M.A. in English from Texas State University-San Marcos. Her research interests include brain-based learning theory and educational support for at-risk and underprepared students.

Kathryn Crisostomo is the Assistant Director of the Academic Enhancement Center at the University of Rhode Island. She holds a B.S. in biology from the University of Connecticut and an M.S. in counseling, with a focus on student development in higher education, from Central Connecticut State University.

Anna Z. Crockett (B.A., M.A.T., German, University of Illinois, Champaign-Urbana), formerly directed College of Liberal Arts Advising, Texas A&M University. At Virginia Military Institute in Lexington, VA, Anna is Associate Director of the Miller Academic Center, responsible for College Reading and Learning Association-certified tutoring and mentoring and other supporting programs. Her major area of interest is Executive Function Processes.

Pamela Czapla, Ph.D., is Director of Tutorial Services and Associate Professor in the Department of Academic Development and Counseling at Lock Haven University. She also teaches library skills to graduate students as an adjunct at University of Maryland University College. Her research interests are data collection, communication, and distance education.

Breana Sylvester Dacy works for The University of Texas at Austin as an institutional researcher, collaborating with multiple departments across the University. Breana earned her Ph.D. in educational psychology from The University of Texas at Austin. Her research focuses primarily on teacher attrition, learning, and motivational well-being.

Mark F. Daddona is Associate Vice President for Enrollment Management an Academic Success and Assistant Professor of Psychology at Clayton State University. He holds a Ph.D. in counseling and student personnel services and is a Licensed Professional Counselor (LPC) in the State of Georgia.

Randy E. Dale, J.D., is a Ph.D. candidate in education at Texas State University-San Marcos. His main research interests lie in the education of older adults about successful aging concepts. He has taught as an adjunct at the University of Mary Hardin-Baylor in Belton, TX, where he practices criminal defense law.

Jeremy K. Dearman is a graduate student at The University of Texas at Austin. He is currently working on a doctorate in the Department of Educational Psychology. His research focuses on strategic and self-regulated learning, motivation, and college student achievement and retention.

Carol Dochen is currently the Director of the Student Learning Assistance Center (SLAC) in the Division of Academic Affairs at Texas State University in San Marcos. She received her Ph.D. in Higher Education Administration from The University of Texas at Austin.

Eric Dunker (B.A., Bucknell University; M.S. in Student Affairs, Colorado State University) has experience in learning support, assessment, and residence life and is currently Director of Assessment and Testing at Metropolitan State College of Denver. He is also completing a Ph.D. at the University of Denver, focusing his dissertation on emerging Hispanic-serving institutions.

Johanna Dvorak directs Academic Support Services at the University of Wisconsin-Milwaukee. She earned her B.A. in English at Drake University, M.Ed. at The University of Texas at Austin, and Ph.D. in Urban Education and Information Science at the University of Wisconsin-Milwaukee, with a focus on learning assistance in higher education.

Anita H. Ens is a doctoral candidate in education at the University of Manitoba. Her background includes working with adults in adult education and postsecondary settings, particularly regarding learning strategies and writing pedagogy. Anita's research interests include collaborative writing, sustainability in education, multiple literacies, and diversity.

Katherine Firkins is a Lecturer in Deaf Studies and English and Tutor Coordinator for the Student Learning Program under the National Center on Deafness at California State University, Northridge. She has a B.A. and M.A. in English and is a certified National Tutoring Association Tutor Trainer.

Peggy J. Fish-Oliver (B.A., M.A., A.B.D. in English, Purdue; A.B.D. in Higher Education Administration, University of Houston) is a retired English professor from San Jacinto College South in Houston, TX. She focused on teaching composition and literature in traditional and online classes for 27 years and tutored in the San Jacinto South Writer's Center.

Carlton J. Fong is a doctoral student in the Department of Educational Psychology and William Powers, Jr., Graduate Fellow at The University of Texas at Austin. His research is focused on understanding the contextual and personality factors that influence motivation, self-regulation, and academic achievement.

Patricia Fullmer is the Director of the Learning Resource Center at Lincoln University, PA. She earned an Ed.D. from Wilmington University and a Master's and Bachelor's from Temple University. Her research interests are in the assessment of student support programs.

Rebekah Haddock has studied at academic institutions in several countries, obtaining a B.A. in Scandinavian Area Studies from the University of East Anglia in England; a certificate in fluency in the Norwegian language from the University of Oslo, Norway; and an M.A. in English Literature at the University of Alabama in Huntsville, USA.

Cheon-woo Han is an assistant instructor and Ph.D. student in the Department of Educational Psychology at The University of Texas at Austin. He has interests in achievement goal orientation, learning environments to enhance intrinsic motivation, and neuroscience.

Jacqueline Harris, Ed.D., is the Writing and Study Strategies Coordinator in Ball State University's Learning Center. She has taught online and on campus at Anderson University, Indiana Wesleyan University, Ball State University, and the Prince of Songkla University (Thailand). Jackie has been president of the National College Learning Center Association and a reading consultant for the Indiana Department of Education.

Barbara Ryan Hausman coordinates disability services at DeSales University and serves as an adjunct professor in the Department of Education. She specializes in assistive technology and has a passion for teaching freshmen how to apply Covey's "7 Habits" to ensure success during their first year at college. Barbara received her master's degree from Adelphi University.

David Hayes is Director of the University of Rhode Island's Academic Enhancement Center. David has an Ed.M. from Harvard University with a concentration on adult learning and teaching and is working toward a Ph.D. in education at the University of Rhode Island. His current research focuses on institutional racism and inclusive pedagogy in higher education.

Janice B. Heerspink (M.A., Michigan State University) is Associate Director of Student Academic Services, Emerita, at Calvin College in Grand Rapids, MI. For 29 years Jan provided academic support to students in higher education, including tutoring support as well as a learning strategies course, which during her tenure became a three-credit course.

Jeanne L. Higbee serves as Professor and Director of Graduate Studies in the Department of Postsecondary Teaching and Learning in the College of Education and Human Development at the University of Minnesota, Twin Cities. Her higher education experience spans student development, teaching, and advising from 1974 to today.

Jodi Patrick Holschuh (Ph.D., University of Georgia) is an Associate Professor at Texas State University and co-author of *Effective College Learning, College Success Strategies, Active Learning,* and *College Rules! How to Study, Survive, and Succeed in College.* Her research interests include epistemological beliefs, self-regulated learning, strategic learning, and motivation.

Timothy A. Hopp is an Associate Professor of Language and Humanities at Trine University. He earned a B.A. in Technical Theatre and in English from Rocky Mountain College, an M.A. in Theatre from the University of Maine, and a Ph.D. in English from Texas A&M University-Commerce.

DeLandra M. Hunter is the Director of the First-Year Advising and Retention Center at Clayton State University. He completed his B.S.Ed. and M.Ed. at Jacksonville State University, AL, and has many years of experience as an educator teaching secondary English, coordinating college academic and mentoring programs, and advising college students.

Monique Idoux coordinates the Writing Center and teaches composition at Northeastern State University in Broken Arrow, OK. Passionate about teaching and tutoring, Monique encourages students to see themselves as writers and scholars making important contributions to their fields of study and to see the power and opportunity that writing well provides.

Lisa M. Johns earned her M.A. in psychology from Texas A&M University-Kingsville and her B.A. in psychology from Texas State University-San Marcos. She has established student leadership programs and continues to supervise mentors. Lisa is currently the Director for Learning Assistance and Assessment in the Tomás Rivera Center of The University of Texas at San Antonio.

Richard George Johnson (M.S., education and human resource development, Texas A&M University) is Director of Academic Support Programs in the Student Learning Center at Texas A&M University. Richard is a fellow of the Wakonse South Conference on College Teaching and has served on that conference's planning committee for 10 years. His interests include critical thinking, peer education, and enjoying life with his loving family.

Leah Allen Jones holds an M.A. from East Carolina University and a Certificate as a Developmental Education Specialist from Appalachian State University. She was a 2007 Kellogg Institute participant. Currently Leah is an Assistant Professor of Reading and English at College of the Albemarle and is pursuing a doctorate from Grambling State University.

Michelle E. Jordan is an Assistant Professor in the Mary Lou Fulton Teachers College at Arizona State University. Michelle earned her Ph.D. in educational psychology from The University of Texas at Austin. Her research focuses on how peers influence one another's learning and how students self-regulate in academic contexts.

JaeHak Jung is a doctoral student in the Department of Educational Psychology at The University of Texas at Austin. His research interest is in learning strategies, including self-regulative, cognitive, metacognitive, and motivational strategies.

Kimberly K. Kelley is Director of Testing Services at Heartland Community College in Normal, IL. Kim currently serves on the National Association for Developmental Education Certification Council. She attended the Kellogg Institute and On Course Workshop I. Kim earned her Master's degree in college student personnel administration at Illinois State University, where she also earned her Bachelor's degree.

Loren Kleinman (B.A., English literature, Drew University; M.A., creative and critical writing, University of Sussex, UK) is Assistant Director of the New Jersey Academic Support Centers at Berkeley College. She studies Writing Across the Curriculum, online learning, learning communities, critical vs. divergent thinking, and creative writing. Loren wrote *Flamenco Sketches* and owns LK Editorial.

Ann M. Koefer, M.Ed., coordinates the Gateway to Success and tutorial programs at DeSales University in Center Valley, PA. Her work focuses on providing services to bridge the transition from high school to university life. Areas of specialization include peer mentoring, tutoring, retention studies, and academic advising.

Jaimie M. Krause is an assistant instructor and doctoral candidate in the Department of Educational Psychology at The University of Texas at Austin. She also teaches Learning Frameworks courses for Texas State University Round Rock Campus and Austin Community College. Her dissertation research examines the role of academic-specific self-compassion with first-generation college students.

Holly Arnold Laue (M.A. English, University of Alabama in Huntsville), former adjunct for the English Department and Freshman Composition instructor, is the Academic Programs manager and an Academic Coach for the Student Success Center at the University of Alabama in Huntsville. She also teaches the First Year Experience seminar.

Jennifer Kay Leach is a doctoral student in educational psychology at The University of Texas at Austin, where she is also an assistant instructor of Individual Learning Skills. Her research is focused on motivation, academic entitlement, and academic major choice and satisfaction among college students.

Ali Mageehon (Ph.D., higher education and adult studies) directs Adult Basic Studies Development at Umpqua Community College in Roseburg, OR. She has taught in a county jail and community colleges in the Marshall Islands and rural New Mexico. Ali's articles focus on technology, women's education in incarceration, and writing center space issues.

Patricia A. Maher holds a Ph.D. in adult education and is the Director of Tutoring and Learning Services, part of the University of South Florida Learning Commons. She oversees tutoring, the Writing Center, learning courses, and other academic support services for both undergraduate and graduate students.

Howard Y. Masuda is Director of the University Tutorial Center at California State University, Los Angeles. He received his Ph.D. in educational psychology (learning and instruction) at the University of California, Los Angeles. Howard is a long-time member of the College Reading and Learning Association (CRLA) and reviewer for CRLA's International Tutor Training Program Certification.

James Mathews is the retired Learning Lab Coordinator for the Student Learning Assistance Center (SLAC) at Texas State University in San Marcos, TX. James earned his M.A. in developmental and adult education at Texas State University-San Marcos.

Mark S. May is Associate Professor of Communication at Clayton State University. Mark's experience includes student retention, First Year Experience courses, developmental education, and learning assistance. He served as President of the National College Learning Center Association and is currently researching tutoring philosophies and the 1895 Cotton States Exposition.

Darla H. McCann, M.S. in education, Moorhead State University, serves on the executive board of the Association for the Tutoring Profession (ATP). Under her direction, Anoka-Ramsey Community College's Cambridge Campus Academic Support Center achieved national recognition with the Diana Hacker Enhancing Developmental Education Award and ATP Tutoring Program Award of Excellence.

M. E. McWilliams directs the Academic Assistance and Resource Center at Stephen F. Austin State University. The Center has won the Texas Higher Education Coordinating Board's Star Award, National Association for Developmental Education's Distinguished Certification, Texas Association for Developmental Education's Distinguished Program Award, and the John Champagne Memorial Award for Outstanding Developmental Education Program.

Julianne Messia is Director of Academic Learning Services at Albany College of Pharmacy and Health Sciences. She has worked in academic support for nearly 10 years managing tutoring programs, advising students, and teaching workshops. Julianne's interests are peer assistance programs and cognitive psychology.

Nancy F. Mills teaches reading and study strategies and manages the tutoring program for St. Cloud State University's Department of Academic Support. Her Ph.D. is from the University of South Florida, with a focus on college teaching. Nancy's research interests include student academic acclimation and faculty responses to teachable moments.

Annemarie Mulkey earned a B.A. in English and M.A. in English with an emphasis in rhetoric and composition at The University of Texas at San Antonio (UTSA) She has worked at UTSA for several years in various positions including student mentor, writing consultant, academic coach, first-year seminar instructor, and currently academic advisor.

Jan Norton (M.A., Educational Research; National College Learning Center Association lifetime Learning Center Leadership Certification) has extensive experience as a learning assistance center manager. She reviews applications for National Association for Developmental Education program certification and assists colleagues with data collection, assessment, evaluation, and research. Jan also is a consultant on program development and evaluation.

Carol E. O'Hara directs the Writing/Resource Center at Friends University in Wichita, KS. She is an Assistant Professor of English and earned her Master's degree from Wichita State University. As Coordinator of the Composition Program, Carol is also involved in the First Year Experience Program and the Retention Taskforce.

Jody L. Owen is Coordinator of Academic Advising for the University College at South Dakota State University. She is interested in research on predictors of degree attainment and the impact of interventions designed to improve degree completion rates. Jody is pursuing an Ed.D. in educational administration.

Eric J. Paulson, Ph.D., is a professor in the graduate program in developmental education at Texas State University-San Marcos. His teaching background and research interests center on post-secondary literacy instruction in developmental education domains, and he has taught in a variety of institutions in several states and countries.

Emily Miller Payne (Ed.D. in reading education) is Associate Professor of Developmental Education and Director of The Education Institute at Texas State University. She researches adult student college transition and developmental literacy. Emily is a former editor of the *Journal of College Reading and Learning (JCRL)* and current College Reading and Learning Association Media Advisory Board and *JCRL* Editorial Board member.

Todd S. Phillips was named Director of the Student Success Center at Truman State University in 2008. He was a Kellogg Institute alumnus and a mentor for Technology Institute for Developmental Educators. Todd served as president of the Midwest Regional Association for Developmental Education and chaired the Political Liaison Committee of the National Association for Developmental Education at the time of his death on March 31, 2011.

Jan R. Pomeroy earned a B.A. in business management and M.A. in organizational leadership from Bethel University, MN. She served Anoka-Ramsey Community College Coon Rapids Campus as Director of the Academic Support Center and subsequently as curriculum and instructional architect for the Experiential Learning Program. Jan's interests include the success and empowerment of college students.

Suzanne Ponicsan serves Hodges University as the Director of Academic Achievement Services. She holds an M.Ed. degree in adult education from The Pennsylvania State University and is currently pursuing an Ed.D. degree in higher education leadership at Northcentral University.

David L. Reedy is Program Coordinator for Tutoring at Columbus State Community College. He earned degrees in music education as well as an M.S. in educational administration and Ph.D. in adult education. David served as President of the National College Learning Center Association and has research interests in students with special needs and at-risk students.

Kevin Roessger is a doctoral student at the University of Wisconsin-Milwaukee. He served as a vocational instructor prior to his current positions as project assistant and instructional design instructor at UWM. His research interests include adult motor learning, applications of behavioral learning theory in adult education, and reflective practice in instrumental learning.

Aileen M. Rolon earned a B.A. in sociology at the University of California, Los Angeles, and an M.S. in counseling with an emphasis in higher education at the University of La Verne. She also earned certification as a tutor trainer from the National Tutoring Association. Aileen is Academic Advisor and Tutor Supervisor for the Student Learning Program of the National Center on Deafness at California State University, Northridge.

Colleen Rustad-Sampson is pursuing a doctorate in clinical psychology at the American School of Professional Psychology, Argosy University, Seattle. She earned her M.C. in counseling at Arizona State University, where she was the Coordinator Senior for the Success Coaching Program. Colleen's research interests include media psychology and health psychology.

Michael Ruwe is the Learning Services Coordinator at the University of North Carolina Wilmington (UNCW). His research interests include metacognition, critical thinking, and tutor development. Michael received B.A. degrees in music and English from Northern Kentucky University and an M.A. in English from UNCW.

Roberta T. Schotka (Ed.M., instructional media and technology; B.S., elementary education) is Director of Programs, Pforzheimer Learning and Teaching Center, Wellesley College. Roberta has expertise developing and directing tutoring programs, academic support services, retention initiatives, and First Year Experience courses. She is Assistant Coordinator of Certified Programs for College Reading and Learning Association International Tutor Training Program Certification.

Candice Kaup Scioscia is Learning Coordinator for the Paramus campus of Berkeley College. She earned an M.A. in English at Rutgers University and a B.A. in creative writing at New York University. Candice is currently pursuing an Ed.M. in English education at Teachers College, Columbia University.

Anne Vermont Shearer has an M.Ed. in higher education and student affairs from the University of South Carolina and worked several years at the University of South Carolina at Aiken as Coordinator of Tutoring. She is temporarily retired from academia to explore the beautiful metropolis of San Francisco and the ever-evolving finance industry.

Rick A. Sheets, Ed.D., is retired from 27+ years in learning centers and computer commons in the Maricopa Colleges. He has mentored professionals in learning assistance and technology since the mid-1980's at Winter Institute and Technology Institute for Developmental Educators. Rick co-founded of the Learning Skill Centers in Higher Education (LSCHE) website with Frank Christ and serves on the College Reading and Learning Association (CRLA) executive board.

Rita Smilkstein (Ph.D., educational psychology with neuroscience minor, University of Washington) is a retired Professor, Seattle Community College, currently teaching brain-compatible curriculum and pedagogy at Western Washington University's Woodring College of Education. Awards include the Robert Griffin Award (College Reading and Learning Association's highest honor) and Fellow of the Council of Learning Assistance and Developmental Education Associations.

Jennifer L. Smith holds an M.Ed. in college and university student personnel administration. She is the program coordinator for the College of Natural Sciences Peer Leader Academy and the Texas Interdisciplinary Plan Academic Peer Mentor Academy at The University of Texas at Austin. Jenny's doctoral research centers on uncovering the undergraduate peer mentor experience.

Kathleen Speed, Ph.D., is a lecturer in the Student Learning Center at Texas A&M University, where she teaches the Learning Frameworks course. She loves teaching and working with students and is often invited to speak to various student groups about how to be a successful student.

Linda Stedje-Larsen is Director of Support Services at Wingate University. In addition to holding an Educational Specialist degree from Appalachian State University, she completed the Kellogg Institute's Certified Developmental Educator program. Her academic interests are in learning disabilities and learning support.

Lorraine Steiner, Ph.D., is Associate Professor of Mathematics at Newman University in Wichita, KS. She is also Newman University's Math Center liaison and offers statistical consulting, primarily for dissertations. Her research and teaching interests include statistics, mathematics for the liberal arts, and math tutor training.

Thomas C. Stewart is Professor of Academic Enrichment at Kutztown University, where he is the Director of Tutoring Services and Academic Support for student athletes. He has a Ph.D. from The Pennsylvania State University and has taught at colleges in Pennsylvania, New York, and Hong Kong.

Melissa Thomas, J.D., is Assistant Director of Learning Assistance at The University of Texas at San Antonio, where she focuses on improving the academic success of graduate students through academic coaching, workshops, and in-depth programs. Her research interests include graduate student success, writing anxiety, and conflict resolution.

Elizabeth J. Threadgill teaches first-year composition at Texas State University-San Marcos, where she received her M.F.A. in creative writing (poetry) with a minor in developmental and adult education. Elizabeth's interests lie in the intersections of disciplines particularly as they affect learning and writing.

Marcia L. Toms is the Associate Director for the Undergraduate Tutorial Center at North Carolina State University. She is the author of *Put the Pencil Down: Essentials of Tutoring* and is currently working on her Ph.D. in educational research and policy analysis at North Carolina State University.

Nicole Foreman Tong, Assistant Professor of Developmental English at Northern Virginia Community College-Annandale, has an M.F.A. from George Mason University. A poet nominated for a Pushcart Prize, Nicole enjoys her students as much as she does hiking, distance running, and reading in her favorite chair.

Reyna I. Torres is the Administrative Coordinator at the University Tutorial Center, California State University, Los Angeles, where she also received her B.S. degree in business administration.

Roseann Torsiello teaches composition and literature at Berkeley College. Her research interests include first-year students, adult learning, and writing for all ages. She has facilitated workshops in writing, communication skills, and adult learning theory. Roseann has served as Director of the Academic Support Center and Chair of the English Department.

G. Mason Tudor, is the Academic Support Center Coordinator at West Kentucky Community and Technical College. He earned a B.A. in creative writing and literature and an M.A. in English at Murray State University. His research interests include peer tutoring, brain dominance learning, and mentoring/coaching.

Penny Turrentine, Director of the West Campus Learning Center at Pima Community College in Tucson, AZ, is a National College Learning Center Association Level 4 Certified Learning Assistance Professional. Penny has worked with student athletes for 22 years, developing programs to facilitate academic success. The Scouting Report will be featured in her upcoming book, *Champions in the Classroom*.

Diane Van Blerkom is retired from the University of Pittsburgh at Johnstown. She serves on the Media Advisory Board of the College Reading and Learning Association (CRLA) and *Journal of College Reading and Learning (JCRL)* Editorial Board. Diane has authored several articles and three textbooks on learning strategies and co-authored the Outstanding *JCRL* Article of 2006-2007. In 2009 she received CRLA's Robert Griffin Award for Long and Outstanding Service.

Preston C. VanLoon received his Ed.D. in educational psychology from Northern Illinois University and has additional graduate studies in human development, curriculum and instruction, and special education. With an interest in developmental education, Preston is a professor, learning center director, author, conference speaker, and Certified Master Reviewer for the College Reading and Learning Association International Tutor Training Certification Program.

Kathryn Van Wagoner has managed the Math Lab at Utah Valley University since 2001. She has degrees in math education and public administration and is currently pursuing a Ph.D. in curriculum and instruction with an emphasis in math education. Her research focus is in targeting and preventing math anxiety. She has presented at numerous conferences.

Jane E. Varakin is a Certified Rehabilitation Counselor, with an M.Ed. in rehabilitation counseling from Kent State University. In 2006–2011 she served the Knox College Center for Teaching and Learning as Academic Coordinator/Learning Specialist and advised Knox College's new Project Eye to Eye Mentoring Program. She gives special acknowledgement to Dr. Donald Varakin and Dr. John Haslem.

Nathalie M. Vega-Rhodes is currently the Math Lab Supervisor at San Jacinto College South, where she also teaches and conducts tutor training each semester. She has authored, developed, and maintained the tutoring program's certification through the College Reading and Learning Association's International Tutor Training Program Certification. Nathalie is also certified through the Association for the Tutoring Profession as a Master Tutor Trainer.

Cindy Walker has an M.A. in English composition and Teaching English to Speakers of Other Languages (TESOL) and taught English as a Second Language before becoming a full-time faculty instructional specialist at Chaffey College in Rancho Cucamonga, CA, in 2001. She currently runs the Language Success Center, serves as faculty tri-chair of Student Success, and leads efforts in Learning to Learn and Accelerated Learning.

Pamela Way, Ph.D., oversees the Appointment Tutoring program for The University of Texas at Austin's Sanger Center, whose 200 tutors deliver almost 19,000 appointments a year. Pam also leads assessment and evaluation efforts for the Sanger Center, provides academic counseling, and serves on the editorial board of the Center's newsletter, *The Learning Curve*.

Sara Weertz (B.A., English; M.Ed., instructional technology with program assessment emphasis, Wayne State University) wrote and edited library and school reference materials. In 2005, she came to Angelo State University as founding director of Supplemental Instruction and tutoring. In July 2010, Sara became Executive Director of First Year Experience at Angelo State University.

Claire Ellen Weinstein is Professor of Educational Psychology at The University of Texas at Austin, author of the Learning and Study Strategies Inventory (LASSI), Director of the Cognitive Learning Strategies Project, and principal investigator of the Community College Longitudinal Retention Study. Her research focuses on strategic and self-regulated learning and on developing diagnostic/prescriptive assessments of students' academic readiness.

Amanda L. F. Weyant has a B.A. in English from Shippensburg University of Pennsylvania and an M.A.Ed. in higher education administration from The University of Akron. Amanda is the Student Accessibility Services Coordinator at Kent State University at Stark and previously worked in Learning Support Services at The University of Akron Wayne College.

Nancy Effinger Wilson has a B.A. in English from the University of Oklahoma, an M.A. in English from Texas State University-San Marcos, and a Ph.D. in English from The University of Texas at San Antonio. She has been tutoring in writing centers since 1986 and currently directs the Texas State University Writing Center. Nancy is author of "Bias in the Writing Center: Tutor Perceptions of African American Language."

Wendy L. Wilson is Assistant Director for Academic Support in the University College at the University of North Texas at Dallas. She received her Ph.D. in college student personnel administration from the University of Maryland, College Park. Wendy also served as President of the National College Learning Center Association in 2005–2006.

Karin E. Winnard, San José State University, has 20+ years of innovative experience in learning assistance, student development, and first-year programs. She authored "Codependency and Tutoring: Training Our Tutors Not to Rescue," co-authored *The Tutor Revue* and *The First-Year Revue*, and served as reviewer from 1988 to 2008 for the College Reading and Learning Association International Tutor Training Program Certification.

Robin Redmon Wright is currently an Assistant Professor of Adult Education at The Pennsylvania State University at Harrisburg. She holds both B.A. and M.A. degrees in English from the University of Tennessee and a Ph.D. in educational human resource development from Texas A&M University. Robin's research interests include critical feminist approaches to adult identity development.

About the Editors

Karen S. Agee, Ph.D., is Reading and Learning Coordinator Emerita of the University of Northern Iowa. She served the College Reading and Learning Association (CRLA) as secretary, president, and executive assistant to the Board. Karen currently represents CRLA on the Council of Learning Assistance and Developmental Education Associations (CLADEA) and on the Board of Directors of the Council for the Advancement of Standards in Higher Education (CAS) and serves on the editorial board of the *Journal of College Reading and Learning*. She has received CRLA's Robert Griffin Award for Long and Outstanding Service and Special Recognition Award, UNI's Exemplary Service Award, and the Iowa Board of Regents' Award for Staff Excellence. Karen previously collaborated with Russ Hodges on the program management chapter in *Handbook of College Reading and Study Strategy Research* (2nd ed., edited by Rona F. Flippo and David C. Caverly, 2008, Routledge).

Russ Hodges, Ed.D., is an associate professor in the College of Education at Texas State University where he co-created and now teaches graduate courses in the new doctoral and master's program in developmental education. Russ is a past president and treasurer of CRLA and is currently serving a third term as chair of CLADEA. Russ serves on the editorial boards for the *Journal of Developmental Education* and the *Journal of College Reading and Learning*. Russ has received many honors throughout his career, including the College Academic Support Programs (CASP) Lifetime Achievement Award, CRLA's Robert Griffin Award for Long and Outstanding Service, and CRLA's Special Recognition Award. He was named CLADEA Fellow—the field's most prestigious honor—in 2009. His books include *Academic Transformation: The Road to College Success* (with De Sellers and Carol W. Dochen, 2011, Pearson Education) and *Teaching Study Strategies in Developmental Education: Readings on Theory, Research, and Best Practices* (with Michele L. Simpson and Norman A. Stahl, 2012, Bedford St. Martin's).

Index